CANADIAN EDITION

# BASIC MARKETING RESEARCH

**ALVIN C. BURNS** ◎ **RONALD F. BUSH** ◎ **JUDITH NASH**

Louisiana State University    University of West Florida    Southern Alberta Institute of Technology (SAIT)

## USING MICROSOFT® EXCEL DATA ANALYSIS

**Pearson Canada**
Toronto

**Library and Archives Canada Cataloguing in Publication**

Burns, Alvin C.
Basic marketing research: using Microsoft Excel data analysis / Alvin C. Burns, Ronald F. Bush, Judith Nash.—Canadian ed.

Includes bibliographical references and index.
ISBN 978-0-13-506384-2

1. Marketing research—Canada.  2. Microsoft Excel (Computer file).  I. Bush, Ronald F  II. Nash, Judith, 1951–  III. Title.

HF5415.2.B77 2011          658.8'30285554          C2011-900327-9

ISBN 978-0-13-506384-2

Vice-President, Editorial Director: Gary Bennett
Editor-in-Chief: Nicole Lukach
Acquisitions Editor: Nick Durie
Sponsoring Editor: Don Thompson
Marketing Manager: Leigh-Anne Graham
Senior Developmental Editor: Eleanor MacKay
Supervising Developmental Editor: Suzanne Schaan
Project Manager: Imee Salumbides
Production Editor: Rachel Stuckey
Copy Editor: Tara Tovell
Proofreader: Susan Broadhurst
Compositor: Aptara®, Inc.
Photo and Permissions Researcher: Heather Jackson
Art Director: Julia Hall
Cover Designer: Anthony Leung
Interior Designer: Quinn Banting
Cover Image: Shutterstock Images

For permission to reproduce copyrighted material, the publisher gratefully acknowledges the copyright holders listed on pages 495–496 and throughout the text, which are considered an extension of this copyright page.

Statistics Canada information is used with the permission of Statistics Canada. Users are forbidden to copy the data and redisseminate them, in an original or modified form, for commercial purposes, without permission from Statistics Canada. Information on the availability of the wide range of data from Statistics Canada can be obtained from Statistics Canada's Regional Offices, its World Wide Web site at www.statcan.gc.ca, and its toll-free access number 1-800-263-1136.

1 2 3 4 5      15 14 13 12 11


Printed and bound in the United States of America.

# Brief Contents

# Contents

# Chapter 3 **Research Design**   79

## Chapter 4 Using Secondary Data and Online Information Databases   113

# Chapter 14 **Communicating the Research Results   462**

# Preface

## You Asked. We Listened!

### The Canadian Edition of *Basic Marketing Research: Using Microsoft® Excel Data Analysis* Offers All This and More!

Based on the second U.S. edition, *Basic Marketing Research: Using Microsoft® Excel Data Analysis*, Canadian edition, uses the framework of the successful, time-tested, 11-step approach to marketing research. The Canadian edition of this book also offers:

- A Canadian perspective including many different examples
- Canadian sources to increase the relevancy of the chapter on secondary data
- An in-depth discussion of customer relationship management and data mining
- Emphasis on the role of online research and online polling, especially as a quantitative survey technique
- An entire chapter on qualitative research that includes social media as a data source
- Many real-life examples to illustrate the text content, including three types of text box in each chapter: Marketing Research in Action, Online Application, Ethics in Marketing Research.

The focus is on the process of marketing research so that students will be better users of marketing research. The book teaches students to evaluate the need for marketing research and determine the adequacy of research proposals. At the same time, students are given the tools they need to conduct basic analysis.

## Features of the Canadian Edition

- The 11-step framework for marketing research is highlighted at the beginning of each chapter with the **Where We Are** feature in the margin.

**Where We Are**
1. Establish the need for marketing research
2. Define the problem
3. Establish research objectives
4. Determine research design
5. Identify information types and sources
6. Determine methods of accessing data
7. Design data collection forms
8. Determine sample plan and size
9. Collect data
10. Analyze data
11. Prepare and present the final research report

**MARKETING RESEARCH IN ACTION 11.1**
**How to Estimate Market Potential Using a Survey's Findings**

A common way to estimate total market potential is to rely on the definition of a market. A market is people with the willingness and ability to pay for a product or a service. This definition can be expressed somewhat like a formula, in the following way:

8470 students. When asked how much they expect to spend on internet purchases in that time period, we found the average to be $63.71. We can use the lower and upper boundaries of the 95% confidence interval for this average to calculate a pessimistic (lower boundary) and an

**ONLINE APPLICATION 1.1**

Online panel surveys are becoming more popular. They appeal to people who resist telephone surveys but whose opinions are valuable to businesses today. You will have the opportunity to experience first-hand what an online survey is all about by going to any of the following websites and following the instructions for joining its online panel for free. (Note: To avoid the possibility of receiving

- Harris/Decima eVox Panel: https://evox.decima.com/evox/en/index.php
- Angus Reid Forum (ARF): www.angusreidforum.com/Portal/p.aspx
- CRC Research Panel: www.consumerresearchpanel.ca

**ETHICS IN MARKETING RESEARCH 2.1**
**Which Company Are You Going to Choose?**

Chris was the marketing research director for a large department in the federal government. Often, Chris needed to hire a marketing research company to undertake large sample surveys costing $150 000 or more.

Typical of buying services for the government, the

private industry. Many market research companies wanted to get the government contracts. Not only were they worth money, but they were also good opportunities for networking and looked good on the company's client list.

Some marketing research firms purposely undercut

**How to Obtain a 95% Confidence Interval for an Average with XL Data Analyst™**

Figure 11.5 illustrates the two options possible from "Generalize—Confidence Interval." One is for a percentage confidence interval, while the other is for an average confidence interval. The Average option opens up a Selection window that can be seen in Figure 11.5. You select your metric variable(s) by highlighting each in the left-hand pane and using the "Add>>" button to move it into the right-hand selection

**Case 2.3 YOUR INTEGRATED CASE**
**Student Life E-Zine**

*This is the second case in our integrated case series. If you have not already done so, please read Case 1.2 (in Chapter 1) before reading this case.*

**ORS Marketing Research**
Sarah, Anna, Wesley, and Don were now firmly

we're going to try to make some accurate estimates of the entire campus population," Bob replied.

**Determining Feasibility**
Anna asked how ORS could determine "feasibility." Bob explained that the word had many differ-

- **Marketing Research in Action** boxes provide discussions of real situations pertinent to topics in each chapter.

- **Online Application** boxes provide online exercises for the reader to explore different marketing research tools and information sources.

- **Ethics in Marketing Research** boxes include discussions of real situations illustrating ethical concerns pertinent to chapter topics.

- A special feature explains the functions of **XL Data Analyst™**, a software package that runs using Microsoft® Excel 2007 or later versions. This Excel add-in can be downloaded from the text Companion Website. It opens Excel's computing capabilities for marketing research applications in an easy-to-use format.

- An **Integrated Case**, complete with a data set, gives students an experiential learning exercise throughout the course. "Student Life E-Zine" is a case about four post-secondary graduates who want to start an e-zine targeting the post-secondary population.

- The end-of-chapter summary is segmented according to the chapter-opening learning objectives.

- The end-of-chapter questions represent a balance between definitions, concepts, and application questions.

# Why Excel for Data Analysis?

By having this book, students will have continuing access to the Excel add-in program, XL Data Analyst™. With this text, students will learn how to use this powerful software program, which they can access as long as they can access Excel. Faculty said they want to teach students a software program that they will have and use in the future. Once students learn to use XL Data Analyst™ they can use it with their Excel software for years to come.

A powerful computing tool, Excel is widely used and understood by students. To increase the usage of Excel, add-ins are commonly developed to address many applications far beyond the intentions of the original Excel spreadsheet. Our add-in, XL Data Analyst™, opens up Excel's computing capabilities for marketing research applications in an easy-to-use format. Many features of XL Data Analyst™ make it more desirable than some of the most widely used dedicated stat packages.

## Features of XL Data Analyst™

XL Data Analyst™ is unique in that it only requires Excel, to which many students have access, and it is written expressly for the purpose of conducting marketing research data analysis. The program operates without statistical terms that are difficult for students to navigate and is written in a user-friendly format. Output is generated in a way that allows students to interpret the results correctly and easily. The XL Data Analyst™ has both traditional and classical statistical formats, as well as output in the new easy-to-interpret format. This helps students to focus on using marketing research to make decisions.

Students may download XL Data Analyst™ at **www.pearsoncanada.ca/burns**.

## A New Approach to Teaching Data Analysis

Because students struggle with levels of measurement, measurement is presented here in terms of categorical or metric variables. And because many students are baffled by data analysis, data analysis is presented in an easy-to-learn six-step process. Data analysis keystrokes are illustrated through colourful, annotated screen captures. Experience has shown that students using XL Data Analyst™ quickly learn the tools of data analysis and complete their projects much faster than with traditional software programs. They focus more on getting the answers and writing their reports rather than staring at hard-to-interpret output.

# Supplementary Materials

## For Students

**Companion Website (www.pearsoncanada.ca/burns):** This site allows students to take self-study quizzes for each chapter and have them automatically graded. XL Data Analyst™ and the data files required for cases in the text can also be downloaded from this site.

**CourseSmart for Students:** CourseSmart goes beyond traditional expectations—providing instant, online access to the textbooks and course materials you need at an average savings of 60 percent. With instant access from any computer and the ability to search your text, you'll find the content you need quickly, no matter where you are. And with online tools like highlighting and note taking, you can save time and study efficiently. See all the benefits at **www.coursesmart.com/students**.

## For Instructors

**Instructor's Resource CD-ROM (978-0-13-231121-2)** *Basic Marketing Research* is accompanied by an Instructor's Resource CD-ROM with the following supplements.

Most of these can be downloaded from Pearson Canada's online catalogue at vig.pearsoned.ca.

- **Instructor's Manual:** The Instructor's Manual can be used to prepare lecture or class presentations and find answers to end-of-chapter questions.
- **Test Item File:** This test bank provides questions in both multiple-choice and true or false format. The test bank is provided in both Microsoft Word and MyTest formats (see below).
- **PowerPoints:** PowerPoint slides complement chapter content and highlight the key concepts.
- **Image Library:** Selected figures and tables from the text are provided in electronic format.

**MyTest (www.pearsonmytest.com)** MyTest from Pearson Canada is a powerful assessment generation program that helps instructors easily create and print quizzes, tests, exams, as well as homework or practice handouts. Questions and tests can all be authored online, allowing instructors ultimate flexibility and the ability to efficiently manage assessments at anytime, from anywhere. MyTest for *Basic Marketing Research,* Canadian Edition, includes approximately 50 multiple-choice and true or false questions per chapter.

**Technology Specialists** Pearson's Technology Specialists work with faculty and campus course designers to ensure that Pearson technology products, assessment tools, and online course materials are tailored to meet your specific needs. This highly qualified team is dedicated to helping schools take full advantage of a wide range of educational resources, by assisting in the integration of a variety of instructional materials and media formats. Your local Pearson Canada sales representative can provide you with more details on this service program.

**CourseSmart for Instructors** CourseSmart goes beyond traditional expectations—providing instant, online access to the textbooks and course materials you need at a lower cost for students. And even as students save money, you can save time and hassle with a digital eTextbook that allows you to search for the most relevant content at the very moment you need it. Whether it's evaluating textbooks or creating lecture notes to help students with difficult concepts, CourseSmart can make life a little easier. See how when you visit www.coursesmart.com/instructors.

# Acknowledgments

This edition could not have been written without the support of the people at Pearson Canada. First, I wish to thank the sponsoring editor, Don Thompson, and the vice president and editorial director, Gary Bennett, for their help and support in getting this project off the ground. I also wish to thank Christina Lee, assistant editor, and Eleanor MacKay, senior developmental editor, for their skill and patience in moving this project along. I wish to also thank Imee Salumbides, project manager, for her management of the final stages of the project, Tara Tovell, copy editor, for her great questions, and Rachel Stuckey, production editor, for her efficiency in getting the project to the finish line. This book would not be a reality without the great team at Pearson Canada!

Finally I wish to thank all the reviewers for their excellent and detailed feedback:

Joseph W. Chang, Vancouver Island University
Magdalena Cismaru, University of Regina
Tulsi Dharel, George Brown College
Victor Emerson, Queen's University
Cynthia Gibson, Trinity Western University
Makarand Gulawani, Grant MacEwan University
Rosalie Hilde, College of New Caledonia
Tim Jones, Memorial University
Tom Jopling, British Columbia Institute of Technology
Irene Kirby-Frith, NAIT
Steve Letovsky, McGill University
David MacLeod, New Brunswick Community College–Moncton
Helen Mallette, Mount Saint Vincent University
David Nowell, Sheridan College Institute of Technology and Advanced Learning
Karen Plesner, British Columbia Institute of Technology
Carla Gail Tibbo, Douglas College
Maria Vincenten, Red River College
Bettina West, Ryerson University
Alison Yacyshyn, University of Alberta

Judith Nash
*Southern Alberta Institute
of Technology*

# About the Authors

**Alvin C. Burns** is the Ourso Distinguished Chair of Marketing and Chairperson of Marketing in the E.J. Ourso College of Business at Louisiana State University. He received his doctorate in marketing from Indiana University and an MBA from the University of Tennessee. Professor Burns has taught undergraduate and master's level courses and doctoral seminars in marketing research for over 35 years. During this time period, he has supervised a great many marketing research projects conducted for business-to-consumer, business-to-business, and not-for-profit organizations. His articles have appeared in the *Journal of Marketing Research, Journal of Business Research, Journal of Advertising Research,* and others. He is a Fellow in the Association for Business Simulation and Experiential Learning. He resides in Baton Rouge, Louisiana, with his wife Jeanne and Yellow Labrador Retriever, Shadeaux (it's a Louisiana thing).

**Ronald F. Bush** is Distinguished University Professor of Marketing at the University of West Florida. He received his B.S. and M.A. from the University of Alabama and his Ph.D. from Arizona State University. With over 35 years of experience in marketing research, Professor Bush has worked on research projects with firms ranging from small businesses to the world's largest multinationals. He has served as an expert witness in trials involving research methods, often testifying on the appropriateness of research reports. His research has been published in leading journals including the *Journal of Marketing, Journal of Marketing Research, Journal of Advertising Research, Journal of Retailing, Journal of Business,* among others. In 1993 he was named a Fellow by the Society for Marketing Advances. He and his wife, Libbo, live on the Gulf of Mexico where they can often be found playing "throw the stick" with their Scottish Terrier, Maggie.

**Judith Nash** is an energetic lifelong learner with a passion for teaching; she started teaching at SAIT in 1998. Her philosophy of teaching and learning is focused on self-discovery and the challenge to be the best person one can be. Since completing doctorate work at the University of Surrey, England, she has worked in the corporate world, provincial government, and post-secondary education. Her professional career began in the advertising business, where she provided marketing research for the development of new products and new communications. Moving to the "client" side of the industry, she was a senior member of the marketing team for the Toronto

Transit Commission (TTC). Here she provided marketing intelligence for developing, executing, and evaluating marketing and advertising strategies and customer service initiatives. Throughout her life, Judith Nash has remained committed to amateur sport, participating in the planning and execution of several provincial, national, and international sporting events. She is also an avid traveller and has been to all parts of the world. Her world experiences have helped her to connect with her diverse students from home and abroad.

## *A Great Way to Learn and Instruct Online*

The Pearson Canada Companion Website is easy to navigate and is organized to correspond to the chapters in this textbook. Whether you are a student in the classroom or a distance learner you will discover helpful resources for in-depth study and research that empower you in your quest for greater knowledge and maximize your potential for success in the course.

[ **www.pearsoncanada.ca/burns** ]

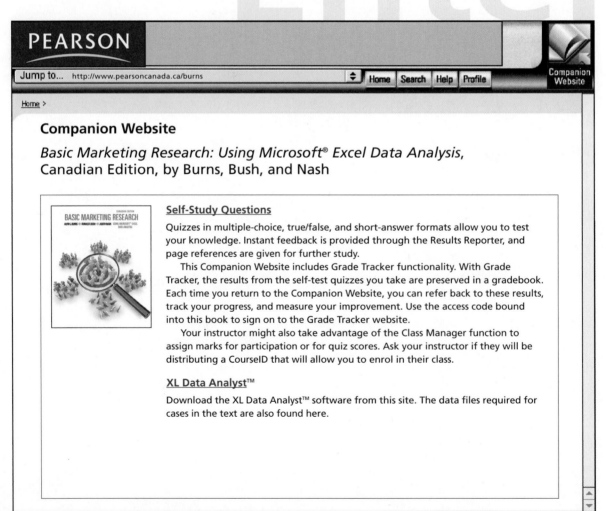

**PEARSON**

Jump to...  http://www.pearsoncanada.ca/burns   ▲▼   Home | Search | Help | Profile   Companion Website

Home >

### Companion Website

### *Basic Marketing Research: Using Microsoft® Excel Data Analysis*, Canadian Edition, by Burns, Bush, and Nash

#### Self-Study Questions

Quizzes in multiple-choice, true/false, and short-answer formats allow you to test your knowledge. Instant feedback is provided through the Results Reporter, and page references are given for further study.

This Companion Website includes Grade Tracker functionality. With Grade Tracker, the results from the self-test quizzes you take are preserved in a gradebook. Each time you return to the Companion Website, you can refer back to these results, track your progress, and measure your improvement. Use the access code bound into this book to sign on to the Grade Tracker website.

Your instructor might also take advantage of the Class Manager function to assign marks for participation or for quiz scores. Ask your instructor if they will be distributing a CourseID that will allow you to enrol in their class.

#### XL Data Analyst™

Download the XL Data Analyst™ software from this site. The data files required for cases in the text are also found here.

# Introducing Marketing Research

## LEARNING OBJECTIVES

1. Describe the role of marketing research in the marketing process.

2. Classify marketing research activities.

3. Examine the evolution of marketing research in Canada.

4. Discover the MRIA and its role in the Canadian marketing research industry.

5. Identify challenges faced by the Canadian marketing research industry today.

## Why Do We Love the Movies?

There are many factors that go into making a great movie: good scripts, directors, producers, actors, and support staff are fundamental. For many years, movies have been improved by using marketing research to gather consumers' reactions. Two of the earliest users of marketing research, though in a primitive form, were Carl Laemmle and Adolph Zukor. In the early 1900s, small neighbourhood theatres called nickelodeons showed films of the day for an admission price of only a nickel. Laemmle observed audience and sales data for movies shown in these theatres. He made notes on what types of people saw the films and determined the most popular screening hours among moviegoers. Zukor, a nickelodeon operator in New York, watched audience faces to see their responses to different parts of the films and claimed he learned to read the reactions of amusement, pleasure, and boredom. Both Laemmle and Zukor must, indeed, have learned something, for they created the film production studios Universal and Paramount—both large motion picture giants even today.

Over the years, marketing research played an ever greater role in movie making.[1] When research conducted by the Gallop poll in the 1930s predicted a huge market success for the movie *Gone With the Wind,* MGM decided to price the movie at between $0.75 and $2.20, at a time when the average movie ticket of the day was 25 cents! The result was higher profits for MGM because the Gallop predictions turned out to be correct.

Market research continues to be used to predict the success of movie scripts, rate the attractiveness of actors, profile various movie-going market segments, and determine which type of movie ending an audience prefers. Today, marketing research is used extensively by Hollywood studios to help make movies you love to see!

Welcome to the exciting world of marketing research! Even in the motion picture industry, marketing research can provide information to help managers make decisions. Marketing research is introduced in this chapter by (1) examining how marketing research helps marketers plan, (2) outlining the evolution of marketing research in Canada, and (3) investigating the role of the Marketing Research and Intelligence Association (MRIA), the self-governing association of the Canadian marketing research industry.

This is an exciting time to learn about marketing research because many innovations are taking place in the field. One change that affects marketing research is the widespread everyday use of the internet and social media such as Facebook and Twitter. This technology impacts how marketing researchers collect and report data.

Another change that is affecting marketing research is the development of new software technology for inputting, analyzing, and reporting data. This text uses XL Data Analyst™, a software program that easily taps the power of Microsoft Excel for marketing research analysis and reporting.

## Marketing and Its Relation to Marketing Research

### What Is Marketing?

Marketing research helps marketers make decisions throughout the marketing process. To understand the role of marketing research in this process, it is important to first agree on what marketing is.

**Marketing** is defined by the Canadian Marketing Association (CMA) as a set of business practices designed to plan for and present an organization's products or services in ways that build effective customer relationships.[2]

Marketing is shifting away from the sequential approach of focusing on a physical product and *then* optimizing profits by making efficient promotion, distribution, and pricing decisions (e.g., the idea that Honda creates value just by virtue of

Calgary-based WestJet continues to grow its domestic market share because WestJet uses its core competencies to create a real threat to Air Canada in the home market.

building cars). Current thinking, proposed primarily by Vargo and Lusch (2004),[3] goes beyond the "manufacturing a tangible product" view of marketing. Firms must be *more* than customer oriented (making and selling what firms think customers want and need). Now firms are expected to *collaborate with* and *learn from* customers and adapt to their changing needs.

In addition, products are not viewed as separate from services. For example, Second Cup is really marketing a service, a service that happens to include a by-product called coffee. Decision makers need information in order to know what their real core competencies are; create meaningful relationships with customers; create, communicate, and deliver value to customers; gauge customer acceptance; and determine appropriate responses to the feedback.

Think about the information needed by these successful firms: Tim Hortons, which holds 75% of the coffee and baked goods sector in Canada; Lululemon Athletica, which creates and delivers such good value in their fitness lifestyle clothing that customers are willing to pay a high price for them; or Apple, which has been so successful with non-computer products such as its iPod and iTunes that it has dropped the word *computer* from its corporate name. To make marketing decisions necessary for success, consumer information is paramount. Marketing research provides this information to decision makers.

Not all firms experience marketing success. Products and services fail. Sometimes this is because a company fails to find out who its target market is, or what its target market wants. In other words, decisions are made without proper marketing research information. In other situations, marketing research results are misleading: research respondents give support for a new product, but few people actually purchase it once the product becomes available. There are thousands of examples of product failures, including the examples below of Sears' reopening of the Eaton's stores, and Cadbury Adams' attempt to market Trident Sugarless Gum, cappuccino flavour.

An eatons store, rebranded by Sears Canada. Sears eventually converted the rebranded stores into traditional Sears stores.

Sears Canada purchased many of the stores owned by the bankrupt Eaton's Co. in an attempt to fill the gap in the Canadian retail environment with a department store offering price points between those of the Hudson's Bay Company and the Holt Renfrew Co. Ltd., an upscale retail store. Sears re-introduced the Eaton's store by changing the inventory and the atmosphere to appeal to an urban, younger demographic, and by rebranding it as "eatons." Unfortunately, the approach did not achieve the desired result. Members of the new target group were turned off by the still visible "Eaton's" brand while members of the older, core target group were turned off by the new look. Sears had to convert the new concept into traditional Sears stores soon afterwards.

Trident's cappuccino flavour did not succeed in the Canadian market alongside fruit- and mint-flavoured gum.

In an attempt to be innovative, Cadbury Adams Canada added the cappuccino flavour to their successful line of Trident Sugarless Gum. A similar coffee-mint flavoured gum was successful in Mexico. Unfortunately, Canadians were not impressed. Most people said they want gum to help remove coffee breath, not create it!

Peter Drucker wrote books on how firms can avoid failure. He noted that successful companies know and understand the customer so well that the product conceived, priced, promoted, and distributed by the company is ready to be bought as soon as it is available.[4] (Note how this is consistent with Vargo and Lusch's view of collaborating and learning from the consumer.) To practise marketing correctly, managers must have information not only about the customer but also about how to deliver value to the customer. This is the purpose of marketing research, and it explains why marketing research is a part of marketing. Marketing research provides the necessary information to enable managers to *properly* market ideas, goods, and services. In addition to having the right information, managers should have the right philosophy to guide their daily decisions; they should adopt the marketing concept.

## The "Right Philosophy": The Marketing Concept

A philosophy may be thought of as a system of values, or principles, by which one lives. For example, students likely have a personal philosophy similar to this: "I believe that higher education is important because it will provide the needed knowledge to enable me to enjoy the standard of living I desire." This philosophy affects students' daily lives and the decisions students make every day. The same is true for business managers. A manager's philosophy affects how he or she makes day-to-day decisions in running a firm. There are many different philosophies that managers may use to guide them in their decision making. A current marketing philosophy is called the marketing concept. One of the leaders in marketing thought, Philip Kotler, defines the **marketing concept** as follows:

> *The marketing concept is a business philosophy that holds that the key to achieving organizational goals consists of the company's being more effective than competitors in creating, delivering, and communicating customer value to its chosen target markets.*[5]

For many years, business leaders have recognized that this is the "right philosophy." Although the *marketing concept* is often used interchangeably with other terms such as *customer oriented* or *market driven*, the key point is that this philosophy puts the customer first. Time has proven that such a philosophy is superior to one in which company management focuses on production, the product itself, or some promotional or sales gimmick. If customers are satisfied with a company, they go out of their way to do business with that company. Think of the lineups to purchase Apple products on the launch dates!

Having the right philosophy is an important first step in being successful. Still, just appreciating the importance of satisfying consumer wants and needs is not enough. Firms must put together the "right strategy."

## The "Right Marketing Strategy"

The term *strategy* is borrowed from military jargon that stressed developing plans of attack to minimize the enemy's ability to respond. **Marketing strategy** consists of selecting a target market and designing the "mix" (product/service, price, promotion, and distribution) necessary to satisfy the wants and needs of that target market and to do so more quickly and better than the competition.

This definition *assumes* the marketing concept is adopted. A manager not having the marketing concept, for example, would not be concerned that his or her plan addressed any particular market segment and certainly would not be concerned with consumers' wants and needs. Because of the marketing concept, the right strategy allows a company to truly meet the wants and needs of the consumers within the market segment chosen. Note that customers can be either individual end users of a product or service, or other organizations such as a distributor or manufacturer that needs a particular product or service.

Many questions must now be answered: Who is the market? How is the market segmented? What are the wants and needs of each segment? How large is each market segment? Who are the competitors, and how are they meeting the wants and needs of each segment? Which segment(s) should be targeted? Which model of a proposed product will best suit the target market? What is the best price? Which promotional method will be the most efficient? How should the product be distributed?

In order to make the right decisions, managers must have objective, accurate, and timely information. Not only do managers need information to implement the right strategy now, but because environments are forever changing, this means marketers constantly need updated information about those environments. Managers must have the right information to understand when and how to modify their company's strategies. To make the right decisions, managers continuously need information. Marketing research supplies much of this information.

## What Is Marketing Research?

**Marketing research** is the process of designing, gathering, analyzing, and reporting information that may be used to solve a specific marketing problem. As noted by the MRIA, this process encompasses many activities,[6] including market intelligence and survey research, competitive intelligence, data mining, insight, and knowledge management.

Sometimes managers say "market research" when they mean "marketing research." Note that **market research** refers to applying marketing research to a specific market area. One definition of market research is "the systematic gathering, recording, and analyzing of data with respect to a *particular market, where 'market' refers to a specific customer group in a specific geographic area.*"[7]

## What Is the Purpose of Marketing Research?

The purpose of marketing research is to link the consumer to the marketer by providing information that can be used in making marketing decisions. As such, the information provided by marketing research for decision making should represent the consumer. Marketing research is consistent with the marketing concept because it "links the consumer . . . to the marketer." Even though focus is on the consumer, marketing research information is also collected on entities other than the

Marketing research is not always right. *Seinfeld* was predicted to be a failure by marketing researchers.

consumer. Information is routinely gathered on members of distribution channels, employees, and competitors as well as the economic, social, technological, and other environments.[8] Such marketing intelligence helps managers understand their consumers.

In their book *Counterintuitive Marketing: Achieve Great Results Using Uncommon Sense,* well-known authors Kevin Clancy and Peter C. Krieg argue that many failures can be attributed to managers just making "intuitive" decisions. Clancy and Krieg implore managers to use marketing research in order to make better decisions. One could argue that the point of all this research is to do a better job of satisfying consumers.

Sometimes marketing research studies lead to the wrong decisions.[9] The fact that a manager uses marketing research does not mean that the decisions based on the research are error-proof. In fact, marketing research results are never perfect. Choosing an acceptable level of accuracy is within control of the researcher. Sometimes, though, the research is wrong for other reasons. For example, it may be difficult for respondents to imagine a product or service that does not yet exist, so the answers they provide on a survey are not "real."

Wrong results do not always bring negative consequences, however. There are plenty of examples in which marketing research said that a product would fail, yet the product turned out to be a resounding success. Jerry Seinfeld's popular TV program in the 1980s, *Seinfeld*, is a good example. Marketing research on the pilot for *Seinfeld* stated the show was so bad that executives gave up on the idea. It was six months before another manager questioned the accuracy of the research and brought back the show, which became one of the most successful programs in television history.[10] Likewise, marketing research studies predicted that hair-styling mousse and answering machines would fail if brought to market.[11]

On the other hand, there are plenty of examples of failure where marketing research predicted success. Most of these failures are removed from the shelves with as little fanfare as possible. A classic example of this was Beecham's cold-water wash product, Delicare. The new product failed even though marketing research predicted it would unseat the category leader, Woolite. When this happened, there was a great deal of publicity because Beecham sued the research company that had predicted success.[12]

The goal of most marketing research studies is to try to understand and predict consumer behaviour, and this is a difficult task. The fact that the marketing research industry has been around for many years and is still growing means that it has passed the toughest of all tests to prove its worth—the test of the marketplace. If the industry did not provide value, marketing research would no longer exist.

## What Are the Applications of Marketing Research?

### Identify Market Opportunities and Problems

The identification of market opportunities and problems is one use of marketing research. Brand360°, a Canadian consumer marketing research company, looks for opportunities for new brands as well as identifying problems for existing brands. Some of its success stories include the relaunch of a financial services brand in a highly competitive "me too" marketplace, and its identification of a successful way for a large retailer to revitalize its brand.[13] Also, many research studies are being conducted today to determine the health effects of ingredients such as omega-3s, lecithin, and soy.[14] Results of these studies are used as a basis for new product development, to provide products that can satisfy consumer health concerns.

Brand360° is a marketing research firm that specializes in helping firms find opportunities in the marketplace.

# BRAND360°

## Generate, Refine, and Evaluate Potential Marketing Actions

Marketing research can also be used to generate, refine, and evaluate a potential marketing action. For example, as Telus Communications Inc. grew from being "the government telephone company" to participating in all forms of the fast-paced telecommunications industry, it wanted a brand image of a user friendly, dynamic, and fast-moving company with advanced products and services in many areas. Research that generated its "The Future is Friendly" branding campaign was undertaken. Then the company conducted research to evaluate the effectiveness of the campaign.[15]

## Monitor Marketing Performance

Marketing research can be used to monitor marketing performance. Everyone talks about the Super Bowl commercials in which companies spend millions of dollars for a 30-second spot during the most-watched TV event of the year. Bruzzone Research Company in the United States monitors the effectiveness of these high-priced ads in order to provide information to companies that want to monitor the impact of their investment.[16]

Another example of monitoring research is called tracking research. Tracking research is used to monitor how well products or services are performing in the marketplace over time. "Consumer packaged-goods" firms, such as P&G Canada and Johnson & Johnson Canada, want to monitor the sales of their brands and the sales of their competitors' brands as well. The Environics Research Group and TNS Canadian Facts are two of several firms monitoring the performance of consumer packaged-goods products in Canada. ACNeilsen is another research company that monitors how many units of consumer packaged-goods products are being sold, through which chains, at what retail price, and so on.

## Improve Marketing as a Process

Some marketing research is conducted to expand basic knowledge of marketing. Typical of such research are attempts to define and classify marketing phenomena and to develop theories that describe, explain, and predict marketing phenomena. Such knowledge is often published in journals such as the *Journal of Marketing Research,* published by the American Marketing Association. There is also an international publication, the *International Journal of Marketing Research.* (The *Canadian Journal of Marketing Research* exists but is not currently being published. The MRIA is reviewing how the journal can best serve the Canadian marketing research community.) Much of this research is conducted by marketing professors at universities. Such research can be described as the only part of marketing research that is basic. **Basic research** is conducted to expand our knowledge rather than to solve a specific problem. Research conducted to solve specific problems is called **applied research**, and this represents the vast majority of marketing research studies.

# The Marketing Information System (MIS)

A **marketing information system (MIS)** is a structure consisting of people, equipment, and procedures to gather, sort, analyze, evaluate, and distribute needed, timely, and accurate information to marketing decision makers.[17]

The four subsystems of an MIS are the internal reports system, marketing intelligence system, marketing decision support system (DSS), and marketing research system. The **internal reports system** gathers information generated by internal reports, which includes orders, billing, receivables, inventory levels, sales-call records, and so on. The **marketing intelligence system** is defined as a set of procedures and sources used by managers to obtain everyday information about pertinent developments in the environment. With the growth of social media and online research, marketing research is becoming more accessible. The **marketing decision support system** consists of collected data that may be accessed and analyzed to help marketers make decisions. The **marketing research system** provides information not available from other components of the MIS. Marketing research studies provide information to solve specific problems and are sometimes referred to as "ad hoc studies." Because they have a beginning and an end, they are sometimes referred to as "projects."

# The Marketing Research and Intelligence Association (MRIA)

To maintain professional standards among various practitioners and buyers of marketing research in Canada, three professional bodies were formed in the latter half of the twentieth century: the **Professional Marketing Research Society (PMRS)**; the **Canadian Association of Market Research Organizations (CAMRO)**; and the **Canadian Survey Research Council (CSRC)**.

PMRS was formed in 1960 to provide a community for users and practitioners of marketing research. Opportunities to share information were created through chapters across the country. The members were individuals rather than companies.

CAMRO was formed in 1975 to "foster high standards of quality and professionalism." The membership of CAMRO was composed of the larger full-service marketing research firms. The organization's main purpose was to maintain a standard code of ethics and practice. Member companies were regularly audited to ensure that they were upholding the code of ethical practice.

CRSC was founded in 1992 as a self-regulating tool for the marketing research industry. This was in response to government pressure regarding threats to the privacy of Canadian individuals, which resulted from growing complaints from Canadians about aggressive and deceptive telemarketing. The main goals of the CRSC were to develop a registration system for market and research firms, a government relations program, and a public relations program.

On November 21, 2004, members of these three associations voted overwhelmingly to create one organization to represent the industry. Thus began the Canadian **Marketing Research and Intelligence Association (MRIA)**, responsible for all aspects of the industry.

The MRIA's mission is "to promote a positive environment that enhances the industry's ability to conduct affairs effectively and to the benefit of the public and members."[18] The products and services the association offers include certification, professional development, publications, advocacy and lobbying, ethical and practice standards, career support services, and annual conferences/trade shows.

Membership of the MRIA is open to corporate as well as individual members. Currently, there are over 1800 practitioner members as well as many corporate buyers of marketing research, including representatives from the government and from manufacturing and insurance industries. An annual general meeting is held each spring, at which accomplishments, challenges, and issues in the marketing research industry are reviewed and resolved.

The MRIA recognizes that respect and cooperation of Canadians as potential research subjects form the core of the marketing research industry. Consequently, privacy of individuals is a main concern. One mechanism for advancing this is *VoxPop*, "Voice of the People." This online survey forum has the mission to "build public understanding of the power of opinion research."

In addition, the MRIA recognizes the importance of standardized education among marketing researchers in order to raise and maintain the high quality of service expected of all practitioners. Thus, there is ongoing development of industry standards through accreditation.

A main publication of the MRIA is the annual *Research Buyer's Guide*. This directory includes only member marketing research companies. A marketing research company that is listed must adhere to the association's code of ethics and practice in order to maintain MRIA membership in good standing.

# Classifying Marketing Research Activities

Table 1.1 classifies the major types of activities in the marketing research industry. Details about any of these categories can be found with the Google search engine.

**Table 1.1** A Classification of Marketing Research Activities

### A. Identifying Market Opportunities and Problems

As the title implies, the goal of these activities is to find opportunities or problems with an existing strategy. Examples of such studies include the following:

- Market-demand determination
- Market segments identification
- Marketing audits SWOT (Strengths, Weaknesses, Opportunities, and Threats) analysis
- Product/service-use studies
- Environmental analysis studies
- Competitive analysis

### B. Generating, Refining, and Evaluating Potential Marketing Actions

Marketing research activities may be used to generate, refine, and then evaluate potential marketing actions. Marketing actions could be as broad as a proposed marketing strategy or as narrow as a tactic (a specific action taken to carry out a strategy). Typically, these studies deal with one

*(Continued)*

**Table 1.1** (Continued)

or more of the marketing-mix variables (product, price, distribution, and promotion). Examples include the following:

- Proposed marketing-mix evaluation testing
- Concept tests of proposed new products or services
- New-product prototype testing
- Reformulating existing product testing
- Pricing tests
- Advertising pretesting
- In-store promotion effectiveness studies
- Distribution effectiveness studies

### C. Monitoring Marketing Performance

These studies are control studies. They allow a firm that already has a marketing mix placed in the market to evaluate how well that mix is performing. Examples include the following:

- Image analysis
- Tracking studies
- Customer satisfaction studies
- Employee satisfaction studies
- Distributor satisfaction studies
- Website evaluations

### D. Improving Marketing as a Process[a]

Some marketing research is conducted to expand our knowledge of marketing as a process rather than to solve a specific problem faced by a company. By having the knowledge generated from these studies, managers may be in a much better position to solve a specific problem within their firms. This type of research is often conducted by institutes, such as the Marketing Science Institute, or universities. Examples include the following:

- How managers learn about the market
- Consumer behaviour differences in e-business transactions
- Determining the optimal amount that should be spent on e-business and measuring success in e-business
- Predictors of new-product success
- The impact of long-term advertising on consumer choice
- Measuring the advantage to being the first product in the market
- Marketing-mix variable differences over the internet

[a]These study topics were taken from the Marketing Science Institute's research priorities list and former award-winning research papers. See **www.msi.org** for additional studies designed to improve marketing as a process.

# Evolution of the Canadian Marketing Research Industry

## The Beginnings

The history of North American marketing research really begins in the United States. Robert Bartels, a marketing historian, wrote that the earliest questionnaire surveys were used in the United States as early as the nineteenth century. In 1879, a study was conducted by N. W. Ayers and Company to examine grain production by state

Read more about Charles Coolidge Parlin by going to **www.advertisinghalloffame.org.** (Go to Members, and search under "P".)

for a client. However, Bartels believes the first continuous and organized research was started in 1911 by **Charles Coolidge Parlin**, a schoolmaster from a small city in Wisconsin. Parlin was hired by the Curtis Publishing Company to gather information about customers and markets to help Curtis sell advertising space. The information he gathered led to increased advertising in Curtis's *Saturday Evening Post* magazine.[19] Parlin is recognized today as the "Father of Marketing Research."

## Growth of the Need

Prior to the Industrial Revolution, businesses were located close to their customers. In an economy based upon artisans and craftsmen involved in barter exchange with their customers, there was not much need to "study" consumers because business owners saw their customers daily. They knew customer needs and wants. However, when the Industrial Revolution led to manufacturers producing goods for distant markets, the need for marketing research emerged.

A. C. Nielsen started his firm in 1922. In the 1930s, colleges began to teach courses in marketing research, and during the 1940s, Alfred Politz introduced statistical theory for sampling in marketing research;[20] and Robert Merton introduced focus groups for exploring customer needs.

In Canada, by the end of World War Two in 1945 there were only five marketing research companies.[21] Marketing research not only had gained acceptance in the business world by the 1960s but also was recognized as being a key to understanding distant and fast-changing markets. It was needed for survival!

Since the 1960s, the marketing research industry has seen technological advances that have increased productivity in the industry. In the 1970s, the Canadian companies Environics Research and Angus Reid were established and have since grown into the largest two marketing research companies in Canada. Many other companies have been established in the intervening decades, and today there are over 400 marketing research companies listed on the MRIA website.[22]

## The Industry Today

### Competition

In the twenty-first century, competition in marketing research is very keen. Inefficient or ineffective firms are quickly removed by market forces. There has been a growth in strategic alliances among competitor firms in recent years. **Strategic alliances** allow firms with strong expertise in one area (for example, data collection) to form partnerships with firms offering expertise in another area (for example, data analysis). This increases competition within the industry. ACNielsen acquired 61% of Net Ratings, which now gives ACNielsen a leadership role in internet audience measurement.[23] In 2000, Angus Reid sold his company to Ipsos SA, a Paris-headquartered marketing research company. Ipsos now owns over 40 other companies. Mergers and acquisitions are commonplace. For instance, Vision Critical, a revolutionary and fast-growing online panel company, merged with Angus Reid Strategies in 2004. This merger is the focus of Marketing Research in Action 1.1, below.

# MARKETING RESEARCH IN ACTION 1.1
## Vision Critical Joins Angus Reid

## Angus Reid Strategies

In November 2009, Vancouver-based Angus Reid Strategies announced its merger with global company Vision Critical Technologies, which became a strategic business unit of Angus Reid. The merger benefited both parties: the interactive technology designed and guided by Angus Reid's researchers, combined with Vision Critical's global panels, provides the company's clients with a faster, cost-effective, and cutting-edge way to interact with consumers.

Vision Critical is an innovative interactive marketing research company that collects data through the use of social media and global panels. The techniques not only reduce marketing research costs but also engage the participating consumers. The company now provides buyers of their services with access to insight from hundreds of thousands of consumers around the world through partnerships with select global partners.

Some of the services Vision Critical offers include virtual shopping, customer satisfaction, media assessment, advertising assessment, and concept screening. The company's Global Partner Program provides other marketing research companies with access to their award-winning technology.

Vision Critical's new website (**www.visioncritical.com**) continues to utilize technology necessary to capture and maintain attention of the new consumer. "Our site focuses on thought leadership and engagement, with blogs containing analysis and advice from industry

experts," says Vision Critical's Senior Vice President of Marketing, Brian Mitchinson. "We took this approach because we believe today's business consumer wants fast access to insights about who we are, what we do and what makes us unique, while also having the ability to engage directly with our thought leaders."

## Dr. Angus Reid

Dr. Angus Reid is a highly awarded marketing researcher whose company evolved from a consulting firm to the largest research company in Canada. The company is known as the leading analyst of social research and public opinion in Canada. Not only marketers but also political parties and government agencies pay close attention to his analysis of Canadian and global attitudes, trends, and market forces.

CEO Dr. Angus Reid says of the merger: "We've got a toolbox that combines interactive technologies, strategic researchers and our own global panels and communities. One of the reasons we've streamlined our technology and research is so we can provide faster and more cost-effective options for clients while engaging respondents in a richer, more interactive way."

Find out more about this merger and what Angus Reid Strategies offers at **www.angusreidstrategies.com**.

### Globalization

Today the marketing research industry is truly global in scope. In recent decades, as firms spread their business throughout the markets of the world, the marketing research industry followed those firms to their distant markets. In addition, technology has resulted in an explosion of online panel research on the World Wide Web, which can be accessed by the international community.

The marketing research industry is growing. In 2006 the world's top 25 marketing/advertising/public opinion firms accounted for over $15 billion of revenue. This represents a 5.1% growth rate from 2005 to 2006. The top 25 global firms account for a major share of total industry revenues due to the increase of acquisitions made by these top 25 companies. Jack Honomichl compiles the list of these companies (known as the Honomichl Global Top 25) and reports it annually in *Marketing News*.[24] Mr. Honomichl's report is widely regarded as the most reliable measure of revenue and change in the marketing research industry.

# Classifying Firms in the Marketing Research Industry

Providers of marketing research information are known as **research suppliers**. In Figure 1.1, modified from a classification by Naresh Malhotra, suppliers are classified as either internal or external.[25]

## Internal Suppliers

An entity within a firm that supplies marketing research is known as an **internal supplier**. Firms having internal suppliers spend about 1% of sales on marketing

**Figure 1.1** Classification of Marketing Research Suppliers
Note: The categories are not necessarily mutually exclusive. Some categories overlap.

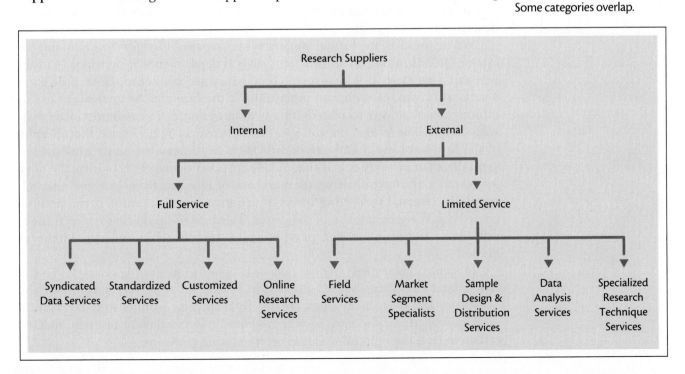

research.[26] General Mills and the Toronto Transit Commission have research departments of their own. Companies that are part of the media, such as the CBC or the Montreal *Gazette*, have internal online panels.

Internal suppliers of marketing research can elect several methods to provide the research function. They may (1) have their own formal departments, (2) have no formal department but place at least a single individual or a committee in charge of marketing research, or (3) assign no one responsibility for conducting marketing research. Anyone in the company can be called upon to do it.

Most large organizations have the resources to staff their own formal marketing research departments. Firms with higher sales volumes (over $500 million) tend to have their own formal marketing research departments, and many large advertising agencies have their own formal research departments. Companies with their own research department must justify the large fixed costs of supporting the personnel and facilities. The advantage is that staff has the opportunity to be fully aware of the firm's operations and the changes in the industry. This may give them better insight into identifying opportunities and problems suitable for marketing research action.

Marketing research departments are usually organized according to one or a combination of the following functions: *area of application, marketing function,* or *the research process.* By "area of application," we mean that these companies organize the research function around the "areas" to which the research is being applied. For example, some firms serve both ultimate consumers as well as industrial consumers. Therefore, the marketing research department may be organized into two divisions: consumer and industrial. Other areas of application may be brands or lines of products or services. Or, marketing research may be organized around *functional areas* (the 4 P's) such as product research, ad research, pricing research, channel of distribution research, and so on. Finally, the research function may be organized around the *steps of the research process* such as data analysis or data collection.

When there is no formal department, *responsibility for research may be assigned to existing organizational units* such as departments or divisions. A problem with this method is that research activities are not coordinated; a division conducts its own research, and other units of the firm may be unaware of useful information. One way to remedy this is to have a *research committee or an individual responsible for the company's marketing research.* This ensures that all units of the firm have input and can benefit from any research activity undertaken. Typically, their primary role is that of helping other managers recognize the need for research and coordinating the purchase of research from external research suppliers. Internal marketing research can give an organization a competitive edge. With the growing use of databases, a dedicated marketing research function inside the company can provide up-to-the-minute knowledge whenever needed.

In some organizations, *no one may be assigned* to marketing research. This is rare in large companies but not unusual in smaller firms. In very small firms, the owner/manager plays many roles, ranging from strategic planner to salesperson to security staff. He or she must also be responsible for marketing research, making certain to have the right information before making decisions.

## External Suppliers

**External suppliers** are outside firms hired to fulfill a firm's marketing research needs. In most cases, internal suppliers of marketing research also purchase research from external suppliers. Both large and small firms, for-profit and not-for-profit, and government and educational institutions purchase research information from external suppliers.

These research firms range in size from one-person proprietorships to the large, international corporations found in the **Honomichl Global 25**. The type, number, and specialties of these firms can be discovered by looking at some online directories of marketing research firms. Figure 1.2 illustrates the list in which the MRIA organizes member marketing research firms (see **www.mria-arim.ca**).

The American Marketing Association has a directory called the *Greenbook* (available at **www.greenbook.org**), in which many U.S. head offices of Canadian branches are listed. A number of other directories can be accessed at **www.quirks .com**. The American Marketing Research Association also publishes a member list called the *Bluebook*, which can be viewed at **www.bluebook.org**. Global company listings are presented on the Honomichl company website at **www.marketingpower .com** (type "Honomichl Top50" in the site's search engine).

External supplier firms organize themselves in different ways: by function (data analysis, data collection, etc.), by type of research application (customer satisfaction, advertising effectiveness, new-product development, etc.), by geography (domestic versus international), by type of customer (health care, government, telecommunications, etc.), or by some combination of these categories. Research companies evolve with changing marketing environments. For example, as a result of increased online research during the last several years, many companies, such as Abbott Research and Consultants, a division of ARC, now offer online focus groups and discussion boards.

### Full-Service Supplier Firms

**Full-service supplier firms** have the ability to conduct the entire marketing research project for the buyer firms. Full-service firms often define the problem, specify the research design, collect and analyze the data, and prepare the final written report. Typically, these are larger firms that have the expertise as well as the necessary facilities to conduct research studies in their entirety. For example, ACNielsen offers services in more than 100 countries and has 41 000 employees. The company can provide marketing research services in any area and has divisions for tracking

---

The Research Buyer's Guide is a comprehensive directory, listing companies and organizations that provide marketing research services and products in Canada. This Directory is the only one of its kind in Canada.

**The Research Buyer's Guide comprises eight sections as follows:**

1. Full Service
2. Field/Tab
3. Sampling/Data Analysis/Software
4. Moderators
5. Recruiters
6. Focus Group Facilities
7. Omnibus/Panels/Syndicated Studies
8. Other

**Figure 1.2** A Classification of External Suppliers for the MRIA's *Research Buyer's Guide*

Source: Courtesy of Marketing Research and Intelligence Association. www.mria-arim.ca.

retail sales, consumer panels, modelling and analytical services, and customized research that can be tailored to the individual needs of the client. Environics Research Group is a Canadian company with branch offices in the Unites States. It currently has three strategic business units: Environics Research Group, Environics Communications Inc., and Environics Analytics. Environics is also a member of ESOMAR, an international association of marketing research firms with its head office in Amsterdam, Netherlands.

All members of ESOMAR share a belief in the importance of high-quality marketing research to effective business decision making. Their mission is to enable "better research into markets, consumers and societies."

### Syndicated Data Service Firms

**Syndicated data service firms** collect information that is made available to multiple subscribers. The information, or data, is provided in standardized form (not tailored to meet the needs of any one company) to a large number of companies, known as a syndicate. Corporate Research Associates Inc. offers the syndicated *Boomer Monitor* and the *Canadian SME Report*. The *Boomer Monitor* reports the most comprehensive market research results on baby boomers. Data are collected using a standardized form twice per year. Clients who purchase the service are allowed to ask their own add-on questions related to the baby boomer sample—questions that are not made available to other clients. The *Canadian SME Report* is based on results collected in a similar way except that the sample is composed of decision makers in small- and medium-sized companies across Canada. The questions asked pertain to the respondents' attitudes and opinions regarding their business decisions. Again, clients who purchase the service can add their own questions to the standardized form with assured discretion.

### Standardized Service Firms

**Standardized service firms** provide omnibus surveys. Client members receive different data, but the process used to collect the data is standardized. Several clients share the cost of implementing the standardized questionnaire and all clients receive the same report. Each client can add four to five of its own questions to the survey and will be the only client on the omnibus survey to see the answers to those questions. This is a far less costly research activity than that of a customized research project. Ipsos Reid offers the Canadian Telephone Express Omnibus, which measures brand advantages and usage.

### Customized Service Firms

**Customized service firms** offer a variety of research services that are tailored to meet a client's specific needs. Each client's problem is treated as a unique research project. Customized service firms spend considerable time with a client firm to determine the problem and then design a research project specifically to address the particular client's problem. Full-service research companies usually provide this service. These studies are often quite extensive and can cost over $100 000 to complete.

### Online Research Services Firms

**Online research services firms** specialize in providing services online. Virtually all research firms today use online research—they make use of online technology in at least one or more phases of the research process. Most of these firms could also be placed in one of the categories shown in Figure 1.1. However, there are many firms that specialize in online services; their "reason for being" is to provide such services in online context. ResearchByNet, a global company, has online panels that access more than 270 000 Canadian households and over six million households across 200 countries. In Canada, Harris/Decima offers a national survey online.

Have you ever participated in a marketing research survey? Why not join an online panel? An online panel is a group of prescreened individuals who are willing to participate in online research surveys. (See Online Application 1.1.)

### Limited-Service Supplier Firms

**Limited-service supplier firms** specialize in one or a few marketing research activities. Firms can specialize in types of marketing research techniques such as eye-testing (tracking eye movements in response to different promotional stimuli) or mystery shopping (using researchers to pose as shoppers to evaluate customer service), or specific market segments such as senior citizens, or certain sports segments such as golf or tennis. Limited-service suppliers can be further classified on the basis of their specialization. These include field services, market segment specialists, sample design and distribution services, data analysis, and specialized research technique service suppliers. Many of these limited-service firms specialize in some form of online research.

**Field service firms** specialize in collecting data. These firms typically operate in a particular territory, conducting telephone surveys, focus-group interviews, mall-intercept surveys, or door-to-door surveys. One such firm is Canadian Viewpoint Inc. Some firms conduct only in-depth personal interviews; others conduct only mall-intercept surveys. Firms such as Market Dimensions are known as **phone banks** because they specialize in telephone surveying. Market Dimensions uses multilingual staff who work around the clock administering international surveys.

## ONLINE APPLICATION 1.1
# Join an Online Panel

Online panel surveys are becoming more popular. They appeal to people who resist telephone surveys but whose opinions are valuable to businesses today. You will have the opportunity to experience first-hand what an online survey is all about by going to any of the following websites and following the instructions for joining its online panel for free. (Note: To avoid the possibility of receiving unwanted spam, you may wish to first sign up for a new web-based email account.)

- Harris/Decima eVox Panel: **https://evox.decima.com/evox/en/index.php**
- Angus Reid Forum (ARF): **www.angusreidforum.com/Portal/p.aspx**
- CRC Research Panel: **www.consumerresearchpanel.ca**

Market Alert Ltd., a Canadian company, provides strategic mystery shopping.

Other limited-service firms, called **market segment specialists**, specialize in collecting data for special market segments. ASDE Survey Sampler Inc. is an example of a limited-service firm that specializes in **sample design and distribution**. It is not uncommon for a company with an internal marketing research department to buy its sample from a firm specializing in sampling and then send the samples and a survey questionnaire to a phone bank for completion of the survey. This way, a firm may quickly and efficiently conduct telephone surveys using a probability sample plan in markets all over the country. SM Research Technologies Inc. uses its unique software called Instant Sampler, an online self-serve tool, to meet most of its clients' sampling needs.

Canadian Viewpoint Inc. is an example of a field services firm.

Some limited-service marketing research firms offer **data analysis services**. Their contribution to the research process is to provide the technical assistance necessary to analyze and interpret data using the more sophisticated data analysis techniques such as conjoint analysis. For example, Just Dicta offers transcription services, and Lucid Data offers quantitative data analysis.

**Specialized research technique firms** provide a service to their clients by expertly administering a special technique. Such services are more widely used in the United States than in Canada. Examples of such firms include Eye Tracking, Inc., a San Diego company that specializes in eye movement research. Eye movements are used to determine the effectiveness of ads, direct-mail pieces, and other forms of visual promotion. Other firms specialize in mystery shopping, taste tests, fragrance tests, creating brand names, generating new ideas for products and services, and so on.

Many full-service firms fit neatly into one of these categories. However, some do not. Environics Research, for example, is a large full-service firm, but it also offers specialized services in political and social polling. In addition, there are other entities supplying research information that do not fit neatly into one of our categories. For example, universities and research institutes supply research information. Universities sponsor a great deal of research that could be classified as basic marketing research.

# Challenges to the Marketing Research Industry

## Marketing Researchers Should Be More Involved with Their Clients

Studies evaluating entire industries are conducted from time to time. These reviews indicate that although the marketing research industry is doing a reasonably good job, there is room for improvement.[27] Here are some striking examples indicating that marketing research needs improving: Sony, Chrysler, and Compaq did not use marketing research when they introduced the Walkman, minivan, and PC network servers—all very successful products. Coca-Cola's first attempt at New Coke and McDonald's McLean Burgers both failed but, in each case, were supported by extensive marketing research.[28] Critics Vijay Mahajan and Yoram Wind suggest, however, that marketing research is not fundamentally flawed but that many executives misapply research by not having research professionals involved in high-level, strategic decision making. Instead, too many executives view marketing research as a commodity to be outsourced to "research brokers" who are hired to conduct a component of the research process when they should in fact be involved in the entire process. To remedy the situation, Mahajan and Wind, highly regarded in academics and business consulting, recommend that researchers (1) focus on diagnosing problems, (2) use information technology to increase speed and efficiency, (3) take an integrative approach, and (4) expand the strategic impact of marketing research.[29]

A report by AgencyLink, a company specializing in client–agency relationship management, suggests that Canadian companies spend far less money on research than do firms in many other countries. Nearly three-quarters of agency leaders surveyed (71%) mentioned that strategic direction and briefings with clients could be improved. About one-third mentioned quality of decision making and need to streamline approval levels (38%), quality of judgment and ability to undertake agency recommendations (34%), and sharing information (33%) as areas to address in order to improve the client–agency relationship. One-quarter (25.5%) mentioned client marketers could be better trained in marketing and marketing research.[30]

## Marketing Researchers Should Focus on Diagnosing the Market

Mahajan and Wind suggest that marketing researchers should stop using marketing research only to test solutions, such as testing a specific product or service. Instead, researchers should diagnose the market. As an example, consider that customers did not "ask" for a Sony Walkman or a minivan. Marketing researchers would not have known about these products by asking customers what they wanted. Without having ever seen these products, it is unlikely that customers would have been able to articulate the product characteristics. But had marketing researchers focused on diagnosing the market in terms of unsatisfied markets and unarticulated needs in those markets, they may have produced these products. The Walkman was successful because it met an unsatisfied market's need for portable entertainment. The minivan was successful because it met an unsatisfied market's need for additional space in family vehicles. Marketing research can improve by properly diagnosing the market first, then testing alternative solutions to meet the needs discovered in the market.

## Marketing Researchers Should Speed Up Marketing Research by Using Information Technology

It has long been recognized that there is a trade-off between quickly producing marketing research information and doing research in a thorough manner. Marketing researchers want time to conduct projects properly. However, Mahajan and Wind point out that researchers must remember that time is money. Companies face real dollar losses when they are late in introducing products and services to the marketplace. So much so, in fact, that many of them cut corners in the research they conduct or do not conduct any marketing research at all. This, of course, often leads to disaster and has been labelled "death-wish" marketing.[31] The suggested prescription is for marketing researchers to make use of information technology (IT) for speed and economic efficiency. This is exactly why online research has become such a significant part of the research industry. Decision Analyst, Inc. allows companies to test product concepts quickly, using online respondents. Affinnova is a new firm that allows a company to actually design new products online. Harris/Decima, Ipsos Reid, and many others allow surveys to be conducted online. All of these firms use IT to speed up and reduce the cost of research.

## Marketing Researchers Should Take an Integrative Approach

Marketing researchers have created "silos," or individual compartments, which separate and isolate different types of information. For example, by separating research into qualitative and quantitative research, researchers tend to use one or the other when, in fact, more insights may be gained by integrating the two approaches. Other silos are created when decision support systems in organizations are not linked with marketing research. Firms should integrate studies they conduct instead of conducting one-shot projects that investigate a single issue. Mahajan and Wind also suggest greater integration of marketing research with existing databases and other information sources such as customer complaints, other studies of product/service quality, and external databases. Marketing researchers would improve their results by taking a closer look at all existing information instead of embarking on isolated research projects to solve a problem.

## Marketing Researchers Should Expand Their Strategic Impact

In some companies, marketing research has become too comfortable with providing standard reports using simple measures. This information, although useful, does not allow marketing research to contribute to the important central issues of determining overall strategy. Research becomes relegated to a lower-level function providing information for lower-level decisions. As an example, Mahajan and Wind refer to marketing research that periodically provides a report on market shares. Although this information is useful for making tactical decisions for each brand, marketing research should be providing such services as defining the market. Questions addressing broader strategic issues such as developing a company's market or product diversification should be looking at marketing research for answers. These are broader, more strategic issues that, if addressed properly, would add value to the function of marketing research.

## Other Criticisms

Over the years, reviews of the marketing research industry and its contribution to marketing have been made. Criticism has focused on the following areas of concern:

- the industry lacks creativity;
- the industry is too survey oriented;
- the industry does not understand the real problems that need studying;
- market researchers show a lack of concern for respondents;
- the industry does not really care about the effects of nonrespondents on the results;
- the price of the research is high relative to its value; and
- academic marketing research should be more closely related to actual marketing management decisions.[32]

One entire issue of the *Canadian Journal of Marketing Research*, edited by Chuck Chakrapani, was devoted to a number of articles questioning customary practices in marketing research.[33] The debate these articles stirred is good for the industry, and the the basic conclusion of the evaluations is that the industry has performed well, but there is room for improvement.

## Improvements: Certification, Auditing, and Education

Even though there have been criticisms of the marketing research industry, the industry has performed well by the toughest of all standards, the test of the marketplace.

Revenues in the Canadian marketing research industry have been increasing. Clients obviously see value in the marketing research that is being generated. However, the industry is not immune from problems. Many suggest that the problems are created by a very small minority of firms, most of which simply are not qualified to deliver quality marketing research services. There is obviously a concern among buyers and suppliers about the lack of uniformity in the industry as well. In a study of buyers' and suppliers' perceptions of the research industry, Dawson, Bush, and Stern found that the key issue in the industry is a lack of uniform quality; there are good suppliers and there are poor suppliers.[34]

### Certification and Education

Over the years, many have argued that marketing research attracts practitioners who are not fully qualified to provide adequate service to buyer firms. No formal requirements, no education level, no degrees, no certificates, no licences, and no tests of any kind were required to open up a marketing research business. **Certification** is a designation that indicates the achievement of some minimal standard of performance, and it is a definite sign of improvement that marketing researchers can now be certified. Certainly, the vast majority of research firms have staff who are thoroughly trained in research methods and have years of excellent performance. However, some say it is those few firms with unqualified personnel and management that tarnish the industry's image.

In March 2009, the MRIA announced the opening of the Institute for Professional Development. The Institute was developed from the School of Marketing Research by adding more course offerings for junior researchers as well as educational opportunities for veteran practitioners.

The Institute facilitates the acquisition of the Certified Marketing Research Professional (CMRP) designation or Professionnel agréé en recherche marketing (PARM). This industry designation demonstrates that the holder is committed to following the MRIA Code of Conduct and adheres to MRIA standards. Individuals can obtain this designation either by writing the Comprehensive Marketing Research Exam (CMRE) or by successfully completing the ethics course after at least eight years of practical experience. The exam can be taken after successful completion of nine core courses and two years of practical experience. The courses are offered through the Institute.

Most post-secondary institutes require at least one successfully completed course in marketing research in order to achieve a degree or diploma in business with a major in marketing.

Classes are offered by the MRIA Institute for Professional Development.

Source: Courtesy of Marketing Research and Intelligence Association. www.mria-arim.ca.

### Auditing

**Auditing** has also been suggested as a means of improving the industry. The concept is to have marketing research firms' work subject to an outside, independent review for the sake of determining the quality of their work. An audit would involve procedures such as retabulation from raw data of a random sample of descriptive surveys, validation of a sample of questionnaires, and even checking questionnaires for evidence of selling under the guise of marketing research.[35]

Though proposed several years ago for the Canadian marketing research industry, in particular through CAMRO, the audit concept has lain dormant and, now, with a certification program in place, auditing is not likely to gain industry acceptance. However, auditing is important in such areas as media research because the cost of media placement is very dependent on the stated reach of the medium (the number of people potentially exposed to it). The Audit Bureau of Circulations (ABC), the auditor of magazine and other periodical circulation for many years, formed ABCi (ABC Interactive) in 2001 for the purpose of auditing traffic on websites.[36] Canadian Outdoor Measurement Bureau (COMB) verifies the potential number of people who will pass a specific outdoor medium (the medium's reach).

## Ethics and Marketing Research

**Ethics** may be defined as a field of inquiry into determining what behaviours are deemed appropriate under certain circumstances. Ethical behaviour is prescribed by codes of behaviour set by society. In some cases, this is formalized by institutions into behaviours that are considered legal or illegal. There are other behaviours that are considered by some groups to be unethical but that are not illegal—for example, having an abortion in Canada. When the legality of these types of behaviours is not spelled out by some societal institution (such as the justice system, legislature, and regulatory agencies such as the Canadian Radio-television and Telecommunications Commission [CRTC], etc.), then determination of whether the behaviours are ethical or unethical is open to debate.

Most marketing associations around the world have codes of ethical behaviour. The Canadian Marketing Association (**www.the-cma.org**) has a code of ethical norms and standards of practice for all marketers, as does the American Marketing Association (**www.marketingpower.com**). The European-based ESOMAR, the European Society for Marketing Research (**www.esomar.org**), has a code of ethics that is adopted by many marketing research organizations around the world, including Australia. All over the world, marketing research organizations strive to achieve ethical behaviour among practitioners of marketing research.

Prior to 2004, the PMRS and CAMRO had separate codes of practice, and when the market research associations merged to form the MRIA, the combined standards were adopted. More recently (December, 2007), the revised Code of Conduct and Good Practice for Members of the MRIA was established. Figure 1.3 outlines the code's 10 core principles. The code in its entirety can be examined by going to the MRIA website (**www.mria-arim.ca**) and clicking on "Standards."

Some of the key issues in the latest MRIA code centre on the following:

- rights of the respondent, especially with regard to privacy and interviewing children;
- maintaining research integrity; and
- fair treatment of both buyers and practitioners of research.

## Rights of the Respondent

With the growing negative reaction of the public to telemarketing and invasion of privacy, respondent rights are a priority in the MRIA's revised Code of Conduct and Good Practice. The MRIA Charter of Respondent Rights (2006) must be upheld by all members. The most urgent issue is with regard to random calling to obtain telephone interviews (see Ethics in Marketing Research 1.1). A researcher cannot use client-supplied lists from one project for any other project. Any call-backs after a first refusal must be done with the respondent's permission only. In addition, the acceptable number of monitored telephone interviews has increased to ensure the respectable treatment of respondents and unbiased collection of information. Respondents are also entitled to know the length of an interview. With regard to online surveys, any survey longer than 30 minutes is considered too long. In a case where a client may wish to receive feedback from customer satisfaction surveys, subjects must give permission to the researcher for their identities to be disclosed to the client. The Research Registration System is a 1-800 number the public can call to verify if a caller is legitimate and/or to register a complaint.

In the case of qualitative research involving focus groups, an individual cannot participate in more than five groups or in-depth interviews within a five-year period. Advertising cannot be used to recruit subjects, and if taste tests are being conducted, subjects have the right to be informed of the ingredients in the tested product. Furthermore, all names of participants must be registered with the Qualitative Research Registry (QRR).

For a customer database survey, the source of the list must be disclosed to the respondents, as well as the identity of the client. All lists must be permission based only. Email addresses are considered private information and are protected by the Canadian Privacy Commission.

With regard to youth under the age of 13, parental permission must be acquired prior to participation.

## Research Integrity

Marketing research information is often used in making significant decisions. The outcome of the decision may impact future company strategy, budgets, jobs, organization, and so forth. With so much at stake, the opportunity is ripe for a lack of total objectivity in the research process. The loss of **research integrity** may take the form of

# Ten Core Principles

The following principles summarize the ideas enshrined in the MRIA Code of Conduct. These principles are founded upon the history of practice of marketing research in Canada, the ICC/ESOMAR Code of Marketing and Social Research and the principles underlying the Personal Information Protection and Electronic Documents Act (PIPEDA).

### PRINCIPLE 1: CONSENT

Contact with members of the public is at all times to be undertaken with their consent and with observance of their right to withdraw at any time.

### PRINCIPLE 2: PUBLIC CONFIDENCE

Members should act in a manner that serves to promote and augment, not diminish, the confidence of the public in research in general.

### PRINCIPLE 3: PUBLIC'S RIGHT TO PRIVACY

The use of research data should extend only to those purposes for which consent was received. The public's desire for privacy and anonymity is to be respected.

### PRINCIPLE 4: ACCURACY

Members agree to recommend those research methods which are appropriate to the research goals, and to avoid conducting research which would be inaccurate or misleading. Members must be accurate in all aspects of research and refrain from purporting or suggesting levels of accuracy which are greater than is warranted by the nature of the research. Members shall report and interpret their results in a manner that represents these results accurately and acknowledges such limitations on the research which, in the absence of such acknowledgement, might mislead.

### PRINCIPLE 5: ETHICAL PRACTICE

Members shall at all times act honestly, ethically and fairly in their dealings with all members of the public, clients, employers, sub-contractors and each other. They will refrain from activities which show disrespect or otherwise unjustifiably demean, criticize or disparage others.

### PRINCIPLE 6: CLIENT RIGHTS

Members shall protect the interests of their clients and clients' rights to confidentiality. Members shall ensure that records of research will be held for the appropriate periods and that these will be protected from theft, misuse and inadvertent destruction.

### PRINCIPLE 7: LAWFULNESS

Members, in their conduct of research, shall abide by the prevailing provincial, national and international legislation which applies to the research they conduct.

### PRINCIPLE 8: COMPETENCY

Members agree to uphold high standards of general competency in the design, execution, analysis, reporting, interpretation and consulting phases of all research.

### PRINCIPLE 9: FAMILIARITY

Members will undertake to keep themselves, their co-workers and clients informed about the code of conduct to avoid breaches of it, and will undertake also to inform themselves of any recent changes made by assessing, where necessary, such sources as the MRIA website or other material.

### PRINCIPLE 10: PROFESSIONALISM

Members commit themselves to the goal of seeking to continuously improve themselves in their chosen profession.

**Figure 1.3** The MRIA's 10 Core Principles

Source: Courtesy of Marketing Research and Intelligence Association. www.mria-arim.ca/STANDARDS/PDF/TenCorePrinciples.pdf

## ETHICS IN MARKETING RESEARCH 1.1
## "Do- Not-Call" Controversy

One of the growing concerns among marketers and the public alike is the unwelcome telephone calls received from telemarketers and market researchers. In response to growing complaints, the Canadian Radio-television and Telecommunications Commission (CRTC) launched the Do-Not-Call Registry on September 30, 2008, to protect Canadians from unwanted telephone and fax solicitations. Individuals who do not wish to be telephoned by marketers or researchers can add their name to the registry. It is accessible to companies, so they should not be calling the numbers listed. Rumours regarding the effectiveness of the program were quick to surface. One belief circulating was that the list is sold to telemarketers so that numbers on the list are actually called more often!

In an attempt to find out how effective this list actually was, MRIA's *VoxPop* surveyed a random sample of 2035 Canadians across the country, aged 18 years and over. The survey was conducted by telephone in the early part of 2009.[37]

Results showed that 80% of Canadians who placed their phone numbers on the Do–Not-Call Registry received fewer calls from telemarketers. However, 13% said they receive more calls than before registering their number on the list.

Most complaints to the CRTC regarding an increase in telemarketing calls refer to calls from American companies. The recession is probably causing American telemarketers to expand their call base to include Canadians. Also, the increased use of computerized random dialling by telemarketers is a likely cause. Unfortunately, the computer is not intelligent enough to recognize random numbers that are on the Do-Not-Call Registry.

The *VoxPop* survey also found that 33% of adult Canadians registered their home phone numbers and 12% registered their cellphone numbers.

The survey is important as it informs the public of the facts about the success of the Do-Not-Call Registry and alerts the CRTC to its challenges in making the registry more effective. As well, the survey is an important public relations tool for the marketing research industry, since it demonstrates how important public opinion research is to the policy and programs initiated by the government.

withholding information, falsifying data, altering research results, or misinterpreting the research findings in a way that makes them more consistent with predetermined points of view.

The source of a compromise in research integrity may come from either the supplier or the buyer. If a research supplier knows that a buyer will want marketing research services in the future, the supplier may alter a study's results or withhold information so that the study will support the buyer's wishes. Breaches of research integrity need not be isolated to those managing the research project. Interviewers have been known to make up interviews and to take shortcuts in completing surveys. In fact, there is some evidence that this is more of a problem than was once thought.[38] Maintaining research integrity is regarded as one of the most significant ethical issues in the research industry. To strengthen the integrity of research reporting, the MRIA states that researchers must include possible sources of error caused by respondents not in the sample. Assumptions the researcher made about data accuracy must also be declared. In the case of nonprobability samples, margins of error cannot be used, since they are misleading.

## Treating Others Fairly

Several ethical issues that centre around how others are treated may arise in the practice of marketing research. Suppliers, buyers, and the public may be treated unethically.

### Buyers

*Passing hidden charges* to buyers, *overlooking study requirements* when subcontracting work out to other supplier firms, and *selling unnecessary research* are examples of unfair treatment of buyer firms. By overlooking study requirements, such as qualifying respondents on specified characteristics or verifying that respondents were interviewed, the supplier firm may lower its cost of using the services of a subcontracting field service firm. A supplier firm may oversell research services to naive buyers by convincing them to use a more expensive research design.

*Sharing confidential and proprietary information* raises ethical questions. Virtually all work conducted by marketing research firms is confidential and proprietary. Researchers build up a storehouse of this information as they conduct research studies. Most ethical issues involving **confidentiality** revolve around how this storehouse of information, or "background knowledge," is treated. It is common practice among research supplier firms to check their existing list of buyer-clients to ensure that there is no conflict of interest before accepting work from a new buyer.

### Suppliers

Buyers also abuse suppliers of marketing research. A major problem exists, for example, when a firm having internal research capabilities issues a **request for proposals (RFP)** from external supplier firms. External firms then spend time and money developing research designs to solve the stated problem, estimating costs of the project, and so on. Having collected several detailed proposals outlining research designs and costs, the abusing firm decides to do the job internally. Issuing a call for proposals from external firms with no intention of doing the job outside is unethical behaviour.

Often buyer firms have obligations such as agreeing to meetings or the provision of materials needed for the research project. Supplier firms must have these commitments from buyers in a timely fashion in order to keep to their schedules. Buyer firms sometimes abuse their agreements to deliver personnel or these other resources in the time to which they have agreed. Also, buyers sometimes do not honour commitments to pay for services. Although this happens in many industries, research suppliers do not have the luxury of repossession; they do, however, have legal recourses.

### The Public

Sometimes researchers are asked to do research on products thought to be dangerous to society. Ethical issues arise as researchers balance marketing requirements with social issues. This is particularly true in the areas of product development and advertising. For example, some advertising attempts to increase the total consumption of refined sugar among children via advertising scheduled during Saturday morning TV programs. Marketing researchers have expressed concern over conducting research on advertising to children. Other ethical concerns arise when conducting research on products researchers feel are dangerous to the public, such as certain chemicals and cigarettes.

To overcome some of these issues, the MRIA created the *VoxPop* online forum. The forum's mission is to build confidence in the value of marketing research for all. One of the things the site does is educate the public about respondent rights.

### Respondents

Market research firms are working hard to protect the privacy of their respondents. Firms in the industry realize that they rely on consumer cooperation for information requests. In order to achieve a cooperative pool of potential respondents, marketing researchers must attempt to separate themselves from telemarketers. This is challenging when "**sugging**" (selling under the guise of research) and "**frugging**" (fundraising under the guise of research) occurs. In both cases, a marketer pretends to be a market researcher conducting a legitimate survey when, in fact, it is actually trying to sell the product in question or solicit funds.

In addition, the future is cloudy in terms of how legal actions against invasion of privacy by marketing researchers will affect the collection and analysis of collected data. Research firms, realizing that respondents are their lifeblood, are moving in the direction of recruiting their own panels of willing respondents. Recruiting and maintaining a panel requires considerable investment. Panel equity, the value of readily available access to willing respondents, is becoming increasingly important. Marketing research firms have to make even greater efforts to ensure fair and ethical treatment of their valuable panel respondents.

## Summary

**1.  Describe the role of marketing research in the marketing process.**
Marketing research is part of marketing. Marketers attempting to practise the marketing concept need information in order to determine wants and needs and to design marketing strategies that will satisfy customers in selected target markets. Environmental changes mean that marketers must constantly collect information to monitor customers, markets, and competition.

Marketing research is defined in this chapter as "*the process of designing, gathering, analyzing, and reporting information that may be used to solve a specific problem.*" The purpose of marketing research is to link the consumer to the marketer by providing information that can be used in making marketing decisions. Not all firms use marketing research and sometimes marketing research leads companies to make the wrong decisions. But marketing research has been used for many years and is growing—it has passed the "test of the marketplace."

**2.  Classify marketing research activities.**
Applications of marketing research are to (1) identify and define marketing opportunities and problems; (2) generate, refine, and evaluate marketing actions; (3) monitor marketing performance; and (4) improve the process of marketing. Marketing research studies are classified according to these four applications.

Marketing research is one of four subsystems making up a marketing information system (MIS). Other subsystems include internal reports, marketing intelligence, and decision support systems. Marketing research gathers information not available through the other subsystems; it provides information for the specific problem at hand.

### 3.  Examine the evolution of marketing research in Canada.

Charles Coolidge Parlin is given credit for conducting the first marketing research, beginning in 1911, for the Curtis Publishing Company. Parlin is recognized as the "Father of Marketing Research." Prior to the Industrial Revolution, there was little need for formal marketing research. Business proprietors—artisans who bartered with their customers—knew their customers' needs and preferences. However, once mass production led to producing goods for distant markets, managers needed information about these distant markets. By the 1930s, the marketing research industry was becoming widespread, and by the 1960s, the practice of marketing research gained wide approval as a method for keeping abreast of fast-changing, distant markets.

Technology has transformed marketing research to include data collection techniques such as social media monitoring and database mining. Access to online results is now readily available.

Today, marketing research is a US$15+ billion global industry. In Canada, there are over 400 firms generating a total of US$750 million annually. Strategic alliances in the industry make it a very competitive arena.

The marketing research industry is composed of research suppliers. Suppliers may be broadly classified as internal (research is provided by an entity within the firm) or external (research is provided by an entity outside the firm). Internal suppliers may be found in for-profit as well as not-for-profit firms and in service firms as well as product firms. Internal suppliers organize by having their own formal departments, by having a marketing research committee or a designated individual responsible for research, or by not having anyone responsible. Internal suppliers often work with external suppliers. External suppliers organize by function, research application, geography, type of customer, or some combination of these qualities. External suppliers may be classified as full-service or limited-service firms. Each of these types may be further subclassified.

### 4.  Discover the MRIA and its role in the Canadian marketing research industry.

The Canadian Marketing Research and Intelligence Association (MRIA) is responsible for all aspects of the industry in Canada. Formed in 2004, the MRIA is a fusion of the Canadian Association of Market Research Organizations (CAMRO), the Canadian Survey Research Council (CSRC), and the Professional Marketing Research Society (PMRS).

The MRIA's mission is "to promote a positive environment that enhances the industry's ability to conduct affairs effectively and to the benefit of the public and members."[39] The products and services it offers include certification, professional development, publications, ethical standards, and annual conferences/trade shows. The association's website address is **www.mria-arim.ca**. Included on the website is a listing of marketing research companies in Canada for interested purchasers of marketing research.

### 5.  Identify challenges faced by the Canadian marketing research industry today.

The marketing research industry's performance is periodically evaluated. In general, these reviews show that the industry is doing a reasonably good job but that there is room for improvement. Suggestions are made for how improvement can be made. Some industry leaders have called for an auditing system to ensure consistency of performance across the industry. The marketing research industry has started several professional development programs for its members in recent years. In March 2009, the MRIA announced the Institute for Professional Development, where members can receive certification in marketing research—the CMRP (Certified Marketing Research Professional) designation or PARM (Professionnel agréé en recherche marketing). In addition, some postsecondary schools in Canada offer diplomas or a degree in marketing research.

Ethical issues in marketing research are more important today than ever, as the public is highly informed about companies' practices. Ethics is defined as a field of inquiry into determining what behaviours are deemed appropriate under certain circumstances as prescribed by codes of behaviour that are set by society. The MRIA has a code of ethical behaviour for both buyers and suppliers of research. Ethical issues include research integrity and treating others (buyers, suppliers, the public, and respondents) fairly. Issues related to respondent fairness include deception, confidentiality, and invasions of privacy. Unsolicited telephone calls and email spam are considered an invasion of privacy. In the future, we can probably expect more legislation affecting access to respondents, such as the Canadian federal government's Do-Not-Call Registry. Research companies, faced with a declining pool of willing respondents in the general public, will rely more heavily on recruiting their own panel members. *VoxPop*, the online survey forum run by the MRIA, functions to educate and uphold the rights of respondents in an effort to create and maintain positive relations between the marketing research industry and the public.

## Key Terms

Applied research   (p. 9)
Auditing   (p. 24)
Basic research   (p. 9)
Canadian Association of Market Research Organizations (CAMRO)   (p. 10)
Canadian Survey Research Council (CSRC)   (p. 10)
Certification   (p. 24)
Charles Coolidge Parlin   (p. 13)
Confidentiality   (p. 29)
Customized service firms   (p. 18)
Data analysis services   (p. 21)
Ethics   (p. 25)
External suppliers   (p. 17)
Field service firms   (p. 19)
Frugging   (p. 30)
Full-service supplier firms   (p. 17)
Honomichl Global 25   (p. 17)
Internal reports system   (p. 10)
Internal supplier   (p. 15)
Limited-service supplier firms   (p. 19)
Market research   (p. 6)

Market segment specialists   (p. 20)
Marketing   (p. 2)
Marketing concept   (p. 5)
Marketing decision support system   (p. 10)
Marketing information system (MIS)   (p. 10)
Marketing intelligence system   (p. 10)
Marketing research   (p. 6)
Marketing Research and Intelligence Association (MRIA)   (p. 10)
Marketing research system   (p. 10)
Marketing strategy   (p. 5)
Online research services firms   (p. 18)
Phone banks   (p. 19)
Professional Marketing Research Society (PMRS)   (p. 10)
Request for proposals (RFP)   (p. 29)
Research integrity   (p. 26)
Research suppliers   (p. 15)

Sample design and distribution    (p. 20)    Strategic alliances    (p. 14)

Specialized research technique    Sugging    (p. 30)

firms    (p. 21)    Syndicated data service firms    (p. 18)

Standardized service firms    (p. 18)    *VoxPop*    (p. 30)

# Review Questions

**1.1** Explain the role of marketing research in the marketing process.

**1.2** Distinguish between market research and marketing research.

**2.1** Provide two examples of marketing research studies for each of the four types of marketing research activities.

**3.1** Explain why marketing research was not popular before the Industrial Revolution.

**3.2** Distinguish among full-service supplier firms, limited-service supplier firms, syndicated data service firms, standardized service firms, customized service firms, and online research services firms. Give situations where you would use each type.

**3.3** What advantages does a company enjoy through maintaining its own internal marketing research department?

**4.1** How is the MRIA an important organization for the marketing research industry in Canada? Be specific.

**5.1** Describe four main challenges the Canadian marketing research industry currently faces.

**5.2** Comment on the ethical nature of each practice presented in the following list. Give reasons for your answers.

   a.  A research company conducts a telephone survey and gathers information that it uses later to send a salesperson to the homes of potential buyers for the purpose of selling a product. It makes no attempt to sell the product over the telephone.

   b.  Would your response to the preceding case change if you found out that the information gathered during the telephone survey was used as part of a legitimate marketing research report?

   c.  A door-to-door salesperson finds that by telling people that he is conducting a survey, they are more likely to listen to his sales pitch.

   d.  Greenpeace sends out a direct-mail piece described as a survey and includes a request for donations as the last question.

   e.  In the appendix of the final report on a survey, the researcher lists the names of all respondents who took part in the survey and places an asterisk beside the names of those who indicated a willingness to be contacted by the client's sales personnel.

   f.  A list of randomly generated telephone numbers is drawn up in order to conduct a telephone survey.

   g.  A list of randomly generated email addresses is created using a "spambot" (an electronic "robot" that searches the internet looking for and retaining email addresses) in order to conduct a random online research project.

   h.  Students conducting a marketing research project randomly select email addresses of other students from the student directory in order to conduct their term project.

## Case 1.1

# Choosing a Marketing Research Company

Sue Evans is the Marketing Director of Jones & Jones, a large Canadian soft package goods manufacturer. One day last week, she was approached by Ajay Rupinder, Manager of Operations. It seems that one of his laboratory technicians has come up with a new formula that could be used for washing hair. Before investing money in developing this formula, Sue wanted to see if there was an opportunity in the marketplace for a new shampoo, and if there was, she wanted further to discover what the new product should look like to appeal to the target audience, find out what would be a good name for the product, discern what price the target market would be willing to pay for it, figure out the best strategy for distributing the new product, and develop a communications plan that would efficiently and effectively introduce the new product to the target audience.

Within the marketing department that Sue manages is a marketing research coordinator, Bob James. Although Bob is a highly trained marketing researcher, he has only two staff members reporting to him. Sue would like to involve him in her quest to develop this new product.

Sue has been the Marketing Director at Jones & Jones for 10 years and has managed the new product development process for other products in the company. The most successful new products were the ones developed on the basis of consumer research at every stage:

- Idea generation in stage 1
- Screening and evaluation in stage 2
- Business analysis in stage 3
- Development of the idea in stage 4
- Market testing in stage 5
- Commercialization in step 6

## Questions

1. How should Sue proceed with the new product development process? What role could Bob take in this?
2. Identify which marketing research studies would be most appropriate for each stage of the new product development process, giving reasons for your selections. Check Table 1.1, page 11.
3. Examine the Buying Research page of the MRIA website. Which marketing research companies do you think could help Sue reach her goal, and why?

## Case 1.2 YOUR INTEGRATED CASE

# Student Life E-Zine

Sarah Stripling, Anna Fulkerson, Wesley Addington, and Don Cooper were good friends who had met while students at City University. All four graduated with majors in marketing five years ago and found careers in the same city in which City University was located. Sarah worked for a large firm that published books and periodicals, including magazines targeted to special market segments ranging from seniors seeking vacation resorts to avid teenage tennis players. Wesley and

Anna had both taken elective courses in computer technology and internet marketing, and both worked for a local consulting firm that specialized in creating e-commerce systems for small and medium-sized firms. Don had started his career with the local newspaper in sales. He had a talent for writing and wrote short articles for the newspaper about new business openings. The editor of the paper recognized Don's talent and moved him into a writing position. Don had just been promoted to editor of the entertainment section of the newspaper. The four were still good friends and often socialized together.

One thing the four friends had in common was a desire to develop their own business. Each had dabbled with a few business ideas and shared them among the other three friends, but, thus far, no one had had an idea that succeeded in generating significant interest. Still, the four constantly talked about potential ways to serve the market's wants and needs. Two more years passed. Each person was successful in his or her line of business and had seven years of good experience in a chosen field.

As the four gathered for a Saturday afternoon of watching City U football and grilling burgers, Sarah suggested a new business idea. "Hey, guys. I've been thinking about a business idea for us. I've been watching the sales of our magazines that are targeted at special markets. Their growth rates surpass all our other publications. Also, our online subscriptions, our 'e-zines,' have been growing each year, especially in publications targeted at younger audiences."

"Yeah," Anna said, "I subscribe to three e-zines myself. I like them because I can read them wherever I have access to a computer, and if I want the actual hard copy, I can always print out an article. But what's your point, Sarah?"

With everyone's attention on her, Sarah replied, "I think there is a huge market that has been missed by all the publishers, the postsecondary student market."

Don argued, "Postsecondary students have their own student newspapers, and when they want more, they can read our newspaper."

Not deterred, Sarah said, "Of course they have their own student newspapers, but those newspapers offer stories and information mostly about what's happening at the college or university. I think postsecondary students want more than just knowing the dates for early withdrawal from classes. They want the news and entertainment stories targeted for postsecondary students. And Don, no disrespect for the newspaper—you guys do a great job—but how many of us read the local newspaper when we were in school?"

"I guess you're right, we sure didn't read the newspaper!" Don replied. As Don recalled his postsecondary school days his creative juices were beginning to flow. He asked, "What would postsecondary students today want to know about? They'd want to know the inside story about sports: teams, players, coaches . . . The major media cover the major sports events. They don't cover City U's championship games, and lots of students would like to watch the basketball games but don't go to the game . . . Also, they want more than what the mass media provides in terms of politics and foreign policy. Political stories are intriguing, but they aren't written for students in the major media. I didn't get interested in politics until I was older and read the paper daily. You could write the stories of politics with a different slant for postsecondary students. I would think the students want to know the basics of the political stories and they want visuals. They want to know more about the people themselves. A *People* magazine approach may appeal to them. They don't want the standard line they read in all the other publications." As Don talked aloud, his rising voice level clearly indicated that his excitement about the idea was growing.

Wesley, sensing everyone's attention turning to the new business idea, mentioned that he and Anna could easily put the concept online in the form of an e-zine targeted to postsecondary students. Sarah, now taking the burgers off the grill, set the plate down and said in a serious tone, "Listen up! We may have something here that uses all of our talents. I know the publishing

*(Continued)*

business, and Don has a flair for writing and creating features, and Anna and Wesley can handle the technical aspects needed to make an e-zine a reality. What should we do to follow up on this idea?"

The four friends have decided they may need the services of a research firm to help them with their business idea. Wesley and Anna are both concerned about exposing their business idea. They worry about telling a marketing research firm about their idea and the firm "selling" their idea to another party.

Don is much less concerned about this. He says, "Those firms are in the marketing research business. They're not magazine publishers and they don't want to be. At the newspaper, our local advertisers confide in us frequently about new business ventures they are considering. They know we're in the newspaper business and we aren't going to steal their business idea."

"That's not what I'm concerned about," says Anna. "What worries me is that the research firm we confide in may already have a big magazine publisher as a client. What's to keep them from sharing our idea with their long-time, big-money customer?"

Don agrees but suggests they ask the research firm what its policy is on this. "Let's confront them with it right up front and see what they say. If we're still concerned, we'll talk to other research firms until we find one we can trust."

Now the friends have to select the "right" research firm. Wesley says, "Let's call our old marketing research professor at City U, Dr. Smith. He can tell us where to start."

The next day, they call Dr. Smith. He tells them, "Well, you can take a look in the Yellow Pages for starters, but you may want to also go to some internet sites to learn more about the companies. I would recommend you take a look at the website for the MRIA. They maintain a directory of research firms. Take a look at their search screens and the types of research firms available. You should be able to make some decisions about the type of firm you want depending on the nature of your project."

They also asked Dr. Smith about the issue of the confidentiality of their business plans. Dr. Smith told them, "There is always a chance you will deal with someone who is unethical. This is just one of several reasons you should take some care in selecting the research firm. I recommend you take a look at some of the codes of ethics to which these firms should adhere.

"On the website for the MRIA, look for the code of ethics posted there. All of their members will be familiar with that code. Check it to see if it deals with confidentiality of client business plans. Good luck and let me know if I can help you in any other way."

## Questions

1. Do you think it was a good idea for the four friends to conduct marketing research? Why, or why not?
2. What questions regarding their business should they seek to answer through the services of a marketing research firm?
3. Go to the MRIA website. Can you find anything in the code of ethics that addresses the four friends' concern about the confidentiality of their business plans?
4. On the MRIA website, search for the list of types of marketing research firms. Take a look at the various services offered by firms in the research industry. Develop some criteria the four friends should use in selecting a research firm.

# Careers in Marketing Research

Sandra Wong received her BA diploma with a marketing major from the Southern Alberta Institute of Technology. While doing her diploma, Sandra discovered she had an interest in marketing research, and upon graduation, she searched for an entry level position in research.

Sandra accepted her first position as a Research Assistant with the Calgary Police Services. She helped plan and implement research studies. While employed, Sandra elected to take additional courses in marketing research at the Institute for Professional Development. In a short time, she received her Certified Marketing Research Professional designation.

After two years with the Calgary Police Services, Sandra accepted another position as marketing research analyst with the Alberta government. In this job, Sandra continued to develop her analytical skills using Exel and other software programs. She also became an active member in the Alberta chapter of the Marketing Research and Intelligence Association.

Currently, Sandra is a market research associate with the Toronto Dominion Bank in the Toronto head office. She is responsible for managing a staff of 15 research analysts who help her provide information to other team members in the marketing department.

Maybe you have been thinking about marketing research as a career choice. Information about possible options on this career path is provided in this appendix. Sources from which to pursue additional information about a career in the marketing research industry are also included.

## Marketing Research Industry Outlook

A good place to find information about job potential within a specific industry is the Government of Canada's "Working in Canada" website: **www.workingincanada.gc.ca**. In the search box, enter "marketing research." Click on "Business Development Officers and Marketing Researcher Consultants." Click continue after the statement "This describes my occupation." Choose a location, then select an area. A list of local job opportunities in this area will appear.

During the recent economic growth cycle, wages in research grew at an above-average rate. Hourly wages for this industry are above the national average for other industries. Also, average unemployment in this industry is less than half the average for all occupations. The percentage of self-employment (23%) in the research sector is higher than the 2004 national average.[40]

The largest number of jobs in the marketing research industry is available to the marketing research analyst. As shown in Figure 1.4, the median salary for this position is reported to be $41 554. The next largest number of jobs in the industry is available to the marketing research manager. Figure 1.4 shows the median salary

**Figure 1.4** Median Salary in the Marketing Research Industry, by Job

Source: PayScale Canada, www.payscale.com/research/CA/ Industry=Market_Research/Salary

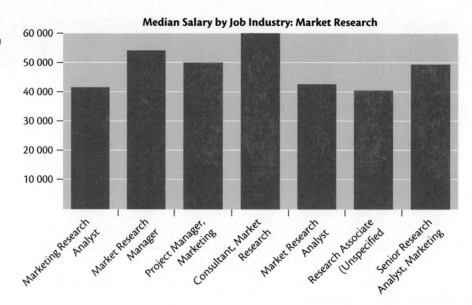

for this position is almost $54 000. Consultants in marketing research have a median salary of $60 000, while the reported median salary for directors of marketing research is $91 000.

As shown in Figure 1.5, the median salary for people with less than 1 year of experience is about $38 000, while the median salary of those with over 20 years of experience is reported to be around $86 000.[41]

Visit the MRIA website (**www.mria-arim.ca**) and click on "About MRIA." Click on "Membership" and then on "Tips for Practitioners Re/Entering Marketing Research." Here you will find some useful information on how to find a job in the industry.

**Figure 1.5** Median Salary in the Marketing Research Industry, by Years of Experience

Source: PayScale Canada, www.payscale.com/research/CA/ Industry=Market_Research/Salary/ by_Years_Experience

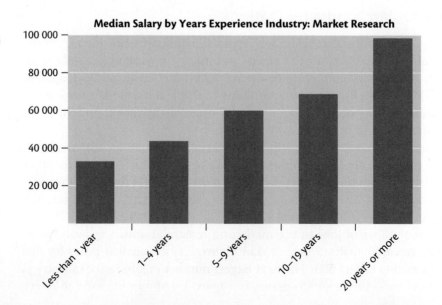

Click on "Research Buyers Guide" to see a listing of marketing research companies in Canada. Most of these sites have "Careers" links that you should explore.

To see a listing of current job offerings in the industry, go to **http://jobsearch.monster.ca.** In the "Search Jobs" bar, enter "marketing research." Click on any of the jobs listed to get a fuller description of the job as well as the job requirements.

Do you have what it takes? The traits associated with the most successful and effective marketing researchers include curiosity, high intelligence, creativity, self-discipline, good interpersonal and communication skills, the ability to work under strict time constraints, and proficiency in working with numbers. About 60% of all new researchers are women.[42] Although an undergraduate degree or diploma is required, there has been a trend toward requiring post-graduate degrees in some firms. Thus, an M.B.A. with a marketing major is one of the more common combinations for people employed in marketing research. Other possibilities are degrees in quantitative methods, sociology, or economics. Undergraduate training in mathematics or the physical sciences is a very suitable (and employable) background for anyone considering a career in marketing research.

# The Marketing Research Process

## LEARNING OBJECTIVES

1. Describe the 11 steps of the marketing research process.

2. Explain the importance of proper problem definition.

3. Identify two sources of research problems.

4. Describe two processes for defining the research problem and generating research objectives.

5. List the contents of a marketing research proposal.

## Bluetooth SIG Uses Marketing Research to Assess Brand Name Awareness

Though many people are familiar with the Bluetooth brand, many probably do not know that Bluetooth SIG does not make wireless headsets in sunglasses or wireless printers. Rather, the Bluetooth SIG coordinates the design of wireless technology among manufacturers of wireless-capable products, so wireless products from different manufacturers can "talk to each other." The Bluetooth Special Interest Group (SIG) is a privately held, not-for-profit trade association composed of over 8000 member companies that are leaders in the telecommunications, computing, automotive, music, apparel, industrial automation, and network product industries. The Bluetooth SIG has a small group of dedicated staff in Hong Kong, Sweden, and the USA, and the global headquarters are in Bellevue, Washington, USA.

The Bluetooth SIG staff is composed of a small team of marketing, engineering, and operations professionals. While they are responsible for coordinating the development of future versions of Bluetooth technology, they also are responsible for creating a high level of public awareness of the Bluetooth brand and maintaining a positive image toward the brand.

The Bluetooth brand is the primary asset of the Bluetooth SIG. Strong customer demand for licensed and qualified Bluetooth products allows the Bluetooth SIG to hold manufacturers to a high standard in qualifying their products, ensuring that licensed products work properly together.

While the SIG's member companies contribute to brand awareness by actively marketing their own products, the Bluetooth SIG's marketing team works to ensure that consumers are aware of the fact that Bluetooth products from different manufacturers work together. SIG marketing efforts highlight all of the possible uses for Bluetooth technology, from hands-free calling to wireless printing, and work to ensure that the Bluetooth brand continues to stand for reliability, interoperability, and ease of use.

As with any new technology, Bluetooth wireless technology experienced growing pains, and some early Bluetooth products worked together less reliably than manufacturers and users had hoped. Marketing research studies that measured brand awareness and image, along with diligent monitoring of print and online media, gave the SIG early warning of potential problem areas and allowed the marketing staff to adjust its communications strategy while the SIG's technical staff worked to address these initial shortcomings. These early efforts paid off, and today Bluetooth name recognition stands at well over 80 percent in many countries.

With the image of the Bluetooth headset now firmly ingrained in the popular culture, current SIG marketing initiatives focus on building awareness that Bluetooth technology means more than just talking hands-free. Other scenarios include printing photos wirelessly from a camera phone to a printer, streaming stereo music to wireless headphones, sharing files between a laptop and PDA, or connecting a laptop PC to the internet wirelessly using a mobile phone's data service.

The Bluetooth vignette illustrates how a company used marketing research to recognize they had a problem and to ensure the problem was corrected in the eyes of consumers.

Bluetooth SIG hired Millward Brown, a global research company, to design and implement the marketing research. In proceeding with the marketing research, Millward Brown undertook steps that make up the marketing research process. The different roles and responsibilities between Bluetooth SIG and Millward Brown were respected as they went through this process.

Marketing research can take place internally, as an in-house marketing research group or department, or externally, as in the Bluetooth example. In the former case, the marketing manager is the "client" to the researcher. In the opening vignette, Bluetooth SIG is the client. This chapter examines the steps of the marketing research process and discusses the respective roles between the "client" and the marketing researcher as they undertake this process.

## The Marketing Research Process

### An 11-Step Process

The 11 **steps in the marketing research process** are shown in Figure 2.1. The steps are: (1) establishing the need for marketing research, (2) defining the problem, (3) establishing research objectives, (4) determining research design, (5) identifying information types and sources, (6) determining methods of accessing data, (7) designing data collection forms, (8) determining the sample plan and size, (9) collecting data, (10) analyzing data, and (11) preparing and presenting the final research report. We will discuss each of these steps in the following para-

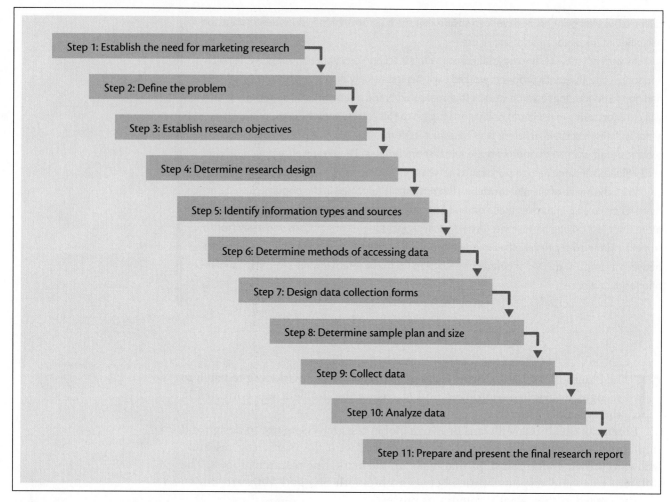

**Figure 2.1** 11 Steps in the Marketing Research Process

graphs, but first it is important to understand there are some caveats associated with using a step-by-step approach to understanding the process of marketing research.

In this text, the marketing research process comprises 11 steps. Others may present the process in fewer steps or even more steps. There is nothing sacred about the 11 steps. Marketing research could be presented as three steps—defining the problem, collecting and analyzing data, and presenting the results—but this over-simplifies the research process. Or, marketing research could be presented as 20-plus steps, but this would provide more detail than is needed. The 11 steps are explicit enough without being overly detailed.

Not all studies follow all 11 steps. Sometimes, for example, a review of secondary research alone may allow the researcher to achieve the research objectives. The 11 steps assume that the research process examines secondary data and continues on to collect primary data.

Most research projects do not follow an orderly, step-by-step process. Sometimes, after beginning to gather data, it may be evident that the research objectives should be changed. Researchers do not move, robotlike, from one step to the next. Rather, as they move through the process, they make decisions as to how to proceed in the future. This may involve going back and revisiting a previous step.

The 11 steps are very useful for understanding the marketing research process. In the opening vignette, the researchers benefit greatly by knowing the steps of the research process. Knowing the steps in the process helps researchers design a better research project for their client. At the beginning of each chapter, a list of the 11 steps is provided, and "where we are" on the list is highlighted, depending on the topics covered in the chapter.

## Step 1: Establish the Need for Marketing Research

The need for marketing research arises when managers must make decisions and they have inadequate information. Not all decisions will require marketing research. Research takes time and costs money. Managers must weigh the value possibly derived from conducting marketing research and having the information at hand against the cost of obtaining that information. Fortunately, most situations do not require research, for if they did, managers would be mired down in research instead of making timely decisions.

## Step 2: Define the Problem

If it is decided to conduct marketing research, the second step is to define the problem. This is the most important step, because if the problem is incorrectly defined, all else is wasted effort. The problem could be specific and narrowly defined or very general. Examples of specific problems are: "Which of three proposed television advertisements will generate the highest level of sales of our running shoes? What message should be used in our promotions to gain sales of our running shoes?" Examples of general problems are: "What should be our overall marketing strategy for our running shoes? Should we be in the running shoe business?" Problems stem from two primary sources: gaps between what is *supposed* to happen and what *did* happen and gaps between what *did* happen and what *could* be happening.

## Step 3: Establish Research Objectives

**Research objectives** state what the researcher must do in order to carry out the research and solve the manager's problem. Figure 2.2 illustrates this relationship between the manager's problem and the researcher's establishment of objectives. For example, if the problem is specifically stated as "What product improvements could be made to gain sales of our running shoes?", then a research objective would be to describe the qualities people look for in running shoes. To collect descriptive information, the researcher would design a survey that asks questions of people who buy running shoes. The questions would include qualities they look for in running shoes, occasions for wearing running shoes, length of time they would wear the running shoes, the importance of brand of running shoe, and so on. The information collected would tell the manager which feature of his running shoes he should focus on developing new versions of the running shoes.

**Where We Are**
1. Establish the need for marketing research
2. Define the problem
3. Establish research objectives
4. Determine research design
5. Identify information types and sources
6. Determine methods of accessing data
7. Design data collection forms
8. Determine sample plan and size
9. Collect data
10. Analyze data
11. Prepare and present the final research report

**Figure 2.2** Relationship between Marketing Manager's Problem and Marketing Researcher's Objectives

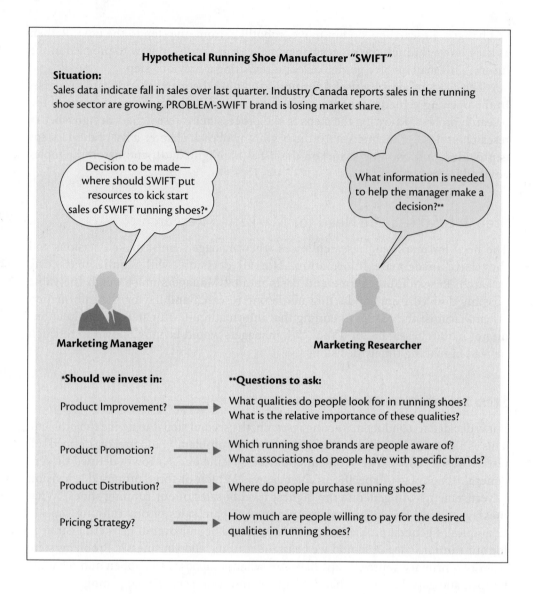

## Step 4: Determine Research Design

*Research design* is the research approach undertaken to meet the research objectives. There are three widely recognized research designs: exploratory, descriptive, and causal designs. Exploratory research, as the name implies, is a form of casual, informal research that is undertaken to learn more about the research problem, learn terms and definitions, or identify research priorities. Going to the library and looking for background information on a topic is an example of exploratory research. Descriptive research describes the phenomena of interest. A marketing executive who wants to know what type of people buy the company's brand wants a study *describing* the demographic profile of heavy users of the company brand. Many surveys are undertaken to describe important aspects of marketing for a company: level of awareness of advertising, intentions to buy a new product, satisfaction level with service, and so on. The last type of research design is causal research. Causal studies attempt to uncover what factor or factors *cause* some event. Will a change in the package size of our detergent cause a change in sales? Causal studies are achieved from a class of studies called *experiments*.

## Step 5: Identify Information Types and Sources

Since research provides information to help solve problems, researchers must identify the type and sources of information they will use in step 5. There are two types of information: primary (information collected specifically for the problem at hand) and secondary (information already collected).

Secondary information should always be sought first, since it is much cheaper and faster to collect than primary information. A company franchising car washes, for example, may use secondary data to make decisions as to where to locate new car washes based on the number of vehicles per square kilometre and the number of existing car washes in different market areas. This is information that has been collected and is available in published sources for a small fee. Sometimes research companies collect information and make it available to all those wishing to pay a subscription to get the information. Neilsen Media Research's TV ratings, which report the numbers of persons who watch different TV programs, are an example of this type of data.

However, sometimes secondary data are inadequate. What if our car-wash franchiser wanted to know how car owners in Halifax, Nova Scotia, would respond to a one-price ticket good for as many car washes as needed in a year? This information is not available. Primary data must be collected specifically for this problem.

## Step 6: Determine Methods of Accessing Data

Primary data are acquired through a variety of methods. While secondary data are relatively easy to collect, gathering primary data is much more complex. Primary data can be collected by exploring information using qualitative methods such as conducting focus groups, observing consumer behaviour, or monitoring online forums and blogs. Qualitative measures are extremely useful in exploring a research problem, and are less expensive than survey methods. Qualitative measures cannot, however, describe the population from which the sample was derived; nor can the cause of observed behaviour be determined since the sample is not statistically representative of the population.

Primary data can also be collected through quantitative methods that examine statistically representative samples. Information is collected using such techniques as face-to-face interviewing, telephone interviewing, and online panels. With the growth of technology, and consumer mistrust of telemarketing, more and more research is conducted online.

## Step 7: Design Data Collection Forms

Step 7 is designing the form used to gather the data. If researchers communicate with respondents (ask them questions), the form is called a *questionnaire*. If researchers observe respondents, the form is called an *observation form*. In either case, great care must be given to designing the form properly. Care must be taken to ensure that the questions asked can generate answers that satisfy the research objectives and that can therefore be used to solve the problem. The questions must be worded properly so that they are clear and unbiased. Care must also be taken to design the questionnaire so as to reduce refusals to answer questions and to get as much information as desired from respondents. Given the care required, data collection forms should not be developed *until* steps 1 to 6 are completed.

### Step 8: Determine Sample Plan and Size

Typically, marketing research studies are undertaken to learn about populations by taking a sample of that population. A population consists of the entire group that the researcher wishes to know about based upon information provided by the sample data. A population could be "all department stores within the greater Vancover area" or it could be "college students enrolled in the School of Business at XYZ College." Populations should be defined by the research objectives. One firm, for example, defines its survey population as individuals between 17 and 70 years old who make buying decisions for the household regarding technology products.

A sample is a subset of the population. A sample frame is a list of the population elements or units. Sample plans describe how each sample element, or unit, is to be drawn from the total population. The objectives of the research as well as the sample frame determine which sample plan is to be used. The type of sample plan used determines whether or not the sample is representative of the population. The size of the sample determines how accurately the sample results reflect values in the population. Marketing Research in Action 2.1 profiles a company that provides sampling solutions.

## MARKETING RESEARCH IN ACTION 2.1
## Survey Sampling International Solves Sampling Problems for Marketing Researchers

Survey Sampling International (SSI) is the premier global provider of sampling solutions for survey research. SSI reaches respondents in 72 countries via Internet, telephone, and mobile/wireless. Client services include questionnaire design consultation, programming and hosting, and data processing.

SSI serves more than 2000 clients, including 48 of the top 50 research organizations. Founded in 1977, SSI has an international staff of more than 400 people representing 50 countries and 36 languages. The company has offices in Beijing, Frankfurt, London, Los Angeles, Madrid, Mexico City, Paris, Rotterdam, Seoul, Shanghai, Shelton (Connecticut), Singapore, Stockholm, Sydney, Timisoara

(Romania), Tokyo, and Toronto, with additional representatives in Hong Kong. For more information, visit **www. surveysampling.com**. By permission.

## Step 9: Collect Data

Errors in collecting data may be attributed to fieldworkers or to respondents, and they may be either intentional or unintentional. What is important is that the researcher knows the sources of these errors and uses controls to minimize them. For example, fieldworkers, those collecting the data, may fabricate data they report. Researchers minimize this from happening by undertaking a control referred to as "validation." Validation means that 10% (the industry standard) of all respondents in a marketing research study are randomly selected, recontacted, and asked if they indeed took part in a research study.

## Step 10: Analyze Data

Marketing researchers transfer data from data collection forms to software packages that help them analyze the data. The objective of data analysis is to use tools to interpret the information collected so that the research objectives can be met. If data are qualitative, analysis can involve monitoring word or concept mentions. For example, electronic search engines such as Google Alerts can be used to analyze social media data for brand mentions. Data from focus groups are in the form of transcribed taped sessions. These tapes are examined for underlying trends. If data are quantitative, analysis usually involves searching for statistical patterns to describe and perhaps test hypotheses about consumers. For example, if the research objective is to see if there are differences in intention to purchase a new product depending on income level, then data analysis on the sample data would determine if there is a relationship between the two variables (intent to purchase and income level) and if any differences found in the sample actually exist in the population from which the sample came. This text comes with XL Data Analyst™, a software program that analyzes data, including simple descriptive analysis, hypothesis testing, determining relationships among variables, and predicting consumer behaviour.

## Step 11: Prepare and Present the Final Research Report

The last step in the research process is preparing and presenting the marketing research report. The report is very important because it is often the client's only record of the research project. In most cases, marketing research firms prepare a written research report and make an oral presentation to the client and staff. Marketing researchers follow a fairly standard report-writing format. Care must be taken to write clearly and to present data accurately using the most appropriate figures and tables.

# Establishing the Need for Marketing Research

## When Is Marketing Research Not Needed?

### The Information Is Already Available

Managers make many decisions. Many of these are routine and the manager has the experience to make a decision without any additional information. When decisions do require additional information, the manager may use the internal reports system, the marketing intelligence system, or the decision support system. All of these information systems are ongoing sources of information. Marketing managers can quickly and inexpensively access this information. Consider the following examples: A manager at Research In Motion (RIM) wants to make a decision regarding the need to spend more dollars on R&D technology. She consults the marketing intelligence system to see what new technology breakthroughs have been brought to market by RIM's competitors. A manager at Wampole, the Canadian nutrition and herbal product manufacturer, needs to make a decision regarding expansion of the sales force. He consults the company's decision support system to do an analysis of which colleges and universities produced the salespeople who most consistently meet or exceed their sales quota so that he can recruit from these institutions. Marketing Research in Action 2.2 discusses further examples. But when information is *not* available, the manager should consider conducting marketing research.

### The Timing Is Wrong to Conduct Marketing Research

Time often plays a critical role in decision making, and that is true with marketing research as well. It may be that there is not enough time to conduct marketing research and remain competitive in a fast-moving market. For example, the telephone mobile service industry is highly competitive. Rogers introduces a new low-priced data package and the number of new customers soars. The company's market share is gained at the expense of Telus and Bell. Managers at Telus and Bell do not have time to conduct research on launching competitive data packages to win back their customers. Instead, they need to rely on internal knowledge and experience to come up with data packages that bring back customers lost to Rogers.

Time may also be a factor for products that are nearing the end of their life cycle. When products have been around for many years and are reaching the decline stage of their life cycle, it may be too late for research to produce valuable results.

### Funds Are Not Available for Marketing Research

Small firms or firms that are having cash flow problems may not conduct marketing research simply because they cannot afford it. Research, if conducted properly, can be expensive. A study gathering primary data for a representative sample can cost hundreds of thousands of dollars. In many cases the total cost of the research project is not calculated. Conducting the research is one cost, but firms must also consider what it may cost to *implement* the research recommendations. The owner of a pizza restaurant saved money for a research project but was then unable to fund the resulting recommendations (that the restaurant offer drive-through and delivery service). In this case, the research money was wasted.

### Costs Outweigh the Value of Marketing Research

Managers should always consider the cost of research and the value they expect to receive from conducting the research. While costs of doing research are readily estimated, it is much more difficult to estimate the value research is likely to add. As an example, consider a decision about how best to package a new brand of toothpaste. The toothpaste must sit on a shelf among many other brands, a number of which have packaging that is easily recognized by brand-loyal customers. Chances are that consumers quickly scanning the toothpaste section will see their favourite brand and make the purchase without even being aware of the existence of the new brand. If research can identify a package design that will cause greater attention and

## MARKETING RESEARCH IN ACTION 2.2
## Do Not Conduct Research If the Information Is Already Available

Marketing researchers John Goodman and David Beinhacker point out that in many cases companies execute surveys and collect data when they already have the information they need and that clients can save money by not doing research to measure variables that are known to be stable and when performance is high. Goodman and Beinhacker also state that firms should not conduct marketing research when internal metrics are already available.

In one financial services firm, management had commissioned research to measure customer satisfaction and quality. Over a period of time, the company had developed and was administering 80 different surveys covering all of the possible customer transactions in the firm. However, upon examination, data showed that in about 30 of the 80 transactions, customer expectations were being met from 98% to 99.5% of the time. Should the company be using marketing research to measure transactions in which it is consistently near-perfect? Goodman and Beinhacker concluded that relying on a traditional complaint system would be a wiser method to monitor these transactions.

Goodman and Beinhacker also tell the story of a major home repair services company that was spending large amounts on surveying customers to determine whether the repair technicians showed up on time. However, the company's call centre already had data that tracked how many times customers were calling to complain about technicians who either were late or did not show up at all. For a high-involvement event like having someone in one's home, the authors reported that 90% of customers will call when the technician is late. So, they ask, why conduct marketing research to collect data when you already have the information needed to make the decision? In another example, a bank was surveying customers about their satisfaction with the readiness of ATMs, since

all ATMs must have some "down time" for maintenance, repair, and daily reloading of cash. But the bank already had internal metrics showing how often the ATMs were down, with data accurate to four decimal places.

Goodman and Beinhacker recommend that if 8 of 10 transactions are being executed with few or no errors, research should not be conducted on all 10 transaction types. The focus should be on those that are done poorly. For example, Neiman Marcus Direct, the U.S. retail giant, has a good reputation for handling telephone customer service. However, management identified two types of transactions that caused problems. Therefore, surveys of customers focus on these two transactions, enabling Neiman to continuously monitor and improve these trouble spots. Firms should also make certain they do not already have the data they need before they undertake to collect more of the same. Goodman and Beinhacker point out that they find that many departments operate in silos; other departments in the same company already have internal metrics that will provide the information needed to make an informed decision.

awareness of the brand on the shelf, sales will go up. This gives value to the research. Managers must try to estimate what impact there will be on sales if 2 out of 10 shoppers are aware of the brand instead of 1 out of 20. Though placing a dollar figure on value is difficult, value *can* be estimated and a more informed decision may be made as to whether or not marketing research is justified. Some managers fail to compare research cost with its value, which is a mistake.[1]

Research is more likely to have greater value in the following situations: It helps clarify problems or opportunities; it identifies changes occurring in the marketplace among consumers or competitors; it clearly identifies the best alternative to pursue among a set of proposed alternatives; it helps a brand establish a competitive advantage.[2] Once a decision is made that research is needed, managers (and researchers) must properly define the problem and the research objectives.

## The Impact of Online Research and Determining the Need to Conduct Marketing Research

A primary advantage of online research is speed. Managers today use an online research company to obtain information in a matter of days, whereas traditional research requires weeks or even months to gather the information. Online research can lead to more decisions to use research in situations where timing ruled out research in the past. Managers at Molson, for example, may want to introduce a new low-calorie beer. By using online research, they would be able, during the short time it would take to develop the proper formula and tool up for production, to quickly test several marketing-mix decisions related to the new beer before introducing it to the market. They could test brand names, package designs, effectiveness of new promotional materials, and the like.

Another favourable point to be made about online research is that, in many circumstances, it is less costly than traditional research. Savings in time and money mean managers can look to online marketing research projects when, in the past, they may have felt traditional research took too much time or did not offer enough value for the cost.

# Define the Problem

## The Importance of Properly Defining the Problem

Sometimes problems are easy to define; for example, "What are the media habits of the heavy users of our brand?" Sometimes problems are very difficult to define; for example, "Our sales are increasing but our market share is going down. Is there a problem and, if so, what is it?" Regardless of how difficult or easy it is to define the problem, properly defining the problem is *the* most important step in the marketing research process. If the wrong problem is defined, *everything* that follows in the research process is wrong! It does not matter if data are properly collected, analyzed, and reported if the research process addresses the *wrong* problem. Great care must be exercised in properly defining the problem.

### How Can We Beat Burger King?

McDonald's conducted marketing research for a new burger, the McDonald's Arch DeLuxe. The burger, targeted to adults, received a less-than-hoped-for result even though McDonald's spent large sums of money on marketing research. The analysis points to "improper problem definition." McDonald's management was eager to match the Burger King Deluxe burger. All research was focused on measuring consumer preferences for different sizes and tastes of hamburgers. McDonald's researchers would have been better off by not defining the problem as "How can we beat Burger King?" but, instead, focusing on *adult* fast-food customers' preferences, including nutritional content. They may have produced a product that was better tasting than the Burger King product, but they did not come up with a product that appealed to adults. Improperly defining the problem results in lost time and money.[3]

### How Can We Win a Taste Test?

Coke was continually losing in taste tests against Pepsi, a cola with a sweeter taste than Coke. Though Coke had significant market share and an established brand name, its executives defined their problem as not having a product as tasty as that of their major competitor. This led to over four years of research in which they developed a sweet-tasting cola. The new flavoured beverage beat the competitor's cola in taste test after taste test. Thinking they had solved the "taste test problem," Coke management dropped its old product and introduced the new, sweeter-tasting cola. To their surprise, sales plummeted and consumers, missing their old drink, protested by the thousands. Many believe Coke did not define the problem correctly. They defined the problem as "How can we beat the competitor in taste tests?" instead of "How can we gain market share against our competitors?" They already had a sizeable share of the market with their non-sweet-flavoured cola. When they stopped producing the old drink, their customers only had the sweet-flavoured beverage to buy, which they did not want; they had already shunned sweeter-tasting Pepsi in favour of Coke. Losing the taste tests led Coke to improperly define the problem; they wanted to beat their competitors in taste tests. They did, but by dropping their existing product in favour of the new "better-tasting" cola, they lost their own customers. With 20/20 hindsight, they should have kept their existing Coke product and introduced a new brand to compete for the market preferring a sweeter cola. Eventually they did re-introduce the old cola as Coke Classic and they kept the new, sweeter version. By not focusing research on the right problem, management learned a hard lesson and wasted much time and millions of dollars.[4]

These examples illustrate the importance of properly defining the problem. Not only does improper problem definition waste valuable resources such as time and money, it also prevents proper marketing research information from setting management on the right track sooner and as we saw in the case of Coke, from losing brand-loyal customers.

Lawrence D. Gibson, a recognized marketing research authority says, "A problem well defined is a problem half solved." It is an old but still valid adage. How a problem is defined sets the direction for the entire project. A good definition is necessary if marketing research is to contribute to the solution of the problem. A bad definition dooms the entire project from the start and guarantees that subsequent marketing and marketing research efforts will prove useless. Nothing researchers can do has much leverage on profit as helping marketing define the right problem."[5]

## Two Sources of Problems

Problems may come from two different sources. A **problem** exists when there is a gap between what was *supposed* to happen and what *did* happen.[6] Failure to meet an objective, for example, creates a gap between what was *supposed* to happen and what actually *did* happen. This situation is what we normally think of when we use the term *problem*. The manager must now determine what course of action to take in order to close the gap between the objective and actual performance. The second type of problem is not often immediately recognized as a "problem." This second type of problem, called an **opportunity**, occurs when there is a gap between what *did* happen and what *could have* happened. This is an opportunity because the situation represents a favourable circumstance or chance for progress or advancement.[7] Put another way, a **marketing opportunity** is defined as an area of potential interest in which a company can perform profitably.[8] For example, if running shoe sales were $X but *could have been* $Y, a marketing opportunity exists. Managers still have a problem in determining how to take advantage of the opportunity, or even whether the company should pursue it.

## Recognizing the Problem

Good managers will be aware of problems or they will soon cease to hold management positions. For managers to recognize a problem, they must be knowledgeable of objectives and actual performance. They should be setting objectives and have a control system in place to monitor performance. Many experienced managers would agree that what is worse than discovering you have a problem is continuing to operate in ignorance of the problem. Unless managers have a control system, they will not likely identify problems arising from failure to meet objectives. Managers must also be aware of opportunities, and unless they have a system for monitoring opportunities, sometimes referred to as a process of **opportunity identification**, it is not likely they will identify these problems.[9] Table 2.1 shows the sources of problems and the systems needed to recognize them.

**Table 2.1** Problem Recognition

| Sources of Problems | Examples | System Required in Order to Recognize Gap |
|---|---|---|
| **Failure to Meet Objectives** | | |
| Gap between what was *supposed* to happen and what *did* happen | Sales calls below target number<br>Sales volume below quota.<br>Return on investment (ROI) below goal | Control system based on setting objectives and evaluating them against actual performance |
| **Opportunities** | | |
| Gap between what *did* happen and what *could* happen. (Should we take advantage of opportunities, and how?) | Basic research opens up new technology in data transmission speed.<br>New demographic analysis shows rapid increases in population and incomes in markets where a firm has no current distribution. | System for identification of opportunities |

Some marketing management problems come from a failure to meet objectives, and other problems stem from determining if and how to take advantage of opportunities. In either case, managers must select the proper course of action from several alternatives.

## The Role of Symptoms in Problem Recognition

The classic statement "We have a problem . . . we are losing money" illustrates how researchers and managers often confuse symptoms with problems. The problem is not that "we are losing money." This is the symptom. Rather, the problem may be found among all those factors that *cause* a company to make (or lose) money, and the manager, with help from the researcher, must identify all those possible causes in order to find the right problem or problems.

**Symptoms** are changes in the level of some key monitor that measures the achievement of an objective; for example, our measure of customer satisfaction has fallen 10% in each of the last two months. In this case, the role of the symptom is to alert management to a problem; there is a gap between what should be happening and what is happening. A symptom may also be a perceived change in the behaviour of some market factor that implies an emerging opportunity. A pharmaceutical company executive sees a demographic forecast that the number of teenagers will increase dramatically over the next 10 years. This may be symptomatic of an opportunity to create new drugs designed for teen problems such as acne or teenage weight problems. Note that symptoms may be *negative* but still bring about opportunities; for example, say that the forecast for teens is that their numbers will *shrink* in the next 10 years. Should the company shift R&D from developing new drugs for teens to the growing aging–baby boomer market? Both types of symptoms should be identified by either the control system (objectives/ monitoring) or the system in place for opportunity identification. The key lesson is that symptoms are not problems; symptoms should be used to alert managers to recognize problems.

## Types of Problems

Not all problems are the same. Sources of problems may differ: Some arise through recognition of a failure to meet an objective, and others from a recognition of an opportunity. Problems can also be described in terms of being specific or general. Some problems are very specific: The director of marketing research at McCain Foods may want to know "What is the best package design to create awareness and interest in our frozen food line?" Sometimes the problem can be very general: "Should we change our entire marketing plan?" "Should we even be in the frozen food business?" Clearly, these two extremes illustrate there are wide differences in the types of problems confronting managers. Generally, the more specific the problem, the easier the marketing researcher's task. When a problem is defined very narrowly and in specific terms by management, it is much easier for the researcher to transform this type of problem into well-defined and specific research objectives. The researcher has a much more challenging task when presented by management with a vague, general problem.

## The Role of the Researcher in Problem Definition

Regardless of the type of problem, the researcher has an obligation to help managers ensure they are defining the problem correctly. This is particularly true when the researcher is called in by the manager who already has the problem defined in very specific terms. The manager who thinks that the problem is coming up with a better cookie recipe may be startled to learn that total cookie sales have been falling for the last five years. Perhaps the researcher should ask the manager the question "Are you sure you should be in the baked cookie business?" Problem definition expert Lawrence Gibson wrote, "Researchers must resist the temptation to 'go along' with the first definition suggested. They should take the time to conduct their own investigation and to develop and consider alternative definitions."[10] This additional investigation may take the form of a situation analysis. A **situation analysis** is a form of preliminary research undertaken to gather background information and gather data pertinent to the problem area.

The researcher should be interested in the long-term welfare of the client. Because researchers are accustomed to dealing with problem definition, they should help managers define the problem accurately. By doing so, their research should add real value to the client's bottom line, helping to ensure the long-term relationship.

## Hurdles to Problem Definition

Attempts to properly define the problem may be hampered by two factors: (1) Managers may fail to communicate and interact closely with researchers, and (2) the differences between researchers and managers may limit communication.

### Failure to Communicate for Problem Definition Situations

Managers sometimes fail to recognize that they need to change their normal behaviour in order to properly define the problem. Managers are accustomed to dealing with outside suppliers efficiently. Suppliers are asked to present their products or services, they are evaluated against established purchasing criteria, and a decision is made. A minimum of interaction and involvement is required to make most purchasing decisions, and this is viewed as desirable; it leads to accomplishing business activities efficiently. Unfortunately, this behaviour is not desirable when dealing with an external supplier of marketing research. To find possible causes of for changing symptoms or to identify and determine the likelihood of success of opportunities requires in-depth communications between marketing managers and marketing researchers over an extended period of time. Often, to be effective, this process is slow and tedious. Managers often are unaware of the need to communicate and this causes problems in identifying the real problem. Veteran researchers are well aware of this situation, and it is up to them to properly inform management of their expected role and the importance of this initial step in the research process.

### Differences between Managers and Researchers

Marketing managers and marketing researchers see the world differently because they have different jobs to perform and their backgrounds differ markedly. For example, managers possess line positions; researchers are in staff positions. Managers are responsible for generating profits; researchers are responsible for generating information. Managers historically have been generalists; and researchers have been technical specialists. These differences hinder communications between the two parties at a time when in-depth, continuous communications and trust are required. However, these differences have improved over the years and are growing smaller. The reason is that college students today, tomorrow's managers, are in a better position to have greater appreciation for the technical side of marketing research. Many of the analyses using XL Data Analyst™, for example, were once available only to computer specialists who could write the code required to run these analyses on mainframe computers. Today, this knowledge is available to all.

## The Role of ITBs and RFPs

**ITBs** are "**invitations to bid**" and **RFPs** are "**requests for proposals.**" Companies use these documents to alert research firms that they would like to receive bids or proposals to conduct research to solve a particular problem. When a company uses an ITB or RFB, it has already defined the problem and, in some cases, the research objectives. At the very least, management has thought through many of the issues revolving around defining the problem. This means that much of the dialogue normally necessary between researchers and managers may be avoided. For example, managers in a firm decide they need to assess customer satisfaction in a way that will allow them to prescribe remedial actions. The problem has been defined. They submit an ITB or RFP to several research firms, who now bid on doing the necessary research.

Although RFPs and ITBs are all different, they contain some common elements. Commonly found sections are:

- *Introduction.* Identification of the company or organization that originates the RFP, with background information about the company.
- *Scope of Proposal.* Description of the basic problem at hand.
- *Deliverables.* Specification of the tasks to be undertaken and products to be produced and delivered to the company soliciting the proposal or bid. For example, the deliverable may be "a survey of 1000 representative recent users of the company's services, described in a report with text, tabulations, figures, and relevant statistical analyses."

---

## ONLINE APPLICATION 2.1
## Look at Real-Life Requests for Research

Take a look at real "invitations to bid" (ITBs) or "requests for proposals" (RFPs) by going to a search engine such as google.ca or yahoo.ca. Check only Canadian sites to find examples from Canada.

Choose one RFP and one ITB that you find interesting.

1. Identify the introduction, scope, evaluation criteria, deadline, and bidding specifics. Disregarding the dif-

ference in subject matter, describe any differences you see in the two approaches.

2. Focusing on one of the documents, identify the research problem. Do you feel that research is warranted? Explain your answer.

- *Evaluation Criteria.* The criteria or standards that will be used to judge the proposals, often set up as a point system in which the proposal is awarded a number of points for each area based on the quality of the work that is proposed.
- *Deadline.* The date by which the deliverables must be delivered.
- *Bidding Specifics.* Necessary items such as the due date for the proposal or bid, specific information required about the bidding company, proposal length and necessary elements (such as sample questions that may appear on the questionnaire), intended subcontract work, payment schedule, contact individual within the origination company, and so on.

ITBs and RFPs are sensitive issues in terms of appropriate ethical behaviour. A firm that sends out phony ITBs (or RFPs) simply to get ideas for research is practising highly unethical behaviour.

## A Process for Defining the Problem and Establishing the Research Objectives

There is no universally accepted, step-by-step approach used by marketing researchers to define the problem and establish research objectives. In fact, Lawrence D. Gibson, a recognized authority on defining the problem, wrote that "defining problems accurately is more an art than science."[11] Although there are a number of problem-solving techniques that individual managers can use,[12] a process that works for the manager–researcher situation is described in Figure 2.3. Recall that there are *two* sources of problems: one when there is a failure to meet an objective and the other when there is an opportunity. The process for defining these two problems is different, though they both end up determining research objectives. The major difference is that, for opportunities, the firm must do research to determine the attractiveness and probability of success of any opportunity. This process Kotler refers to is **market opportunity analysis (MOA).**[13] After a company conducts an MOA it now has a problem choosing from among several alternative opportunities or evaluating different alternative means to take advantage of the opportunity selected. It is at this point that the two types of problems are similar, and therefore we are going to discuss only the process involved when there is a failure to meet an objective. The problem definition process results in definitions of the research objectives.

### Assess the Background and the Manager's Situation

At this stage, the researcher has considerable homework to do after the first meeting with the manager. The researcher must conduct some exploratory research to learn about the industry, the company, and its competitors and markets. The researcher should also find out the manager's unique situation, including constraints he or she is operating under, and what particular objective he or she is trying to achieve. Researchers should not accept a manager's stated problem without question. By ensuring the proper problem is being addressed, researchers add value to the research activity.

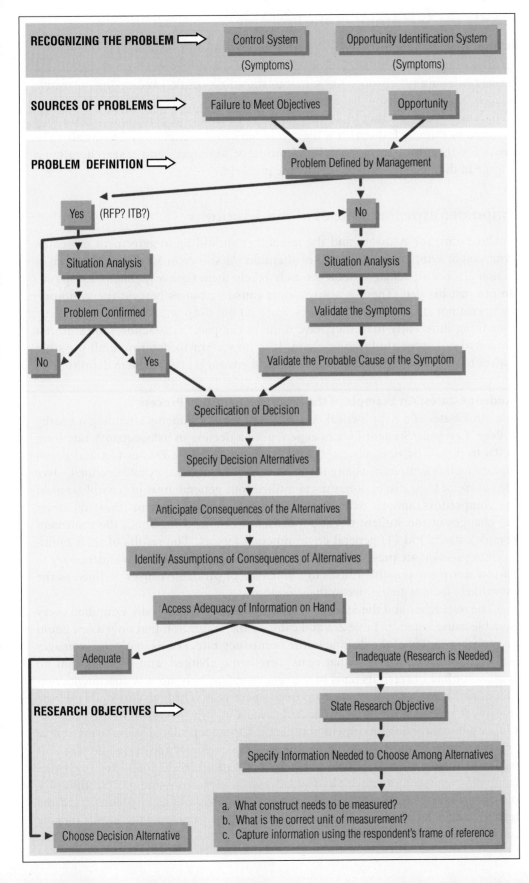

**Figure 2.3** Defining the Problem and Determining the Research Objectives: Assuming the Use of Marketing Rresearch

## Clarify the Symptoms of the Problem

Without symptoms, problem definition is virtually impossible. The researcher needs to understand what control system is in place. Companies vary greatly in terms of defining their objectives, monitoring their results, and taking corrective action. Does the company have an adequate control system? Is the manager alert to symptoms? What are they? Are they accurate measures of performance? Are they reported in a timely fashion? It is the researcher's role to explore and to question, in order for the problem to be defined properly. Managers and researchers must engage in diologue to properly define the problem.

## Pinpoint Suspected Causes of the Symptom

At this point, the manager and the researcher should be in agreement on which symptom or symptoms are in need of attention. As shown in Marketing Research in Action 2.3, not all managers want research to help them resolve problems. Symptoms do not just happen. There is always some **cause** or causes beyond the symptom. Profits do not go down by themselves. Sales do not drop without customers doing something differently than they have done in the past. Satisfaction scores do not drop without some underlying cause. It is important to determine all **possible causes** to correctly identify the real cause and ensure proper problem definition.

### Student Estates: An Example of the Problem Definition Process

Student Estates is a hypothetical complex that targets students attending a nearby college. Last year, Student Estates experienced a decline in its occupancy rate from 100% to 80%. The researcher and the manager of Student Estates met and began discussing this symptom, asking themselves why the occupancy rate declined. Over the course of their discussion, they identified four general areas of possible causes: (1) competitors' actions, which had drawn prospective student residents away; (2) changes in the student target population; (3) something about the apartment complex itself; and (4) general environmental factors. The results of their brainstorming session are presented in Table 2.2. Given this long list, it was necessary to narrow down the possible causes to a small set of **probable causes**, defined as the most likely factors giving rise to the symptom.

The researcher and the Student Estates manager systematically examined every possible cause listed in Table 2.2 and came to the realization that only a few could be probable causes of the decline in the occupancy rate. For example, the manager was vigilant in monitoring what rents were being charged, and he knew that no competitor had lowered its rents in the past year. Similarly, no new apartment complexes had been built or opened up in the past year. Through this dialogue, the researcher and the Student Estates manager narrowed the list down to two probable causes: (1) competing apartment complexes had added digital cable television in every apartment, and (2) some apartment complexes had added on-site workout facilities. With a little more background investigation, it was found that only one competing apartment complex had added a workout facility, and most of the complexes, including Student Estates, did not have any workout facility. Thus, the cable television deficiency of Student Estates was narrowed down as the most probable cause for its occupancy decline.

**Table 2.2** Possible Causes
for Student Estates
Occupancy Rate Decline

### Competitors' Actions

- Reduced rents
- New or additional competitors
- New services
- New facilities
- Better advertising
- Financial deals such as no deposit

### Consumers (Current and Prospective Student Renters)

- Loss of base numbers of students
- Change in financial circumstances
- Better living opportunities elsewhere
- Concern for personal safety
- Gravitating to condominiums
- Want more value for the money
- Negative word-of-mouth publicity

### Student Estates Itself

- Traffic congestion
- Noisy neighbours
- Advertising cutback, change
- Aging facilities and equipment
- Image as "old" apartments
- Upkeep issues

### The Environment

- Less student financial aid
- Increased crime rate
- Housing market oversupply
- Change in students' preferences
- Cost of commuting increase
- Other living alternatives

## Specify Possible Solutions That May Alleviate the Symptom

Managers have at their disposal certain resources, and these resources may provide the solutions needed to address the probable cause of the symptom. Essentially, possible **solutions** include any marketing action that the marketing manager thinks may resolve the problem, such as price changes, product modification or improvement, promotion of any kind, or even adjustments in channels of distribution. It is during this phase that the researcher's marketing education and knowledge fully come into play; often both the manager and the researcher brainstorm possible solutions.

Once again, it is for the manager to specify *all* of the solutions needed to address the probable cause of the symptom. In fact, one marketing research consultant has gone on record with this bold statement: "Unless the entire range of potential solutions is considered, chances of correctly defining the research problem are poor."[14]

Returning to the Student Estates example, the manager realized that he needed to look into *all* types of television-delivery systems. After a thorough review of the alternatives, the manager was not content to just match the competition, so he began considering a satellite television system such as Show Direct Residential Multi Dwelling Complex Package with 470 channels, HDTV, and pay-per-view as one of his likely plans of action. In fact, the manager was quite pleased with his discovery that he could offer satellite television connections in every apartment because the satellite programming seemed far superior to basic cable television.

## Speculate on Anticipated Consequences of the Solutions

Research on anticipated **consequences**, or most likely outcomes, of each action under consideration will help determine whether the solution is correct or not. Even though a solution might resolve the problem, it might intensify the problem if the solution is not the correct action. To avoid resolving the problem incorrectly, the manager asks "what if" questions regarding possible consequences of each marketing action being considered. These questions include:

- What will be the impact on the problem at hand and throughout the marketing program if a specific marketing action is implemented?
- What additional problems will be created if a proposed solution is implemented?

Typically, the consequences of possible marketing actions is apparent. For example, if a company's advertising medium is changed from *Maclean's* magazine to *Canadian Business* magazine, customers will either see less, more, or the same amount of advertising. If a nonsudsing chemical is added to a swimming pool treatment, customers will like it more, less, or have no change in their opinions about it. Most marketing research investigates consumer consequences of marketing solutions, but it is also possible to research dealers' reactions or even suppliers' reactions, depending on the nature of the problem.

It seemed reasonable to the Student Estates manager to speculate that if Student Estates added a satellite television system connection in each apartment, the residences would be seen as more attractive than other competitive apartment complexes.

## Identify the Manager's Assumptions about the Consequences of the Solutions

As they attempt to define the problem, the manager and the researcher make certain **assumptions** that certain conditions exist or that certain reactions will take place if the considered solutions are implemented. For example, the manager may say, "I am positive that our lost customers will come back if we drop the price to $500," or "Our sales should go up if we gain more awareness by using advertising inserts in the Sunday paper." However, if a researcher questions a manager about his or her beliefs regarding the consequences of certain proposed actions, it may

## MARKETING RESEARCH IN ACTION 2.3
# The Decision[a]

When researchers, either internal or external, are called upon, it is because management has information needs. Managers are responsible for increasing shareholders' wealth by increasing the value of their company or brand. They should request information when they need to make decisions and need additional information in order to make a good decision. They cannot (should not!) request information just because they "want to know something." Of course, we recognize that, in some cases, managers do exactly this, and we discuss this situation below.

## Not All Research Is Conducted Because Managers Want to Make a Decision

Sometimes managers want research conducted because they want to know "what is going on." This often happens when there are unplanned changes in the marketing environment—for example, gasoline prices soar, the stock market plunges, and so on—or managers may want to know the current level of customer satisfaction. In our earlier discussion of the uses of research, one use was to "monitor marketing performance." Churchill and Brown have labelled the decision driving this type of research as "discovery-oriented decision problem," and they note that the accompanying research rarely solves a problem. Rather, the research conducted in this situation leads to insights that may help managers make better decisions.[b] But, managers do not always clearly specify decision alternatives. To illustrate this, let us look at some typical examples of decisions managers make.

## Examples of Decisions

Most research is conducted because managers wish to make a decision. First, understand that you cannot formulate the decision without specifying the alternatives that allow the decision. If there are no alternatives, there is no decision to be made. The following examples illustrate that managers sometimes clearly specify the alternatives and sometimes do not. The researcher's task is to clearly state the decision alternatives.

1.  *Example:* "I want to choose the better of two proposed advertising claims." Here the decision and alternatives are clear to the researcher. When the researcher specifies the research objective, the decision can still be improved on by specifying additional information, such as what makes one proposed claim "better" than another.

2.  *Example:* "I want to choose between two formulations for my product. One formulation is more expensive but provides greater benefit to the customer. Because this is a very mature category with a very small range of prices, we believe we would have to substantially increase volume at the current price to warrant the more expensive formulation." Here the alternatives are not provided to the researcher, but they are clear.

3.  *Example:* "I want to choose the best way to express my product's benefit to this target market." Here it is implicitly expressed that alternatives could exist, but they are not stated. The researcher will have more difficulty specifying the alternatives and may need to do exploratory research to determine exactly what the alternatives are.

[a] Much of this material was adapted from a conversation with Ron Tatham.
[b] Churchill, G.A., Jr. and Brown, T.J. (2004). *Basic Marketing Research.* Mason, OH: Thomson/South-Western, 62.

turn out that the manager is not really as certain as he or she sounds. Conversely, the manager may be quite certain and cite several reasons why his or her assumption is valid. It is imperative, therefore, that the manager's assumptions be analyzed for accuracy.

Assumptions deserve researcher attention because they are the glue that holds the decision process together. Given a symptom, the manager assumes that certain causes are at fault and further assumes that by taking corrective actions (solutions) the problem will be resolved and the symptoms will disappear. Research will help to eliminate a manager's uncertainty and therefore aid in decision making.

### The Role of Hypotheses in Defining the Problem

**Hypotheses** are statements that are taken for true for the purposes of argument or investigation. In making assumptions about the consequences of solutions, managers are making hypotheses. For example, a successful restaurant owner uses a hypothesis that he must serve X amount of food in an entrée portion in order to please his customers. This restaurant owner bases his decisions on the validity of this hypothesis; he makes sure that a certain quantity of food is served on every plate regardless of the menu choice. Businesspeople make decisions every day based upon statements they believe to be true. Sometimes those decisions are very important, and the businessperson may not be confident in making the hypothesis. Sometimes, the manager makes a specific statement (an assumption) and wants to know if there is evidence to support the statement. The term *hypothesis* is used to describe this "statement thought to be true for purposes of a marketing research investigation." Note that not all research is conducted through hypotheses. A research question is often used to guide research. In this case, the question, not being a statement, is not considered a hypothesis. When a manager makes a statement believed to be true and wants the researcher to determine if there is support for the statement, these types of statements are called *hypotheses*.

The key assumptions underlying the Student Estates manager's proposed solution are that students (1) know about and understand the advantages of satellite television over basic cable TV and (2) want satellite television more than they want cable television in their apartments. The manager was also assuming that (3) installing a satellite television connection in each apartment would make Student Estates more desirable than the other apartment complexes targeting university students that do not offer this service.

## Assess the Adequacy of Information on Hand to Specify Research Objectives

Recall that it is the researcher's responsibility to provide information to the manager that will help resolve the manager's problem. Obviously, if the manager knows something with a high degree of certainty, it is of little value for the researcher to conduct research to repeat that knowledge. It is vital, therefore, that the researcher assess the existing **information state,** which is the quantity and quality of evidence a manager possesses for each assumption mode. During this assessment, the researcher should ask questions about the current information state and determine the desired information state. Conceptually, the researcher seeks to identify **information gaps,** which are discrepancies between the current information level and the desired level of information at which the manager feels comfortable resolving the problem at hand. Ultimately, information gaps are the basis for establishing research objectives.

With the Student Estates situation, the manager felt quite confident about the accuracy of his information that cable television was offered by his competitors because they had advertised this new feature as well as announced this new service with signs outside the apartment complexes. He was also confident that students were interested in cable television; however, he was not sure about how much they desired the additional programming available on satellite television. Thus, the manager had an information gap because he was unsure of what the reactions of prospective Student Estates residents would be if the satellite program package was included in the apartment package. Would they see it as competitive to the other apartment complexes that had cable television? Would they want to live at Student Estates more than at an apartment complex that had only basic cable?

In the Student Estates example, whenever an information gap that is relevant to the problem at hand is apparent to the manager, the manager and researcher come to agree that it is a research objective. **Research objectives** are set to gather specific bits of knowledge that need to be gathered in order to close the information gaps. Research objectives become the basis for the marketing researcher's work. In order to formulate the research objectives, the marketing researcher considers all of the current information surrounding the marketing management problem. Table 2.3 identifies the information gaps and appropriate research objectives in the case of Student Estates.

The entire time that the dialogue is going on between the manager and the researcher, the manager is fixed on one goal: "How can I solve this problem?" The researcher, on the other hand, is fixed on a different but highly related goal: "How can I gather information relevant to the problem that will help the manager solve his or her problem?" The researcher knows that if the right information is provided to the manager, the problem will be solved. The problem and the research objectives are "intertwined."

## The Role of the Action Standard

An **action standard** is the predesignation of some quantity of a measured attribute that must be achieved in order for a predetermined action to take place. The purpose of the action standard is to define what action will be taken given the results of the research findings.

| Information Gap | Research Objective(s) |
|---|---|
| How will prospective residents react to the inclusion of the satellite television programming package with the base price of the apartment? | To what extent do prospective student residents want satellite television? |
| Will Student Estates be more competitive if it adds a satellite television package? | Will Student Estates be more attractive than competing apartment complexes if it has the satellite television progamming package? |

**Table 2.3** Information Gaps and Research Objectives for Student Estates

Action standards require the researcher to make important decisions before collecting information. They serve as clear guidelines for action once the research is over. Ron Tatham, former CEO of Burke, Inc. and a veteran of the problem definition process with many clients, told the authors, "The action standard is an important component of the problem definition and research objective formulation process because it requires the client to focus on predetermining what information he or she will need in order to take action. Using action standards helps the

# MARKETING RESEARCH IN ACTION 2.4
# Decision Analyst Uses Action Standards

Decision Analyst has a database that helps it determine appropriate action standards. The following quote, supplied to us by Decision Analyst, explains the role that action standards play when the company conducts research for its clients on the effectiveness of a given advertisement. Through the use of an "action standard," Decision Analyst's clients know, after an advertising test, whether to run a proposed ad or kill it.

*Advertising testing systems have long relied on normative data to help determine if a given advertisement is likely to be successful. "Normative data" simply means historical averages of how other advertisements in the same or similar product category have scored. If a company's new ad scores above the "norm," or average, then the advertising agency is happy and the client's marketing director is happy. However, it is Decision Analyst's position that normative data are insufficient as benchmarks. A simple average of historical test scores sets too low a standard, because the normative data include many failed advertisements (i.e., low-scoring commercials), which pull down the historical averages. Normative data set the bar too low.*

*That is why Decision Analyst focuses on "normative action standards" as the appropriate benchmarks. One might think of an "action standard" as normative data with the low-scoring advertisements removed (at a minimum). The search for a meaningful action standard is the goal of an advertising testing program. As advertisements for a brand are tested and then run or put "on air," actual sales responses are monitored to see if the ads appear to be working. Over time, through trial and error, a company will begin to develop an understanding of the testing scores that correlate with positive sales response. This*

*point at which the testing scores begin to signal an effective advertisement is where the action standard should be set. Advertisements that score near or above the action standard go forward, while ads that score below the action standard are killed.*

Source: By permission, Decision Analyst.

## ETHICS IN MARKETING RESEARCH 2.1
# Which Company Are You Going to Choose?

Chris was the marketing research director for a large department in the federal government. Often, Chris needed to hire a marketing research company to undertake large sample surveys costing $150 000 or more.

Typical of buying services for the government, the process Chris had to follow involved advertising a request for proposals, objectively analyzing the proposals received, interviewing the short list of winning proposals, and hiring the company with the winning proposal. The process took Chris some time, as he needed not only to develop criteria for the research but also to develop objective criteria for evaluating alternative proposals. The process also took a great deal of time for the market research firms since they had to develop the proposal.

Even though Chris was always careful to choose the best proposal, he had to keep within budget. Budgets for government research were less flexible than were budgets in private industry. Many market research companies wanted to get the government contracts. Not only were they worth money, but they were also good opportunities for networking and looked good on the company's client list.

Some marketing research firms purposely undercut the cost of the research in order to win the bid. This really frustrated other marketing research firms who knew that they had to spend a minimum amount in order to do the research properly and were not willing to take shortcuts.

Chris always stayed within budget and this usually meant choosing the least expensive proposal.

1. Was it unethical for marketing research firms to take shortcuts in order to win the bid?
2. Did Chris make the right decision in choosing the proposal that was within budget?
3. What would you do if you were Chris?

researcher determine the appropriate research objective because the specification of the action standards tells the researcher what information and in what format they must provide the client. Secondly, action standards allow clients to take action on research results. Without action standards, managers will often say, 'The results of the research are interesting. I learned a lot about the market but I am not sure what to do next.'[15] Marketing Research in Action 2.4 outlines the role of action standards in assessing advertising effectiveness.

## Formulate the Marketing Research Proposal

The research objectives are the all-important results of the dialogue between the manager and researcher in their quest to specify the problem. With the problem statement agreed upon, the marketing researcher develops the research objectives and quickly moves to the formulation of a marketing research proposal. A **marketing research proposal** is a formal document prepared by the researcher, and it serves three important functions: (1) it states the problem, (2) it specifies the research objectives, and (3) it details the research method proposed by the researcher to accomplish the research objectives. Proposals also contain a timetable and a budget.

## Problem Statement

The first step in a research proposal is to describe the problem. This is normally accomplished with a single statement, rarely more than a few sentences long, called the *problem statement*. The problem statement typically identifies four factors: (1) the company, division, or principals involved; (2) the symptoms; (3) the probable causes of these symptoms; and (4) the anticipated uses of the research information to be provided. The problem statement section of the formal marketing research proposal is necessary to confirm that the researcher and the manager fully agree on these important issues.

## Research Objectives

After describing the problem in the marketing research proposal, the marketing researcher must state the specific research objectives. The research objectives specify what information will be collected in order to address information gaps that must be closed in order for the manager to go about resolving the problem. The proposal ensures that the manager and researcher agree as to exactly what information will be gathered by the proposed research.

In creating research objectives, researchers must keep in mind four important qualities. Each research objective must be *precise*, *detailed*, *clear*, and *operational*. To be precise means that the terminology is understandable to the marketing manager and that it accurately captures the essence of each item to be researched. Detail is provided by elaborating each item perhaps with examples. The objective is clear if there is no doubt as to what will be researched and how the information will be presented to the manager. Finally, the research objective must be **operational**: the research objective should define how the construct being evaluated is actually measured. These definitions are referred to as operational definitions. An **operational definition** is a definition of a construct, such as intention to buy or satisfaction (see next section), that describes the operations to be carried out in order for the construct to be measured empirically.[16] For example, students' preference for apartment complex characteristics can be measured with a 7-point rating scale for each characteristic, which ranges from 1 = Strongly Not Preferred to 7 = Strongly Preferred.

### The Role of Constructs

A construct is an abstract idea inferred from specific instances that are thought to be related.[17] For example, marketers refer to the specific instances of someone buying the same brand 9 out of 10 times as a construct entitled "brand loyalty." A construct provides a mental concept that represents real-world phenomena. When a consumer sees an ad for a product and states "I am going to buy that new product X," marketers would label this with the construct "intention to buy." Marketers use a number of constructs to refer to phenomena that occur in the marketplace. Preference, awareness, recall, satisfaction, and so on are examples. Marketing researchers find constructs very helpful because, once it is determined that a specific construct is applicable to the problem, there are customary ways of operationalizing, or measuring, these constructs. This knowledge becomes very useful in developing the research objectives. Additionally, many constructs have relationships that are explained by models, and these relationships can be useful in solving problems. For example, Table 2.4 illustrates how certain constructs are related using a model referred to as the "hierarchy of effects." Note how useful this would be to the researcher in the Student Estates example.

## Detail the Proposed Research Method

Finally, the research proposal details the proposed **research method**. The proposal describes the data collection method including data collection forms. If the research design is exploratory and qualitative data collection methods such as focus groups or observation are to be used, then details of what information is sought and how it will be gathered are provided. If the research design is

| Hierarchy Stage | Description | Research Question |
|---|---|---|
| **Unawareness** | Not aware of your brand | What percentage of prospective student residents are unaware of satellite television? |
| **Awareness** | Aware of your brand | What percentage of prospective student residents are aware of satellite television? |
| **Knowledge** | Know something about your brand | What percentage of prospective student residents who are aware of it know that satellite television has (1) 150 channels, (2) premium channels, and (3) pay-per-view? |
| **Liking** | Have a positive feeling about your brand | What percentage of prospective student residents who know something about satellite television feel negatively, positively, or neutral about having it in their apartment? |
| **Intention** | Intend to buy your brand next | What percentage of prospective student residents who are positive about having satellite television in their apartment intend to rent an apartment with it? |
| **Purchase*** | Have purchased your brand in the past | What percentage of the market purchased (tried) your brand in the past? |
| **Repurchase/Loyalty*** | Purchase your brand regularly | What percentage of the market has purchased your brand more than other brands in the last five purchases? |

Table 2.4 How the "Hierarchy of Effects" Model Can Frame Research for Student Estates' Satellite Television Decision

*Not applicable to Student Estates, as the satellite television feature is not currently available.

descriptive, then questionnaire design and sampling plan are described in detail. If causal research is proposed, then details of the controls in the testing situation are provided in addition to a sampling plan and data collection form. Proposals vary greatly in format and detail, but most share the basic components: problem

## MARKETING RESEARCH IN ACTION 2.5
# Marketing Research Proposal for Student Estates
### Proposal to Determine the Attractiveness of Satellite Television to Prospective Residents of Student Estates

## Introduction

This proposal responds to a request on the part of the principals of Student Estates to assist in its decision of adding satellite television to attract prospective student residents.

## Background

Student Estates is experiencing an occupancy drop from 100% to 80%. This decline coincides with the addition of cable television now available in all Student Estates competitors. Student Estates principals are contemplating the addition of a satellite television system that will include 470 channels, HDTV, and pay-per-view. Information is needed to assess prospective student residents' reactions to this possible additional service.

### Research Objectives

Discussion with Student Estates managers suggests that answers are desired to the following questions:

- To what extent do prospective student residents want satellite television?
- Will Student Estates be more attractive than competing apartment complexes if it has the satellite television programming package?

## Research Framework

Based on Research Associates' understanding of the decision facing Student Estates principals, and further using the company's experience in these types of questions, the company proposes to use the "hierarchy of effects" model as a framework in which to cast the research questions to be used in the proposed survey.

This framework addresses the decision by identifying factors that may facilitate or hamper the attractiveness of the satellite progamming package.

Using this model, the research questions are:

- What percentage of prospective student residents are aware of satellite television?
- What percentage of prospective student residents who are aware of it know that satellite television (1) has 470 channels, (2) HDTV and (3) pay-per-view?
- What percentage of prospective student residents who know something about satellite television have a positive feeling (as opposed to negative or neutral feelings) about having it in their apartment?
- What percentage of prospective student residents who are positive about having satellite television in their apartments intend to rent an apartment with it?
- Is Student Estates with satellite television more attractive than competing apartment complexes with cable television?

Action standards are to be determined for each question above.

## Research Method

Research Associates proposes to undertake a telephone survey of 500 full-time students who live off-campus. Research Associates will prepare and pretest the survey questionnaire, subcontract the telephone survey work, analyze the data, and present the findings to Student Estates principals within six weeks of the execution of a contract. The cost of the proposed survey work is $20 000.

statement, research objectives, and proposed research method, including time frame and costs.

What does a marketing research proposal look like? We have prepared Marketing Research in Action 2.5, which is the proposal written for Student Estates based on the way it has been described in this chapter.

# Summary

1.  **Describe the 11 steps of the marketing research process.**
This chapter begins with a description of an 11-step marketing research process. Keep in mind that not everyone agrees that there are 11 steps, not all studies use all 11 steps, and few studies follow the steps in the exact order. The steps are: (1) establishing the need for marketing research, (2) defining the problem, (3) establishing research objectives, (4) determining research design, (5) identifying information types and sources, (6) determining methods of accessing data, (7) designing data collection forms, (8) determining the sample plan and size, (9) collecting data, (10) analyzing data, and (11) preparing and presenting the final research report.

Establishing the need for marketing research, step 1, involves knowing when to conduct marketing research. Marketing research is not needed when information to make a decision is already available, the timing is wrong, there are insufficient funds, or when costs outweigh the value of doing research. Several reasons are provided to illustrate when one should conduct marketing research so that the research is likely to have great value. These situations include when research will help clarify problems or opportunities, identify changes in the marketplace, identify the best alternative to action, and establish a competitive advantage.

2.  **Explain the importance of proper problem definition.**
Defining the problem, step 2, is the most important of all of the steps. A problem well defined is a problem half solved, and a bad problem definition will doom the entire project.

Problems may be general or specific, and the researcher is responsible for ensuring that management has properly defined the problem. In some cases, a situation analysis is required to help define the problem. Problem definition is sometimes impeded because (1) managers fail to change their normal behaviour in order to interact closely with researchers, and (2) managers are usually generalists and researchers tend to be technical. ITBs are "invitations to bid." Alternatively, some firms use RFPs, which stands for "requests for proposals." Companies use these documents to alert research firms that they would like to receive bids or proposals to conduct research.

3.  **Identify two sources of research problems.**
There are two sources of problems. One arises when there is a gap between what was supposed to happen and what did happen. This type of problem is attributed to failure to meet an objective. The second type of problem arises when there is a gap between what did happen and what could have happened. We refer to this type of problem as an opportunity. Managers recognize problems through either monitoring

control systems or monitoring systems to recognize opportunities. Symptoms are changes in the level of some key monitor that measures the achievement of an objective. Symptoms alert managers to problems.

**4.   Describe two processes for defining the research problem and generating research objectives.**

The process for defining the problem when the source of the problem is a failure to meet objectives is: (1) assess the background and the manager's situation, (2) clarify the symptoms of the problem, (3) pinpoint suspected causes of the symptom, (4) specify solutions that may alleviate the symptom, (5) speculate on anticipated consequences of the solutions, (6) identify the manager's assumptions about the consequences of the solutions, and (7) assess the adequacy of information on hand to specify research objectives. When faced with an opportunity, management should conduct a market opportunity analysis to determine which opportunities to further pursue with additional marketing research. Both problem definition processes lead to generating research objectives. Research objectives gather the specific bits of knowledge needed to close information gaps. Action standards help researchers determine the appropriate research objectives and their format. Action standards also determine client actions.

**5.   List the contents of a marketing research proposal.**

Marketing research proposals are formal documents prepared by the researcher and serve the functions of stating the problem, specifying research objectives, detailing the research method, and specifying a timetable and budget. Research proposals typically identify marketing constructs and the operational definitions specifying how the constructs will be measured.

## Key Terms

Action standard    (p. 63)

Assumptions    (p. 60)

Cause    (p. 58)

Consequences    (p. 60)

Hypotheses    (p. 62)

Information gaps    (p. 62)

Information state    (p. 62)

Invitations to bid (ITBs)    (p. 55)

Marketing opportunity    (p. 52)

Market opportunity analysis (MOA)    (p. 56)

Marketing research proposal    (p. 65)

Operational    (p. 66)

Operational definition    (p. 66)

Opportunity    (p. 52)

Opportunity identification    (p. 52)

Possible causes    (p. 58)

Probable causes    (p. 58)

Problem    (p. 51)

Research method    (p. 67)

Research objectives    (p. 43 and p. 63)

Requests for proposals (RFPs)    (p. 55)

Situation analysis    (p. 54)

Solutions    (p. 59)

Steps in the marketing research process    (p. 41)

Symptoms    (p. 53)

## Review Questions

1.1 Which step in the 11-step process is the most important step? Why?

1.2 Which steps in the 11-step process are sometimes eliminated? Why?

**2.1** What is the impact of online research in terms of determining the need for marketing research?

**2.2** Give an example of a research project that was conducted with the wrong problem definition.

**2.3** Write at least three different definitions that indicate how a researcher might form a question in a survey to assess the degree of television channel loyalty. One example is, "Channel loyalty is determined by a stated preference to view a given channel for a certain type of entertainment."

**3.1** Explain how research problems may vary, and give some examples.

**3.2** What is the process for determining the problem and establishing research objectives?

**4.1** Explain how the process for determining the problem and establishing research objectives differs when a manager is faced with an opportunity instead of a failure to reach an objective.

**4.2** Sony is thinking of expanding its line of flat-screen televisions. It thinks there are three situations in which this line would be purchased: (1) as a gift, (2) as a set to be used by children in their own rooms, and (3) for use at sporting events. How might the research objective be stated if Sony wished to know what consumers' preferences are with respect to these three possible uses?

**4.3** The local Lexus dealer thinks that the company's four-door sedan with a list price in excess of $80 000 should appeal to BMW 500 Series owners who are thinking about buying a new automobile. He is considering a direct-mail campaign with personalized packages to be sent to owners whose BMW 500 Series are over two years old. Each package would contain a professional video of all of the Lexus sedan's features and end with an invitation to visit the Lexus dealership. This tactic has never been tried in this market. State the marketing problem and indicate what research objectives would help the Lexus dealer understand the possible reactions of BMW 500 Series owners to this campaign.

**5.1** Which part of a marketing research proposal is the most critical? Why?

# Case 2.1

# Washington Suites

Montagne is a small hypothetical community in northeastern Quebec, with a population of 20 000. The average age is 35. Most people who live there are young families with two to four children. Income levels are average, with most people working in the local paper mill. The Montagne Community Centre was a small facility typical of such centres built in the 1950s. It was one large recreation room attached to the "arena." The arena was a simple ice rink. The children came to practise such activities as hockey, ringette, or figure skating while their parents cheered them on. Whenever there was a civic holiday, the centre was used as the home for the celebrations. The centre was a non-profit organization funded mainly by the town of Montagne and by a subsidy from the Quebec government. The facility was small relative to today's standards, but the residents of Montagne could easily make do.

*(Continued)*

Not long ago, the Montagne Community Centre burned to the ground as a result of a tragic accident. Thankfully, no one was hurt in the fire. The centre's volunteer board learned that the insurance company would provide the replacement cost for a new centre. The board members felt that they had a real opportunity to build a new centre that was modern and had more specialized activity spaces such as a gym and a hockey rink. Board members felt that if they could present a solid business case to the town, additional funds could be found for this new, bigger, more expensive centre. They could even subsidize the operating costs of the new centre by asking for user fees.

To build the business case for a larger, expanded facility, much information was needed. The board developed an RFP and published it in several Quebec newspapers. Weeks later, they received 10 proposals from various marketing research companies. One company, Community Research Inc., provided a proposal that seemed to satisfy the board's needs.

1. How was the board's problem stated?
2. What was the source of the problem? What process did the marketing researchers undertake to ensure accurate problem identification?
3. What were the research objectives? What research methods were proposed, and why?

# Case 2.2

# AJResearch

Five years ago, when Allison James started her marketing research firm, she had no idea she would be working with so many clients at one time. You are her new research assistant. She asks you to review her five new clients to determine the research objectives to each of their problems. The five new clients and their marketing research problems are as follows:

1. Wired, Inc., an electronics firm, has developed a new flat-screen television that will sell for one-third of the price of those currently on the market. Problem: Will there be enough demand to offset the large fixed costs of retooling to make the new television sets?
2. Wacky Znacks, a large snack foods firm, has made a name for itself with wild-flavoured snacks like licorice cookies and jalapeño sunflower seeds. Problem: They feel that customers expect even wilder flavours. Wacky Znacks wants to know what consumer reactions would be to even more unusual flavoured snacks (e.g., watermelon-flavoured corn chips and barbecue-flavoured chewing gum).
3. Wild About Toys is a large toy firm that enjoys surprising consumers with innovative new toys. They have developed an edible clay for children. Problem: Will parents want to purchase a toy that their children can also eat?
4. Jimmy Roberts wants to start a small catalogue business that caters to new parents. He wants to offer a variety of high-quality, higher-priced items. Problem: So many different baby products exist. Roberts needs to start with a limited product line. Which products should he start his business with?
5. The Better Butter company has spent many years researching and developing a butter product that the company believes is truly superior to other butters on the market. Problem: There is a plethora of butter products. How can Better Butter package its product to call attention to it while portraying the idea of a superior product?

Using the information above, determine the research objectives for each client.

## Case 2.3 YOUR INTEGRATED CASE

# Student Life E-Zine

*This is the second case in our integrated case series. If you have not already done so, read Case 1.2 (in Chapter 1) before reading this case.*

### ORS Marketing Research

Sarah, Anna, Wesley, and Don were now firmly committed to their business idea of providing an e-zine targeted to postsecondary students. They had scheduled their second appointment with Bob Watts of ORS Marketing Research. ORS stands for Online Research Solutions, and the firm was committed to providing high-quality online research. It had the capability of conducting online survey research as well as conducting research using traditional data collection methods such as focus groups, person-to-person interviews, and telephone surveys.

### The Need for Primary Data

Bob described some of the secondary data collected by ORS. It was clear that e-zines were growing, especially among younger and more educated segments of the market. All of this was very favourable for the new business venture. "However," Bob stated, "we have no secondary data to tell us if an e-zine targeted specifically to postsecondary students will be feasible." Bob went on to explain the need to collect primary data. "We'll need to get some feedback from the students at City U to tell us whether or not to proceed with this business idea and, if we do proceed, how to design the e-zine so that we maximize its appeal. We're going to need to construct the research project so that we can project the findings to the entire student population at City U with an accurate level of precision."

"You're talking about using those sample size formulas we learned in school to give us the margin of error we want, aren't you?" asked Wesley.

"Exactly. I think that it'll be important to have a representative sample and the right sample size if

we're going to try to make some accurate estimates of the entire campus population," Bob replied.

### Determining Feasibility

Anna asked how ORS could determine "feasibility." Bob explained that the word had many different meanings and that they themselves would have to determine what was feasible and what was not feasible. "The four of you will have to make the 'go/no-go' decision. Obviously you want to earn a reasonable return on the savings you're going to invest, so one definition of 'feasible' would be for the business to project a return on equity (ROE) at the level you desire. But, before we get too far, maybe we should do some work to determine how many subscriptions you will need to break even. We often recommend this to clients so they can make an early decision as to whether to continue or drop the project idea."

"That makes a lot of sense," said Don. "We were always working on break-even analysis in school. If we project that we will need more students to subscribe than there are students at City U, we're in trouble."

Laughing, Bob agreed. "Yes, you remember your school work well. Break-even analysis is a tool for helping us to determine if the demand required to break even is a reasonable demand level for us to achieve. It doesn't tell us how many people will actually buy the e-zine."

They all agreed break-even analysis would be a great tool to help them begin determining feasibility.

"You all have majors in marketing," said Bob. "Why don't the four of you work the break-even analysis and call me when you're ready to go over it?"

"That'll be no problem," said Sarah. "We can get together tonight at my house and start trying to determine our expenses."

All agreed that that would be a great start.

*(Continued)*

### Estimating Expenses, Determining a Price, and Calculating the Break-Even Point

That evening, the group met at Sarah's to begin working on the break-even analysis. Fortunately, given their work experience, they had little difficulty in estimating most of the expenses. Determining the price they would charge was more difficult. Since the e-zine would be updated often and because it contained "interactive" components, it was not comparable to a regular monthly magazine. Also, they knew from their work experiences that many advertisers would offer the students many specials to get their business and, at least for the students who used the specials and coupons, this would represent a significant value. After much discussion, the group decided on a price of $15 per month that could be billed automatically to a credit card. They would offer six-month subscriptions. Wesley was concerned that this was too expensive.

"That's why we're conducting marketing research," said Anna. "We can do some focus groups first to determine students' reactions to this price once they fully understand the concept. If those focus groups tell us we're way out of line, we can revisit the price."

Wesley felt relieved they were doing the research to help them make this important decision.

At a price of $15 per month for a subscription, the break-even analysis indicated they needed 6000 subscriptions. Now the four friends were not sure what this meant to them in terms of a "go/no-go" decision. They agreed that at least it was not a number like 30 000, which they knew they could never achieve. On the other hand, it was not a small number, like 2000, which they felt they could more easily achieve. After some discussion they agreed that they needed to ask Bob at ORS if they could obtain research information that would help them make the decision to "go or not go" with the e-zine business. The next day, they called and set up another meeting with Bob Watts to discuss their break-even point of 6000 subscriptions.

### Information Needed to Confirm Meeting the Break-Even Point

At the meeting, Bob asked to see their analysis. The group discussed the assumptions they had made, and Bob approved of the decisions they used in the break-even analysis. He then asked the group, "Okay, so now what do you think?"

Sarah spoke up and said, "Well, since City U has 35 000 students, the four of us felt that 6000 subscriptions could be achieved, but we are very uncertain about that assumption. We need some kind of information that will help us confirm our decision that we can reach at least 6000 subscriptions."

Bob replied, "Yes, I agree that you need that information. Once you get it you'll really see the value of doing marketing research."

"You bet we will," Wesley said, "but what information can ORS gather that will help us with this uncertainty?"

Bob said, "We can conduct research that tells us what percentage of the campus population is intending to purchase a subscription." He went on to discuss how they could measure the construct of "intention to subscribe" with a scale ranging from "very likely" to "very unlikely." "Of course," Bob continued, "people don't always do what they say they intend on doing, but if we use only the respondents who say they are 'very likely' to subscribe, this may give us a pretty good estimate of the percentage of students who actually will subscribe." Bob then explained that they would not count on the "somewhat likely" or "undecided" respondents even though they knew some of them would subscribe.

Wesley said, "I see. We need to know what percentage of 35 000 students equals 6000 students?" As they all nodded in agreement, Wesley was already entering the figures in his calculator. "If we divide 6000 by 35 000, we get 17.14%. So, we should be pretty confident in our decision to continue on as long the percentage of those saying they are 'very likely' to subscribe is better than, say, 18%."

"Yes," said Bob. "If the number turns out to be 3%, we know the e-zine is probably ahead of its time. On the other hand, if it exceeds 18%, you should be in good shape, at least from a break-even standpoint."

The friends agreed that this would give them a good criterion upon which they could make a decision to move forward or not. Once they knew exactly what percent was willing to subscribe, they would be able to get a better estimate of total sales revenue, expenses, profits, and, eventually, ROE.

### Accuracy of the Estimate of the Percentage "Very Likely" to Subscribe

Sarah, after quietly listening, said, "Okay, I understand trying to determine the percentage of the students in the sample you're going to study who want to subscribe, but I'm having trouble understanding how we're going to apply that percentage to the entire campus population. How do we know that the percentage you calculate from your one sample study is *the* correct percentage of students who are 'very likely' to subscribe? Would that percentage change if you did the study again the next day?"

Bob replied, "You are exactly right, Sarah. The percentage we get from the sample data will be our best estimate of the percentage of the campus that we expect to subscribe. But it's only an estimate. There is a statistical tool that we can use that will help us identify a range within which the real population value is likely to fall. And we'll be able to say we're 95% confident that the true population percentage falls within that range. I'll go over that tool with you later, but you have an excellent point. For now, please understand that ORS will be able to provide you with that information, which really gives you greater confidence in using the estimate we get from the sample."

## Other Revenue Sources: Advertising, Affiliated Marketing, and Pay-Per-View

After the group finished discussing the break-even analysis, Bob reminded them that they had intentionally prepared a conservative break-even analysis in that they had assumed revenues flowing only from subscriptions. Now it was time to discuss the

other potential revenue sources: (1) advertising, (2) affiliated marketing programs with online vendors, and (3) "pay-per-view" revenues for special events provided through the e-zine. The group had intentionally omitted these revenues from their break-even analysis because they all agreed that it would take time to generate ad revenue, since advertisers would not want to place money in the e-zine until they were confident that it was an established product. Also, they were not sure if the student subscribers to the e-zine were purchasing over the internet, so they did not want to base any revenue on affiliated marketing. (Affiliated marketing is an e-commerce arrangement whereby a webpage owner, A, establishes a link for webpage owner B's webpage. If a webpage visitor clicks through A's webpage to B's webpage and buys something, B provides A with a fee. Sometimes this fee can be 15% of the sale, and it can result in substantial revenues.) Finally, they did not want to use pay-per-view revenues without having any idea as to whether students would be willing to pay extra for these events.

All five members of the group felt that if subscription fees could carry the costs of the e-zine, the other sources of revenue would just add icing on the cake. "I agree with your thinking wholeheartedly," said Bob. "In fact, most of the time, we have to discourage would-be entrepreneurs at this stage. Usually, they want to count every conceivable revenue source and we try to bring them back to reality. I think your conservative estimate, based solely on subscription revenue, is a good idea. But in planning the research we're going to conduct, we need to think about what information you're going to need in order to help you make the decisions you'll need to make concerning these other revenue sources. When we conduct our research, we want to be sure we gather that information for you."

### Information Needed for Potential Advertisers

"Let's focus first on what information we need for potential advertisers in the e-zine," said Bob.

Don, being very familiar with ad revenue for publications, noted that the group should consider

(Continued)

local advertisers such as the movie theatres, restaurants, pizza parlours, and entertainment spots that surrounded City U. He also reminded the group that City U was only the first of what they hoped would be a national market of colleges and universities and that national advertisers seeking to target the postsecondary student market would likely be very interested in advertising in the e-zine.

Bob then made this statement: "Okay, Don and Sarah both work for publishers that earn their living by selling advertising space. What information do we need to collect in order to appeal to potential advertisers in our e-zine?"

Both Sarah and Don agreed that their advertisers first want to know if their customers, the people who buy the advertisers' goods and services, read their publications. Don said, "I would have to say that is the foremost criterion our advertisers use. They want to make certain that the types of people who are their potential customers are actually reading the newspaper."

Sarah agreed and pointed out that the reason many of their specially targeted magazines had been so successful was that they allowed advertisers to target the most likely buyers of their goods and services.

Bob said, "Great, this gives us direction. Now, let's determine what kinds of advertisers we want to gather this information for."

The five brainstormed and came up with the following: soft drinks, non–fast-food restaurants, fast-food restaurants, pizza delivery chains, automobile dealers, real estate (for local student apartments), clothing stores, and local night entertainment spots.

## Information Needed for Potential Affiliated Marketing Programs

"Okay, team," Bob said, "we can generate the information you're going to need to help you attract advertisers. Now, let's talk about what information we can provide that will help you establish good affiliated marketing contracts."

Again, everyone launched into a discussion of what potential affiliated partners would want them to demonstrate. First, they agreed that affili-

ated partners would want to know if subscribers to e-zines are e-commerce users. In other words, do they make purchases over the internet? Second, for those e-zine subscribers that do make purchases, on which types of products and services do they spend their money? Looking ahead to the research, Bob said it would be beneficial if they could come up with categories, as they had with advertising, of products or services bought over the internet. The five-member team did some exploratory research by searching the internet and came up with the following: books, gifts for weddings and other special occasions, music CDs, financial services such as insurance and loans, clothing, and general merchandise for home and car. Bob assured the group that he could design the research project so that they would have that information.

## Information Needed for Potential Pay-Per-View Programs

Bob also told them they needed to decide if they wanted a flat fee for everything or if there was a market that would pay extra for pay-per-view events.

Don immediately threw in, "Yes, like streaming video of the school's sporting events."

The group talked about costs, and they were a little uncertain as to what the cost would be to get into pay-per-view offerings. Nevertheless, they all felt strongly that there was great potential in pay-per-view and it could be a way of differentiating their offering from competitors. Don said, "If we are the first in the market and we get the contracts with the schools to video their sports events, we'll have a definite strategic advantage over competitors, who are bound to arise if we are successful."

Bob advised, "Okay, I'm hearing a lot of enthusiasm about the potential of pay-per-view in the future. For now, let's see what kind of response we get if we ask potential subscribers their preference for a type of pay-per-view event. How they answer that question will tell you how much you should pursue this idea after you get the basic e-zine up and running."

Sarah, speaking softly to Anna, said, "Am I glad we hired ORS. I'm feeling much better about these tough decisions we are going to have to make."

Anna nodded her agreement.

## Related Advertising/Affiliated/Pay-Per-View Decisions

Anna said, "Back to measuring this construct you called intentions. Aren't we going to have to adequately describe the concept to them first? I can't tell you if I'm going to buy something until I know what the 'something' is."

Bob agreed and stated that he realized the four had not decided on what the features and articles would actually be but told them, "We can describe the general idea to them and get their likelihood to subscribe. This is pretty standard in marketing research. Once we determine who intends to subscribe and who doesn't, we can examine some relationships to get a better understanding of profiling our subscriber target market."

Sarah said, "We'll want to have a good profile of our subscribers. Not only will this help us make better marketing decisions, but it will be necessary when we try to sell other companies on advertising in our e-zine or establishing affiliated marketing partners." Bob agreed.

## What Features Should Be Included in the E-Zine?

Bob stated that ORS could also provide information that would help determine potential subscribers' preferences for various types of features in the e-zine.

Don said, "Some hard data would be very helpful to us in making those decisions. We have to remember not to put ourselves in the place of our customers. We haven't been students for several years now! I've been thinking about the different types of features we can offer, and I'll bring the list of ideas to our work session tonight."

Bob said, "That sounds great. We may also want to consider doing some focus groups right away with postsecondary students. They're likely to have some great ideas about exactly what they would like to see in the e-zine. Focus groups may

give you some good ideas on what to name your e-zine as well, and they'll give us some idea about students' willingness to accept the $15-per-month subscription fee."

## Are All Postsecondary Students the Same?

Anna spoke up: "All this sounds great, but I keep thinking we shouldn't treat all postsecondary students alike. I lived at home my first two years of school, and I doubt I would have been interested in an e-zine about college and universities. I was too busy watching my parents' big-screen TV and going to the movies with my old high school buddies. But when I moved to campus, my life changed. I think I would have loved an e-zine."

"Good point!" Bob said. "We'll want to know if there is a difference in preferences for the e-zine between on-campus and off-campus students, and we may find some differences between part-time and full-time students."

Wesley added, "I'll bet we find that first-year students will have different preferences for reading material and topics covered than second-, third-, or fourth-year students. As a first-year student, my world revolved around the latest Britney Spears CD. By the time I was in third year, I was hooked on world affairs!"

Bob assured the group that the marketing research project could be constructed so as to help them make the proper decisions regarding differences between these groups.

## Expanding Beyond City U

Everyone agreed that the real potential in the e-zine was in expanding the concept to other colleges and universities. Since many of the features in the e-zine would remain the same, this would lower the incremental costs of adding other postsecondary schools. Targeting the right colleges and universities would be very important to the success of the e-zine. Bob said ORS could design the research so that they could use the information gathered to determine other schools with the best potential. He explained, "For example, if we find

(*Continued*)

that a large proportion of, say, engineering students subscribe, we'll target schools with large engineering departments. Or, if we find that most subscribers live on campus, we can target universities with large on-campus enrolments. Colleges and universities publish this type of information, so we'll be able to select those schools that have the greatest potential."

Later that evening, the four friends met at Wesley's home. Everyone was pleased with the meeting at ORS, and Don said, "I'm very pleased with Bob Watts. I feel like hiring ORS to help us has been a smart decision."

Anna agreed, "Yes, it was a good idea, and when we get the results of the research, we'll have the information that we need to make several decisions."

The group spent a couple of more hours discussing the various features and their contents. They knew that, as entrepreneurs, their work had only just begun.

## Questions

1. Define the problem or problems.
2. What are the research objectives?

# Research Design

## Research Design at Momentum Market Intelligence

Momentum Market Intelligence (MMI) supplies strategic research to customers in the information technology, financial services, health care/life sciences, public utilities, and consumer packaged goods (CPG) industry sectors. Doss Struse is senior partner and CEO. Doss has several years of high-level marketing research experience with firms such as Oscar Mayer, Carnation/Nestlé, and General Mills. He has also served as an executive with ACNielsen, Research International, and Knowledge Networks. In the following paragraphs, Doss describes several client problems and how knowledge of research design would enable him to make advance decisions regarding methods and procedures needed to solve the problems.

*Research design refers to a set of advance decisions that make up the master plan specifying the methods and procedures for collecting and analyzing the information needed to solve a problem. The benefit of knowledge of research design is that by knowing which research design is needed to solve a client's problem, a good researcher can predetermine certain procedures that will likely be needed. This not only leads to a more efficient research planning process, but it enables a good researcher to advise the client early on as to the advantages and disadvantages that will be experienced with the chosen design. Let me give you some examples to illustrate my point.*

*Let us assume we have a client that is a consumer packaged goods manufacturer with a well-established brand name. The client has focused on manufacturing and distribution for years while the marketing program has been set on "auto pilot." All had worked fine though there was a hint of emerging problems when, in the preceding year, market share had fallen slightly. Now, let us assume our client is reviewing the current market share report and notices that over the previous 12 months their*

Doss Struse, Senior Partner
and CEO, Momentum Market
Intelligence

*share has gradually eroded 15%. When market share falls clients are eager to learn why and to take corrective action. In these situations, we know immediately the problem is that we don't know what the problem is: There are many possible causes for this slippage. In this situation, we would follow a research design known as exploratory research which means exactly what the name implies. We would begin to explore by examining secondary data about the industry, the market, submarkets served, and competitors. We would likely conduct some focus groups, often used in exploratory research, of both consumers and distributors. In quick order, the client's problem (or problems) would begin to emerge and, once identified, we could begin solving the problem. By knowing we needed to know more about the problem itself, we would know we would be using an exploratory research design. By knowing we needed this research design, the researcher would be in a position to select from a variety of procedures used with this design, such as secondary information search or focus groups and make advanced decisions early in the life of the project. The client could also be apprised of the advantages and disadvantages of the procedures early on in the project.*

*As another example, let us assume we have a manufacturer of several baked goods products sold in grocery stores throughout the country. Marketing is divided up into five regional divisions in the United States. The five divisions have had total autonomy over their advertising though all of them have used TV advertising almost exclusively. Each division has tried several different TV ad campaigns; some were thought to be successful and others not as successful, but no one had ever formally evaluated the ad expenditures. A new Marketing VP now wants to evaluate the advertising. She's interested in knowing not only the sales of the client's products during the different campaigns, she also wants to know what happened to sales of competitors' brands. In this case, the client needs us to describe sales by SKU in the client's product category for each TV market and for each time period associated with each ad campaign. When we need to describe something, such as consumers' level of satisfaction with brand X or the percentage of the target population that intends to buy a new product, we turn to descriptive research design. Again, by knowing we are going to be doing descriptive research, we are in a better position to determine, in advance, what methods and procedures we will be using to solve the client's problem.*

*To complete our discussion, let's look at one more situation. Imagine a client that is in a very competitive category with equal market share of the top three brands. Assume the client is convinced that they have changed every marketing mix variable possible except for package design. Since the three competitive brands are typically displayed side-by-side, they want us to determine what factors of package design (i.e., size, shape, color, texture, and so on, cause an increase in awareness, preference for, and intention to buy the brand). When clients want to know if they change x what happens to y, we know the appropriate research design is causal research. By knowing this we know we will be using experimental design research and, once again, this helps us plan many decisions in advance. You will learn more about research design by reading this chapter. After you've read the chapter, come back to this page and reread the examples I've given you. You will have a better appreciation of how important research design is to those of us in the marketing research profession.*

Doss Struse, Momentum Market Intelligence

You can visit MMI at **www.mointel.com**.    By permission, Momentum Market Intelligence.

D oss Struse's discussion of research design at MMI provides an excellent introduction to the concept of research design. While they do many types of studies, these studies fall into one of three categories: exploratory, descriptive, or causal (experiments). Thus, they use all three types of research design that will be discussed in this chapter.

## Research Design

Marketing research methods vary widely. For example, there are experiments of food tasting held in kitchen-like labs; there are focus groups to explore new product concepts; there are simulated test markets or large, nationally representative sample surveys to back consumer attitudes. Some research objectives require only library research, whereas others require thousands of personal interviews; other studies require observation of consumers in supermarkets, while another may involve two-hour-long, in-depth, personal interviews in respondents' homes.

Each type of study has certain advantages and disadvantages. There are some basic marketing research designs that can be successfully matched to given problems and research objectives. In this way, they serve the researcher much like the blueprint serves the builder. After thoroughly considering the problem and research objectives, researchers select a **research design**, which is a set of advance decisions that makes up the master plan, specifying the methods and procedures for collecting and analyzing the needed information.

**Where We Are**

1. Establish the need for marketing research
2. Define the problem
3. Establish research objectives
4. Determine research design
5. Identify information types and sources
6. Determine methods of accessing data
7. Design data collection forms
8. Determine sample plan and size
9. Collect data
10. Analyze data
11. Prepare and present the final research report

## The Significance of Research Design

Marketing researcher David Singleton of Zyman Marketing Group, Inc., believes that good research design is the first rule of good research.[1] Every research problem is unique. In fact, one could argue that, given each problem's unique customer set, area of geographical application, and other situational variables, there are so few similarities among research projects that each study should be completely designed as a new and independent project. In a sense, this is true; almost every research problem is unique in some way or another, and care must be taken to select the most appropriate set of approaches for the unique problem and research objectives at hand.

Although every problem and research objective may seem unique, there are usually enough similarities among problems and objectives to allow us to make some decisions in advance about the best plan to use to resolve the problem. There are some basic marketing research designs that can be successfully matched to given problems and research objectives. In this way, they serve the researcher much like the blueprint serves the builder.

Once the problem and the research objectives are known, the researcher selects a research design. The proper research design is necessary for the researcher to achieve the research objectives. Sometimes the wrong research design is formulated, leading to disaster.

# Three Types of Research Design

Research designs are classified into three traditional categories: exploratory, descriptive, and causal. The choice of the most appropriate design depends largely on the objectives of the research. In general, research has one of three objectives: (1) to gain background information in order to develop hypotheses, (2) to measure the state of a variable of interest (for example, level of brand loyalty), or (3) to test hypotheses that specify the relationships between two or more variables (for example, level of advertising and brand loyalty). The choice of research design is dependent on how much is already known about the problem and research objective. The less that is known, the more likely it is that exploratory research will be used. **Causal research**, on the other hand, should only be used when a fair amount about the problem is known and the researcher is looking for causal relationships among variables associated with the problem or the research objectives. Table 3.1 shows the three types of research design and the basic research objective that would prescribe a given design.[2] Possible research methodologies for each design are also shown.

## Research Design: A Caution

It is incorrect to think of research design in a step-by-step fashion. The order in which the designs are presented—that is, exploratory, descriptive, and causal—is not the order in which these designs should necessarily be carried out. In some cases it may be legitimate to begin with any one of the three designs and to use only that one design. Research is an "iterative" process: By conducting one research project, it may be necessary to do additional research. This may mean that multiple research

| Research Objective | Appropriate Design | Research Methods (partial list) |
|---|---|---|
| To gain background information, to define terms, to clarify problems and hypotheses, to establish research priorities | Exploratory | Secondary data analysis, focus groups, observation |
| To describe and measure marketing phenomena | Descriptive | Cross-sectional survey, longitudinal survey |
| To determine causality, to make "if–then" statements | Causal | Experiments, test markets |

**Table 3.1** The Basic Research Objective, Research Design, and Research Method

designs be used. For example, after conducting descriptive research, one might need to go back and conduct exploratory research. If multiple designs are used in any particular order (if there is an order), it makes sense to first conduct exploratory research, then descriptive research, and finally causal research. The only reason for following this order is that each subsequent design requires greater knowledge about the problem and research objectives on the part of the researcher. Therefore, exploratory research may give one the information needed to conduct a descriptive study, which, in turn, may provide the information necessary to design a causal experiment.

## Exploratory Research

**Exploratory research** is most commonly unstructured, informal research that is undertaken to gain background information about the general nature of the research problem. Exploratory research is unstructured because it does not have a formalized set of objectives, sample plan, or questionnaire. It is usually conducted when the researcher does not know much about the problem and needs additional information or desires new or more recent information. Often exploratory research is conducted at the outset of research projects. It is considered informal because, unlike some research designed to test hypotheses or measure the reaction of one variable to a change in another variable, exploratory research can be accomplished by simply reading a magazine or even observing a situation. For example, in the late 1990s an 18-year-old University of British Columbia student named Brian Scudamore, while sitting in his car in line at a fast-food drive-through, saw an old dilapidated truck loaded with junk. This observation gave Brian the idea to start a junk moving company, and he did so. He watched what his competitors were doing and asked informally for feedback. Now, more than a decade later, his company, known as 1-800-Got-Junk, continues to grow and is franchised in more than 300 locations across Canada, the United States, and Australia. The company is consistently named one of Canada's top employers.[3] As this example demonstrates, exploratory research is very flexible in that it allows the researcher to investigate any and all available sources in order to gain a good feel for the problem at hand.

## Uses of Exploratory Research

Exploratory research is used in a number of situations: to gain background information, to define terms, to clarify problems and hypotheses, or to establish research priorities.

### Gain Background Information

When very little is known about the problem or when the problem has not been clearly formulated, exploratory research may be used to gain much-needed background information. Even for very experienced researchers, some exploratory research is usually undertaken to gain current, relevant background information. There is far too much to be gained from exploratory information to ignore it.

### Define Terms

Exploratory research helps to define terms and concepts. For example, conducting exploratory research to define a question such as "What is 'bank image'?" the researcher quickly learns that bank image is composed of several components: perceived convenience of location, loan availability, friendliness of employees, and so on. Not only would exploratory research identify the components of bank image, but it could also demonstrate how these components may be measured.

### Clarify Problems and Hypotheses

Exploratory research allows the researcher to define the problem more precisely and to generate hypotheses for the upcoming study. For example, exploratory research on measuring bank image reveals that different groups of bank customers have different ways of looking at banks. Retail customers see banks differently than do commercial customers. This information is useful in clarifying the problem of the measurement of bank image because it raises the issue of which customer segment's version of bank image should be measured.

Exploratory research can also be beneficial in the formulation of **hypotheses**, which are statements taken for true for the purpose of argument or investigation. Hypotheses often describe the speculated relationships among two or more variables.

Formally stating hypotheses prior to conducting a research study is very important to ensure that the proper variables are measured. Once a study has been completed, it may be too late to state which hypotheses are desirable to test. The data collected and analyzed may not be appropriate for testing the "right" hypothesis.

### Establish Research Priorities

Exploratory research can help a firm prioritize research topics in order of importance. For example, a summary account of complaint letters by retail store may tell management where to devote its attention. One furniture store chain owner decided to conduct research on the feasibility of offering office furniture after some exploratory interviews with salespeople revealed that customers in their stores often asked for directions to stores selling office furniture.

## Methods of Conducting Exploratory Research

A variety of methods are available for conducting exploratory research. These include secondary data analysis, experience surveys, case analysis, focus groups, and projective techniques.

### Secondary Data Analysis

**Scondary data analysis** is the process of searching and interpreting existing information relevant to the research objectives. Secondary data are data that have been collected for some other purpose. The library and the internet are full of secondary data, which include information found in books, journals, magazines, special reports, bulletins, newsletters, and so on. An analysis of secondary data is often the "core" of exploratory research.[4] This is because there are many benefits to examining secondary data, and the costs are typically minimal. Furthermore, the costs for search time of such data are being reduced every day as more and more computerized databases become available. Knowledge of and ability to use these databases are already mandatory for marketing researchers.

### Experience Surveys

The term **experience surveys** refers to gathering information from those thought to be knowledgeable on the issues relevant to the research problem. Volvo, believing that autos have been designed by and for men, asked 100 women what they wanted in a car. Based on some major differences they discovered, Volvo introduced a "Volvo for women."[5] Experience surveys differ from surveys conducted as part of descriptive research in that there is usually no formal attempt to ensure that the survey results are representative of any defined group of subjects. Useful information can be gathered by this method of exploratory research.

### Case Analysis

**Case analysis** is a review of available information about former situations that have some similarities to the present research problem.[6] Even when the research problem deals with a radically new product, there are often some similar past experiences that may be observed. For example, when cellular telephones were invented but not yet on the market, many companies attempted to forecast the rate of adoption by

Exploratory research in the form of discussions with employees led a furniture store owner to add office furniture.

looking at adoption rates of consumer electronic products such as televisions and VCRs. A wireless communications company, 21st Century Telesis, used data from a low-power neighbourhood phone system that was very successful in Japan to help it market cellular phones to young people in Japan.[7] Researchers must be cautious in using former case examples for current problems. For example, cases dealing with technology-based products just a few years ago may not be relevant today. Since the advent of the internet and the widespread use of computers, the public's use of and attitudes toward technical products and services have changed completely.

### Focus Groups

A popular method of conducting exploratory research is the use of **focus groups**. Focus groups are small groups of people brought together and guided by a moderator through an unstructured, spontaneous discussion for the purpose of gaining information relevant to the research problem.[8] Although focus groups should encourage openness on the part of the participants, the moderator's task is to ensure the discussion is focused on some general area of interest. For example, Passport Canada held focus groups across Canada in the fall of 2009. The focus groups helped Passport Canada to better understand public opinions, expectations, and preferences regarding passport security features, the new validity period, and service standards. This is a useful technique for gathering some information from a limited sample of respondents. The information can then be used to generate ideas, to learn the vocabulary respondents' use when relating to a certain type of product, or to gain some insights into respondents' basic needs and attitudes.[9] Marketing Research in Action 3.1 explores the use of focus groups.

## MARKETING RESEARCH IN ACTION 3.1
## Understanding Focus Groups

Companies and organizations constantly update, reposition, redesign, or add totally new items to what they offer their constituents so that they might better serve the needs and interests of those on whom they rely. Whether they are looking for consumers to buy their products, association members to re-up for another year, stockholders to add them to their portfolios, patrons to donate, or patients to bring their maladies, corporate types have long known that either you grow and flourish or you die.

The cost of innovation is high, but the cost of errant innovation is even higher. So, today, most institutions rely on some sort of face-to-face marketing research to help them touch base with their target market from time to time to make sure whatever they are working on is as compelling as they would like it to be.

Touching base, however, is easier said than done. Who, exactly, is it that you want to talk to? Where can you gain open access to such individuals? What sort of environment should you provide to make them comfortable talking about their preconceptions, desires, and honest reactions to your ideas? Is it possible to have an environment with all the technology that's required today to present one's case (teleconferencing, AV-display, presentation space) that's emotionally warm enough to keep ordinary people at ease for some time?

How do you record the details of those conversations so that you can analyze what they say in pursuit of your own understanding?

Fieldwork, Inc. is a company devoted to helping corporate entities of all sorts reach and relate to their constituents in a comfortable but efficient and purposeful manner.

Fieldwork has three divisions. One of those divisions is composed of a collection of focus group facilities (16) found in major cities throughout the United States.

So, what is a focus group facility, and how does it work? A focus group facility is an office composed of interviewing suites, each of which is approximately 1000 square feet (two large hotel rooms). Each suite has a conference room where focus groups take place and a "back room" where interested parties can observe and listen (via piped-in sound system). Video and audio recording equipment is hardwired into the suite so that a record of what transpires can be taken. That record goes to the client to be analyzed later. The personal identities of respondents (last names, addresses, phone numbers, etc.) are not made available unless permission has been granted ahead of time.

Finding the right people to talk to is frequently a complex task. Let me cite an example. A major restaurant chain is introducing a new line of barbequed entrées, but before it goes to the enormous expense of contracting with its meat vendors, printing up new menus, developing advertising, and so forth, it hires a research firm to do some focus groups regarding how appealing this new line is and how well it "fits" under the current brand umbrella.

Who does the research firm want us to recruit? First of all, we need people who eat out with some regularity. People who go to casual dining restaurants (the type the client has). People who aren't vegetarians. Perhaps, people who have been to one of the client's restaurants in the past six months, so they aren't totally clueless as to what the current brand umbrella really is. Furthermore, clients don't want people who are involved in any way with industries related to their own; they don't want to deal with "experts" or alert their competitors as to what they have in mind.

But there are more issues than that. The client needs people who are articulate in English. The client needs people who aren't such focus group habitués that their point of view has become more like a professional respondent's than a "real" consumer's might be. But most importantly, the client wants people who represent a broad range of demographic, psychometric, or sociometric characteristics from that geographic area.

Keeping it all straight is the business of Fieldwork. Getting the right people to show up at the right time in the right frame of mind to talk openly with strangers and doing so without violating their need for privacy is perhaps the biggest challenge a focus group facility has. Along the way, we have to maintain separation between client and respondent since clients frequently require that respondents be uninformed about who is sponsoring the research, not because they want to be clandestine about it, but because they don't want responses to be biased by the participants' knowing who is behind the mirror listening in.

In fact, much of what takes place in a focus group needs to be held in confidence. Every day we are dealing in intellectual property that is not only proprietary but, because these are new ideas just being considered, also very susceptible to being picked up and perhaps used by competitive institutions. One of our primary tasks, then, is to have a high level of security throughout every aspect of our organization.

The recruiting process is an iterative one. The nature of the recruit may, itself, give insights and force changes into the nature of the recruiting process. We may find, for example that when we ask people in Chicago (where there is a strong Southern influence) about barbecued food, they have a totally different take on what it means than do those in Seattle (where there's a strong Asian influence). Part of our job is to keep in daily contact with our clients

*(Continued)*

to let them know how the recruiting process is going. It's not at all uncommon for a client to direct us to change one or more of our recruiting specifications midstream in response to what's happened so far.

After the recruiting is accomplished, we play host to various constituencies ourselves. Clients may represent a manufacturer, an ad agency and public relations associates, a design firm and a research house each represented by one or two people often flying in from several different cities. Then we have respondents who arrive hungry and need to be fed before they go in to chat for a few hours. It's a major logistical effort but the truth is, it's our favourite part of the process—it's where we get to meet clients, hear about their efforts—it's that point in time when we get to see our hard work begin to pay off.

A focus group facility is a social place. It's full of life, and interesting ideas float around. Respondents may arrive with a little trepidation the first time they come to a focus group but they almost always leave with a smile and a request that they be considered in the near future for another opportunity to be a focus group participant.

Source: Molly Turner-Lammers, Fieldwork Seattle, Inc.; adapted with permission, Fieldwork Seattle, Inc.

### Other Techniques

**Qualitative research** involves collecting, analyzing, and interpreting data by observing what people do and say. Observations and statements are in a qualitative or nonstandardized form. Qualitative data can be quantified but only after a translation process has taken place. While focus groups make up a large percentage of qualitative studies, other methods include **depth interviews**, in which probing questions are posed one-on-one to a subject by a trained interviewer so as to gain ideas as to what the respondent is thinking or why he or she behaves in a certain way; **protocol analysis**, in which respondents are placed in a decision-making setting and asked to verbalize everything they consider when making a purchase decision; **projective techniques**, in which consumers' hidden motives when buying are explored; and **ethnographic research**, in which a detailed, descriptive observation study of a group and its behaviour, characteristics, culture, and so on, is undertaken.[10] Qualitative research techniques, including focus groups and observation research are discussed in detail in Chapter 5.

Exploratory research should almost always be used because it is fast, inexpensive, and may help in designing the proper descriptive or causal research study.

## Descriptive Research

**Descriptive research** is undertaken to describe answers to questions of who, what, where, when, and how. When a company wants to know *who* their customers are, *what* brands they buy and in what quantities, *where* they buy the brands, *when* they shop, and *how* they found out about products, descriptive research is used. This type of research is also desirable when projecting a study's findings to a larger population. If a descriptive study's sample is representative, the findings may be used to predict some variable of interest such as sales.

## Classification of Descriptive Research Studies

Figure 3.1 illustrates the classification of descriptive research studies. Two basic descriptive research studies are available to the marketing researcher: cross-sectional

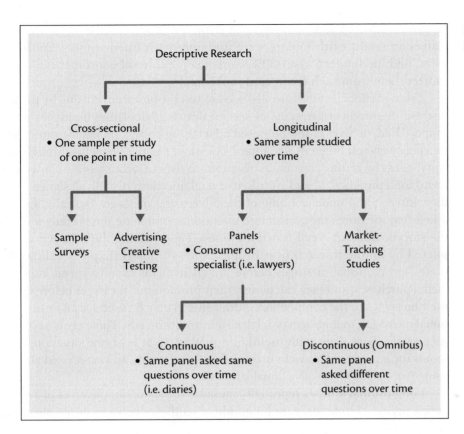

**Figure 3.1** Types of Descriptive Research

and longitudinal. **Cross-sectional studies** measure units from a sample of the population at only one point in time.

A study measuring attitude toward adding a required course in a degree program, for example, would be a cross-sectional study. Attitude toward the topic is measured at *one point in time*. Cross-sectional studies are very prevalent in marketing research, outnumbering longitudinal studies and causal studies. Because cross-sectional studies are one-time measurements, they are often described as "snapshots" of the population.

Many magazines survey a sample of their subscribers to ask questions such as their age, occupation, income, educational level, and so on. These sample data, taken at one point in time, are used to describe the readership of the magazine in terms of demographics. Cross-sectional studies normally employ fairly large sample sizes, so many cross-sectional studies are referred to as sample surveys.

**Sample surveys** are cross-sectional studies whose samples are drawn in such a way as to be representative of a specific population. *Marketplace*, an investigative consumer television program on CBC, conducts surveys on topics of interest. The surveys' samples are drawn from a random sample of 1000 Canadians aged 18 and above so that the results are representative of the Canadian population and have a stated margin of error of ±3%. Sample surveys require that samples be drawn according to a prescribed plan and to a predetermined number. (Sampling plans and sample size techniques are discussed in detail in Chapter 9.) For example, *Marketplace* hired EKOS Research Associates to undertake a cross-sectional study of Canadian credit card holders. EKOS used the hybrid internet telephone research panel Pro*bit* to interview 1036 Canadians 18 years old or older. The sample was randomly selected and the margin of error was ±3%. The research indicated that Canadian credit card holders were unhappy with interest rates, confusing fine print, and hidden fees. Over 80% wanted some form of consumer bill of rights to protect them from such credit card problems.[11]

Cross-sectional studies are also used to test proposed advertising by using "storyboards." A storyboard consists of several drawings depicting the major scenes in a proposed ad, as well as the proposed advertising copy. Companies can quickly and inexpensively test different ads' appeal, copy, and creative elements through the use of storyboards by getting consumers' reactions to them. Consumers are shown the storyboard for a proposed ad and are asked several questions, usually designed to measure their interest and understanding of the advertising message. Typically, a question is asked that measures the consumer's intention to purchase the product after viewing the storyboard. Dirt Devil tested a proposed ad by using the AdInsights[SM] service offered by online research firm InsightExpress®. InsightExpress® allows firms to pretest promotional messages before the client firms have to spend large sums on media purchases, and they can perfect their promotional messages before they expose their messages to the competition. AdInsights[SM] may be used for all forms of promotional messages, including radio, television, and print ads. These cross-sectional studies provide client firms with useful information. In at least one situation, evaluation scores for a proposed ad were increased 219% after the ad was revised as a result of using AdInsights[SM] cross-sectional studies.

**Longitudinal studies** repeatedly measure the same sample units of a population over a period of time. Because longitudinal studies involve multiple measurements,

By showing a sample of online consumers proposed ads and getting their evaluations, client firms may use Insight-Express®'s AdInsights[SM] to modify promotional materials before placing them in the media. AdInsights[SM] studies are examples of cross-sectional research. Visit InsightExpress® at **www.insightexpress.com.**     By permission, InsightExpress®.

they are often described as "movies" of the population. To ensure the success of the longitudinal study, researchers must have ongoing access to the same members of the sample, called a panel, so as to take repeated measurements. **Panels** represent sample units who have agreed to answer questions at periodic intervals. Maintaining a representative panel of respondents is a major undertaking.

Several commercial marketing research firms develop and maintain consumer panels for use in longitudinal studies. Typically, these firms attempt to select a sample that is representative of some population. Firms such as CRC Research and ACNielsen have maintained panels consisting of hundreds of thousands of households for many years. In many cases, these companies will recruit panel members such that the demographic characteristics of the panel are proportionate to the demographic characteristics found in the total population according to Canadian census statistics. Sometimes these panels will be balanced demographically not only with the Canadian population as a whole but also with the population of each of the various geographical regions. In this way, a client who wishes to get information from a panel of households in the West can be assured that the panel is demographically matched to the total population in the provinces making up the western region. Many companies maintain panels to target market segments such as Canadian teens (**www.tns-cf.com/services/panel.html/#teen**). Note that panels are not limited to member of consumer households. Panels may consist of building contractors, supermarkets, physicians, lawyers, universities, or other entities.

## ETHICS IN MARKETING RESEARCH 3.1
# Is Digital Fingerprinting Unethical/Illegal?

Digital fingerprinting is a tool used to identify an online panel member. The technology works within a respondent's browser and assigns a unique ID to the respondent's computer, based on publicly available information about that computer. The fingerprinting digital tool was widely adopted by online panel researchers to prevent fraudulent and duplicate respondents from participating in a survey. Digital fingerprinting filters out suspects at the start of a survey, through the use of security controls defined by the researcher. Research indicates that fingerprinting does work at reducing the number of unwanted survey completions.

There is a snag, though. Questions regarding a possible violation of the Canadian Personal Information Protection and Electronic Documents Act (PIPEDA) have emerged. In particular, since individuals' computers are identified, are respondents truly anonymous? In anticipation of legal actions, the Marketing Research and Intelligence Association (MRIA) is offering legal counsel to members who may be exposed to liability suits by using digital fingerprinting in their marketing research.

Source: James Verrinder, "Digital fingerprinting 'may be unlawful' in Canada, warns MRIA," *Research*, September 29, 2009. Retrieved August 16, 2010, from www.research-live.com/news/legal/digital-fingerprinting-may-be-unlawful-in-canada-warns-mria/4001050 .article

Online research created the opportunity for several new companies to emerge offering panels recruited to respond to online queries. One such company is Lightspeed Research, Canada, which offers clients access to panels of consumer households. Survey Head is another firm that offers clients access to its online panel of consumers. Many of these online panels offer money for participation in surveys. Check out **www.internetpaidsurveys.com/Canada/Survey1.htm** for a list.

There are two types of panels: continuous and discontinuous. **Continuous panels** ask panel members the same questions over a period of time. Continuous panel examples include many of the syndicated data panels that ask panel members to record their purchases using diaries or scanners. Panel members are asked to record the same information (for example, grocery purchases) over and over. Firms are interested in data from continuous panels because they can gain insight into changes in consumer attitudes and behaviour over time. **Brand-switching studies** can use continuous panels to collect data in order to show how panel members switched brands from one time period to another.

**Discontinuous panels** vary questions from one panel measurement to the next. They are sometimes referred to as **omnibus panels** because each panel survey covers many things. The primary usefulness of a discontinuous panel is that it represents a large group of willing research subjects who are demographically matched for representativeness. As such, these panels provide clients with information that can be accessed quickly and for a wide variety of purposes.

To illustrate the difference between using continuous panel longitudinal data and cross-sectional surveys to gain insights into how consumers change brands, compare data from the two methods. Figure 3.2 shows data collected from two separate cross-sectional studies, each having a household sample size of 500. (Cross-sectional data are referenced as "Survey 1" or "Survey 2.") Look at how many families used each brand in Survey 1 (red) and then see how many families used each brand in Survey 2 (blue). It is clear that Pooch Plus has lost market share because only 75 families indicated that they purchased Pooch Plus in the second survey as opposed to 100 Pooch Plus families in the first survey; and, apparently, Pooch Plus has lost out to Milk Bone dog treat brand, which increased from 200 to 225 families. Note that Beggar's Bits remained the same. This analysis would lead most brand managers to focus on the strategies that had been used by Milk Bone (since it is "obvious" that Milk Bone took share from Pooch Plus) to increase market share for Pooch Plus.

Examining the longitudinal data leads to quite a different conclusion from the one reached by looking at the two cross-sectional studies. Look at the Panel 1 totals (red) and Panel 2 totals (blue) in the two cross-sectional surveys. The Panel 1 totals show that Pooch Plus had 100 families, Beggar's Bits had 200 families, and Milk Bone had 200 families. (This is exactly the same data found in the first cross-sectional survey.) Return for a second measurement of the *same families* in Panel 2, and the totals are Pooch Plus, 75 families; Beggar's Bits, 200 families; and Milk Bone, 225 families. (Again, the same totals as shown by the Survey 2 data.) But the real value of the continuous panel longitudinal data is found in the changes that occur between the Panel 1 and Panel 2 measurements. With longitudinal data, we can examine how each family changed from Panel 1 to Panel 2. To see how the families changed, look again at the Panel 1 totals (red), and then look *inside the figure*

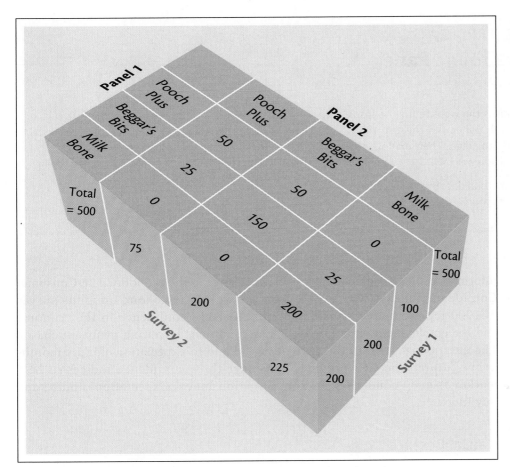

**Figure 3.2** The Advantage of Longitudinal Studies versus Cross-Sectional Studies

(green) at the Panel 2 results. In Panel 1 (red) 100 families used Pooch Plus. Looking at the data on the inside of the figure (green) and reading across for Pooch Plus, 50 families stayed with Pooch Plus, 50 switched to Beggar's Bits, and none of the original Panel 1 Pooch Plus families switched to Milk Bone. Now look at the 200 families in Panel 1 (red) who used Beggar's Bits. In the Panel 2 data (green), 25 of those 200 families switched to Pooch Plus, 150 stayed with Beggar's Bits, and 25 switched to Milk Bone. Finally, all of the 200 Milk Bone families in Panel 1 stayed loyal to Milk Bone in Panel 2. It is clear that Pooch Plus is competing with Beggar's Bits and not with Milk Bone. Milk Bone's total shares increased but at the expense of Beggar's Bits, not Pooch Plus. The brand manager should direct his or her attention to Beggar's Bits, not Milk Bone. This is quite different from the conclusion reached by examining cross-sectional data. Since longitudinal data allow measures of the change by each sample unit between time periods, much richer information for analysis purposes is gained. This type of brand-switching data may be obtained only by using the continuous panel.

Another use of longitudinal data is that of market tracking. **Market-tracking studies** are those that measure some variable(s) of interest—that is, market share or unit sales over time. By having access to representative data on brand market shares, for example, a marketing manager can track how a brand is doing relative to a competitive brand's performance. Every month, TNS Canadian Facts tracks

## ONLINE APPLICATION 3.1
# Join an Online Panel

Go to **www.i-say.com**. This is the website for the Ipsos i-Say online market research panel. On the top right, choose your country and language. Then explore the website and join the panel if you wish.

1.  What type of research method does this site represent? What evidence supports your answer?

2.  What type of data will this method yield?
3.  Given the type of data gathered, what type of research design does this method best serve?
4.  If you did join the panel, what do you like about being on the panel? What do you dislike?

information on Canadian consumers' confidence in the economy. The Consumer Confidence Index (CCI) is based on a biweekly telephone omnibus survey of 1000 representative Canadian adults. It tracks confidence in the economy and the employment situation as well as conditions favouring major purchases. The questions pertain to the current period and to expectations for six months in the future. The CCI provides consumer three confidence indices to help marketers and economists: Present Situation Index, Expectations Index, and Buy Index. [12]

## Causal Research

**Causality** may be thought of as understanding a phenomenon in terms of conditional statements of the form "If $x$, then $y$." These "if–then" statements become a way of manipulating variables of interest. For example, if the thermostat is lowered, then the air will get cooler. If a car is driven at lower speeds, then the gasoline mileage will increase. If more is spent on advertising, then sales will rise. As humans, we are constantly trying to understand the world in which we live. Likewise, marketing managers are trying to determine what will cause a change in consumer satisfaction, a gain in market share, or an increase in sales. In one experiment, marketing researchers investigated how colour versus noncolour and different quality levels of graphics in Yellow Pages ads caused changes in consumers' attitudes toward the ad itself, the company doing the advertising, and perceptions of quality. The results showed that colour and high-photographic graphics cause more favourable attitudes. However, the findings differ depending on the class of product being advertised.[13] This example illustrates how complex cause-and-effect relationships are in the real world. Consumers are bombarded on a daily basis and sometimes even hourly basis by a vast multitude of factors, all of which could cause them to act in one way or another. Thus, understanding what causes consumers to behave as they do is extremely difficult. Nevertheless, there is a significant reward in the marketplace for even partially understanding causal relationships. Causal relationships are determined by the use of experiments, which are special types of studies. Many companies are now taking advantage of conducting experiments online.

# Experiments

An **experiment** is defined as the manipulation of an independent variable to see how it affects a dependent variable, while the effects of additional extraneous variables are also controlled. **Independent variables** are those variables that the researcher has control over *and* wishes to manipulate. Some independent variables include level of advertising expenditure, type of advertising appeal (humour, prestige), display location, method of compensating salespersons, price, and type of product. **Dependent variables**, on the other hand, are those variables over which there is little or no direct control, yet in which the researcher has a strong interest. These variables cannot be changed in the same way independent variables can be changed. A marketing manager, for example, can easily change the level of advertising expenditure or the location of the display of a product in a supermarket but cannot easily change sales, market share, or level of customer satisfaction. To the extent that marketers can establish causal relationships between independent and dependent variables, they enjoy some success in influencing the dependent variables.

**Extraneous variables** are those that may have some effect on a dependent variable but that are not independent variables. To illustrate, let us say you and a friend wanted to know if brand of gasoline (independent variable) affected gas mileage in automobiles (dependent variable). The experiment consists of each of you filling up your car, one with Brand A, the other with Brand B. At the end of the week, Brand A achieves 18.6 miles per gallon and Brand B achieves 26.8 miles per gallon. Does Brand B get better gas mileage than Brand A, or could the difference in the dependent variable (gas mileage) be due to factors other than gasoline brand (independent variable)? Possible extraneous variables may be: (1) One car is an SUV and the other is a small compact; (2) one car was driven mainly on the highway and the other was driven in the city in heavy traffic; and (3) one car has never had a tune-up and the other was just tuned up.

Imagine that a supermarket chain conducts an experiment to determine the effect of type of display (independent variable) on sales of apples (dependent variable). Management records sales of the apples in its regular produce bin's position and then changes (manipulates the independent variable) the position of the apples to end-aisle displays and measures sales once again. Assume that sales increased. Does this mean that change in display position of apples from the produce bins to end-aisle displays causes sales to increase? What would happen to apple sales if the weather changed from rainy to fair? What if the apple industry began running ads on TV? As this example illustrates, it would be difficult to isolate the effects of independent variables on dependent variables without controlling for the effects of the extraneous variables. Unfortunately, it is not easy to establish causal relationships, but it can be done. Different experimental designs control extraneous variables.

## Experimental Design

An **experimental design** is a procedure for creating an experimental setting such that a change in a dependent variable may be attributed solely to the change in an independent variable. In other words, experimental designs are procedures that allow experimenters to control for the effects on a dependent variable by an extraneous variable. In this way, the experimenter is assured that any change in the dependent variable is due only to the change in the independent variable.

Symbols of experimental design can be used to show how such designs work:

$O$ = The measurement of a dependent variable

$X$ = The manipulation, or change, of an independent variable

$R$ = Random assignment of subjects (consumers, stores, and so on) to experimental and control groups

$E$ = Experimental effect, that is, the change in the dependent variable due to the independent variable

When a measurement of the dependent variable is taken *prior to* changing the independent variable, the measurement is sometimes called a **pretest**. When a measurement of the dependent variable is taken *after* changing the independent variable, the measurement is sometimes called a **posttest**.

There are many research designs available to experimenters. Our purpose is to illustrate the logic of experimental design, and we can do this by reviewing three designs, of which only the last is a true experimental design. A **"true" experimental design** is one that truly isolates the effects of the independent variable on the dependent variable while controlling for effects of any extraneous variables. The three designs we discuss are after-only; one-group, before-after; and before-after with control group.

## Quasi-experimental Design: After-Only Design

The **after-only design** is achieved by changing the independent variable and, after some period of time, measuring the dependent variable. It is diagrammed as follows:

$$X \quad O_1$$

where $X$ represents the change in the independent variable (moving all of the apples to end-aisle displays) and $O_1$ represents the measurement, a posttest, of the dependent variable (recording the sales of the apples). Since there is no measure of sales prior to changing the display location, it is not known if sales have gone up or down. There *may* have been other extraneous variables that have had an effect on apple sales. Managers are constantly changing things "just to see what happens" without taking any necessary precautions to properly evaluate the effects of the change. Hence, the after-only design does not really measure up to the requirement for a true experimental design.

Designs that do not properly control for the effects of extraneous variables on the dependent variable are known as **quasi-experimental designs**. Note that in the after-only design diagram, there is no measure of $E$, the "experimental effect" on the dependent variable due solely to the independent variable. This is true in all quasi-experimental designs.

## Quasi-experimental Design: One-Group, Before-After Design

The **one-group, before-after design** is achieved by first measuring the dependent variable, then changing the independent variable, and, finally, taking a second measurement of the dependent variable. This design is symbolized as:

$$O_1 \quad X \quad O_2$$

The obvious difference between this design and the after-only design is that there is a measurement of the dependent variable prior to and following the change in the independent variable. Also, as the name implies, there is only one group (a group of consumers in one store) on which the study is conducted.

As an illustration of this design, go back to the previous example. In this design, our supermarket manager measured the dependent variable, apple sales, prior to changing the display location. The change in the dependent variable from time period 1 to time period 2 is known. Sales went up, down, or stayed the same. However, it is not possible to attribute the change in the dependent variable solely to the change in the independent variable. Numerous extraneous variables, such as weather, advertising, or time of year, could have caused an increase in apple sales. With the one-group, before-after design, it is not possible to measure E, the "experimental effect," because this design does not control for the effects of extraneous variables on the dependent variable. Hence, the one-group, before-after design is also not a true experimental design; it is a quasi-experimental design.

Control of extraneous variables is typically achieved by the use of a second group of subjects, known as a control group. A **control group** is a group whose subjects have not been exposed to the change in the independent variable. The **experimental group**, on the other hand, is the group that has been exposed to a change in the independent variable. Having these two groups as part of the experimental design enables the researcher to overcome many of the problems associated with the quasi-experimental designs. The following true experimental design illustrates the importance of the control group.

## Experimental Design: Before-After with Control Group

The **before-after with control group** design may be achieved by randomly dividing subjects of the experiment (in this case, supermarkets) into two groups: the control group and the experimental group. A pretest measurement of the dependent variable is then taken on both groups. Next, the independent variable is changed only in the experimental group. Finally, after some time period, posttest measurements are taken of the dependent variable in both groups. This design may be symbolized as follows:

$$\text{Experimental group } (R) \quad O_1 \quad X \quad O_2$$
$$\text{Control group } (R) \qquad\qquad O_3 \qquad O_4$$
$$\text{where } E = (O_2 - O_1) - (O_4 - O_3).$$

In this true experimental design, there are two groups. Assume there are 20 supermarkets in the supermarket chain. Theoretically, if the stores are randomly divided into two groups—10 in the experimental group and 10 in the control group—then the groups should be equivalent. That is, both groups should be as similar as possible, each group having an equal number of large stores and small stores, an equal number of new stores and old stores, an equal number of stores in upper-income neighbourhoods and lower-income neighbourhoods, and so on.

$R$ indicates that the supermarkets have been randomly divided into two equal groups—one a control group, the other an experimental group. Pretest measurements of the dependent variable, apple sales, were recorded at the same time for both groups of stores as noted by $O_1$ and $O_3$. The $X$ symbol indicates that only in the experimental group of stores were the apples moved from the regular produce bins to end-aisle displays. Finally, posttest measurements of the dependent variable were taken at the same time in both groups of stores, as noted by $O_2$ and $O_4$.

$(O_2 - O_1)$ tells how much change occurred in the dependent variable during the time of the experiment. $(O_2 - O_1)$ tells how many dollars in apple sales may be attributed to (1) the change in display location and (2) other extraneous variables, such as the weather, apple industry advertising, and so on. Because it cannot account for changes in apple sales due to a change in display location (the display was not changed), then any differences in sales as measured by $(O_4 - O_3)$ must be due to the influence of other extraneous variables on apple sales. Therefore, the difference between the experimental group and the control group, $(O_2 - O_1) - (O_4 - O_3)$, results in a measure of $E$, the "experimental effect." If apple display locations are changed, then apple sales will change by an amount equal to $E$.

There are many other experimental designs, and almost limitless applications of experimental designs to marketing problems. An experimenter, for example, could use the before-after with-control-group design to measure the effects of different types of music (independent variable) on total purchases made by supermarket customers (dependent variable). Although experimentation can be valuable in providing knowledge, not all experiments are valid.

What type of experimental design is being used in the test described in Marketing Research in Action 3.2?

## How Valid Are Experiments?

An experiment is valid if (1) the observed change in the dependent variable is, in fact, due to the independent variable, and (2) the results of the experiment apply to the "real world" outside the experimental setting.[14] Two forms of validity are used to assess the validity of an experiment: internal and external.

**Internal validity** is concerned with the extent to which the change in the dependent variable was actually due to the independent variable. This is another way of asking if the proper experimental design was used and implemented correctly. To consider an experiment that lacks internal validity, return to the apple example. In the before-after with control group experimental design, the design assumes that the experimental group and the control group are, in fact, equivalent. What would happen if the researcher did not check the equivalency of the groups? Suppose that, by chance, the two groups of supermarkets had customers who were distinctly different regarding a number of factors such as age and income. This difference in the groups, then, would represent an extraneous variable that had been left uncontrolled. Such an experiment would lack internal validity because it could not be said that a change in apple sales was due solely to the change in the location of apples. Experiments lacking internal validity have little value because they produce misleading results. Lack of internal validity suggests that the researcher is not measuring what he or she thinks is being measured. Sometimes organizations will conduct studies and present them as experiments in order to intentionally mislead others.

**External validity** refers to the extent that the relationship observed between the independent and dependent variables during the experiment is generalizable to the "real world." In other words, can the results of the experiment be applied to units (consumers, stores, and so on) other than those directly involved in the experiment? There are several threats to external validity. How representative is the

# MARKETING RESEARCH IN ACTION 3.2
# Online Data Collection: Are We There Yet?

For many years, NADbank has been using RDD (random digit dialling) telephone-based methodology to collect data on newspaper readership and consumer behaviour of adults in urban markets across Canada. However, the decline in response rates (45% in 2006) and the increase in cellphone-only households (5% in 2006) have motivated NADbank to explore alternatives to its traditional methodology.

Parallel with its 2006 fieldwork, NADbank conducted an online survey using the questionnaire applied in their telephone research. The purpose of the test was to obtain top-line estimates of similarities and differences between online and traditional telephone survey methodologies. The test compared the results of the TNS Canadian Facts online panel (Toronto members only) with the NADbank telephone research in the Toronto market. Observations from the test are reported below.

## Differences in Sample Composition

Generally speaking, the online panel was composed of more male respondents, fewer 18- to 24-year-old respondents, and more 35- to 64-year-olds than the sample collected via telephone survey. Compared with the respondents in the telephone survey, those in the online test tended to have a higher level of education, particularly at the "some post-secondary" level, but lower average household incomes. They were also less likely to own their own home and were more likely to speak English. The online panel had fewer respondents classified as blue-collar workers compared with the telephone sample.

## Differences in Media Exposure

Generally speaking, online respondents said they spent about 50% more time (hours per week) with individual media than those in the telephone sample and also more time online than the "wired" respondents in the telephone sample (i.e., those who accessed the internet in the past three months). Compared with the full telephone sample and the wired respondents in the telephone sample, the online respondents typically read more weekday issues of a newspaper (4.7 issues per week versus 4.0 for the "wired" group) and more weekend issues (4.5 issues per week versus 3.6 for the "wired" group).

Readership of "any" and specific daily newspaper titles was higher for the online panelists than for those in the telephone sample. The differences were not consistent across titles or metrics. Even when the demographic profile of the online panel was adjusted to match the telephone-based sample using weighting, the differences in readership persisted.

## Test Conclusions

NADbank concluded that there were behavioural differences between those participating in the online panel and those reached via RDD telephone sampling. Further, it was concluded that such differences could not be overcome by simply adjusting or weighting the panel to match known demographics. Differences in results gleaned from traditional versus online panels are likely due, in part, to the fundamental differences in the research platforms.

## Next Steps

NADbank will continue its research into issues relating to web-based panels. A second test with four panels in three markets was conducted last fall in order to look at consistency of survey-to-survey results, ability to conduct research in markets outside of Toronto, and comparability of different panels. NADbank will continue to conduct its study using the traditional telephone-based protocol.

Source: Anne Crassweller, President, NADbank, Toronto. Presented to the CARF (The Canadian Advertising Research Foundation) Seminar—Market Research Surveys: Online versus Traditional, January 18, 2008. (First presented at the Worldwide Readership Research Symposia, Vienna, October 21–24, 2007.) Courtesy of Canadian Advertising Research Foundation.

sample of test units? Is this sample really representative of the population? There are many examples of the incorrect selection of sample units for testing purposes. For example, some executives, headquartered in large cities in cold winter climates, have been known to conduct experiments in warmer, tropical climes during the winter. Although the experiments they conduct may be internally valid, it is doubtful that the results will be generalizable to the total population.

Another threat to external validity is the artificiality of the experimental setting itself. In order to control as many variables as possible, some experimental settings are far removed from real-world conditions.[15] If an experiment is so contrived that it produces behaviour that would not likely be found in the real world, then the experiment lacks external validity.

## Types of Experiments

Experiments can be classified into two broad classes: laboratory and field. **Laboratory experiments** are those in which the independent variable is manipulated and measures of the dependent variable are taken in a contrived, artificial setting. This is done to control the many possible extraneous variables that may affect the dependent variable.

To illustrate, consider a study whereby subjects are invited to a theatre and shown test ads, copy A or copy B, spliced into a TV "pilot" program. Such a setting is used to control for variables that could affect the purchase of products other than those in the test ads. By bringing consumers into a contrived laboratory setting, the experimenter is able to control many extraneous variables. It is important to have equivalent groups (the same kind of people watching copy A as those watching copy B commercials) in an experiment. By inviting preselected consumers to the TV pilot showing in a theatre, the experimenter can match (on selected demographics) the consumers who view copy A with those who view copy B, thus ensuring that the two groups are equal. By having the consumers walk into an adjoining "store," the experimenter easily controls other factors such as the time between exposure to the ad copy and shopping, as well as the consumers' being exposed to other advertising by competitive brands. Any one of these factors, left uncontrolled, could have an impact on the dependent variable. By controlling for these and other variables, the experimenter can be assured that any changes in the dependent variable are due solely to differences in the independent variable, ad copy A and ad copy B. Laboratory experiments, then, are desirable when the intent of the experiment is to achieve high levels of internal validity.

There are other advantages to laboratory experiments. First, they allow the researcher to control for the effects of extraneous variables. Second, compared with field experiments, lab experiments may be conducted quickly and with less expense. The disadvantage is the lack of a natural setting and, therefore, there is concern for the generalizability of the findings to the real world. For instance, blind taste tests of beer have found that a majority of beer drinkers favour the older beers such as Pabst, Michelob, or Coors, yet new beer brands are introduced regularly and become quite popular.[16] It appears the generalizability of blind taste tests to the real world is questionable.

**Field experiments** are those in which the independent variables are manipulated and the measurements of the dependent variable are made on test units in their natural setting. Many marketing experiments are conducted in natural settings, such as in supermarkets, malls, retail stores, and consumers' homes. Assume that a marketing manager conducts a *laboratory* experiment to test the differences between ad copy A, the company's existing ad copy, and a new ad copy, copy B. The results of the laboratory experiment indicate that ad copy B is far superior to the company's present ad copy A. But, before spending the money to use the new copy, the manager wants to know if ad copy B will create increased sales in the real world. She elects to actually run the new ad copy in Red Deer, Alberta, a city noted as being representative of the average characteristics of the Canadian population. By conducting this study in the field, the marketing manager will have greater confidence that the results of the study will actually hold up in other real-world settings. Red Deer, Alberta, is an example of a test market. Note, however, that even if an experiment is conducted in a naturalistic field setting in order to enhance external validity, the experiment is invalid if it does not also have internal validity.

The primary advantage of the field experiment is that of conducting the study in a naturalistic setting, thus increasing the likelihood that the study's findings will also hold true in the real world. Field experiments, however, are expensive and time consuming. Also, the experimenter must always be alert to the impact of extraneous variables, which are very difficult to control in the natural settings of field experimentation.

Much of the experimentation in marketing is conducted as field experiments in specific locales known as *test markets*.

## Test Marketing

**Test marketing** is the phrase commonly used to indicate an experiment, study, or test that is conducted in a natural setting. Companies may use one or several test-market cities, which are selected geographical areas in which to conduct the test. Test market uses may be divided into two broad classes: (1) to test the sales potential for a new product or service, and (2) to test variations in the marketing mix for a product or service.[17]

Although test markets are very expensive and time consuming, the costs of introducing a new product on a national or regional basis routinely amount to millions of dollars. The costs of the test market are then justified if the results of the test market can improve a product's chances of success. Sometimes the test market results will be sufficient to warrant further market introductions. Sometimes the test market identifies a failure early on and saves the company huge losses. The GlobalPC, a scaled-down computer targeted to novices, was tried in test markets. The parent company, MyTurn, concluded that the test market sales results would not lead to a profit, and the product was dropped before the company experienced further losses.[18] Test markets are conducted not only to measure sales potential for a new product but also to measure consumer and dealer reactions to other marketing-mix variables. A firm may use only department stores to distribute the product in one test-market city and only specialty stores in another test-market city in order to gain some information on the best way to distribute the product. Companies can also test media usage, pricing, sales promotions, and so on through test markets.

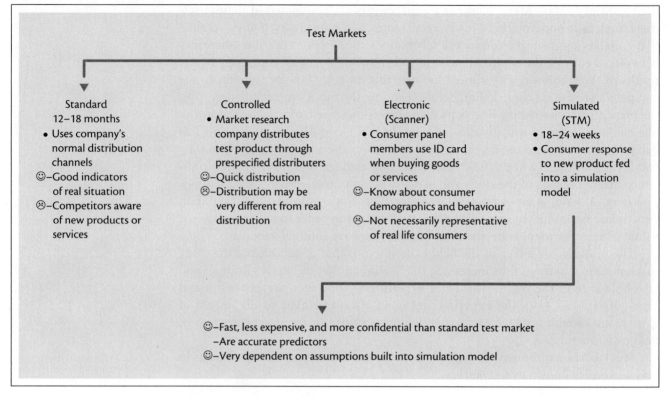

**Figure 3.3** Types of Consumer Test Markets

## Types of Test Markets

Test markets have been classified into four types: standard, controlled, electronic, and simulated (see Figure 3.3).[19] The **standard test market** is one in which the firm tests the product or marketing-mix variables through the company's *normal* distribution channels. A disadvantage of this type of test market is that competitors are immediately aware of the new product or service. However, standard test markets are good indicators as to how the product will actually perform because they are conducted in real settings.

**Controlled test markets** are conducted by outside research firms that guarantee distribution of the product through prespecified types and numbers of distributors. Companies specializing in providing this service, such as ACNielsen, provide dollar incentives for distributors to provide them with guaranteed shelf space. Controlled test markets offer an alternative to the company that wishes to gain fast access to a distribution system set up for test-market purposes. The disadvantage is that this distribution network may or may not properly represent the firm's actual distribution system.

**Scanner (electronic) test markets** are those in which a panel of consumers has agreed to carry scannable cards that each consumer presents when buying goods and services. These tests are conducted only in a small number of cities in which local retailers have agreed to participate. The advantage of the card is that as consumers buy (or do not buy) the test product, demographic information on the consumers is automatically recorded. In some cases, firms offering scanner test markets may also have the ability to link media viewing habits to panel members as well.

In this way, firms using the electronic test market also know how different elements of the promotional mix affect purchases of the new product. North American firms offering this service include Information Resources, Inc. and ACNielsen. Obviously, the electronic test market offers speed, greater confidentiality, and a lower cost than standard or controlled test markets. However, the disadvantage is that the test market is not the real market. By virtue of having agreed to serve as members of the electronic panel, consumers in electronic test markets may be atypical. A user firm must evaluate the issue of representativeness. Also, electronic test markets are not common in Canada.

**Simulated test markets (STMs)** are those in which a limited amount of data on consumer response to a new product is fed into a simulation model containing certain assumptions regarding planned marketing programs. The computer model generates likely product sales volume. It is claimed that IBM has suffered business failures such as the ill-fated Aptiva line of PCs because it failed to use STM research.[20] Typical STMs share the following characteristics: (1) Respondents are selected to provide a sample of consumers who satisfy predetermined demographic characteristics; (2) consumers are shown commercials or print ads for the test product as well as ads for competitive products; (3) consumers are then given the opportunity to purchase, or not to purchase, the test product in either a real or a simulated store environment; (4) consumers are then recontacted after they have had an opportunity to use the product in an effort to determine likelihood of repurchase, as well as other information relative to use of the product; and (5) information from the preceding process is fed into a computer program that is calibrated by assumptions of the marketing mix and other elements of the environment. The program then generates output such as estimated sales volume, market share, and so on.[21]

There are many advantages to STMs. They are fast relative to standard test markets. STMs typically take only 18 to 24 weeks, compared with as many as 12 to 18 *months* for standard test markets. STMs cost only 5% to 10% of the cost of a standard test market. STMs are confidential; competitors are less likely to know about the test. Different marketing mixes may be tested, and results of STMs have shown that they can be accurate predictors of actual market response. The primary disadvantage is that STMs are not as accurate as full-scale test markets. They are very dependent on the assumptions built into the models.[22]

## Consumer versus Industrial Test Markets

The use of test marketing has been increasing in the industrial market, sometimes called the B2B (business-to-business) market. Although the techniques are somewhat different between consumer and industrial test markets, the same results are sought: the timely release of profitable products.

In consumer test markets, multiple versions of a more-or-less finished product are tested by consumers. In industrial test markets, the key technology is presented to selected industrial users, who offer feedback on desired features and product performance levels. Given this information, product prototypes are then developed and are placed with a select number of users for actual use. Users again provide feedback to iron out design problems. In this way, the new product is tried and tested under actual conditions before the final product is designed and produced for the total market. The downside of this process is the time it takes to test the product from the beginning stages to the final, commercialized stages. During this time period, information on the new product is leaked to competitors, and the longer the product is being tested, the more investment costs increase without any revenues being generated. U.S. automakers, for example, take 48 to 60 months to design, refine, and begin production of a new car model. Japanese companies are able to do it in 30 months by having a development team made up of a combination of marketing and production people. 3M has experimented with this concept. In many firms, future industrial test marketing will be fully integrated with the new-product development process.

## "Lead Country" Test Markets

A **lead country test market** is test marketing conducted in specific foreign countries that seem to be good predictors for an entire continent. As markets have become more global, firms are no longer interested in limiting marketing of new products and services to their domestic markets.

Colgate-Palmolive used lead country test marketing when it launched its Palmolive Optims shampoo and conditioner. The company tested the product in the Philippines, Australia, Mexico, and Hong Kong. A year later, distribution was expanded to other countries in Europe, Asia, Latin America, and Africa.[23] Colgate used two countries as test markets in 1999 to test its battery-powered Actibrush for kids. These two countries brought in $10 million in sales. Colgate moved into 50 countries in 2000 and earned $115 million in sales.[24] South Korea is being used as a lead country test market for digital products and services. Seongnam is a middle-class Seoul suburb with a mix of high-rise apartment blocks, restaurants, and malls. During the next three years, municipal officials plan to transform the town of 930 000 into the world's first digital city. Multiple broadband connections will seek to do away with analog concepts—like cash and credit cards. Seongnam will start equipping citizens with digital cellphones that, in effect, pay for purchases at every store in the city. Cash-free Seongnam is one of many on-the-ground tests being launched in South Korea, a nation preoccupied with all things digital. More than half of South Korea's 15 million households have broadband service and more than 60% of Koreans carry cellphones. The country is now so wired that many companies can use entire urban populations as test markets for their latest digital products and services.[25]

## Selecting Test-Market Cities

There are three criteria that are useful for selecting test-market cities: **representativeness**, **degree of isolation**, and **ability to control distribution and promotion**. Because one of the major reasons for conducting a test market is to achieve external validity, the test-market city should be representative of the marketing territory in which the product will ultimately be distributed. Consequently, a great deal of effort is expended to locate the "ideal" city in terms of comparability with characteristics of the total Canadian population. The "ideal" city is, of course, the city whose demographic characteristics most closely match the desired total market. Based on the 2006 Canadian census, Environics Analytics identified the top 10 "anytowns" that best represent the Canadian population. They are as follows:

1. Red Deer, Alberta
2. Waterloo, Ontario
3. Guelph, Ontario

4. Kingston, British Columbia (B.C.)
5. Kelowna, B.C.
6. Maple Ridge, B.C.
7. Grande Prairie, Alberta
8. London, Ontario
9. Calgary, Alberta
10. Langley, B.C.

The ability to control distribution and promotion depends on a number of factors. Are the distributors in the city being considered available and willing to cooperate? If not, is a controlled-test-market service company available for the city? Will the media in the city have the facilities to accommodate the test-market needs? At what costs? All of these factors must be considered before selecting the test city. Fortunately, because city governments often consider it desirable to have test markets conducted in their city because it brings in additional revenues, they as well as the media typically provide a great deal of information about their city to prospective test marketers.

## Pros and Cons of Test Marketing

The advantages of test marketing are straightforward. Testing product acceptability and marketing-mix variables in a field setting provides the best information possible to the decision maker prior to actually going into full-scale marketing of the product. Because of this, Philip Kotler has referred to test markets as the "ultimate" way to test a new product.[26] Test marketing allows for the most accurate method of forecasting future sales, and it allows companies the opportunity to pretest marketing-mix variables. Marketing Research in Action 3.3 explores how companies can use test marketing to reduce risks.

There are, however, several disadvantages to test marketing. First, there have been many instances in which test-market results have led to decisions that proved wrong in the marketplace. No doubt there have probably been many potentially successful products withheld from the marketplace due to poor performances in test markets. Much of this problem, however, is not due to anything inherent in test marketing; rather, it is a reflection of the complexity of consumer behaviour. Accurately forecasting consumer behaviour is a formidable task. Also, competitors intentionally try to sabotage test markets. Firms will often flood a test market with sales promotions if they know a competitor is test marketing a product. When PepsiCo tested Mountain Dew Sport drink in Minneapolis in 1990, Quaker Oats Company's Gatorade counterattacked with a deluge of coupons and ads. Mountain Dew Sport was yanked from the market, although Pepsi says Gatorade had nothing to do with the decision.[27] These activities make it even more difficult to forecast the normal market's response to a product.

Another problem with test markets is their cost. Estimates are that the costs exceed several hundred thousand dollars even for limited test markets. Test markets involving several test cities and various forms of promotion can easily reach well over six figures. Finally, test markets bring about exposure of the product to the competition. Competitors get the opportunity to examine product prototypes and to see the planned marketing strategy for the new product via the test market. If a company spends too much time testing a product, it runs the risk of allowing enough time for a competitor to bring out a similar product and to gain the advantage of being first in the market. In spite of these problems, the value of the information from test marketing makes test marketing a worthwhile endeavour.

Finally, test markets may create ethical problems. Companies routinely report test-marketing results to the press, which allows them access to premarket publicity. Companies, eager to get good publicity, may select test-market cities that they feel will return favourable results. *The Wall Street Journal* has addressed these issues, and the Advertising Research Foundation in the United States has published the document "Guidelines for Public Use of Market and Opinion Research" in an attempt to make reporting of test markets more candid.[28] In Canada, the MRIA now offers a core course on Ethical Issues and Privacy in Marketing Research.

## MARKETING RESEARCH IN ACTION 3.3
# Companies Can Reduce Risks by Test Marketing First

### Snoring While Driving May be Hazardous to Your Health

Specialists estimate that 20% of accidents are caused by drivers who are tired or not paying attention to the road. Moreover, statistics show that thousands of people die every year because of drivers falling asleep at the wheel. With the objective of reducing this problem, Saab is launching an in-car system called Driver Attention Warning System (DAWS) that is supposed to determine when the driver is tired or not paying enough attention to the road and to advise the driver to stop for a rest. The system consists of two cameras focused on the driver's eyes to detect when eye movements indicate drowsiness. DAWS is an innovative product in that it focuses on detecting the onset of drowsiness or inattention. Competitive products have focused on the immediate consequences of falling asleep. Saab is test marketing the system on its 9-3 Sport Wagon in Sweden; if it is successful, the idea is to introduce DAWS in other Saab models across Europe.[29]

### e.l.f. Testing Online

Eyes. Lips. Face. (e.l.f.) is the brand of a company that offers good-quality, low-priced products for the eyes (shadows, liners, mascara), lips (plumpers, glosses, lipsticks), and face (powder, blusher, concealer). An urban legend had it that the company would be acquired by the retailer Nordstrom and that the new owner would sell all e.l.f. products for $1 at the website **www.eyeslipsface.com**. The story was not true, but the news spread quickly and resulted in an

avalanche of business at the website. Now the company is using the well-known website as a test-marketing medium, trying out new products and colours before it sends products to big retail stores like Target and Kmart.[30]

### Want to Stop by for Some Snacks, a Beer, and a Paternity Test?

Soreson Genomics Company has developed a do-it-yourself DNA test that allows people to discover the identity of a baby's father in a cheaper and faster way than ever before. The kit costs $29.99 and the laboratory costs are $119, representing a total cost of less than $150 instead of the $2000 or more charged for the traditional test. The company also guarantees the results within five business days; the traditional test averages six months. The test has 99.9% certainty of establishing paternity or proving genetic links between siblings.

After a good response to the test marketing done in U.S. states on the Pacific coast, Sorenson rolled out its Identigene paternity kits nationally in March 2008. Even though the test is not admissible in court (because the identity of those taking part in the at-home test cannot be verified), demand for it is high. People take the test for different reasons, but often to avoid the need to go to court. The company is promising to provide a legally sound test for about $350.[31]

## McCoffee Anyone?

The number of consumers who buy a coffee drink during a quick-service food visit grew to 6.6% in 2007 from 3.5% in 2006. Looking at the fast growth of coffee consumption during snack occasions, McDonald's has launched McCafé Specialty Coffees. The company started the launching by test marketing in six major markets, including Grand Rapids, Michigan; California's Central Coast; Kansas City, Missouri; and parts of Georgia, North Carolina, and Texas. Initial results were above expectations, but after some time had passed espresso drink sales fell off their initial pace. McDonald's moved ahead with the new product line with the goal of adding $125 000 a year in sales per restaurant. The company planned to expand the rollout from the stores that started the test marketing to its 14 000 stores during 2009.[32]

# Summary

**1. Describe the role of research design in the marketing research process.**
*Research design* refers to a set of advance decisions about the plan for conducting the research project. There are three general types of research designs: exploratory, descriptive, and causal. Each one of these types has its own inherent approaches. By matching the research objective with the appropriate research design, a host of research decisions may be predetermined. Therefore, a research design serves as a "blueprint" for researchers. Selecting the appropriate research design depends, to a large extent, on the research objective and how much information is already known about the problem.

**2. Characterize exploratory research design.**
If very little is known, exploratory research is appropriate. Exploratory research is unstructured, informal research that is undertaken to gain background information; it is helpful for more clearly defining the research problem. Exploratory research is used in a number of situations: to gain background information, to define terms, to clarify problems and hypotheses, and to establish research priorities. Reviewing existing literature, surveying individuals knowledgeable in the area to be investigated, relying on former similar case situations, conducting focus groups, and using projective techniques are methods of conducting exploratory research. Focus groups are conducted by having a small group of people guided by a moderator through a spontaneous, unstructured conversation that focuses on a research problem. Focus-group research is a type of qualitative research. Other forms of qualitative research include in-depth interviews, protocol analysis, projective techniques, observation, and ethnographic research. Focus groups should be used when there is information that needs to be described. However, when information needs to be predicted, focus groups should not be used. Exploratory research should be used in almost all cases because it is fast, inexpensive, and sometimes classifies the research objective or is helpful in carrying out descriptive or causal research.

3.  **Characterize descriptive research design.**

If concepts, terms, and background information are already known and the research objective is to describe and measure phenomena, then descriptive research is appropriate. Descriptive research measures marketing phenomena and answers the questions of who, what, where, when, and how. Descriptive studies may be conducted at one point in time (cross-sectional), or several measurements may be made on the same sample at different points in time (longitudinal). Longitudinal studies are often conducted using panels. Panels represent sample units of individuals who have agreed to answer questions at periodic intervals. Continuous panels are longitudinal studies in which sample units are asked the same questions repeatedly. Brand-switching tables may be prepared based on data from continuous panels, and market-tracking studies may be conducted using data from such panels.

The second type of panel used in longitudinal research is the discontinuous panel. Discontinuous panels, also called omnibus panels, are those in which the various sample units are asked different questions. The main advantage of the discontinuous panel is that research firms have a large sample of persons who are willing to answer whatever questions they are asked. The demographics of panel members are often balanced to the demographics of the larger geographical areas they are to represent, such as a region. Widespread use of the internet has led to the growth of online panels. Marketing research firms such as CRC Research and ACNielsen have maintained panels for many years. Online survey research firms such as Lightspeed and Survey Head offer clients the use of online panels of respondents.

4.  **Characterize causal research design.**

Sometimes the research objective requires the researcher to determine causal relationships between two or more variables. Causal relationships provide relationships such as "If $x$, then $y$." Causal relationships may be discovered only through special studies called experiments. Experiments allow us to determine the effects of one variable, known as an independent variable, on another variable, known as a dependent variable. Experimental designs are necessary to ensure that the effect observed in a dependent variable is due, in fact, to the independent variable and not to other variables known as extraneous variables. The validity of experiments may be assessed internally, by measuring what one thinks is being measured, and externally, by extrapolating results to the population as a whole.

Laboratory experiments are particularly useful for achieving internal validity, whereas field experiments are better suited for achieving external validity. Test marketing is a form of field experimentation. Test-market cities are selected on the basis of their representativeness, isolation, and the degree to which market variables such as distribution and promotion may be controlled. Various types of test markets exist (standard, controlled, electronic, simulated, consumer, industrial, and lead country). Although test markets provide much useful information, they are expensive and not foolproof.

# Key Terms

| | |
|---|---|
| Ability to control distribution and promotion   (p. 104) | Before-after with control group   (p. 97) |
| After-only design   (p. 96) | Brand-switching studies   (p. 92) |

# Review Questions

**1.1** What criteria would you use to select the best research design?

**1.2** In order to enhance the options they currently offer, Google is interested in researching how people use its service. What is the research problem, and what type of research design would you recommend?

**2.1** Describe two example scenarios where it is best to use exploratory research.

**2.2** To which type of research design are focus groups best suited? Why do you say that?

**3.1** What are the differences between longitudinal and cross-sectional studies?

**3.2** In what type of situation would a continuous panel be more suitable than a discontinuous panel? In what type of situation would a discontinuous panel be more suitable than a continuous panel?

**4.1** What is the objective of good experimental design? Explain why certain designs are called quasi-experimental.

**4.2** Design an experiment. Select the independent and dependent variables. Identify the extraneous variables. Explain how you would control for the effects these variables may have on your dependent variable. Is your experiment valid?

4.3 Describe the two types of validity in experimentation and explain why different types of experiments are better suited for addressing one type of validity than another.

4.4 The Maximum Company has invented an extra strong instant coffee brand called "Max-Gaff." It is positioned to be stronger tasting than competing brands. Design a taste test experiment that compares Max-Gaff with the two leading instant coffee brands to determine which brand consumers consider to taste the strongest. Indicate how the experiment is to be conducted. Assess the internal and external validity of your experiment.

4.5 Coca-Cola markets Powerade as a sports drink that competes with Gatorade. Competition for sports drinks is fierce where they are sold in coolers of convenience stores. Coca-Cola is thinking about using a special holder that fits in a standard convenience store cooler but moves Powerade to eye level and makes it more conspicuous than Gatorade. Design an experiment that determines whether the special holder increases the sales of Powerade in convenience stores. Assess the internal and external validity of your experiment.

# Case 3.1

# Quality Research Associates

Sam Fulkerson of Quality Research Associates reviewed notes of meetings with his clients during the last week.

*Monday/A.M.* Discussion with Janey Dean, director of marketing for the Toronto Dominion Bank. Dean is interested in knowing more about a bank image study. Informed her that we had not conducted such a study but that I would meet with her in a week and discuss how to proceed. Dean wants to hire us for advice; her own staff may actually do the image study. Next meeting set for 15th at 2:30 p.m.

*Tuesday/P.M.* Met with Cayleigh Rogers, business manager for Appleton College. College is considering a football team, and the president wants some indication from alums if they favour it and if they will be willing to send in a donation to help with start-up costs. The president of the college also wants to know if present students will support the football team. Call him back for follow-up meeting.

*Wednesday/A.M.* Met with Lawrence Brown of Effan Foods. Brown is brand manager for a new chocolate bar, and he needs advice on promotional methods in the chocolate bar business. Specifically, he would like to know what promotional methods have been used over the last five years by chocolate bar brands and how those promotions impacted sales. Advised Brown I would contact some other research suppliers and get back to him.

*Wednesday/P.M.* Tom Greer visited office. Tom also with Effan Foods. Company interested in going into cereal line and wants information fast on how consumers will react to chocolate-flavoured cereal that company has developed. Company's own taste tests have been favourable, but Greer wants reaction from a larger sample of consumers from around the country. Would like this information within a month. Important: Company already has the samples ready for mailing.

*Thursday/A.M.* Meeting with Phyllis Detrick of Sobeys. Sobeys has a chain of 1300 stores in 10 provinces. Company is spending several million dollars a year on print advertising. Detrick wants to know what she can do with the advertising copy and layout of the ads that will generate the most attention. She conducted some exploratory research and found that potential consumers who were reading the newspapers never even recalled seeing the Sobeys ads. Specifically, she wants to know if adding colour is worth the expense. Will colour ads generate greater attention? We set up a joint meeting with the Sobeys advertising manager, who will bring in all of the company's newspaper ads from the last six months.

*Thursday/P.M.* Meeting with Carolyn Phillips, French Yarbrough, and Jeff Rogers. All three are part of a start-up company that has been working on a new toothbrush storage and sanitation device.

The new product steam-sanitizes the toothbrushes overnight to make them virtually germ free. Two years ago we conducted exploratory research in the form of focus groups. We followed that up with a survey of a representative sample of households within the city. The survey showed the respondents a picture of the device and asked them if they would be willing to pay $x to buy it. Thus far, all had gone well and all studies indicated "go." Now, Phillips, Yarbrough, and Rogers think they are ready to introduce the product to the country. They have had several discussions with large retail chains. All of the chain buyers are interested, but they want more evidence that the market will accept the devices. One chain buyer said, "I want to know if people will walk into our stores and really buy these off the shelf." Also, Phillips, Yarbrough, and Rogers have narrowed their national promotion campaigns down to two options, but they aren't certain which one will gain them the most customers.

*Friday/A.M.* No client meetings. Work on research designs.

1. Which research design do you think Sam Fulkerson should select for each of his clients?
2. For each research design you specify in question 1, describe the reason(s) you selected it.

# Case 3.2

# Future Oriented

Future Oriented is a hypothetical, small marketing consulting firm in Halifax. It was started 15 years ago by the current president, Jane Ferguson. The company specializes in developing new products in the soft package goods industry. Stuart Campbell of Halifax is the founder and president of the OH SO GOOD! candy company. He approached Jane recently with a request. It appears that one of the candy master cooks in the OH SO GOOD! laboratories had developed a new candy formula but was not certain what specific candy product this formula could be developed into.

1. Outline the various research activities Future Oriented should follow in order to develop the final new product idea. First, identify the research problem at every step of the new product development process.
2. Next, identify the research design appropriate for each step.
3. Finally, describe the research method most appropriate for each step in the development of the new OH SO GOOD! product, giving reasons for your choices.

# Case 3.3 YOUR INTEGRATED CASE

# Student Life E-Zine

*In Chapter 2, we presented the second instalment of the Student Life E-Zine case to you. Here, we return to a portion of that instalment:*

Bob stated that ORS could also provide information that would help determine potential subscribers' preferences for various types of features in the e-zine.

Don said, "Some hard data would be very helpful to us in making those decisions. We have to remember not to put ourselves in the place of our customers. We haven't been students for several years now! I've been thinking about the different types of features we can offer, and I'll bring the list of ideas to our work session tonight."

Bob said, "That sounds great. We may also want to consider doing some focus groups right away with students. They're likely to have some great ideas about exactly what they would like to see in the e-zine. Focus groups may give you some good ideas on what to name your e-zine as well, and they'll give us some idea about students' willingness to accept the $15-per-month subscription fee."

## Questions

1. Explain why it may be beneficial to conduct qualitative research, such as focus groups, prior to conducting quantitative research, such as the survey of students at City U.

2. Explain why you believe this particular problem—determining the types of features for the e-zine—would be suitable for a focus group.

3. What limitations do you think focus-group research will have in this situation?

# Using Secondary Data and Online Information Databases

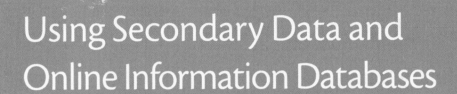

## LEARNING OBJECTIVES

1. Classify types of secondary data and demonstrate their uses.

2. Discuss advantages and disadvantages of secondary data.

3. Discover how to find secondary data, including strategies for searching online information bases.

4. Examine major sources of external secondary data, including standardized information sources.

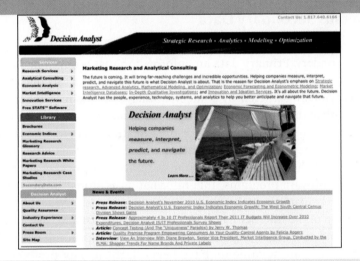

## Marketing Researchers Use Secondary Data

Here at Decision Analyst® we make certain we are fully aware of all existing information about an industry, a product category, and a company before we decide on the research objectives and methodology for a research project. Even when we are dealing with a client in an industry in which we have conducted dozens of marketing research projects, a review of current secondary data can alert us to any recent developments. Any good marketing researcher should be adept at searching for and analyzing secondary data. Secondary data analysis is fast and inexpensive compared with collecting primary data. Sometimes, secondary data are all we need in order to provide the necessary information to solve our client's problem. Also, when we need to collect primary data for our clients, we provide current, relevant secondary data to help our client better understand the implications of the primary data. We strive to add value for our clients and secondary data helps us accomplish that goal.

The internet has been a catalyst for allowing faster searches and giving us access to more information than we thought possible just a few years ago. However, we are cautious in accepting any secondary data. Sometimes information is disseminated to serve special interests. At Decision Analyst® we use secondary data from known and trusted sources. Go to our website at **www.decisionanalyst.com** and click on Secondary Data.com.

Jerry W. Thomas, President/CEO, Decision Analyst
By permission

Marketing researcher Jerry W. Thomas's comments demonstrate the importance of secondary data and online databases to marketing researchers. As he points out, even when the project involves collecting primary data, marketing researchers also consult secondary data. He also points out how online information databases have made this task much easier for the researcher.

# Secondary Data

## Primary versus Secondary Data

Data needed for marketing management decisions can be grouped into two types: primary and secondary. **Primary data** are information that is developed or gathered by the researcher specifically for the research project at hand. **Secondary data** are information previously gathered by someone other than the researcher and/or for some purpose other than the research project at hand. As commercial firms, government agencies, or community service organizations record transactions and business activities, they are creating a written record of these activities in the form of secondary data. When consumers fill out warranty cards or register their boats, automobiles, or software programs, this information is stored in the form of secondary data. It is available for someone else's secondary use.

The evolution of the internet has done more to bring fast and easy access to secondary data to end users than anything since Gutenberg's printing press. Since the mid-1980s, virtually all documents have been electronically produced, edited, stored, and made accessible to users. For several years, firms have concentrated on bringing this information to users through specialized services, and today many of these firms offer these services via the internet. Although some information is available only through a subscription, the Internet provides an incredible stock of free secondary data. Google®, Yahoo®, Live Search®, and ASK® account for millions of searches per day, and specialized search engines are devoted to such areas as business, real property, health, careers, news, and so on. Search engines no longer publicize how many searches are conducted daily, but Google is thought to be the largest.[1] Secondary data access through the internet continues to grow and becomes more and more important in the marketing researcher's toolbox.

## Uses of Secondary Data

There are so many uses of secondary data that it is rare for a marketing research project to be conducted without including it. Some projects may be totally based on secondary data. The applications of secondary data range from predicting very broad changes in a culture's "way of life" (see Marketing Research in Action 4.1) to very specific applications, such as selecting a street address location for a new car wash. As noted in our opening vignette, Decision Analyst, Inc., a marketing research firm, has a website devoted entirely to secondary data. Another very useful website is **www.statcan.gc.ca**, the website of Statistics Canada, Canada's national statistical agency. Statistics produced by the agency, along with a variety of reports on subjects of interest to Canadians, are found throughout the website. Suggested applications include economic trends forecasting, among others.

Marketers are very interested in having secondary demographic data to help them forecast the size of the market in a newly proposed market territory. A researcher may use secondary data to determine the population and growth rate in almost any geographical area. Government agencies are interested in having secondary data to help them make public policy decisions. The Department of Education needs to know how many five-year-olds will enter the public school system next year. Healthcare planners need to know how many senior citizens will be eligible for public health care during the next decade. Sometimes, secondary data can be used to evaluate market performance. For example, since data on gasoline and fuel taxes are available in public records, petroleum marketers can easily determine the volume of fuels consumed in a province. Articles on virtually every topic are published, and this storehouse of secondary data is available to marketers who want to understand a subject more thoroughly.

A large amount of secondary data is available concerning the lifestyles of demographic groups, including their purchasing habits. Marketing researchers have identified certain **demographic and psychographic groups** as market segments, in that they tend to make similar purchases, have similar attitudes, and have similar media habits. The most significant of these demographic groups for decades has been the "**baby boomer**" population, defined as those born between 1946 and 1964. As the boomers enter middle-age and senior status, marketers have turned to studying other demographic groups, such as **Gen Xers**[2] and **Gen Yers**. Marketing Research in Action 4.1 discusses some psychographic groups developed by Environics to give marketers more marketing intelligence than is provided by demographics alone.

# Classification of Secondary Data

Given that the amount of secondary information available can be overwhelming, marketing researchers must learn to handle it properly. A basic understanding of the classification of secondary data is helpful. The advantages and disadvantages of each classification and how to evaluate the information available are also worth knowing.

## Internal Secondary Data

Secondary data are broadly classified as either internal or external. **Internal secondary data** are data that have been collected within the firm. Such data include sales records, purchase requisitions, and invoices. Obviously, a good marketing researcher always determines what internal information is already available. Internal data analysis is part of the internal reports system of a firm's marketing information system (MIS). Today, a major source of internal data is databases containing information on customers, sales, suppliers, and any other facet of business a firm may wish to track. Philip Kotler defines **database marketing** as "the process of building, maintaining, and using customer (internal) databases and other (internal) databases (products, suppliers, resellers) for the purpose of contacting, transacting, and building relationships [italics added]."[3] The use of internal databases continues to grow dramatically.

## MARKETING RESEARCH IN ACTION 4.1
# What Does Sex Have to Do with Marketing Research?

*Sex in the Snow: Canadian Social Values at the End of the Millennium* is a book about the "psychographic geography of Canada." Written by Michael Adams, the founder and previous president of the Environics Research Group, the book examines the values, attitudes, and lifestyles of Canadian adults. Environics is one of the leading marketing intelligence companies in Canada and a pioneer in social values research. The author argues that knowledge of the psychographics of Canadians arms businesses with stronger market intelligence than do demographic measures alone.

Psychographics is a very valuable tool used by marketers to help segment their markets while developing their marketing plans. Psychographics developed as a result of the application of social science research to the marketing research industry. In the early 1960s, Daniel Yankelovitch looked at evolving social values by analyzing extensive one-on-one interviews. By the early 1970s, quantitative questions and scales were developed to examine "socio-cultural currents" (3SC). Environics Research Group and CROP, a Canadian polling firm, brought the 3SC system to Canada in 1983.

Over the years, Environics developed refined research tools based on the 3SC system. Data were collected from adult Canadians using a detailed questionnaire. Analysis of the responses included clustering the responses according to individual versus social inclinations and traditional versus modern values. The clusters thus formed were composed of individuals who share common responses on these dimensions. Adams identified 12 psychographic groups (or "tribes," as they are termed by Adams) classified under three major categories: the Elders, the Boomers, and the Gen Xers. Gen Xers are made up of Thrill-Seeking Materialists (25%), Aimless Dependants (27%), Social Hedonists (15%), Autonomous Post-Materialists (20%), and New Aquarians (13%).

So, what does this have to do with sex, and what does sex have to do with marketing research? "Sex" represents the self-indulgent, pleasure-seeking behaviour that Canadians engage in today, while still holding on to values that are

uniquely Canadian. This knowledge about Canadian behaviour helps marketers plan added value for their customers. For example, smart marketers will offer their self-indulgent customers the same product with a different "stripe" so that they will want to buy more of the same. Apple is very successful at marketing the iPod through this approach. The iPod comes in several shapes and sizes, and many customers have more than one, even when the differences between the products may not warrant it. The UGG company is also successful at producing different variations of the same theme for their sheepskin boots. Many customers own several pairs at a time. Other marketers offer products that enable customers to individualize their possessions (for example, GelSkin covers for iPods).

To find out which psychographic tribe you fit into, visit the Environics website, **http://research-environics-net.sitepreview.ca**. Click on "Environics Research Group"; then click on the "Social Values Survey" icon, and answer the questions.

## Internal Databases

A **database** refers to a collection of data and information describing items of interest.[4] Each unit of information in a database is called a **record**. A record could represent a customer, a supplier, a competitive firm, a product, an individual inventory item, and so on. Records are composed of subcomponents of information called **fields**. As an example, a company maintaining a database of customers would have records representing each customer. Typical fields in a customer database would include name, address, telephone number, email address, products purchased, dates of purchases, locations of purchase, warranty information, and any other information of importance. The majority of databases are computerized because they contain large amounts of information and their use is facilitated by the computer's capability to edit, sort, and analyze the mass of information. Indeed, most information today is gathered electronically, such as customer purchases on a Safeway or Visa card.

**Internal databases** are databases consisting of information gathered by a company during the normal course of business transactions. Marketing managers normally develop internal databases about customers, but databases may be kept on any topic of interest, such as products, members of the sales force, inventory, maintenance, and supplier firms. Companies gather information about customers when customers inquire about a product or service, make a purchase, or have a product serviced. Think about the information a customer may have provided to marketing firms: their name, address, telephone number, fax number, email address, credit card number, banking institution and account number, and so on. The products one has purchased in the past, coupled with other information provided by government and other commercial sources, give companies quite a bit of information about customers. Companies use their internal databases for purposes of direct marketing and to strengthen relationships with customers. This is called **customer relationship management (CRM)**.[5]

Internal databases can be quite large. Dealing with the vast quantities of data and managing the information in internal databases has been challanging, especially, since there are many database silos within an organization. **Data mining** is analyzing data for trends or patterns. Data mining software programs are designed to gain insight for helping managers make decisions. Anthony Lea, an instructor for the data mining techniques course at the Marketing Research and Intelligence Assoication (MRIA) Institute for Professional Development, states that "the value of data mining can be to increase the efficiency and/or decrease the cost of marketing by increasing customer loyalty, cross-sell, up-sell, or by decreasing churn or credit risk."[6] While looking for specific trends, data miners find other things of interest during the search. Traditional statistical techniques, discussed in later chapters of this text, are used in data mining as well as "new" methods such as regression trees and artificial intelligence.

Internal databases can also be developed through company websites and can include company blogs, online forums, and other forms of social media originating from the company such as accounts on Facebook and Twitter. **Text mining** is a growing type of data mining analysis. It includes text from both internal and external data sources. Text is scanned from websites, online blogs, Facebook, and other social media. Anderson Analytics uses a variety of text mining software to analyze verbatim concepts written by customers as well as emotional content software, "which looks at the words people choose to use" as a way of understanding their emotional needs.[7] However, not all databases are massive, and even simple ones in small businesses can be invaluable. One study showed that almost half of retail firms have some sort of database containing information about their customers.[8]

Internal databases, built with information collected during the normal course of business, can provide invaluable insights to managers. Databases can tell them which products are selling, report inventories, and profile customers by stock keeping unit (SKU). Coupled with geodemographic information systems (GIS), databases can provide maps of where the most profitable and least profitable customers reside by postal codes.

What companies do with the information collected for their internal databases can present ethical problems. Should a credit card company share information on what types of goods and services a customer bought with anyone who wants to buy that information? Should an internet service provider be able to store information about the internet sites a customer visits? As more consumers have grown aware of these privacy issues, more companies have adopted privacy policies.[9] Ethics in Marketing Research 4.1 provides a summary of the MRIA Privacy Code and outlines how the marketing research industry in Canada deals with these issues.

---

 ## ETHICS IN MARKETING RESEARCH 4.1
# The MRIA Privacy Code

## Introduction

At the MRIA, respecting privacy has always been important to us and is why we have developed the MRIA Privacy Code. The MRIA Privacy Code is a statement of principles and guidelines regarding our management of personal information. The objective of the MRIA Privacy Code is to promote responsible and transparent personal information management practices in a manner consistent with the provisions of applicable privacy laws such as the Personal Information Protection and Electronic Documents Act (Canada). The MRIA will continue to review The MRIA Privacy Code to make sure that it remains current with changing industry standards, technologies, and laws.

## Summary of Principles

### Principle 1: Accountability

The MRIA is responsible for personal information under its control and will designate one or more persons who are accountable for the MRIA's compliance with the following principles.

### Principle 2: Identifying Purposes for Collection of Personal Information

The MRIA will identify the purposes for which personal information is collected at or before the time the information is collected.

### Principle 3: Obtaining Consent for Collection, Use, or Disclosure of Personal Information

The knowledge and consent of an individual are required for the collection, use or disclosure of personal information, except where exempted by applicable law.

### Principle 4: Limiting Collection of Personal Information

The MRIA will limit the collection of personal information to that which is necessary for the purposes identified by the MRIA. The MRIA will collect personal information by fair and lawful means.

### Principle 5: Limiting Use, Disclosure, and Retention of Personal Information

The MRIA will not use or disclose personal information for purposes other than those for which it was collected, except with the consent of the individual or as required or permitted by law.

### Principle 6: Accuracy of Personal Information

Personal information will be as accurate, complete, and up to date as is necessary for the purposes for which it is to be used.

### Principle 7: Security Safeguards

The MRIA will protect personal information by security safeguards appropriate to the sensitivity of the information.

### Principle 8: Openness Concerning Policies and Procedures

The MRIA will make readily available to individuals specific information about its policies and procedures relating to the management of personal information.

### Principle 9: Access to Personal Information

The MRIA will inform an individual of the existence, use, and disclosure of his or her personal information upon request and will provide the individual access to that information. An individual will be able to challenge the accuracy and completeness of the information and have it amended as appropriate.

### Principle 10: Challenging Compliance

An individual will be able to address a challenge concerning compliance with the above principles to the designated person or persons accountable for the MRIA's compliance with the MRIA Privacy Code.

## Scope and Application

The 10 principles that form the basis of The MRIA Privacy Code are interrelated and the MRIA will adhere to the 10 principles as a whole. Each principle should be read in conjunction with the accompanying commentary. As permitted by applicable privacy laws such as the Personal Information Protection and Electronic Documents Act (Canada), the commentary in the MRIA Privacy Code has been drafted to reflect personal information issues specific to the MRIA.

The scope and application of the MRIA Privacy Code are as follows:

- The MRIA Privacy Code applies to personal information collected, used, or disclosed by the MRIA.
- The MRIA Privacy Code applies to the management of personal information in any form whether oral, electronic, or written.
- The MRIA Privacy Code does not impose any limits on the collection, use, or disclosure of the following information by the MRIA:

  a. as per applicable privacy laws, certain business contact information such as an individual's name, title, business address, or telephone number;

  b. other information about an individual that is publicly available and is specified by regulation pursuant to applicable law; or

  c. as otherwise exempted by the MRIA Privacy Code and/or applicable law.

- The MRIA Privacy Code will not typically apply to information regarding organizations that deal with the MRIA. However, such information may be protected by other MRIA policies and procedures or through contractual arrangements.
- The application of the MRIA Privacy Code is subject to the requirements and provisions of the Personal Information Protection and Electronic Documents Act (Canada), the regulations enacted thereunder, and other applicable legislation or regulation.

Find out more about this important privacy code by going to **www.mria-arim.ca** and moving your cursor over "Standards" on the left navigation bar. On the pop-up menu, scroll down to "Privacy" and click.

Source: The Marketing Research and Intelligence Association Privacy Code, www.mria-arim.ca/STANDARDS/Privacy.asp. Retrieved June 20, 2010. Courtesy of Marketing Research and Intelligence Association.

## External Secondary Data

**External secondary data** are data obtained from outside the firm. There are three general sources of external data: (1) published, (2) **syndicated services data**, and (3) databases. **Published sources** are those prepared for public distribution and are normally found in libraries or provided by a variety of other entities, such as trade associations,

## MARKETING RESEARCH IN ACTION 4.2
# A Published Source of Secondary Information
## Quirk's Marketing Research Review

After 20 years of marketing research experience, Tom Quirk started *Quirk's Marketing Research Review* in 1986. The mission of the magazine has remained steadfast: to provide practical, valuable, and useful information to the marketing research industry. Each issue contains cases, practical examples, expert advice on research techniques, and information on the latest new-product information, as well as on survey findings. Special issues address topics such as advertising research, B2B research, customer satisfaction, health care research, international research, internet research, and technology, among others. In addition to publishing *Quirk's Marketing Research Review*, Quirk's also publishes nine specialty directories of research providers and a directory of all marketing research providers in the *Researcher SourceBook™*.

Tom Quirk's vision to provide information to marketing research professionals has grown to become a significant source of secondary information for researchers. Quirk's has over 16 000 subscribers in countries all over the world. You can visit Quirk's at **www.quirks.com**.

Courtesy of *Quirk's Marketing Research Review*.

professional organizations, or companies. Published sources are available in a number of formats, including print and online (via the internet). Many publications that were formerly available in print only are becoming available in electronic format; for example, magazines appear as e-zines and journals as e-journals. Providers of published secondary information are the government (e.g., Statistics Canada publications), non-profit organizations (e.g., chambers of commerce, colleges and universities), trade and professional associations (e.g., CASRO, CMA, IMRO, MRIA), and for-profits (e.g., *Marketing Magazine*, book publishers such as Prentice Hall and McGraw-Hill Ryerson, and research firms). Many research firms publish secondary information in the form of books, newsletters, white papers, special reports, magazines, or journals (e.g., see Marketing Research in Action 4.2 on *Quirk's Marketing Research Review*). GD Sourcing is a web-based directory that has helped "Canadians find stats online since 1987." It is a directory of websites that provide free Canadian data.

## ONLINE APPLICATION 4.1
# How to Find Publications from Statistics Canada

Go to **www.statcan.gc.ca** andclick on your language of preference. On the right side of the screen, lists are provide of the latest indicators, such as population estimates, CPI annual inflation rates, and unemployment rates.

In the "Search the Site" box, type "publications" in the search bar. Click on any publication of interest to explore the wealth of information available from Statistics Canada.

The sheer volume of published sources makes searching this type of secondary data difficult. However, understanding the functions of the different types of publications can be of great help in successfully searching published secondary information sources. Table 4.1 depicts the different types of publications, their functions, and an example of each type.

**Table 4.1** Understanding the Function of Different Types of Publications Can Make You a Better User of Secondary Data

1. **Reference Guides**

   Function: Refer to types of other reference sources and recommended specific titles. Guides tell you where to look to find different types of information.
   Examples: Blue Book of Canadian Business, **www.bluebook.ca;** Business.com, **www.business.com**

2. **Indexes and Abstracts**

   Function: List periodical articles by subject, author, title, keyword, etc. Abstracts also provide summaries of the articles. Indexes allow you to search for periodicals by topic.
   Examples: Canadian Business Index (Micromedia Ltd.); AMICUS (Canadian National Catalogue)

3. **Bibliographies**

   Function: List various sources such as books, journals, etc. on a particular topic. Tell you what is available, in several sources, on a topic.
   Example: The Apparent Per Capita Food Consumption in Canada (Statistics Canada).

4. **Almanacs, Manuals, and Handbooks**

   Function: These types of sources are "deskbooks" that provide a wide variety of data in a single handy publication.
   Examples: *Corpus Almanac and Canadian Sourcebook* (Southern Business Information and Communications Group Inc.)

5. **Dictionaries**

   Function: Define terms and are sometimes specialized by subject area.
   Example: *The Canadian Dictionary of Business and Economics*, David Crone

6. **Encyclopedias**

   Function: Provide essays, usually in alphabetical order, by topic.
   Example: *The Canadian Encyclopedia*, **www.thecanadianencyclopedia.com**

7. **Directories**

   Function: List companies, people, products, organizations, etc., usually providing brief information about each entry.
   Example: Industry Canada Company Directories, **www.ic.gc.ca/eic/site/ic1.nsf/eng/h_00070 .html**

8. **Statistical Sources**

   Function: Provide numeric data, often in tables, pie charts, and bar charts.
   Example: Statistics Canada, **www.statcan.gc.ca**

9. **Biographical Sources**

   Function: Provide information about people. Useful for information on CEOs, etc.
   Example: *Canadian Who's Who* (University of Toronto Press) **www.utppublishing.com/ _search.php?page=1&q=Canadian+Who%27s+Who**

10. **Legal Sources**

    Function: Provide information about legislation, regulations, and case law.
    Example: Supreme Court of Canada, **www.sec-csc.gc.ca**

Today, many libraries list their holdings of books and other publications in electronic records with fields that are searchable electronically. This allows researchers to search secondary data quickly, conveniently, inexpensively, and thoroughly. The information in most electronic libraries is available in catalogues and indexes. A **catalogue** consists of a list of a library's holdings of books. (Catalogues sometimes also list the periodicals to which the library subscribes.) Therefore, catalogues are useful for finding books by subject, author, title, date of publication, or publisher. **Indexes** are records compiled from periodicals and contain information on the contents of periodicals recorded in fields such as author, title, keywords, date of publication, name of periodical, and so on. Sometimes an index contains the entire contents of the periodical (called full-text indexes). Such indexes are not normally constructed by a library. Rather, they are provided by companies that make them available to libraries or other organizations.

**Standardized data** are provided by firms that collect data in a standard format. A branch of this is syndicated data. Such data are typically highly specialized and are not available in libraries for the general public. The suppliers syndicate (sell) the information to multiple subscribers, thus making the costs more reasonable for any one subscriber.

**External databases** are databases supplied by organizations outside the firm and may be used as sources of secondary data. Some of these databases are available in printed format, but in recent years many have become available online. These **online information databases** are searchable by search engines. Some are available free of charge and are supplied as a service by a host organization. However, many online databases are compiled by commercial sources that provide subscribers password (or IP address identification) access for a fee. The number of these databases has grown dramatically since the 1980s. Larger firms can offer subscribers access to billions of records of information. Such services, sometimes called "aggregators" or "databanks," include Factiva, Gale Group, ProQuest, First Search, LexisNexis, and Dialog, among others. Business databases comprise a significant proportion of these databanks. Figure 4.1 illustrates the types of secondary data available to marketing researchers.

# Advantages of Secondary Data

## Secondary Data Are Obtained Quickly

Secondary data can be obtained quickly, in contrast to collecting primary data, which may take several months from beginning to end. A great deal of secondary data can be found on the internet for free.

## Secondary Data Are Inexpensive Relative to Primary Data

Collecting secondary data is inexpensive when compared with collecting primary data. Primary data collection is seldom achieved without spending at least a few thousand dollars or, depending on the research objective, hundreds of thousands or even millions of dollars. Even purchasing secondary data from commercial vendors is inexpensive relative to collecting primary data.

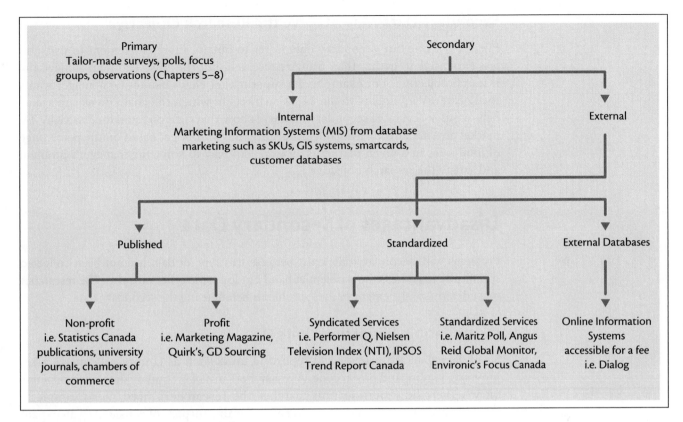

**Figure 4.1** Data in Marketing Research

## Secondary Data Are Usually Available

Secondary data are usually available. Availability is one reason that many predict secondary data will grow in importance in marketing research applications. Not only is the amount of data growing but the ability to search billions of records to find the right data is improving with technology.

## Secondary Data Enhance Primary Data

Secondary data enhance existing primary data. A secondary data search can familiarize the researcher with the industry, including its sales and profit trends, major competitors, and the significant issues facing the industry.[10] A secondary data search can identify concepts, data, and terminology that may be useful in conducting primary research. For example, a bank's management hired a marketing research firm. Together, management and the research team decided to conduct a survey measuring the bank's image among its customers. A check of the secondary data available on the measurement of bank image identified the components of bank image for the study. Also, the research team, after reviewing secondary data, determined there were three sets of bank customers: retail customers, commercial accounts, and other, correspondent banks. When the researchers mentioned this to bank management, the original objectives of the primary research were changed in order to measure the bank's image among all three customer groups.

## Secondary Data May Achieve the Research Objective

Finally, not only are secondary data faster to obtain, more convenient to use, and less expensive to gather than primary research, but they also can help achieve the research objective! For example, if a supermarket chain marketing manager wants to allocate TV ad dollars to the 12 TV markets in which the chain owns supermarkets, a quick review of secondary data will show that data on retail food sales by TV market area are already available. Allocating the TV budget based on the percentage of food sales in a given market is an excellent way to solve the manager's problem and satisfy the research objective.

# Disadvantages of Secondary Data

Problems with secondary data exist because this type of data has not been collected specifically to address the problem at hand but for some other purpose. The researcher must determine the extent of these problems before using the secondary data.

## Incompatible Reporting Units

Secondary data are provided in reporting units such as county, city, metro area, province, region, and postal code. A researcher's use of secondary data often depends on whether the reporting unit matches the researcher's need. For example, a researcher wishing to evaluate market areas for the purpose of considering an expansion may be pleased with data reported at the city level. But what if another marketer wishes to evaluate a three-kilometre area around a street address proposed as a site location for a retail store? City data would hardly be adequate. Another marketer wishes to know the demographic makeup of each postal code in a major city in order to determine where to target a direct-mail campaign. Again, city data would be inappropriate. Inappropriate reporting units are often a problem in using secondary data, but more and more data are available today in multiple reporting units. Geodemographic information systems offer marketers access to data in arbitrarily defined reporting units. The latter would be very useful to the marketer wishing to know the demographics within a three-kilometre ring around a street address.

## Measurement Units Do Not Match

Sometimes measurement units reported in secondary data sources do not match the researcher's needs. For example, household income may be reported when the researcher needs per capita income. Or consider a research project that needs to categorize businesses by size in terms of square footage. Many secondary data sources classify businesses in terms of size, according to sales volume, number of employees, profit level, and so on.

## Class Definitions Are Not Usable

The class definitions of the reported data may not be usable by a researcher. Secondary data are often reported by dividing a variable among different classes and reporting the frequency of occurrence in each class. For example, there is a problem when the researcher needs to know the percentage of households having income over $80 000 but the highest income category in the secondary data source is $50 000 and over. Often, with continued searching, the information sought can be found eventually.

## Data Are Outdated

Sometimes a marketing researcher will find information reported with the desired unit of measurement and the proper classifications; the data, however, are "out of date." Some secondary data are published only once. But even with secondary data published at regular intervals, the time that has passed since the last publication can pose a problem when the data are applied to a current problem.

# Evaluating Secondary Data

In order to properly use secondary data, information must be evaluated before it isused as a basis for making decisions. This is done by answering the following five questions:

- What was the purpose of the study?
- Who collected the information?
- What information was collected?
- How was the information obtained?
- How consistent is the information with other information?[11]

## What Was the Purpose of the Study?

Studies are sometimes conducted to advance the special interest of those conducting the study. Many years ago, chambers of commerce were known for publishing data that exaggerated the size and growth rates of their communities. They did this to "prove" that their communities were a good choice for new business locations. However, after a few years, they learned that few people trusted chamber data, and today chambers of commerce publish reliable and valid data.

## Who Collected the Information?

Even when it appears that there is no bias in the purpose of the study, it is important to question the competence of the organization that collected the information. First, ask others who have more experience in a given industry. Typically, creditable organizations are well known in those industries for which they conduct studies. Second, examine the report itself. Competent firms almost always provide carefully written and detailed explanations of the procedures and methods used in collecting the information contained in the report. Third, contact previous clients of the firm. Have they been satisfied with the quality of the work performed by the organization?

## What Information Was Collected?

Many studies claim to provide information on a specific subject but, in fact, measure something quite different. Consider a study conducted by a transit authority

## ETHICS IN MARKETING RESEARCH 4.2
# Sabotage? Francophones May Be Lying about English Abilities on Census

OTTAWA—Thousands of francophones across Canada are believed to have lied about their ability to speak English in a seemingly co-ordinated attempt to manipulate the 2006 census in order to guarantee federal funding of programs for French speakers.

Statistics Canada has taken the unusual step of posting a warning on its website to caution users that the data on bilingualism rates for francophones outside Quebec may not be reliable. The suspected cause is an anonymous French-language email that circulated widely across Canada prior to the census, encouraging francophones to say they could not speak English even if they could. The email went on to say that this would ensure that the federal government would not cut services to francophones.

The resulting statistics showed for the first time an inexplicable decrease in the number of francophones outside Quebec who said they could speak English, reversing a long trend of increasing rates of bilingualism for francophones outside Quebec.

The number of bilingual francophones in Ontario, for example, has been on the rise by between 1% and 3% in every census since 1991. However, in 2006 the number fell to 88.4% from 89.4% in 2001—an unexpected drop of one percentage point.

Jean Pierre Corbeil, a chief specialist in the language statistics section, said they have studied the trend reversal and the email appears to be the only factor that may have produced this aberration to the trend.

"How can you explain people living in a minority situation, even in really strong minority situations, that they would become less bilingual? This is almost impossible," said Corbeil.

Even if the actual number of bilingual francophones had risen by only 1%, confirming the long-standing trend, the number of Franco-Ontarians who may have lied in the census would be about 10 000.

It wasn't just Ontario bucking the trend. Fewer francophones said they could speak English in 2006 in Nova Scotia, New Brunswick, Ontario, Manitoba, Saskatchewan, and Alberta. The percentage of francophones outside Quebec who said they could speak English dropped 2.5 percentage points to 83.6% in 2006. The rate of bilingualism for francophones also dropped in Quebec.

The Statistics Act says anyone who lies when participating in a Statistics Canada survey is liable for a $500 fine, but Marc Hamel, manager of the 2011 census, said efforts are never made to track the liars down.

"We rely on Canadians to provide accurate information, but we have no means of verifying," said Hamel.

The unreliability of data concerning the number of bilingual francophones in Ontario comes on the heels of a controversial decision last year by Ottawa-based provincial politician Madeleine Meilleur, Ontario's minister responsible for francophone affairs, to change the provincial definition. Previously, a francophone was someone whose mother tongue was French. Now, it can be anyone whose mother tongue is neither English nor French, but who at least understands French. Statistics Canada says this will artificially increase the number of French speakers in the province, likely by about 50 000, and include some people who may not even be able to speak French.

Source: David Gonczol, *Ottawa Citizen*, May 30, 2010. Material reprinted with the express permission of "POSTMEDIA NEWS," a division of Postmedia Network Inc.

on the number of riders on its bus line. Upon examination of the methods used in the study, the number of riders was not counted at all. Rather, the number of tokens was counted. Since a single rider may use several tokens on a single destination route requiring transfers to other buses, the study overestimated the number of "riders." The user should discover exactly what information was collected.

## How Was the Information Obtained?

Be aware of the methods used to obtain information reported in secondary sources. It is not always easy to find out how the secondary data were gathered. However, as noted earlier, most reputable organizations that provide secondary data also provide information on their data-collection methods.

## How Consistent Is the Information with Other Information?

Ideally, if two or more independent organizations report the same data, there is a greater confidence in the validity and reliability of the data. Demographic data, for example, for metropolitan areas (MAs) and most municipalities are widely available from more than one source. If you are evaluating a survey that is supposedly representative of a given geographic area, compare the characteristics of the sample of the survey with the demographic data available on the population. It is indeed rare, however, for two organizations to report exactly the same results. Look at the magnitude of the differences and determine what to do.

# Locating Secondary Data Sources

To locate secondary data sources:

**Step 1 Identify what you wish to know and what you already know about your topic.** This is the most important step when searching for information. Without having a clear understanding of what you are seeking, you will undoubtedly have difficulties. Clearly define your topic: relevant facts, names of researchers or organizations associated with the topic, key papers and other publications with which you are already familiar, and any other information you may have.

**Step 2 Develop a list of key terms and names.** These terms and names will provide access to secondary sources. Unless you already have a very specific topic of interest, keep this initial list long and quite general. Use business dictionaries and handbooks to help develop your list. Be flexible. Every time a new source is consulted, you may have to develop a new list of terms.

In printed sources as well as online databases, it is important to use correct terminology to locate the most relevant resources. In many cases, the researcher must think of related terms or synonyms for a topic. For example, one database may use the term *pharmaceutical industry*, whereas another may use the term *drug industry*. In addition, the source may require a broader term. *Pharmaceutical industry* may be listed as part of the *chemical industry*. However, a narrower term might be required. For example, if one is researching a database on the *drug industry*, it would be foolish to search on the term *drugs* because almost everything in that database would include that term. Perhaps using a specific drug may be a wiser choice.

Many databases list the terms or subject headings they assign to records of information in such sources as books or articles. These lists are called *thesauri*, dictionaries, or subject headings lists. In most library catalogues, subject headings are used, which are standard (sometimes called *controlled*) terms for describing a particular subject. For example, the term *real property* is standard in the subject headings instead of the term *real estate*. Using a standard subject heading should result in a more efficient search.

For searching a database, keyword searching is usually available, but using a keyword often retrieves too many false results. A keyword search means that the computer will retrieve a record that has that word anywhere in the record. For example, if someone is searching on the word *banks*, that could turn up the name of a person, a business, a type of bank, a bank of dirt (hill), or any other use of the word. Sometimes, to avoid false results, the searcher may simply want to search one field in the record. Keywords may also be used to lead to better terms to search on. If a long list of sources is generated, it is wise to select an item that is relevant and examine its record to identify the standard subject heading assigned to that item. Submitting that subject heading should retrieve a much more relevant list of sources (see Online Application 4.2).

**Step 3  Begin your search using several of the library sources, such as those listed in Table 4.1 on page 121.**

## Search Strategies Used for Searching Online Information Databases

To better understand how to search online databases, the researcher should understand how databases are organized. A common vendor, also known as an aggregator or databank, may provide many databases. For example, the vendor ProQuest provides ABI/INFORM Global and *The Wall Street Journal*. An actual hierarchy exists in the organization of these databases. For example:

> Top level—Databank (sometimes called "aggregator") = ProQuest
> Second level—Databases = ABI/INFORM Global
> Third level—Records = the units describing each item in the database
> Fourth level—Fields = parts of the record, such as author, title, Standard Industrial Classification (SIC) number, and so on
> Fifth level—Words or numbers = the text of the fields

Usually, all databases from the same databank are searched similarly and several methods (basic, advanced, and command) of searching the databases may be available. A basic search is often sufficient when searching for books in a catalogue or when searching small databases; however, it is often advisable to use the advanced mode when searching for journal articles or complex ideas so that search refinements can be used.

Most databanks use the same search features, but other databanks may use different symbols or interfaces to retrieve results. An interface is the "look and feel" of the database that actually helps the searcher know how to submit a search. Each

## ONLINE APPLICATION 4.2
# Improve Your Searching Skills by Finding a Standard Subject Heading

Finding information on Alternative Fuel AND Automobile OR Car

How many times have you used an online information service database only to end up frustrated that you could not find what you really needed? Problems of two types occur. First, you get thousands of "hits," which requires that you read through huge amounts of information still searching for what you wanted to find in the first place. Second, you get information about articles that contain your key search terms, but the articles have nothing to do with what you really want. Sound familiar? You need to learn an important skill in searching online information databases: finding the standard subject heading.

Imagine that you had available several persons who were well trained in evaluating and interpreting the contents of information sources such as books, manuals, special reports, magazine articles, journal articles, and so on. Next, imagine if you told these well-trained persons to look through everything that has been published and to place all the books, articles, reports, and so on that pertained to your topic in one stack. So, you now have all the publications on your topic in one category. Now imagine that this information is all scanned into an electronic database that can be searched using any one or a combination of search strategies. Wow! Think this would improve your information search skills? The good news is that this has already been done for you. You just need to learn how to take advantage of what we shall call standard subject headings.

Databases have a field called the subject field. When a new piece of information arrives, be it a book, journal article, or whatever, that information is evaluated to determine its subject matter. For example, let's say there is an article entitled "The Pod Squad." The title can be very misleading. In fact, if someone were doing a search about police squads or iPods, this article would appear in a results list (along with thousands of other irrelevant information sources).

But why is it misleading? Because the subject of the article is a recent upscale restaurant design phenomenon!

Keywords are often not in the title or even the abstract of an article. If you were searching for information about restaurants, chances are you would not find the pod article using key terms in the title field of your database search engine. But because those "people who are working for you" have looked over this article and correctly placed it in the category of restaurants, we are going to find it. So, **standard subject headings** are specific words or phrases that are used to properly categorize the subject matter of records as they are entered into databases. Let's see how you would do it using ABI/INFORM Global, a popular online database owned by ProQuest.

### ProQuest

| Basic | Advanced | Topics | Publications | My Research 0 marked items |

Databases selected: ABI/INFORM Global

**Advanced Search**                    Tools: Search Tips  Browse Topics

| | Subject | Look up subjects |
| AND | Citation and abstract | |
| AND | Citation and abstract | |

Add a row | Remove a row     Search   Clear

In ABI/INFORM Global, you can use the "Basic Search" if you don't really know much about your topic. However, basic searches are not very productive if you know enough about your topic to conduct a more efficient search. In fact, if you enter "automobiles" in a basic search you will get over 95 000 hits! So, how do you find a "standard subject heading" in ABI/INFORM Global? First, go to "Advanced Search." Then click on the drop-down menu on the right of the first row where it presently reads "Citation and abstract." (This refers to the citation and abstract fields of the records in the database.) From the drop menu, select the "Subject" field. You will then see a new choice on the right—"Look up subjects." Clicking "Look up subjects" opens a dialog box that allows you to enter the words that you suspect may identify the predetermined subject category—what we call a "standard subject heading." Experiment by entering "fuel efficient autos"

(Continued)

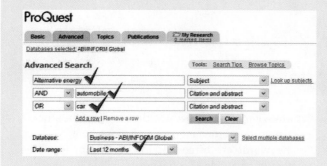

or "high mpg cars." You will find that these are NOT standard subject headings. You know this because when you click "Find term," your search words are not listed. But if you enter "alternative energy," you find this is a standard subject heading! Now click "Add to search" and then close the "Look up Subjects" dialog box. Notice you are now back to the advanced search screen.

If you conduct this search, you will find that you have discovered ALL records in the database that have a subject classified as "alternative fuel," even though they may not have anything to do with automobiles. To drill down and get a more focused search, let's go back to "Advanced

Search" and add to "alternative energy" in the Subject field "automobile" OR "car" in the two fields each covering "Citation and Abstract." Now our search will reveal a subset of articles in the "alternative energy" subject field that have either "automobile" OR "car" either in the citation of the articles or in the article abstracts. Finally, let's limit the search to include only articles written in the last 12 months (see "Date Range").

We are now ready to begin our search. Instead of over 95 000 hits, we now have a very manageable list of 59 articles. Note the titles of some of the articles in the search; they appear to be "right on target." One is "The Car of the Perpetual Future" and another is a study of alternative fuels in vehicles. Another method of refining your search is to scroll down once you find an article that meets your search requirements and examine the Subject field from which it was drawn. You may find another standard subject heading that is even more on target than the one you've already discovered. Happy searching!

---

1. **Electric Car Sets Sights On Network in Australia**
   John Murphy. **Wall Street Journal (Eastern edition).** New York, N.Y.: Oct 29, 2008.
   📄 Abstract | 📄 Full text

2. **The Election Choice: Energy**
   Joseph Rago. **Wall Street Journal (Eastern edition).** New York, N.Y.: Oct 28, 2008. p. A.17
   📄 Abstract | 📄 Full text

3. **Thais Lead Drive to Natural-Gas Cars; Subsidies, Volatility of Oil Prices Spur Move Even as a Campaign Starts in U.S. to Get Americans to Switch**
   Patrick Barta. **Wall Street Journal (Eastern edition).** New York, N.Y.: Oct 21, 2008. p. B.1
   📄 Abstract | 📄 Full text

4. **ALTERNATIVE BATTERIES**
   Vahan Janjigian. **Forbes.** New York: Oct 13, 2008. Vol. 182, Iss. 7; p. 134
   📄 Abstract | 📄 Find a copy

5. **THE TOP 100**
   Richard Yerema. **Maclean's.** Toronto: Oct 13, 2008. Vol. 121, Iss. 40; p. 56 (4 pages)
   📄 Abstract | 📄 Full text

6. **MARKET TRENDS: Fleet management**
   Nic Paton. **Employee Benefits.** London: Oct 9, 2008. p. 71
   📄 Abstract | 📄 Full text

7. **Coping with a Persistent Oil Crisis**
   Jeffrey D Sachs. **Scientific American.** New York: Oct 2008. Vol. 299, Iss. 4; p. 38
   📄 Abstract | 📄 Find a copy

8. **Eyes on the Road: What the U.S. Should Do To Cut Oil Consumption**
   Joseph B. White. **Wall Street Journal (Eastern edition).** New York, N.Y.: Sep 16, 2008. p. D.2
   📄 Abstract | 📄 Full text

9. **The car of the perpetual future;**
   Anonymous. **The Economist.** London: Sep 6, 2008. Vol. 388, Iss. 8596
   📄 Abstract | 📄 Full text

database has a help screen, which is always useful. Try finding a standard subject reading by following the directions in Online Application 4.2.

## Boolean Logic

**Boolean logic** allows the establishment of relationships between words and terms in most databases. Typical words used as operators in Boolean logic are AND, OR, and NOT. The following examples illustrate:

| Operator | Requirements | Examples | |
|---|---|---|---|
| AND | Both terms are retrieved | chemical AND Industry | Exxon AND financial |
| OR | Either term is retrieved | drug OR pharmaceutical | outlook OR forecast |
| NOT | Eliminates records containing the second term | Cherokee NOT jeeps | drugs NOT alcohol |

## Field Searching

**Field searching** refers to searching records in a database by one or more of its fields. Databases are collections of records that consist of fields designated to describe certain parts of the record. Searching "by field" may make a search more efficient. For example, if a title is known, a search of the title field should find the desired record. Terms entered as "subjects" may be restricted to specific subject headings depending on the database. Most databases also allow the use of keyword searching, which searches every word in a record.

Most electronic databases use the same search strategies for searching databases, but they often vary in the keystrokes designated to perform the search. For example, on the internet, the keyword "real estate" should be submitted with quotes surrounding the phrase so that the exact sequence of words will be searched. However, to search on the same keyword phrase in some library catalogues, "real ADJ estate" would be submitted. ADJ means *adjacent*.

## Proximity Operators

The preceding "real estate" example demonstrates one of the proximity operators that are available to enhance keyword searching. **Proximity operators** allow the searcher to indicate how close and in which order two or more words are to be positioned within the record. Examples of proximity operators are as follows:

| Operator | Requirements | Examples |
|---|---|---|
| ADJ | Adjoining words in order | Electronic ADJ Commerce |
| NEAR | Adjoining words in any order | Bill NEAR Gates |
| SAME | Both terms are located in the field of the record | Microsoft SAME legal |

## Truncation

Another feature of database searching is **truncation**, which allows the root of the word to be submitted, retrieving all words beginning with that root. The term "forecast?" would retrieve "forecasting," "forecasts," "forecaster," and so on. The question mark is the truncation symbol in some databases; others may use an asterisk, a plus sign, a dollar sign, or other symbol. In some cases, truncation symbols may not be useful. For example, searching "cat" by submitting "cat?" would retrieve "cat," "cats," "catch," "catastrophe," and so on. Using the search "cat OR cats" is preferable.

## Nesting

**Nesting** is a technique that indicates the order in which a search is to be done. For example, to search for microcomputers or personal computers in Alberta, submit "Alberta AND (microcomputer? OR personal ADJ computer?)," indicating that "Alberta" should be combined with either term. The parentheses nest the two terms as one. Without the parentheses, "Alberta" would be combined with "microcomputer," and every instance of the words "personal computer" would be added to the results. In search engines, there are text boxes that serve much like parentheses to aid in keeping similar terms together.

## Limiting

**Limiting** allows restricting searches to only those database records that meet specified criteria. For example, searches may be limited to a search of records containing a specific language, location, format, and/or date. These limitations are usually available on the database advanced search screen. When searching for current materials, the date limitation is most important in retrieving the correct results.

**Step 4  Compile the literature you have found and evaluate your findings.** Rework your list of keywords and authors. If you have had little success or your topic is highly specialized, consult specialized directories, encyclopedias, and so on, such as the ones listed in this chapter. The librarian may be able to recommend the most appropriate source for your needs.

**Step 5  If you are unhappy with what you have found or are otherwise having trouble and the reference librarian has not been able to identify sources, use an authority.** Identify some individual or organization that might know something about the topic. Publications such as *Canadian Who's Who* may help you identify people or organizations that specialize in your topic. University faculty, government officials, and business executives may also be helpful.

There are several keys to a successful search. First, be well informed about the search process. Second, do not expect information to fall into your lap; be committed to finding it. Finally, there is no substitute for a good, professional librarian. Do not be afraid to ask for advice.

**Step 6  Report results.** You may be successful in locating data, but if the information is not properly transmitted to the reader, the research is worthless. It is important to outline the paper or report, correctly compose it, and accurately reference the sources that were used.

# Key Sources of Secondary Data for Marketers

## The Census of the Population

The Canadian census, the Census of Canada, is considered the "granddaddy" of all market information. Since the first census under Confederation was taken in 1871, several changes have taken place to better serve providers and users of the information. In 2006, when the last census was taken, all Canadians could complete the survey online. There were two forms of the survey. The short version was completed by 80% of households and asked for mainly demographic information. The long version asked the same questions as well as 53 new ones. Information from the longer version is of great use to Statistics Canada. Permission for the public use of information collected was also asked. Find out more details about the 2006 census by going to **www.statcan.gc.ca** and clicking on the "Census" icon.

Several surveys are conducted by Statistics Canada on a regular basis, generating many reports for the public. Examples include:

- Survey of Household Spending (SHS)—annual survey
- Ethnic Diversity Survey (EDS)—2002
- Labour Force Survey—monthly, annual, and occasional
- Participation and Activity Limitation Survey (PALS)—occasional
- Consumer Price Index (CPI)—monthly

There are many Canadian government publications available online. Explore the Statistics Canada website to view several of these.

## North American Industry Classification System (NAICS)

The **North American Industry Classification System (NAICS)**, pronounced "nakes," is a coding system that can be used to access information. The system allows reports conducted by the Mexican, Canadian, and U.S. governments to share a common language for easier comparisons of international trade, industrial production, labour costs, and other statistics. NAICS classifies businesses based on similar production processes, with special attention given to classifying emerging industries such as services and high technology. More classifications are assigned to certain industry groups such as eating and drinking places.

NAICS groups the economy into 20 broad sectors and a six-digit classification code. The three countries agreed on a standard system using the first five digits. The sixth digit is used by each country allowing for special user needs. Note that the NAICS code does not tell anything specific. Knowing a NAICS number for a type of business can help researchers find all kinds of secondary information about the firms in that business.

# Standardized Information

**Standardized information** is a type of secondary data in which the data collected and/or the process of collecting the data are standardized for all users. There are two broad classes of standardized information: syndicated data and standardized services. **Syndicated data** are data that are collected in a standard format and made available to all subscribers. Marketing Evaluations, Inc., for example, offers several Q Scores® services. One of its services measures the familiarity and appeal of performers in a number of categories, such as actors, actresses, authors, athletes, sportscasters, and so on. This information is used by companies to help choose the most appropriate spokesperson for their company or help a movie producer select a performer for an upcoming movie. **Performer Q®** is the service for ratings of approximately 700 performers. Data for all 1700 performers studied is the same—standardized—regardless of who uses the data. Data are collected two times a year for all performers based on a sample of nearly 2000 persons and are made available to all who subscribe (advertisers, TV and movie production companies, licensing companies, talent and public relations companies, among others). Nielsen Media Research's **Nielsen Television Index (NTI)**, another example of a syndicated data provider, supplies subscribers with data on TV viewing. The data are standardized in the sense that the same data are made available to anyone wishing to purchase it.

On the other hand, **standardized services** refers to a standardized marketing research *process* that is used to generate information for a particular user. The Maritz Poll uses a standardized *process* to ensure that consumer attitudes and opinions are properly measured and represented. **ESRI's Tapestry™ Segmentation** is a standardized service that uses a *process* to profile residential neighbourhoods. This information is purchased by clients desiring to better understand who their customers are, where they are located, how to find them, and how to reach them. Each poll addresses a different topic and, therefore, supplies different data; these polls are examples of a standardized service.

Syndicated data are a form of external, secondary data supplied from a common database for a service fee to subscribers. Firms in the marketing research industry providing such data are called *syndicated data service firms*. These firms provide specialized, routine information needed by a given industry in the form of ready-to-use, standardized marketing data to subscribers. Firms supplying syndicated data follow standard research formats that enable them to collect the same standardized data over time. Ipsos Canada, for instance, offers a range of syndicated studies. Table 4.2 illustrates a partial list. Well-known studies include the *Ipsos Trend Report Canada* and *Canadian Corporate Reputation Monitor (I-Rep)*. The *Trend Report* is conducted six times per year and tracks consumer thoughts and public opinion to help Canadian decision makers. *I-Rep* provides a comparative measure of a company's reputation relative to a norm in their market and against their competitors. With syndicated data, both the process of collecting and analyzing the data and the data itself are standardized; neither is varied for the client. On the other hand, standardized services rarely provide clients with standardized data. Rather, it is the *process* they are marketing. The application of that standardized process will result in different data for each client. For example, a standardized service may be measurement of customer satisfaction. Instead of a user firm trying to "reinvent the wheel" by developing its own process for measuring customer satisfaction, it may elect to use a standardized service to do so. Several other marketing research services, such as test marketing, naming new brands, pricing a new product, or using mystery shoppers, are also purchased from standardized service firms.

**Table 4.2** Syndicated
Studies Offered by
Ipsos Canada

### Canadian Business Media Relations Review

The *Canadian Business Media Relations Review* is an elite survey of top business and financial print, online, and broadcast editors and journalists. Ideal for media, corporate, and public relations professionals, this report provides candid and current opinions about communications approaches, tools, and issues of interest to the business and financial media today.

### Canadian Corporate Reputation Monitor (I-Rep)

The *Canadian Corporate Reputation Monitor* is Canada's premier reputation measurement syndicated study for leading corporations. Since 1994, organizations have used this study to gain valuable intelligence to further their business strategies and to assess themselves against the marketplace, their competitors, and *I-Rep* norms.

### Canadian Donors and You

*Canadian Donors and You* has been designed to help charities better understand their donor market and help grow their donor dollars. This comprehensive report features customized proprietary profiles of each subscribing organization's past donors and potential future donors, as well as a psychographic donor segmentation and overview of the Canadian donor market, with donor demographics, motivations for giving, and communication and solicitation preferences.

### Global @dvisor Reputation Risk Identifier

The **Global @dvisor Reputation Risk Identifier** research service enables companies to proactively understand and manage the potential risk to their reputations. It is a 22+–country, online, monthly syndicated research service that is specifically constructed to understand the reputation risk environment that is critical to protecting the goodwill and equity—both financial and public—of a company's brand.

### Government Service and Satisfaction

To better understand how Canadians obtain and perceive government service and information, Ipsos Canada interviews 2400 Canadians, including 1200 who have not contacted the federal government in the three months prior to doing the survey and 1200 who have. This study, *Government Service and Satisfaction*, offers a unique look at how different channels of government service delivery (internet, telephone, in-person, and mail) impact the behaviour and attitudes of Canadians, and particularly which elements of service drive levels of satisfaction when Canadians interact with their government.

### Municipal Quality of Life and Financial Planning

The *Municipal Quality of Life and Financial Planning* study is designed to help local governments better understand their citizens' satisfaction levels, attitudes, needs, and priorities. This study provides municipal leaders with actionable information to track citizens' satisfaction levels, plan future budgets, develop new programs and services, and establish effective communication strategies.

### Municipal Recreation and Physical Fitness

The *Municipal Recreation and Physical Fitness* study is designed to help local governments better understand their citizens' recreation behaviours and needs. This study provides municipal leaders with actionable information to track their citizens' current fitness behaviours and satisfaction with municipal recreation offerings, as well as to help plan future recreation services for the community.

*(Continued)*

**Table 4.2** (Continued)

### Municipal Solutions for a Greener Earth

The *Municipal Solutions for a Greener Earth* study is designed to help local governments better understand their citizens' attitudes toward the environment by providing municipal leaders with actionable information to manage and respond effectively to their citizens' needs, concerns, and perceptions around environmental issues.

### Public Opinion and First Canadians

The *Public Opinion and First Canadians* syndicated study series is designed to provide subscribers with a better understanding of the attitudes and opinions of First Canadians as citizens and stakeholders.

### Public Opinion and New Canadians

The *Public Opinion and New Canadians* syndicated study series is designed to provide subscribers with a better understanding of the attitudes and opinions of new Canadians as citizens and stakeholders.

### Reconnecting with Older Canadians

As Canada's population ages, governments and businesses are confronted with new challenges in meeting the needs of older Canadians and how best to meet them. The *Reconnecting with Older Canadians* syndicated study explores attitudes of Canadians aged 55 and older toward leaving the workforce; crime, justice, and security; housing; health; society, governments, and governance; communications and media; and travel and leisure.

### Reconnecting with Youth

Since 1997, Ipsos Canada has conducted a unique, annual study aimed at better understanding the relationship between Canada's youth and government and the nature of Canadian youth engagement in public life. *Reconnecting with Youth* surveys over 2000 Canadians between the ages of 12 and 30. The study explores youth attitudes toward education and careers, society, governments and governance, communications and media, internet usage, and diversity.

Source: See **www.ipsos.ca** for a list of syndicated services offered by Ipsos Canada.

## Advantages and Disadvantages of Standardized Information

### Syndicated Data

One of the key advantages of syndicated data is shared costs. Many client firms may subscribe to the information; thus, the cost of the service is greatly reduced to any one subscribing firm. Because syndicated data firms specialize in the collection of standard data and because their usefulness depends on the validity of the data, the quality of the data collected is typically very high. With several companies paying for the service, the syndicating company can go to great lengths to gather a great amount of data.

Another advantage of syndicated data comes from the routinized systems used to collect and process the data. Data are normally disseminated very quickly to subscribers because the syndicated data firms set up standard procedures and methods for collecting the data over and over again on a periodic basis. The more current the data, the greater their usefulness.

Although there are several advantages to syndicated data, there are some disadvantages. First, buyers have little control over what information is collected. Since the research is not customized, the buyer firm must be satisfied that the information received is the information needed.

A second disadvantage is that buyer firms often must commit to long-term contracts when buying syndicated data. Finally, there is no specific strategic information advantage in purchasing syndicated data because all competitors have access to much of the same information. However, in many industries, firms would suffer a serious strategic disadvantage by not purchasing the information.

## Standardized Services

The key advantage of using a standardized service is taking advantage of the experience of the research firm offering the service. Often, a buyer firm may have a research department with many experienced persons but no experience in the particular process that it needs. Imagine a firm setting out to conduct a test market for the very first time. It would take the firm several months to gain the confidence needed to conduct the test market properly. A second advantage is the reduced cost of the research. Because the supplier firm conducts the service for many clients on a regular basis, the procedure is efficient and far less costly than if the buyer firm tried to conduct the service itself. A third advantage is speed, which is usually much faster than if the buyer firm were to conduct the service on its own. The efficiency gained by conducting a service over and over translates into reduced turnaround time from start to finish of a research project.

There are disadvantages to using standardized services as well. "Standardized" means "not customized." Although some firms offer some customization, generally they cannot design a service specifically for the project at hand. Second, the client is burdened with the responsibility of ensuring that the standardized service fits the intended situation. Client firms need to be very familiar with the service, including what data are collected on which population, how the data are collected, and how the data are reported, before they purchase the service.

# Applications of Standardized Information

Although many forms of standardized information have many applications, five major applications are discussed here.

## Measuring Consumer Attitudes and Opinion Polls

There are several "high-profile" firms that offer measurement of consumer attitudes and opinions. These firms are the most recognized and respected by the media, the government, and the public. Emerging social and political issues are polled "on demand," typically with a random sample of 1000 to 2000 Canadians. This can be done with telephone surveys or online. These firms also provide standardized polls in which data collected over decades are analyzed for trends and themes regarding developing issues. Today, much of this data is collected using online polling panels. Daily and specialized reports are generated from these standardized polls, in which analysis is integrated with information from a variety of sources. The home websites of these companies offer daily headlines about emerging themes in the public's attitudes and opinions.

Environics Research Group monitors the Canadian public's attitudes and opinions about political, economic, and social issues through "on demand" public opinion polls. It also provides **Focus Canada**, a quarterly survey of 2000 Canadians. Focus Canada is the longest-running survey report of attitudes toward political, social, and economic issues.

Results from Environics Research Group polling surveys are frequently reported in the Canadian media.

Angus Reid is another key player in the polling of Canadian opinions and attitudes. Aside from frequent on demand polls, the company offers the **Angus Reid Global Monitor**, a daily report from its online global database of political and social issues.

EKOS Research Associates, another well-known Canadian polling company, offers a suite of syndicated surveys called "Rethinking." EKOS's current line of Rethinking studies includes *Rethinking Government*, *Rethinking the Information Highway*, *Rethinking Citizen Engagement*, *Rethinking North American Integration*, *Rethinking Science and Society*, *Rethinking Energy and Sustainable Development*, and *Rethinking Canada's Aging Population*. Analysis is based on a wealth of standardized information collected over the years.

Gallup is one of the oldest and largest social research companies in the world. The company has many strategic business units and produces many syndicated reports on people's thoughts on political, social, and economic issues. Perhaps the best known is the **Gallup Poll**. The Canadian version of the poll is one of many used globally to discover people's attitudes about political, social, and economic issues. Gallup Daily News reports daily on emerging issues discovered through analysis of these ongoing polls.

Harris Interactive Inc. produces the **Harris Poll Online**, which reports results from respondents from around the globe, including Canada. The **Maritz Poll** is a global poll produced by Maritz Research, which focuses on opinions regarding consumer products and services, such as financial services.

## Defining Market Segments

Defining market segments entails placing customers sharing certain attributes (age, income, stage in the family life cycle, etc.) into homogeneous groups or market segments. Marketers gather information about the market members, compiling profiles of the attributes of the consumers that make up each segment. Marketers can then decide which segments are currently being served or not served by the competition. They can also determine the size, growth trends, and profit potential of each segment. Using these data, a segment, or group of segments, can be targeted for marketing.

Several standardized information sources provide marketers with information about customers in markets. Some concentrate on members of the industrial market, and others provide information on members of the consumer market.

A great deal about the industrial market in North America can be learned by using the North American Industry Classification System (NAICS), the governments' method of classifying business firms. It allows users to identify, classify, and monitor standard statistics about member firms. Industry Canada also provides market segmentation reports on many industries in Canada.

One global standardized information service firm, Dun & Bradstreet (D&B), supplies additional information that allows subscribers to make even better use of government classification systems. **Dun & Bradstreet's D-U-N-S®** (Data Universal Numbering System) is a nine-digit classification system that assigns an identification number to all firms. This gives D&B the ability to identify over 100 million companies around the globe. Since D&B originated as a credit reporting firm, companies willingly supply it with detailed information about their companies and their operations. This allows D&B to create databases containing a wide array of information on businesses for which it reported a credit rating. These databases allow D&B to offer more services, such as **Dun's Market Identifiers®** (DMI), which provides information on over four million firms and is updated monthly. The real benefit of DMI is its use of eight-digit codes to classify businesses. With more digits than other government classification systems such as the NAICS, the service can break firms down into many more categories than other classification systems. This is important if a marketer is trying to target specific business firms, however narrow their classification.

Many standardized information services are available to help marketers understand the consumer market. As mentioned earlier in this chapter, Environics founder Michael Adams developed the concept of social values tribes, which divides respondents to the company's social values survey into segments based on shared values and lifestyle. The process of segmention is based on the belief that people express themselves through their underlying behaviour. Therefore, the tribe a consumer belongs to will predict which brand choices he or she will make. Knowing such psychographic characteristics of a segment can help marketing managers plan a product and its promotion, pricing, and distribution to match the needs of the segment. The segments Environics uses are Autonomous Rebels, Connected Enthusiasts, Disengaged Darwinists, and Anxious Communitarians. If you have not already done so, discover which tribe you belong to by taking the short online survey at the Environics website. Go to **http://research-environics-net .sitepreview.ca**, and click on the 3SC Social Values icon.

A similar segmentation tool is the **VALS™ Survey**, created by Strategic Business Insights (SBI). To discover which segment you belong to in this system, go to **www.strategicbusinessinsights.com/vals/presurvey.shtml**. Like Environics' system, VALS™ segments consumers by psychographics.[12] The essential logic of VALS™ is that people express their personalities through their behaviours. Consumers' selections of TV programs, magazines, toothpaste brand, automobile brand, stores to patronize—all are motivated by their personalities. On the basis of their answers to the VALS™ Survey, consumers are placed in one of eight personality segments. The segments are Innovators, Thinkers, Believers, Achievers, Strivers, Experiencers, Makers, and Survivors. (Read about the differences among these

Find out which VALS segment you belong to by completing the online survey at www.strategicbusinessinsights.com/vals/presurvey.sthtml

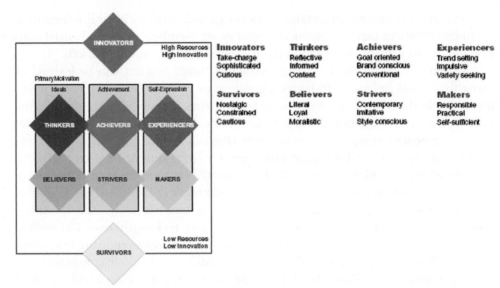

eight segments at **www.strategicbusinessinsights.com/vals/ustypes.shtml** under "The VALS™ Types.") SBI can help a client firm determine which VALS™ segments tend to purchase its goods or services. Knowledge of these segments helps the client firm develop a deeper understanding of its target consumer market.

**Geodemographics** is the term used to describe the classification of arbitrary, usually small, geographic areas in terms of the characteristics of their inhabitants. Aided by computer programs called **geodemographic information systems (GIS)**, geodemographers can access huge databases and construct profiles of consumers residing in the geographic areas of interest to the geodemographer. Geodemographers can produce information about geographic areas thought to be relevant to a given marketing application (such as a proposed site for a fast-food restaurant).

Firms specializing in geodemographics combine census data with their own survey data or data that they gather from other sources. The U.S.company Nielsen Claritas (formerly Claritas Inc.) is the firm that pioneered geodemography. By accessing zip codes and census data regarding census tracts, census block groups, or blocks, which make up a firm's trading area(s), Nielsen Claritas can compile much information about the characteristics and lifestyles of the people within these trading areas. Or, a firm may give Nielsen Claritas a descriptive profile of its target market and Nielsen Claritas can supply the firm with geographic areas that most closely match the prespecified characteristics. This service is referred to as **PRIZM** (potential ratings index for zip markets). Environics Analytics partners with Nielsen Claritas to produce **PRIZM C2**. This service classifies Canadians into 66 segments (see Marketing Research in Action 4.3).

ESRI Canada is a fully Canadian-owned company whose affiliate is in the United States. The parent company leads the world in the application of GIS technology. Its ArcGIS software program is designed to analyze markets and customers to categorize them into demographic segments. ESRI's Business Analyst Online program applies these data to help marketers plan their direct marketing communications, and Tapestry Community, a community coder, is a lifestyle segmentation and geographic location tool.

## MARKETING RESEARCH IN ACTION 4.3
## From Mainstream Marketing to Cutting-Edge Innovation

Consumer segmentation systems originated 30 years ago when Claritas Inc. developed the first geodemographic-based model for the U.S. It worked on the sociological premise that "birds of a feather flock together," that is, that people with similar demographic traits tend to behave in the same way in the marketplace. Years of research have taken this concept further, confirming that residents in neighbourhoods with similar demographics tend to have similar marketplace preferences regardless of where those neighbourhoods are located. As PRIZM C2 from Environics Analytics proves, the residents of Nouveaux Riches, a cluster of prosperous suburban francophone families, share a fondness for bicycling and cross-country skiing, whether they live in St-Bruno, Lac Beauport, Lorraine, or Boucherville. These principles are expanded with PRIZM C2, integrating psychographic data with geodemographics to show that the residents of the same cluster tend to share the same value systems as well.

Social values analysis provides much deeper answers about why consumers make the choices that they do. With its social values component, PRIZM C2 helps companies and not-for-profits understand how their target consumers think, in order to tailor marketing messages for the greatest impact.

Most marketers are familiar with the concepts of social values from reading Michael Adams' award-winning books *Sex in the Snow, Fire and Ice,* and *American Backlash*. PRIZM C2 enables organizations to take the values at the national level and apply them to customers and markets at the neighbourhood level.

For example, geodemographic analysis tells us that Young Digerati segments consist of tech-savvy singles and couples living in fashionable urban neighbourhoods in a handful of large cities. But by adding social values data, marketers learn that the values of Young Digerati are as cutting-edge as their laptops. These young Canadians see themselves as belonging to the global village and show their recognition of the shrinking world in their global ecological consciousness. While they are eager to succeed, they do not want to climb an outdated corporate hierarchy to do so; any marketing campaign should highlight

Source: Copyright 2010 Environics Analytics, www. environicsanalytics. ca. PRIZM and selected PRIZM C2 nicknames are registered trademarks of Nielsen Claritas Services, The Nielsen Company (U.S.) and are used with permission.

their independent spirit, working on their own outside the cubicles of a large corporation.

Through a strategic partnership, PRIZM C2 is also linked to PRIZM NE, the U.S. system developed by Claritas Inc., which is the best-known cluster system in the world. Sixteen segments in both systems share the same name and similar demographic profile—clusters such as Money & Brains, Back Country Folks, and Big Sky Families. As a result, PRIZM C2 permits clients from Canada and the U.S. to accomplish a variety of business applications—customer profiling and acquisition, cross-selling and site selection, strategic planning, and media buying—to reach consumers on both sides of the border. Sixteen clusters are the same, but 50 are different. Understanding those differences can make Canada a more lucrative market for U.S. businesses.

Source: Courtesy of Environics Analytics.

## Conducting Market Tracking

**Tracking studies** are those that monitor, or track, a variable such as sales or market share over time. Tracking studies can tell a firm how well its products are selling in retail outlets around the world and also provide sales data on competitors' products.

### Scanning Studies

**Nielsen Scantrack Services**    The Scantrack service is based on syndicated retail **scanning data** and is recognized as an industry standard in terms of providing tracking data gathered from stores' scanners. Each week, Nielsen collects information on purchases of items from thousands of stores: 14 000+ food stores, 18 000+ drugstores, 3000+ mass merchandisers, 2500+ convenience stores, 450+ liquor stores, 140+ warehouse/club stores, 35+ dollar stores, plus many more collected through retailer censuses. **Nielsen Scantrack Services** allows brand managers to monitor sales and market share and to evaluate marketing strategies. Scantrack reports can be provided at many different levels of information. For example, a report may be ordered for just one category of products across Canadian and global markets. Alternatively, a report can be generated for one brand in a single market.

The primary advantage of scanning data is that data are available very quickly to decision makers. There is a minimum delay from the time the data are collected to the time the information is available. The disadvantage is that a company may have products distributed through smaller stores that do not have scanners. This was the case a few years ago when demand for natural and organic foods began to grow. These foods were distributed through small stores, mostly independently owned and without scanners. Since this emerging market was not served by the large scanner-based services, a new firm, SPINS, emerged to track sales of natural and organic foods. Today, these foods are distributed through traditional food retailers and SPINS is associated with The Neilsen Company.

**Nielsen Homescan Panel**    The Nielsen Homescan® Panel recruits panel members who use handheld scanners to scan all bar-coded products purchased and brought home from all outlets, from grocery stores to wholesale clubs to convenience stores. Panel members also record the outlet at which all merchandise was purchased and which family member made the purchase, as well as price and promotion information such as coupon usage. The Homescan® Panel consists of households that are demographically and geographically balanced and projectable to the total United States. In addition, local markets can be tracked. Nielsen's Worldwide Panel Service also provides home tracking services for 26 countries around the world, including Canada.

**IRI ScanKey Consumer Network Household Panel**    Owned by Symphany ICI, the **IRI ScanKey Consumer Network Household Panel** maintains a panel of consumer households that record purchases at outlets by scanning UPC codes on the products purchased. Using IRI's handheld ScanKey scanning wand, panel members record their purchases, and this information is transmitted via telephone link to IRI. In the summer of 2005, IRI had 70 000 shoppers as part of its consumer panel. Like many panels, an advantage is that not only information on products purchased is gathered, but also purchase data that are linked to the demographics of the purchasers.[13]

**Retail-Store Audits**    Some tracking services do not rely solely on data collected in retail stores by scanners. They use **retail-store audits** as well. In retail-store audits, auditors are sent to stores to record merchandising information needed for tracking studies. Store audits are particularly useful for smaller stores that do not have scanner equipment. Sales are estimated by calculating the following:

$$\text{Beginning Inventory} + \text{Purchases Received} - \text{Ending Inventory} = \text{Sales}$$

Auditors not only record this information for many products but also note other merchandising factors, such as the level and type of in-store promotions, newspaper advertising, out-of-stock products, and shelf facings of products. Like data collected by scanning services, data collected by audit are stored in a common database and made available to all who subscribe.

Information is gathered in homes using scanning devices and diaries. In the United States, in-home scanner devices are provided to panel members who agree to scan the UPC codes on products they have purchased. Other services ask panel members to record purchases in diaries that are subsequently mailed back to the research firm. Almost all of these methods rely on consumer household panels whose members are recruited for the purpose of recording and reporting their household purchases to one of the standardized data services firms.

NPD Group provides a retail tracking service in Canada using aggregate sales figures in conjunction with consumer panel tracking. Ipsos Canada offers the **Households Panel**, an online panel of respondents who record their retail purchases.

### Diaries

The use of diaries to collect data appears to be decreasing. This is likely due to falling response rates. Consumers seem to be less willing to complete diaries recording their purchases or media habits. However, some companies still offer tracking data collected in this way. Each panel member is asked to complete a **diary** containing such information as the type of product, name brand, manufacturer or producer, model number, description, purchase price, store from which the item was purchased, and information about the person making the purchase. This information can then be used to estimate important factors such as market share, brand loyalty, brand switching, and demographic profile of purchasers. The panel members are typically balanced geographically across Canada.

## Turning Market Tracking Information into Intelligence

One of the disadvantages of today's information technology is that a user of information can easily be swamped with information, producing "information overload." As previously mentioned, various companies have created a host of products to help decision makers use vast quantities of information to make intelligent decisions. Variously labelled "decision support systems," "data mining systems," "expert systems," and the like, these systems use analytical tools to attach meaning to data, allowing managers to make decisions in response to quickly changing market conditions.

**Nielsen's Category Business Planner** is a web-based category planning tool that aids managers in making better decisions based on sales information about products in the consumer packaged goods industry. What is unique about Category Business Planner is that it allows a manufacturer to move from retailer to retailer to view how its product is performing. This allows a manufacturer to evaluate product performance in the same way a retail customer would evaluate the manufacturer's product. In turn, this enables the manufacturer to better collaborate with retailers when developing business plans for each product category.

## Monitoring Media Usage and Promotion Effectiveness

To serve the need for objective measure of promotional effectiveness, several syndicated data service companies supply such information to subscribing firms. Some of these services specialize in a particular medium; a few others conduct studies on several forms of media.

Monitoring media usage is particularly important in the advertising industry since advertising space is sold at a price determined by exposure to the target audience. CARD is a monthly database used by media planners that provides this information.

### Tracking Downloaded Music, Videos, and Recorded Books

Nielsen's **SoundScan** tracks music and music video products downloaded online from several online music stores, such as Apple's iTunes, throughout the United States and Canada. Likewise, Nielsen's sister company **VideoScan** integrates point-of-sale data collected by both companies to provide information on sales of VOD (video on demand). Nielsen VideoScan's sales charts are currently published in *Billboard*, *The Hollywood Reporter*, the *Los Angeles Times*, *The New York Times*, and others. **BookScan U.S.A.**, part of The Nielsen Company, tracks the sale of over 300 000 titles weekly. The company also has global operations as **BookScan United Kingdom, BookScan Australia**, and **BookScan New Zealand**.

### Radio and Television

The Broadcast Bureau of Measurement Canada (BBM Canada) is one of the major providers of TV viewing and radio data in Canada. BBM Analytics collects and analyzes data about Canadian television and radio audiences. Nielsen Media Research also provides data for Canadian markets. The two companies use similar techniques. The information collected is used by media industry. Ratings help television networks and studios decide which programs to retain and which ones to cancel, and also help them price and sell space for advertisers. As well, media research helps media planners decide which specific advertising space they should purchase based on who watches or listens to which programs, and when.

Both BBM and Nielsen Media Research use the diary method to collect data. Selected households are asked to record their television viewing habits in 15-minute intervals each day over a one-week period, using a hard-copy diary provided by the company. In a few markets in Canada, a "**people meter**" is used to collect information. This is an electronic device that automatically measures when a television set is on and who is watching which channel. Data from the people meter are transmitted directly back to BBM or Nielsen, allowing the company to develop estimates of audience size for each program. Consumer information is also collected, and the data allow advertisers to choose specific space that matches their target audience requirements. A similar method is used for radio listening.

### Print

**MRI's Starch Readership Service** is known as the most widely used source for measuring the extent to which magazine ads are seen and read. Starch conducts personal interviews on a given issue of a magazine, trade publication, or newspaper. Starch readership studies are not designed to determine the number of readers who read a particular issue of a magazine. Rather, Starch determines what readers saw and read in a study issue when they first looked through it. MRI (Mediamark Research & Intelligence) Starch allows advertisers to measure impact, branding, and reader involvement. The service also allows access to several other services that provide clients with feedback about the performance of individual ads.

Starch also analyzes the impact of many other variables on readership, such as ad size, number of pages, effect of black and white and colour, special position (cover, centre spread, etc.), and product category. To further help marketers make decisions about what comprises a good ad, Starch provides another syndicated data service called **Adnorms**, which provides readership scores by type of ad. For example, Adnorms could calculate the average readership scores for one-page, four-colour computer ads appearing in *Business Week*. This allows advertisers to compare their ad scores with the norm. Adnorms lists rankings of magazines based upon engagement criteria and identifies the publications likely to generate word of mouth. In this way, subscribers can assess advertising effectiveness. Users learn the effect of ad size, colour, and even copy on readership. MRI Starch also does **cover testing** and **editorial tracking**, which identifies whether the types of editorial matter or columns read are closely aligned with a client's target market. MRI Starch conducts studies of **internet advertising** as well.

## Single-Source Data

**Single-source data** are data that contain information on several variables such as promotional message exposure, demographics, and buyer behaviour. Single-source data can help managers determine causal relationships between types of promotions and sales.

Several technological developments have led to the growth of single-source data, including the universal product code (UPC) and scanning equipment that electronically records and stores data gathered at the point of purchase. When coupled with computer and MIS technology, powerful "single-source" databases can be built that are capable of providing a wealth of information on consumer purchases down to the UPC level.

Although scanner-based databases can provide up-to-the-minute reports on the sale of virtually any consumer product by store, date, time of day, price, and so on, these databases cannot tell anything about *who* bought the product. There are several marketing research services in the United States, such as IRI's **BehaviorScan**, that can supply demographic data on purchasers. Although single-source data services do not replace traditional marketing research studies, there is a growing demand for them in the United States.

**MARKETING RESEARCH IN ACTION 4.4**
# What Is the *Buzz* about Your Company's Brand?
# Nielsen Online's BuzzMetrics® Service Can Tell You!

What is CGM? It is consumer-generated media. It is the name given by Nielsen to describe the tremendous growth of online content, opinion, recommendations, word-of-mouth behaviour, and buzz! CGM has been recognized as the fastest-growing medium and it is unique in that consumers create it and share it among themselves. Powerful messages are mediated through the web in the form of blogs, recommendations on websites, viral videos, discussion forums, and so on. But how can a company keep track of what is being said about them and their products? Are there negatives being disseminated? Are there advocates for the company and its products? Nielsen provides this information through a joint venture with McKinsey & Company called NM Incite®, which offers a suite of products such as the My Buzzmetrics Dashboard® and Brand Association Maps®; as well as a suite of consulting solutions, including: Marketing Optimization, New Product Innovation, Threat Tracking, Building Advocacy and Increasing Customer Value.

By using its proprietary data-mining technology, NM Incite® can draw on millions of forums, discussion boards, and blogs to answer important questions for clients, such as:

How do consumers feel about your brand—across a time horizon and in real time?

How many consumers are talking online, and how many other consumers are influenced by the conversation?

What specific issues are being discussed? What issues are coming around the corner?

Nielsen and McKinsey & Company's NM Incite® can help firms identify threats as well as opportunities. For example, a Brand Association Map® can identify hostile threats associated with a client's brand or positive associations with the brand being made by third parties about whom the client has no knowledge. BlogPulse® allows client firms to track trends in the conversations occurring over millions of blogs. Through My Buzzmetrics Dashboard®, client firms can keep up with what is going on in the world of CGM not only for their products and brands but also for those of their competitors.

Source: www.nmincite.com. Used with permission.

## Summary

1.  **Classify types of secondary data and demonstrate their uses.**
Secondary data should be examined in virtually all marketing research projects. Data may be grouped into two categories: primary and secondary. Primary data are gathered specifically for the research project at hand. Secondary data are data that have been previously gathered for some other purpose. Access to and availability of secondary data have been greatly enhanced by the internet. Online secondary data analysis is now an important tool in the marketing researcher's toolbox. There are many uses of secondary data in marketing research, and sometimes secondary data are all that is needed to achieve research objectives.

Marketing researchers should be fully aware of the classifications of secondary data and their advantages and disadvantages, and researchers must know how to evaluate the information available to them. Secondary data may be internal—that is, data already gathered within the firm for some other purpose. Electronic data collected and stored from sales receipts—customer names; types, quantities, and prices of goods or services purchased; delivery addresses; shipping dates; salesperson making the sale; and so on—are considered to be internal secondary data. Companies use information recorded in internal databases for purposes of direct marketing and to strengthen relationships with customers. This is known as customer relationship management (CRM). Data mining is the name for software available to help managers make sense out of the seemingly unconnected masses of information contained in databases. What companies do with information collected for their internal databases can present such ethical problems as violating privacy laws.

External secondary data are data obtained from sources outside the firm. These data may be classified as (1) published, (2) syndicated services data, and (3) online databases. The different types of published secondary data include reference guides, indexes and abstracts, bibliographies, almanacs, manuals, and handbooks. Understanding the different functions of each type is useful in researching secondary data. Syndicated services data are provided by firms that collect data in a standard format and make them available to subscribing firms. Online information databases are sources of secondary data searchable by search engines. When several databases are offered under one search engine, the service is called either an aggregator or a databank.

## 2.   Discuss advantages and disadvantages of secondary data.

Secondary data have the advantages of being quickly gathered, readily available, and relatively inexpensive. They are helpful in gaining insights should primary data be needed. Disadvantages are that the data are often reported in incompatible reporting units; measurement units do not match researchers' needs, class definitions are incompatible with the researchers' needs, and the data may be out of date. Evaluation of secondary data is important. Not all organizations are ethical in terms of reporting secondary information objectively.

## 3.   Discover how to find secondary data, including strategies for searching online information bases.

To find secondary data, indexes and bibliographies may be consulted first; they list sources of secondary information by subject. Computerized data searches from databases, if available, should be conducted. Knowing how to find standard subject headings within a database is a key to successful information searching. Understanding the logic of database organization as well as being familiar with database search techniques, including Boolean logic, field searching, proximity operators, truncation, nesting, and limiting, are helpful.

## 4.   Examine major sources of external secondary data, including standardized information sources.

Examples of secondary data sources widely accessed for business are Statistics Canada census information and Industry Canada's reports. Regular reports are generated to provide such timely information as the annual Survey of Household Spending (SHS), the monthly Labour Force Survey, and the monthly Consumer Price Index (CPI).

NAICS is a coding system of business firms and can be used by researchers to access information stored in databases according to the NAICS codes. NAICS groups businesses into 20 sectors and uses codes of up to 6 digits to classify businesses.

Standardized information is a type of secondary data in which the data collected or the process of collecting the data is standardized for all users. There are two classes of standardized information. Syndicated data are collected in a standard format and made available to all subscribing users. An example would be the Nielsen television ratings. Standardized services offer a standardized marketing research process that is used to generate information for a particular user. PRIZM C2 is a system of classifying residential neighbourhoods into different segments. The process is standardized; it is the same for all users. The information from the process is then applied to generate different data for each user. Syndicated data are the same for each user; standardized services use the same process of generating data for each user.

Syndicated data have the advantages of sharing the costs of obtaining data among all those subscribing to the service, high data quality, and the speed with which data are collected and distributed to subscribers. Disadvantages are that buyers cannot control what data are collected, must commit to long-term contracts, and gain no strategic information advantage because the information is available to all competitors.

The advantages of standardized services are the supplier firm's expertise in the area, reduced cost, and speed with which supplier firms can perform the service. The disadvantages of standardized services are that the process cannot easily be customized, and the supplier firm may not know the idiosyncrasies of the industry in which the client firm operates.

Five major areas in which standardized information sources may be applied are measuring consumers' attitudes and opinions, defining market segments in both the industrial/business-to-business markets and the consumer market, conducting market tracking studies, turning market tracking information into intelligence, and monitoring media usage and promotion effectiveness. Focus Canada (Environics), the Global Monitor (Angus Reid), and the Gallup Poll (Gallup) are examples of syndicated data sources providing information on Canadians' attitudes and opinions. Many firms offer standardized services that define consumer market segments, such as PRIZM C2 (Environics/Nielsen Claritas) and the VALS® Survey (SBI). Examples of syndicated data sources for monitoring media exposure include the Broadcast Bureau of Measurement, the Print Media Bureau, and the Canadian Outdoor Measurement Bureau.

# KEY TERMS

Adnorms   (p. 145)

Angus Reid Global Monitor   (p. 138)

Baby boomer   (p. 115)

BehaviorScan   (p. 145)

BookScan Australia   (p. 144)

BookScan New Zealand   (p. 144)

BookScan United Kingdom   (p. 144)

BookScan U.S.A.   (p. 144)

Boolean logic   (p. 131)

Catalogue   (p. 122)

Cover testing   (p. 145)

Customer relationship management   (CRM)   (p. 117)

Data mining   (p. 117)

Database   (p. 117)

Database marketing   (p. 115)

Demographic and psychographic groups   (p. 115)

Diary   (p. 143)

Dun & Bradstreet's D-U-N-S   (p. 139)

Dun's Market Identifiers (DMI)   (p. 139)

Editorial tracking   (p. 145)

ESRI's Tapestry™ Segmentation   (p. 134)

External databases   (p. 122)

External secondary data   (p. 119)

# Review Questions

1.1 Describe how secondary data may add value to primary data.

1.2 Describe some uses of secondary data.

1.3 What are the various types of secondary data?

1.4 What is database marketing and what is customer relationship management (CRM)?

1.5 Go online to your favourite search engine (e.g., Google, Yahoo, etc.), and enter "demographics." Go to some of the sites you find, and describe the kind of information you are receiving. Why would this information be considered secondary data?

2.1 What are the five advantages of secondary data? Discuss the disadvantages of secondary data.

2.2 How would you go about evaluating secondary data? Why is evaluation important?

2.3 What are online information databases? Name three of them.

3.1 Discuss how you would go about locating secondary data in your own library.

3.2 What is a standard subject heading? Explain why knowing how to find a standard subject heading would help increase your information searching skills when using online information databases.

3.3 Access the Statistics Canada website and find information relevant to any topic you are currently studying in your coursework.

3.4 Select an industry and go to the NAICS website at **www.mediacorp.ca/ find_naics.html**. Find the NAICS number that represents your industry. Discuss how you could use this number.

3.5 Suppose you were the marketing director for a luxury car manufacturer. Discuss what information you would consider in building the next marketing plan. Identify secondary information sources you would use.

4.1 Briefly identify some sources of secondary data.

4.2 Distinguish between syndicated data and standardized services. Consider advantages and disadvantages of each.

4.3 Name four broad types of applications of standardized information, and give an example of each.

4.4 Explain how "information overload" of tracking information can be minimized through the use of software also offered as standardized services.

4.5 Explain how a marketer of boats could use the VALS™ Survey.

4.6 Go to the website of three marketing research companies. Review their lists of products and services offered. Which of these are standardized services? Syndicated data? Custom research offerings?

4.7 Review the kinds of information gathered by Gallup. Go to the website (**www.gallup.com**) and take a look at some of the studies they report. How could a marketing manager use some of this information?

4.8 Given what you know about syndicated services, which firm would you call on if you had the following information needs?

a. You want to know which magazines have the heaviest readership among tennis players.

b. You have decided to conduct a test market but you have no research department within your firm and no experience in test marketing.

c. You need to know how a representative sample of households would answer seven questions about dental hygiene.

d. You are thinking about a radically new advertising theme, but you are very concerned about consumer reaction to the new theme. You want some idea as to how the new theme will impact sales of your frozen dinners.

# Case 4.1

# Pure- Aqua Systems

Ronny McCall and Lucy Moody were considering a new business of supplying residential homes with bottled water. They knew the public was growing wary of tap water, and they also knew that many consumers were aware that about one-third of the bottled water purchased in stores was actually bottled tap water. They investigated a new distillation system based upon heating water and collecting the condensation. Such a system has the advantage of producing the cleanest water. Even water taken from sewage water, once heated and recondensed, was perfectly clean. Traditional distillation systems operated at high costs, but McCall and Moody had developed a new system that could distill large quantities of water at costs comparable with other water-filtering systems. The two entrepreneurs scanned secondary information for clues as to how the public opinions were changing in terms of their attitudes toward tap water. The problem with some of the information they found was that the secondary information was reported for markets outside their proposed area of operation, Northern Saskatchewan.

Lucy, always searching secondary information sources, found an article in the local newspaper about a new study conducted by the local university in a joint venture with a marketing research firm. The two had worked together to create a panel of consumers that were reportedly representative of Northern Saskatchewan that Lucy and Ronny had targeted as their market. Excited, Lucy told Ronny about the story and, together, they went online to search for the original study. They found results of a study conducted in November 2009 that asked a key question important to Lucy and Ronny's bottled-water venture. The question asked the respondents to rate the tap water quality in their home. The two were startled at the results. In one community, almost 24% had rated the tap water as either "bad" or "poor." They knew that home-delivered water companies were successful in other markets for which they had discovered secondary data showing that as little as 10% of the population rated the tap water as "bad" or "poor."

McCall and Moody discussed what the survey results meant to them. Was this an indication that there was a need for their service in the Northern Saskatchewan market area? "Wait a minute," said Ronny. "Before we go ahead and invest our nest egg in this project, how do we know these secondary data are really representative of the population?"

## Questions

1. How would you evaluate the need for the secondary data referred to in this study?

2. Go online and search for information that would help you evaluate the secondary data reported. What can you find to either support or refute the representativeness of the data?

3. Given your answers to questions 1 and 2 above, do you think Ronny McCall and Lucy Moody should continue to investigate their proposed bottled-water venture?

# Case 4.2

# Apple Supermarkets, Inc.

Bow Wow Dog Treats are sold all over Canada. Distribution is through grocery stores and a few large mass-merchandising chains such as Walmart. Mike Hall is V.P. of marketing for the company. Hall has been concerned with the level of competition in dog treat brands in the last few months. More and more competitors are trying innovative marketing programs. Mike has commissioned an ad agency to develop a national promotional campaign. The agency has presented four different sets of TV ads. To be integrated with the TV ads is a series of in-store promotions. The four in-store

(Continued)

promotion campaigns are each stand-alone campaigns. In other words, any one of them may be run simultaneously with any one of the four proposed TV ad campaigns.

The agency made its final presentation to Mike and the other officers of the company. Essentially, they must choose between the four different TV ad/in-store promotion campaigns. Hall and the other officers are very pleased with the creative work conducted by the ad agency. All four campaigns are equally appealing. All four campaigns are consistent with the key benefits of Bow Wow treats: Dogs like them, and they have high nutritive value. The officers know that the selection of the right campaign is important, since they are going to allocate several million dollars to the campaign. They also know it is important because they believe it is crucial for them to maintain or increase market share in light of the extreme, recent competition.

"This is a case where even a very small difference in effectiveness may play a major role in the success of our brand," says Hall. After several hours of debate it was clear that no one, even with many years in the dog treat business, could clearly determine which of the four campaigns should be selected. Finally, the Executive V.P., Jack Russell, stated, "We need to run this by Ron Spiller. He's responsible for marketing research. Maybe Ron can help us decide what to do."

The following day the officers met with Ron Spiller and reviewed the four TV ad campaigns and the four in-store promotion campaigns. Ron agreed that even a small difference in the effectiveness of the campaigns could make a significant difference in market share, profits, and return on investment. Spiller also pointed out that it was possible that there could be a significant "interaction" effect between the TV campaigns and the in-store promotions. In other words, they might find that a particular TV campaign performs significantly better when it is run with a particular in-store promotion.

Bow Wow did not have their own marketing research department. However, Spiller was responsible for assisting managers in determining whether research was needed and in selecting the right outside supplier firm and service to use. Spiller stated that he would make some calls and gather some information from different research suppliers. A meeting was set up for the following Friday morning to consider Spiller's proposed suggestions for conducting marketing research.

## Questions

1. Do you think it is appropriate to conduct marketing research?
2. Should Ron Spiller consider a standardized information service? What are the arguments for and against using a standardized information service?
3. Should Ron Spiller consider standardized data or a standardized service?
4. Which particular standardized information service discussed in this chapter do you think Ron Spiller should recommend? Why?

# Qualitative Research Methods

## Identifying and Filling Gaps between the Marketing Promise and Consumer Perceptions

*The Canadian Marketing Association hosts the Canadian Marketing Blog, an initiative of its Digitial Marketing Council. The excerpt below is a post from Jim Estill, author and social media and marketing expert.*

Measuring media has been a challenge of business for a long time. I even wrote a controversial blog entry here on The Fallacy of Return On Investment in Marketing.

Now with internet, social media and Web 2.0, the challenge is even greater. This new media has "democratized" the press and proliferation is huge. Tracking this new media and combining it with "old media" measurement is the new goal.

Let's first remember how much the media world has changed. Media was formally shout box from Brands to Consumers: TV, Radio, and Print: that was about it. Then technology and the Internet came along with a major curveball.

The world went online. All the news, weather, sports—everything went online. The sources of information increased dramatically. Blogs, Twitter, Facebook, Linkedin, etc. became easily accessible to all. Plus, these media had influence. But their influence varied based on the number and character of each site. They are not all of equal value. It depends on the quantity and quality of the readership. Measuring the sentiment and changes in sentiment became a challenge.

Listen carefully. The noise on the internet is your customers. Your place is determined by your competitors. You need to see where you stand. Measuring it is the new challenge. Twitter, blogs, and websites can make and break companies. And there is no professional editor checking facts. But the media value still impacts. Measuring social media is not like measuring the news. These are your very customers, the most passionate of the bunch, talking about the very products you are trying to sell. Listen to nuances, the qualitative component of discussion. Discover the context, associated topics and sentiment-laden words. And then check for volume, exposure, and statistical relevance. Your focus groups are fine, but this is better.

The world has shifted from a few huge media sources to a multitude of small ones. The tough challenge is—how do you measure all this new media? What is the value of it. The new term is Media value. Measuring it is the new challenge.

Marketing Impact Measurement—Whether it's a product launch, public relations push, or advertising campaign, you need a yardstick to measure the reaction. In today's world, Media are leveraged such that you may pay for your first set of eyeballs, but the rest come as word-of-mouth. Media Value is a new way of attributing impact and measuring the success or failure of marketing initiatives. Your tracking studies can work, but this is better (and cheaper).

Brand awareness is the key. Where does your brand stand? Where do you stand compared to the competition? And importantly, is the perception changing positively or negatively? Knowing what people feel about brands is important. Or trying to get a brand onto the radar. Not only awareness, perception, sentiment. All these are key components.

It is good to have an early warning system. Something that can tell you if sentiment is changing for or against you or for or against a trend. It is also great to know and understand the value of that media.

Measuring marketing impact is the key. Social media can give valuable feedback on the success (or failure) of a media campaign. Having the public comments and weighing them can provide critical decision-making data.

Marketers are turning to things like media value reports by General Sentiment to try to figure out the value of various social media mentions and to determine the trending—whether it is positive or negative.

The opening vignette provides an example of a qualitative technique using online blogs. In this specific online chat, the participants have illustrated the types of findings from qualitative research, provided you with a brief overview of some of the qualitative research methods, and offered the rationale for why firms use qualitative research. Qualitative research methods are sometimes referred to as the "soft side" of marketing research simply because the findings are not quantitative. However, qualitative research is an important tool that provides clients with insights not found in quantitative research. Each qualitative method has its place in the marketing research process and each has its unique advantages and disadvantages.

# Quantitative, Qualitative, and Pluralistic Research

Methods for collecting data during the research process can be classified into three broad categories: quantitative, qualitative, and pluralistic.

Quantitative research, the traditional mainstay of the research industry, is sometimes referred to as "survey research." **Quantitative research** is defined as research involving the use of structured questions in which the response options have been predetermined and a large number of respondents are involved. When you think of quantitative research, you might envision a nationwide survey conducted by telephone interviews. That is, quantitative research involves a representative sample of the population and a formalized procedure for gathering data. The purpose of quantitative research is very specific, and it is used when the client and researcher have agreed that precise information is needed. Data format and sources are clear and well defined. The compilation and formatting of the data gathered follows an orderly procedure that is largely numerical in nature. One way to think of it is that *quanti*tative research *quanti*fies information.

**Qualitative research**, in contrast, involves collecting, analyzing, and interpreting data by observing and listening to what people do and say. Observations and statements are in a nonstandardized form. Qualitative data can be quantified, but only after a translation process has taken place. For example, if five people were asked to express their opinions on a topic such as gun control or promoting alcoholic beverages to post-secondary students, each would probably give a different answer. But after studying each response, one could characterize each one as "positive," "negative," or "neutral." This translation step would not be necessary if you instructed them to choose predetermined responses such as "yes" or "no." Any study that is conducted using an observational technique or unstructured questioning can be classified as qualitative research. Qualitative research is becoming increasingly popular in a number of research situations,[1] especially in the application of social media (as illustrated in our opening vignette).

As a testament to the usefulness of qualitative research in Canada, the MRIA has a Qualitative Research Division. Also, the U.S.-based international Qualitative Research Consultants Association has a Canada chapter and a Canada Eastern chapter.

The importance of properly executed qualitative research is recognized by the marketing research industry in Canada. To gain certification as a Canadian marketing research professional (CMRP), a quantitative methods course is required. For those seeking an advanced designation by writing the CMR exam, there is an advanced qualitative methods course. Why would you want to use such a "soft" approach? Occasionally, marketing researchers find that a large-scale survey is inappropriate. For instance, Procter & Gamble may be interested in improving its Tide laundry detergent, so it invites a group of homemakers to join an online forum and brainstorm how Tide could perform better or how its packaging could be improved, or to discuss other features of the detergent. Listening to the market in this way can generate excellent packaging, product design, or even product positioning ideas. As another example, if the Procter & Gamble marketing group were developing a special end-of-aisle display for Tide, they might want to test one version in an actual supermarket environment. They could place a display in a Safeway grocery store located in a Vancouver suburb and videotape shoppers as they encountered it. The marketing group would then review the videotape to see if the display generated the types of responses they hoped it would. For instance, did shoppers stop there? Did they read the copy on the display? Did they pick up the displayed product and look at it? Qualitative research techniques afford rich insight into consumer behaviour.[2]

In the rush toward conducting online quantitative research that produces huge amounts of data, qualitative research is sometimes overlooked.[3] **Pluralistic research** is defined as the combination of qualitative and quantitative research methods in order to gain the advantages of both. In pluralistic research, it is common to begin with exploratory, qualitative techniques—for example, a series of focus group discussions with customers in order to understand how they perceive a product and service compared with those of competitors. Qualitative research often helps clarify and define a problem or otherwise open researchers' eyes to factors and considerations that might have been overlooked if they rushed into a full-scale survey. The qualitative phase serves as a foundation for the quantitative phase of the research project; it provides the researcher with first-hand knowledge. Armed with this knowledge of the problem, the researcher's design and execution of the quantitative phase are superior to what they might have been without the qualitative phase. Thus, the qualitative phase serves to frame the subsequent quantitative phase.

In some cases, qualitative methods are used *after* a quantitative study because they help the researcher understand the quantitative findings. For example, Mountain Equipment Co-op (MEC) needed to distinguish itself from competitors on the basis of its long-time use of sustainability marketing. Through a pluralistic approach involving depth interviews, ethnography, online groups, and surveys, the company redeveloped its sustainability strategy.

The pluralistic approach is becoming increasingly popular, especially for examining emerging and complex marketing phenomena such as online shopping behaviour. Marketing Research in Action 5.1 shows how a pluralistic program com-

## MARKETING RESEARCH IN ACTION 5.1
## Pluralistic Research Identifies Online Buyer Segments and Distinct Purchasing Behaviours

Because online purchasing behaviour is an emerging phenomenon, a pluralistic approach that uses both qualitative research techniques and quantitative methods is the most appropriate way to investigate it. Accordingly, market researchers combined the following research techniques in a strategy to reveal online buyer market segments.

Focus groups, which are moderated discussions conducted with groups of 8 to 12 online buyers, were used to gain a basic understanding of online buying, such as why, where, when, and how often. The focus groups uncovered basic differences between male and female online buyers.

Depth interviews, which are personal interviews lasting from 30 to 45 minutes, were then used in order to probe motivations for online purchasing, including func-

tional as well as emotional reasons for buying online. These depth interviews also sought to tap into personal styles for online information search and processing.

An online survey was conducted via email invitations to about 40 000 internet users. The survey contained questions about demographics, lifestyle, internet usage, preferences for internet delivery formats, and importance of various internet content types (such as news, entertainment, travel, family, etc.).

The online survey data were subjected to various analyses, and they resulted in the discovery of five distinct female online user segments as well as five separate male online user segments. The segments and their key differences are noted in the table on the next page.

## Online Segments and Key Differences Revealed by Pluralistic Research

| Segment | Percent | Demographics | Key Online Usage | Online Favourites |
|---|---|---|---|---|
| **Female Segments** | | | | |
| Social Sally | 14% | 30–40, college educated | Making friends | Chat and personal web space |
| New Age Crusader | 21% | 40–50, highest income level | Fighting for causes | Books and government information |
| Cautious Mom | 24% | 30–45, with children | Nurturing children | Cooking and medical facts |
| Playful Pretender | 20% | Youngest, many are students | Role playing | Chat and games |
| Master Producer | 20% | Tends to be single | Job productivity | White pages and government information |
| **Male Segments** | | | | |
| Bits and Bytes ` | 11% | Young and single | Computers and hobbies | Investments, discovery, software |
| Practical Pete | 21% | 40-ish, some college, above-average income | Personal productivity | Investments, company listings |
| Viking Gamer | 19% | Young or old, least college education | Competing and winning | Games, chat, software |
| Sensitive Sam | 21% | Highest education and income of males | Helping family and friends | Investments, government information |
| World Citizen | 28% | 50 and older, most with college education | Connecting with world | Discovery, software, investments |

These are only thumbnail descriptions of these 10 different online market segments. Much more detail is provided in the original descriptions.[4] It is important to note that such complete understanding of these emerging online segments was possible only through the use of pluralistic research.

bined qualitative and quantitative research techniques to yield an understanding of the differences between male and female shopping behaviour online and to identify gender differences in online market segments.

The marketing research industry borrowed the qualitative research approach from such social sciences as anthropology and sociology. During the 1970s and 1980s, the usefulness of qualitative research to consumer research was recognized—for understanding consumer reactions to new products, product positioning, and advertising. Due to growing criticism about the reliability and validity of qualitative research, new methods evolved in the 1980s and 1990s.

Marketing researchers use a variety of popular types of qualitative methods, which can be organized into three categories: observation techniques, social media techniques, and focus groups. Focus group analysis is the most commonly used qualitative method in Canada, but with the evolution of technology, social media are fast becoming another popular form of data collection. Although commonly used in the United States, observation methods are less popular in Canada, mainly because of the Personal Information Protection and Electronic Documents Act

(PIPEDA), which governs the privacy rights of Canadians. Mystery shopping is a popular observation technique in the Canadian retail sector. These three types of qualitiative research are discussed in detail below.

Several other qualitative research techniques not included in the above three categories include ethnographic research and projective techniques. As we shall see, these methods are becoming more popular among Canadian marketing researchers.

## Observation Techniques

In using **observation methods**, the researcher relies on observation rather than on communication in order to obtain information. Researchers depend on recording devices such as videotapes, audiotapes, handwritten notes, or some other tangible record of what is observed.

In order for the observations to be consistent and for comparisons or generalizations to be made, it is important to adhere to a plan for data collection. There are four types of observation studies: (1) direct versus indirect, (2) disguised versus undisguised, (3) structured versus unstructured, and (4) human versus mechanical.

Observing behaviour as it occurs is called **direct observation**. For example, if interested in finding out how much shoppers squeeze tomatoes to assess tomato freshness, researchers observe people actually picking up the tomatoes. Direct observation has been used by Kellogg to understand breakfast rituals, and by a Swiss chocolate maker to study the behaviour of "chocoholics."[5] It has also been used by General Mills to understand how children eat breakfast, leading to the launch of Yoplait Tubes, a mid-morning snack for schoolchildren.[6]

To observe types of hidden behaviour, such as past behaviour, indirect observation is used. With **indirect observation**, the researcher studies the effects or results of the behaviour rather than the behaviour itself. Types of indirect observations include archives and physical traces.

**Archives** are secondary sources, such as historical records, that can be applied to the present problem. These sources contain a wealth of information and should not be overlooked or underestimated. There are many types of archives. For example, records of sales calls may be inspected to determine how often salespersons make cold calls. Warehouse inventory movements can be used to study market shifts. Scanner data may give insight into the effects of price changes, promotion campaigns, or changes in package size.

**Physical traces** are tangible evidence of some event. For example, "garbology" (observing the trash of subjects being studied) is used as a way of finding out how much recycling of plastic milk bottles occurs. A soft-drink company might do a litter audit in order to assess how much impact its aluminum cans have on the countryside. A fast-food company such as Wendy's might measure the amount of graffiti on buildings located adjacent to prospective sites as a means of estimating the crime potential for each site.[7]

With **disguised observation**, the subject is unaware that he or she is being observed. An example of this method might be a "mystery shopper" who is used by a retail store chain to record and report on sales clerks' assistance and courtesy. One-way mirrors and hidden cameras are other ways used to prevent subjects from awareness of being observed. Hiding the fact of observation is important because if subjects were aware of it they might behave differently than they normally would. The use of mystery shopping can improve customer service, evaluate retail operations, and increase customer satisfaction. Disguised observation has proved illuminating in studies of parents and children shopping together in supermarkets.[8]

When the respondent knows he or she is being observed, the technique is called **undisguised observation**. Laboratory settings, observation of a sales representative's behaviour on sales calls, and people meters (Nielsen Media Research's device attached to a television set to record when and to what station a set is tuned) must all be used with the subject's knowledge. Because people might be influenced by knowing they are being observed, it is wise to always minimize the presence of the observer to the maximum extent possible.

The use of observation raises ethical questions. Should people being observed be informed of the observation and, if so, what changes might they make in their behaviour in order to appear "normal" or conform to what they think is expected? The researcher wants to observe behaviour as it actually occurs, even if it is unusual or out of the ordinary. However, those being observed might feel uncomfortable about their habits or actions and try to act in more conventional ways. For instance, if a family agrees to have its television set wired so a researcher can track what programs the family watches, will the parents make sure that the children watch mainly wholesome shows? Sometimes, researchers resort to deceit in order to observe people without their knowledge. The ethical thing to do is to inform people ahead of time and give them an "adjustment period" or, if such a period is not feasible, to fully debrief them about the observation afterwards. Ethics in Marketing Research 5.1 shows a press release from ESOMAR, the global organization for marketing research, announcing its guide on passive data collection, observation, and recording, which deals with these issues.

When using **structured observation** techniques, the researcher identifies beforehand which behaviours are to be observed and recorded. All other behaviours are "ignored." Often a checklist or a standardized observation form is used to focus the observer's attention on specific factors.

**Unstructured observation** places no restriction on what the observer will record. All behaviour in the episode under study is monitored. The observer just watches the situation and records what seems interesting or relevant. Of course, the observer has been thoroughly briefed about the area of general concern. Unstructured observation is often used in exploratory research. For example, Black and Decker might send someone to observe carpenters working at various job sites as a means of better understanding how the tools are used and to help generate ideas on how the tools can be designed for increased safety.

**Human observation**, where a real person observes a situation, can be costly and prone to error. **Mechanical observation** involves replacing a live person with some form of device to observe behaviour. For instance, auto traffic counts may be more accurate and less costly when recorded by machines that are activated by car tires rolling over them. Besides, during rush hour, a human observer could not accurately count the number of cars on most major metropolitan commuter roads. Nor would it be possible to count the number of fans entering a gate at a professional hockey title game, so turnstile counts are used instead. Typically, scanning devices are used to count the number and types of products sold, for inventory management.

AMSTERDAM, 12 November 2010—ESOMAR, the world association for enabling better research into markets, consumers and societies, is issuing new guidelines to ensure that researchers who are using the latest technologies, continue to protect the rights of respondents who participate in market, social and opinion research.

Research via mobile phone is becoming more common in many countries due to the falling use of landline phones and a decrease in gaining a representative research sample using fixed line coverage alone.

In response to this trend, ESOMAR has issued a new Guideline on Research via Mobile Phone which covers contacts with respondents by voice or text message (SMS) and includes subjects such as respondent safety and confidentiality, calling times and duration of the interview.

It does not cover the use of interactive mobile services for research purposes as this will be included in ESOMAR's soon-to-be released Guideline on Online Research. This will also cover the use of online identification and tracking technologies in research and will list practices that research companies should adopt as well as practices that are unacceptable. An expanded section on notification highlights the need for clear and understandable privacy notices about the information being collected, and assurances regarding its confidentiality.

These two guidelines are designed to promote respectful relationships with respondents, ethical and professional standards and best practices. Integral to each of these guidelines and a core principal of market research and the ICC/ESOMAR International Code on Market and Social Research is that the rights of respondents as private individuals must be protected and they should never be harmed or adversely affected as a direct result of cooperating in a market research project.

The ICC/ESOMAR Code and the ESOMAR guidelines clearly state that when personally identifiable data is collected for research purposes, the respondent must know about the nature of the data collected, the reasons for processing it and what will be done with it.

"People have to be confident that if they talk to a market researcher, the information will only be used for research purposes and they will not be personally identified" said Adam Phillips, chair of ESOMAR's legal and professional standards committees. "The two important pillars of privacy are transparency and trust."

David Stark, former President of the Canadian Market Research and Intelligence Association also noted "The key lesson is: one should not design and implement new services, applications or technologies without first conducting privacy impact assessment."

Both guidelines should be read in conjunction with the ICC/ESOMAR International Code on Market and Social Research, which is designed to strengthen consumer protection and confidence. All ESOMAR members have undersigned to uphold the ICC/ESOMAR Code which has been adopted or endorsed by 56 associations in 46 countries worldwide.

Source: Courtesy of ESOMAR

Mechanical observation has become a high-technology research tool through the combination of telecommunications, computer hardware, and software programs.

## Appropriate Conditions for the Use of Observation

Certain conditions must be met before a researcher can successfully use observation as a marketing research tool: The event must occur during a short time interval, the observed behaviour must occur in a public setting, and the possibility of faulty recall rules out collecting information by directly asking the person.

*Short time interval* means that the event must begin and end within a reasonably short time span. Examples include shopping in a supermarket, waiting in a line at a bank, purchasing a clothing item, or observing children as they watch a television program. Some decision-making processes can take a long time (e.g., buying a home), and it would be unrealistic in terms of the time and money required to observe the entire process.

Because of this factor, observational research is usually limited to scrutinizing activities that can be completed in a relatively short time span or to observing certain phases of activities that have a long time span. *Public behaviour* refers to behaviour that occurs in a setting the researcher can readily observe. Actions such as cooking, playing with one's children at home, or private worshipping are not public activities and are, therefore, not suitable for observational studies such as those described here.

*Faulty recall* occurs when actions or activities are so repetitive or automatic that the respondent cannot recall specifics about the behaviour in question. For example, people cannot recall accurately how many times they looked at their wristwatch while waiting in a long line to buy a ticket to a best-selling movie, or which FM radio station they listened to last Thursday at 2 pm. Observation is necessary under circumstances of faulty recall to fully understand the behaviour of interest. Faulty recall is one of the reasons that companies have for many years experimented with mechanical devices to observe these behaviours.[9]

## Advantages of Observational Data

Ideally, the subjects of observational research are unaware they are being studied, so they react in a natural manner, giving the researcher insight into actual, not reported, behaviours. As previously noted, observational research methods also eliminate recall error. The subjects are not asked what they remember about a certain action; instead, they are observed while engaged in the act. In some cases, observation may be the only way to obtain accurate information. For instance, children who cannot yet verbally express their opinion of a new toy will do so by simply playing or not playing with the toy. Retail marketers commonly gather marketing intelligence about competitors by hiring the services of "mystery shoppers."[10] In some situations, data can be obtained with better accuracy and less cost by using observational methods. For example, observational techniques can often obtain counts of in-store traffic more accurately and less expensively than can survey techniques.

Even though there are several advantages to observational research, observation techniques should not be used without considering other research methods. A resourceful researcher will use observation techniques to supplement and complement other methods.

## Limitations of Observational Data

One disadvantage of observational research is that it normally observes only a few persons. Researchers must be concerned about how accurately those observed represent all consumers in the target population. This factor, plus the subjective quality of the interpretation required to explain the observed behaviour, usually forces researchers to consider their conclusions as tentative. The greatest drawback to all observational methods is that motivations, attitudes, intentions, and other internal conditions cannot be observed. Only when these feelings are relatively unimportant or are readily inferred from the behaviour is it appropriate to use observational research methods. For example, facial expression might be used as an indicator of a child's attitudes or preferences for various types of fruit drink flavours because children often react with conspicuous physical expressions. However, adults and even children usually conceal their reasons and true reactions in public, and this fact necessitates direct questioning. Observation alone cannot give a complete picture of why and how people act the way they do.

# Social Media Research

**Social media research** is becoming an increasingly popular method for understanding consumer views. As more and more people choose to join online social communities to share their views and experiences about companies, products, and services, companies are realizing the value of mining these data that are so readily available. Social media research is less expensive than other forms of data collection (it is essentially "free" with an internet account), and the information is obtained in real time—as it is happening.

There are many opportunities for marketing researchers to listen to the conversations consumers engage in online. A partial list of avenues includes social networks (e.g., LinkedIn; Facebook), blogs (e.g., CMA blog), social bookmarking (e.g., StumbleUpon; Delicious), content communities (e.g., Flickr; YouTube), user groups and forums, podcasts, online focus groups, and internet depth interviews. Needless to say, there is an explosion of information on an enormous array of topics. In order to be useful to marketers, engine tools are used to search, monitor, and analyze the wealth of information from these conversations.

Google and Bing are two popular search engines that allow marketing researchers to discover sites containing content on topics of their choice. Google Alerts can send an email to a subscriber to notify him or her of new sites carrying a specific topic. A limitation to this service is that only public sites are accessible and the data discovered are only as good as an individual's internet searching techniques.

Another useful search tool is StumbleUpon. Once a topic is submitted for a search, this program will generate a list of sites related to the topic, including a sample of people who are participating in threaded conversations about it. One can find out about the demographics of those interested in the topic, and about other topics of interest to any user of the site by clicking on the user's posted comment.

LinkedIn is a growing social network that lists people and their professional information. Information about any company listed on the site, such as job titles, average employee age, and gender ratio, can be provided simply by generating a company profile. LinkedIn Answers is a tool that allows users to direct questions to a targeted group of LinkedIn users.

Twitter is another social network that contains conversations about many topics. To find out what people are saying about any of these topics, the Twitter search tool Summize can present real-time conversations.

Forums are earlier types of social networks, such as Twitter, and are still very popular. Forums on any topic can be visited by typing in the topic and adding the word *forum* on a Google search bar. There are an increasing number of niche social sites that deal with specific subjects such as pets. By joining these sites, users gain access to a wealth of information on what people think about that niche topic.

It is important to keep in mind that the information collected through social networks is a biased representation of all available social media conversations on that one topic. It does not represent a statistically generated sample of all individuals in the population of interest.

Once social media are tapped for information, the next step is for the marketing researcher to segment the conversations into meaningful categories and issues. Through review of approximately 100 conversations, these categories can be developed. The next step is to join some of the conversations by asking well-thought-out questions based on the categories of interest. If the questions developed are standardized, the responses can be standardized for analysis.

For example, if a camera manufacturer is interested in improving one of its digital cameras, the marketing researcher can monitor social media for mentions of the product. Examination of 100 conversations can yield categories of interest such as ease of use, weight, and quality of pictures. Now probing questions can be developed: for example, "Would you sacrifice quality of picture for ease of use?" This question can be posted on the media monitored. Answers can then be analyzed from across the various social media conversing about the product.

Tom Webster is the author of a blog called BrandSavant. This blog is dedicated to developing the use of social media in marketing research. He discusses "six degrees of social media monitoring." The first degree, or simplest form, is the monitoring of brand mentions, followed by the more in-depth monitoring of sentiment—consumer reactions, positive or negative, to a brand. The third degree involves tracking conversations about the competition. Armed with all of the information monitored so far, in the fourth degree a more in-depth analysis of direct consumer need can be made. This analysis is done by segmenting the conversations into coded "buckets" or categories of issues. The fifth degree of monitoring moves to the consideration of indirect consumer need, and entails listening to consumers' experience with the product. Finally, the sixth degree of social media monitoring examines the underlying psychological and social meaning behind consumer interaction with specific social media.[11]

# Focus Groups

A popular method of conducting exploratory research is through **focus groups**. Focus groups are small groups of people brought together and guided by a moderator through an "unstructured," spontaneous discussion for the purpose of gaining information relevant to the research problem. Although focus groups are intended to encourage openness on the part of the participants, the moderator's task is to ensure that the discussion is "focused" on some general area of interest. For example, ING Direct conducts focus groups. The conversation may seem "freewheeling," but the purpose of the focus group is to learn about people's preferences regarding financial services.

**Figure 5.1** A Sample of Focus Group Facilities in Ontario

Source: www.greenbook.org. Courtesy of GreenBook Directories, New York American Marketing Association.

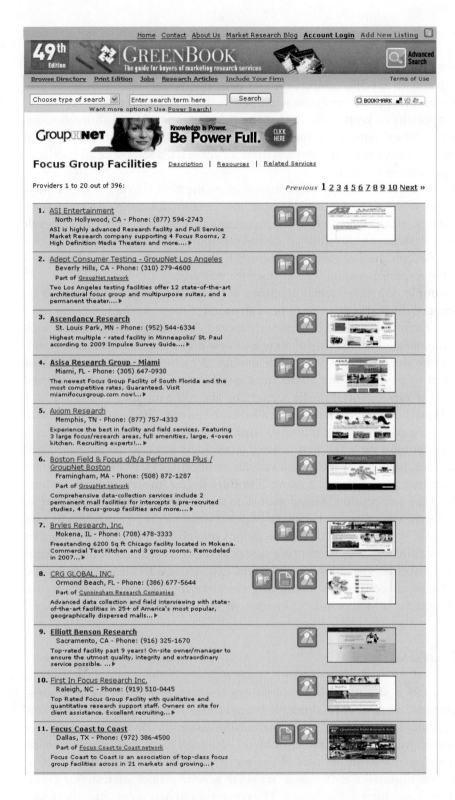

Focus groups are a useful technique for gathering information from a limited sample of respondents. The information can be used to generate ideas, to learn the respondents' "vocabulary" in relation to a certain type of product, or to gain some insights into basic needs and attitudes. Of the total amount of money spent on qualitative research in the United States, 85% to 90% is spent on focus groups.[12] They have become so popular in marketing research that every large city has a number of companies that specialize in performing focus group research. Figure 5.1 shows a partial list of focus group facilities in Ontario. "Almost nothing gets done without them," says Bill Hillsman, a successful advertising executive.[13] Focus groups are very helpful for learning about new customer groups.

## How Focus Groups Work

Focus groups can be of several types. **Traditional focus groups** select about 6 to 12 persons and meet in a dedicated room, with a one-way mirror for client viewing, for about 2 hours. Recent years have seen the emergence of **nontraditional focus groups**.[14] In this format, the groups may be online and clients may observe on computer monitors from distant locations; the groups may have as many as 25 or even 50 respondents; clients may interact with participants; and sessions may last 4 or 5 hours and occur outside traditional facilities, such as in a park.

A marketing research firm offering traditional focus groups typically will have a **focus group facility**, which is a set of rooms especially designed for focus groups. The meeting is conducted in a room that seats about 10 people (optimal size is thought to be somewhere between 6 and 12 participants) and a moderator. A wall in the room has a one-way mirror, which allows clients in the adjoining room to watch the focus group without influencing what the group members say or do. Some facilities have video cameras in the focus group room, which allow clients to observe the group from another room or even a distant location. Microphones are built into the walls or ceiling or otherwise set in the centre of the table, and videotape equipment often operates from an inconspicuous location.

In the past, some companies tried to hide or disguise the equipment they used to record respondents' reactions. However, such a practice is unethical. Now it is a requirement to let participants know about the recording when they are recruited. If they have any objections, they can decline at that time.

Focus group participants are interviewed by **moderators**, often referred to as **Qualitative Research Consultants** (QRs or QRCs).[15] The training and background of the moderator or QRC are extremely important to the success of the focus group.[16] The MRIA's Qualititative Research Division guides professional standards in QRCs. QRCs are responsible for creating an atmosphere that is conducive to openness, yet they must make certain the participants do not stray too far from the central focus of the study. A good moderator must have excellent observational, interpersonal, and communication skills to recognize and overcome threats to a productive group discussion. He or she must be prepared, experienced, and armed with a detailed list of the topics to be discussed.[17] It is also helpful if the focus group moderator can eliminate any preconceptions about the topic from his or her own mind. The best moderators are experienced, enthusiastic, prepared, involved, energetic,

Coastal Views is an example of a Canadian focus group facility.

and open-minded. An incompetent moderator can create a disaster of the focus group. Some trade secrets of successful moderators may be found in Table 5.1.

QRCs also must prepare a **focus group report** that summarizes the information provided by the participants relative to the research questions. When analyzing the data, two important factors must be kept in mind. First, the qualitative statements of participants must be translated into categories and then the degree of consensus apparent in the focus groups must be assessed. Second, the demographic and buyer behaviour characteristics of focus group participants should be judged against the target market profile to assess to what degree the groups represent the target market. Information from the focus group is evaluated by an analyst who carefully observes the recorded tapes several times, transcribing any relevant statements. These statements are then subjected to closer evaluation. The evaluation is based on the analyst's knowledge of the history and statement of the problem plus his or her own interpretation of the responses. A detailed report is prepared for the client's review. To see an example of a focus group report, go to **www.ppt.gc.ca/consultations/rop-por/2009-10-eng.pdf**.

The focus group report reflects qualitative research. It lists all of the themes that have become apparent, and it notes any diversity in opinions or thoughts expressed by the participants. Numerous verbatim excerpts may be included as evidence. In fact, some reports include complete transcripts of the focus group discussion. This information is then used as the basis for further research studies or even for additional focus groups. The client uses the first group as a learning

| Question | Tricks of the Trade |
|---|---|
| **How do you make your groups great every time?** | ■ Be prepared.<br>■ Be energized.<br>■ Be nice but firm.<br>■ Make sure everything about the experience is comfortable. |
| **How do you build rapport quickly?** | ■ Make meaningful eye contact during each person's introduction.<br>■ Learn and remember names.<br>■ Let them create their own name cards.<br>■ Welcome participants as they come into the room, and use small talk. |
| **How do you bring a drifting group back into focus?** | ■ Tell them the topic is "for another group" and that they need to focus on the topic for this group.<br>■ Make a note and tell them that they will come back to this topic if there is time.<br>■ Tell them the topic is "interesting" but not the subject at hand, and refer to the next question.<br>■ Suggest that they can talk about it on their own after the focus group is over. |
| **How do you get them to talk about deeper things rather than top-of-the-mind answers?** | ■ Play naive or dumb, and ask them to help you understand by explaining.<br>■ Use probes such as "Tell us more about that," or "Can you go deeper on that?"<br>■ Ask for specifics such as "Tell me about the last time that you...."<br>■ Pair them up, and give them 10 minutes for each pair to come up with a solution or suggestion. |
| **What about management of the "back room" where your clients are observing?** | ■ Orient clients with a 10-minute overview of focus groups, research objectives, and what to expect.<br>■ Check with the client(s) during breaks, written exercises, and so on to make sure things are going well.<br>■ Have an associate or colleague there to work with the client(s).<br>■ If you do not have an associate for the back room, ask the client to select one person to be the point person to communicate with you. |

**Table 5.1** Focus Group Moderators' "Tricks of the Trade"

The above trade secrets were divulged by experienced focus group moderators at a recent panel at the annual conference of the Qualitative Research Consultants Association.[18]

experience, making any adjustments to the discussion topics as needed to improve the research objectives. Although focus groups alone may be used to tackle a marketing problem or question, they are also used as a starting point for quantitative research.

## Online Focus Groups

The **online focus group**, a form of "nontraditional" focus group, is one in which the respondents and/or the clients communicate and/or observe over the internet. Typically, online focus groups allow participants the convenience of sitting at their own computers while the moderator operates out of an online focus group company. The online focus group is "virtual" in that it communicates electronically, and there is no face-to-face contact in the traditional focus group sense. Although some experts hold that online focus groups are not equivalent to traditional focus groups, they offer many advantages and few disadvantages. The Qualitative Research Consultants Association's Online Qualitative Research Task Force published its investigations into online focus groups;[19] its major conclusions are listed in Table 5.2.

Online focus groups have the following advantages over traditional focus groups: (1) No physical setup is necessary, (2) transcripts are captured on electronic files in real time, (3) participants can be in widely separated geographic locations, (4) participants are comfortable in their home or office environments, and

**Table 5.2** Online Focus Groups FAQs[20]

| Question | Answer |
| --- | --- |
| Can online focus groups substitute for face-to-face ones? | Yes, as long as the online environment is consistent with the study's objectives. |
| For what situations are online focus groups best suited? | Some are:<br>  Low-incidence respondents<br>  Geographically dispersed respondents<br>  Business-to-business (B2B) professionals |
| What is "lost" with online focus groups? | You cannot:<br>  See body language<br>  Show prototypes or models of products<br>  Conduct taste tests |
| Can I recruit online focus group participants via email invitation? | Yes, if they have valid email accounts that they use regularly. |
| What incentives should I use to recruit my focus group participants? | The going rate is about $40 in cash or the equivalent, but B2B participants may require twice this amount. |
| How many participants should I plan for in my online focus group? | A common number is 15 to 20. |
| How long should it last? | Up to 90 minutes is typical. |
| How secure is the online focus group environment? | If you use a commercial chat program, password systems can be used to maintain security. |
| Can my clients observe the online focus group? | Yes, there are systems in which the client(s) can observe the focus group while online at their own computers. The clients can communicate privately with the moderator online as well. |
| Are the moderator's skills different with an online focus group? | In addition to basic focus group moderator skills, the moderator needs to take more care in preparing the wording of the discussion topic guide to avoid misinterpretation, phrase probes to include all participants, have good typing ability, and be familiar with chat room slang. |
| Are participants more or less candid with online focus groups? | Participants tend to be more candid because they have anonymity. Also, they tend to compose answers to topic questions without reading others' responses, so the comments are unique to each participant. |

(5) the moderator can exchange private messages with individual participants. Innovative approaches are possible, as some researchers combine online with telephone communications for maximum effectiveness.[21] On the flip side, there are some disadvantages, such as (1) observation of participants' "body language" is not possible, (2) participants cannot physically inspect products or taste food items, and (3) participants can lose interest or become distracted.[22] As Table 5.2 indicates, both traditional and online focus groups require recruitment and compensation of participants, scheduling and notification, and a prepared and skilled moderator.

A variation of the online focus group is one conducted in a traditional setting, but with the client watching online. ActiveGroup has pioneered this research technique using streaming media and high-speed internet connections. The focus group is conducted at a traditional focus group facility with the participants and moderator present. Several members of the client firm can observe the focus group at their own location, which saves the client firm travel expense and time. ActiveGroup provides clients with reports and a CD-ROM of the focus group. Since their introduction a few years ago, online focus groups have grown in popularity. Although they will not replace traditional focus groups, they offer a viable research method.[23] Marketing Research in Action 5.2 summarizes results of a comparison between online and offline qualitative research methods.

## MARKETING RESEARCH IN ACTION 5.2
## Comparing Online and Offline Qualitative Research Methods

### The Company
Three companies came together for this product positioning study: Pierre Bélisle, President of Bélisle Marketing Limitée; Gillian Humphreys of NFO CF Group; and Joanne McNeish of Canada Post. They conducted qualitative research on product positioning and benefits for a new web-based service from Canada Post. They were looking at differences between online and offline research methods and the results achieved from each.

### The Need
The researchers used three different types of qualitative methodologies and compared the procedures and the results from each.

1. A face-to-face (FTF) mini-group allowed observation of reactions to gauge if a better understanding of the service's features and operations needed to be addressed.

2. A Real-Time Online Focus Group was decided to be an efficient way to assess alternative names in an online context (in which this service's name would be used).

3. An Online Bulletin Board was required to give insight into the usefulness of the service by allowing participants to experiment with it online.

*(Continued)*

## The Solution

Because comparing qualitative research methods is a challenge, the researchers opted for two approaches:

- A brief quantitative comparison of outputs (words)
- A qualitative analysis of each method and its strategic implication

Itracks software and services were used to provide an online environment for both the virtual chat group (Online Focus Group) and the extended time frame group (through the Bulletin Board Focus Group software). The FTF mini-group was conducted along traditional lines. Using the Itracks' suite of virtual solutions, researchers explored the degree to which online qualitative research differs from FTF research.

## The Outcome

**Outputs:** The five-day Bulletin Board Focus Group (BBFG) yielded nearly three times the number of citations than did either the chat or the FTF sessions. These BBFG citations comprised over 20 000 words, about twice the volume generated by the FTF session, and nearly seven times that of the chat session.

**Communication:** Online participants type their answers and do so carefully, forcefully, and honestly. They may even reveal more of themselves through writing than FTF participants do through speaking. It may be that online participants are inherently more expressive or that writing allows one to better communicate concepts and emotions. (Note, however, that modulation of emotions may be more difficult online.)

**Comprehension:** Understanding the concept was not affected by method, but price was. Online, the service was seen as expensive, while FTF participants saw it as inexpensive. Brand image also varied. Online participants saw the brand as positive and desirable, while FTF participants did not necessarily feel this way.

**Skill Sets:** Many offline qualitative skills are portable to the virtual world, and nonmoderating skills (problem definition, analysis, and report writing) are completely portable. Even moderating skills, such as knowing what questions to ask, how to phrase them, and when and how to probe, transfer well to the virtual environment. However, some moderating skills, such as "Performance Skills," are not needed online.

**Importance of Internet Savvy:** Keyboard skills are critical in real-time chat groups. Reliable computer systems and fast internet access are also important, as is the ability to download and install the various applications and plug-ins that are often the subject of virtual qualitative research. To fully participate in discussions it is also important to understand internet slang and emoticons.

**Anonymity:** It can be advantageous to not know how people in your group look, sound, or even smell. For example, in conducting a group with participants who mentioned that they "had a problem with weight," anonymity may assist the researcher to focus on their comments and not on their girth (which might have influenced the analysis). Virtual qualitative research would thus work well with sensitive groups, such as the disabled or those with other medical conditions.

**Bringing the World to Your Office:** Virtual qualitative research may do away with the need to repeat similar sessions in different cities.

**Time Conquered:** Bulletin Board Focus Groups are asynchronous. Participants log on, read messages, and post comments at their convenience. This suggests applications across time zones and with hard to attract audiences (such as IT managers and professionals).

**Richer Data:** The research resulted in a richer data set, either because it was online, and/or because of multiple lines of enquiry.

"Virtual qualitative is an exciting new addition to the researcher's toolkit"
    Pierre Bélisle
    Gillian Humphreys
    Joanne McNeish

To explore this company, visit its website at **www.itracks. com.**

Source: www.itracks.com/index.php?option=com_k2&view=item&layout=item&id=122&Itemid=179. Courtesy of Itracks Online Data Collection.

## Advantages and Disadvantages of Focus Groups

The four major advantages of focus groups are (1) they generate fresh ideas; (2) they allow clients to observe the participants; (3) they may be directed at understanding a wide variety of issues, such as reactions to a new food product, brand logo, or television ad; and (4) they allow fairly easy access to special respondent groups, such as lawyers or doctors, from whom it may be very difficult to collect a representative sample.

There are three major disadvantages to focus groups. First, focus groups do not constitute representative samples and therefore caution must be exercised in generalizing the findings. Second, it is sometimes difficult to interpret the results of focus groups; the moderator's report is based on a subjective evaluation of what was said during the session. Finally, the cost per participant is high, though the total spent on focus group research is generally a fraction of what might be spent on quantitative research.

## When to Use Focus Groups

When the research objective is to describe or explore ideas, rather than to predict, focus groups may be an alternative to using quantitative methods. Consider the following situations: A company wants to know "how to speak" to its market, by using language the customers use. A company wants to explore new ideas for an advertising campaign or wants to get a feel for consumer reaction to new product concepts. Because focus groups are composed of a small number of persons who are not representative of some larger population, care must be exercised. If the research objective is to predict, focus groups should not be used. For example, if 12 persons in a focus group are shown a new-product prototype and 6 say they are going to buy it, one cannot predict that 50% of the population will buy the product. Likewise, if the results of the research are going to drive a major, expensive decision for a company, the researcher should not rely solely on focus groups. If the decision is that important, quantitative research methods that are based on some large population and that have some known margin of error should be used.

## Some Objectives of Focus Groups

There are four main objectives of focus groups: (1) to generate ideas; (2) to understand consumer vocabulary; (3) to reveal consumer needs, motives, perceptions, and attitudes about products or services; and (4) to understand findings from quantitative studies.

Focus groups *generate ideas* for managers to consider. For example, the Atlantic Lottery Corporation (ALC) replaced its Lotto Super 7 with Lotto Max and was interested in attracting a younger demographic to the new lottery. Focus groups carried out with 15- to 34-year-olds helped them to come up with a new idea on how to promote the new lottery. The focus groups revealed that a demonstration of Lotto Max had to be engaging as well as have the prospective customer at the centre of attention. The ALC ended up using "sphering" events. At each event, two participants were asked to wear head cams while they rolled down a five-metre ramp in a giant transparent bubble. The tape of the ride was posted at the Going to the Max website, and friends of participants could vote for their favourite video via Twitter, Facebook, or email. The participant with the top-rated video was awarded a $500 prize. In this instance, focus group research was very useful in devising the best way to reach the target audience.

Focus groups also help marketers *understand consumer vocabulary* and stay abreast of the words and phrases consumers use when describing products so as to improve communication with them about products or services. Such information may help in designing advertising copy or in preparing an instruction pamphlet, in refining the definition of a research problem, and also in structuring questions for use in later quantitative research.

Focus groups *reveal consumer needs, motives, perceptions, and attitudes* about products or services. They inform the marketing team of what customers really feel or think about a product or service and give managers early customer reactions to changes being considered in products or services. Thus focus groups are commonly used during the exploratory phase of research, where they are useful in generating objectives to be addressed by subsequent research.[24]

Focus groups help marketers *understand findings from quantitative studies.* Sometimes a focus group can reveal why the findings came out a particular way. For example, a bank image survey showed that a particular branch consistently received lower scores on "employee friendliness." Focus group research identified the problem as being several front-line employees who were so concerned with efficiency that they appeared to be unfriendly to customers. The bank revised its training program to remedy the problem.

Warner-Lambert has successfully used focus groups to accomplish all four of the preceding objectives. Its consumer health products group, which markets over-the-counter health and beauty products such as Wilkinson Sword, Silk Effects, and Personal Touch as well as nonprescription drugs, makes extensive use of focus groups.[25] In fact, Warner-Lambert uses a combination of qualitative research techniques to gain background information, to reveal needs and attitudes related to health and beauty products, to interpret the results of qualitative studies, and to stimulate the brainstorming of new ideas. Focus groups have been useful to the company for understanding basic shifts in consumer lifestyles, values, and purchase patterns.

## Operational Considerations

Before a focus group is conducted, certain operational questions should be addressed. It is important to decide how many people should take part, who they should be, how they will be selected and recruited, and where they should meet.

According to industry wisdom, the optimal size of a traditional focus group is 6 to 12 people. A small group (fewer than six participants) is not likely to generate the energy and group dynamics necessary for a truly beneficial focus group session. With fewer participants, one or two of the participants do most of the talking in spite of the moderator's efforts. At the same time, a small group often produces awkward silences and forces the moderator to take too active a role in the discussion just to keep it alive. Similarly, a group with over a dozen participants is too large to be conducive to a natural discussion. As a focus group becomes larger, it tends to become fragmented. Those participating may become frustrated by the inherent digressions and side comments. Conversations may break out among two or three participants while another is talking. This situation places the moderator in the role of disciplinarian, in which he or she is constantly calling for quiet or order rather than focusing the discussion on the issues at hand.

Unfortunately, it is often difficult to predict the exact number of people who will attend the focus group interview. Ten may agree to participate and only 4 show up; 14 may be invited in the hope that 8 will show up, but all 14 may arrive. If this occurs, the researcher must make a judgment call as to whether to send some participants home. In the worst case, no one attends, despite promises to the contrary. There is no guaranteed method that will ensure a successful participation ratio. Incentives (which will be discussed later) are helpful but definitely not a sure way of gaining acceptance. Although 6 to 12 is the ideal focus group size, it is not uncommon to have some groups with fewer than 6 and some with more than 12.

It is generally believed that the best focus groups are ones in which the participants share homogeneous characteristics. For instance, the focus group may be composed of executives who use satellite phones, it may involve building contractors who specialize in building residences over $500 000 in value, or it may involve a group of salespeople who are experiencing some common customer service difficulty.

Focus group participants are typically strangers. In most cases, they are not friends or even casual acquaintances, and many people feel intimidated or at least hesitant to voice their opinions and suggestions to a group of strangers. However, participants typically feel more comfortable once they realize they have similarities such as their age (they may all be in their early 30s), job situations (they may all be junior executives), family composition (they may all have preschool children), purchase experiences (they may all have bought a new car in the past year), or even leisure pursuits (they may all play tennis). Furthermore, by conducting a group that is as homogeneous as possible with respect to demographics and other characteristics, the researcher is assured that differences in these variables will be less likely to confuse the issue being discussed.

The selection of focus group participants is determined largely by the purpose of the group. For instance, if the purpose is to generate new ideas for improvements in digital cameras, the participants must be consumers who have used a digital camera. If the focus group is intended to elicit building contractors' reactions to a new type of central air-conditioning unit, it is necessary to recruit building contractors. Companies often provide customer lists for focus group recruiters to work from. For instance, with building contractors, the list might come from the local Yellow Pages or the membership roster of a building contractor trade association. In the case of traditional focus groups, it is necessary to initially contact prospective participants by telephone to qualify them and then to solicit their cooperation in the focus group. Occasionally, a focus group company may recruit by requesting shoppers in a mall to participate, but this approach is rare. Recruitment for online focus groups is an ongoing process. A database of prospective participants is generated and maintained by companies offering online focus groups.

As we noted earlier, "no-shows" are a problem with focus groups; researchers have at least two strategies with which to entice prospective participants: incentives and callbacks. Incentives range from monetary compensation for the participants' time to free products or gift certificates. Many focus group companies use callbacks during the day immediately prior to the focus group to remind prospective participants that they have agreed to take part. If one prospective participant indicates that some conflict has arisen and he or she cannot be there, it is then possible to recruit a replacement. Neither approach works perfectly. Some focus group companies have a policy of overrecruiting; others have lists of people they can rely on to participate, given that they fit the qualifications.

The difficulties encountered by focus group companies in recruiting focus group participants have led to some unethical practices. Some people like to participate in focus groups, and a focus group company may keep them on a list of willing participants. Other participants may want to take part simply for the monetary compensation, and their names may be on the focus group company's list as well. In either case, the inclusion of people who have previously participated in numerous focus groups can lead to serious validity problems. Some researchers will explicitly forbid a focus group company to use these participants because of this concern. In 2007, the Qualitative Research Division of the MRIA set up the Qualitative Research Registry (QRR). See Ethics in Marketing Research 5.2 for details of its launch.

Focus groups are held in a variety of settings and ideally are conducted in large rooms set up in a format suitable to the research objective. In some cases in which it is important to have face-to-face interaction, a round-table format is ideal. Other formats are more suitable for tasting foods or beverages or for viewing video. An advertising company conference room, a moderator's home, a respondent's home, the client's office, hotels, and meeting rooms at churches are all locations in which focus groups can be held. Aside from a seating arrangement in which participants can all see one another, the second critical requirement in selecting a meeting place is to find one quiet enough to permit an intelligible audiotaping of the sessions. Marketing research firms with focus group facilities offer ideal settings for focus groups.

The focus group's success depends on the participants' involvement in the discussion and in their understanding of what is being asked of them. Productive involvement is largely a result of the moderator's effectiveness, which, in turn, is dependent on the moderator's understanding of the purpose and objectives of the interview. Unless the moderator understands what information the researcher is after and why, he or she will not be able to phrase questions effectively. It is good policy to have the moderator be part of the development of the project's goals so as to be able to guide the discussion topics. By aiding in the formation of the topics (questions), the moderator will be familiar with them and be better prepared to conduct the group.

When formulating questions, it is important that they be organized into a logical sequence and that the moderator follows this sequence to the furthest extent possible. The moderator's introductory remarks are influential; they set the tone of the entire session. All subsequent questions should be prefaced with a clear explanation of how the participants should respond—for example, how they really feel personally, not how they think they should feel. This allows the moderator to establish a rapport with participants and to lay the groundwork for the interview's structure.

Focus groups report some of the subtle and obscure features of the relationships between consumers and products, advertising, and sales efforts. They provide qualitative data on things such as consumer language; emotional and behavioural reactions to advertising; lifestyle; relationships; the product category and specific brand; and unconscious consumer motivations relative to product design, packaging, promotion, or any other facet of the marketing program under study. Focus group results are qualitative and not perfectly representative of the general population.

The focus group approach is firmly entrenched in the world of marketing research as a mainstay technique. Focus groups are an appealing qualitative research method because their total cost is reasonable compared to that of large-scale quantitative

## ETHICS IN MARKETING RESEARCH 5.2
# New Qualitative Research Registry Launched

**January 30, 2007**

This week, MRIA and its Qualitative Research Division (QRD) launched the Qualitative Research Registry (QRR), or Registre de la recherche qualitative (RRQ) in French, as a new and improved successor to Qualitative Central.

Tracking qualitative research study participants is a vitally important Standards-based self-regulatory initiative for our industry, and the time was ripe to revamp and rebrand Qualitative Central into something new that will deliver better service to members.

By way of historical recap: in 2004—with Canada's federal privacy legislation, the Personal Information Protection and Electronic Documents Act (PIPEDA), coming into full force—the QRD Division of PMRS realized that it was time to re-look at the old "Central Files" system that had been in place for many years. Central Files and Qualitative Central were designed to assist those who recruited for qualitative market research by registering respondents and thereby helping to ensure that the then-PMRS standards for participation in qualitative research were upheld.

Respondents are only allowed to participate once in a six-month period, five times in total, and never more than once on the same topic.

We have all heard "horror stories" of respondents who "cheat and repeat"; and we recognize that it is important in our industry that a reliable and well-used registry is in force. Cheaters and repeaters reflect poorly on our industry and have more than once been the subject of a disparaging article about our industry.

While unscrupulous recruiters are occasionally the issue and should be avoided by all moderators, the main source of the problem seems to be respondents who register with several recruiters and deny previous participation. We see them at our facilities and do our best to dismiss them and then ensure they don't show up in the future.

Only with a strong "registry" system will we be able to really take control of this problem and improve our reputation as a credible part of the industry.

With MRIA's launch of our new Charter of Respondent Rights in October, respondents are guaranteed to be treated well and with the respect they deserve. In return, we as an industry must do our part to make sure that those few who try to cheat are "weeded out."

Some of the country's leading recruiters (most notably Alana Richman, Gini Smith and Dawn Smith) have worked hard along with the MRIA staff to get the new Qualitative Research Registry underway. These recruiters have outlined the elements of the new system that will provide us, as an industry, with the information we need and the ability to track respondent participation.

Administrative responsibility for QRR has been assumed by the MRIA staff, under Executive Director Brendan Wycks. This will help ensure the delivery of consistent, quality service and support to QRR participants—through a central staff contact in the MRIA office—as compared to operating the system through an outside supplier or member of the industry.

MRIA and QRD are committed to ensuring that the Qualitative Research Registry becomes an increasingly recognized, well-utilized, and user-friendly tracking vehicle. QRR builds upon QualCentral's foundation as a comprehensive "Do-Not-Call" list of those who have recently participated in qualitative research studies, those who have asked not to be contacted further, and those felt by recruiters and moderators to be best served by not being contacted.

MRIA's Standards require that recruiters should provide accurate data to the Qualitative Research Registry on a consistent basis and check all respondents against the Registry. Similarly, our Association's Standards require that moderators buying recruiting services should give primary consideration to recruiting agencies which submit to the Qualitative Research Registry on a regular and ongoing basis.

Source: Courtesy of Marketing Research and Intelligence Association. www.mria-arim.ca/QRD/NEWS02.asp.

surveys involving a thousand or more respondents. They are adaptable to managers' concerns, and they can yield immediate results. They are a unique research method because they permit marketing managers to see and hear their customers. It is common for marketing managers to come away from an observation of a focus group session stimulated and energized to respond to the market's desires.

# Other Qualitative Research Techniques

Although focus group interviews and many of the observation methods described are the most frequently used qualitative research techniques, there are other qualitative methods, including depth interviews, protocol analysis, projective techniques, ethnographic research, and physiological measurement.

## Depth Interviews

A **depth interview** is defined as a set of probing questions posed one-on-one to a subject by a trained interviewer to gain an idea of what the subject thinks about something or why the subject behaves in a certain way. The interview is conducted in the respondent's home or possibly at a central interviewing location such as a mall-intercept facility, where respondents can be interviewed in depth in a relatively short time.

Interviewers have the ability to probe, asking many additional questions. In-depth responses may be more revealing in some research situations than, say, responses to the predetermined, yes–no questions typical of a structured survey. If used properly, depth interviews can offer great insight into consumer behaviour. The disadvantage of in-depth interviewing is the lack of structure in the process. Unless interviewers are well trained, the results can be too varied to give sufficient insight into the problem. Depth interviews are especially useful when the researcher wants to understand decision making on the individual level, how products are used, or the emotional and sometimes private aspects of consumers' lives. Respondents in a depth interview are not influenced by others, as they might be in a focus group.

Depth interviews should be conducted by a trained fieldworker who is equipped with a list of topics or, perhaps, open-ended questions. The interviewer can record responses or can take detailed notes. Although depth interviews are typically conducted face to face, they can be done over the telephone when interviewees are widely dispersed. Depth interviews are versatile, but they require careful planning, training, and preparation. **Laddering**, a technique used in in-depth interviews, attempts to discover how product attributes are associated with consumer values. Essentially, values important to consumers, such as "good health," are first identified. Next, researchers determine which routes consumers take to achieve their values, such as exercise, eating certain foods, stress reduction, and so on. Finally, researchers attempt to find out which specific product attributes are viewed as a means of achieving the desired value. Through depth interviews researchers may learn that low-sodium foods or "white meats" are instrumental in achieving "good health."[26] The term *laddering* comes from the notion of establishing the linkages, or steps, leading from product attributes to values.

## Protocol Analysis

**Protocol analysis** involves placing people in a decision-making situation and asking them to verbalize everything they consider when making a decision. It is a special-purpose qualitative research technique that has been developed to peek into the consumer's decision-making processes. Often a recorder is used to maintain a permanent record of the person's thinking. After several people have provided protocols, the researcher reviews them and looks for commonalities, such as evaluative criteria used, number of brands considered, types and sources of information, and so forth.

Protocol studies are useful in two different purchase situations. First, they are helpful in studying purchases in which several decision factors must be considered, such as when buying a house. By having people verbalize the steps they went through, a researcher can piece together the whole process. Second, when the decision process is very short, recall may be faulty and protocol analysis can be used to slow the process down. For example, most people do not give much thought to buying chewing gum, but if Dentyne wanted to find out why people buy spearmint gum, protocol analysis might provide some important insights regarding this purchasing behaviour.

## Projective Techniques

**Projective techniques** involve situations in which participants undergo (are projected into) simulated activities in the hope that they will divulge things about themselves that they might not reveal under direct questioning. Projective techniques are appropriate in situations in which the researcher is convinced that respondents will be hesitant to relate their true opinions. Such situations may include behaviours such as tipping waitresses, socially undesirable behaviours such as smoking or alcohol consumption, questionable actions such as littering, or even illegal practices such as betting on hockey games. See Marketing Research in Action 5.3 for an example of the use of projective techniques with focus groups.

Five projective techniques are commonly used by marketers: the word-association test, the sentence-completion test, the picture test, the cartoon or balloon test, and role-playing activity.

A **word-association test** involves reading words to a respondent, who then answers with the first word that comes to mind. These tests may contain over 100 words and usually combine neutral words with words being tested for ads or words involving product names or services. The researcher then looks for hidden

# MARKETING RESEARCH IN ACTION 5.3
## Using Projective Techniques to Discover New Insights
### Turbo Charge Focus Groups with Projective and Interactive Exercises!

Focus group moderators are charged with discovering actionable insights. Marketers understand that most purchase decisions are made subconsciously and steeped with emotional imagery—both positive and negative associations. Marketers are keenly aware of the power of perception. So, how do moderators bypass the rational controls of consumers and strike up a meaningful dialogue that elicits emotions, perceptions, biases, and true buying motivations? Projective techniques and interactive exercises are the prescription here, tapping respondents' subconscious emotions and values that drive purchase behaviour and shape brand relationships.

It is not enough to gather only rational thoughts in qualitative research. The challenge with pure questioning is that language is based in the left brain, the part of the brain that also processes logic, analysis, science, and math. Yet, brand relationships live in the human right brain, the part of the brain responsible for intuition, creativity, imagination, art, and music. In *How Customers Think*, author Gerald Zaltman asserts that 95% of purchase decisions are made subconsciously.

Using only structured dialogue, respondents often have difficulty expressing the sum total of their perceptions, opinions, and feelings. In a focus group that relies solely on structured dialogue, respondents can become too analytical. Therefore, moderators can use projective techniques and interactive exercises to aid respondents' verbalizing of their subconscious motivations. Interactive exercises can also uncover issues and opinions that respondents may not otherwise be able to fully verbalize, or of which they might be unaware. By increasing the variety of communication methods and modes, respondents can more easily express the whys behind their needs and feelings. As much of the imagery associated with purchase techniques are tactile in nature, they promote insights from multiple senses, thus painting rich customer profiles.

According to *Qualitative Market Research* by Hy Miriampolski, projective techniques, which try to circumvent rational thinking, were adopted by the Freudians as

another means of channelling into the unconscious mind. His book goes on to define projective techniques as a category of exercises that provoke imagination and imagery. Other practitioners more narrowly define projective techniques as unstructured techniques used to project emotions onto unrelated stimuli. However, in practice, both true projective techniques and the wider class of interactive exercises bring forth deep-rooted emotions and imagery associated with purchase decisions and provide marketers with exceptional, actionable insights.

Not only do projective and interactive exercises allow marketers to uncover fresh insights, but they result in a deeper level of understanding about target buyers. Further, on a tactical level, they create more engaging and productive rapport with respondents, which, in turn, inspires new marketing learning. By injecting creativity into the moderating process, projective and interactive exercises keep the discussion moving and the energy level up in the room, which are also goals of the moderator. Field research has proven that when respondents are more engaged in the focus group, they are more willing and more able to open up, speak honestly, and express their inner thoughts, feelings, motivations, and biases. For the most part, respondents find these exercises to be fun, which further promotes their brains into stimulating new connections and thus provides additional learning for marketers.

Nearly all focus groups, regardless of the topic or respondent base, can benefit from at least one projective or interactive exercise. Depending upon the research objectives, some focus groups can include more. Exercises can be designed for respondents to work individually, for the group to work as a whole, or for the group to be split into several smaller teams.

While there are literally hundreds of these types of exercises suitable for qualitative research, below you will find a few techniques that have wide applicability to different types of studies, objectives, and respondent types. Of course, each exercise should be customized, so that it is germane to the research at hand. Nonetheless, the more generic descriptions and instructions that follow are a great primer to introduce these exciting qualitative modalities.

## Sort Me Up™

**Sort Me Up** is great for determining how target brands relate to their competition. This exercise uncovers similarities and differences across brands, product types, and product segments. It is valuable for segmentation studies, as it reveals frames of reference, thus allowing marketers to really understand what products the target brand most and least competes with. After several sorts (i.e., several focus groups), a purchase decision hierarchy emerges, which not only helps marketers understand consumer attitudes and usage patterns across different product segments but also provides an understanding of how consumers shop and consume the category under study.

To begin, the moderator places about 25 actual products on the table and asks respondents to work together as a team to sort the products into groups that make sense to them. Respondents are encouraged to create as many product groupings as they see fit. They are also instructed to give each group of items they've placed together a descriptive title. Note that for product categories where the size or shape of individual products or services is not easily brought into the focus group room (e.g., large appliances, online banking sites), Sort Me Up

can be executed with cards imprinted with brand names, logos, package graphics, etc. This exercise engages respondents in a tangible way. There is visual stimulation as well as physical activity (i.e., moving the products around the table). The ensuing lively, post-exercise discussion and probing provides marketers with key insights largely unattainable through direct questioning.

## Sort Me Straight™

**Sort Me Straight** is a variation of Sort Me Up. This variation is best implemented when the goal is to determine how the target brand and its competition perform on specific attributes. In brief, it assesses how the products being studied are perceived on these specific attributes, relative to each other. It also assesses how brands perform relative to the specific attributes. Unlike Sort Me Up, this exercise is an aided technique, where consumers determine product rankings on a continuum based upon predetermined attributes. To begin, the moderator places 5 to 10 preselected products from the category on the table. The moderator then places pole cards on the table—opposite each other, leaving adequate room for the respondents to build the continuum. Pole cards are simply cards printed with the attributes—for example, Most Natural to Least Natural, Most Expensive to Cheapest, Masculine to Feminine, and For Guests versus For Everyday.

## Picture This, Picture That™

If a research goal is to learn about imagery and emotional associations for target brands, then **Picture This, Picture That** is a particularly insightful projective technique. In this exercise, pictures become metaphors for respondents to describe their perceptions. In brief, this technique allows respondents to think more broadly, frame their ideas, and get over their inhibitions. The images trigger key perceptions and give consumers permission to divulge their innermost thoughts (as they project their real attitudes onto the image).

This exercise begins with about 50 preselected images that represent a wide range of emotions. It's important that the images be rich, but they can be from almost any source: magazine ads, art books, furniture catalogues, etc. It's imperative that images that are related to the topic under discussion are not included (e.g., soup for a soup study, honeymoon vacation if researching online

*(Continued)*

dating). The moderator places these images on the table and asks respondents to individually select a picture that depicts how they feel about the brand, category, or situation. Of course, the question should be crafted to be consistent with study goals. An easy variation is to ask each respondent to select two images—for example, one that depicts the best thing and one that depicts the worst thing about the brand, category, or situation or one that depicts how they feel about shopping at Store A and one that depicts how they feel about Store B.

The tangible aspects of implementing this exercise, combined with the intangible aspects of the deep-seated imagery, yield insightful stories for marketers. The discussion and active probing surrounding the emotional underpinnings of these images and how they relate to the target brand reveal fresh insights, which can greatly aid the advertising team's ability to create more engaging campaigns.

## Color My World™

**Color My World** is similar to Picture This, Picture That. Rather than using rich images, this projective technique uses colour as keys to uncovering consumer attitudes and perceptions. Here, colours become the metaphors for respondents to describe their thoughts and feelings. This quick and easy-to-implement exercise provokes storytelling and gives consumers considerable opportunity to verbalize positive and negative associations for the brand, category, or situation being studied.

To start, the moderator places several dozen paint chips on the table. Be sure to use a wide range of assorted colours. Again, it's imperative to exclude any category-related colours (e.g., exclude red and deep purple for a wine study). Ask respondents to choose a colour that depicts how they feel when they buy or consume a brand or category, when they encounter a specific situation, etc. While this engaging exercise is suitable for almost any juncture in the discussion guide, as a warm-up exercise it has the added benefit of setting the stage for a deeper, more revealing conversation.

## Dot, Dot, Dot™

This quali-quant technique helps marketers understand preferences among a set of brands, flavours, advertisements, etc. **Dot, Dot, Dot** yields weighted rankings, allowing marketers to iteratively narrow the range of ideas and concepts being researched. Most importantly, this exercise uncovers the functional and emotional rationale behind consumer perceptions.

This easy-to-implement technique begins with the moderator presenting respondents with a short list of choices (e.g., brands, flavours, advertisements) and 10 small, round dot stickers (think purchase tokens). Respondents are instructed to allocate the dots according to their preferences, placing as many dots as they feel appropriate (or even zero dots) on each option. Of course, they should place a greater number of dots on their preferred option(s), but how many is up to them. While the results are not statistically significant, they can be considered directional. The ensuing discussion following Dot, Dot, Dot provides fresh insights about customer preferences. When "forced" to vote their preferences, it is often easier for respondents to later divulge their needs, emotions, and biases underlying these preferences.

## About Talking Business

**Talking Business**, LLC delivers the truth behind brands and what motivates purchase behaviour—vital insights decision makers need to drive competitive marketing solutions. Offering more than focus group moderating, we specialize in innovative marketing research and strategic brand development. Our category expertise includes consumer, financial, pharmaceuticals, technology, and hospitality, with clients such as GlaxoSmithKline, Princess Cruises, and Experian. Exceeding client expectations for 14 years, Talking Business connects with target audiences to better understand brands, loud and clear. You can visit Talking Business at **www.TalkingBusiness.net**.

Source: Courtesy of Talking Business, LLC

meanings or associations between responses and the words being tested on the original list to uncover people's real feelings about these products or services, brand names, or ad copy. The time taken to respond, called "response latency," and/or the respondents' physical reactions may be measured and used to make inferences. For example, if the response latency to the word duo is long, it may mean that people do not have an immediate association for that word.

Decision Analyst, Inc. uses word-association tests in its battery of qualitative online research services. Anywhere from 50 to 75 words are given to online respondents as stimuli. Respondents then type the first word, association, or image that comes to mind. Sample sizes are typically 100 to 200 persons, and the entire process lasts about 30 minutes. Decision Analyst states that this projective technique is very helpful in determining awareness or exploring the imagery or other associations that are linked to brands.[27]

With a **sentence-completion test**, respondents are given incomplete sentences and asked to complete them in their own words. The researcher then inspects these sentences to identify themes or concepts. The notion here is that respondents will reveal something about themselves in their responses. For example, suppose that Lipton Tea was interested in expanding its market to teenagers. A researcher might recruit high school students and instruct them to complete the following sentences:

Someone who drinks hot tea is _____

Tea is good to drink when _____

Making hot tea is _____

My friends think tea is _____

The researcher would attempt to identify central themes from the written responses. For instance, the theme identified from the first sentence might be "healthy," which would signify that tea is perceived as a drink for those who are health conscious. The theme from the second sentence might be "hot," indicating that tea is perceived as a cold-weather drink, whereas the theme from the third sentence may turn out to be "messy," denoting the students' reaction to using a tea bag. Finally, the theme from the last sentence might be "okay," suggesting there are no peer pressures that would cause high school students to avoid drinking tea. Given this information, Lipton might deduce that there is opportunity to capitalize on the hot-tea market with teens. Decision Analyst, Inc. also conducts sentence-completion tests online by giving 50 to 75 respondents 50 to 60 incomplete sentences.[28]

In a **picture test**, participants are given a picture and are instructed to describe their reactions by writing a short story about it. The researcher analyzes the content of these stories to ascertain feelings, reactions, or concerns generated by the picture. Such tests are useful when testing images being considered for use in brochures, advertisements, and on product packaging. For example, a test advertisement might show a man holding a baby, and the ad headline might say, "Ford includes driver and passenger airbags as standard equipment because you love your family." A picture test may well divulge something about the picture that is especially negative or distasteful to respondents. Perhaps male respondents who are not parents cannot relate to the ad because they do not have children and have not experienced strong feelings for children. On the other hand, it may turn out that the picture has a much more neutral tone than Ford's advertising agency intended. It may be that the picture does not generate feelings of concern and safety for the family in respondents who have young children.

A **balloon test** is a line drawing with an empty "balloon" above the head of one of the figures. Subjects are instructed to write in the balloon what the figure is saying or thinking. The researcher then examines these responses to find out how subjects feel about the situation depicted in the cartoon. For example, when shown a line drawing of a situation in which one of the characters is making the statement "Ford Explorers are on sale with a discount of $4000 and 0% interest for 48 months," the participant is asked how the other character in the drawing would respond. Feelings and reactions of the subject are judged based on their answers.

In a **role-playing** activity, participants are asked to pretend they are a "third person," such as a friend or neighbour, and to describe how they would act in a certain situation or react to a specific statement. By reviewing their comments, the researcher can spot latent reactions, positive or negative, conjured up by the situation. This method reveals some of the respondents' true feelings and beliefs because they are pretending to be another individual. For example, if Ray-Ban is thinking about introducing a new "Astronaut" sunglasses model with superior ultraviolet light filtration, space-age styling, and a price of about $200, it might use role-playing exercises to discover what consumers' initial reactions would be. Subjects could be asked to assume the role of a friend or close workmate and indicate what that person would say to a third person when learning that their friend had purchased a pair of Astronaut sunglasses. If consumers felt the Astronaut model was overpriced, this feeling would quickly surface. On the other hand, if the space-age construction and styling are consistent with the consumers' lifestyles and product desires, this fact would be divulged in the role-playing comments.

As with depth interviews, all of these projective techniques require highly qualified professionals to interpret the results. This increases the cost per respondent compared to other survey methods. Thus, projective techniques are not used extensively in commercial marketing research, but each has its value in its special realm of application.

## Ethnographic Research

**Ethnographic research**, a technique borrowed from anthropology, is a detailed, descriptive study of a group and its behaviour, characteristics, culture, and so on. *Ethno-* means "people" and *-graphy* means "to describe." Anthropologists have gained insights into human behaviour by living among their subjects (a process called *immersion*) for prolonged periods to study their emotions, behaviours, and reactions to the demands of everyday events. Ethnography uses several different types of research, including immersion, participant observation, and informal and ongoing depth interviewing. Ethnographers pay close attention to words, metaphors, symbols, and stories people use to explain their lives and communicate with one another. The use of ethnographic research techniques in marketing research is growing (see Marketing Research in Action 5.4). In ethnographic marketing research, researchers use direct observation, interviews, and audio and video recordings of consumers conducted over time instead of at one point in time. One researcher, Ann-Marie McDermott of Quaestor Research, who was working on a new chicken burger project, decided to spend time with consumers instead of using the standard research techniques. She visited their homes and watched them shop, cook, and eat.[29]

Ethnographic research is an area of ethical sensitivity. Researchers immersing themselves in others' homes, schools, and places of work and play in order to record the behaviours, comments, reactions, and emotions of persons who do not know the purposes of the research is unethical. As the technique grows more common

## MARKETING RESEARCH IN ACTION 5.4
## Ethnography Enjoying Resurgence as Important Qualitative Tactic

More and more companies are mandating that the marketing, research, and R&D staff get to know their consumers "up close and personal" on a regular basis. Ethnography—qualitative research that studies people in their own natural habitat—is enjoying resurgence among marketers because it provides that real-life, first-hand observation of experiences.

Ethnography differs from laboratory-based research (focus groups) because it allows the interviewer the opportunity to observe and study subjects in their own surroundings and around family and friends, if applicable. Describing how someone cleans a floor and actually watching how it is done is a completely different experience. In a Q&A format, participants may be reluctant to "spill the beans" on how much they rely on convenience food, that their kids eat sugary cereal, or that they love to eat chocolate while watching TV in the afternoon. In their homes, however, you see what is in their cupboards and refrigerator.

Some other examples of ethnographic qualitative research are:

1. Moms at home to see what they make for dinner.
2. Men at breakfast to observe what they eat and why.
3. Shopping with people at supermarkets and retail stores to observe how they shop and how they make brand decision choices.
4. "Hanging out" with teen girls as they shop and socialize in the mall.

5. Walking with seniors in their walking groups and listening to them discuss their hopes, fears, worries, health, and family/friends.
6. Watching people use a product they have been given days ago to find out how it fits into their routine (test product or a competitive product).
7. The "before and after" of someone taking a medication to observe how it makes or does not make a difference in their life.

Source: Qualitative Research Consultants Association. By permission: QRCA

in marketing research, researchers must become adept in the skills necessary to be "present and known" without interfering with normal behaviour. Fortunately, most behaviours that marketers are interested in are public behaviours—shopping and eating, for example. Such public behaviours are easily observed.

## Physiological Measurement

**Physiological measurement** involves monitoring a respondent's involuntary responses to marketing stimuli via the use of electrodes and other equipment. Most people who are monitored find the situation strange, and they may experience uneasiness during the monitoring. This measurement technique is rarely used in marketing research. Two physiological measures are described the pupilometer and the galvanometer. The **pupilometer** is a device that attaches to a person's head and determines interest and attention by measuring the amount of dilation in the pupil of the eye. It actually photographs the movement of the pupil as the subject views different pictures. The theory is that a person's pupil enlarges more when viewing an interesting image than when viewing an uninteresting one. Eye-tracking has a new application in internet marketing. For example, AT&T uses eye-tracking coupled with depth interviewing to understand how AT&T customers interact with its customer service website.[30] The **galvanometer** is a device that determines excitement levels by measuring the electrical activity in the respondent's skin. It requires electrodes or sensing pads to be taped to a person's body in order to monitor this activity. When encountering an interesting stimulus, the electrical impulses in the body become excited.

Physiological measures are useful under special circumstances, such as testing sexually oriented stimuli. Their disadvantages are that the techniques are unnatural, and subjects may become nervous and emit false readings. Even though the respondent reacts to the stimulus, there is no way to tell if the response is positive or negative.

# Summary

**1.   Identify circumstances where qualitative research is applicable.**
Quantitative research involves predetermined structured questions with predetermined structured response options, normally with large samples. Qualitative research is much less structured than quantitative approaches. Qualitative research involves collecting, analyzing, and interpreting data by observing what people do or say. The observations and statements are in a qualitative or unstructured, nonstandardized form. The advantage of qualitative research is that it allows researchers to gather deeper, richer information from respondents. Pluralistic research involves using both qualitative and quantitative research methods.

**2.   Discuss applications of the observation qualitative research technique.**
Observation is a qualitative research technique in which researchers observe what consumers do rather than communicate with them. The four general types of observation are direct versus indirect, disguised versus undisguised, structured versus unstructured, and human versus mechanical. The circumstances most suitable to observational studies are instances of (1) short time interval, (2) public behaviour, and (3) lack of recall. Ethical issues arise in observation studies when respondents are not aware they are being observed. The primary advantage of observation is that researchers record what respondents actually do instead of relying on their recall of what they think they have done. The limitations of observation studies are that they often rely on small samples, so representativeness is a concern. Another disadvantage is that subjective interpretation is required to explain the behaviour observed. Researchers do not know consumers' motives, attitudes, or intentions.

**3.   Discuss emerging applications of social media as a data source.**
A legitimate form of qualitative research involves social media. Social media such as online blogs, Facebook, Twitter, and online forums provide acceptable ways for a

company to get in touch with its customers. As with other types of qualitative research, the information thus gathered does not represent the thoughts of a statistically significant sample but does provide clues as to what marketers need to pay attention to. Used in conjunction with other types of research, social media can provide very useful, up-to-date information.

**4.   Discover why focus groups are so popular in the marketing research industry.**
Focus groups, moderated small-group discussions, are a very popular form of research. The major task of the moderator is to ensure freewheeling and open communication that is focused on the research topic. Traditional focus groups are made up of about 6 to 12 persons who meet in a dedicated room with a one-way mirror for client viewing. In recent years, many innovations have been introduced, comprising what we call nontraditional focus groups. Online focus groups, in which clients may observe a focus group from a distant location via video streaming over the internet, are one example of such innovations. Another form of online focus group allows the group members to participate from their homes or any remote location where they can observe and respond to others in the focus group via chat rooms. Focus groups have the following advantages: (1) They generate fresh ideas; (2) they allow clients to observe the participants; and (3) they may be directed at understanding a wide variety of issues. Disadvantages include lack of representativeness, subjective evaluation of the meaning of the discussions, and high cost per participant. Focus groups should be used when the researcher needs to describe marketing phenomena. They should not be used when the researcher needs to predict a phenomenon, such as how many persons will actually buy a new product evaluated by focus groups. Four main objectives of focus groups are to generate ideas; to understand consumer vocabulary; to reveal consumer needs, motives, perceptions, and attitudes about products or services; and to better understand findings from quantitative studies.

The chapter presented several operational issues involved in running focus groups. Participants should share similar characteristics and recruiting and selection may be problematic because of "no-shows." Focus group facilities exist in most major cities, but any large room with a central table can be used. The moderator's role is key to a successful focus group, and the moderator should be involved early on in the research project.

**5.   Examine other types of qualitative methods used by marketing researchers.**
Descriptions of some of the other qualitative techniques used in marketing research were presented. Depth interviews, for instance, have been adapted to probe consumer motivations and hidden concerns. Protocol analysis induces participants to "think aloud" so the researcher can map the decision-making process being used while a consumer goes about making a purchase decision. Projective techniques, such as word association, sentence completion, or role-playing, are also useful in unearthing motivations, beliefs, and attitudes that subjects may not be able to express well verbally. Ethnographic research involves observing consumers in near-natural settings to record their behaviours, relations with others, and emotions. Finally, some physiological measurements, such as pupil movement or electrical skin activity, can be used in special circumstances to better understand consumer reactions.

# Key Terms

| | |
|---|---|
| Archives    (p. 158) | Physiological measurement    (p. 183) |
| Balloon test    (p. 181) | Picture test    (p. 181) |
| Color My World    (p. 180) | Picture This, Picture That    (p. 179) |
| Depth interview    (p. 176) | Pluralistic research    (p. 155) |
| Direct observation    (p. 158) | Projective techniques    (p. 177) |
| Disguised observation    (p. 158) | Protocol analysis    (p. 177) |
| Dot, Dot, Dot    (p. 180) | Pupilometer    (p. 184) |
| Ethnographic research    (p. 182) | Qualitative research    (p. 155) |
| Focus group facility    (p. 165) | Qualitative Research Consultants    (p. 165) |
| Focus group report    (p. 166) | |
| Focus groups    (p. 163) | Quantitative research    (p. 154) |
| Galvanometer    (p. 184) | Role-playing    (p. 182) |
| Human observation    (p. 159) | Sentence-completion test    (p. 181) |
| Indirect observation    (p. 158) | Social media research    (p. 162) |
| Laddering    (p. 176) | Sort Me Straight    (p. 179) |
| Mechanical observation    (p. 159) | Sort Me Up    (p. 179) |
| Moderators    (p. 165) | Structured observation    (p. 159) |
| Nontraditional focus group    (p. 165) | Traditional focus group    (p. 165) |
| Observation methods    (p. 158) | Undisguised observation    (p. 159) |
| Online focus group    (p. 167) | Unstructured observation    (p. 159) |
| Physical traces    (p. 158) | Word-association test    (p. 177) |

# Review Questions

**1.1** Identify circumstances where qualitative research is applicable.

**1.2** Sony wants to find gaps in the netbook market. The findings will help Sony research and develop new product ideas. Outline which research methods Sony could use for this purpose.

**2.1** Indicate why disguised observation would be appropriate for a study on how parents discipline their children when dining out.

**2.2** A national retail company wants to ensure that its sales staff are well trained and doing a good job. Outline an observation technique it could use to investigate this.

**3.1** One of your customers lets you know about an online forum he came across, on which participants are discussing your company's products and your competitors' products. Describe how this information can be used in a productive way for your company.

**3.2** Your school has a presence on Facebook. All applicants are automatically invited to join whether or not they end up at your school. Let us say your school wants to know how people find the design of the school's homepage. Describe how your school could use Facebook to gather useful information to help improve the design of its homepage.

**4.1** Indicate how a focus group moderator of a traditional focus group should handle each of the following cases: (a) a loud, dominating participant; (b) a participant who has coughing fits every few minutes; (c) two participants who persist in having a private conversation about their children throughout the focus group meeting; (d) a situation in which the only visible minority participant feels uncomfortable and refrains from talking.

4.2 A prominent chocolate manufacturer is thinking of launching a new product. The product would be available in several flavours and shapes and will be named "chocolates." The company decides to test the concept with focus groups. Describe in detail how participants of the focus groups should be recruited and what topics the moderator of each group should cover.

5.1 Discuss how a marketing researcher could get into an ethically sensitive situation using ethnographic research.

5.2 A large national grocer has noticed that competitors are offering reusable bags to customers. The grocer is not certain to what extent their own customers are conscientious about recycling. Select two projective techniques and describe how they could be used to address this concern.

# Case 5.1

# The College Experience

The College of Business is a full-service business school at a mid-size regional university. It specializes primarily in undergraduate business education with selected graduate programs. While the college emphasizes mostly professional education, it does so within a liberal arts context. Business majors range from standards such as accounting, marketing, and finance to unique offerings such as the highly successful manufacturing and supply chain management degree.

The college is committed to a student-centred style of education, which emphasizes students not as customers per se but as equal stakeholders in the process of education. As part of its commitment to involving students as true partners, the college has recently begun the process of conducting focus groups of undergraduate and graduate students. The objective of these focus groups is to identify negative and positive attitudes about the college and develop new ideas to improve the college.

The following is an excerpt from the transcript of the first undergraduate focus group. This group was composed of 14 students with the characteristics found in the charts on the next page.

**Moderator:** So what do you guys think are some ways that the college (not the university) can be improved?

**Jeff:** I really like the fact that professors are accessible, willing to help and a lot of them let us call them by their first name. Something that I think could be better is that we don't spend enough time learning how to do things but instead professors spend too much time talking about theory.

**Sarah:** Yea, Yea, I agree totally. It seems like most of the time we aren't learning practical skills but just talking about what we "should" do, not really learning how to do it.

**Moderator:** Interesting points, how would you suggest the college try to increase the amount of practical learning?

**Todd:** It would really be cool if we could do more real-life professional work in our classes. Things like skill-based projects that focus on doing what we would really do in our profession.

*(Continued)*

**Tim:** I think we should all have to do a mandatory internship as part of our major. Right now, some majors let you do it as an elective but they are really hard to find and get.

**Moderator:** Good ideas. Are there other things you think we could improve?

**Rhonda:** I agree that the professors try really hard to be open to students but the advising is really not very good. I don't know how to fix it but I know my advisor is pretty much useless.

**Ariel:** I know, I know. It is so frustrating sometimes. I go to my advisor and she tells me to just fill in my degree planning sheet and she'll sign it. It's like they don't even know what I should be taking or why.

**Jon:** My advisor is kind of funny, he just tells me that he doesn't really know that much about classes he doesn't teach and my guess is as good as his. At least he's honest anyway.

**Moderator:** Ok, Ok, so the advising you are getting from the faculty leaves a little to be desired. What do you guys do to figure out how to plan your degrees if your advisors aren't helping much?

**Sarah:** I just ask my friends who are further along in the major than I am.

**Mark:** Yea, me too. In the Student Marketing Association we all give each other advice on what

professors are good, what classes go well together, which have prerequisites and stuff like that. It would be cool if we could have something like that for the whole college.

**Moderator:** Don't you think the college could be improved if we developed some sort of peer-advising program?

Using these excerpts as representative of the entire focus group transcript, answer the following questions.

## Questions

1. Do you think focus groups were the appropriate research method in this case, given the research objectives? What other type(s) of research might provide useful data?
2. Evaluate the questions posed by the moderator in light of the research objectives/question: (a) Are any of them leading or biasing in any way? (b) Can you think of any additional questions that could/should be included?
3. Examine the findings. How is the College of Business perceived? What are its apparent strengths and weaknesses?
4. Can we generalize these findings to all of the college's students? Why, or why not?

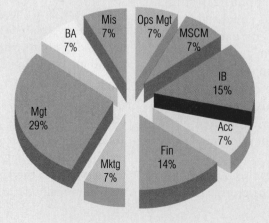

**Distribution of Majors**

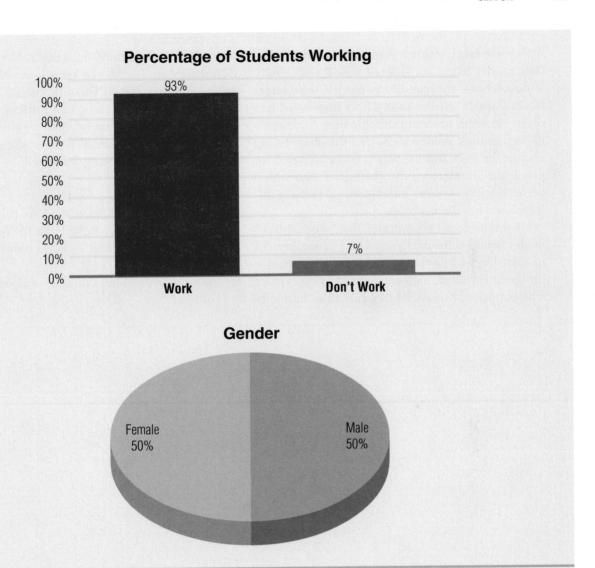

# Case 5.2

# Advanced Automobile Concepts

Nick Thomas, CEO of Advanced Automobile Concepts, has begun formulating some concepts in terms of the types of car models to pursue to bring ZEN Motors' product line back to life. He has been using a cross-functional approach to new-product development involving finance, production, R&D, marketing, and advertising in his planning. Recently, Ashley Roberts, from advertising, discussed some of the general plans for the new car models with Thomas. Nick told Ashley that he will need more marketing research information on customer preferences for different types of cars. However, he told her the broad choices will come down to different-sized vehicles

*(Continued)*

with some much smaller than ZEN had ever built. One model being considered was a very small, almost scooter-like car. Other models were larger but still much smaller than ZEN's traditional line of cars in order to obtain suitable mpg (miles-per-gallon) ratings. Ashley knew that this meant a big change for ZEN and the way it had advertised for years. She wondered if the customers who would prefer the new, smaller models would possess different sets of salient values.

Perhaps those who prefer the "scooter-like" model would value excitement and entertainment in their lives while those expressing a preference for the larger-sized, high-mpg models would place a higher priority on social recognition or harmony with the environment or some other value. If differences are found, the agency would alter the values emphasized in the ad's visuals and copy (e.g., depicting an exciting life, thrill of the drive, or sense of accomplishment, or recognition of contributing to environmental problems, etc.) to suit the model of the car being promoted.

## Questions

1. What techniques identified in this chapter would help Ashley Roberts decide on the best advertising approach? Describe how they could be used.

2. Why did you choose these techniques and not others?

# Quantitative Data Collection Methods

## LEARNING OBJECTIVES

1. Evaluate each of the four basic survey modes for gathering data.

2. Describe different types of survey data collection methods.

3. Express major concerns in choosing a particular survey method.

## On-site Consumer Research . . . It's All in the Details

*by David Kay*

Purchase decisions are made in the store, the showroom, the restaurant. This is where the action happens. This is where consumer research should be conducted.

When the premises (the store, the restaurant, the shopping mall) are the subject of the research, or when the purchase decision is made with one eye on the shelf and one hand on the shopping cart, then the research should be conducted on premises using the five types of interviews described below.

When the task is to improve the design of the facility, the look, the atmosphere, the image, the traffic pattern, the on-premises merchandising, the shelving, signage, counters, washrooms, menu board, promotions, etc., it is best to have the customer go through a realtime, real eating/shopping/buying/browsing experience. Then interview him or her on the spot.

Shoppers, travellers, restaurant-goers react to the whole experience. But they are most influenced by the details. And they can recall and discuss these details most effectively during a real shopping, eating, travelling experience—not one week later in a focus group facility or at home during a telephone interview.

Here are the five types of information that can best be obtained through on-site research. The interview pattern is always from least directed to most directed, but not all types of interviews will be conducted in every study.

## 1. Stream of Consciousness Interview

A stream of consciousness interview is a conversation rather than a grilling. The interview questions are designed to elicit what the respondent is experiencing at every moment of the shopping/restaurant/airline trip.

Stream of consciousness interviews were used when we travelled with and interviewed frequent flyer business travellers on long-haul flights (over three hours). We invited them to describe their travel experiences, their thoughts and feelings as they were happening.

By letting them talk freely, we learned that travellers were frustrated and angry at the loss of control over the process, from the moment they entered the limo, to waiting at the check-in counter, going through security, sitting in the departure lounge, standing in the loading bridge and tripping over the other guy's carry-on in the aircraft aisle. A key response from the airline was to give travellers better control over the process.

## 2. Spontaneous Reaction Interview

Spontaneous reaction interviews invite spontaneous, minimally prompted reactions of customers to their environment (prompting comes later). The key question, after walking around the shop, is "Tell me about this restaurant/store/mall, etc." By avoiding specific prompting, the respondent will share with the interviewer the most important influence on attitude.

A national bank built offices with glass walls for customer contact staff who provide non-teller services (loans, mortgages, investment products, etc.). It believed that glass offices would demonstrate that it is approachable. Instead it robbed customers of a sense of privacy. Also, the staff was always on view and felt the need to acknowledge other customers who waved to them as they walked through the branch, which made the customer feel even more on view.

When we asked customers to tell us, in the most general terms, what it feels like doing business in that bank, the spontaneous customer reaction was "I'm not comfortable in this office." Every transaction was a distraction. The bank changed its glass walls.

## 3. Directed General Response Interview

Directed general response interviews are a good way to determine whether a strategy has been met. The key questions are general, but are directed to the strategy—for example, "Is this restaurant friendly? Is this store easy to shop in? Does this seem like a good value store? Why? Are the uniforms casual, professional, modern, formal? Why?" In one study, respondents told us that a new restaurant restored did not feel welcoming. Instead, it felt threatening because it was too open (floor-to-ceiling glass wall). Customers felt exposed.

Instead of talking to us about window shades, decals on the glass, or plants in the windows, our respondents told us they wanted protection from drive-by shootings. They wanted real walls.

A new design model was developed for the rest of the chain.

## 4. Directed Specific Response Interview

Once the consumers' pattern of response and general attitude have been established, the next task is to determine why they feel the way they do, using directed specific response questions such as "What makes this racetrack modern and up to date?" Respondents can answer in a focused manner.

## 5. Prompted Reaction to Execution Elements

The one constant in nearly all on-site research is the requirement to investigate response to the specific executional elements—for example: "Tell me about the restaurant's artifacts. Do they convey elegance?" "Tell me about the uniforms. Do they suggest that . . ."

In one study, consumers told us that the artifacts in a restaurant with a European theme looked Mexican. The effect jarred. The artifacts were changed.

Two types of research can only be obtained through on-site research. These are:

- Impulse purchase research
- Constructs, i.e., building new products "on the floor"

Consumers buy many types of purchases on impulse. They can only tell us what prompted the impulse purchase at the time and place of the purchase. Memory is least reliable in this circumstance. On-site research is the only reliable way to determine what generated the impulse purchase.

Finally, "constructs," i.e., working with consumers to build new products, is one of the most exciting types of consumer research that works especially well on the premises. Consumers can actually create new product concepts while walking through a store with a moderator, by combining aspects of different products seen on shelf. "I like that type of package. I like that other type of product. Why can't they combine the two?"

On-site consumer research can be conducted almost anywhere. During the past 15 years, we have conducted research in:

- Stores ranging from a lottery kiosk, to small boutiques, to box stores
- Supermarkets
- Restaurants
- Bank branches
- Racetracks
- Airports
- On board aircraft
- Cars during a test drive
- Shopping centres

We've interviewed householders while they cleaned their bathrooms.

We've interviewed children in classrooms about a new Junior Achievement program.

Consumer reaction to an environment is influenced by all of the elements. In a store or restaurant, reaction is influenced by lighting, colours, decoration, signage, merchandising, ceiling patterns, packaging, counters, traffic pattern, staff attitude, end aisle displays, etc. But the interplay and the key influences are not always obvious or remembered. To determine the overall effect and the influences, the research should be conducted on-site.

David Kay is principal and founding partner of Research Dimensions.

I n this vignette, David Kay illustrates how researchers select methods of data collection depending on the research objectives of a given project. There are many different ways of conducting marketing research studies. Respondents' behaviour is observed and recorded by the researcher in observation studies. Some studies use physiological measurements, such as eye-movement-tracking devices. Other studies may use passive electronic means to gather data, such as Arbitron's PPM or the Pretesting Company's "WhisperCode," which is a device that is placed in respondents' homes and automobiles and that automatically records TV, radio, or internet commercials to which respondents are exposed. However, in many studies, marketers must communicate with large numbers of respondents in order to collect a large enough sample of subgroups or to ensure that the study accurately represents some larger population. A **survey** involves interviews with a large number of respondents using a predesigned questionnaire. In this chapter, the various methods used to collect data for surveys are presented.

## Four Data Collection Modes

There are four major modes of collecting survey information from respondents: (1) Have a person ask the questions, either face-to-face or on the telephone, without any assistance from a computer; (2) have a computer assist or direct the questioning in a face-to-face, voice-to-voice, or other survey; (3) allow respondents to fill out the questionnaire themselves, without computer assistance; (4) use some combination of two or more of the above three modes. These four alternatives are person-administered, computer-administered, self-administered, and mixed-mode surveys, respectively. Each one has special advantages and disadvantages. Technology has had a large impact on these methods (see Figure 6.1). The various types of surveys are discussed later.

**Figure 6.1** Impact of Technology on Data Collection Methods

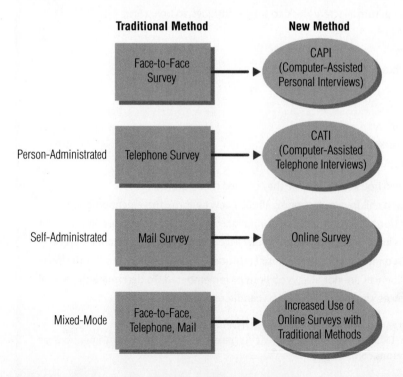

## Person-Administered Surveys (without Computer Assistance)

A **person-administered survey** is one in which an interviewer reads questions, either face-to-face or over the telephone, to the respondent and records his or her answers. Although the primary administration method for many years, its popularity has fallen off as communications systems have developed and computer technology has advanced.

### Advantages of Person-Administered Surveys

Person-administered surveys have four unique advantages: They offer feedback, rapport, quality control, and adaptability.

1. **Feedback.** Interviewers often must respond to direct questions from respondents during an interview. Sometimes respondents do not understand the instructions, or they may not hear the question clearly, or they might become distracted during the interview. A real person interviewer may be allowed to adjust his or her questions according to verbal or nonverbal cues. When a respondent begins to fidget or look bored, the interviewer can say, "I have only a few more questions." Or if a respondent makes a comment, the interviewer may jot it down as a side note to the researcher.

2. **Rapport.** Some people distrust surveys in general, or they may have some suspicions about the survey at hand. It is often helpful to have another human present to develop some rapport with the respondent early on in the questioning process. Another person can create trust and understanding that nonpersonal forms of data collection cannot.

3. **Quality control.** An interviewer sometimes must select certain types of respondents based on gender, age, or some other distinguishing characteristic. Personal interviewers may be used to ensure respondents are selected correctly. Alternatively, some researchers feel that respondents are more likely to be truthful when they respond face-to-face.

Personal interviewing is not used as much as it was in the past but still should be used if the situation calls for it. A good personal interviewer can create trust and rapport with respondents.

4. **Adaptability.** Personal interviewers can adapt to respondent differences. It is not unusual, for instance, to find an elderly person or a very young person who must be helped step by step through the answering process in order to understand how to respond to questions. Interviewers are trained, however, to ensure that they do not alter the meaning of a question by interpreting the question to a respondent. In fact, interviewers should follow precise rules on how to adapt to different situations presented by respondents.

Marketing Research in Action 6.1 illustrates how useful person-administered surveys are in selected situations.

---

## MARKETING RESEARCH IN ACTION 6.1
## Situations Where Personal Interviewing Is Needed to Collect Data

TAi Companies specialize in collecting data. Their facilities allow for focus groups and other marketing research studies. They have locations in New Jersey, Tampa, and Denver. OPS, Opinion Polling Service, is a division of TAi Companies that specializes in on-site (or on-location) personal interviewing when the situation dictates using personal interviewers. We asked Hal Meier, owner, to give some examples when it is best to personally interview consumers.

- XYZ chain restaurant regularly tests new menu items to discover if any can replace current offerings. Respondents fill out a survey form at the conclusion of their meal, so the survey is completed by real customers in the same setting in which the product is consumed commercially. Refusal rates are very low. It is impossible to duplicate this direct taste test in an artificial setting.

- XYZ bank asks its own customers why/whether they are using a new service (e.g., holiday layaway). Since the target population is its own customers they can easily be recruited in the bank. The incidence rate is nearly 100%; almost all intercepts qualify.

- XYZ paint company distributes through a local mass merchandiser and wants to know how its paint compares with other brands, broken down by professional painters vs. home owners. By interviewing on the premises of the mass merchandiser, it is easy to identify respondents and brands they select at the paint department.

Hal Meier's basic philosophy is that, in many situations, it should be a great advantage to interview the respondent in the same setting in which they will consume or purchase the product and to have them see and hold the product instead of looking at an image on a computer screen.

ON-SITE INTERCEPT/ INTERVIEWING BY PEOPLE WITH BOTH FEET ON THE GROUND

**O**pinion **P**olling **S**ervice

Opinion Polling Service (OPS) is the TAi division for out-of-the office on-site intercepts and interviewing. OPS is located in each TAi facility and utilizes a core group of TAi staff and specially trained "outsiders" just for this work.

OPS conducts customer surveys in banks, restaurants, stores, theme parks and many other venues. Ask for details on electronic data collections and real-time data retrieval with our "handy" PDAs.

**TAi** Companies       *We Measure Our Success In Client Satisfaction*

Visit TAi Companies at **www.taicompanies.com.**

By permission, TAi Companies.

### Disadvantages of Person-Administered Surveys

The drawbacks to using human interviewers are human error, slowness, cost, and interview evaluation.

1. **Humans make errors.** Interviewers might ask questions out of sequence; they might change the wording of a question, consequently changing the meaning of the question altogether, or they might incorrectly record the information provided by the respondent.
2. **Slow speed.** Collecting data using human interviewers is slower than other modes. Although pictures, videos, and graphics can be handled by personal interviewers, they cannot accommodate them as quickly as, say, computers. Often personal interviewers simply record respondents' answers using pencil and paper, which necessitates a separate data-input step to build a computer data file. But increasing numbers of data collection companies have shifted to the use of laptop computers that immediately add the responses to a data file.
3. **High cost.** The use of a face-to-face interviewer is more expensive than mailing the questionnaire to respondents. This is partially due to the cost of each interviewer. Personal interviewers are trained and skilled. A less expensive person-administered survey is a telephone interview.
4. **Interview evaluation.** Another disadvantage of person-administered surveys is that the presence of another person may create apprehension, called "**interview evaluation**," among certain respondents.

## Computer-Administered Surveys

Computer technology represents a viable option with respect to survey mode, and new developments occur almost every day. Although person-administered surveys are still the industry mainstay, the use of computer-administered survey methods is growing very rapidly and will rival person-administered surveys in the foreseeable future. Computer-assisted surveys are in an evolutionary state, and they are spreading to other survey types. For instance, a computer may house questions asked by a telephone interviewer, or a questionnaire may be posted on the internet for administration. Basically, a **computer-administered survey** is one in which computer technology plays an essential role in the interview work. Either the computer assists an interview or it interacts directly with the respondent. In the case of internet-based questionnaires, the computer acts as the medium through which potential respondents are approached, and it is the means by which respondents submit their completed questionnaires. As with person-administered surveys, computer-administered surveys, including random telephone dialling, have their advantages and disadvantages.

### Advantages of Computer-Administered Surveys

There are variations of computer-administered surveys. At one extreme, the respondent answers the questions on his or her computer, often online, and the questions are tailored to his or her responses to previous questions. At the other end, there are computer programs in which a telephone or personal interviewer is prompted by the computer as to what questions to ask and in what sequence. Regardless of which variation is considered, at least five advantages of computer-administered surveys are evident: speed; error-free interviews; use of pictures, videos, and graphics;

real-time capture of data; and reduction of anxieties caused by "interview evaluation" (respondents' concern they are not answering "correctly").

1.  **Speed.** The computer-administered approach is much faster than the human interview approach. Computers can quickly jump to questions based on specific responses, they can rapidly dial random telephone numbers, and they can easily check on answers to previous questions to modify or otherwise custom-tailor the interview to each respondent's circumstances. The speed factor translates into cost savings, and there is a claim that the cost of internet surveys is about one-half that of mail or phone surveys.[1]

2.  **Error-free interviews.** Properly programmed, the computer-administered approach guarantees zero interviewer errors such as inadvertently skipping questions, asking inappropriate questions based on previous responses, misunderstanding how to pose questions, recording the wrong answer, and so forth. Also, the computer, unlike humans, neither becomes fatigued nor cheats.

3.  **Use of pictures, videos, and graphics.** Computer graphics can be integrated into questions as they are viewed on a computer screen. Rather than have an interviewer pull out a picture of a new type of window-unit air conditioner, for instance, computer graphics can show it from various perspectives. High-quality video windows may be programmed to appear so the respondent can see the product in use or can be shown a wide range of visual displays.

4.  **Real-time capture of data.** Because respondents are interacting with the computer, the information is entered directly into a computer's data storage system and can be accessed for tabulation or other analyses at any time. Once the interviews are finished, final tabulations can be completed in a matter of minutes. This feature is so beneficial that some interview companies have telephone interviewers directly linked to computer input when they conduct their interviews. Such interviews are known as computer-assisted telephone interviews, or CATI.

5.  **Reduction of "interview evaluation" concern in respondents.** When involved in responding to questions in a survey, some people become anxious about the possible reaction of the interviewer to their answers. They may be concerned as to how the interviewer evaluates their responses. This may be especially present when the questions deal with personal topics such as personal hygiene, political opinions, financial matters, and even age. The presence of a human interviewer may cause them to answer differently than they would in a nonpersonal data collection mode. Some respondents, for example, try to please the interviewer by saying what they think the interviewer wants to hear. In any case, some researchers believe that respondents will provide more truthful answers to potentially sensitive topics when interacting with a machine.

The advantages of using computers have created a growing demand for the use of online survey research. This has led to the growth of firms specializing in assisting companies in planning and conducting online surveys. Canadian Viewpoint is a leading market research company specializing in data collection through the use of tools such as the online panel, Survey Lion. The company provides clients with the option to design their own surveys or useits programming services. It can target a sample from its online panel of a quarter million households

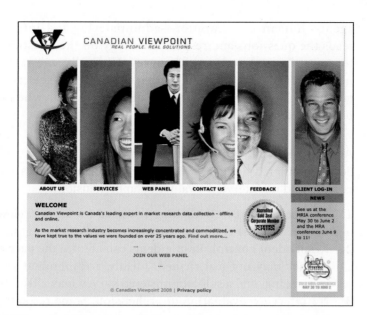

Canadian Viewpoint is a leading market research company that uses online tools.

and businesses, including subgroups such as consumers, business-to-business (B2B), health care, technology professionals, and students. If necessary, Canadian Viewpoint can use mixed modes and call on partner panels to gain the needed responses.

### Disadvantages of Computer-Administered Surveys

The primary disadvantages of computer-assisted surveys are that they require some level of technical skill, and setup costs may be significant.

1. **Technical skills required.** There is a wide range of computer-assisted methods available to marketing researchers. However, even the simplest options require some technical skills, and many of them require considerable skill to ensure the systems are operational and free of errors. Viruses, software bugs, and hardware breakdowns must be diagnosed and remedied immediately.
2. **High setup costs.** Although computer technology can result in increases in productivity, there are usually high setup costs associated with getting the systems in place and operational. Programming and debugging costs must be incurred with each survey. One software evaluator implied that two days of setup time by an experienced programmer was fairly efficient.[2] Depending on what type of computer-administered survey is under consideration, these costs, including the time factor associated with them, can render computer-administered delivery systems for surveys less attractive than other data collection options. There are a growing number of moderate- to low-cost computer-administered options, such as web-based questionnaires with user-friendly development interfaces that are fuelling the rush toward more and more online research around the world.

## Self-Administered Surveys

A **self-administered survey** is one in which the respondent completes the survey on his or her own. It is different from other survey methods in that there is no agent—human or computer—administering the interview. The respondent reads the questions and responds directly on the questionnaire. This is the prototypical "pencil-and-paper" survey. Normally, the respondent goes at his or her own pace, and in most instances he or she selects the place and time to complete the interview. He or she also may decide when the questionnaire will be returned.

### Advantages of Self-Administered Surveys

Self-administered surveys have three important advantages: reduced cost, respondent control, and no interview-evaluation apprehension.

1. **Reduced cost.** By eliminating the need for an interviewer or an interviewing device such as a computer program, there can be significant savings in cost.
2. **Respondent control.** Respondents can control the pace at which they respond, so they may not feel rushed. Ideally, a respondent should be relaxed while responding, and a self-administered survey may affect this state.
3. **No interview-evaluation apprehension.** Some respondents feel apprehensive when answering questions, or the topic may be sensitive.[3] Self-administered surveys reduce or eliminate interview-evaluation apprehension.

The self-administered approach takes the administrator, whether human or computer, out of the picture, and respondents may feel more at ease. Self-administered questionnaires have been found to elicit more insightful information than face-to-face interviews.[4]

### Disadvantages of Self-Administered Surveys

The disadvantages of self-administered surveys are respondent control, lack of monitoring, and high questionnaire requirements.

1. **Respondent control.** Self-administration places control of the survey in the hands of the prospective respondent. As such, this type of survey is subject to the possibility that respondents will not complete the survey, will answer questions erroneously, will not respond in a timely manner, or will refuse to return the survey at all.
2. **Lack of monitoring.** With self-administered surveys, there is no opportunity to monitor or interact with the respondent during the course of the interview. Respondents who do not understand the meaning of a word or who are confused about how to answer a question may answer improperly or get frustrated and refuse to answer at all. A monitor can offer explanations and encourage the respondent to continue.
3. **High questionnaire requirements.** Due to the absence of the interviewer or an internal computer check system, the burden of respondent understanding falls on the questionnaire itself. Not only must it have perfectly clear instructions, examples, and reminders throughout, the questionnaire must also entice the respondents to participate and encourage them to continue answering until all questions are complete. Questionnaire design is important regardless of the data collection mode. However, with self-administered surveys, the questionnaire must be thoroughly checked for clarity and accuracy before data collection begins.

## Mixed-Mode Surveys

**Mixed-mode surveys**, sometimes referred to as "hybrid" surveys, use multiple data collection methods. In recent years, it has become increasingly popular to use mixed-mode surveys because of the increasing use of online survey research. As more and more respondents have access to the internet, the online survey, a form of computer-assisted survey, is often combined with some other method such as telephone surveying, a form of person-administered surveying.

### Advantage of Mixed-Mode Surveys

**Multiple advantages to achieve data collection goal.** The advantage of mixed-mode surveys is that researchers are able to take the advantages of each of the various modes to achieve their data collection goals. For example, a quarterly administered panel of households uses a randomly selected sample of 800 households. Since 50% of these households have internet service, they may be surveyed each quarter via an online survey. This gives the panel administrators the advantage associated with online surveys: access to all panel households with a touch of the computer key. Also, responses are automatically downloaded to the panel's statistical package for analysis. In order to achieve a representative sample, households without internet service must be contacted each quarter via telephone surveys. With this mixed-mode approach, the panel administrators benefit from the advantage of the speed and low cost of online surveying as well as the advantage of reaching the total household population through telephone surveys.[5] Marketing Research in Action 6.2 illustrates how a Canadian company is able to satisfy its clients using mixed-mode surveys.

### Disadvantages of Mixed-Mode Surveys

There are two primary disadvantages of using mixed-mode, or hybrid, data collection methods.

1.  **Mode affects response?** One of the reasons researchers in the past were reluctant to use mixed modes for gathering data was concern that the mode used might affect responses given by consumers. In a study conducted by Professors Green, Medlin, and Whitten, two methods of data collection were compared: online surveys versus a traditional mail survey. The study showed no difference in the data quality, or in response rates. This is surprising since one of the major disadvantages of mail surveys is a low response rate.[6] Several other studies were conducted to assess differences among data collection methods in mixed-mode applications.[7] Questionnaire authors must assess differences in data collected to determine if the data collection mode explains differences in responses to the research questions.

2.  **Additional complexity.** Using mixed modes of data collection adds to the complexities of data collection. For example, if conducting a survey online and by telephone, the wording of the instructions must be different to accommodate those reading instructions they themselves are to follow (for online respondents) versus someone else reading the instructions to the respondent (for telephone respondents). Further, data from the two sources will need to be integrated and care must be taken to ensure data are compatible. Responses must be coded in exactly the same way.

# Descriptions of Data Collection Methods

There are 11 different data collection methods used by marketing researchers (see Table 6.1):

**Person Administered**

1. In-home interview
2. Mall-intercept interview
3. In-office interview
4. "Traditional" telephone interview
5. Central location telephone interview

**Computer Administered**

6. Computer-assisted telephone interview (CATI)
7. Fully computerized interview
8. Online and other internet-based surveys

## MARKETING RESEARCH IN ACTION 6.2
## Mixed-Mode Surveys Have Their Advantages

The influence of technology on data collection methods is staggering. Computers not only can aid in finding the right numbers and types of respondents but also can help respondents to complete surveys.

Voxco is a global, Montreal-based software company specializing in collecting and processing data. The company has developed "fully featured multi-mode survey software for gathering high-quality, reliable and pertinent data, in single or mixed collection mode." One such product is Voxco Interviewer™, which enables three types of computer-assisted interview methods: CATI (telephone), CAWI (web), and CAPI (personal). Researchers can use Voxco Interviewer CATI to perform telephone interviewing, or use Interviewer Virtual Call Center™ to conduct online computer interviews. Interviewer Web™, allows for web surveying (CAWI), and Interviewer CAPI enables personal (face-to-face) interviewing with its Web CAPI Manager.

The advantage of mixed-mode interviewing options is that they allow respondents to complete the survey online. It also gives the researcher control over data layout. According to Voxco, "The look and feel of Interviewer Web surveys is fully customizable, and even gives you an exclusive tool to ask unaided awareness questions on the web."

Voxco also offers a predictive dialler, Pronto™, which manages all of the researcher's sample needs, including quotas, as well as callback rules. The company even has a tool for central management of international surveys, called Interviewer Virtual Call Center™.

Fullyweb-based reporting tools for predefined or periodic reporting are also offered by Voxco.

Explore what else this company does at **www.voxco.com.**

## Self-Administered

9. Group self-administered survey
10. Drop-off survey
11. Mail survey

| Data Collection Type | Data Collection Method | Description |
| --- | --- | --- |
| Person-Administered | In-home interview | The interviewer conducts the interview in the respondent's home. Appointments may be made ahead by telephone. |
| | Mall-intercept interview | Shoppers in a mall are approached and asked to take part in the survey. Questions may be asked in the mall or in the mall-intercept company's facilities located in the mall. |
| | In-office interview | The interviewer makes an appointment with business executives or managers to conduct the interview at the respondent's place of work. |
| | "Traditional" telephone interview | Interviewers work out of their homes to conduct telephone interviews with households or business representatives. |
| | Central location telephone interview | Interviewers work in a data collection company's office using cubicles or work areas for each interviewer. Often the supervisor has the ability to "listen in" to interviews and to check that they are being conducted correctly. |
| Computer-Administered | Computer-assisted telephone interview | With a computer-assisted telephone interview, the questions are programmed for a computer screen and the interviewer then reads them off. Responses are entered directly into the computer program by the interviewer. |
| | Fully computerized interview | A computer is programmed to administer the questions. Respondents interact with the computer and enter in their own answers by using a keyboard, by touching the screen, or by using some other means. |
| | Online or other internet-based survey | Respondents fill out a questionnaire that resides on the internet, or otherwise accesses it via the internet such as by receiving an email attachment or downloading the file online. |
| Self-Administered | Group self-administered survey | Respondents take the survey in a group context. Each respondent works individually, but they meet as a group and this allows the researcher to economize. |
| | Drop-off survey | Questionnaires are left with the respondent to fill out. The administrator may return at a later time to pick up the completed questionnaire, or it may be mailed in. |
| | Mail survey | Questionnaires are mailed to prospective respondents who are asked to fill them out and return them by mail. |

**Table 6.1** Ways to Gather Data

## Person-Administered Interviews

There are at least four variations of person-administered interviews, and their differences are largely based on the location of the interview. These variations include the in-home interview, the mall-intercept interview, the in-office interview, and the telephone interview (which includes the "traditional" and central location telephone interviews).

### In-Home Interviews

Just as the name implies, an **in-home interview** is conducted in the home of the respondent. It takes longer to recruit participants for in-home interviews, and researchers must travel to and from respondents' homes. Therefore, the cost per interview is very high. Two important factors justify the high cost of in-home interviews. First, the marketing researcher must believe that personal contact is essential to the success of the interview. Second, the researcher must be convinced that the in-home environment is conducive to the questioning process. In-home interviews are useful when the research objective requires respondents' physical presence to see, read, touch, use, or interact with the research object (such as a product prototype) *and* the researcher believes that the security and comfort of respondents' homes is an important element affecting the quality of the data collected.

Some research objectives require the respondents' physical presence in order to interact with the research object. A company develops a new type of counter top toaster oven that is designed to remain perfectly clean. However, in order to get the benefit of clean cooking, the oven must be configured differently for different cooking applications, and the throwaway "grease-catch foil" must be placed in just the right position to work properly. Will consumers be able to follow the instructions? This is an example of a study that would require researchers to conduct surveys in the home kitchens of the respondents. Researchers would observe respondents open the box, unwrap and assemble the device, read the directions, and cook a meal. All of this may take an hour or more. Respondents may not be willing to travel somewhere and spend an hour on a research project, but would be more likely to do this in their own homes.

### Mall-Intercept Interviews

Although the in-home interview has important advantages, it has the significant disadvantage of cost. The expense of in-home interviewer travel is high, even for local surveys. Less costly and more convenient for the researcher is the **mall-intercept interview**. The respondent is encountered and questioned while he or she is visiting a shopping mall. A mall-intercept company generally has its offices located within a large shopping mall, usually one that draws from a regional rather than a local market area. Typically, the interview company negotiates exclusive rights to do interviews in the mall and, thus, forces all marketing research companies that wish to do mall intercepts in that area to use that interview company's services. Shoppers are intercepted in the pedestrian traffic areas of shopping malls and either interviewed on the spot or asked to move to a permanent interviewing facility located in the mall office. Although some malls do not allow marketing research interviewing because they view it as a nuisance to shoppers, many do permit mall-intercept interviews and may rely on these data themselves to fine-tune their own marketing programs.

In addition to low cost, mall-intercept interviews have most of the advantages associated with in-home interviewing. Perhaps the most important advantage is the presence of an interviewer who can interact with the respondent. However, there are disadvantages specifically associated with mall interviewing. First, sample representativeness is an issue. If researchers are looking for a representative sample of some larger area than that in which the mall is located, they should be wary of using the mall intercept. Some people shop at malls more frequently than others and therefore have a greater chance of being interviewed. Recent growth of nonmall retailing concepts such as catalogues and stand-alone discounters such as Walmart means that more mall visitors are recreational shoppers rather than convenience-oriented shoppers, resulting in the need to scrutinize mall-intercept samples as to what consumer groups they actually represent.[8] Also, many shoppers refuse to take part in mall interviews for various reasons. Nevertheless, special selection procedures called quotas, described in Chapter 9, may be used to counter the problem of nonrepresentativeness.

A second shortcoming of mall-intercept interviewing is that a shopping mall does not offer a comfortable home environment that is conducive to rapport and close attention to details. The respondents may feel uncomfortable because passersby stare at them; they may be pressed for time or otherwise preoccupied by various distractions outside the researcher's control. These factors may adversely affect the quality of the interview. As indicated earlier, some interview companies attempt to counter this problem by taking respondents to special interview rooms located in research facilities in mall offices. This procedure minimizes distractions and encourages respondents to be more relaxed. Some mall-interviewing facilities have kitchens and rooms with one-way mirrors. Marketing Research in Action 6.3 examines the current status of mall-intercept interviewing.

## In-Office Interviews

Although the in-home and mall-intercept interview methods are appropriate for a wide variety of consumer goods, marketing research conducted in the business-to-business or organizational market typically requires interviews with business executives, purchasing agents, engineers, or other managers. Normally, **in-office interviews** take place in person while the respondent is in his or her office, or perhaps in a company lounge area. Interviewing businesspeople face-to-face has essentially the same advantages and drawbacks as in-home consumer interviewing. For example, if Hewlett-Packard wanted information regarding user preferences for different features that might be offered in a new ultra-high-speed laser printer designed for business accounting firms, it would make sense to interview prospective users or purchasers of these printers. It would also be logical to interview these people at their places of business.

As you might imagine, in-office personal interviews are costly. Those executives qualified to give opinions on a specific topic or individuals who would be involved in product purchase decisions must first be located. Sometimes names can be obtained from sources such as industry directories or trade association membership lists. More frequently, screening must be conducted over the telephone by calling a particular company that is believed to have executives of the type needed. However, locating those people within a large organization may be time consuming. Once a qualified person is located, the next step is to persuade that person to agree to an interview and then set up a time for the interview. This may require a sizable incentive. Finally, an interviewer must go to the particular place at the appointed time. Even with appointments, long waits are sometimes encountered and cancellations are not uncommon because businesspeople's schedules sometimes shift unexpectedly.

## MARKETING RESEARCH IN ACTION 6.3
# Has the Mall Intercept Become a Dinosaur?

The status and use of mall data collection companies are declining. This is the conclusion of a recent panel composed of a number of data collection professionals.[9] Historically, the popularity of mall-intercept data collection, whereby face-to-face interviewers had permission to roam the mall and ask shoppers to take part in surveys, crested in the 1990s. Thus, the heyday of mall-intercept data collection in Canada occurred in the 1980s, a time when large numbers of consumers flocked to huge regional shopping malls. During this decade, prospective mall-intercept survey respondents were plentiful and mall-intercept companies proliferated.

The 1990s, however, saw a turnaround in the mall-intercept business. Three trends converged to greatly diminish the importance of mall intercepts. First, malls themselves became less desirable shopping venues because of travel costs, the advent of online shopping, and the desire of shoppers to have a "shopping experience." Second, the marketing research industry came to realize that online surveys had significant cost and other advantages.

Third, the technique became more complex and difficult as marketing researchers increasingly used it for surveys that were longer and had more stringent participant qualifications and faster turnaround requirements. As a consequence, the number of mall-intercept interviews fell dramatically.

So, are mall intercepts now dinosaurs? The panel members did not believe this to be the case. They did agree that mall intercepts have an "image" problem now, precisely for the reasons just listed. However, mall-intercept companies can adopt some strategies to make this data collection method more attractive to the marketing research industry. These strategies include:

1.  Adopt and keep pace with mobile data collection technology, such as laptops, tablets, electronic pads, and handheld devices.
2.  Establish kiosk locations in malls where they are more visible and more in tune with the "shopping experience" atmosphere desired by mall shoppers.
3.  Work with marketing research buyers to make incentives more substantial and attractive to mall shoppers, thus recruiting higher-quality respondents.
4.  Work with marketing research buyers to reduce interview length and/or create an understanding of the amount of time necessary to obtain high-quality mall intercept interviews.
5.  Partner with full-service marketing research companies and thus become the preferred provider of mall-intercept interviews.
6.  Tighten quality assurance systems for interviewers, interview quality, time management, and close communications with marketing research buyers.
7.  Publicize the fact that respondents typically experience more enjoyment and involvement with face-to-face interviews compared to self-administered ones.

Added to these cost factors is that interviewers who specialize in businessperson interviews are more costly in general because of their specialized knowledge and abilities. They have to navigate around gatekeepers such as secretaries, learn technical jargon, and be conversant on product features when the respondent asks pointed questions or even criticizes questions as they are posed to him or her.

### Telephone Interviews
The need for a face-to-face interview is often determined by the need of the respondents to actually see a product, advertisement, or packaging sample. It may be vital

that the interviewer watch the respondent to ensure that correct procedures are followed or otherwise to verify something about the respondent or his or her reactions. If, however, physical contact is not necessary, telephone interviewing is an attractive option. There are a number of advantages as well as disadvantages associated with telephone interviewing. First, the telephone is a relatively inexpensive way to collect survey data. Long-distance telephone charges are much lower than the cost of a face-to-face interview. A second advantage of the telephone interview is that it has the potential to yield a very high-quality sample. If the researcher employs random-dialling procedures and proper callback measures, the telephone approach may produce a better sample than any other survey procedure. A third and very important advantage is that telephone surveys have very quick turnaround times. Most telephone interviews are of short duration anyway, but a good interviewer may complete several interviews per hour. Conceivably, a study could have the data collection phase executed in a few days with telephone interviews. In fact, in political polling, in which real-time information on voter opinions is essential, it is not unusual to have national telephone polls completed in a single night.

Unfortunately, the telephone survey approach has several inherent shortcomings. First, the respondent cannot be shown anything or physically interact with the research object. A second disadvantage is that the telephone interview does not permit the interviewer to make the various judgments and evaluations that can be made by the face-to-face interviewer. For example, judgments regarding respondent income based on the homes they live in and other outward signs of economic status cannot be made. Similarly, the telephone does not allow for the observation of body language and facial expressions, nor does it permit eye contact. On the other hand, some argue that the lack of face-to-face contact is helpful. Self-disclosure studies have indicated that respondents provide more information in personal interviews, except when the topics are threatening or potentially embarrassing. Questions on alcohol consumption, contraceptive methods, racial issues, or income tax reporting probably generate more valid responses when asked in the relative anonymity of a telephone call than when administered face-to-face.[10]

A third disadvantage of the telephone interview is that the marketing researcher is more limited in the quantity and types of information that he or she can obtain. Very long interviews are inappropriate for the telephone, as are questions with lengthy lists of response options that respondents will have difficulty remembering when they are read over the telephone. Respondents short on patience may hang up during interviews, or they may utter short and convenient responses just to speed up the interview. The telephone is a poor choice for conducting an interview with many open-ended questions.

A last problem with telephone interviews is the growing threat to its existence by the increased use of answering machines, caller ID, and call-blocking devices being adopted by consumers. The research industry is concerned about these gatekeeping methods, and it is just beginning to study ways around them.[11] Another difficulty is that legitimate telephone interviewers must contend with the negative impression people have of telemarketers. As a result of telemarketing survey scams, potential respondents are not as willing to participate in telephone interviews as they once were. (Read Ethics in Marketing Research 6.1 to learn more about "sugging" and "mugging.") It is too early to judge the effects of the Do-Not-Call legislation discussed in Chapter 1. There are two types of telephone interviews: traditional and

# ETHICS IN MARKETING RESEARCH 6.1
## Telemarketing Survey Scams Widespread, *VoxPop* Survey Finds
### Almost 4 in 10 Canadians Report Being Victimized by Telemarketers Posing as Survey Researchers

**Toronto, May 5, 2009**—Canadians are being victimized at an alarming rate by fraudulent telemarketers illegally posing as survey researchers to sell products or raise money, according to a national *VoxPop* (Voice of the People) survey by the Marketing Research and Intelligence Association (MRIA), which governs and regulates Canada's opinion research industry.

The poll found that, over the past year, 38% of Canadian adults were contacted to participate in a research survey that actually turned out to be an attempt to sell them a product or service or ask for a donation.

"Legitimate survey researchers never, under any circumstances, sell or ask for money, and they always give the research company's name and information on the nature of the research at the beginning of the call," says VoxPop spokesperson Brendan Wycks, Executive Director of MRIA. "Any attempt to sell or raise money following a survey request is a scam. People who receive such calls should immediately report the company's name and, if possible, its phone number to PhoneBusters, a national anti-fraud call centre jointly operated by the Competition Bureau, Royal Canadian Mounted Police and the Ontario Provincial Police."

Canadians who are victimized by fraudulent telemarketers posing as survey researchers can reach PhoneBusters by calling toll-free 1-888-495-8501.

These illegal practices, known in the opinion research industry as "sugging" (soliciting under the guise of interviewing) and "mugging" (marketing under the guise of interviewing), carry a maximum penalty of up to five years in prison under the federal Competition Act. That penalty may be increased to up to 14 years in prison, under a review of the Competition Act currently underway.

The frequency of fraudulent telemarketer calls was highest in Alberta (44%) followed by Quebec (40%), Manitoba/Saskatchewan (39%), Ontario (36%), Atlantic Canada (35%), and British Columbia (33%).

Under the Competition Act, telemarketers are required by law to identify their company and disclose their true purpose at the beginning of a call. The Personal Information Protection and Electronics Documents Act (PIPEDA) also requires business organizations to obtain valid consent from Canadians before collecting, disclosing, or using their personal information.

The MRIA has worked diligently with Canadian legislators to stop sugging and mugging, with significant success. A similar study by MRIA in 2007 found that 41% of Canadians had experienced mugging or sugging in the previous year.

"The modest decrease in these destructive telemarketing practices over the past year is good news, but what is needed now is greater public awareness of the problem and how to stop it," says Wycks. "First and foremost, survey respondents need to know their rights and how they can protect themselves."

The MRIA's Charter of Respondent Rights, established in 2006, enforces a strict code of conduct upon the Association's members to protect the time and privacy of survey respondents, and makes Canadians aware that they can verify the legitimacy of research projects via MRIA's Canadian Research Registration System.

People can verify the legitimacy and nature of the research they are being asked to participate in by asking for the survey's registration code or calling a toll-free number (1-800-554-9996) for information on the research project. MRIA member research firms will provide this information upon request, along with contact information for the research director who is conducting the study.

Canadians can also visit **www.mria-arim.ca** to learn more about their rights as survey respondents and about MRIA's *VoxPop* (Voice of the People) information campaign, the purpose of which is to educate Canadians about the value of opinion research and encourage participation in surveys.

The most recent *VoxPop* survey also examined attitudes toward opinion research, and revealed that a strong majority of Canadians believe survey research creates economic and social value by giving individuals direct influence over decisions made by governments and corporations.

More than 8 in 10 respondents (84%) felt surveys and polls serve a useful purpose; 79% agreed participation in surveys gives people the opportunity to influence public policy issues; and 75% agreed that public opinion surveys lead to products, services, and public policies that better meet consumer needs and wants.

"Canadians overwhelmingly maintain a high regard for survey research, as evidenced by the belief of 63% of respondents that opinion research strengthens Canada's democracy by giving people a say in important decisions by governments and corporations," says Wycks. "No other vehicle offers such influence, or delivers such tangible benefits to all Canadians. That's why, when telemarketer scams victimize research respondents, we all lose."

MRIA's *VoxPop* survey studying the incidence of mugging and sugging was conducted by Harris-Decima via telephone between January 29 and February 15, 2009, with a national random sample of 2035 adult Canadians and is considered accurate within $\pm 2.2\%$, 19 times out of 20.

This survey is part of a series from *VoxPop*, a campaign to give voice to Canadians and encourage participation in opinion research. ***VoxPop:*** **You speak. We listen. *Things improve.***

Source: Courtesy of Marketing Research and Intelligence Association. www.mria-arim.ca/VOXPOP/NEWS/PDF/VoxPopMay5-2009.pdf.

central location. Telephone interviewing has been and continues to be greatly affected by advances in telephone systems and communications technology. The traditional telephone approach has largely faded away, whereas the central location approach has embraced technological advances in telephone systems.

**Traditional Telephone Interviewing**  Technology has radically changed telephone surveys; however, it is worthwhile to describe this form of telephone interviewing as a starting point. Prior to central location and computer-assisted telephone interviewing, these **traditional telephone interviews** were those that were conducted either from the homes of the telephone interviewing staff or from telephone stalls located in the data collection company's offices. Everything was done mechanically. That is, interviewers dialled the telephone number manually, they read questions from a printed questionnaire, they were responsible for following special instructions on how to administer the questions, and they checked off the respondent's answers on each questionnaire. Quality control was limited to training sessions, sometimes in the form of a dress rehearsal by administering the questionnaire to the supervisor or another interviewer, and to callback checks by the supervisor to verify that the respondent had taken part in the interview.

The traditional telephone-interview method has great potential for errors. In addition to the possibilities of misdialling and making mistakes in administering the questions, there are potential problems of insufficient callbacks for not-at-homes, and a host of other problems. Also, because the actual hours worked while performing telephone interviews are difficult to track, most interview companies opt for a "per completion" compensation system. That is, the interviewer is compensated for each questionnaire delivered to the office that is completely filled out. Although most traditional telephone interviewers are honest, only minimal control and supervision can be used with this method. Recording of all telephone interviews can be challenging since this could violate PIPEDA, Canada's privacy law. Consequently, there are temptations to cheat by, for example, turning in bogus completed questionnaires or conducting interviews with respondents who do not qualify for the survey at hand. When traditional telephone interviewing is used, checks should be more extensive and may include the following:

1.  Have an independent party call back a sample of each interviewer's respondents to verify that they took part in the survey. In Canada, a minimum of 50% of each interviewer's completed interviews must be monitored.
2.  Have interviewers submit copies of their telephone logs to validate that the work was performed on the dates and in the time periods required.
3.  If long-distance calls were made, have interviewers submit copies of their telephone bill with long-distance charges itemized to check that the calls were made properly.
4.  If there is a concern about a particular interviewer's diligence, request that the interviewer be taken off the project.

A researcher should always check the accuracy and validity of interviews, regardless of the data collection method used.

**Central Location Telephone Interviewing**   This form of telephone interviewing is in many ways the research industry's standard. With **central location telephone interviewing**, a field data collection company installs several telephone lines at one location, and the interviewers make calls from the central location. Usually, interviewers have separate enclosed workspaces and lightweight headsets that free both hands so they can record responses. Everything is done from this central location. There are many advantages to operating from a central location. For example, resources are pooled, and interviewers can handle multiple surveys, such as calling plant managers in the afternoon and households during the evening shift.

The reasons for the popularity of the central location phone interview are cost savings and quality control. To begin with, recruitment and training are performed uniformly at this location. Interviewers can be oriented to the equipment, they can

Trained interviewers conduct telephone interviews at MRSI. Visit MRSI at **www.mrsi.com**.

study the questionnaire and its instructions, and they can simulate the interview among themselves over their phone lines. Also, the actual interviewing process can be monitored. Most telephone-interviewing facilities have monitoring equipment that permits a supervisor to listen in on interviewing as it is being conducted. Interviewers who are not doing the interview properly can be spotted and the necessary corrective action taken. Ordinarily, each interviewer will be monitored at least once per shift, but the supervisor may focus attention on newly hired interviewers to ensure they are doing their work correctly. The fact that each interviewer never knows when the supervisor will listen in guarantees more overall diligence than would be seen otherwise. Also, completed questionnaires are checked on the spot as a further quality control; interviewers can be immediately informed of any deficiencies in filling out the questionnaire. Finally, there is control over interviewers' schedules. That is, interviewers report in and out and work regular hours, even if they are evening hours, and make calls during the time periods stipulated by the researcher as appropriate interviewing times.

## Computer-Administered Interviews

Computer technology has affected the telephone data collection industry significantly. There are two variations of computer-administered telephone-interview systems. In one, a human interviewer is used, but in the other a computer, sometimes with a synthesized or tape-recorded voice, is used. At the same time, there are important computer-assisted interview methods that have recently emerged.

### Computer-Assisted Telephone Interviews (CATI)

The most advanced companies have computerized the central location telephone-interviewing process, creating **computer-assisted telephone interviews (CATIs)**. Each interviewer is equipped with a hands-free headset and is seated in front of a computer screen that is driven by the company's computer system. Often the computer dials the prospective respondent's telephone automatically, and the computer screen provides the interviewer with the introductory comments. As the interview progresses, the interviewer moves through the questions by pressing a key or a series of keys on the keyboard. Some systems use light pens or pressure-sensitive screens. The questions and possible responses appear on the screen one at a time. The interviewer reads the question to the respondent and then enters the response code. Then, the computer moves on to the next appropriate question. For example, an interviewer might ask if the respondent owns a dog. If the answer is "yes," there could appear a series of questions regarding what type of dog food the dog owner buys. If the answer is "no," these questions would be inappropriate. Instead, the computer program skips to the next appropriate question, which might be "Do you own a cat?" In other words, the computer eliminates the human error potential that would exist if this survey were done in the traditional paper-and-pencil telephone-interview mode. The human interviewer is just the "voice" of the computer.

The computer can even be used to customize questions. For example, in the early part of a long interview, a respondent might be asked the years, makes, and models of all cars he or she owns. Later in the interview, questions are asked about each specific car owned. The question might come up on the interviewer's screen as follows: "You said you own a Lexus. Who in your family drives this car most often?" Other questions about this car and others owned would appear in similar fashion. Questions like this can be dealt with in a traditional or central location manual interview, but they are handled much more efficiently in the computerized version because the interviewer does not need to physically flip questionnaire pages back and forth or remember previous responses.

The CATI approach also eliminates the need for editing completed questionnaires and creating computer data files by later manually entering every response with a keyboard. There is no checking for errors in completed questionnaires because there is no physical questionnaire. More to the point, in most computerized interview systems it is not permitted to enter an "impossible" answer. For example, if a question has three possible answers, with codes "A," "B," and "C," and the interviewer enters a "D" by mistake, the computer will ask for the answer to be re-entered until an acceptable code is entered. If a combination or pattern of answers is impossible, the computer will not accept an answer, or it may alert the interviewer to the inconsistency and move to a series of questions that will resolve the discrepancy. Data entry for completed questionnaires is eliminated because data are entered directly into a computer file as the interviewing is completed.

This second operation brings to light another advantage of computer-assisted interviewing. Tabulations may be run at any point in the study. Such real-time reporting is impossible with pencil-and-paper questionnaires, which often entail a wait of several days following interviewing completion before detailed tabulations of the results are available. Instantaneous results available with computerized telephone interviewing provide some real advantages. Based on preliminary tabulations, certain questions may be dropped, saving time and money in subsequent interviewing. If, for example, over 90% of those interviewed answered a particular question in the same manner, there may be no need to continue asking the question.

Tabulations may also suggest the addition of questions to the survey. If an unexpected pattern of product use is uncovered in the early interviewing stages, questions can be added to further delve into this behaviour. Thus, the computer-administered telephone survey affords an element of flexibility unavailable in the traditional paper-and-pencil survey methods. Finally, managers may find the early reporting of survey results useful in preliminary planning and strategy development. Sometimes survey project deadlines run very close to managers' presentation deadlines, and early indications of the survey's findings permit managers to organize their presentations in advance rather than all in a rush the night before. The many advantages and quick turnaround of CATI and CAPI (computer-assisted personal interviewing) make them mainstay data collection methods for many syndicated omnibus survey services.[12]

Computer-administered telephone interviewing options are very attractive to marketing researchers because of the advantages of cost savings, quality control, and time savings over the paper-and-pencil method.

## Fully Computerized Interviews (Not Online)

Some companies have developed **fully computerized interviews**, in which the survey is administered completely by a computer, but not online. With one such system, a computer dials a phone number and a recording is used to introduce the survey. The respondent then uses the push buttons on his or her telephone to make responses, thereby interacting directly with the computer. In the research industry, this approach is known as **completely automated telephone survey (CATS)**. CATS has been successfully employed for customer satisfaction studies, service quality monitoring, election day polls, product/warranty registration, and even in-home product tests with consumers who have been given a prototype of a new product.[13]

In another system, the respondent sits or stands in front of the computer unit and reads the screen. Each question and its various response options appear on the screen, and the respondent answers by pressing a key or touching the screen. The computer could be programmed to beep when an inappropriate response is offered and instruct the respondent to make another entry.

All of the advantages of computer-driven interviewing are found in this approach and human interviewer expense is eliminated. Because respondents' answers are saved in a file during the interview itself, tabulation can take place on a daily basis. Even if the interviews are conducted in remote locations, it is a simple matter to download the files to the central facility for daily tabulations. Some researchers believe that the research industry should move to replace pen-and-paper questionnaires with computer-based ones.[14]

### Online and Other Internet-Based Interviews

Online research may take on a number of forms, but the **internet-based question-naire**, in which the respondent answers questions online, is becoming the industry standard for online surveys. Internet-based online surveys are fast, easy, and inexpensive.[15] These questionnaires accommodate all of the standard question formats, and they are very flexible, as they have the ability to present pictures, diagrams, or displays to respondents. This ability is a major reason why researchers tracking advertising effects prefer online surveys to telephone surveys.[16] The researcher can check the website for current tabulations whenever he or she desires, and respondents can access the online survey at any time of the day or night. Online data collection has had and will continue to have a profound impact on the marketing research landscape. For instance, in the case of customer satisfaction, instead of "episodic" research in which a company does a large study one time per year, it allows for "continuous market intelligence" in which the survey is posted permanently on the web and modified as the company's strategies are implemented. Company

## ONLINE APPLICATION 6.1
# Be Part of a Global Online Survey

Go to **www.surveygarden.com**. SurveyGarden has many online surveys for clients of Dobney, a full-service international marketing research consultancy firm based in Britain and Spain. The site also offers ready-made online surveys for small to medium-sized businesses.

    Once at the website, click on "Consumer Demo" and complete the survey.

    Now that you have participated in an online survey, you can offer some insight about this research methodology.

### Questions
1. What type of research design lends itself to surveys online? Why do you say this?
2. What advantages for a marketing researcher does this type of survey offer?
3. What are some disadvantages of this method?

managers can click up tabulated customer reactions on a daily basis. Some researchers refer to this advantage of online surveys as "real-time research."[17]

Debbie Davis, Director of Market Research, BMO, Toronto, compared online surveys with traditional data collection methods. She found that online surveys have important advantages of speed (half the time) and low cost (20% less) plus real-time access of data; however, there are drawbacks of sample representativeness, respondent validation, and difficulty in asking probing types of questions. Sample representativeness is most troublesome when global market research is involved, and firms are finding that considerable investments are required to achieve sampling goals.[18] Nevertheless, as internet connectivity becomes more commonplace and integrated into daily life, and as software becomes more flexible for web-based questionnaires, online surveys are becoming the most prevalent data collection mode. In fact, companies such as Ipsos Reid are overcoming the sample representativeness problem by recruiting online panels whose demographic and purchasing profiles are consistent with target markets. Its Canadian online panel is randomly recruited and includes 35 000 Canadian households. Such online panels provide accurate research data very quickly.[19] You can do an online survey by following the instructions given in Online Application 6.1.

A disadvantage of online surveys is not being able to validate who is answering the survey. i.think_inc. can validate the members of its online panel. By permission, i.thinkinc.

ithinkinc.com

**Just who really is answering your online survey?**

With 7 years of online panel experience, we know our ithinkers

> Our panel was built one person at a time — Never through webmaster referral programs, co-registrations or mass web-site intercepts

> Respondent survey answers are validated against stored demographic information for consistency and accuracy

> Security, privacy and double opt-in best practices are strictly enforced

> Approximately 1.4 million US household members

> Survey programming and hosting also available for start-to-finish fielding solutions

**[i.think_inc.]**

www.ithinkinc.com   2811 McKinney Ave., Suite 218   Dallas, TX 75204   [214] 855-3777

## Self-Administered Surveys

Online surveys are also taken by respondents alone, but the following survey modes are, for the most part, all paper-and-pencil situations in which the respondent fills out a static copy of the questionnaire. Types of self-administered surveys are the group self-administered survey, drop-off survey, and mail survey.

### Group Self-Administered Surveys

Basically, a **group self-administered survey** entails administering a questionnaire to respondents in groups, rather than individually, for convenience or to gain certain economies. One way to be more economical is to have respondents self-administer the questions. For example, 20 or 30 people might be recruited to view a TV program sprinkled with test commercials. All respondents would be seated in a viewing-room facility, and a video would run on a large television projection screen. Then they would be given a questionnaire to fill out regarding their recall of test ads, their reactions to the ads, and so on.

Variations for group self-administered surveys are limitless. Students can be administered surveys in their classes; church groups can be administered surveys during meetings; social clubs and organizations, company employees, movie theatre patrons, and any other group can be administered surveys during meetings, work, or leisure time. Often the researcher will compensate the group with a monetary payment as a means of recruiting the support of the group's leaders. In all of these cases, each respondent works through the questionnaire at his or her own pace. A survey administrator may be present, so there is some opportunity for interaction concerning instructions or how to respond, but the group context often discourages respondents from asking all but the most pressing questions.

### Drop-off Surveys

Another variation of the self-administered survey is the **drop-off survey**, in which the survey representative approaches a prospective respondent, introduces the general purpose of the survey to the prospect, and leaves it with the respondent to fill out on his or her own. Essentially, the objective is to gain the prospective respondent's cooperation. The respondent is told the questionnaire is self-explanatory and it will be left with him or her to fill out at leisure, typically online. Drop-off surveys are especially appropriate for local market research undertakings in which travel is necessary but limited. They have been reported to have quick turnaround, high response rates, minimal interviewer influence on answers, and good control over how respondents are selected. They are also inexpensive.[20]

Variations of the drop-off method include handing out the surveys to people at their places of work and asking them to fill them out online. Some hotel chains have questionnaires in their rooms with an invitation to fill them out and turn them in at the desk on checkout. Stores sometimes have short surveys on customer demographics, media habits, purchase intentions, or other information that customers are asked to fill out at home, online. A gift certificate drawing may even be used as an incentive to participate. The term *drop-off* can be stretched to cover any situation in which the prospective respondent encounters the survey as though it were "dropped off" by a research representative.

### Mail Surveys

A **mail survey** is one in which the questions are mailed to prospective respondents, who are asked to fill them out and return them to the researcher by mail. Part of its attractiveness stems from its self-administered aspect: There are no interviewers to recruit, train, monitor, and compensate. Similarly, mailing lists are readily available from companies that specialize in this business, and it is possible to access very specific groups of target respondents. For example, it is possible to obtain a list of physicians specializing in family practice who operate clinics in cities with populations larger than 500 000. Also, one may opt to purchase computer files, printed labels, or even labelled envelopes from these companies. In fact, some list companies will even provide insertion and mailing services. There are a number of companies—for example, infoCanada—that sell mailing lists, and most, if not all, have online purchase options.[21] On a per-respondent basis, mail surveys are very inexpensive. In fact, they are almost always the least expensive survey method in this regard. But mail surveys incur all of the problems associated with not having an interviewer present, which we discussed earlier in this chapter.

Despite the fact that the mail survey is described as "powerful, effective, and efficient," this type of survey is plagued by two major problems.[22] The first is **nonresponse**, which refers to questionnaires that are not returned. The second is **self-selection bias**, which means that those who do respond are probably different from those who do not fill out the questionnaire and return it. Therefore, the sample gained through this method is nonrepresentative of the general population. To be sure, the mail survey is not the only survey method that suffers from nonresponse and self-selection bias. Failures to respond are found in all types of surveys, and marketing researchers must be constantly alert to the possibility that their final samples are somehow different from the original list of potential respondents because of some systematic tendency or latent pattern of response. Whatever the survey mode used, those who respond may be more involved with the product, they may have more education, they might be more or less dissatisfied, or they may even be more opinionated in general than the target population of concern.

When informing clients of data collection alternatives, market researchers should inform them of the nonresponse problems and biases inherent in each one being considered. For example, mail surveys are notorious for low response, and those respondents who do fill out and return a mail questionnaire are likely to be different from those who do not. Further, there are people who refuse to answer questions over the telephone, and consumers who like to shop are more likely to be encountered in mall-intercept interviews than are those who do not like to shop. Each data collection method has its own nonresponse and bias considerations, and a conscientious researcher will help his or her client understand the dangers represented in the methods under consideration. Thus, nonresponse and the danger of self-selection bias are greatest with mail surveys because mail surveys of households typically achieve response rates of less than 20%. Researchers have tried various tactics to increase the response rate, such as using registered mail, colour, money, personalization, reminder postcards, and so on.[23] Even with these incentives, however, response rates are low for mail surveys.[24] Despite this situation, mail surveys are viable in countries with high literacy rates and dependable postal systems.[25] Remember, however, that consumers and business respondents are constantly changing, and the inducement that works today may not necessarily work the same way in the future. One way in which research companies have sought to cope with the low response rate for mail surveys is to create a mail panel in which respondents agree to respond to several questionnaires mailed to them over time.[26] Others are shifting to internet communication systems that are faster and cheaper. Of course, the panel members are carefully prescreened to ensure that the mail panel represents the company's target market or consumers of interest.

# Choice of the Survey Method

The marketing researcher is faced with the problem of selecting the one survey mode that is optimal in a given situation. Each data collection method has unique advantages, disadvantages, and special features (see Table 6.2). How do you decide which is the best survey mode for a particular research project? When answering this question, the researcher should always have as a foremost objective the quality of the data collected. Even the most sophisticated techniques of analysis cannot make up for poor data. "Garbage in, garbage out" is the time-worn phrase that reflects this concern for quality data. In selecting a data collection mode, the researcher balances quality against cost, time, and other special considerations.

## The Survey Data Collection Time Horizon

Sometimes data must be collected within a very short time frame. For example, a national campaign is set to kick off in four weeks and a survey of the awareness of the company's trademark is needed. Or, an application for a radio licence from the Canadian Radio-Television and Telecommunications Commission (CRTC) requires that a listenership study of other stations in the area be conducted, and the deadline for the licence application is in five weeks. Traditionally, if there was a very short time horizon, telephone surveys were often selected due to their speed. If the respondent had to interact with the research object, such as a product prototype, mall-intercept studies were a top choice. Today, online surveys are exceptionally fast and can accommodate all but physical handling of research objects. Magazine ads, logos, and other marketing stimuli may be evaluated in online surveys.

When time is a factor in doing research, online surveys are fast. As online surveying has matured, marketing researchers find better-quality data by collecting data from established panels consisting of respondents who have previously agreed to provide information. Panels have been widely used in the research industry to ensure high response rates. However, recruiting panel members is costly and time consuming. e-Rewards® Market Research is an example of a firm that provides online panel access to clients worldwide with over three million panel members. The e-Rewards panel members are recruited into the panel by invitation only and are offered valuable rewards for their time spent taking and responding to survey requests.[27]

## The Survey Data Collection Budget

A very inexpensive method of collecting data is the mail survey. However, it is used infrequently due to the low response rate. Online survey research is another option.

| Method | Key Advantages | Key Disadvantages | Comment |
|---|---|---|---|
| In-home interview | Conducted in privacy of the home, which facilitates interviewer–respondent rapport | Cost per interview can be high; interviewers must travel to respondents' homes | Often much information per interview is gathered |
| Mall-intercept interview | Fast and convenient data collection method | Only mall patrons are interviewed; respondents may feel uncomfortable answering questions in the mall | Mall-intercept company often has exclusive interview rights for that mall |
| In-office interview | Useful for interviewing busy executives | Relatively high cost per interview; gaining access is sometimes difficult | Useful when respondents must examine prototypes or samples of products |
| Central location telephone interview | Fast turnaround; good quality control; reasonable cost | Restricted to telephone communication | Long-distance calling is not a problem |
| Computer-assisted telephone interview (CATI) | Computer eliminates human interviewer error; simultaneous data input to computer file; good quality control | Setup costs can be high | Losing ground to online surveys and panels |
| Fully computerized interview | Respondent responds at his or her own pace; computer data file results | Respondent must have access to a computer or be computer literate | Many variations and an emerging data collection method with exciting prospects |
| Online questionnaire | Ease of creating and posting; fast turnaround; computer data file results | Respondent must have access to the internet | Fastest-growing data collection method; very flexible; online analysis available |
| Group self-administered survey | Cost of interviewer eliminated; economical for assembled groups of respondents | Must find groups and secure permission to conduct the survey | Prone to errors of self-administered surveys; good for pretests or pilot tests |
| Drop-off survey | Cost of interviewer eliminated; appropriate for local market surveys | Generally not appropriate for large-scale national surveys | Many variations exist with respect to logistics and applications |
| Mail survey | Economical method; good listing companies exist | Low response rates; self-selection bias; slow | Many strategies to increase response rate exist |

**Table 6.2** **Key Advantages and Disadvantages of Alternative Data Collection Methods**

There are some online survey companies that allow the client to design the questionnaire and select the target sample type and number. Surveys can be completed for a few hundred or a few thousand dollars. All online surveys enjoy the advantage of being less expensive than many of the other data collection methods. Companies using online surveys must ask themselves if they can use data generated only from people with online access. There are companies that can supply online access to representative samples made up of people who would not normally have online

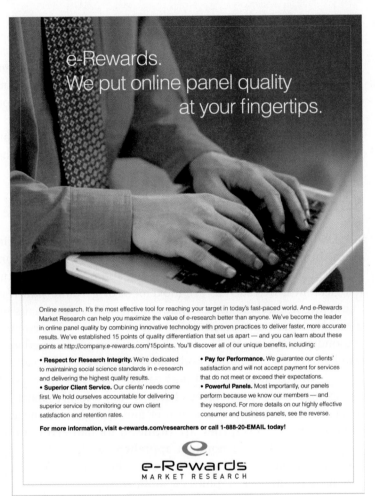

e-Rewards has implemented 15 points of quality differentiation to its panel management in order to ensure the integrity of its panel. Read e-Rewards' 15 points of quality differentiation at **http://researcher.e-rewards.com/15points**.

By permission, e-Rewards, Inc.

access but have been supplied with it by the research firm. If neither of these methods, mail or online, will work, probably the next least expensive method would be the use of telephone surveying.

## Incidence Rate

**Incidence rate** is the percentage of the population that possesses some characteristic necessary to be included in the survey. For example, the study may be targeted only to registered voters, or persons owning and driving their own automobile, or persons 16 years of age and older, and so on. Sometimes the incidence rate is very low.

A drug company may want to interview only men over the age of 50 with medicated cholesterol above 250. A cosmetics firm may want to interview only women who are planning facial cosmetic surgery within the next six months. In low-incidence situations such as these, certain precautions must be taken in selecting the data collection method. For example, in either of the above examples, it would be foolishly expensive to send out interviewers door-to-door looking for members who have the qualifications to participate in the study. A data collection method that can easily and inexpensively screen respondents is desirable. Online surveys, telephone surveys, and, to a lesser extent, mall surveys may be good choices.

## Cultural/Infrastructure Considerations

Cultural diversity has increasingly become an important issue as more and more marketing research companies operate around the globe. For example, in Scandinavia, residents are uncomfortable allowing strangers into their homes. Therefore, telephone and online surveying is more popular than door-to-door interviewing. Door-to-door interviewing is used often where online access at home is low.[28] When a firm plans to conduct a study in a culture about which they know little, they should consult local research firms before making the data collection method decision.

# Summary

1.  **Evaluate each of the four basic survey modes for gathering data.**

With the exception of observation studies, in which respondents' behaviour is observed and recorded by the researcher, and physiological studies, in which physiological measures such as eye movement or galvanic skin response are measured, marketing researchers must communicate with respondents in order to gather primary data. Marketing researchers refer to the process of communicating with study respondents as surveys. The four basic survey modes used are (1) person-administered surveys, (2) computer-administered surveys, (3) self-administered surveys, and (4) mixed-mode, sometimes called "hybrid," surveys. Person-administered survey modes are advantageous because they allow feedback, permit rapport building, facilitate certain quality controls, and capitalize on the adaptability of a human interviewer. However, they are prone to human error, are slow and costly, and sometimes produce respondent apprehension known as "interview evaluation." Computer-administered interviews, on the other hand, are faster, are error-free, may have pictures or graphics capabilities, allow for real-time capture of data, and may make respondents feel more at ease because another person is not listening to their answers. Disadvantages are that technical skills are required, and there may be high setup costs. Self-administered survey modes have the advantages of reduced cost, respondent control, and no interview-evaluation apprehension. The disadvantages of self-administered surveys are respondent control (in that respondents may not complete the task or may make errors), lack of a monitor to help guide respondents, and the need to have a perfect questionnaire. Finally, mixed-mode surveys use multiple data collection methods. The advantage of mixed-mode surveys is that researchers are able to take the advantages of each of the various modes to achieve their data collection goals. Disadvantages are that different modes may produce different responses to the same research question, and researchers must evaluate this difference. Second, mixed-mode methods result in greater complexities as researchers must design different questionnaires and be certain that data from different sources all come together in a common database for analysis.

2.  **Describe different types of survey data collection methods.**

Survey data collection methods include (1) in-home interviews, which are conducted in respondents' homes; (2) mall-intercept interviews, conducted by approaching shoppers in a mall; (3) in-office interviews, conducted with executives or managers in their places of work; (4) telephone interviews, conducted by an interviewer working in his or her home; (5) telephone interviews, conducted from a central location in a telephone-interview company's facilities; (6) computer-assisted telephone interviews, in which the interviewer reads questions off a computer screen and enters responses directly into the program; (7) fully computerized interviews, in which the respondent interacts directly with a computer; (8) online and other internet-based surveys; (9) group self-administered surveys, in which the questionnaire is handed out to a group for individual responses; (10) drop-off surveys, in which the questionnaire is left with the respondent to be completed and picked up or returned at a later time; and (11) mail surveys, in which questionnaires are mailed to prospective respondents, who are requested to fill them out and mail them back. Each data collection method has specific advantages and disadvantages.

**3.  Express major concerns in choosing a particular survey method.**
Researchers must take into account several considerations when deciding on a survey data collection method. The major concerns are (1) the survey time horizon, (2) the survey data collection budget, (3) incidence rate of the population, (4) cultural and infrastructure considerations, and (5) the type of respondent interaction required. Ultimately, the researcher should select the data collection method that will result in the highest quality and quantity of information without exceeding time or budget constraints.

## Key Terms

Central location telephone interviewing (p. 210)

Completely automated telephone survey (CATS)    (p. 213)

Computer-administered survey (p. 197)

Computer-assisted telephone interviews (CATI)    (p. 211)

Drop-off survey    (p. 215)

Fully computerized interviews (p. 212)

Group self-administered survey (p. 215)

Incidence rate    (p. 219)

In-home interview    (p. 204)

In-office interviews    (p. 205)

Internet-based questionnaire    (p. 213)

Interview evaluation    (p. 197)

Mail survey    (p. 216)

Mall-intercept interview    (p. 204)

Mixed-mode surveys    (p. 201)

Nonresponse    (p. 216)

Person-administered survey    (p. 194)

Self-administered survey    (p. 199)

Self-selection bias    (p. 216)

Survey    (p. 194)

Traditional telephone interviews (p. 209)

## Review Questions

**1.1** What are the advantages of person-administered surveys over computer-administered ones?

**1.2** Discuss why a researcher would or would not use a mixed-mode survey. Give an example to illustrate your points.

**2.1** Why are telephone surveys popular?

**2.2** What advantages do online surveys have over telephone surveys?

**3.1** What are the major factors to be considered in the choice of the survey method?

**3.2** Car Parts Inc. is a fictional retail chain specializing in stocking and selling both domestic and foreign automobile parts. The company is interested in learning about its customers, so the marketing director sends instructions to all 2000 store managers telling them that whenever a customer makes a purchase of $150 or more, they are to write down a description of the customer who made that purchase. They are to do this just for the second week in October, writing each description on a separate sheet of paper. At the end of the week, they are to send all sheets to the marketing director. Comment on this data collection method.

3.3 Discuss the feasibility of each of the types of survey modes for each of the following cases:

a.   Fabergé, Inc. wants to test a new fragrance called "Lime Brut."

b.   Kelly Services needs to determine how many businesses expect to hire temporary support staff to replace secretaries who go on vacation during the summer months.

c.   The *Encyclopedia Britannica* requires information on the degree to which mothers of elementary school–aged children see encyclopedias as worthwhile purchases for their children.

d.   Rogers is considering an iPhone "stick" modem and wants to know people's reaction to it.

3.4 Compu-Ask Corporation has developed a stand-alone computerized interview system that can be adapted to almost any type of survey. The respondent directly answers questions once the interviewer has turned on the computer and started up the program. Indicate the appropriateness of this interviewing system in each of the following cases, giving reasons for your answers:

a.   A survey of plant managers concerning a new type of hazardous-waste disposal system

b.   A survey of high school teachers to see if they are interested in a company's videotapes of educational public broadcast television programs

c.   A survey of consumers to determine their reactions to a nonrefrigerated variety of yogurt

3.5 A researcher is pondering what survey mode to use for a client who markets a home security system for apartment dwellers. The system comprises sensors that are pressed onto all windows and magnetic strips that are glued to each door. Once plugged into an electric socket and activated with a switch box, the system emits a loud alarm and simulates a barking guard dog when an intruder trips one of the sensors. The client wants to know how many apartment dwellers in Canada are aware of the system, what they think of it, and how likely they are to buy it in the coming year. Which survey method should be used and why?

# Case 6.1

# Steward Research, Inc.

Joe Steward is president of Steward Research, Inc. The firm specializes in customized research for clients in a variety of industries. The firm has a centralized location telephoning facility, and it has a division, "Steward Online," that specializes in online surveys. However, Joe often calls on the services of other research firms in order to provide his clients with the most appropriate data collection method. In a meeting with four project directors, Joe discusses each client's special situation.

*Client 1:* A small tools manufacturer has created a new device for sharpening high-precision drill bits. High-precision drill bits are used to drill near-perfect holes in devices such as engine blocks. The bits can be resharpened and used in as many as a dozen applications. After testing the device and conducting several focus groups in order to get modifications suggestions, the client is now ready for more information on presentation methods. The project director and the client have developed several different presentation formats. The client wishes to have some market evaluation of these presentations before launching a nationwide training program of the company's 125-salesperson salesforce.

*Client 2:* A regional bakery markets several brands of cookies and crackers to supermarkets throughout Canada. The product category is very competitive and competitors use a great deal of newspaper and TV advertising. The bakery's vice-president of marketing wants more information to make the promotional decisions for the firm. She spends several million dollars a year on promotions and she has no research with which to evaluate the effectiveness of the expenditures. Steward's project director has recommended a study that will establish some baseline measures of attitudes, preferences, and top-of-mind brand awareness (called TOMA, this measure of awareness is achieved by asking respondents to name the first three brands that come to mind when thinking of a product or service category, such as "cookies").

*Client 3:* An inventor developed a new device that sanitizes a toothbrush each time the brush is used and replaced in the device. The device uses steam to sanitize the brush, and lab tests have shown the mechanism to be very effective at killing virtually all germs and viruses. The inventor approached a large manufacturer who is interested in buying the rights to the device but would like some information first. The manufacturer wants to know if people have any concerns about toothbrush sanitization and whether they would be willing to purchase a countertop plug-in device to keep their toothbrushes sterile. It wants to know what only a few hundred people think about these issues. The inventor is anxious to supply this information very quickly before the manufacturer loses interest in the idea.

## Questions

1. For each of the three clients, suggest one or more data collection methods that would be appropriate.
2. For each data collection method you select in question 1, discuss the rationale for your choice.
3. What disadvantages are inherent in the data collection methods you have recommended?

# Case 6.2

# Coca-Cola Official Drink at the Vancouver 2010 Winter Olympic Games

Coca-Cola was one of the main sponsors of the Vancouver 2010 Olympic Games. Nicole Kettlitz, Coca-Cola's general manager for the Vancouver 2010 Olympic Games, knew that Canadians thought poorly of the company's green agenda.

For one thing, Canadians felt that too much water is wasted in making Coke. For another, Canadians threw out many plastic bottles containing Coke product, not realizing that the container was recyclable.

In the meantime, archrival PepsiCo Inc. was gaining ground with Canadians because of its announcement of using 20% less plastic content in the bottles used for Aquafina water. Coca-Cola, producer of Dasani bottled water, knew it had to catch up, especially in the eyes of younger consumers, who tend to be skeptical, especially about superficial solutions to greening the planet.

Coca-Cola introduced its new PlantBottle, used for Dasani, at the Vancouver 2010 Olympic Games. It was announced that the bottle was made of natural ingredients in combination with plastic, and produced one-quarter fewer carbon dioxide emissions than standard plastic bottles. The green components were listed on the bottle's labels, and an integrated marketing communication campaign was carried out online and in stores.

Coca-Cola likely monitored the situation closely as it unfolded its green agenda at the Vancouver 2010 Olympic Games.

**Questions**

1. Outline the various survey data collection methods Coca-Cola could use to monitor Canadian reaction to its green agenda. Consider a minimum of four methods.
2. For each method chosen, give reasons for your choice.
3. What are some of the limitations of each of the methods you selected?

Sources: http://cokenews.ca/2010/02/coca-cola-canada-opens-happiness-at-the-vancouver-2010-olympic-winter-games; http://adage.com/article?article_id=141839

# Case 6.3 Your Integrated Case

# College Life E-Zine: Determining the Data Collection Method

*This is the fourth installment in our integrated case series. You will find the previous E-Zine cases in Chapters 1, 2, and 3.*

Bob Watts of ORS Research sat alone in his office late on Friday afternoon. He knew he needed to be thinking more about the research design for the e-zine project he had been working on. Specifically, he gave some thought to the data collection method that should be used. He sketched out some considerations.

*Population targeted?* The entire student body should be considered the population. Key factor to determine is the percentage of the total students who are "very likely" to subscribe.

*Timing?* We need to go ahead and proceed with collecting this information as soon as we can. Data from the survey will allow us to estimate a number of potential subscribers, and this figure will tell us whether to proceed or not. Somewhat urgent to get this primary data collected.

*Costs?* A budget to collect data has not been confirmed . . . but we are talking about a few thousand dollars. We are constrained by the investment potential of the four investors. Not dealing with large, multinational corporation that could invest hundreds of thousands if need be.

*Cultural considerations?* Does it matter what time during the year we conduct the survey? Should not conflict with midterms or final exams. Other special considerations of college student life?

*Infrastructure considerations?* A very high percentage, nearly 100%, of the students have telephone service. On-campus students have access to high-speed internet service. University can not tell us what percentage of the students actually are online, though they think it is fairly high. All students have an email account.

*Respondent interaction?* We need to adequately describe the concept of the e-zine before we ask respondents for their intention to subscribe.

We will also want their preferences for different types of e-zine features as well as information on students' buying habits, their classification, and so on. It would be nice, for "tweaking" a proposed magazine feature, to allow students to actually interact with the magazine.

*Special situations?* The university will allow us permission to use its electronic directory that has all registered students' names, telephone numbers, and email addresses.

## Questions

1. What data collection modes do you think should be considered?
2. What are the advantages and disadvantages of these modes?
3. Which one method do you think Bob Watts should recommend? Why?

# Survey Measurement Scales

## LEARNING OBJECTIVES

1. Examine question response formats commonly used in marketing research.

2. Distinguish among the different levels of measurement.

3. Explain four types of measurement scales used by marketing researchers.

4. Explain validity and reliability in measurement.

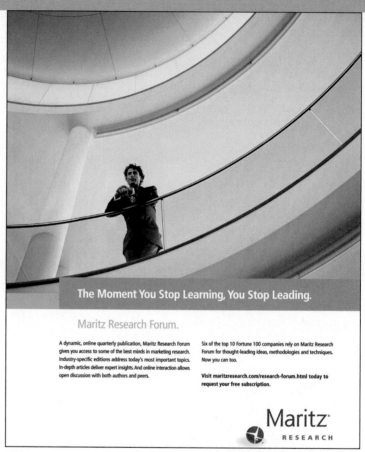

**The Moment You Stop Learning, You Stop Leading.**

Maritz Research Forum.

A dynamic, online quarterly publication, Maritz Research Forum gives you access to some of the best minds in marketing research. Industry-specific editions address today's most important topics. In-depth articles deliver expert insights. And online interaction allows open discussion with both authors and peers.

Six of the top 10 Fortune 100 companies rely on Maritz Research Forum for thought-leading ideas, methodologies and techniques. Now you can too.

**Visit maritzresearch.com/research-forum.html today to request your free subscription.**

Maritz® RESEARCH

## Measuring Customer Loyalty

Walt Disney once said: "Do what you do so well that they will want to see it again and bring their friends." Walt Disney understood the value of retaining customers, and today's successful companies understand that it costs much less to keep a customer than to attract new customers. Firms seek to increase customer loyalty. But companies must measure customer loyalty as one of the first steps in trying to understand it and to develop strategies to increase it. As you will read in this chapter, measurement is defined as quantifying some quality or attribute of an object. For example, marketers have attempted to quantify the construct "customer loyalty" among their present customers.

There are different ways customer loyalty is measured. Almost everyone agrees that there are degrees of customer loyalty; customers do not just "have" or "not have" customer loyalty. So, most everyone agrees the construct should be measured not with a closed-ended "yes" or "no" response but, rather, with a scaled response such as a 5-point or 10-point scale. However, there is disagreement as to how many scale points should be used, how many questions should be asked, and which questions should be asked in order to measure customer loyalty properly.

A common method for measuring customer loyalty is by creating a loyalty index by averaging three scaled response questions. The three questions measure overall satisfaction, willingness to recommend, and likelihood to return or buy again. The three questions are normally asked using a 5-point rating scale and the average score on these three questions is used to measure customer loyalty.

Colloquy is a global company that specializes in customer loyalty. In 2008, it developed the Colloquy Retail Loyalty Index, a tool that measures which retailers in the grocery, personal care, and mass merchant sectors consumers say they are most loyal to and why. Consumers were asked to measure their experiences with retailers at which they shopped, using a 10-point scale ranging from "not loyal" to "very loyal." To find out more about the research this company does, visit its website at **www.colloquy.com**.

A second method has been suggested by Fred Reichheld, who wrote *The Ultimate Question: Driving Good Profits and True Growth*. In the book, Reichheld recommends asking only one question ("The Ultimate Question"): "How likely is it that you would recommend Company X to a friend or colleague?" and the responses are recorded on a scale ranging from 0, "Not at all likely," to 10, "Extremely likely."[1] Reichheld believes this is the only question needed to measure customer loyalty.

Maritz Research also specializes in customer loyalty. Its researchers believe the 5-point rating scales do not adequately discriminate among those who are loyal and those who are not. Most customers give only positive ratings; there are few negative ratings. Through researching how to best measure customer loyalty, Maritz researchers developed the "Probability Allocation" measure, which consists of the key question: "Of the next 10 times you make a purchase of <insert product class here>, how many times will you buy <insert client's brand here>?"[2]

What characteristics should we look for in "good" measurement? First, does the method used to measure the construct actually measure what it is intended to measure? If so, the measurement is said to have "validity." Second, will the measurement method provide a reliable result? That is, if the method identifies a customer as loyal in one measurement setting, assuming the customer does not change, will the customer be identified as loyal in a second measurement? There are many other issues to look for in good measurement. Does the measure actually predict loyal and nonloyal customers?

**Where We Are**

1. Establish the need for marketing research
2. Define the problem
3. Establish research objectives
4. Determine research design
5. Identify information types and sources
6. Determine methods of accessing data
7. Design data collection forms
8. Determine sample plan and size
9. Collect data
10. Analyze data
11. Prepare and present the final research report

This chapter is the first of two devoted to the questionnaire design phase of the marketing research process. Its primary goal is to develop the foundation for understanding measurement in marketing research.

**Figure 7.1** A Diagram of the Six Question–Response Format Options

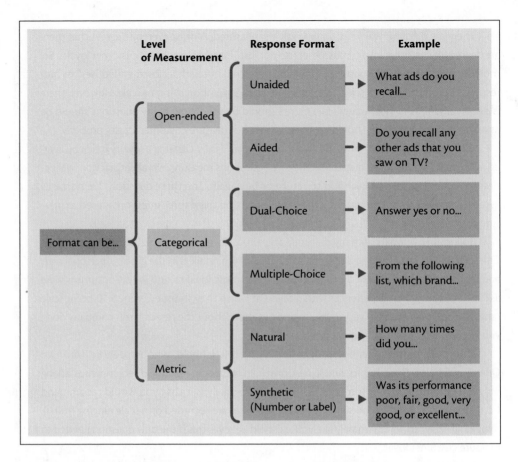

## Question–Response Format Options

While it takes skill and experience to become a proficient questionnaire designer, there are some basic building blocks. One basic building block is question–response formats. There are three basic question–response formats from which to choose: open-ended, categorical, and scaled response. Within each format are two options. Figure 7.1 illustrates the six response format options.

### Open-Ended Response Format Questions

With an **open-ended response format** question, the subject is asked to respond in his or her own words. This format is useful when the researcher does not want respondents to limit their answers. For example, in exploratory research situations, it is often useful to just let respondents say what is on their minds about the topic. Even in descriptive research studies, it is sometimes valuable to gather respondents' comments or answers. An **unaided open-ended format** does not prompt or probe the respondent beyond the initial question. When the researcher uses an **aided open-ended format**, there is a **response probe** in the form of a follow-up question instructing the interviewer to ask for additional information, saying, for instance, "Can you think of anything else you took the last time you had a bad cold?" The intent is to encourage the respondent to provide information beyond the initial and possibly superficial first comments.[3]

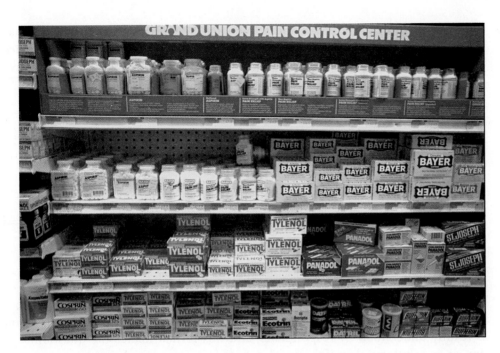

An aided open-ended response format can be used to help respondents remember what medicine they took the last time they had a cold.

## Categorical Response Format Questions

The **categorical response format** question provides answer options on the questionnaire. Students are familiar with this type of format. It is used on exams and quizzes. Categorical response formats are used when the researcher already knows the possible response to a question.[4] A **dual-choice question** is an instance where the respondent must select one answer from only two possible alternatives, such as "yes or no" or "true–false." With a **multiple-choice category question** format, there could be several options, such as a list of several cola brands, and the respondent indicates the one that answers the question posed.

Both the dual-choice and multiple-choice categorical question formats are very common on questionnaires because coding and analysis of responses are easier for the researcher. Also, respondents have a clearer idea of the type of answer the researcher is looking for. The **"check all that apply" question** is a special case. What appears to be a multiple-choice category question is really a dual-choice question. Consider the following question:

---

When you are purchasing a new pair of casual shoes, what features do you take into consideration? (Check all that apply.)

_____ Style

_____ Price

_____ Comfort

_____ Fit

_____ Construction

---

This question looks like a multiple-choice category question because it has several categories listed as possible responses. However, it is really a dual-choice category question because the respondent is actually answering the following five separate questions.

---

When you are purchasing a new pair of casual shoes, what features do you take into consideration? (Check "Yes" or "No" for each one.)

**a.** Style          _____ Yes          _____ No

**b.** Price          _____ Yes          _____ No

**c.** Comfort          _____ Yes          _____ No

**d.** Fit          _____ Yes          _____ No

**e.** Construction          _____ Yes          _____ No

---

The researcher knows that when a respondent checks an item, it is a "yes"; if the item is not checked, it is a "no" answer. The "check all that apply" instruction is readily understood by respondents, and this format makes the questionnaire appear less cluttered than if the "yes" or "no" format was used.

### Metric/Scaled Response Format Questions

The **metric/scaled-response question** calls for a number to be provided by the respondent or uses a scale developed by the researcher. "Metric" means that the answer is a number that expresses some quantity of the property being measured. With a **natural metric/scaled-response format**, the respondent is asked to give a number that measures the property being investigated such as age, number of visits, number of dollars, and so on. The number is on a continuum from "low" to "high" or "bad" to "good." The **synthetic metric/scaled-response format** uses an artificial number to measure the property. For instance, when respondents are asked to indicate their levels of satisfaction using a scale of 1 to 10, these numbers are assigned artificially by the researcher as a convenient way for respondents to express themselves. Synthetic metric/scaled formats may include scale descriptors such as "poor," "fair," "good," "very good," and "excellent." As you will learn shortly, these labels, or scale descriptors, are assigned artificial numbers (1, 2, 3, and so on) to represent the different gradations of the property being measured. Table 7.1 summarizes the pros and cons of the various response formats.

# Considerations in Choosing a Question–Response Format

All of the six different question formats we have just described are possible response formats for questions on a questionnaire. How does the researcher decide on which option to use? At least four considerations serve to narrow down the choice: (1) the nature of the property being measured, (2) previous research studies, (3) the ability of the respondent, and (4) the scale level desired.

**Table 7.1** Pros and Cons of Various Response Formats

| Response Format | Example Question | Pros | Cons |
|---|---|---|---|
| Unprobed open-ended | *"What was your reaction to the most recent Sony Blu-Ray disc player advertisement you saw on television?"* | + Allows respondent to use his or her own words. | − Difficult to code and interpret.<br>− Respondents may not give complete answers. |
| Probed open-ended | *"Did you have any other thoughts or reactions to the advertisement?"* | + Elicits complete answers. | − Difficult to code and interpret. |
| Categorical dual-choice | *"Do you think that Sony Blu-Ray players are better than Panasonic Blu-Ray disc players?" (Answer yes or no.)* | + Simple to administer and code. | − May oversimplify response options. |
| Categorical multiple-choice | *"If you were to buy a Blu-Ray disc player tomorrow, which brand would you be most likely to purchase? Would it be:*<br>*a. Panasonic*<br>*b. General Electric*<br>*c. Sony*<br>*d. JVC, or*<br>*e. Some other brand?"* | + Allows for broad range of possible responses.<br>+ Simple to administer and code. | − May alert respondents to response options of which they were unaware.<br>− Must distinguish "pick one" from "pick all that apply." |
| Metric natural scale | *"About how many times per week do you use your Blu-Ray disc player?"* | + Respondents can relate to the scale.<br>+ Simple to administer and code. | − Respondents may not be able to give exact answers using the scale. |
| Metric synthetic scale | *"Do you disagree strongly, disagree, agree, or agree strongly with the statement 'Sony Blu-Ray disc players are a better value than General Electric Blu-Ray disc players'?"* | + Allows for degree of intensity/feelings to be expressed.<br>+ Simple to administer and code. | − Scale may be "forced" or overly detailed. |

## Nature of the Property Being Measured

The inherent nature of the property being measured often determines the question–response format. For example, when Alka Seltzer wants to know if respondents have bought its brand of flu relief medicine in the last month, the only answers are "yes," "no," or "do not recall." If we ask marital status, a woman is married, separated, divorced, widowed, or single, or she may be cohabitating in a common-law relationship. But when we ask how much a person likes Cadbury chocolate, we can use a scaled-response approach because "liking" is a subjective property with varying degrees.

## Previous Research Studies

In tracking studies, it is necessary to compare the new findings with the previous survey. In this case, it is customary to simply adopt the question format used in the initial study. In other cases, scales are published or available for use by marketing researchers at no cost. For instance, some research companies specialize in customer satisfaction studies, and they have refined their own scales tapping this construct.[5] In any case, if a researcher believes a question format to be suitable for the purpose of the study at hand, it is good practice to adopt or adapt it rather than invent a new one.

## Ability of the Respondent

It is good practice to match the question format with the abilities of the respondents. For instance, if a researcher feels that the respondents in a particular study are not articulate or that they will be reluctant to verbalize their opinions, the open-ended option is not a good choice. Similarly, if the respondent, such as a child, is unable to rate objects on natural scales, it is appropriate to use a dual-choice categorical question format in which the respondent simply indicates "agree" or "disagree."[6]

## Scale Level Desired

Certain statistical analyses incorporate assumptions about the nature of the measures being analyzed. The researcher must bear these requirements in mind when selecting a question format. For example, if the response options are simply "yes" or "no," the researcher can report the percentage of respondents who answered each way, but if the question asks how many times respondents used an ATM machine in the past month, the researcher could calculate an average number of times. An average is different from a percentage, one reason being that a dual-choice "yes" or "no" response option is less informative than a scaled-response option such as "0," "1," "2," and so on. If a researcher desires to use higher-level statistical analyses, the question must have a scaled-response format. This point brings us to the concepts involved with measurement.

# Basic Concepts in Measurement

Questionnaires are designed to collect information gathered via **measurement**. Measurement determines if a property is possessed by an object and, if so, how much of it. For instance, a marketing manager may wish to know how a person feels about a certain product, or how much of the product he or she uses in a certain time period. This information, once compiled, can help answer specific research objectives such as determining product opinions and usage.

What are really being measured are properties—sometimes called *attributes* or *qualities*—of objects. Objects include consumers, brands, stores, advertisements, or whatever is of interest to the researcher working with a particular manager. **Properties** are the specific features or characteristics of an object that can be used to distinguish it from another object. For example, assume the object is a consumer.

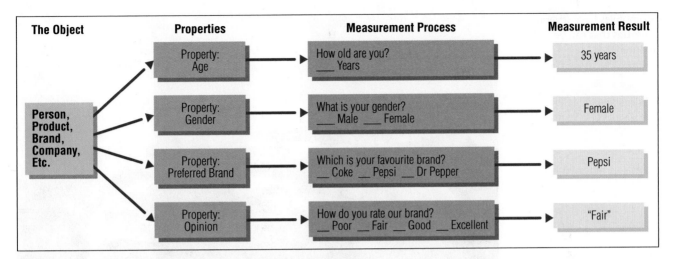

**Figure 7.2** How Measurement Works in Marketing Research

As depicted in Figure 7.2, the properties of interest to a manager who is trying to define who buys a specific product are a combination of demographics, such as age and gender, as well as buyer behaviour, which includes such things as the buyer's preferred brand and perceptions of various brands. In the figure, note that the measurement process is embodied in the response format presented in the question dealing with each property. Once the object's value on a property has been determined, the object has been measured on that property. Measurement underlies marketing research to a very great extent because researchers are keenly interested in describing marketing phenomena. Furthermore, researchers are often given the task of finding relevant differences in the profiles of various customer types, and measurement is a necessary first step.

Measurement is a very simple process as long as **objective properties**—which are physically verifiable characteristics such as age, income, number of bottles purchased, store last visited, and so on—are being measured. They are observable and tangible. Typically, objective properties, such as gender, are the ones that are preset as to appropriate response options, such as "male" or "female." However, marketing researchers often desire to measure **subjective properties**, which cannot be directly observed because they are mental constructs, such as a person's attitude or intentions. Subjective properties are unobservable and intangible. In this case, the marketing researcher must ask respondents to translate their mental constructs onto a "continuum of intensity", which is not an easy task. To do this, the marketing researcher must adapt or develop rating-scale formats—referred to as "metric synthetic" scales in Table 7.1—that are very clear and that are used identically by the respondents. This process is known as "scale development."

## Scale Characteristics

**Scale development** consists of designing questions and response formats to measure the subjective properties of an object. There are various types of scales, each of which possesses different characteristics. There are four characteristics of scales: description, order, distance, and origin.

Automobiles have several properties that can be measured.

## Description

**Description** refers to the use of a unique descriptor, or label, to stand for each designation in the scale. For instance, "yes" and "no," "agree" and "disagree," and the number of years of a respondent's age are descriptors of three different scales. All scales include description in the form of unique labels that are used to define the response options in the scale.

## Order

**Order** refers to the relative sizes of the descriptors. Here, the key word is *relative,* which includes such distinctions as "greater than," "less than," and "equal to." Respondents' least-preferred brand is "less than" their most-preferred brand, and respondents who check the same income category are the same ("equal to"). Not all scales possess order characteristics. For instance, is a "buyer" greater than or less than a "nonbuyer?"

## Distance

A scale has the characteristic of **distance** when differences between the descriptors are known and may be expressed in units. The respondent who purchases three bottles of diet cola buys two more than the one who purchases only one bottle; a three-car family owns one more automobile than a two-car family. Note that when the characteristic of distance exists, order is also given. Not only does the three-car family have "more than" the number of cars of the two-car family but also the distance between the two is known (the three-car family has *1 car* more).

## Origin

A scale is said to have the characteristic of **origin** if there is a true zero point for the scale. Thus, 0 is the origin for an age scale just as it is for the number of miles

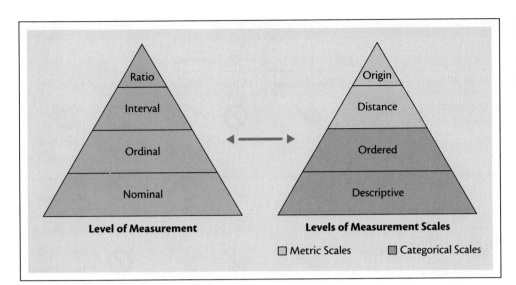

**Figure 7.3** Relationship between Levels of Measure and Levels of Measurement Scales

travelled to the store or for the number of bottles of soda consumed. Not all scales have a true zero point for the property they are measuring. In fact, many scales used by marketing researchers have arbitrary neutral points, but they do not possess origins. For instance, when a respondent says, "No opinion," to the question "Do you agree or disagree with the statement, 'The Lexus is the best car on the road today'?" it is nonsensical to say the person has a true zero level of agreement.

Each scale characteristic builds on the previous one. That is, description is the most basic and is present in every scale. If a scale has order, it also possesses description. If a scale has distance, it also possesses order and description, and if a scale has origin, it also has distance, order, and description. In other words, if a scale has a higher-level property, it also has all lower-level properties. This hierarchy of scales is illustrated in Figure 7.3. But the opposite is not true, as is explained in the next section.

## Levels of Measurement Scales

The characteristics possessed by a scale determine that scale's level of measurement. It is very important for a marketing researcher to understand the level of measurement of the scale selected. There are four levels of measurement: nominal, ordinal, interval, and ratio. Table 7.2 shows how each scale type differs.

A **categorical scale** is one that is typically composed of a small number of distinct values or categories, such as "male" versus "female," or "married" versus "single" versus "widowed." As you can see in Table 7.2, there are two categorical scale types: nominal and ordinal. The other concept is a **metric scale**, which is composed of numbers or labels that have an underlying measurement continuum. In this hierarchy of scale, ratio scales are the "highest" and nominal scales are the "lowest" (see Figure 7.3).

**Table 7.2** Measurement Scales Differ by The Scale Characteristics They Possess

| Level of Measurement | | Scale Characteristic | | | | Example |
|---|---|---|---|---|---|---|
| | | Description | Order | Distance | Origin | |
| **Categorical scale** | Nominal | ✔ | ⊘ | ⊘ | ⊘ | Which brand or brands do you use? |
| | Ordinal | ✔ | ✔ | ⊘ | ⊘ | Rank the brands as to 1st, 2nd, etc. choice. |
| **Metric scale** | Interval | ✔ | ✔ | ✔ | ⊘ | Rate each brand on a scale of 1 to 7. |
| | Ratio | ✔ | ✔ | ✔ | ✔ | How many times do you use each brand? |

✔ = does possess this characteristic      ⊘ = does not possess this characteristic

## Nominal Scales

**Nominal scales** are defined as those that use only labels; that is, they possess only the characteristic of description. Examples include designations of race, religion, type of dwelling, gender, brand last purchased, buyer/nonbuyer; answers that involve yes–no, agree–disagree; or any other instance in which the descriptors cannot be differentiated except qualitatively. If respondents in a survey are described according to their occupation—banker, doctor, computer programmer—a nominal scale is used. Note that these examples of a nominal scale only label the consumers. They do not provide other information such as "greater than," "twice as large," and so forth. Examples of nominal-scaled questions are found in Table 7.3A.

## Ordinal Scales

**Ordinal scales** permit the researcher to rank-order the respondents or their responses. For instance, if respondents are asked to indicate their first, second, third, and fourth choices of brands, the results would be ordinally scaled. Similarly, if one respondent checked the category "Buy every week or more often" on a purchase-frequency scale and another checked the category "Buy once per month or less," the result would be an ordinal measurement. Ordinal scales indicate only relative size differences among objects. They possess description and order. How far apart the descriptors are on the scale is unknown because ordinal scales do not possess distance or origin. Examples of ordinal-scaled questions are found in Table 7.3B.

A. **Nominal-Scaled Questions (descriptors with no order, distance, or origin)**

1. Please indicate your gender: ___Male ___Female

2. Check all the brands you would consider purchasing. (Check all that apply.)

   _____ Sony

   _____ LG

   _____ RCA

   _____ Samsung

3. Do you recall seeing a Delta Airlines advertisement for "carefree vacations" in the past week?

   _____ Yes _____No

B. **Ordinal-Scaled Questions (descriptors with order, but no distance or origin)**

1. Please rank each brand in terms of your preference. Place a "1" by your first choice, a "2" by your second choice, and so on.

   _____ Arrid

   _____ Right Guard

   _____ Mennen

2. For each pair of grocery stores, circle the one you would be more likely to patronize.

   Kroger versus First National

   First National versus A&P

   A&P versus Kroger

3. In your opinion, would you say the prices at Walmart are

   _____ Higher than Sears,

   _____ About the same as Sears, or

   _____ Lower than Sears?

C. **Interval-Scaled Questions (descriptors with order and distance but no origin)**

1. Please rate each brand in terms of its overall performance.

| | Rating (Circle One) | | | | | | | | | |
|---|---|---|---|---|---|---|---|---|---|---|
| **Brand** | **Very Poor** | | | | | | | | | **Very Good** |
| Mont Blanc | 1 | 2 | 3 | 4 | 5 | 6 | 7 | 8 | 9 | 10 |
| Parker | 1 | 2 | 3 | 4 | 5 | 6 | 7 | 8 | 9 | 10 |
| Cross | 1 | 2 | 3 | 4 | 5 | 6 | 7 | 8 | 9 | 10 |

2. Indicate your degree of agreement with the following statements by circling the appropriate number.

| **Statement** | **Strongly Agree** | | | | **Strongly Disagree** |
|---|---|---|---|---|---|
| a.  I always look for bargains. | 1 | 2 | 3 | 4 | 5 |
| b.  I enjoy being outdoors. | 1 | 2 | 3 | 4 | 5 |
| c.  I love to cook. | 1 | 2 | 3 | 4 | 5 |

3. Please rate Pontiac Vibe by checking the line that best corresponds to your evaluation of each item listed.

**Table 7.3** (*Continued*)

Slow pickup _____ _____ _____ _____ _____ _____ _____ Fast pickup

Good design _____ _____ _____ _____ _____ _____ _____ Bad design

Low price _____ _____ _____ _____ _____ _____ _____ High price

**D. Ratio-Scaled Questions (descriptors with order, distance, and origin)**

1. Please indicate your age.

   _____Years

2. Approximately how many times in the last month have you purchased something over $10 in price at a 7-Eleven store?

   0 1 2 3 4 5 More (specify:____)

3. How much do you think a typical purchaser of a $250 000 term life insurance policy pays per year for that policy?

   $_____

4. What is the probability that you will use a lawyer's services when you are ready to make a will?

   _____ %

## Interval Scales

**Interval scales** are those in which the distance between each descriptor is known. For adjacent descriptors, the distance is normally defined as one scale unit. For example, a coffee brand rated "3" in taste is one unit away from one rated "4." Sometimes the researcher must impose a belief that equal intervals exist between the descriptors. That is, if asked to evaluate a store's salespeople by selecting a single designation from a list of "extremely friendly," "very friendly," "somewhat friendly," "somewhat unfriendly," "very unfriendly," or "extremely unfriendly," the researcher would probably assume that each designation was one unit away from the preceding one. In these cases, the scale is "assumed interval." As shown in Table 7.3C, these descriptors are evenly spaced on a questionnaire; as such, the labels represent a continuum and the check lines are equal distances apart. By wording or spacing the response options on a scale so they appear to have equal intervals between them, the researcher achieves a higher level of measurement than ordinal or nominal. A higher-level measure allows the researcher to see finer distinctions among respondents' properties.

## Ratio Scales

**Ratio scales** are ones in which a true zero origin exists—such as an actual number of purchases in a certain time period, dollars spent, miles travelled, number of children in the household, or years of college education. This characteristic allows the use of ratios when comparing results of the measurement. One person may spend twice as much as another or travel one-third as far. Such ratios are inappropriate for interval scales, since we cannot say that one store was one-half as friendly as another. Examples of ratio-scaled questions are presented in Table 7.3D.

# Why the Measurement Level of a Scale Is Important

It is extremely important to know which level of measurement to use. First, the level of measurement determines what information is collected about the object of study; it determines what can be said and what cannot be said about the object. For example, nominal scales measure the lowest information level, and therefore they are sometimes considered the crudest scales. Nominal scales allow nothing more than to identify the object of study on some property. Ratio scales, however, contain the greatest amount of information; many things about our object can be said such as how different it is from another object quantitatively. Secondly, the level of measurement dictates what type of statistical analyses may or may not be done. Low-level scales necessitate low-level analyses, such as simple percentages, whereas high-level scales permit much more sophisticated analyses, such as correlations. In other words, the amount of information contained in the scale dictates the limits of statistical analysis.

As a general recommendation, it is desirable to use a scale at the highest appropriate level of measurement. Appropriateness is determined by the properties of the object being measured. As pointed out, some characteristics are inherently qualitative and can be measured only with a nominal scale, while other characteristics can be quantified and measured with a metric scale. Figure 7.3 on page 235 illustrates the relationship between data analysis, data presentation, and type of measurement scale used. Marketing Research in Action 7.1 illustrates how data collection using interval scales allows researchers to perform appropriate statistical analysis to confirm a relationship between event marketing and brand choices.

## MARKETING RESEARCH IN ACTION 7.1
## Measuring Brand Attitudes and Emotions with a Marketing Event

A rapidly growing phenomenon is special-event marketing where a company, brand, or group of companies sponsors some sort of short-term happening that attracts a significant number of potential customers. This event can take on any of a variety of forms; it can be as large as a festival or a fair; it can be as exciting as a concert with famous music stars; it can be as small as a reception before a sports event; or it can be as local as a company picnic. Regardless of the event, it will have the potential to stir some emotions and to change attitudes in consumers. That is, it will affect subjective properties of the attendees, and there is good reason to believe that these unobservable changes will translate into opinions about the brand and/or intentions to purchase the sponsoring brand.

*(Continued)*

Here is a diagram of the possible factors associated with and affected by a marketing event that were investigated in a recent study on event marketing.[7]

On the top half of the diagram is the "brand-attitude route"; in the bottom half is the "event-related route." Both routes are composed of unobservable constructs that are suspected to have some role in the consumer's intention to buy the sponsoring brand (buying intentions). The brand-attitude route is the typical way that traditional marketing efforts work. Specifically, through advertising, free samples, coupons, and the like, consumers become interested in the brand (brand involvement) and this leads to brand-related emotions and attitudes. These, in turn, affect intentions to buy the brand. In the study, all of the constructs were measured with 5- or 7-point synthetic metric interval scales. Brand involvement was measured by interest such as degree of importance of the brand to the person; brand emotion was feelings such as degree of joy or worry about the brand; and brand attitude was the degree of "goodness" of the brand. As can be seen by looking at the arrows in the figure, traditional marketing efforts heighten brand involvement, which stimulates brand emotion and increases brand attitude. Brand emotion, in turn, affects brand attitude, which increases intentions to buy the brand.

The marketing event path takes place when the brand or company sponsors some special event. Here, a critical consideration is the fit of the event with the brand's identity. For example, if there is a natural and logical connection—such as the John Deere company, which markets mainly argicultural equipment, sponsoring a tractor pull—the perceived fit is high; whereas if John Deere sponsored a golf tournament, the fit would surely be low. Fit and event involvement (importance of the event to the person) affect event emotions (how much happiness or excitement was experienced), and these affect the person's attitudes and opinions about how good the event was. Note that the event-related route directly affects the brand attitude in its route. In other words, if the event successfully fits the image of the sponsoring brand, and it is important, exciting, and valuable to the consumer, experiencing the event will increase the consumer's opinions of the goodness of the sponsoring brand, and we already know that increased brand attitude will generate more intentions to buy the brand.

So, by mapping and measuring unobservable, subjective properties of fit, involvement, emotions, attitudes, and intentions with interval scales, the researchers were able to investigate the relationships indicated by the arrows in the diagram. Using interval scales allowed the reseachers to apply sophisticated statistical techniques to confirm these relationships and to expand our understanding of how event marketing affects consumers' ultimate brand choices.

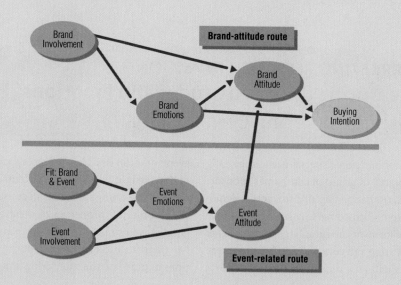

# Commonly Used Synthetic Metric Scales in Marketing Research

Marketing researchers often measure the subjective properties of consumers. There are many variations of these properties, but usually they are concerned with the psychological aspects. Various terms and labels are given to these constructs: attitudes, opinions, evaluations, beliefs, impressions, perceptions, feelings, and intentions. Because these constructs are unobservable, the marketing researcher must develop some means of allowing respondents to express the direction and the intensity of their impressions in a convenient and understandable manner. To do this, the marketing researcher uses scaled-response questions. As noted in Figure 7.1, these are called "synthetic metric or scale-response" format questions because the researcher uses a tailor-made scale. In this section, the basic synthetic metric/scale formats that are most common in marketing research practice are described. These scale formats are used time and again on questionnaires; they are called "**workhorse scales**" because they do the bulk of the measurement work in marketing research.

## The Intensity Continuum Underlying Workhorse Scales

Because most psychological properties exist on a continuum ranging from one extreme to another in the mind of the respondent, it is common practice to use metric scaled-response questions with an interval scale format. Sometimes numbers are used to indicate a single unit of distance between each position on the scale. Usually, but not always, the scale ranges from an extreme negative, through a neutral, and to an extreme positive designation. The neutral point is not considered zero, or an origin; instead, it is considered a point along a continuum, from extremely negative to extremely positive with a "no opinion" position in the middle of the scale(see Table 7.4).

As noted, it is not good practice to invent a novel scale format with every questionnaire. Instead, marketing researchers often fall back on standard types used by the industry. These workhorse scales include the Likert scale, the lifestyle inventory, and the semantic differential.

Workhorse scales are standard ones that marketing researchers rely on time and again.

**Table 7.4** The Intensity Continuum Underlying Scaled-Response Question Forms

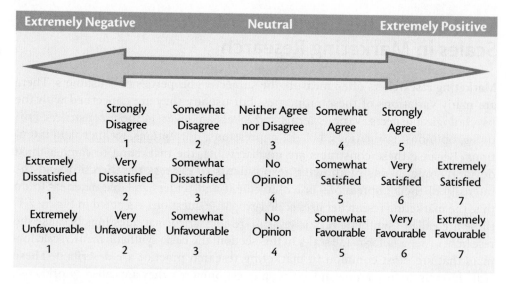

| Extremely Negative | | | Neutral | | | Extremely Positive |
|---|---|---|---|---|---|---|
| | Strongly Disagree | Somewhat Disagree | Neither Agree nor Disagree | Somewhat Agree | Strongly Agree | |
| | 1 | 2 | 3 | 4 | 5 | |
| Extremely Dissatisfied | Very Dissatisfied | Somewhat Dissatisfied | No Opinion | Somewhat Satisfied | Very Satisfied | Extremely Satisfied |
| 1 | 2 | 3 | 4 | 5 | 6 | 7 |
| Extremely Unfavourable | Very Unfavourable | Somewhat Unfavourable | No Opinion | Somewhat Favourable | Very Favourable | Extremely Favourable |
| 1 | 2 | 3 | 4 | 5 | 6 | 7 |

## The Likert Scale

A synthetic metric scaled-response form commonly used by marketing researchers is the **Likert scale**. Respondents are asked to indicate their degree of agreement or disagreement on a symmetric agree–disagree scale for each of a series of statements. The scale is "symmetric" because there are the same number of units to the left of a neutral point as there are to the right. With this scale, it is best to use "flat" or plain statements and let respondents indicate the intensity of their feelings by using the agree–disagree response continuum position. Table 7.5 presents an example of this scale in a telephone interview. You should note the directions given by the interviewer to ensure proper administration of this scale.

**Table 7.5** The Likert Question Format Can Be Used in Telephone Surveys, but Respondents Must Be Briefed on Its Format or Otherwise Prompted

(INTERVIEWER: READ) I have a list of statements that I will read to you. As I read each one, please indicate whether you agree or disagree with it.

Are the instructions clear? (IF NOT, REPEAT)

(INTERVIEWER: READ EACH STATEMENT. WITH EACH RESPONSE, ASK) Would you say that you (dis)agree STRONGLY or (dis)agree SOMEWHAT?

| Statement | Strongly Agree | Agree | Neutral | Disagree | Strongly Disagree |
|---|---|---|---|---|---|
| Levi's Engineered jeans are good-looking. | 1 | 2 | 3 | 4 | 5 |
| Levi's Engineered jeans are reasonably priced. | 1 | 2 | 3 | 4 | 5 |
| Your next pair of jeans will be Levi's Engineered jeans. | 1 | 2 | 3 | 4 | 5 |
| Levi's Engineered jeans are easy to identify on someone. | 1 | 2 | 3 | 4 | 5 |
| Levi's Engineered jeans make you feel good. | 1 | 2 | 3 | 4 | 5 |

The Likert-type of response format, borrowed from Rensis Likert's formal scale development approach, has been extensively modified and adapted by marketing researchers, so much, in fact, that its definition varies from researcher to researcher. Some assume that any intensity scale using descriptors such as "strongly," "somewhat," "slightly," or the like is a Likert variation. Others use the term only for questions with agree–disagree response options.

## The Lifestyle Inventory

There is a special application of the Likert question form called the **lifestyle inventory**. Lifestyle inventories measure a person's activities, interests, and opinions with a Likert scale, toward their work, leisure time, and purchases. The technique was originated by advertising strategists who wanted to obtain descriptions of groups of consumers as a means of developing more effective advertising. The underlying belief is that knowledge of consumers' lifestyles, or psychographics as opposed to just demographics, offers direction for marketing decisions. Many companies use psychographics as a market targeting tool.[8]

Lifestyle questions measure consumers' unique ways of living. These questions can be used to distinguish among types of purchasers, such as heavy versus light users of a product, store patrons versus nonpatrons, or other customer types. They can assess the degree to which a person is, for example, price-conscious, fashion-conscious, an opinion giver, a sports enthusiast, child-oriented, home-centred, or financially optimistic. These attributes are measured by a series of statements, usually in the form presented in Table 7.6.[9] Each respondent indicates degree of agreement or disagreement by responding to the scale positions. In some applications, the questionnaire may contain a large number of different lifestyle statements, ranging from very general descriptions to very specific statements concerning particular products, brands, services, or other items of interest to the marketing researcher.

## The Semantic Differential Scale

A specialized scaled-response question format that has sprung directly from the problem of translating a person's qualitative judgments into metric estimates is the **semantic differential scale**. Like the Likert scale, this one has been borrowed from another area of research, namely, semantics. The semantic differential scale contains a series of bipolar adjectives for the various properties of the object under study, and respondents indicate their impressions of each property by indicating locations along its continuum. The focus of the semantic differential is on the measurement of the meaning of an object, concept, or person. Because many marketing stimuli have meaning, mental associations, or connotations, this type of synthetic scale works very well when the marketing researcher is attempting to determine brand, store, or other images.[10]

The construction of a semantic differential scale begins with identifying a concept or object to be rated. The researcher then selects bipolar pairs of words or phrases that could be used to describe the object's salient properties. Depending on the object, some examples might be "friendly–unfriendly," "hot–cold," "convenient–inconvenient," "high quality–low quality," or "dependable–undependable." The opposites are positioned at the endpoints of a continuum of intensity, and it is customary to use five or seven separators between each point.

**Table 7.6 Examples of Lifestyle Statements on a Questionnaire**

Please respond by circling the number that best corresponds to how much you agree or disagree with each statement.

| Statement | Strongly Disagree | Disagree | Neither Agree Nor Disagree | Agree | Strongly Agree |
|---|---|---|---|---|---|
| I shop a lot for "specials." | 1 | 2 | 3 | 4 | 5 |
| I usually have one or more outfits that are of the very latest style. | 1 | 2 | 3 | 4 | 5 |
| My children are the most important thing in my life. | 1 | 2 | 3 | 4 | 5 |
| I usually keep my house very neat and clean. | 1 | 2 | 3 | 4 | 5 |
| I would rather spend a quiet evening at home than go out to a party. | 1 | 2 | 3 | 4 | 5 |
| It is good to have a charge account. | 1 | 2 | 3 | 4 | 5 |
| I like to watch or listen to baseball or football games. | 1 | 2 | 3 | 4 | 5 |
| I think I have more self-confidence than most people. | 1 | 2 | 3 | 4 | 5 |
| I sometimes influence what my friends buy. | 1 | 2 | 3 | 4 | 5 |
| I will probably have more money to spend next year than I have now. | 1 | 2 | 3 | 4 | 5 |

Respondents then check their evaluation of the performance of the object, say a brand, by checking the appropriate line. The closer respondents' checks are to an endpoint on a line, the more intense their evaluation is of the object being measured.

Table 7.7 shows how this was done in a survey for Red Lobster. Respondents also rated Jake's Seafood Restaurant on the same survey. You can see that each respondent has been instructed to indicate his or her impression of various restaurants, such as Red Lobster, by checking the appropriate line between the several bipolar adjective phrases. The phrases have been randomly flipped to avoid having all of the "good" ones on one side. This flipping procedure is used to avoid the **halo effect**,[11] which is a general feeling about a store or brand that can bias a respondent's impressions of its specific properties.[12] For instance, if a respondent had a very positive image of Red Lobster and all of the positive items were on the right-hand side (with all of the negative ones were on the left-hand side) the respondent might be tempted to just check all of the answers on the right-hand side without reading each characteristic carefully. But it is entirely possible that some specific aspect of the Red Lobster might not be as good as the others. Perhaps the restaurant is not located in a very convenient place, or the menu is not as broad as desired. Randomly flipping favourable and negative ends of the descriptors in a semantic

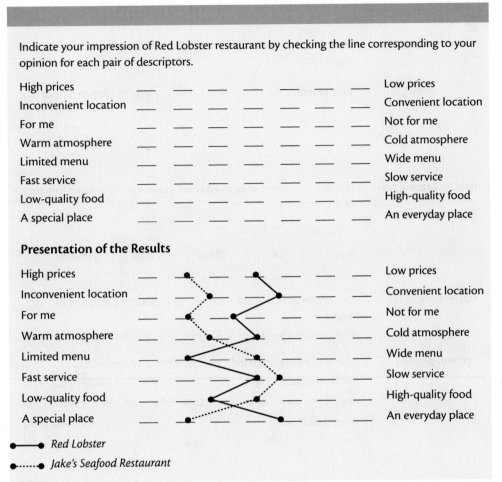

Indicate your impression of Red Lobster restaurant by checking the line corresponding to your opinion for each pair of descriptors.

| High prices | Low prices |
| Inconvenient location | Convenient location |
| For me | Not for me |
| Warm atmosphere | Cold atmosphere |
| Limited menu | Wide menu |
| Fast service | Slow service |
| Low-quality food | High-quality food |
| A special place | An everyday place |

**Presentation of the Results**

| High prices | Low prices |
| Inconvenient location | Convenient location |
| For me | Not for me |
| Warm atmosphere | Cold atmosphere |
| Limited menu | Wide menu |
| Fast service | Slow service |
| Low-quality food | High-quality food |
| A special place | An everyday place |

● ● Red Lobster

●······● Jake's Seafood Restaurant

differential scale minimizes the halo effect.[13] Also, there is some evidence that when respondents are ambivalent about the survey topic, it is best to use a balanced set of negatively and positively worded questions.[14]

One of the most appealing aspects of the semantic differential scale is that the researcher can compute averages and then plot a "profile" of the brand or company image. Each check line is assigned a number for coding. Usually, the numbers are 1, 2, 3, and so on, beginning from the left side. Because a metric scale is used, an average may be computed for each bipolar pair. The averages are plotted as you see them in Table 7.7. The marketing researcher has a very nice graphic with which to report the findings to the client.

## Other Synthetic Metric Scaled-Response Question Formats

A great many variations of synthetic scaled-response question formats are used in marketing research. Each marketing research company or marketing research department tends to rely on "tried-and-true" formats that they apply in study after study. Several examples are provided in Table 7.8.

**Table 7.8 Scaled-Response Question Formats Can Have Various Forms**

| Scale Name | Description and Examples |
|---|---|
| **Graphic rating scale** | Use of a line or pictorial representation to indicate intensity of response:<br><br>unimportant ◄-------------------► extremely important<br><br>☺ ☺ ☺ ☺ ☺ |
| **Itemized rating scale** | Use of a numbered or labelled continuous scale to indicate intensity of response:<br><br>___1　　___2　　___3　　___4　　___5<br><br>　　　　　　　　　　　　Very<br>Poor　　Fair　　Good　　Good　　Excellent<br><br>_____　　_____　　_____　　_____　　_____ |
| **Stapel scale** | Use of numbers, usually −5 to +5 to indicate the intensity of response:<br><br>Fast checkout service　−5 −4 −3 −2 −1 +1 +2 +3 +4 +5 |
| **Percentage scale** | Use of percentages to indicate the intensity of response:<br><br>Unlikely to purchase　　　　　　　　　　　Likely to purchase<br>0% 10% 20% 30% 40% 50% 60% 70% 80% 90% 100%<br>Very dissatisfied　　　　　　　　　　　　Very satisfied<br>0%　　　　25%　　　　50%　　　　75%　　　　100% |

There are very good reasons for this practice of adopting a preferred question format. First, it streamlines the questionnaire design process. By selecting a standardized scaled-response form that has been used in several studies, there is no need to be creative and to invent a new form. This saves both time and money.[15] Second, by testing a synthetic scaled-response format across several studies, there is opportunity to assess its reliability as well as its validity. Both of these topics are discussed in detail in the next sections of this chapter.

## Nonsymmetric Synthetic Scales

A symmetric scale is sometimes called "balanced," as it has equal amounts of positive and negative positions. But not all constructs that researchers deal with have counteropposing ends.[16] For example, suppose respondents are asked to indicate how important having jail bail bond protection was as a feature when purchasing automobile insurance. It is doubtful that a respondent would differentiate between "extremely unimportant," "very unimportant," or "somewhat unimportant," but could indicate how important it was with the response options of "not important" to "somewhat important," "very important," and "extremely important." That is, a nonsymmetric, or unbalanced, scale would be more appropriate because most

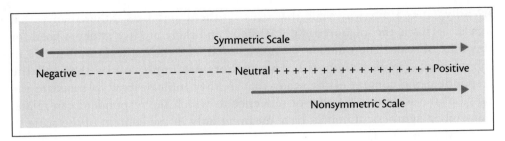

**Figure 7.4** Comparison of a Symmetric Synthetic Scale to a Nonsymmetric Synthetic Scale

people do not think in degrees of negative importance. As you can see in Figure 7.4, the symmetric scale includes the same ranges of negative as ranges of positive, and includes the neutral position on the scale. However, a nonsymmetric scale typically begins at the lowest positive position and extends to the highest positive position, plus it does not include the neutral, or "no opinion," position on the scale.

The **one-way labelled scale** allows the researcher to measure some construct attribute with the use of labels that restrict the measure to the "positive" side. The importance scale that ran from "not important" to "extremely important" just described is a one-way labelled scale, as it is primarily degrees of importance. Granted, there is a "not important" position on the scale, but this is the only instance of unimportance, and the rest of the positions on the scale are differing levels of importance. Ideally, respondents should respond to a one-way labelled scale as having equal intervals.[17]

*Example of a One-Way Labelled Scale*

How important is each of the following to you when you are deciding on a dentist?

| Factor | Not Important | Somewhat Important | Quite Important | Very Important | Extremely Important |
|---|---|---|---|---|---|
| Lowest prices in town | ____ | ____ | ____ | ____ | ____ |
| Close to my home | ____ | ____ | ____ | ____ | ____ |
| Guaranteed painless procedures | ____ | ____ | ____ | ____ | ____ |
| Will see me right away | ____ | ____ | ____ | ____ | ____ |

The ***n*-point scale**, meaning a 5-point, 7-point, or 10-point scale format, is a popular choice for researchers measuring constructs on nonsymmetric attributes. For example, consider rating the friendliness of the wait staff at Olive Garden Restaurant, where 1 means "not friendly" and 5 means "extremely friendly." It is a one-way scale that uses synthetic numbers rather than verbal labels.[18] This is the **anchored *n*-point scale**, and there are two anchors used for this type of scale. The number "1" is anchored, and the highest number, "5" in our example, is also anchored. The anchors are important as they tell the respondent the context of the scale; that is, they indicate how to translate the range of the scale into a frame of reference to which the respondent can relate. Remember, synthetic numbers have meaning only in the context of the scale in which they are used.

Below is an example of an anchored 5-point scale. It is critical to have good instructions that communicate the anchors and the numbers in the scale.

**Example of a 5-Point Anchored Scale**

Rate the performance of your book bag from 1 to 5, where 1 means "poor" and 5 means "excellent."

| Performance Factor | Poor | | | | Excellent |
|---|---|---|---|---|---|
| | | | Your Rating | | |
| Appearance | 1 | 2 | 3 | 4 | 5 |
| Roominess | 1 | 2 | 3 | 4 | 5 |
| Waterproofing | 1 | 2 | 3 | 4 | 5 |
| Easy to carry | 1 | 2 | 3 | 4 | 5 |

Occasionally, a researcher will opt to not provide the anchors, in which case it will be **an unanchored *n*-point scale**. An example is "On a scale of 1 to 5, how do you rate the friendliness of Olive Garden's wait staff?" As a general rule, anchors are desirable as they define concrete ends of the scale to respondents, but anchors are not mandatory.

*Reader's Digest* conducts an annual consumer-trust survey each year in 18 European countries to identify the most-trusted consumer brands in each country for at least 30 different product categories. To accomplish this end, the survey instrument asks each respondent to indicate his or her most-trusted brand in each product category. Respondents are then asked to rate each brand on an unanchored 5-point scale. The ratings are gathered for each of four aspects of trust: (1) quality, (2) value, (3) strong image, and (4) understanding customer needs.

**Trusted Brands Survey**
**www.rdtrustedbrands.com**

Because of the diversity of languages in Europe and because *Reader's Digest* is published in many languages, the questionnaire is printed in 20 languages. The ability of a 5-point unanchored scale to span so many languages is its strong point and places it high on the choice list of marketing researchers doing multi-national or single-country surveys. *Reader's Digest's* use of the simple 5-point scale of intensity demonstrates that it is applicable across Western cultures. Here is a sample of the findings of the most-trusted consumer brands in the United Kingdom in 2007. By the way, almost 28 000 people completed and returned the mail survey.

| Category | Brand |
|---|---|
| Car | Ford |
| Kitchen Appliance | Hotpoint |
| PC | Dell |
| Mobile Phone | Nokia |
| Camera | Canon |
| Holiday Company | Thomson |
| Bank/Building Society | Lloyds TSB |
| Credit Card | Visa |
| Insurance Company | Norwich Union |
| Airline | British Airways |
| Internet Company | BT |
| Petrol Retailer | Tesco |
| Vitamins | Boots |
| Pain Relief | Nurofen |
| Cold Remedy | Beechams |
| Cereal | Kellogg's |
| Hair Care | Pantene |
| Cosmetic | Boots |
| Skin Care | Nivea |
| Soap Powder | Persil |

The **graphic rating scale** is another nonsymmetric synthetic scale. Instead of labels or numbers, a graphic rating uses symbols such as smiley faces, dollar signs, thermometers, or anything else that is appropriate to the construct being measured. Typically, as one moves along a graphic rating scale, the symbols increase in size to connote differences in degree. On some relevant part of the symbol—such as the smile in the smiley face or the level of the mercury in the thermometer—changes can indicate the differences in degree. Because the graphic rating scale is a picture scale, it can be used for respondents who have reading difficulties, such as children, or it might be used by a researcher to break up the monotony of labelled and numbered scales on the questionnaire.

**Example of a Graphic Rating Scale**

How did you feel the last time your parents bought you a Learning Tree book?

## Issues in the Use of Synthetic Scaled-Response Formats

When using synthetic scaled-response formats the researcher should consider whether to include the middle, neutral response option. The Likert scale, lifestyle, and semantic differential examples all have a neutral point, but some researchers prefer to leave out the neutral option on their scales. There are valid arguments for both options.[19] Those arguing for the inclusion of a neutral option believe that some respondents have not formed opinions on that item, and they must be given the opportunity to indicate their ambivalence. Proponents of not including a neutral position, however, believe that respondents may use the neutral option as a way to hide their opinions.[20] Eliminating the neutral position forces these respondents to indicate their opinions or feelings.

Also, the researcher should decide whether to use a completely symmetric scale. Sometimes, common sense suggests only the positive side is appropriate. For example, when thinking how important something is people do not usually think in terms of degrees of "unimportance." In fact, for many constructs symmetric scales are awkward or nonintuitive and should not be used.[21] Consequently, some scales contain only the positive side, because very few respondents would make use of the negative side.

When in doubt, a researcher can pretest both the balanced and the one-sided versions to see whether the negative side will be used by respondents. As a general rule, it is best to pretest a scale to make sure it is being used in its entirety.

A sometimes troublesome issue that global marketing reseachers encounter is cultural differences among respondents. In some cultures extremism is valued, and in some others moderation or "going along with the crowd" is expected. Marketing Reseach in Action 7.2 describes what researchers found when they examined how respondents in 26 different countries compared with respect to their use of the full range of a scale.[22]

---

## MARKETING RESEARCH IN ACTION 7.2
## How Cultural Differences Affect Respondents' Use of the Extreme Ends of Scales

Whenever a marketing researcher undertakes global studies, a host of considerations must be considered. Typically, language differences alone are a great concern, for often a literal translation of questions fails to include nuances, idioms, and subtleties that are built into the initial question's wording. Often two or three iterations of translations, interpretations, and pretests are necessary for the researcher to feel confident that the various language versions are equivalent.

However, even when the questions are equivalent, there is the possibility that cultural response styles will come into play. A cultural response style is a tendency among members of a cultural group to use the scale in a particular way. For instance, cultures where individualism and dogmatism are valued are perhaps more likely to use the extreme ends of scales than are cultures where collectivism and cooperation are valued. In the collective cultures, extremism is avoided, and one would expect that respondents in these cultures would tend to respond with more "middle-of-the-road" responses to the scales posed on a questionnaire.

This line of thinking was validated to some extent by a study. As can be seen in the following figure, respondents from Thailand and Taiwan, which are collective, communal cultures, exhibited a relatively strong middle-of-the-road response tendency. That is, they tended not to use the extreme end response options such as "very strongly agree" or "very strongly disagree" in the test surveys. Chinese respondents, also representing a communal society, were found to have middle-of-the-road response propensities as well. In contrast, Russian respondents displayed very pronounced extreme response tendencies, meaning that they used the "very strongly agree" and "very strongly disagree" endpoints of the scales in the study a great deal, and much more so than respondents in any other countries. Romanian and Argentinian respondents also displayed extreme response tendencies, although these were somewhat less pronounced.

The majority of countries in the study fell into a range of response moderation rather than response extremism, as can be seen by the clustering of many countries close to the "0" response-style demarcation in the figure, which indicates neither high numbers of extreme responses nor unusually large numbers of middle-of-the-road responses were found.

This figure and findings from other studies that have corroborated these differences in cultural response tendencies are a cautionary warning to any researcher undertaking global marketing research, and the warning is especially relevant to marketing researchers who are investigating countries whose cultures are strongly individualistic or largely collective in nature.

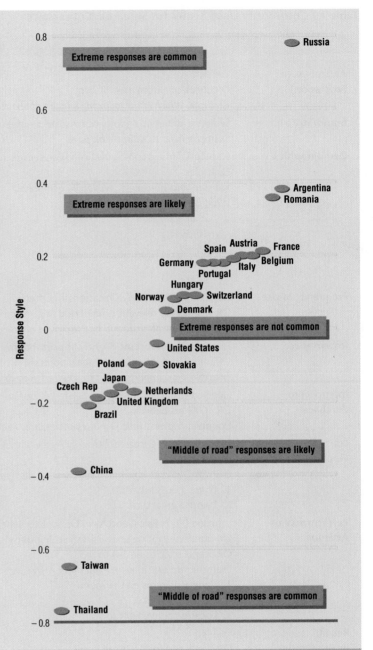

## What Scale to Use When

Market researchers use "constructs," or standard marketing concepts. They typically have a mental vision of how each construct will be measured. This mental vision is called an **operational definition.**

Table 7.9 is a quick reference on appropriate scales to use for the constructs most often measured by market researchers. Most of the scales are interval scaled because most of the constructs are attitudinal or intensity scales. The general

**Table 7.9 Commonly Used Scales for Selected Constructs**

| Construct | Response Scale |
|---|---|
| Awareness (or Possession) | Yes–No<br>OR check one from a list of items<br>Example: *Which of the following kitchen appliances do you own? (check all that apply.)* |
| Brand/Store Image | Semantic differential (with 4 or 7 scale points) using a set of bipolar adjectives<br>Example: *Refer to example on page ___.* |
| Demographics | Standard demographic questions (gender, age range, income range, etc.)<br>Examples:<br>*Indicate your gender ___ Male ___ Female*<br>*What is your age range?*<br>*___ 20 or younger*<br>*___ 21–30*<br>*___ 31–40*<br>*___ 41–50*<br>*___ 51 or older* |
| Frequency of Use | Labelled (Never, Rarely, Occasionally, Often, Quite Often, Very Often)<br>OR # times per relevant time period (e.g., month)<br>Example: *How often do you buy takeout Chinese dinners?* |
| Importance | Labelled (Unimportant, Slightly Important, Important, Quite Important, Very Important)<br>OR numbered rating using 5 scale points<br>Example: *How important is it to you that your dry cleaning service has same-day service?* |
| Intention to Purchase | Labelled (Unlikely, Somewhat Likely, Likely, Quite Likely, Very Likely)<br>OR 100% probability<br>Example: *The next time you buy cookies, how likely are you to buy a fat-free brand?* |
| Lifestyle/ Opinion | Likert (Strongly Disagree–Strongly Agree with 5 scale points) using a series of lifestyle statements<br>Example: *Indicate how much you agree or disagree with each of the following statements.*<br>1. I have a busy schedule.<br>2. I work a great deal. |
| Performance or Attitude | Labelled (Poor, Fair, Good, Very Good, Excellent)<br>OR numbered rating scale using 5 scale points<br>OR Stapel scale using −3 to +3<br>Example: *Indicate how well you think Arby's performs on each of the following features.*<br>1. Variety of items on the menu<br>2. Reasonable price<br>3. Location convenient to your home |
| Recall or Recognition | Yes–No<br>OR check one from a list of items<br>Example: *Where have you seen or heard an ad for Pets-R-Us in the past month? (check all that apply).* |
| Satisfaction | Labelled (Not at all Satisfied, Slightly Satisfied, Somewhat Satisfied, Very Satisfied, Completely Satisfied)<br>OR 10-point satisfaction scale where 1 = "not at all satisfied" and 10 = "completely satisfied"<br>*Note*: If there is reason to believe that an appreciable number of respondents are not satisfied, the recommendation is for a symmetric balanced scale to measure the degree of dissatisfaction (Completely Dissatisfied; Slightly Dissatisfied; Neither Dissatisfied nor Satisfied; Slightly Satisfied; Completely Satisfied)<br>Example: *Based on your experience with Federal Express, how satisfied have you been with its overnight delivery service?* |

| Not at all Satisfied | Slightly Dissatisfied | Somewhat Satisfied | Somewhat Satisfied | Completely Satisfied |
|---|---|---|---|---|
| ☐ | ☐ | ☐ | ☐ | ☐ |

Figuring out what scale to use and when is challenging for a neophyte marketing researcher.

recommendation is to use the highest-level scale possible.[23] The table is not a complete listing of marketing constructs.

Also included are some nominally scaled constructs—the awareness, possession, recall, and recognition constructs are measured with yes–no scales. If there is a list, and the respondent checks all that apply, the researcher can use a **summated scale**, meaning that the number of checks will be counted for each respondent and that number will stand as the metric measure of the construct. For example, in a list of 10 appliances that a person could have in a kitchen, those respondents with many appliances will have high summated scale numbers; those with few will have low summated scale numbers.

## Reliability and Validity of Measurements

Ideally, a measurement used by a market researcher should be reliable and valid. A **reliable measure** is one in which a respondent answers in the same or in a very similar manner to an identical or near-identical question. Obviously, if a question elicits wildly different answers from the same person, and circumstances have not changed between administrations of the question, there is something very wrong with the question. It is unreliable.[24]

Validity, on the other hand, operates on a completely different plane than reliability; it is possible to have perfectly reliable measurements that are invalid. Validity is defined as accuracy of the measurement: It is an assessment of the exactness of the measurement relative to what actually exists. A **valid measure** is one that is truthful: the question measures what one thinks is being measured. To illustrate this concept and its difference from reliability, think of a respondent who is embarrassed by a question about his income. This person makes under $40 000 per year, but he does not want to tell that to the interviewer. Consequently, he responds with the highest category, "Over $100 000." In a retest of the questions, the respondent persists in his lie by stipulating the highest income level again. Here, the respondent has been perfectly consistent (that is, reliable), but he has also been completely untruthful (that is, invalid). Of course, lying is not the only reason for invalidity. The respondent may have a faulty memory, may have a misconception, or may even be a bad guesser.[25]

When developing a questionnaire, a researcher uses an intuitive form of judgment called **face validity** to evaluate the validity of each question. Face validity is concerned with the degree to which a measurement "looks like" it measures that which it is designed to measure.[26] Often, a researcher will ask colleagues to look at the questions to see if they agree with the researcher's face validity judgments. Revisions strengthen the face validity of the question until it passes the researcher's subjective evaluation. Unfortunately, face validity is considered by academic marketing researchers to be a very weak test, so marketing research practitioners are faced with an ethical dilemma when they work with scales. Ethics in Marketing Research 7.1 examines this dilemma.

---

## ETHICS IN MARKETING RESEARCH 7.1
# Why Marketing Researchers Face Ethical Issues in Scale Development

Scale development poses an ethical dilemma for researchers. The proper development of a scale is a very lengthy and expensive process because several different criteria must be satisfied in assessing the quality of a scale. To meet these criteria, a scale should be developed over a series of administrations. After each one, statistical tests are used to refine the scale, and each subsequent administration tests the new version, which leads to further refinement. It is not unusual for scales that are published in academic journals to go through three or four administrations involving hundreds of respondents. To say this more pointedly, when a marketing researcher must develop a scale to measure a marketing construct, doing it properly may take several months or even years of work.

The few marketing research firms that have pursued scale development have developed proprietary instruments that are protected by copyright. That is, they have invested time and money in scale development so that scale will be part of the marketing research services they offer, and they will enjoy a competitive advantage over other marketing research firms because of the legal protection afforded their work by a copyright.

As you would expect, the vast majority of marketing research practitioners do not have the time, and their clients are unwilling to supply the monetary resources necessary, to thoroughly develop scales. So there is an ethical dilemma when a marketing researcher must measure some marketing phenomenon but does not have the luxury of time nor the resources necessary to do so properly. Proper scale development simply cannot take place because clients do not appreciate the time and cost factors. In fact, they may not even believe these procedures are warranted and will refuse to pay for them, meaning that if such tests are performed, the marketing researcher's profits will be reduced. Consequently, the vast majority of marketing researchers are forced to design their measures by relying on face validity alone, meaning that the researcher, and perhaps the client if inclined to take part, simply judges that the question developed to measure the marketing construct at hand "looks like" an adequate measure.

The unfortunate truth is that most marketing research practitioners cannot concern themselves at all with rigorous scale development that relies on time-consuming reliability or validity measurements. The standard procedure is to use measures that are well known through the company's experience, through the researcher's own experience, or available in the marketing research literature. On the other hand, it is unethical for a researcher to discover reliability or validity problems and not strive to resolve them. A conscientious market researcher will devote as much time and energy as possible to ensure the reliability and validity of the research throughout the entire process.

The formal development of reliable and valid measures is a long and complicated process that is largely entrusted to academic marketing researchers.[27] Marketing professors who work on the cutting edge of research often labour for months and sometimes years to develop reliable and valid measures of the marketing constructs with which they are working. Fortunately, these labours are ultimately published in academic journals, which puts these measures in the public domain. Marketing research practitioners can use them freely. The *Marketing Scales Handbooks* edited by Gordon C. Bruner II, Karen E. James, and Paul J. Hensel contain hundreds of scales (available at their Office of Scales Research, **www.siu.edu/ departments/coba/osr/index.html**). These handbooks save time and effort in searching for scales in journal articles or other similar academic sources.

# Summary

1. **Examine question response formats commonly used in marketing research.**
There are three basic types of question–response formats from which to choose: open-ended, categorical, and scaled response. Within each type are two variations, thus providing six variations of question–response format. For open-ended questions, there is aided and unaided response; for categorical questions, there is dual choice and multiple choice; and for scaled questions, there is natural and synthetic response. Given all of these options, it is challenging for the marketing researcher to design the best questionnaire. It is important to consider the following when making choices: the nature of the property being measured, previous research, ability of the respondent, and the level of statistical analysis desired when the answers have been collected.

2. **Distinguish among the different levels of measurement.**
There are four different levels of measurement. They form a hierarchy from least mathematically robust to most robust. The simplest, or most basic, is the nominal level. It measures objects according to labels. As such, it does not order or assign a value to the property being measured but merely describes it. The next level of measurement is the ordinal. This allows the property to be ordered as better or worse, bigger or smaller, and so on. The next level is the interval measure. Here it is assumed that there is an equal distance between measures. The highest level of measurement is the ratio measure. Ratio measures have a true zero point so that measures represent a real number system. The nominal and ordinal levels are considered to be categorical measures. The interval and ratio levels are considered to be metric measurements.

The level of measurement predetermines the type of statistical analysis that can be done with it. For nominal and ordinal data, not much can be done except to describe the object. Simple analysis, providing frequency of mention, can be performed. With interval and ratio data, more sophisticated analysis can be done including averages and multivariate analysis.

3. **Explain four types of metric measurement scales used by marketing researchers.**
There are four commonly used scales for metric data. They are scales that are used so often in marketing research that researchers know they can trust the type of

data collected and the type of analysis they can perform on the data thus collected. The first two scales are called "symmetric" or "balanced" because there are equal amounts of positive and negative positions between the extremes. The last two scales are called "nonsymmetric" or "unbalanced" because there is no negative side to the scale. Respondents choose from a lowest positive end to the highest positive end.

The Lickert scale is a commonly used symmetric scale that measures the extent to which a respondent agrees or disagrees with a statement. There is usually a central point with an equal number of units to the left of this point as to the right of this point. As such, the Lickert scale is considered to be a balanced, synthetic metric scale. The Lifestyle Inventory is a variation of the Lickert scale that measures the extent to which respondents agree or disagree with statements about attitudes, values, and lifestyle. A multivariate analysis of responses can produce a score that can segment respondents according to the pattern of their answers to the questions in the inventory. Many clients are interested in seeing the relationship between responses to this inventory and choices made by consumers.

The semantic differential is another commonly used symmetric scale made of two bipolar adjectives. The respondent rates an object relative to one extreme or the other. The advantage to using semantic differential scales is that averages can be computed. Averages can be computed because one can think of the degrees between the two bipolar extremes as an ordered, metric scale.

A commonly used nonsymmetric scale is the one-way labelled scale. Respondents are asked to rate factors from least to most on some descriptor such as importance. The $n$-point scale is another commonly used nonsymmetric scale. Again, respondents are asked to rate a factor but there are identified 5 or 7 points between the lowest and the highest.

Which scale to use is dependent on the operational definition of the construct the researcher wishes to measure. Almost all scales measure at least interval level constructs. It is recommended that the highest-level scale possible always be used.

## 4.   Explain validity and reliability in measurement.

Reliability and validity are fundamental to the credibility of marketing research findings. Reliability means that if one were to measure sample after sample from the same population under study, with the same measuring instruments, the results would be the same within a range of statistical acceptance. It also applies to a single respondent. Reliability is the degree to which the respondent's answers are consistent. Validity, on the other hand, means that one is measuring what one believes is being measured. In other words, validity applies to the accuracy of responses. Validity is very challenging since most researchers rely on face validity, or intuitive judgment. This presents an ethical concern since actions are often taken on face validity, which may actually misrepresent the truth of the situation being measured. For instance, you can ask students to measure how they feel about a teacher, keeping their feelings about the course content aside. The responses the students give may not be about the teacher after all, but about the course content. The validity of the answers in this instance is questionable since one is really not certain what is being measured. Taking action to change the course content or to change the teacher based on the responses is therefore unethical. Note that it is possible to have reliable measures that are invalid.

# Key Terms

Aided open-ended format     (p. 228)
Anchored *n*-point scale     (p. 248)
Categorical response format     (p. 229)
Categorical scale     (p. 235)
"Check all that apply" question
    (p. 229)
Description     (p. 234)
Distance     (p. 234)
Dual-choice question     (p. 229)
Face validity     (p. 254)
Graphic rating scale     (p. 249)
Halo effect     (p. 244)
Interval scales     (p. 238)
Lifestyle inventory     (p. 243)
Likert scale     (p. 242)
Measurement     (p. 232)
Metric scale     (p. 235)
Metric/scaled-response question
    (p. 230)
Multiple-choice category question
    (p. 229)
*n*-point scale     (p. 247)
Natural metric/scaled-response
    format     (p. 230)

Nominal scales     (p. 236)
Objective properties     (p. 233)
One-way labelled scale     (p. 247)
Open-ended response format
    (p. 228)
Operational definition     (p. 251)
Order     (p. 234)
Ordinal scales     (p. 236)
Origin     (p. 234)
Properties     (p. 232)
Ratio scales     (p. 238)
Reliable measure     (p. 253)
Response probe     (p. 228)
Scale development     (p. 233)
Semantic differential scale     (p. 243)
Subjective properties     (p. 233)
Summated scale     (p. 253)
Synthetic metric/scaled-response
    format     (p. 230)
Unaided open-ended format
    (p. 228)
Unanchored *n*-point scale     (p. 248)
Valid measure     (p. 253)
Workhorse scales     (p. 241)

# Review Questions

**1.1** Identify at least three considerations that determine the format of a question, and indicate how each one would affect the format.

**2.1** Name the four characteristics that determine the level of measurement of a scale.

**2.2** What is measurement? In your answer, differentiate an object from both its objective and subjective properties. Explain what is meant by a continuum along which a subjective property of an object can be measured.

**2.3** What is an operational definition? Provide operational definitions for the following constructs:

   **a.**   Brand loyalty
   **b.**   Intention to purchase
   **c.**   Importance of "value for the price"
   **d.**   Attitude toward a brand
   **e.**   Recall of an advertisement
   **f.**   Past purchases

**3.1** Distinguish among a Likert scale, a lifestyle scale, and a semantic differential scale.

**3.2** What are the arguments for and against the inclusion of a neutral response position in a symmetric scale?

3.3 Mike, the owner of Mike's Market, a convenience store, is concerned about low sales. He reads in a marketing textbook that the image of a store often has an impact on its ability to attract its target market. He contacts the All-Right Research Company and commissions it to conduct a study that will shape his store's image. You are charged with the responsibility of developing the store image part of the questionnaire.

Design a semantic differential scale that will measure the relevant aspects of Mike's Market's image. In your work on this scale, you must do the following: (1) Brainstorm the properties to be measured, (2) determine the appropriate bipolar adjectives, (3) decide on the number of scale points, and (4) indicate how the scale controls for the halo effect.

3.4 Each of the examples listed next involves a marketing researcher's need to measure some construct. Devise an appropriate scale for each one. Defend the scale in terms of its scaling assumptions, number of response categories, use or nonuse of a "no opinion" or neutral response category, and face validity.

   a.   Mattel wants to know how preschool children react to a sing-along video game in which the child must sing along with an animated character and guess the next word in the song at various points in the video.

   b.   TCBY is testing five new flavours of yogurt and wants to know how its customers rate each one on sweetness, flavour strength, and richness of taste.

   c.   A pharmaceutical company wants to find out how much a new federal law eliminating doctors' dispensing of free sample prescription drugs will affect their intentions to prescribe generic versus brand-name drugs for their patients.

3.5 Harley-Davidson is the largest American motorcycle manufacturer and has been in business for several decades. Several years ago, Harley-Davidson expanded into "signature" products, such as shirts that prominently display the Harley-Davidson logo. Some people have a negative image of Harley-Davidson because it was the motorcycle favoured by the Hells Angels and other motorcycle gangs. There are two research questions here. First, do consumers have a negative feeling toward Harley-Davidson and, second, are they disinclined to purchase Harley-Davidson signature products such as shirts, belts, boots, jackets, sweatshirts, lighters, and key chains? Design a Likert measurement scale that can be used in a nationwide telephone study to address these two issues.

4.1 How does reliability differ from validity? In your answer, define each term.

4.2 In conducting a survey for the Equitable Insurance Company, Burke Marketing Research assesses reliability by calling back a small group of respondents to readminister five questions. One question asks, "If you were going to buy life insurance sometime this year, how likely would you be to consider the Equitable Company?" Respondents indicate the likelihood on a probability scale (0% to 100% likely). Typically, this test–retest approach finds that respondents are within 10% of their initial response. That is, if respondents indicated that they were 50% likely in the initial survey, they responded in the 45% to 55% range on the retest.

The survey has been going on for four weeks, and it will be two more weeks before the data collection is completed. Respondents who are retested are called back exactly one week after the initial survey. In the last week, reliability results have been very different. Now Burke is finding that the retest averages are 20% higher than the initial test. Has the scale become unreliable? If so, why has its previous good reliability changed? If not, what has happened, and how can Burke still claim that it has a reliable measure?

4.3 General Foods Corporation includes Post, which is the maker of Fruit and Fibre Cereal. The brand manager is interested in determining how much Fruit and Fibre consumers think is helping them toward a healthier diet. But the manager is very concerned that respondents in a survey may not be entirely truthful about health matters. They may exaggerate what they really believe so they "sound" more health conscious than they really are, and they may say they have healthy diets when they really do not.

The General Foods Corporation marketing research director has come up with a unique way to overcome the problem. He suggests that they conduct a survey of Fruit and Fibre customers in Pittsburgh, Atlanta, Dallas, and Denver. Fifty respondents who say that Fruit and Fibre is helping them toward a healthier diet and who also say they are more health conscious than the average American will be selected, and General Foods will offer to "buy" their groceries for the next month. To participate, the chosen respondents must submit their itemized weekly grocery trip receipts. By reviewing the items bought each week, General Foods can determine what they are eating and make judgments on how healthy their diets really are. What is your reaction to this approach? Will General Foods be able to assess the validity of its survey this way? Why, or why not?

# Case 7.1

# Metro Toyota

(The following is a hypothetical case.)

The Metro Toyota dealership, located on the south side of a major metropolitan area, wanted to know how people who intended to buy a new automobile in the next 12 months view their purchase. The general sales manager called the marketing department at the local university and arranged for a class project to be undertaken by undergraduate marketing research students. The professor had a large class that semester, so she decided to divide the project into two groups and to have each group compete against the other to see which one designed and executed the better survey.

Both groups worked diligently on the survey over the semester. They met with the Metro Toyota general sales manager, discussed the dealership with his managers, conducted focus groups, and consulted the research literature on brand, store, and company image. Both teams conducted telephone surveys, whose findings are presented in their final reports.

The marketing research professor offered to grant extra credit to each team if it gave a formal presentation of its research design, findings, and recommendations.

*(Continued)*

**Findings of Marketing Research Teams**
**Team One's Findings for Metro Toyota**
**Importance of Features of Dealership in Deciding to Buy There**

| Feature | Percent Indicating "Yes"[a] |
|---|---|
| Competitive prices | 86% |
| No high pressure | 75% |
| Good service facilities | 73% |
| Low-cost financing | 68% |
| Many models in stock | 43% |
| Convenient location | 35% |
| Friendly salespersons | 32% |

[a]Based on responses to the question "Is/are ____(insert feature)____ important to you when you decide on a dealership from which to purchase your new automobile?"

**Perception of Metro Toyota Dealership Percent Responding "Yes"**

| Feature | Percent Indicating "Yes"[b] |
|---|---|
| Competitive prices | 45% |
| No high pressure | 32% |
| Good service facilities | 80% |
| Low-cost financing | 78% |
| Many models in stock | 50% |
| Convenient location | 81% |
| Friendly salespersons | 20% |

[b]Based on responses to the question "Were you satisfied with Metro Toyota's ____(insert feature)____ when you purchased your new automobile there?"

**Team Two's Findings for Metro Toyota**
**Importance and Image of Metro Toyota Dealership**

| Feature | Importance[c] | Satisfaction[d] |
|---|---|---|
| Competitive prices | 6.5 | 1.3 |
| No high pressure | 6.2 | 3.6 |
| Good service facilities | 5.0 | 4.3 |
| Low-cost financing | 4.7 | 3.9 |
| Many models in stock | 3.1 | 3.0 |
| Convenient location | 2.2 | 4.1 |
| Friendly salespersons | 2.0 | 1.2 |

[c]Based on a 7-point scale where 1 = "unimportant" and 7 = "extremely important."
[d]Based on a 5-point scale where 1 = "completely unsatisfied" and 5 = "completely satisfied."

## Questions

1. Describe the different ways these findings can be presented in graphical form to the Metro Toyota management group. Which student team has the ability to present its findings more effectively? How, and why?

2. What are the managerial implications apparent in each team's findings? Identify the implications and recommendations for Metro Toyota that are evident in each team's findings.

# Case 7.2

# Extreme Exposure Rock Climbing Centre Faces The Krag

(The following case is hyphothetical.)

For the past five years, Extreme Exposure Rock Climbing Centre has enjoyed a monopoly. Located in Canmore, Alberta, Extreme Exposure was the dream of Kyle Anderson, an avid participant in freesyle extreme sports of various types, including outdoor rock climbing, hang-gliding, skydiving, mountan biking, snowboarding, and a number of other adrenalin-pumping sports. Now in his mid-30s, Kyle had come to realize at the age of 30 that after three leg fractures, two broken arms, and numerous dislocations, he could not participate on the extreme edge as he used to. So, he found an abandoned warehouse, recruited two investors and a friendly banker, and opened up Extreme Exposure.

Kyle's rock climbing centre has over 6500 square feet of simulated rock walls to climb, with about 100 different routes up to a maximum of 50 vertical feet. Extreme Exposure's design permits the four major climbing types: top-roping, where the climber climbs up with a rope anchored at the top; lead-climbing, where the climber clips a rope to the wall while ascending; bouldering, where the climber has no rope but stays near the ground; and rapelling, where the person descends quickly by sliding down a rope. Climbers can buy day passes or month-long or annual memberships. Shoes and harnesses can be rented cheaply, and helmets are available free of charge as all climbers must wear protective helmets. In addition to individual and group climbing classes, Extreme Exposure has several group programs, including birthday parties, a kids' summer camp, and corporate team-building classes.

A newspaper article has reported that another rock climbing centre, to be called "The Krag," will be built in Canmore in the next six months. Kyle notes the following items about The Krag that are different from Extreme Exposure: (1) The Krag will have climbs up to a maximum of 60 vertical feet, (2) it will have a climber certification program, (3) there will be day trips to outdoor rock-climbing areas, (4) there will be group overnight and extended-stay rock-climbing trips to the Canadian Rockies, and (5) The Krag's annual membership fee will be about 20% lower than Extreme Exposure's.

Kyle chats with Dianne, one of his Extreme Exposure members who is in marketing, during a break in one of her climbing visits. Dianne summarizes what she believes Kyle needs to find out about his current members. Dianne's list follows:

1. What is the demographic and rock-climbing profile of Extreme Exposure's members?
2. How satisfied are the members with Extreme Exposure's climbing facilities?
3. How interested are its members in (a) day trips to outdoor rock-climbing areas, (b) group overnight and/or extended-stay rock-climbing trips to the Rockies, and (c) a climber certification program?
4. What are members' opinions of the annual membership fee charged by Extreme Exposure?
5. Will members consider leaving Extreme Exposure to join a new rock-climbing centre with climbs that are 10 feet higher than the maximum climb at Extreme Exposure?
6. Will members consider leaving Extreme Exposure to join a new rock-climbing centre with climbs that are 10 feet higher than the maximum climb at Extreme Exposure and whose annual membership fee is 20% lower than Extreme Exposure's?

For each of Dianne's questions, identify the relevant construct and indicate how is should be measured.

*January 6, 2010*

### Stampede Accused of Sexist, Homophobic Market Research

*by Canadian Press*

The Calgary Stampede is distancing itself from controversial statements in a survey it commissioned, some of which are being described as sexist and homophobic.

The Stampede hired Illumina Research Partners to conduct a market research study. While it mostly gauged people's knowledge and opinions of the Stampede, one section asks opinions on a number of statements including, "The only acceptable definition of a family is a husband, wife and children," and "Some jobs are best suited to men. Women should just accept this."

Stampede spokesman Doug Fraser said they didn't create the statements "and they do not reflect the opinions of the Calgary Stampede."

However, he called the research "important" and noted the study provides the Stampede with the detailed information it needs to develop programming, marketing and products "that reflect our rapidly changing community."

Yvonne Brouwers, president of the research firm, said the statements are used by reputable market research firms to get insight into the variety of viewpoints that exist in a population.

"The research model is based on identifying opinions that divide people, so that we can get a better understanding of differences and similarities," she said.

"We've used this type of question for more than 15 years," said Brouwers, who added she has not personally encountered complaints about the statements as anti-gay or anti-woman.

"Many market research firm use these kinds of questions."

Human rights lawyer Mellissa Luhtanen said the two statements were "outdated, discriminatory and irresponsible."

"I think it's clear that they've been using these questions for 15 years because . . . the definition of family is no longer a husband, wife and children," said Luhtanen, who works with the Alberta Civil Liberties Research Centre.

She suggested researchers could have reworded or replaced the statements.

"There are other questions they can ask that aren't disrespectful to a community," she said.

Brouwers said the online survey will still be available for a few days, but by Tuesday evening the site was indicating its quota had been reached.

This is the second of two chapters on the questionnaire design phase. Functions of a questionnaire and the process of developing them are described.

## What Is a Questionnaire and What Steps Are Taken to Develop It?

A **questionnaire** is the vehicle used to pose the questions that the researcher wants respondents to answer. As such, the questionnaire serves important functions. It translates the research objectives into specific questions that are asked of the respondents. It standardizes those questions and the response categories so that every participant responds to identical stimuli. By its wording, question flow, and appearance, it fosters cooperation and keeps respondents motivated throughout the interview. Questionnaires serve as permanent records of the research. Finally, depending on the type of instrument used, the questionnaire can speed up the process of data analysis.

Given that it serves all of these functions, the questionnaire is a very important element in the research process. In fact, studies have shown that questionnaire design directly affects the quality of the data collected. Even experienced interviewers cannot compensate for questionnaire defects.[1] The time and effort invested in developing a good questionnaire are well spent.[2] **Questionnaire design** is a systematic process in which the researcher contemplates various question formats, considers a number of factors characterizing the survey at hand, composes the various questions very carefully, and organizes the questionnaire's layout.

Figure 8.1 offers a flowchart of the various phases in a typical marketing research survey. The first two steps in the flowchart have been covered in previous chapters, but there are some specific activities the research must execute

**Where We Are**
1. Establish the need for marketing research
2. Define the problem
3. Establish research objectives
4. Determine research design
5. Identify information types and sources
6. Determine methods of accessing data
7. Design data collection forms
8. Determine sample plan and size
9. Collect data
10. Analyze data
11. Prepare and present the final research report

**Figure 8.1** Steps in the Questionnaire Development Process.

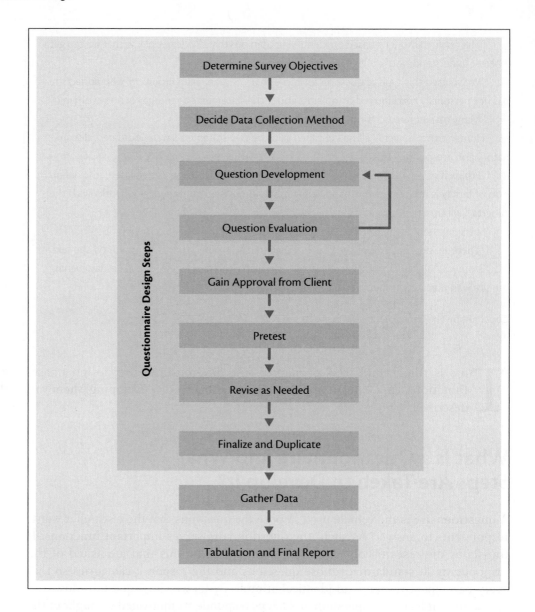

before the questionnaire is finalized. As shown in Figure 8.1, a questionnaire ordinarily goes through a series of drafts before it is in acceptable final form. In fact, even before the first question is constructed, the researcher mentally reviews alternative question formats to decide which ones are best suited to the survey's respondents and circumstances. As the questionnaire begins to take shape, the researcher continually evaluates each question and its response options. Changes are made, and the question's wording is re-evaluated to make sure that it is asking what the researcher intends. Also, the researcher strives to minimize **question bias,** the ability of a question's wording or format to influence respondents' answers.[3]

It is important to know that with a custom-designed research study, the questions on the questionnaire, along with its instructions, introduction, and general layout, are systematically evaluated for potential error and revised accordingly. Generally, this evaluation takes place by the researcher, and the client will not be involved until after the questionnaire has undergone considerable development and evaluation. The client is given the opportunity to review and comment on the questionnaire during the client approval step. This step is essential, and some research companies require the client to sign or initial a copy of the questionnaire as verification of approval. The client may not appreciate all of the technical aspects of questionnaire design but is vitally concerned with the survey's objectives and can comment on the degree to which the questions appear to address these objectives. The first step in questionnaire design is to make a list of information required for each of the research objectives. For example, if the marketing manager for Ombrelle, L'Oréal's line of sun protection products, is interested in consumer awareness of this brand, then a list of information required will include top-of-mind awareness of sun protection products, aided awareness of this brand, and thoughts associated with this brand. Possible questions that could aid in collecting this information are as follows:

1. Thinking about products that are designed to protect your skin from the sun, which ones come to mind?
2. Are there any others? (If Ombrelle is not mentioned, move on to question 3.)
3. Have you heard of Ombrelle?
4. Where have you heard of Ombrelle?
5. How does Ombrelle differ from competitors?
6. If respondent is still unaware of the brand, state that Ombrelle is a line of sun protection products manufactured by L'Oréal, and that it is the sun protection brand most recommended by Canadian dermatologists.[4]

If another research objective was to determine respondents' intent to purchase Ombrelle products, then possible information required includes the price point the respondent is willing to pay for sun protection products, the importance of brand name in the purchase of this product category, and the importance of the key point of difference between this and competitors.

Following client approval, the questionnaire normally undergoes a pretest, which is an actual field test using a very limited sample to reveal any difficulties that might still lurk in wording, instructions, administration, and so on.[5] Revisions are made based on the pretest results, and the questionnaire is finalized.

## Developing Questions

**Question development** is the practice of selecting appropriate response formats for each question and wording questions so that they are understandable, unambiguous, and unbiased. Marketing researchers are very concerned with developing research questions because they measure (1) attitudes, (2) beliefs, (3) behaviours, and (4) demographics,[6] and they desire reliable and valid answers to their questions. Although open-ended questions are valuable when exploring topics, it is desirable to have predefined answer options (closed-ended). This is because open-ended questions can be more time consuming to quantify and analyze. During a pretest, common themes to open-ended questions are discovered. These themes are then translated into predefined answer options. Question development is challenging but absolutely vital to the success of the survey.

Consider the following question:

---

Have you stopped trying to beat red traffic lights when you think you have the chance?

_____ Yes _____ No

---

The wording is ambiguous and biased. A "yes" response means the respondent used to speed up when the traffic light showed yellow. A "no" response means the respondent is still taking chances. Regardless of the answer, one concludes everyone drives recklessly. As this is not true, the question is biased.

Other ambiguous words that should be avoided are *usually*, *normally*, *frequently*, *often*, *regularly*, and *occasionally*.

Developing a question's precise wording is not easy. A single word can make a difference in how study participants respond to a question, and there is considerable research to illustrate this. In one study, researchers changed only one word. They asked, "Did you see *the* broken headlight?" to one group of participants, and asked, "Did you see *a* broken headlight?" to another group. Only the "the" and the "a" were different, yet the question containing the "the" produced more "Don't know" and "Yes" answers than did the "a" question.[7] As little as one word in a question can result in question bias that distorts the findings of the survey. Unfortunately, commonly used words sometimes encourage biased answers when they appear on a questionnaire. Table 8.1 lists 10 words to avoid in question development.[8] While these words are used in everyday language, they can introduce an element of bias into a questionnaire because respondents are using a literal interpretation in their efforts to answer the questions.

"Did you see the broken headlight?"

**Table 8.1** Ten Words to Avoid in Question Development: Example in a Survey Performed with Home Theatre System Purchasers

| Word | Poor Wording | Why the Wording Is Poor | Better Wording |
|------|-------------|------------------------|----------------|
| *All* | Did you consider all options before you decided to purchase your home theatre system? | There may be a huge number of options or too many for a consumer to even know about, let alone consider one by one. | What options did you consider when you decided to purchase your home theatre system? |
| *Always* | Do you always buy audio products from Bose? | "Always" means every purchase every time with no exceptions. | How often do you buy audio products from Bose? |
| *Any* | Did you have any concerns about the price? | Even the smallest concern qualifies as "any," and small concerns are usually insignificant. | To what extent was the price a concern for you? |
| *Anybody* | Did you talk to anybody about home theatre systems before you made your decision? | This includes family, friends, co-workers, sales personnel, neighbours, parents, teachers, and anybody else on the planet. | Which of the following people did you talk with about home theatre systems before you made your decision? (Likely parties such as spouse, co-workers, etc. are listed.) |
| *Best* | What is the best feature on your new home theatre system? | "Best" implies that there is a single feature that stands out, but it is possible that features were of equal importance or that combinations of features are important. | Please rate the following features of our new home theatre system on their performance for you using "poor," "fair," "good," or "excellent." |
| *Ever* | Have you ever seen a home theatre system? | "Ever" means on any occasion in one's past lifetime. | Have you seen a home theatre system in the past 30 days? |
| *Every* | Do you consult *Consumer Reports* every time you purchase a major item? | "Every" means without fail, or otherwise no way without doing this. | How often do you consult *Consumer Reports* when you purchase a major item? |
| *Most* | What was the most important factor that convinced you it was time to make this purchase? | There may not be a single most important factor; there may be factors of equal importance, or there may be combinations of factors that are relevant. | Please rate the following factors on their importance in convincing you it was time to purchase a home theatre system using "unimportant," "slightly important," or "very important." |
| *Never* | Would you say that you never think about an extended warranty when making a major electronics purchase? | "Never" means not ever, without fail. | How often do you consider an extended warranty when making a major electronics purchase? |
| *Worst* | Is the high price the worst aspect of purchasing a home theatre system? | There may not be a single bad or worst factor; there may be ties for last place or combinations of factors that make for "worst" aspects. | To what extent did the high price concern you when you were considering the purchase of your home theatre system? |

Why avoid these words? The words are **extreme absolutes**, meaning that they place respondents in a situation where they must either agree fully or completely disagree with the extreme position in the question.

It is important that questions do not contain subtle cues, signals, or interpretations that lead respondents to give answers that are inaccurate. Not all respondents are influenced by question wording, but if a significant minority is affected, this bias can cause the findings to be distorted or mixed.

In global marketing research, how can a manager avoid question bias when he or she does not speak the language of the respondents? A researcher working with Air Canada might need to design a survey with respondents who speak only one of the following languages: English, French, Spanish, Italian, Dutch, German, or Russian. One solution might be to design the questionnaire in some "universal" language, such as English, that many non–native English speakers can read. This approach is generally unsatisfactory because there are many opportunities for miscommunication. Instead, global marketing researchers use the following when attempting to do across-the-globe research:

- Create the questionnaire in the researcher's native language (e.g., English)
- Translate the questionnaire into the other language (e.g., German)
- Have independent translators translate it back into the native language (e.g., from German to English) to check that the first translation was accurate
- Revise the questionnaire based on the "back translation" (into a better German version)
- If an online survey is used, make certain the words and characters are accurate for the local language (e.g., Chinese, Japanese)
- Carefully pretest the revised questionnaire using individuals whose native tongue is the other language (e.g., natives of Germany)

## Four "Do's" of Question Wording

**Question evaluation** consists of scrutinizing the wording of a question to ensure that question bias is minimized and the wording is such that respondents understand the question and can respond to it with relative ease. Question bias occurs when the phrasing of a question influences a respondent to answer unreliably or inaccurately. Ideally, every question should be examined and tested according to a number of crucial factors known to be related to question bias. Four simple guidelines, or "do's," for question wording are that the question should be (1) focused, (2) brief, (3) simple, and (4) crystal clear.

### The Question Should Be Focused on a Single Issue or Topic

The researcher must stay focused on the specific issue or topic. For example, consider the question "What type of hotel do you usually stay in when on a trip?" The focus of this question is hazy because it does not narrow down the type of trip or when the hotel is being used. Is it a business trip or a pleasure trip? Is the hotel at a place en route or at the final destination? A more focused version of the question is, "When you are on a family vacation and stay in a hotel at your destination, what type of hotel do you typically use?" As a second example, consider how "unfocused" the following question is: "When do you typically go to work?" Does this mean when do you leave home for work or when do you actually begin work once at your workplace? A better question would be, "At what time do you ordinarily leave home for work?"

### The Question Should Be Brief

Unnecessary and redundant words should always be eliminated. This requirement is especially important when designing questions that will be administered verbally, such as over the telephone. Brevity will help the respondent understand the central question and reduce the distraction of wordiness. Here is a question that suffers from too many words: "What are the considerations that would come to your mind while you are confronted with the decision to have some type of repair done on the automatic icemaker in your refrigerator, assuming that you noticed it was not making ice cubes as well as it did when you first bought it?" A better, brief form is, "If your icemaker was not working correctly, how would you fix the problem?"

### The Question Should Be a Grammatically Simple Sentence If Possible

A simple sentence is preferred because it has only a single subject and predicate, whereas compound and complex sentences are busy with multiple subjects, predicates, objects, and complements. The more complex the sentence, the greater the potential for respondent error. There are more conditions to remember and more information to consider simultaneously, so the respondent's attention may wane or he or she may concentrate on only one part of the question. To avoid these problems, the researcher should strive to use only simple sentence structure; however, sometimes two separate sentences are necessary. For example, consider the question: "If you were looking for an automobile that would be used by the head of your household who is primarily responsible for driving your children to and from school, music lessons, and friends' houses, how much would you and your spouse discuss the safety features of one of the cars you took for a test-drive?" A simpler approach is, "Would you and your spouse discuss the safety features of a new family car?" If the respondent answered "yes," a second question could be, "To what extent would you discuss safety?

### The Question Should Be Crystal Clear

All respondents should interpret the question identically. For example, the question "How many children do you have?" might be interpreted in various ways. One respondent might think of only those children living at home, whereas another might include children from a previous marriage. A better question is, "How many children under the age of 18 live with you in your home?" One tactic for clarity is to develop questions that use words in respondents' core vocabularies. The general public does not use marketing jargon such as "price point" or "brand equity." It is best to avoid words that are vague or open to misinterpretations. Question clarity can be obtained with an economical number of words.[9]

## Four "Do Nots" of Question Wording

There are four situations in which question bias is assured. Avoid them or spot them when reviewing a questionnaire draft. Specifically, the question should not be (1) leading, (2) loaded, (3) double-barrelled, or (4) overstated.

### The Question Should Not "Lead" the Respondent to a Particular Answer

A **leading question** is worded or structured in such a way as to give the respondent a strong cue or expectation as to the answer. Consider this question: "Don't you see any problems with using your credit card for an online purchase?" The question wording stresses the negative side of the issue. Therefore, the question "leads" respondents to believe there must be some problems with online purchases. Respondents will likely agree with the question, particularly those who have no opinion. Rephrasing the question as, "Do you see any problems with using your credit card for an online purchase?" is a more objective request of the respondent. Here the respondent is free—that is, not led—to respond "yes" or "no." Examine the following questions for other forms of leading questions:

| | |
|---|---|
| As a Cadillac owner, you are satisfied with your car, aren't you? | This is a leading question because the wording presupposes that all Cadillac owners are satisfied. It places the respondent in a situation where disagreement is uncomfortable and singles him or her out as being different. |
| Have you heard about the satellite radio system that everyone is talking about? | This is a leading question because it can influence the respondent to answer in a socially desirable manner. Few people would want to admit they are clueless about something "everybody is talking about."[10] |

Read Ethics in Marketing Research 8.1 for more examples of leading questions.

## ETHICS IN MARKETING RESEARCH 8.1
# The Many Ways That a Question Can Be Leading

Marketing and public opinion research associations consider deceptive practices such as leading questions to be unethical. Actually, our definition of a leading question is rather simple, and some authors have recently come up with a more complete definition.

*A leading question is an interrogatory making use of a biasing mechanism. This mechanism may come in any one of, or any combination of, three forms: question structure; question content; question delivery.*

This more formal definition of a leading question reveals that there are three different ways that a question can lead or strongly influence the respondent to give a particular answer. It can lead with form, facts, or phonics. Each is described in the following table. For each type, we have provided an example using the subject of fast food and overweight consumers.

As can be seen from the expanded definition of a "leading question" and these examples, there are many obvious as well as many subtle ways a question may lead a respondent to answer in a particular way. From an ethical point of view, it is vital that marketing researchers examine their questions carefully and remove any elements of bias such as these.

### Leading by *Form* (Question Structure)

*Common ways to make the form of the question leading include crafting a question that:*

1. *Includes the answer in the question*

2. *Uses logic or apparent logic to steer the respondent to an answer (parallel examples)*

3. *Presumes the truth of an answer, or the truth of something logically leading to an answer*

*Examples*

1. *Don't you think that fast foods have too many calories?*

2. *Since most fast foods are fried, shouldn't these companies put warnings on their labels?*

3. *Since McDonald's is the largest fast-food company, shouldn't it set the example for more nutritious meals?*

### Leading with *Facts* (Question Content)

*Common ways to use facts to make a question leading would be to include:*

1. *Unsupported assertions presented as facts*

2. *Supported facts (or points presented as supported) presented in an unbalanced fashion*

3. *Loaded words or broadly held beliefs that generate an emotional or cognitive impetus toward an answer*

*Examples*

1. *Since everyone buys fast foods, shouldn't everyone be concerned about nutrition?*

2. *Since studies have shown that overweight children buy fast foods, shouldn't "kids meals" be healthier?*

3. *Do you think that Kentucky Fried Chicken should have warnings for obese people suffering from deadly diseases such as diabetes?*

### Leading with *Phonics* (Question Delivery)

*Common ways to use phonics (or context) to make a question leading include:*

1. *Make respondents aware of the desired outcome of, or "purpose" for, the survey*

2. *Make respondents aware of the sponsor*

3. *Use preceding questions to set up assumptions in the mind of the respondent*

*Examples*

1. *Will you take part in our survey that will alert consumers to the dangers of fast food?*

2. *Our survey is sponsored by the Vegetarian Council.*

3. *Since you have agreed that fast-food consumption contributes to eating disorders, shouldn't fast-food companies take responsibility for correcting them?*

## The Question Should Not Have "Loaded" Wording or Phrasing

Leading questions are biased in that they direct the respondent to answer in a predetermined way. **Loaded questions** have buried in their wording subtle references to universal beliefs or rules of behaviour. For example, a company marketing mace for personal use may use the question: "Should people be allowed to protect themselves from harm by using mace as self-defence?" Most respondents will agree with the need to protect oneself from harm, and self-defence is an acceptable defence. To remove the loading aspect, the question should be rephrased: "Do you think carrying a mace product is acceptable for people who are worried about being attacked?" The phrasing of each question should be examined thoroughly to guard against the various sources of question bias error. Many researchers use "experts" to review drafts of their questionnaires to avoid loaded questions. For example, it is common

"Which one of these questions should I answer?"

for the questionnaire to be designed by one employee of the research company and then given to another employee for a thorough inspection.

### The Question Should Not Be "Double-Barrelled"

A **double-barrelled question** is really two different questions posed in one question. With two questions posed together, it is difficult for a respondent to answer either one directly. Consider a question asked of customers at a restaurant: "Were you satisfied with the food and service?" If they say "yes," does that mean they were satisfied with the food? The service? A combination? The question would be much improved by asking about a single item: one question for food and another question for service. Sometimes double-barrelled questions are not as obvious. Look at the following question designed to ask for occupational status:

> Which term best describes you?
>
> _____ Employed full-time
>
> _____ Full-time student
>
> _____ Part-time student
>
> _____ Unemployed
>
> _____ Retired

How does one who is retired and a full-time student answer the question? An improvement is to ask one question about occupational status and another about student status.[11]

### The Question Should Not Use Words That Overstate the Condition

An **overstated question** is one that places undue emphasis on some aspect of the topic. It uses what might be considered "dramatics" to describe the topic. Avoid using words that overstate conditions. It is better to present the question in a

Asking someone how much they would pay for a pair of sunglasses that would help prevent blindness is an overstatement.

neutral tone rather than in a strong positive or negative tone. Here is an example of an overstated question that might be found in a survey conducted for Ray-Ban sunglasses: "How much do you think you would pay for a pair of sunglasses that will protect your eyes from the sun's harmful ultraviolet rays, which are known to cause blindness?" As you can see, the overstatement concerns the effects of ultraviolet rays, and because of this overstatement, respondents think about how much they would pay for something that can prevent blindness and not about how much they would really pay for the sunglasses. A more toned-down and acceptable question wording would be, "How much would you pay for sunglasses that will protect your eyes from the sun's rays?"

Use common sense in developing questions. For example, it is nonsensical to ask respondents questions about details they do not usually recall ("How many and what brands of pain relievers did you see the last time you bought some?"), questions that invite guesses ("What is the price per gallon of premium gasoline at the gas station on the corner?"), or questions that ask them to predict their actions in circumstances they cannot imagine ("How often would you go out to eat at this new, upscale restaurant that will be built 10 kilometres from your home?").

There are unfortunate cases in which questionnaire designers have deliberately used leading questions, loaded questions, or some other question wording that is biased in order to influence the survey's findings to support a particular point of view. This practice is considered unethical in marketing research. Table 8.2 provides several examples of poor question wording.

## Questionnaire Organization

Normally, the researcher creates questions by taking the research objectives one at a time and developing the questions that relate to each objective. In other words, the questions are developed but not organized. **Questionnaire organization** is the sequence of statements and questions that make a questionnaire. Questionnaire organization is an important concern because the questionnaire's appearance and the ease with which respondents complete the questions have the potential to affect

**Table 8.2 Examples of Do's and Do Nots for Question Wording**

| Do or Do Not Guideline | Bad Question | Better Question |
|---|---|---|
| Do: Be Focused | How do you feel about your automobile's GPS system? | Please rate your automobile's GPS system on each of the following features. (Features are listed.) |
| Do: Be Brief | When traffic conditions are bad, do you or do you not rely on your automobile's GPS system to find the fastest way to work? | Does your autmobile GPS system help you arrive at work on time? (Yes, No, Don't know) |
| Do: Use Simple Structure | If you needed to find your child's best friend's house that was over 10 kilometres from your house for your child to attend a birthday party, would you rely on your automobile GPS system to get you there? | How often would you rely on your automobile GPS system to find a person's house? (Rated scale) |
| Do: Be Crystal Clear | Is your automobile GPS system useful? | How useful is your automobile GPS system for each of the following occasions? (Rated scale for a list of occassions) |
| Do Not: Lead | Shouldn't everyone have a GPS system in their automobile? | How helpful is an automobile GPS system? (Scaled response) |
| Do Not: Load | If GPS systems were shown to help us decrease our depletion of world oil reserves, would you purchase one? | Do you think an automobile GPS system might save you on gasoline? (Yes, No, Don't know) |
| Do Not: Double-Barrel | Would you consider purchasing an automobile GPS system if it saved you time, money, and worry? | Would you consider buying an automobile GPS system if it reduced your commuting time by 10%? (Separate questions about money and worry.) (Yes, No, Don't know) |
| Do Not: Overstate | Do you think that an autobile GPS system can help you avoid traffic jams that may last for hours? | To what extent do you believe an automobile GPS system will help you avoid traffic congestion? (Rated scale) |

the quality of the information that is gathered. Well-organized questionnaires motivate respondents to be conscientious, while those that are poorly organized discourage and frustrate respondents, and may even cause them to stop answering questions in the middle of the survey. Two critical aspects of questionnaire organization are the introduction and the actual flow of questions in the questionnaire body.

## The Introduction

The introduction is very important in questionnaire design. If the introduction is written to accompany a mail survey or online survey, it is referred to as a **cover letter**. If the introduction is to be verbally presented to a potential respondent, as in the case of a personal or telephone interview, it is referred to as the opening comments. Each survey and its target respondent group are unique, so a researcher cannot use a standardized introduction. Table 8.3 lists five functions of the introduction and provides examples of sentences found in a survey on personal money management software.

**Table 8.3** The Functions of the Questionnaire Introduction

| Function | Example | Explanation |
|---|---|---|
| Identifies the surveyor/sponsor. | "Hello, my name is ____, and I am a telephone interviewer working with Nationwide Opinion Research Company here in Ottawa. I am not selling anything." | The sponsor of the survey is divulged, plus the prospective respondent is made aware that this is a bona fide survey and not a sales pitch. |
| Indicates the purpose of the survey. | "We are conducting a survey on money management software used by individuals." | Informs prospective respondent of the topic and the reason for the call. |
| Explains how the respondent was selected. | "Your telephone number was generated randomly by a computer." | Notifies prospective respondent how he or she was chosen to be in the survey. |
| Requests/provides incentive for participation. | "This is an anonymous survey, and I would now like to ask you a few questions about your experiences with money management computer programs. Is now a good time?" | Asks for prospective respondent's agreement to take part in the survey at this time. (Also, here, notes anonymity to gain cooperation.) |
| Determines if respondent is suitable. | "Do you use Quicken or Microsoft Money?" | Determines if prospective respondent is qualified to take part in the survey; those who do not use either program will be screened out. |

First, it is common courtesy to introduce oneself at the beginning of a survey. Additionally, the sponsor of the survey should be identified. There are two options with respect to sponsor identity. With an **undisguised survey**, the sponsoring company is identified, but with a **disguised survey**, the sponsor's name is not divulged to respondents. The choice of which approach to take depends on the survey's objectives and on whether disclosure of the sponsor's name or true intent can in some way influence respondents' answers. Another reason for disguise is to prevent alerting competitors to the survey.

Second, the general purpose of the survey should be described clearly and simply. In a cover letter, the purpose may be expressed in one or two sentences. Typically, communicating specific purposes of the survey is unnecessary as it would be boring and perhaps intimidating to list all of the research objectives. Consider a bank having a survey conducted by a marketing research firm. The actual purpose of the survey is to determine the bank's image relative to that of its competitors. However, the research firm need only say, "We are conducting a survey on customers' perceptions of financial institutions in this area." This satisfies the respondent's curiosity and does not divulge the name of the bank.

Third, prospective respondents must be made aware of how and why they were selected. Just a short sentence to answer the respondent's mental question "Why me?" will suffice. Telling respondents that they were "selected at random" usually is sufficient if this selection method is used. If the selection was not random, the researchers should inform them as to which method was used.

Fourth, prospective respondents must be asked to participate in the survey. With a mail survey, the cover letter might end with, "Please take five minutes to complete the attached questionnaire, and mail it back to us in the postage-paid, preaddressed envelope provided." If you are conducting a personal interview or a telephone interview, you might say something like, "Do you have 10 minutes to answer some questions about...?" You should be as brief as possible yet let the respondent know that you are getting ready for him or her to participate by answering questions. This is also the appropriate time to offer an incentive to participate. **Incentives** are offers to do something for the respondents in exchange for their time and participation. Incentives are found to increase participation. There are various incentives that may be used by the researcher to encourage participation. Examples are offering money, a sample of a product, or a copy of study results. Other incentives encourage participation by letting respondents know the importance of their participation: "You are one of a select few, randomly chosen, to express your views on a new type of automobile tire." Or the topic itself can be highlighted for importance: "It is important that consumers let companies know whether or not they are satisfied."

Privacy is an important incentive to encourage participation. There are two methods of ensuring privacy. One method is **anonymity**, in which the respondent is assured that neither the respondent's name nor any identifying designation will be associated with his or her responses. The second method is **confidentiality**, which means that the respondent's name is known by the researcher, but it is not divulged to a third party—namely, the client. Anonymous surveys are most appropriate in data collection modes where the respondent answers directly on the questionnaire. Any self-administered survey qualifies for anonymity as long as the respondent does not indicate his or her identity and provided the questionnaire does not have any identification-tracing mechanism. However, when an interviewer is used, appointments or callbacks are usually necessary, so there typically is an explicit designation of the respondent's name, address, telephone number, and so forth on the questionnaire. In this case, confidentiality may be required. Often questionnaires have a callback notation area for the interviewer to make notes indicating, for instance, whether the phone is busy, the respondent is not at home, or a time at which to call back when the respondent will be available. In this case, it is vital that the researcher guard against the loss of that confidentiality.

A fifth function of the introduction is to qualify prospective respondents. Respondents are screened for their appropriateness to take part in the survey. **Screening questions** are used to eliminate people who do not meet qualifications necessary to take part in the research study.[12] Whether you screen respondents depends on the research objectives. If the survey's objective is to determine factors used by consumers to select an automobile dealer for purchasing a new car, the researcher might want to screen out those who have never purchased a new car or those who have not purchased a new car within the last two years, by asking, "Have you purchased a new car within the last two years?" For all those who answer "no," the survey is terminated with a polite "Thank you for your time." Some would argue that the screening question should be asked early on so as not to waste the time of the researcher or the respondent. Others feel that screening questions are better placed later in the introduction. Marketing Research in Action 8.1 presents various ways to organize questions in a questionnaire.

# MARKETING RESEARCH IN ACTION 8.1
## Approaches to Question Block Organization on a Questionnaire

The flow of questions we have described in this chapter is generally used by questionnaire designers. Given a great many questions, it is often possible to think of the questionnaire in terms of "blocks" of similar questions, such as demographic questions, usage questions, opinion questions, and so forth. We will describe three of the approaches to block organization: the funnel approach, the work approach, and the sections approach.

The **funnel approach** is the simplest and uses a wide-to-narrow or general-to-specific flow of questions that places general inquiries at the beginning of a topic on the questionnaire and those requiring more specific and detailed responses later on.[13] That is, the questionnaire begins (after the screens) with a block of general and easy-to-answer questions and proceeds to a block of more detailed questions.[14] The most specific questions are personal demographic questions located at the end of the questionnaire.

The **work approach** is employed when the researcher realizes that respondents will need to apply a different amount of mental effort to various blocks of questions. When questions tap responses that are deeper than simple recall, respondents must apply a higher degree of concentration in answering them. As we have specified in our recommendations on question flow, difficult questions are placed deep in the questionnaire. As a rule, nominal-scale questions are easier to answer than either scaled-response or open-ended questions. Open-ended questions are thought to be the most taxing questions for respondents. In fact, some researchers recommend rarely using open-ended questions or using a minimum of open-ended questions.[15] As just noted, when respondents encounter the work question block(s), they should be caught up in the responding mode or otherwise committed to completing the questionnaire. If this is the case, respondents will be more inclined to expend the extra effort necessary to answer them.

Another organization scheme is to arrange the questions in logical sets on the questionnaire, which is referred to as the **sections approach**. A sections approach organizes questions into sets based on the common objective of the questions in the set. This approach is particularly useful when the researcher is investigating several topics with a block of questions for each topic. By using sections, the researcher has a structure to cover all of the topics, and the respondent's focus is concentrated on that topic in the section question block. For example, several questions may measure media habits, others may measure frequency of purchasing different products, and other sets of questions may measure preferences for restaurant services and features. Sometimes the research objectives define the sections. Sections could also be based on question format, for example, placing all Likert questions in one section.

Which approach is best? There is no single format that fits all cases. In fact, the three approaches we have just described are not mutually exclusive, and a researcher may use a combination of approaches in a single questionnaire. A researcher may find that the survey topics influence the placement or approach used in question flow.[16] However, although any one or a combination of these approaches may be used, the guiding principle should be which approach best facilitates respondents in answering the questions. Researchers can analyze questions in any sequence they wish; it is the respondents who are important here.

As we indicated earlier, designing a questionnaire is a blend of creativity and adherence to simple, common-sense guidelines. The most important idea to keep in mind, though, is to design the questionnaire's flow of questions so as to make it respondent-friendly by minimizing the amount of effort necessary to respond while maximizing the probability that each respondent will fill it out reliably, accurately, and completely.[17, 18] To achieve these results, the researcher selects logical response formats, provides clear directions, makes the questionnaire visually appealing, and numbers all sections plus all items in each section.[19]

Developing the introduction should take as much care and effort as developing the questions on the questionnaire. The first words heard or read by the prospective respondent will largely determine whether he or she will take part in the survey. A cover letter or opening should have a maximum chance of eliciting the respondent's willingness to take part in the survey. If the researcher is unsuccessful in persuading prospective respondents to take part in the survey, all of his or her work on the questionnaire itself will have been in vain.

## Question Flow

**Question flow** is the sequencing of questions, including any instructions, on the questionnaire. To facilitate respondents' ease in answering questions, the organization of questions should follow some understandable logic. A commonly used sequence of questions is presented in Table 8.4. To begin, the first few questions are normally screening questions that determine whether the potential respondent qualifies to participate in the survey. They are based on certain selection criteria that the researcher has deemed essential. Of course, not all surveys have screening questions. A survey of all charge account customers for a department store, for example, may not require screening questions. This is true because, in a sense, all potential respondents have already been qualified by virtue of having charge accounts with the store.

**Table 8.4 The Location of Questions on a Questionnaire Should Be Logical**

| Question Type | Question Location | Examples | Rationale |
|---|---|---|---|
| Screens | First questions asked | "Have you shopped at Gap in the past month?" "Is this your first visit to this store?" | Used to select the respondent types desired by the researcher to be in the survey |
| Warm-ups | Immediately after any screens | "How often do you go shopping?" "On what days of the week do you usually shop?" | Easy to answer; shows respondent that survey is easy to complete; generates interest |
| Transitions (statements and questions) | Prior to major sections of questions or changes in question format | "Now, for the next few questions, I want to ask about your family's TV viewing habits." "Next, I am going to read several statements and, after each, I want you to tell me if you agree or disagree with this statement." | Notifies respondent that the subject or format of the following questions will change |
| Complicated and difficult-to-answer questions | Middle of the questionnaire; close to the end | "Rate each of the following 10 stores on the friendliness of their salespeople on a scale of 1 to 7." "How likely are you to purchase each of the following items in the next three months?" | Respondent has committed himself or herself to completing the questionnaire; can see (or is told) that there are not many questions left |
| Classification and demographic questions | Last section | "What is the highest level of education you have attained?" | Questions that are "personal" and possibly offensive are placed at the end of the questionnaire |

Once the individual is qualified by the screening questions, the next questions serve a "warm-up" function. **Warm-up questions** are simple and easy-to-answer questions that spark respondents' interest. They also serve to demonstrate how easy it is to do the survey. Ideally, warm-up questions relate to the research objectives. If the first question dealing with a research objective is difficult, a warm-up question may be used to heighten the respondent's interest so that he or she will be more inclined to deal with the harder questions that follow.

**Transitions** are statements or questions telling the respondent that changes in question topic or format are forthcoming. A statement such as, "Now I would like to ask you a few questions about your family's TV viewing habits," is an example of a transition statement. Such statements help ensure that the respondent understands the line of questioning. Transitions include "skip" questions. A **skip question** is one whose answer affects which question will be answered next. For example, a transition question may be, "The last time you baked a cake, did you do it from scratch, or did you use a box mix?" If the person responds that he or she used a box mix, questions asking more details about baking from scratch are not appropriate, and the questionnaire will instruct the respondent (or the interviewer, if one is being used) to skip over or to bypass inappropriate questions.

It is good practice to "bury" complicated and difficult-to-answer questions deep in the questionnaire. Scaled-response questions such as semantic differential scales, Likert-type response scales, or other questions that require some degree of mental activity such as evaluation, voicing opinions, recalling past experiences, indicating intentions, or responding to "what if" questions are found later for at least two reasons. First, by the time the respondent has arrived at these questions, he or she has answered several relatively easy questions and is now more commited to completing the survey. Second, if the questionnaire is self-administered or online, the respondent can see that only a few sections of questions remain to be answered—the end is in sight, so to speak. If the survey is being administered by an interviewer, the questionnaire will typically have prompts for the interviewer to notify the respondent that the interview is in its last stages. Also, experienced interviewers can sense when respondents' interest levels sag, and they may voice their own prompts, if permitted, to keep the respondent on task.

The last section of a questionnaire is traditionally reserved for classification questions. **Classification questions**, sometimes called demographic questions, are used to classify respondents into various groups for purposes of analysis. For instance, the researcher may want to classify respondents into categories based on age, gender, income level, and so on. The placement of demographic questions at the end of the questionnaire is useful because some respondents will consider certain demographic questions "personal," and they may refuse to give answers to questions about the highest level of education they attained, their income level, or their marital status. If these questions were asked at the very beginning, the interview would begin on a negative vein, perhaps causing the person to think the survey will be asking many personal questions, and the respondent will likely refuse to take part in the survey at that point. Online Application 8.1 directs you to a website where you can evaluate questionnaires designed by students.

## ONLINE APPLICATION 8.1
## Evaluate Student-Designed Questionnaires

Go to **www.my3q.com**. This website hosts several questionnaires designed by students for their research. Under "What's New," click on a title of your choice. Print the questionnaire that pops up.

1.   Identify "do's" of questionnaire wording that the authors may have used in the questionnaire.

2.   Identify any "do nots" of questionnaire wording that the authors may have used in the questionnaire.

Comment on the flow of questions. Is there anything you would change? Give reasons for your suggestions.

## Precoding the Questionnaire

A final task in questionnaire design is **precoding** questions, which is the placement of numbers on the question responses to facilitate data entry after the survey has been conducted. The primary objective of precoding is to associate each possible response with a unique number, because numbers are easier and faster to keystroke into a computer file. Also, computer tabulation programs are more efficient when they process numbers rather than words. Table 8.5 illustrates code designations for selected questions. When words such as "yes" and "no" are used as literal response categories, precodes are normally placed alongside each response and in parentheses. For labelled scales, precoded numbers match the direction of the scale. For example, in question 3 in Table 8.5, the precodes are 1–4, to match the Poor–Excellent direction of the scale. Another example is a Strongly Disagree–Strongly Agree scale where the precodes would be 1–5. With scaled-response questions, the numbers are already on the questionnaire, so there is no need to use precodes for these questions.

Occasionally, a researcher uses an **"all that apply" question** that asks the respondent to select more than one item from a list of possible responses. This is the case in question 4 in Table 8.5. With "all that apply" questions, the standard approach is to have each response category coded with a 0 or a 1. The designation "0" will be used if the category is not checked, whereas a "1" is used if it is checked by a respondent. It is as though the researcher asked each item in the list with a yes/no response (e.g., Do you usually order green pepper as topping? ____ No [0] ____ Yes [1]).

It is becoming less common to see precodes on the final questionnaire as the marketing research industry moves toward more high-tech questionnaire design and administration. There is no need for precodes on a questionnaire using computer-assisted questionnaire design programs, because the codes are embedded in the software instructions. Still, the researcher must know how to code the responses.

**Table 8.5** Examples of Precodes on the Final Questionnaire

1. Have you purchased a Godfather's pizza in the last month?

_____ Yes (1)    _____ No (2)    _____ Not Sure (3)

2. The last time you bought a Godfather's pizza, did you (check only one):

_____ Have it delivered to your house?    (1)

_____ Have it delivered to your place of work?    (2)

_____ Pick it up yourself?    (3)

_____ Eat it at the pizza parlour?    (4)

_____ Purchase it some other way?    (5)

3. In your opinion, the taste of a Godfather's pizza is (check only one):

_____ Poor (1)    _____ Fair (2)    _____ Good (3)    _____ Excellent (4)

4. Which of the following toppings do you typically have on your pizza? (Check all that apply.)

_____ Green pepper    (0;1)

_____ Onion    (0;1)

_____ Mushroom    (0;1)    (Note: The 0;1 indicates the coding system that will be used Typically, no

_____ Sausage    (0;1)    precode such as this is placed on the questionnaire. Each response category

_____ Pepperoni    (0;1)    must be defined as a separate question.)

_____ Hot peppers    (0;1)

_____ Black olives    (0;1)

_____ Anchovies    (0;1)

5. How do you rate the speediness of Godfather's in-restaurant service once you have ordered?

(Circle the appropriate number if a 1 means very slow and a 7 means very fast.)

| Very Slow | 1 | 2 | 3 | 4 | 5 | 6 | 7 | Very Fast |
|---|---|---|---|---|---|---|---|---|

6. Please indicate your age: _____ Years (Note: No precode is used, as the respondent will write in a two-digit number.)

7. Please indicate your gender.

_____ Male (1)    _____ Female (2)

# Computer-Assisted Questionnaire Design

**Computer-assisted questionnaire design** refers to software programs that allow researchers to use computer technology to develop and distribute questionnaires and, in some cases, to retrieve and analyze data gathered by the questionnaire. Several companies have developed computer software that bridges the gap between composing questions on a word processor and generating the final, polished version complete with check boxes, radio buttons, and coded questions. Most of these software programs allow users to publish their questionnaires on the internet and enable respondents to enter responses online. Collected data are then downloaded and made available for analysis. Practically all of these special-purpose personal computer programs generate data files that can be exported in Excel-readable format. Computer-assisted questionnaire design is easy, fast, friendly, and flexible.

## Questionnaire Creation

Typical computer-assisted questionnaire design programs ask the researcher about types of question, number of response categories, if skips are to be used, and how response options will appear on the questionnaire. The survey creation feature sometimes appears on a menu of choices, or it might appear as a sequence of format inquiries for each section of the questionnaire. Usually the program offers a list of question types such as closed-ended, open-ended, numeric, or scaled-response questions. The program may even have a question library feature that provides "standard" questions on constructs that researchers often measure, such as demographics, importance, satisfaction, performance, or usage. An advanced feature allows the researcher to upload graphic files of various types if they are part of the research objectives. Most computer-assisted questionnaire design programs are quite flexible and allow the user to modify question formats, build blocks or matrices of questions with the identical response format, include an introduction and instructions to specific questions, and move the location of questions with great ease. Often the appearance can be modified to the designer's preferences for font, background, colour, and more.

## Data Collection and Creation of Data Files

Computer-assisted questionnaire design programs create online survey questionnaires that are published on the internet. Once there, the survey is ready for respondents who are alerted to the online survey with whatever communication methods the researcher wishes to use. Each respondent accesses the online questionnaire, registers responses to the questions, and, typically, clicks on a "Submit" button at the end of the questionnaire. The submit signal prompts the program to write the respondent's answers into a data file, so the data file grows in direct proportion to and at the same rate as respondents submit their surveys. Features that block multiple submissions by the same respondent, such as requesting an email address, are often available. The data file can be downloaded at the researcher's discretion and, usually, several different formats, including Excel-readable ones, are available.

## Data Analysis and Graphs

Many of the software programs for questionnaire design also have provisions for data analysis, graphic presentation, and report formats of results. Some packages offer only simplified graphing capabilities, whereas others offer different statistical analysis options. It is very useful to researchers to monitor the survey's progress with these features. The graph features vary, and some of these programs enable users to create professional-quality graphs that can be saved or embedded in word processor report files.

# Performing the Pretest of the Questionnaire

Before finalizing the questionnaire, one last evaluation should be conducted on the entire questionnaire. Such an evaluation uses a pretest to ensure that the questions will accomplish what is expected of them. A **pretest** involves conducting the survey on a small, representative set of respondents in order to reveal questionnaire errors before the survey is launched. It is very important that pretest participants are in fact representative—that is, selected from the target population under study. Before the questions are administered, participants are informed of the pretest, and their cooperation is requested in spotting words, phrases, instructions, question flow, or other aspects of the questionnaire that appear confusing, difficult to understand, or otherwise problematic. Normally, between 5 and 10 respondents are involved in a pretest, and the researcher looks for common problem themes across this group.[20] For example, if only one pretest respondent indicates some concern about a question, the researcher probably would not attempt to change its wording, but if three mention the same concern, the researcher should make the revision. Ideally, when making revisions, researchers should place themselves in the respondent's shoes and reflect, "Is the meaning of the question clear?" "Are the instructions understandable?" "Are the terms precise?" and "Are there any loaded or charged words?" Because researchers can never completely replicate the respondent's perspective, a pretest is extremely valuable.[21]

# Summary

1.    **Describe the questionnaire design process.**
Questionnaires do more than translate research objectives into specific questions. The design of the questionnaire can directly affect the quality of the data collected. Therefore it is critical that the questionnaire used in a research project be properly designed. The researcher should follow a step-by-step development process that includes question development, question evaluation, client approval, and a pretest. The chapter also introduces "precoding" as part of the questionnaire development. Software programs that perform questionnaire design are also discussed.

2.    **Identify the "do's" and "do nots" of questionnaire wording.**
The objective of question development is to create questions that minimize question bias. The four "do's" in question development stress that the ideal question is focused, simple, brief, and crystal clear. Question bias is most likely to occur when question wording is leading, loaded, double-barrelled, or overstated. In addition, there are certain words that should be avoided because they are absolute extremes that force respondents to totally agree or totally disagree with the question. For example, words such as *all* or *every* are part of the "top 10 list" of absolute words presented in the chapter.

3.    **Outline the basics of questionnaire organization.**
The organization of questions on the questionnaire is critical, including the first statements, or introduction to the survey. The introduction should identify the sponsor of the survey, relate the survey's purpose, explain how the respondent was selected, solicit the individual's cooperation to take part, and, if appropriate, qualify him or her for taking part in the survey. General guidelines on the flow of questions on the questionnaire are provided in this chapter, including the location and roles of screens, warm-ups, transitions, "difficult" questions, and classification questions.

# Key Terms

"All that apply" questions    (p. 280)
Anonymity    (p. 276)
Classification questions    (p. 279)
Computer-assisted questionnaire
    design    (p. 281)
Confidentiality    (p. 276)
Cover letter    (p. 274)
Disguised survey    (p. 275)
Double-barrelled question    (p. 272)
Funnel approach    (p. 277)
Incentives    (p. 276)
Leading question    (p. 269)
Loaded question    (p. 271)
Overstated question    (p. 272)
Precoding    (p. 280)

Pretest    (p. 282)
Question bias    (p. 264)
Question development    (p. 265)
Question evaluation    (p. 268)
Question flow    (p. 278)
Questionnaire    (p. 263)
Questionnaire design    (p. 263)
Questionnaire organization    (p. 273)
Screening questions    (p. 276)
Sections approach (p. 277)
Skip question    (p. 279)
Transitions    (p. 279)
Undisguised survey    (p. 275)
Warm-up questions    (p. 279)
Work approach    (p. 277)

# Review Questions

**1.1** Why is pretesting a questionnaire so critical in the questionnaire design process?

**2.1** Write two biased questions using the "bad" words in Table 8.1. Rewrite each question without using the problem words.

**2.2** The Marketing Club at your school is thinking about undertaking a money-making project that involves a photo-calendar of 12 women on campus. All photographs will be taken by a professional photographer and tastefully done. Some club members are worried that students might think the calendar is degrading to women. To find out how valid this intuitive thought is, the club decided to undertake a one-question survey of the student population. Using at least two of the "do nots" of question wording, write a question that would tend to support the view that such a calendar would be degrading. Indicate how the question is in error. Provide a "correct" form.

**2.3** Write a clear, focused question for each of the four "do's" of questionnaire development on any topic of interest. Indicate how your questions incorporate the "do's."

**3.1** Indicate the functions of (a) screening questions, (b) warm-up questions, (c) transitions, (d) "skip" questions, and (e) classification questions.

**3.2** A researcher is developing a questionnaire for a study on B.C. tourism. It is to be administered by personal interviewers who will intercept tourists as they are waiting at the Vancouver airport in the seating areas of their departing flight gates. Decribe a logical question flow for the questionnaire using the guidelines in Table 8.4.

- Determine how the respondents selected B.C. as a destination.
- Discover what places they visited in B.C. and how much they liked each one.

- Specify how long they stayed and where they stayed while in B.C.
- Provide a demographic profile of each respondent interviewed.

**3.3** Under what conditions should classification questions go at the beginning of a questionnaire? Why should classification questions otherwise go at the end of the questionnaire?

**3.4** Panther Martin invents and markets various types of fishing lures. In order to survey the reactions of potential buyers, the company hires a research company to intercept fishers at boat launches, secure their cooperation to use three lures under development, and interview them later that day after they have had a chance to use the lures. Each respondent receives five more lures at the end of the interview as a reward for participating in the research. What opening comments should be made when approaching fishers? Draft a script to be used when asking these fishers to take part in the survey.

## Case 8.1

## Moe's Wraps & Subs

Moe's is a submarine sandwich shop that also offers wraps, which are sandwiches made with a tortilla rather than bread. There are seven Moe's units located in the greater metropolitan area, and Moe is thinking about setting up a franchise system to go "big-time" with nationwide coverage. A business associate recommends that Moe first conduct a baseline survey of his seven units to better understand his customers and to spot any weaknesses that he might not be aware of. Moe meets with Bob Watts of OSR Marketing Reseach, and together they agree on the following research objectives. Also, Bob has convinced Moe that a telephone survey of the greater metropolitan area is the best choice.

### Research Objectives for Moe's Wraps & Sub's Survey

1. How often do people purchase a meal at Moe's?
2. About how much do they spend there per visit (per individual)?
3. Overall, how satisfied are they with Moe's?
4. How do they rate Moe's Wraps & Subs' performance on the following various aspects?
   a. Competitive price
   b. Convenience of locations
   c. Variety of sandwiches
   d. Freshness of sandwich fillings
   e. Speed of service
   f. Taste of subs
   g. Taste of wraps
   h. Uniqueness of sandwiches
5. What recent advertising do they recall and where do they recall seeing the advertising? (Moe's uses the following advertising: Yellow Pages, billboards, newspaper ads, coupons, and internet banner ads.)

Obtain a demographic profile of the sample. Design a questionnaire for the Moe's Wraps & Subs survey that will be performed by OSR Marketing Reseach under Bob Watts' direction.

## Case 8.2

# Starbuck's Instant Coffee
## Research Questionnaire Design

(The following is a hypothetical case.)

Chris and Jeff are partnering to undertake a project for their marketing research course. The project requires them to select a research problem, identify the research objectives, choose the research design best suited for their purposes, and design a questionnaire to collect data.

Starbucks Coffee recently introduced VIA Ready Brew, an instant coffee alternative. The coffee is the same price per cup as the company's regular brewed coffee. Its unique selling point is that it is a revolutionary way of getting the same great taste as brewed coffee by just adding water to the instant coffee.

For their research project, Chris and Jeff decided to examine the acceptance of Starbucks instant coffee by current Starbucks drinkers. Their research objectives were to see if there are any differences between drinkers of regular coffee and those who chose instant coffee. They were also interested in knowing if current Starbucks drinkers perceived the unique selling point of the instant coffee. They wondered whether current customers would be reluctant to pay the same price for the instant coffee as for the brewed coffee. They also wanted to know if the instant coffee could become a permanent substitute for some segment of the Starbucks customer base.

Chris and Jeff are at the stage of designing the questionnaire and have developed the following questions:

- How many cups of coffee do you normally drink at Starbucks?
- On average, how much money do you spend at Starbucks?
- Have you tried the new VIA Ready Brew instant coffee? Is it as good as the regular coffee? Would you consider ever switching to instant coffee? Why, or why not?
- How do you feel about paying the same price for a Tall, Grande, or Vente cup of instant coffee as you do for regular brewed coffee?
- How old are you? What is your income? What is the highest degree you achieved? Do all of your friends feel the same as you about instant coffee?

### Questions
1. Do the proposed research questions address the research objectives? Give reasons for your answers.
2. Go through each question and identify questions that follow the do's of questionnaire design and those that do not.
3. Edit the questions so that they are properly designed. Add answer options.

## Case 8.3 YOUR INTEGRATED CASE

# The Student Life E-Zine Survey Questionnaire

Here, you will find the complete Student Life E-Zine survey questionnaire designed by Bob Watts of ORS Marketing Research. Questionnaire organization and other aspects of this questionnaire are explained below.

*Hello, I am ____ with ORS, a marketing research firm. We received permission from City U to call you. We are conducting a survey about possible City U internet services, and you were selected at random from the Student Directory. Your participation is important in that your answers will represent hundreds of your fellow students. To thank you for taking part in this survey, we will send you a coupon for a free drink and dinner entrée of your choice at any one of five local restaurants. May I take a few minutes of your time to ask you some questions?*

1. *Do you have internet access?*
   ____ Yes ____ No **(If no, go to Question 38.)**
2. *What type of internet connection do you have where you live?*
   ____ *High-speed cable*
   ____ *Dial-up modem*
   ____ *DSL*
   ____ *Other (Specify: ____)*

*We are interested in knowing about how you shop and what products and services you are planning on purchasing. Please answer the following questions with "Yes" or "No" or "Not sure."*

| Question | Yes | No | Not Sure |
|---|---|---|---|
| 3. *Do you typically use coupons, "2-for-1 specials," or other promotions you see in magazines or newspapers?* | ____ | ____ | ____ |
| 4. *Will you purchase regular or diet soft drinks during the next week?* | ____ | ____ | ____ |
| 5. *Will you eat out at a local, non–fast-food restaurant during the next week?* | ____ | ____ | ____ |
| 6. *Will you eat out at a local fast-food restaurant during the next week?* | ____ | ____ | ____ |
| 7. *Will you order a pizza to be delivered during the next week?* | ____ | ____ | ____ |
| 8. *Will you purchase an automobile during the next three months?* | ____ | ____ | ____ |
| 9. *Will you be looking for new off-campus housing for next semester?* | ____ | ____ | ____ |
| 10. *Will you purchase new clothes during the next month?* | ____ | ____ | ____ |
| 11. *Will you go out to a night entertainment establishment during the next week?* | ____ | ____ | ____ |

12a. *Will you make a purchase over the internet in the next TWO MONTHS?*
   ____Yes____No____Not Sure

**(If "No" or "Not Sure," skip to Question 14.)**

12b. *(If "Yes" to 12a.) To the nearest $5, about how much do you think you will spend on internet purchases in the next two months?*
   $____

13. *Next, I have six categories below that I will read to you. After I read them, for each one, tell me about how much you spend over the internet on that category out of every $100 you spend on the internet. Are my instructions clear?* **(If not, repeat.)**
   $____ *Books*
   $____ *Gifts for weddings and other special occasions*
   $____ *Music purchases*
   $____ *Financial services (insurance, loans, etc.)*
   $____ *Clothing*
   $____ *General merchandise for your home or car*
   $____ *100 TOTAL*

**(Interviewer: The total must be $100. Work with respondents to achieve this total.)**

14. *Now, I want to read to you the description of an "e-zine," and then ask you some questions about it.*

*An e-zine is a magazine delivered to you online. We want you to think of an e-zine written especially for post-secondary students. The e-zine would include articles about your university or college as well as*
(Continued)

*articles about national and world events thought to be of interest to postsecondary students. The e-zine would use state-of-the-art graphics and would have several interactive features such as interviews with campus leaders, athletes, and well-known celebrities. The e-zine would feature streaming video of local events such as previews of entertainment in some of the local night spots or even college sporting events. Some major events would be available on a "pay-per-view" basis. E-zine readers would have access to a variety of special promotions such as free coupons, admit-2-for-price-of-1 specials, and much more.*

*If the subscription price for this e-zine was $15 per month for a minimum of six months, how likely would you be to subscribe to it? Would you say you are "very unlikely," "somewhat unlikely," "neither*

*likely nor unlikely," "somewhat likely," or "very likely"?*

| Very Unlikely | Somewhat Unlikely | Neither Likely nor Unlikely | Somewhat Likely | Very Likely |
|---|---|---|---|---|
| ___ | ___ | ___ | ___ | ___ |

(Interviewer: For those responding "Unlikely" or "Neither . . . ," go to Question 31. Otherwise, continue.)

*We are considering a number of ideas for our e-zine and we would like some help from you in determining which features will be most preferred by our subscribers. I will read you names and brief descriptions of possible features. For each feature, please indicate your level of preference by saying "strongly do not prefer," "somewhat do not prefer," "no preference," "somewhat prefer," or "strongly prefer."*

| Feature | Strongly Do Not Prefer | Somewhat Do Not Prefer | No Preference | Somewhat Prefer | Strongly Prefer |
|---|---|---|---|---|---|
| 15. The Campus Calendar—*with prompters for important dates like Drop/Add deadlines (and you can specify other important personal dates)* | ___ | ___ | ___ | ___ | ___ |
| 16. Course & Instructor Evaluator —*Inside information about courses and instructors from students who have recently taken the course* | ___ | ___ | ___ | ___ | ___ |
| 17. Your Legislature—*Pending and passed legislative actions that affect college students* | ___ | ___ | ___ | ___ | ___ |
| 18. Popcorn Favourites—*A listing of top video rentals by category of entertainment* | ___ | ___ | ___ | ___ | ___ |
| 19. Online "specials" from local retailing establishments where you can save money by taking advantage of these specials | ___ | ___ | ___ | ___ | ___ |
| 20. World & National News— *Written by college students for college students* | ___ | ___ | ___ | ___ | ___ |

| Feature | Strongly Do Not Prefer | Somewhat Do Not Prefer | No Preference | Somewhat Prefer | Strongly Prefer |
|---|---|---|---|---|---|
| 21. My Major—*Messages from the department that is your major* | ____ | ____ | ____ | ____ | ____ |
| 22. Online Registrar—*Register, drop, add, and pay tuition online* | ____ | ____ | ____ | ____ | ____ |
| 23. My Advisor—*Messages to or from your advisor and other university officials* | ____ | ____ | ____ | ____ | ____ |
| 24. Student Government—*Streaming video of Student Government Association meetings, live and taped replays* | ____ | ____ | ____ | ____ | ____ |
| 25. Cyber-Sports—*Pay-per-view of nontelevised college/university sporting events at about $20 per football game and $10 for other events* | ____ | ____ | ____ | ____ | ____ |
| 26. What's Happen'n?—*Information about entertainment, cultural opportunities in the area for this week* | ____ | ____ | ____ | ____ | ____ |
| 27. Weather Today—*Local weather radar and forecast for the day and week* | ____ | ____ | ____ | ____ | ____ |
| 28. Entertainment News—*Reviews of movies, books, and theatre, and celebrity news* | ____ | ____ | ____ | ____ | ____ |
| 29. Inside Sports—*The "inside scoop" from athletes and coaches throughout the conference; what big media doesn't cover* | ____ | ____ | ____ | ____ | ____ |
| 30. Cyber-Cupid—*An online dating service* | ____ | ____ | ____ | ____ | ____ |

*In the next few questions we want to ask you about your activities, interests, and opinions. Please tell me if you "strongly disagree," "disagree," "neither agree nor disagree," "agree," or "strongly agree" with each of the following statements that I will read:*

| Statement | Strongly Disagree | Disagree | Neither Agree nor Disagree | Agree | Strongly Agree |
|---|---|---|---|---|---|
| 31. *I am a homebody.* | ____ | ____ | ____ | ____ | ____ |
| 32. *I highly value the information I can access through the internet.* | ____ | ____ | ____ | ____ | ____ |

*(Continued)*

| Statement | Strongly Disagree | Disagree | Neither Agree nor Disagree | Agree | Strongly Agree |
|---|---|---|---|---|---|
| 33. Even though I am a post-secondary student, I feel I have enough income to buy what I want. | ____ | ____ | ____ | ____ | ____ |
| 34. I shop a lot for "specials." | ____ | ____ | ____ | ____ | ____ |
| 35. I like to wear the latest styles in clothing. | ____ | ____ | ____ | ____ | ____ |
| 36. Keeping up with the political and economic news is not important to me. | ____ | ____ | ____ | ____ | ____ |
| 37. Keeping up with entertainment news is not important to me. | ____ | ____ | ____ | ____ | ____ |

*Finally, we would like some information for classification purposes only.*

38. What is your academic classification?
   ____ 1st year or 1st semester
   ____ 2nd year or 2nd semester
   ____ 3rd year or 3rd semester
   ____ 4th year or 4th semester
   ____ Grad student
   ____ Other
39. Do you live . . .
   ____ On Campus ____ Off Campus
40. In which year were you born? 19____ .
41. What is your GPA? ____
42. What is your gender? ____ Male ____ Female
43. Do you work? ____ Yes ____ No

(**If "yes," ask**) *How many hours per week?* ____ *hours.*

44. Please tell me what is your academic major or program?
   ____ Arts
   ____ Architecture
   ____ Business
   ____ Computer Technology
   ____ Education
   ____ Engineering
   ____ Music
   ____ Nursing
   ____ Professional Studies
   ____ Sciences

*Thank you very much for your participation in our survey*

## Explanations of Aspects of the Student Life E-Zine Survey Questionnaire

Below, we identify various parts of the questionnaire and provide comments related to our recommendations about questionnaire organization and other specifics.

| Questionnaire Item | Explanation |
|---|---|
| 1. Do you have internet access? | This is a *qualification/skip question* that causes the interviewer to "jump over" questions that are not relevant to respondents without internet access, meaning that they are not qualified to be target-market members. Asking demographic questions of these respondents is a courtesy so they can be entered into the incentive drawing. |
| 2. What type of internet connection do you have where you live? | This is an easy-to-answer *warm-up question*. |

*(Continued)*

| Questionnaire Item | Explanation |
|---|---|
| **Questions 3–11** | All are easy-to-answer *warm-up questions* that also serve to keep the respondent motivated and interested. |
| 13. If you do purchase over the internet, please tell us how you allocate your expenditures. | This is a *difficult-to-answer question* that is "buried" deep in the questionnaire. In fact, it may take a good deal of interviewer–respondent dialogue to effect answers that add to $100. |
| 14. Now, we want you to read the description of an "e-zine" below and then tell us how likely you would be to subscribe to an e-zine if it were available to you. | It is necessary to read this description because the e-zine does not exist. All respondents will have the identical mental picture of the e-zine being researched. |
| *(Interviewer: For those responding "Unlikely" or "Neither . . . ," go to Question 31. Otherwise, continue.)* We are considering a number of ideas for our e-zine and we would like some help from you in determining which features will be most preferred by our subscribers. I will read you names and brief descriptions of possible features. For each feature, please indicate your level of preference by saying "strongly do not prefer," "somewhat do not prefer," "no preference," "somewhat prefer," or "strongly prefer." | First, this is a *skip instruction* for the interviewer. Only those who are "likely" to subscribe are asked the next set of questions. Second, the instructions are transition statements that relate the scale to be used for the next several questions. |
| In the next few questions, we want to ask you about your activities, interests, and opinions. Please tell me if you "disagree strongly," "disagree," "neither agree nor disagree," "agree," or "strongly agree" to each of the following statements that I will read. | This is a standard description of lifestyle questions, and the disagree–agree response scale is related with a *transition statement*. |
| Finally, we would like some information for classification purposes only. | This *transition statement* notifies the respondent that the survey is almost at an end. Also, it strongly implies that the *demographic questions* that follow are not to be taken personally; rather, they are for *classification*. |

Answer the following questions regarding this questionnaire:
1. Does the introduction satisfy all of its necessary functions? Why, or why not?
2. Would you say that the survey was disguised or undisguised? Why do you think Bob Watts chose to indicate who the research survey was designed for?
3. There are no precodes on the questionnaire. Indicate the appropriate precodes.

## LEARNING OBJECTIVES

1. Define sample design terminology.

2. Calculate sample size.

3. Describe four probability sampling methods.

4. Describe four nonprobability sampling methods.

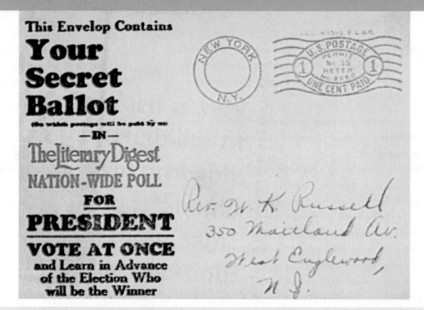

*The Literary Digest's* famous blunder was due to using a poor sampling method.

## A Survey that Changed Survey Sampling Practice

*The Literary Digest,* an influential general interest magazine started in 1890, correctly predicted several presidential campaigns by using surveys. The world was becoming accustomed to viewing surveys as accurate predictors of future events. But the prediction the magazine made in the 1936 election was so bad that it is given credit for not only causing the collapse of the magazine (it was purchased by *Time* in 1938) but also for stirring interest in refining surveying sampling techniques.

Alf Landon, the Republican candidate and governor of Kansas, was running against Democratic president Franklin D. Roosevelt. *The Literary Digest* used three lists as its sample frame for polling American voters. First, it sent a postcard to each of its two million subscribers. Second, it added to this sample with sample frames composed of lists of telephone owners and automobile owners.

The *Digest's* survey predicted Landon would win overwhelmingly. Roosevelt won in a landslide, taking 46 of 48 states. Only Maine and New Hampshire voted for Landon. What went wrong? *The Literary Digest* had used an unusually large sample, yet the results were terribly wrong. The answer: The sampling method was wrong. Remember, 1936 was in the depths of the

Great Depression. Those who could afford a magazine subscription, telephone, or automobile were much better off than the general public, and these "better off" citizens were much more likely to vote Republican. So the *Digest* was surveying, in very large numbers, voters who were mostly Republican. They did not use a sampling method that would guarantee that Democratic voters would be just as likely to be surveyed. What this illustrates is that you must have a good sampling method. With a poor sampling method, even very large sample sizes will not produce good survey results. In contrast, other surveys using much smaller sample sizes predicted Roosevelt would win. They were ridiculed for using small samples, but their predictions were correct because they used sound sampling methods. Among those producing accurate predictions was a young man named George Gallup. The Gallup Company exists today and is still conducting accurate surveys. In this chapter, you will learn how the sample method is important in producing representative results, and how the sample size is important in producing accurate survey results.[1]

I nternational markets are measured in hundreds of millions of people, national markets comprise millions of individuals, and even local markets may constitute hundreds of thousands of households. To obtain information from every single person in a market is usually impossible and obviously impractical. For these reasons, marketing researchers make use of a sample. This chapter describes how researchers go about deciding sample size and taking samples. First definitions of basic concepts such as population, sample, and census are presented. To be sure, sample size determination can be complicated but a simple way to calculate the desired size of a sample is described along with how the XL Data Analyst™ can be used to do these calculations.[2] Four types of probability sampling methods and four types of nonprobability sampling methods are discussed. Lastly, a step-by-step procedure for designing and taking a sample is presented.

**Where We Are**
1. Establish the need for marketing research
2. Define the problem
3. Establish research objectives
4. Determine research design
5. Identify information types and sources
6. Determine methods of accessing data
7. Design data collection forms
8. Determine sample plan and size
9. Collect data
10. Analyze data
11. Prepare and present the final research report

## Basic Concepts in Samples and Sampling

The **population** is the entire group under study as specified by the research project. For example, a researcher may specify a population as "heads of households in those metropolitan areas served by Terminix who are responsible for insect pest control." A **sample** is a subset of the population that should represent that entire group. A **census** is defined as an accounting of everyone in the population. In Canada a census of every 1 in 5 households is taken every five years. Eighty percent of the sample are given the short questionnaire of 8 questions while 20% are given the longer version of 61 questions. Organizations other than Statistics Canada normally use a sample instead of a census because a census is normally unobtainable due to time, accessibility issues, and cost.

There are accuracy concerns that always occur when a sample is taken. **Sampling error** is any error in a survey that occurs because a sample is used. Sampling error is caused by two factors: (1) the method of sample selection and

(2) the size of the sample. Larger samples represent less sampling error than smaller samples, and some sampling methods minimize this error, whereas others do not control it at all regardless of the size of the sample. In order to select a sample, a **sample frame** is needed, which is a master list of all members of the population. For instance, if a researcher had defined a population to be all shoe repair stores in New Brunswick, a master listing of these stores as a frame from which to sample would be needed. Similarly, if the population being researched consisted of all certified chartered accountants (CAs) in Canada, a sample frame for this group would be needed. In the case of shoe repair stores, a list service such as the Canadian Business Directory, which has compiled a list of shoe repair stores, might be used. For CAs, the researcher could use the list of members of the Canadian Institute of Chartered Accountants, located in Toronto, which contains a listing of all accountants who have passed the three-day uniform evaluation (UFE) exam. Lists are not perfect representations of populations because new members are added, old ones drop off, and there may be clerical errors in the list. Researchers understand that **sample frame error**, great or small, exists for sample frames in the forms of mis-, over-, or underrepresentations of the true population. Whenever a sample is drawn, the amount of potential sample frame error should be judged by the researcher.[3] Sometimes the only available sample frame contains much potential sample frame error, but it is used due to the lack of any other sample frame. It is a researcher's responsibility to seek out a sample frame with the least amount of error at a reasonable cost. The researcher should also report to the client the degree of sample frame error involved.

## Determining Size of a Sample

Assume that a sample frame that has an acceptably low level of sample frame error can be found and that a sample that is truly representative of the population can be selected.

### The Accuracy of a Sample

A convenient way to describe the amount of sample error due to the size of the sample, or the **accuracy of a sample**, is to treat it as a plus-or-minus percentage value.[4,5] That is, one can say that a sample is accurate to $\pm x\%$, such as $\pm 5\%$ or $\pm 10\%$. The interpretation of sample accuracy uses the following logic: If a sample size with an accuracy level of $\pm 5\%$ is used, when one analyzes the survey's findings, they will be about $\pm 5\%$ of what one would find if a census was performed. For example, take a sample that is representative of the population of people who bought pizza in the past month. Fifty percent of respondents say "Yes" to the question, "The last time you bought a pizza, did you choose more than one topping?" With a sample accuracy of $\pm 5\%$, one can say that if this question was asked of everyone in the population of our pizza buyers, the percentage that will say "Yes" is between 45% and 55% (or 50% $\pm 5\%$). Think, for a minute, about the incredible power of a sample: A subset of the entire population can be interviewed, and the sample's findings can be generalized to the population with a $\pm x\%$ approximation of what would be found if all the time, energy, and expense to interview every single member of the population were taken.

While directories and phone books are readily available, they may have substantial sample frame error.

The relationship between sample size and sample accuracy is presented graphically in Figure 9.1. In this figure, sample error (accuracy) is listed on the vertical axis and sample size is noted on the horizontal one. The graph shows the accuracy levels of samples ranging in size from 50 to 2000. The shape of the graph shows that as the sample size increases, sample error decreases. However, note that the graph is not a straight line. In other words, doubling sample size does not result in halving the sample error. The relationship is a curved one.

There is another important property of the sample accuracy graph. As you look at the graph note that at a sample size of around 500, the accuracy level drops below ±5% (it is actually ±4.4%), and it continues to decrease at a very slow rate with larger sample sizes. In other words, once a sample is greater than, say, 500, large gains in accuracy are not realized with large increases in the size of the sample. In fact, if it is already ±4.4% in accuracy, not much more accuracy is possible.

With the lower end of the sample size axis, however, large gains in accuracy can be made with a relatively small sample size increase. For example, with a

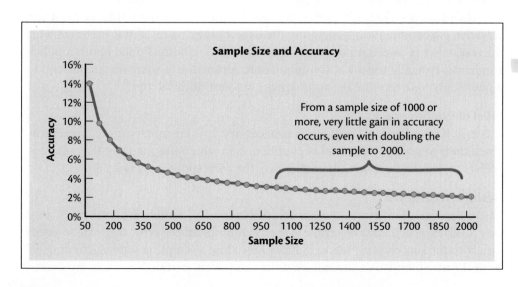

**Figure 9.1** The Relationship Between Sample Size and Sample Accuracy

sample size of 50 the accuracy level is ±13.9%, whereas with a sample size of 250 it is ±6.2%. The accuracy of the 250 sample is roughly double that of the 50 sample. But, as was just described, such huge gains in accuracy are not the case at the other end of the sample size scale because of the nature of the curved relationship.

## How to Calculate Sample Size

The proper way to calculate sample size is to use the **confidence interval formula for sample size** that follows:

$$n = \frac{z^2(pq)}{e^2}$$

**Sample size formula** ▷

where    $n$ = the calculated sample size
         $z$ = standard error associated with the chosen level of confidence (typically, 1.96)
         $p$ = estimated percentage in the population
         $q$ = 100% − $p$
         $e$ = acceptable error (desired accuracy level)

The confidence interval formula for sample size is based on three elements: variability, confidence level, and desired accuracy. We will describe each in turn.

### Variability: *p* times *q*

Variability refers to how much respondents agree in their answer to a question. For instance, when conducting a Domino's Pizza survey, our major concern might be the percentage of pizza buyers who want the same toppings on their pizza. There are two possible answers: "yes" or "no" for each topping. If our pizza buyers population has very little **variability**—that is, if almost everyone, let us say 90%, respond"yes" to all items—then this belief will be reflected in the sample size formula as 90% ($p$) times 10% ($q$), or 900. However, if there is great variability, meaning that no two respondents agree on the type of toppings and we have a 50/50 split (50% of the sample say "yes" to an item and 50% say "no"), $p$ times $q$ becomes 50% times 50%, or 2500, which is the largest $p$ times $q$ number possible.

The use of $p$ = 50%, $q$ = 50% is a research industry standard. It is the most conservative $p$-$q$ combination, generating the largest sample size, so it is preferred when the researcher is uncertain or guessing about the variability. Public opinion polling companies typically use a 50/50 combination. Alternatively, some researchers opt for a pilot study to determine the approximate amount of variability.[6]

### Level of Confidence: *z*

A decision on a **level of confidence** is necessary. It is customary among marketing researchers to use the 95% level of confidence, in which the $z$ is 1.96. If a researcher prefers to use the 99% level of confidence, the corresponding $z$ is 2.58.

### Desired Accuracy: *e*

Lastly, the formula requires that an acceptable level of sample error (the ±% accuracy level) be specified. The term $e$ is the amount of sample error that will be associated with the survey. It is used to indicate how close a sample percentage finding will be to the true population percentage if the study were repeated many, many times.

If everyone wanted the same thing on their pizzas, there would be no variability.

Figure 9.2 on the next page illustrates how the level of confidence figures into sample size accuracy. Theoretically, if the survey were repeated a great many times—several thousands of times—and if the frequency distribution of each $p$ for every one of these repeated samples was graphed, the pattern would appear as a bell curve, as shown in Figure 9.2. Note that 95% of the replications would fall between the population $p$ (50% in our example in Figure 9.2) and $\pm e$.

If the mean number of toppings chosen by our sample of pizza buyers is 3 toppings and the **desired accuracy** level is 95%, then the average number of toppings is $3 \pm 2$ toppings. We can be certain that if we repeated our study several thousands of times, the average number of toppings would be 1 to 5. The number of toppings closen by the true population is 1 to 5 toppings.

Here is an example of a sample size calculation. Assume that there is great expected variability (50%) and that a $\pm3\%$ accuracy level at the 95% level of confidence is desired:

**Sample size computed with $p = 50\%$, $q = 50\%$, and $e = 3\%$**

$$n = \frac{1.96^2(50 \times 50)}{3^2}$$

$$= \frac{3.84(2500)}{9}$$

$$= \frac{9600}{9}$$

$$= 1067$$

Whenever the sample size is calculated, the number of respondents who should participate fully in the survey in order to reach the stipulated level of confidence in the results is determined. Surveys run into two difficulties that require an upward adjustment of the computed sample size. Marketing Research in Action 9.1 illustrates the two problems of "incidence rate" and "nonresponse" and discusses how to adjust the sample size to cope with these two problems. A list of other practical issues that often force researchers to make sample size adjustments is also presented.

**Figure 9.2** How Sample Error and the 95% Level of Confidence Theoretically Operate

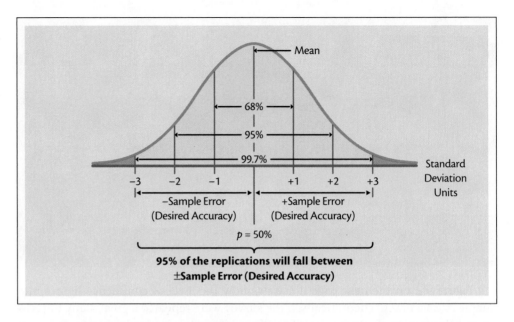

To further see the effect of confidence interval on the sample size, follow the instructions in Online Application 9.1 on page 314.

## MARKETING RESEARCH IN ACTION 9.1
## Adjusting Your Sample Size to Compensate for Incidence Rate, Nonresponse, and More

Suppose that Scope mouthwash wanted to find reactions to a new formula that whitens teeth and controls tartar. The researcher and Scope managers agree on a sample size of 500, so the researcher purchases the names of 500 individuals from a sample supply company. The survey moves along, but the data collection company that is performing the telephone interviews reports only 4 out of 5 people in the sample use mouthwash. In other words, the **incidence rate**, defined as the percent of individuals in the sample who qualify to take the survey, is 80%, meaning that 20%, or 100 names in the sample, are not usable. So, under this situation, the largest final sample size possible is 400.

At the same time, the data collection manager reports to the researcher that potential respondents who qualify are refusing to take the survey. This problem is referred to as **nonresponse**, or failures by qualified respondents to take part in the survey. The data collection company estimates a refusal rate of 40%, meaning that the response rate is 60%. A response rate of 60% means that only 60% of the 400 qualified respondents will be in the final sample.

The researcher is now faced with a final sample size of 240, far smaller than the desired size of 500.

To cope with the realities of incidence rate and nonresponse, researchers must make adjustments on their calculated sample sizes. A simple adjustment formula is as follows:

**Sample size adjustment formula**

$$\text{Adjusted sample size} = \text{Calculated sample size} \times (1/\text{Incidence rate \%}) \times (1/\text{Response rate \%})$$

If you apply this formula to our Scope mouthwash example, the computations are as follows:

**Sample size adjustment example**

$$
\begin{aligned}
\text{Adjusted sample size} &= \text{Calculated sample size} \times (1/\text{Incidence rate}) \times (1/\text{Response rate}) \\
&= 500 \times (1/0.8) \times (1/0.6) \\
&= 500 \times 1.25 \times 1.67 \\
&= 1044
\end{aligned}
$$

So, as seen here, incidence rates and nonresponse can combine to have a tremendous impact on the final sample size of a survey. Astute marketing researchers make estimates of the magnitudes of these problems and adjust the calculated sample size accordingly.

There are other factors that may force sample size adjustments. Susie Sangren, president of Clearview Data Strategy, has contributed the following list of practical constraints that researchers are likely to encounter:

- *Time pressure.* Often research results are needed "yesterday," meaning that the sample size may be reduced to save time.

- *Cost constraint.* A limited amount of money is available for the study, and limited funds translate to reduced sample size.
- *Study objective.* What is the purpose of the study? A decision that does not need great precision can make do with a very small sample size such as a few focus groups or a pilot study.
- *Data analysis procedures.* Some advanced data analysis procedures require much-larger-than-ordinary sample sizes in order to be fully used.*

*Personal communication to the author from Susie Sangren.

# Using the XL Data Analyst™ to Calculate Sample Size

It is time to introduce the XL Data Analyst Excel macro software that accompanies this textbook. The XL Data Analyst is primarily a set of data analysis procedures that are easy to use and interpret.

There is a procedure in the XL Data Analyst that calculates sample size. For now, all you need to do is open up any Excel file that accompanies this textbook. Because the XL Data Analyst is an Excel macro, you will need to set the Excel 2010 Macro Settings via "Excel Options—Trust Center—Trust Center Settings—Macro Settings" to "Disable all macros with notification." With both 2010 and 2007, enable the macro content via the Security Warning feature after the file is loaded. If you have a problem, go to either www.xldataanalyst.com or www.pearsoncanada.ca/burns, and read "Documentation."

After the file is loaded, you will see a "Data" worksheet and a "Define Variables" worksheet, but you can ignore whatever you see on these worksheets. Instead, use the XL Data Analyst to access the "Calculate" function available in its main menu—with Excel 2010 or 2007, you will need to click on "Add-Ins" after you have clicked on "Enable this Content" in your Security Warning. Then click on XL Data Analyst and you will see the menu. The XL Data Analyst will calculate sample size using the confidence sample size formula we have described in this chapter. As you can see in Figure 9.3, we have "pinned" the XL Data Analyst menu item on the Excel 2010 Quick Access tool bar. The menu sequence is Calculate—Sample Size, which opens up the selection window where you can specify the allowable error (desired sample accuracy) and the estimated percent, $p$, value. In our example, we have set the accuracy level at 4% and the estimated $p$ at 50%.

Figure 9.4 reveals that the XL Data Analyst has computed the sample size for the 95% level of confidence to be 600, while for the 99% confidence

*(Continued)*

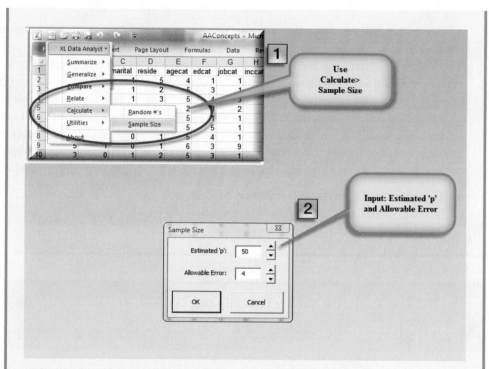

**Figure 9.3** XL Data Analyst Setup for Sample Size Calculation

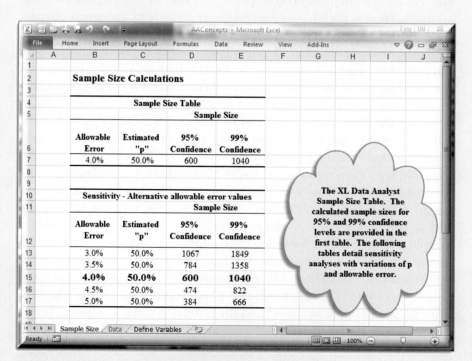

**Figure 9.4** XL Data Analyst Sample Size Calculation Output

level the calculated sample size is 1040. There are two tables following the sample size table that a researcher can use to inspect the sensitivity of the sample size to slight variations of $e$ (with estimated $p$ constant), ranging in our example from 3.0% to 5.0% by 0.5% increments, or variations in the estimated $p$ (with $e$ constant), ranging from 40% to 60% by 5% increments. (Note: This part of the table is not shown in Figure 9.4.) The sensitivity analysis tables are provided so that a researcher who is wrestling with a sample size decision can quickly compare the impact of small differences in his or her assumptions about variability in the population ($p$) as well as slightly loosening or tightening the sample accuracy requirements, or allowable error.

Marketing managers and other clients of marketing researchers do not have a thorough understanding of sample size. In fact, they tend to have a belief in a false "law of large sample size." Often they confuse the size of the sample with the representativeness of the sample. The reality is that the way the sample is selected, not its size, determines its representativeness. Also, gains in accuracy by increasing sample size excessively typically do not justify their increased costs.

It is an ethical marketing researcher's responsibility to try to educate a client on the wastefulness of excessively large samples. Occasionally, there are good reasons for having a very large sample, but whenever the sample size exceeds that of a typical national opinion poll (1200 respondents), justification is required. Otherwise, the manager's cost will be unnecessarily inflated. Unethical researchers may recommend very large samples as a way to increase their profits, set at a percentage of the total cost of the survey. They may even have ownership in the data collection company gathering the data at a set cost per respondent. It is important, therefore, that marketing managers know the reasons behind recommendations of sample size.

# How to Select a Representative Sample

If the sample selection method is faulty or biased, the findings will be compromised regardless of sample size. For example, if Starbucks Coffee wanted to find out how its Canadian customers feel about Starbucks coffee and other food products and it used a sample of customers drawn from those who happened to make a purchase at its Vancouver International Airport location on June 12, this sample would not be truly representative of all Canadian Starbucks Coffee customers. It would only represent Canadian Starbucks Coffee customers of that location in that time period.

## Probability Sampling Methods

A **random sample** is one in which every member of the population has an equal chance, or probability, of being selected into that sample. Sample methods that use random sampling are often termed **probability sampling methods**. Here, the chance of selection can be expressed as a probability. Four probability sampling methods are described: simple random sampling, systematic sampling, cluster sampling, and stratified sampling. Use Table 9.1 as a handy reference.

**Table 9.1** Four Different Probability Sampling Techniques

### Simple Random Sampling

The researcher uses a table of random numbers, random digit dialling, or some other random selection procedure that guarantees each member of the population has an identical chance of being selected into the sample.

### Systematic Sampling

Using a list of the members of the population, the researcher selects a random starting point for the first sample member. A constant "skip interval" is then used to select every other sample member. A skip interval must be used such that the entire list is covered, regardless of the starting point. This procedure accomplishes the same end as simple random sampling and is more efficient.

### Cluster Sampling

The population is divided into groups called clusters, each of which must be considered similar to the others. The researcher can then randomly select a few clusters and perform a census of each one. Alternatively, the researcher can randomly select more clusters and take samples from each one. This method is desirable when highly similar clusters can be easily identified.

### Stratified Sampling

If the population is believed to have a skewed distribution for one or more of its distinguishing factors (e.g., income or product ownership), the researcher identifies subpopulations called *strata*. A random sample is then taken of each stratum. Weighting procedures may be applied to estimate population values such as the mean. This approach is better suited than other probability sampling methods for populations that are not distributed in a bell-shaped pattern.

### Simple Random Sampling

With **simple random sampling**, the probability of being selected into the sample is "known" and equal for all members of the population. This sampling technique is expressed by the following formula:

**Formula for sample selection probability** ▷

$$\text{Probability of selection} = \text{Sample size/Population size}$$

Simple random sampling is like a lottery because everyone has an equal chance of being selected.

With simple random sampling, if the researcher was surveying a population of 100 000 recent iPod buyers using a sample size of 1000 respondents, the probability of selection on any single population member into this sample would be 1000 divided by 100 000, or 1 out of 100, calculated to be 1%. There are some variations of simple random sampling.

The **random numbers technique** is an application of simple random sampling that uses a **table of random numbers**. This table is a list of numbers whose nonsystematic (or random) order is assured. Before computer-generated random numbers were widespread, researchers used physical tables that had numbers with no discernible relationship to each other. Looking at a table of random numbers, there is no systematic sequence of the numbers regardless of where on the table one begins and whether one goes up, down, left, right, or diagonally across the entries.

# Using the XL Data Analyst™ to Generate Random Numbers

You can use the XL Data Analyst to generate your own table of random numbers. Figure 9.5 shows the menu command sequence and setup window to accomplish this end. Note that the menu sequence is "Calculate—Random #'s," and the selection window allows you to specify how many random integer numbers you want (up to 9999). You can also specify the largest possible value (up to 999 999 999).

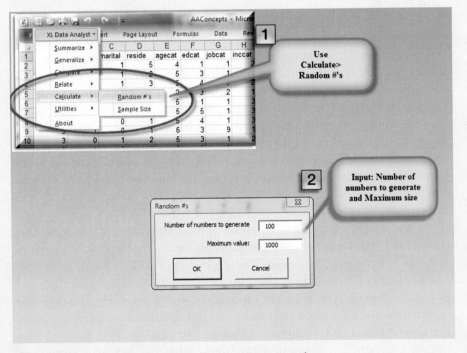

**Figure 9.5** XL Data Analyst Setup for Random Numbers

*(Continued)*

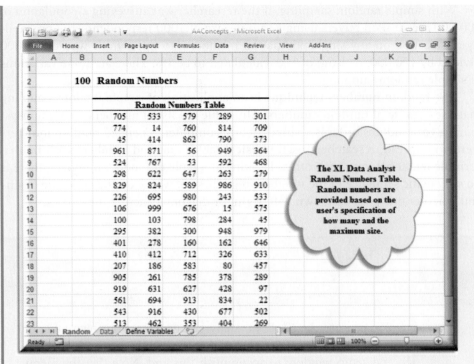

**Figure 9.6** XL Data Analyst Output for Random Numbers

In our example, we have specified 100 random numbers with a maximum value of 1000.

Figure 9.6 displays our random numbers. Note that they are arranged in five columns. You can experiment with the random-number-table-generator function of the XL Data Analyst. You should discover that there is no systematic pattern relating these numbers to one another.

With the random numbers technique, unique number values must be assigned to each of the members of a population. Social insurance numbers are unique to each person and could be used, or a computer could assign unique numbers to them and do the matching to determine which individuals are selected into the sample. Again, the use of random numbers assures the researcher that every population member who is present in the master list or file has an equal chance of being selected into the sample.

If a researcher is using telephone numbers and drawing a sample, this technique is referred to as **random digit dialling**. This approach is used in telephone surveys to overcome the problems of unlisted and new telephone numbers. Unlisted numbers, numbers on the "Do Not Call" list, and population members without land lines are a growing concern for researchers not only in Canada but in all industrialized countries, such as the United States and countries in Europe.[7] In random digit dialling, telephone numbers are generated randomly with the aid of a computer. Telephone interviewers call these numbers and complete the survey once the person has been qualified. However, random digit dialling may result in a large number of calls to nonexisting telephone numbers. A popular variation of random digit dialling that reduces this problem is the **plus-one dialling procedure**, in which numbers are selected from a telephone directory and a digit, such as a "1," is added to each number.

## Systematic Sampling

Before widespread use of computerized databases, researchers used hard-copy lists, such as a phone book. In this situation, **systematic sampling** is a way to select a simple random sample from a directory or list that is much more efficient (uses less effort) than with simple random sampling. With a physical list, the researcher must scan all names to match up each random number. To apply the systematic sampling technique in the special case of a physical listing of the population, such as a membership directory or a telephone book, systematic sampling can be applied with less difficulty and accomplished in a shorter time period than can simple random sampling. Furthermore, in many instances, systematic sampling has the potential to create a sample that is almost identical in quality to samples created from simple random sampling.

To use systematic sampling, it is necessary to obtain a hard-copy listing of the population, but it is not necessary to have a unique identification number assigned to each member on the list. The goal of systematic sampling is to literally "skip" through the list in a systematic way, but to begin at a random starting point in the list. That is, the research calculates a "**skip interval**" using the following formula:

Skip interval = Population list size/Sample size      ◀ **Formula for skip interval**

For example, if the skip interval is calculated to be 100, the researcher will select every 100th name in the list. This technique is much more efficient than searching for matches to random numbers. The use of this skip interval formula ensures that the entire list will be covered. The random sample requirement is implemented by the use of a **random starting point**, meaning that the researcher must use some random number technique to decide on the first name in the sample. Subsequent names are selected by using the skip interval. Because a random starting point is used, every name on the list has an equal probability of being selected into the systematic sample. If drawing a systematic sample from a directory of thousands of names, it is daunting to count to, say, the 44 563rd name. Instead, a single random number from 1 to the number of pages in the directory could be drawn to randomly select a page, then a random number from 1 to the number of columns on the page can be drawn to select the random column, and, finally, a random number between 1 and the number of names in that column can be selected. Thus, three quickly drawn random numbers would effect the random starting point for your systematic sample.

## Cluster Sampling

Another form of probability sampling is known as **cluster sampling**, in which the population is divided into subgroups, called "clusters." Each cluster represents the entire population.[8] The basic concept behind cluster sampling is very similar to the one described for systematic sampling, but the implementation differs. This procedure identifies identical clusters. Any one cluster, therefore, will be a satisfactory representation of the population. Cluster sampling is advantageous when there is no electronic database of the population. It is easy to administer and try to gain economic efficiency over simple random sampling by simplifying the sampling procedure.

In **area sampling**, a type of cluster sampling, the researcher subdivides the population to be surveyed into geographic areas such as census tracts, cities, neighbourhoods, or any other convenient and identifiable geographic designation. The researcher has two options at this point: a one-step approach or a two-step approach. In the **one-step area sample** approach, the researcher may believe the various geographic areas to be sufficiently identical to permit him or her to concentrate on one area and then generalize the results to the full population. But the researcher would need to select that one area randomly and perform a census of its members. Alternatively, he or she may employ a **two-step area sample** approach. For the first step, the researcher could select a random sample of areas, and then, for the second step, he or she could decide on a probability method to sample individuals within the chosen areas. The two-step area sample approach is preferable to the one-step approach because there is always the possibility that a single cluster may be less representative than the researcher believes. The two-step method is more costly because more areas and time are involved.[9]

### Stratified Sampling

All of the sampling methods described thus far implicitly assume that the population has a normal or bell-shaped distribution for its key properties. That is, it is assumed that every potential sample unit is a fairly good representation of the population. Any sample unit that is extreme in one way is perfectly counterbalanced by an opposite extreme potential sample unit. Unfortunately, in marketing research it is common to work with populations that contain unique subgroupings; that is, a population that is not distributed symmetrically across a normal curve. With this situation, unless adjustments in sample design are made, a sample that is inaccurate is generated. One solution is **stratified sampling**, which separates the population into different subgroups and then samples all of these subgroups using a random sampling technique.

For example, take the case of a post-secondary school that is attempting to assess how its students perceive the quality of its educational programs. A researcher has formulated the question, "To what extent do you value your degree?" The response options are along a 5-point scale, where 1 equals "not valued at all" and 5 equals "very highly valued." The population of students is defined by year: first year, second year, third year, and fourth year. It seems reasonable to believe that the averages will differ by the respondent's year status because fourth-year students probably value a degree more than do third-year students, who value a degree more than do second-year students, and so on. At the same time, it is expected that fourth-year students would be more in agreement (have less variability) than would students in other years. This belief is due to the fact that some first-year students are trying out a post-secondary degree, are not serious about completing it, and do not value it highly, while others are intending to carry on. The serious students would value a degree or diploma highly, whereas the less serious ones would not.

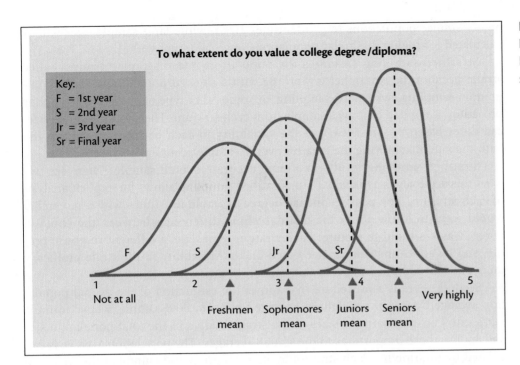

**Figure 9.7** Illustration of Four Strata in a Stratified Population of Post-secondary Students

There is much variability in the first-year students, less variability in second-year students, still less in third-year students, and the least among those in their fourth and final year.

The situation might be something similar to the distributions illustrated in Figure 9.7: The average score for each class is successively higher, with first-year students at the lowest average and fourth-year students at the highest average. Also, the bell-shaped curve for each group, or stratum, is successively narrower, meaning that there is great variability in the first-year stratum but much less in the fourth-year stratum of the population.

What would happen if a simple random sample of equal size were used for each year of study? Because sample accuracy is determined by the variability in the population—regardless of whether variability is assessed by using $p$ times $q$ for categorical questions or by using the standard deviation for metric scales—in the student example, there is least accuracy with first-year students and greatest accuracy with fourth-year students. To state this situation differently, the sample would be statistically overefficient with fourth-year students and statistically underefficient with first-year students because there would be oversampling of the fourth year and undersampling of the first year. To gain overall statistical efficiency, a larger sample of first-year students and a smaller one of fourth-year students should be drawn. This can be done by allocating the sample proportionately based on the total number of first-year, second-year, third-year, and fourth-year students, each taken as a percentage of the whole school population. (Normally, there are fewer fourth-year students than third-years than second-years than first-years in a post-secondary school.) The smallest sample would be drawn from the fourth-year group, who have the least variability in their assessments of the value of their education, and the largest sample would be drawn from the first year, who have the most variability in their assessments. As discussed earlier, smaller sample sizes will occur for highly similar populations (e.g, 90% times 10%), while large sample sizes will be calculated for highly dissimilar populations (e.g., 50% times 50%).

Stratified sampling separates the population into dissimilar groups, called **strata**, because the researcher is working with a **skewed population**. Then simple random sampling, systematic sampling, or some other type of probability sampling procedure is applied to draw a sample from each stratum. The stratum sample sizes can differ based on knowledge of the variability in each population stratum and with the aim of achieving the greatest overall sample accuracy.

Stratified sampling results in a more accurate overall sample. There are two ways this accuracy is achieved. First, stratified sampling allows for explicit analysis of each stratum. The post-secondary degree example illustrates why a researcher would want to know about the distinguishing differences between the strata in order to assess the true picture. Each stratum represents a different response profile, and by allocating sample size based on the variability in the strata profiles, a more efficient sample design is achieved.

Second, there is a procedure that allows the estimation of the overall population average by use of a **weighted average** for a stratified sample, whose formula takes into consideration the sizes of the strata relative to the total population size and applies those proportions to the strata's averages. The population average is calculated by multiplying each stratum by its proportion and summing the weighted stratum averages. This formula results in an estimate that is consistent with the true distribution of the population when the sample sizes used are not proportionate to their shares of the population. Here is the formula that is used for two strata:

**Formula for weighted average** ▶

$$\text{Average}_{\text{population}} = (\text{Average}_A)(\text{Proportion}_A) + (\text{Average}_B)(\text{Proportion}_B)$$

where A signifies stratum A, and B signifies stratum B.

For example, a researcher separated a population of households that rent videos on a regular basis into two strata. Stratum A included families without young children, and stratum B included families with young children. When asked to use a scale of 1 = "poor" and 5 = "excellent" to rate their video rental store on its video selection, the means were computed to be 2.0 and 4.0, respectively. The researcher knew from census information that families without young children

With stratified sampling, the researcher identifies subgroups or strata in the population and samples each stratum.

accounted for 70% of the population, whereas families with young children accounted for the remaining 30%. The weighted mean rating for video selection was then computed as $(0.7)(2.0) + (0.3)(4.0) = 2.6$.

Usually, a **surrogate measure**, which is some observable or easily determined characteristic of each population member, is used to help separate the population members into their various subgroupings. For example, in the instance of the post-secondary school, the year classification of each student is a handy surrogate. With its internal records, the school could easily identify students in each stratum, and this determination would be the stratification method. Of course, there is the opportunity for the researcher to divide the population into as many relevant strata as necessary to capture different subpopulations. For instance, the school might want to further stratify on major of study, gender, or grade point average (GPA) ranges. Perhaps professional-school students value their degrees more than do liberal arts students, female students differently than male students, and high-GPA students more than average-GPA or failing students. The researcher should use some basis for dividing the population into strata that results in different responses across strata. There is no need to stratify if all strata respond alike.

If the strata sample sizes are faithful to their relative sizes in the population, a **proportionate stratified sample** design is used. Here you do not use the weighted formula, since each stratum's weight is automatically accounted for by its sample size. With **disproportionate stratified sampling**, where the strata sizes do not reflect their relative proportions in the population, the weighted formula needs to be used.

## Nonprobability Sampling Methods

The four sampling methods described thus far embody probability sampling assumptions. In each case, the probability of any unit being selected from the population into the sample is known, and it can be calculated precisely given the sample size, population size, and, if used, strata or cluster sizes. With a **nonprobability sampling method**, selection is not based on fairness, equity, or equal chance. One author has noted that nonprobability sampling uses human intervention, while probability sampling does not.[10] In fact, a nonprobability sampling method is inherently biased. The researcher acknowledges that the sample is representative only to the degree the researcher feels is sufficient for the survey. Most nonprobability sampling methods take shortcuts that save effort, time, and money while destroying the equal-chance guarantee of any probability sampling method. The probability of any one person in the population being selected into a nonprobability sample cannot be calculated.

Compared with random sampling techniques, nonrandom ones, that is nonprobability sampling methods, take less effort, are faster, and cost less. These savings have a cost that ethical researchers readily acknowledge, and that cost is diminished representativeness. Nonetheless, there are instances, such as when conducting a pretest or a pilot study, when a nonrandom sampling technique is useful. One should be able to identify when a nonrandom sample has been used, so that informed judgment about the sample representativeness can be made. Marketing Research in Action 9.2 describes several sampling techniques used in marketing research.

## MARKETING RESEARCH IN ACTION 9.2
## Consumer Samples
### Targeting Saves Time and Money

SMART DATA. SMARTER DECISIONS.

Targeting by geography is common to most general population studies. However, for population segment studies, targeting by demographics, lifestyle, or ethnicity will increase the probability of reaching qualified respondents with fewer calls, thereby completing your study in less time with lower cost.

| | |
|---|---|
| **Geographic** | ■ Sample by Province, Municipality, Census Boundaries, Federal and Provincial Electoral Boundaries, Postal Boundaries, Telephone Exchange. |
| **Targeting** | ■ We have all the maps, GIS expertise and staff resources in house, at your disposal. |
| | ■ We can create drive-time zones around your locations or any other custom study area(s) your project requires. |
| **Demographic** | ■ Our sample source is fully linked to all levels of the Canadian Census. |

| | |
|---|---|
| **Targeting** | ■ We have current and historical Census data as well as third party projections and estimates. |
| | ■ Our staff are experts at the nuances, opportunities, and idiosyncrasies of the Census data. |
| **Finding Qualified Consumers** | ■ Consumer lifestyle sampling is available using over 2500 purchasing and leisure behaviour variables. |
| | ■ These targeting variables are derived from the Bureau of Broadcast Measurement (BBM-RTS) study, which annually surveys 60 000 Canadian households. |
| **Finding Ethnic Respondents** | ■ Ethnicity is predicted by overlaying Statistics Canada ethnicity data with our own carefully constructed surname origin database. |

Good targeting reduces time wasted with unqualified respondents, saving time and money, making you more competitive.

Source: Courtesy of SM Research Inc. www.smres.com/Mr_ConsumerData_More_Targeting.aspx.

There are four nonprobability sampling methods: convenience samples, judgment samples, referral samples, and quota samples. Table 9.2 summarizes each method.

### Convenience Samples

A **convenience sample** is a sample drawn at the convenience of the researcher or interviewer. Accordingly, the most convenient areas to a researcher in terms of time and effort turn out to be high-traffic areas such as busy pedestrian intersections or the web. The selection of the place and, consequently, prospective respondents is subjective rather than objective. Certain members of the population are automatically eliminated from the sampling process.[11] For instance, there are those people who may be infrequent or even nonvisitors of the particular high-traffic area being used or there may be those who do not go online frequently. On the other hand, in the absence of strict selection procedures, there are members of the population who may be omitted because of their physical appearance, their general demeanour, or the fact that they

**Table 9.2** Four Different Nonprobability Sampling Techniques

**Convenience Sampling**

The researcher uses a high-traffic location such as a busy pedestrian area or the web to intercept potential respondents. Sample selection error occurs in the form of the absence of members of the population who are infrequent or nonusers of that location.

**Judgment Sampling**

The researcher uses his or her judgment or that of some other knowledgeable person to identify who will be in the sample. Subjectivity enters in here, and certain members of the population will have a smaller chance of selection into the sample than will others.

**Referral Sampling**

Respondents are asked for the names or identities of others like themselves who might qualify to take part in the survey. Members of the population who are less well known, who are disliked, or whose opinions conflict with the respondent have a low probability of being selected into a referral sample.

**Quota Sampling**

The researcher identifies quota characteristics such as demographic or product-use factors and uses these to set up quotas for each class of respondent. The sizes of the quotas are determined by the researcher's belief about the relative size of each class of respondent in the population. Often quota sampling is used as a means of ensuring that convenience samples will have the desired proportions of different respondent classes, thereby reducing the sample selection error but not eliminating it.

are in a group rather than alone. As one author states, "Convenience samples . . . can be seriously misleading."[12]

Mall-intercept companies often use a convenience sampling method to recruit respondents. Shoppers are encountered at large shopping malls and quickly qualified with screening questions. For those satisfying the desired population characteristics, a questionnaire may be administered or a taste test performed. Alternatively, the respondent may be given a test product and asked if he or she would use it at home. A follow-up telephone call some days later solicits his or her reaction to the product's performance. Additionally, large numbers of respondents can be recruited in a matter of days. The screening questions and geographic dispersion of malls may appear to reduce the subjectivity inherent in the sample design, but, in fact, the vast majority of the population was not there and could not be approached to take part. Yet, there are ways of controlling convenience sample selection error using a quota system.

Convenience samples can result from online polling. Individuals who like to do online surveys may sign up for too many of them or respond to the same one multiple times. Measures are being taken to eliminate these problems.

## Judgment Samples

A **judgment sample** is somewhat different from a convenience sample because a judgment sample requires a judgment or an "educated guess" as to who should represent the population. Often the researcher has considerable knowledge about the population and chooses those individuals felt to constitute the sample. Judgment samples are highly subjective and therefore prone to much error.

With a convenience sample, the researcher selects high-traffic locations and interviews individuals who happen to be there.

However, judgment samples do have special uses. For instance, in the preliminary stages of a research project, the researcher may use qualitative techniques such as depth interviews or focus groups as a means of gaining insight and understanding the research problem. Judgment sampling is a quick, inexpensive, and acceptable technique because the researcher does not want to generalize the findings of the sample to the population as a whole. For example, a focus group can be conducted to find the need for a low-calorie, low-fat microwave oven cookbook. Twelve people are selected as representative of the present and prospective market. Six of these individuals owned a microwave oven for 10 or more years, 3 of them owned the oven for less than 10 years, and 3 of them were searching for a microwave oven. In the judgment of the researcher, these 12 individuals represent the population adequately for the purposes of the focus group. The intent of this focus group is far different from the intent of a survey. Consequently, the use of a judgment sample is considered satisfactory for this particular phase in the research process for the cookbook. The focus group findings can serve as the foundation for a large-scale regional survey to be conducted two months later.

### Referral Samples

A **referral sample** is sometimes called a "snowball sample" because it requires respondents to provide the names of additional respondents. Such lists begin when the researcher compiles a short list of potential respondents based on convenience or judgment. After each respondent is interviewed, he or she is asked to refer other possible respondents. As the name implies, the sample grows just as a snowball grows as it rolls downhill.

Referral samples are most appropriate when there is a limited and disappointingly short sample frame and when respondents can provide the names of others who would qualify for the survey. For example, some foreign countries have low telephone penetration or slow mail systems that make these options unsuitable, while a referral approach adds an element of trust to the approach for each new potential respondent. The nonprobability aspects of referral sampling come from the selectivity used throughout. The initial list may also be special in some way, and the primary means of adding people to the sample is by tapping the memories of those on the original list. Referral samples are often useful in industrial marketing research situations.[13]

### Quota Samples

The most commonly used nonprobability sampling method is the quota sample method. The **quota sample** establishes a specific quota for various types of individuals to be interviewed. The quotas are determined through application of the research objectives and are defined by key characteristics used to identify the population. In the application of quota sampling, a fieldworker is provided with screening criteria that will classify the potential respondent into a particular quota cell. For example, if the interviewer is assigned to obtain a sample quota of 50 each for Asian females, Asian males, white females, and white males, the qualifying characteristics would be ethnicity and gender. Assuming the fieldworkers were conducting mall intercepts, each would determine through visual inspection which category the prospective respondent fits into and would work toward filling the quota in each of the four cells. So a quota system overcomes much of the nonrepresentativeness danger inherent in convenience samples.[14]

The popularity of quota samples is attributable to the fact that they combine nonprobability sampling advantages with quota controls that ensure the final sample will approximate the population with respect to its key characteristics. Quota samples are often used by consumer goods companies that have a firm grasp on the features characterizing the individuals they wish to study in a particular marketing research project. The use of quota controls guarantees that the final sample will satisfactorily represent the population. Quota samples are also used in global marketing research where communication systems are problematic. For example, most companies performing research in Latin America use quota samples.[15] When done conscientiously and with a firm understanding of the quota characteristics, quota sampling can rival probability sampling in the minds of some researchers.

# Online Sampling Techniques

Internet surveys are becoming increasingly popular. To be sure, sampling for internet surveys poses special challenges.[16] The cellphone surveys is a special form of internet survey. Ethics in Marketing Research 9.1 on page 315 discusses challenges facing researchers using cellphone surveys, many of which apply to internet surveys as well. For purposes of illustration, three types of online sampling are described: (1) random online intercept sampling, (2) invitation online sampling, and (3) online panel sampling.

**Random online intercept sampling** relies on a random selection of website visitors. There are a number of Java-based or other html-embedded routines that will select website visitors on a random basis, such as time of day or random selection from the stream of website visitors. If the population is defined as website visitors, then this is a simple random sample of these visitors within the time frame of the survey. If the sample selection program starts randomly and incorporates a skip

## ONLINE APPLICATION 9.1
# What Sample Size Should You Use?

Go to **www.macorr.com**. Macorr is a full service marketing research firm specializing in finding samples for online research data collection. Click on the box "Download Free Sample Calculator."

1. Place five in the box for confidence interval. Compare the sample sizes when you have a population size of 1000, 10 000, and 1 million.

2. Graph the different sample sizes by putting sample size on the *y* axis and population size on the *x* axis. Describe the relationship between sample size and population size at a given confidence interval.

3. Place 10 in the box for confidence interval. Compare the sample sizes when you have a population size of 1000, 10 000, and 1 million.

4. Graph the different sample sizes by putting sample size on the *y* axis and population size on the *x* axis. Describe the relationship between sample size and population size at a given confidence interval.

5. Describe any differences you perceive between the graph from item 2 and the graph from item 4. What can you say about the effect of confidence interval on the relationship between sample size and population size?

interval system, it is a systematic sample, and if the sample program treats the population of website visitors like strata, it uses stratified simple random sampling as long as random selection procedures are used faithfully.[17] However, if the population is other than website visitors, and the website is used because there are many visitors, the sample is akin to a mall-intercept sample (convenience sample).

**Invitation online sampling** is when potential respondents are alerted that they may fill out a questionnaire that is hosted at a specific website.[18] For example, a retail store chain may have a notice that is handed to customers with their receipts notifying them that they may go online to fill out the questionnaire. To avoid spam, online researchers must have an established relationship with potential respondents who expect to receive an email survey. If the retail store uses a random sampling approach such as systematic sampling, a probability sample will result. Similarly, if the email list is a truly representative group of the population, and the procedures embody random selection, it will constitute a probability sample. However, if in either case there is some aspect of the selection procedure that eliminates population members or otherwise overrepresents elements of the population, the sample will be a nonprobability one.

**Online panel sampling** refers to respondent panels that are set up by marketing research companies for the explicit purpose of conducting online surveys with representative samples. There are a growing number of these companies, and online panels afford fast, convenient, and flexible access to preprofiled samples.[19] Typically, the panel company has several thousand individuals who are representative of a large geographic area, and the market researcher can specify sample parameters such as specific geographic representation, income, education, family characteristics, and so forth. The panel company then uses its database on its panel members to broadcast an email notification to those panelists who qualify for a study. Although online panel samples are not probability samples, they are used extensively by the marketing research industry.[20] In some instances, the online panel company creates the

## ETHICS IN MARKETING RESEARCH 9.1
## Ethical Considerations in Surveys Using Cellphones

Worldwide, the cellphone generation continues to grow, and, in some cases, it is larger than the land line population of potential survey respondents. On the surface, it might seem that accessing cellphone users would be just the same as accessing land line users for surveys; however, there are at least four thorny ethical aspects accompanying cellphone surveys that marketing researchers should consider as they increasingly rely on cellphone populations.[21]

1. **Cellphone surveys are inherently unsafe.** While the typical land line telephone survey respondent is comfortably situated at home, the typical cellphone survey respondent is more likely to be engaged in some multi-tasking activity: driving a car, negotiating a busy sidewalk or stairway, operating machinery, exercising on a treadmill, or even catching a train. So, it is up to the ethical marketing researcher to include simple questions about the reasonableness of the respondent taking part in a survey that may distract from the primary task. If sufficient danger exists, the survey should be postponed.

2. **Cellphone surveys are unevenly expensive for respondents.** Depending on calling plans and other factors, there may be a cost applied to the cellphone respondent for the time used on the cellphone for the survey. This cost varies by respondent, and the ethical marketing researcher will build into the survey an offer for remuneration of the expense incurred by taking part in the survey. Of course, some respondents will decline this offer because it would require disclosure of personal information such as name and mailing address.

3. **Most cellphone surveys are not brief.** The general use and expectation of cellphone users is that calls will be short and to the point. Granted some cellphone users do not have this expectation, the general belief is that most are not expecting a long phone call. The ethical marketing researcher will therefore strive to make the cellphone survey as brief as possible.

4. **Cellphone users are disproportionately nonadults.** While practically no underaged individuals own land line telephones, the number of underage/nonadult cellphone owners is immense. This situation means that random cellphone calls are guaranteed to access teenagers and even preteens. Nonadults are more susceptible to question bias and far less sophisticated than adults in their approach to surveys. The ethical marketing researcher will take precautions that ensure that interviewers can detect when a nonadult has been contacted and not include such underage individuals if they are not consistent with the objectives of the survey.

questionnaire; at other times, the researcher composes the questionnaire on the panel company's software, or some other means of questionnaire design might be used, depending on the services of the panel company. One of the greatest pluses of online panels is the high response rate, which ensures that the final sample closely represents the population targeted by the researcher. Other online sampling approaches are feasible and limited only by the creativity of the sample designers.

# Summary

1. **Define sample design terminology.**
Common words in the English language have special meaning in marketing research and, in particular, in sample design. For example, a *population* in sampling

is the entire group under study as defined by the research objectives. A sample is defined as a subset of the population that should represent the entire population. Other concepts in sampling that are introduced include *census, sampling error, sample frame,* and *sample error frame.*

**2.  Calculate sample size.**

Sample accuracy depends to some extent on the sample size. As sample size increases, sample error decreases. However, doubling sample size does not result in halving sampling error. This is due to the curved relationship between sample size and sample accuracy. To determine the best sample size for a marketing research activity, the confidence interval formula should be used. The formula requires the researcher to (1) specify a desired sample accuracy level such as ±3% or ±4%, (2) estimate the variability in the population (50%/50% if the researcher is unsure), and (3) use the 95% or 99% level of confidence. Sample size can be calculated with the formula provided in the chapter or computed by XL Data Analyst™.

**3.  Describe four probability sampling methods.**

Probability sampling methods guarantee that each member of the population has an equal chance of being selected into the sample. Four such methods are (1) simple random sampling, where random numbers are employed; (2) systematic sampling, where a skip interval for a sample frame list is used; (3) cluster sampling, where census are taken from a random sample of homogeneous groups in the population; and (4) stratified sampling, where a random sample is taken from each subpopulation in a skewed population.

**4.  Describe four nonprobability sampling methods.**

Nonprobability sampling methods are not based on fairness, equity, or equal chance and are inherently biased. Such sampling methods are also called nonrandom, and they take less effort, less time, and cost less than random sampling methods. Nonetheless, there are circumstances such as pretesting when a nonprobability sample is acceptable. The four methods described are (1) convenience sampling, using a readily available sample such as users of the internet; (2) judgment sampling, in which the researcher uses his or her judgment to specify who will be in the sample— for example, by guessing a subject's income level by the clothes worn; (3) referral sampling, in which a respondent gives the names of friends and acquaintances to increase the number of subjects in the sample; and (4) quota sampling, in which the researcher attempts to minimize sample selection error by restricting certain classes of individuals in proportions believed to reflect their presence in a population.

# Key Terms

Accuracy of a sample    (p. 294)
Area sampling    (p. 306)
Census    (p. 293)
Cluster sampling    (p. 305)
Confidence interval formula for
   sample size    (p. 296)
Convenience sample    (p. 310)
Desired accuracy    (p. 297)

Disproportionate stratified sampling
   (p. 309)
Incidence rate    (p. 298)
Invitation online sampling    (p. 314)
Judgment sample    (p. 311)
Level of confidence    (p. 296)
Nonprobability sampling method
   (p. 309)

# Review Questions

**1.1** What are the differences between a sample and a population?

**1.2** Indicate the sample frame error typically found in the households listing of a telephone book.

**1.3** Below are four populations and a potential sample frame for each one. For each pair, identify: (1) members of the population who are not in the sample frame, and (2) members of the sample frame items who are not part of the population. Also, for each one, would you judge the amount of sample frame error to be acceptable or unacceptable? Give reasons for your answers.

| Population | Sample Frame |
| --- | --- |
| **a.** Buyers of Scope mouthwash | Mailing list of *Consumer Reports* subscribers |
| **b.** Listeners of a particular FM radio classical music station | Telephone directory in your city |
| **c.** Prospective buyers of a new day planner and prospective-client tracking kit | Members of Sales and Marketing Executives International (a national organization of sales managers) |
| **d.** Users of weatherproof decking materials (to build outdoor decks) | Individuals' names registered at a recent home and garden show |

**2.1** Explain the relationship between sample size and sample accuracy.

**2.2** Why is $p$ taken to represent the variability of a population?

**2.3** Crest toothpaste is reviewing plans for its annual survey of toothpaste purchasers. With each case that follows, calculate the sample size pertaining to the key variable under consideration. Where information is missing, provide reasonable assumptions. You can check your computations by using the sample size calculation feature of the XL Data Analyst™.

| Case | Key Variable | Variability | Acceptable Error | Confidence Level |
|------|-------------|-------------|------------------|------------------|
| 1 | Market share of Crest toothpaste last year | 23% share | 4% | 95% |
| 2 | Percentage of people who brush their teeth per week | Unknown | 5% | 99% |
| 3 | How likely Crest buyers are to switch brands | 30% switched last year | 5% | 95% |
| 4 | Percentage of people who want tartar-control features in their toothpaste | 20% two years ago 40% one year ago | 3.5% | 95% |
| 5 | Willingness of people to adopt the toothpaste | Unknown | 6% | 99% |

2.4 An online company selling used textboks to post-secondary students wants to research the growth rate of its market in Canada. The company conducted a survey of used-book buying by students each year for the past four years. In each survey, 1000 randomly selected students were asked to indicate whether they bought a used textbook in the previous year. The results were as follows:

| | Years Ago | | | |
|---|---|---|---|---|
| | 1 | 2 | 3 | 4 |
| Percentage buying used text(s) | 70% | 60% | 55% | 50% |

Assess whether or not the survey should be continued in the coming year with a sample size of 1000. Is the sample size of 1000 adaquate for the company's analysis? Give reasons for your answer.

3.1 Why is a probability sample also a random sample?

3.2 How does cluster sampling differ from stratified sampling?

3.3 Pet Insurers markets insurance to pet owners. It specializes in coverage for pedigreed dogs, cats, and exotic pets such as miniature Vietnamese potbellied pigs. The veterinary care costs of these pets can be high, and their deaths represent substantial financial loss to their owners. A researcher working for Pet Insurers finds that a listing company can provide a list of 15 000 names that includes all current subscribers to *Cat Lovers*, *Pedigreed Dog*, and *Exotic Pets Monthly*. If the final sample size is to be 1000, calculate what the skip interval should be in a systematic sample for each of the following:

a. A telephone survey using drop-down replacement of nonrespondents

b. A mail survey with an anticipated 30% response rate (assume the incidence rate for this sample frame to be 100%)

4.1 Compare a judgment sample with a referral sample. How are they similar? How are they unalike?

4.2 In order to implement a quota sample, what prior knowledge does the researcher need to have about the population?

4.3 A market researcher is proposing a survey for a private country club that is contemplating several changes in its layout to make the golf course more championship calibre. The researcher is considering three different sample designs as a way to draw a representative sample of the club's golfers. The three alternative designs are:

a. Station an interviewer at the first-hole tee on one day chosen at random, with instructions to ask every tenth golfer to fill out a self-administered questionnaire.

b. Put a stack of questionnaires on the counter where golfers check in, and pay for their golf carts. There would be a sign above the questionnaires, and there would be an incentive for a "free dinner in the clubhouse" for three players who fill out the questionnaires and whose names are selected by a lottery.

c. Using the city telephone directory, a plus-one dialling procedure would be used. With this procedure a random page in the directory would be selected, and a name on that page would be selected, both using a table of random numbers. The plus-one system would be applied to that name and every name listed after it until 1000 golfers are identified and interviewed by telephone.

Assess the representativeness and other issues associated with this sample problem. Be sure to identify the sample method being contemplated in each case. Which sample method do you recommend using, and why?

# Case 9.1

# Peaceful Valley: Trouble in Suburbia

(The following case is fictitious.)

Located on the outskirts of a large city, the suburb of Peaceful Valley comprises approximately 6000 upscale homes. The subdivision came about 10 years ago when a developer built an earthen dam on Peaceful River and created Peaceful Lake, a meandering 20-acre body of water. The lake became the centrepiece of the development, and the first 2000 half-acre lots were sold as lakefront property. Now Peaceful Valley is fully developed, with 50 streets, all approximately 2.5 kilometres in length, with approximately 60 houses on each street. Peaceful Valley's residents are primarily young, professional, dual-income families with one or two school-aged children. A unique feature of Peaceful Valley is that there are only two entrances/

exits, which have security systems that monitor vehicle traffic. As a result, Peaceful Valley is considered the safest community in the province.

But controversy has come to Peaceful Valley. The suburb's steering committee has recommended that the community build a swimming pool, tennis court, and meeting room facility on four adjoining vacant lots in the back of the subdivision. Construction cost estimates range from $1.5 million to $2 million, depending on how large the facility will be. Currently, every Peaceful Valley homeowner is billed $100 annually for maintenance, security, and upkeep of Peaceful Valley. About 75% of the residents pay this fee. To construct the proposed recreational facility, each Peaceful Valley household would be expected to pay a one-time fee of $500,

*(Continued)*

and annual fees would increase to $200 based on facility maintenance cost estimates.

Objections to the recreational facility come from various quarters. For some, the one-time fee is unacceptable; for others, the notion of a recreational facility is not appealing. Some residents have their own swimming pools, belong to local tennis clubs, or otherwise have little use for a meeting room facility. Other Peaceful Valley homeowners see the recreational facility as a wonderful addition where they could have their children learn to swim, play tennis, or just hang out under supervision.

The president of the Peaceful Valley Suburb Association has decided to conduct a survey to poll the opinions and preferences of Peaceful Valley homeowners regarding the swimming pool, tennis court, and meeting room facility concept.

## Questions

1. If the steering committee agrees to a survey that is accurate to ±5% and at a 95% level of confidence, what sample size should be used?

2. What sample method do you recommend? In making your recommendation, carefully consider the geographic configuration of Peaceful Valley. Provide the specifics of how each household in the sample should be selected, including what provision(s) to take if a selected household happened to be on vacation or was unwilling to take part in the survey.

3. Should the survey be a sample (of the size you calculated in question 1 or a census of Peaceful Valley homeowners? Defend your choice. Be certain to discuss any practical considerations that enter into your choice.

# Case 9.2

# On-Campus Food: What Do Students Think?

(The following case is fictitious.)

Campus Group Canada is the nation's leading food service management company, providing food services to both public and private corporations as well as to special events such as the Rogers AT&T Cup and Tennis Masters Canada. Stewarts, a member of Campus Group Canada, is the largest food services company on campuses across Canada. Faced with the challenge of satisfying the tastes and preferences of today's highly diverse student population, and faced with the growing number of competitor options available on Canadian campuses, Stewarts decided to undertake marketing research.

The manager of operations needed to more fully understand the needs and wants of the student customers and wanted some feedback on their food experiences while on campus. He decided to undertake a research survey that would sample campuses across Canada and across campus segments. He wanted the sample to be representative of the entire Canadian campus population. He also wanted to be able to make decisions based on a 95% level of confidence.

## Questions

1. What sample size does Stewarts need in order to achieve its goals?

2. Given the company's criteria, what sampling method should be used? Describe how the sample representation would be gathered using this method.

3. What are some of the challenges in using this sampling method?

4. If you could recommend an alternative sampling method to Stewarts, which would you recommend? Explain how your recommended method can solve the research problem that the manager of operations faces.

# Case 9.3 YOUR INTEGRATED CASE

## Student Life E-Zine
### Sample Decisions

This is the sixth installment in our integrated case series. You will find the previous Student Life E-Zine cases in Chapters 1, 2, 3, 6, and 8.

Bob Watts is on the phone with Wesley, one of our hopeful Student Life E-Zine owners, discussing the sample size and selection steps of the survey. Wesley has volunteered to talk with Bob about this as he is the one who remembers most about this topic from his undergraduate studies at City U. "Okay," says Bob, "we need to make some decisions that will have some important consequences about the generalizability of our survey. As you and the others know, we have an agreement with City University officials to have access to their student data files as long as we provide them with the results of this survey, as they are very interested in partnering with the Student Life E-Zine. It could offload a lot of the City U website work that is planned over the next two years. They said they would work with us in any way possible to develop a sample of City U students."

Wesley says, "That's great! I knew they'd be willing to help us, since my cousin works in the City U website tech area, and he told me a year ago that they had so much to do that it might take five years to put it all on City U's website because his area is so underfunded." Wesley continues, "I actually consulted my old marketing research class notes, and I found that the typical opinion poll has a sample accuracy of from ±3% to ±4%. I will leave it to you to make the recommendation, however. And as for the sample selection, I'll trust it to you as well, but since we are using a telephone survey, I found in my notes that random digit dialling is a commonly used technique. But you're the expert, Bob, so whatever you come up with, we'll give it strong consideration."

Bob says, "I'll take all of this under consideration and get back to you and the others next week. So long for now." Upon switching off his phone,

Bob glances at his calendar and notices that the marketing research intern he hired from from City U—he has jotted her first name down—Lori—will meet with him in three days to begin her five-week rotation in his group. Somewhat devilishly, Bob thinks, "I think I'll give this Lori a test. I'll send her an email with the Student Life E-Zine sample decisions that are pending and see what she comes up with for our initial interview."

Here is Bob's email to Lori.

To: Lori Baker, Marketing Research Intern

From: Bob Watts, Division Manager

Subject: Initial Interview

Lori:

*Some time has passed since we met and I hired you as our marketing research intern this semester. You are about to begin your third and last department rotation in the company and into my department. For your initial interview with me on Friday, I am providing you with some information about a current project, and I would like you to be prepared to discuss with me your recommendations for certain sample decisions that must be made very shortly for the E-Zine project (project proposal attached for your perusal—I have also included my notes with relevant communications, including the most recent one concerning sample size and method with the client group).*

1. *What is your recommendation as to the sample size for the survey? I suggest that you use Wesley's telephone conversation comments in deciding on your recommendation.*

2. *What is your reaction to a random-digit-dialling approach to select the sample of City U students? Consider that we will use a data collection company that can generate random-digit-dialling numbers easily. Does this alter your reaction to random digit dialling to any degree?*

*(Continued)*

3.  What if one of our budding Student Life E-Zine entrepreneurs is bullish on having us sample just the technical majors at City U, such as computer science, computer and electrical engineering, information systems/decision sciences, computer graphics, and the like? What is your reaction to this sample design, and why?

4.  City U says it will access its electronic student files to select a sample, but it will only provide us the sample of students based on our instructions as to how to select these students. If I assign you the task of communicating to the City U technical folks how to select the sample, what steps do you propose to tell them to take to effect:

    a.  A simple random sample using electronic records?

    b.  A systematic sample using the City University Student Directory?

Have a good next few days, and I will see you at your interview at 10:00 a.m. on Friday.

Your task in analyzing this case is to take Lori's role and develop answers to each of Bob's four sampling questions for the Student Life E-Zine survey.

# Data Collection and Basic Descriptive Statistics

By permission, DSS Research.

## Data Analysis at DSS Research

At DSS, when a project calls for measuring satisfaction, we often use a five-point response scale with descriptors such as: "Completely Satisfied," "Very Satisfied," "Somewhat Satisfied," "Not Too Satisfied," and "Not at All Satisfied." As you will learn in this chapter, we use data analysis techniques to summarize the results for our clients. For example, while this satisfaction scale is a metric scale and allows us to calculate means and standard deviations, we've learned that many of our clients prefer focusing on the percentages of the sample that fall in the top two categories or the top three categories. We summarize the data for them by reporting the percentages for each category of satisfaction. We also summarize by reporting the means and standard deviations to metric questions. By summarizing the findings we give our clients the basic descriptive statistics they need to interpret the data we have collected for them. These basic descriptive statistics are the "bread and butter" of data analysis. You will learn how to summarize findings in this chapter.

While summarizing data is very important, this is just the beginning of the analytics we provide DSS Research clients. Clients want to know if they can *generalize* the findings from our sample data to their entire population of customers. For example, if we determine that 43% of the sample falls in the "Completely Satisfied" and "Very Satisfied" groups, our clientswant to know if the 43% we are giving them is a reliable estimate of the true percentage of satisfied customers in the population. Calculating a confidence interval around the percentage allows us to answer their concerns. A confidence interval allows us to tell our clients something like: *"Our best estimate of those in the population who are either Completely or Very Satisfied is 43%. In addition, we are 95% confident that the true percentage of those who are Completely or Very*

*Satisfied falls between 40% and 46%."* In this way we can assure the client that the results are *generalizable* to their actual customer population. You will learn how to *generalize* sample findings to the population by constructing confidence intervals in the next chapter.

Clients also need to know if there are any significant *differences* among subgroups. Are males *different* from females? Are "Heavy Usage" customers *different* from "Moderate" or "Light Usage" customers? Are customers at different client locations *different* in terms of satisfaction? To test for significant *differences* between two groups, we use t-tests. Also, when we conduct segmentation analysis for clients, we examine differences between several market segments. To analyze differences between more than two groups, we use a technique known as Analysis of Variance (ANOVA). You will learn about *differences* analysis using both t-tests and ANOVA in Chapter 12.

Clients know that satisfied customers are *related* to sales and sales are *related* to profits. Clients know that intentions of customers to buy their brand or patronize their store in the future are *related* to sales and profits. Clients also know that customers' willingness to recommend their brand or store to others is also related to sales and profits. Since satisfaction, intentions, and willingness to recommend are so important, clients want to know what drives these important variables. What variables are *related* to higher levels of satisfaction? What variables are *related* to increased intention to buy a client's brand? What variables are *related* to increased willingness to recommend a client's brand to others? To answer these questions we find *relationships* between variables that clients can act on and level of satisfaction, intention, and willingness to recommend. In Chapter 14, you will learn how to use cross-tabulations, correlation, and regression analysis to find these *relationships*.

At DSS Research, we are capable of running the most sophisticated data analysis techniques, including multivariate analyses. How do we know which data analysis technique to use? First, we have to be knowledgeable of what data analysis tools are available and the purpose each tool serves. We also must be knowledgeable of the requirements to properly run each analysis technique. Armed with this knowledge, we examine each research objective we have carefully crafted to address the client's problem and we select the most appropriate data analysis technique to reach the research objective. By reading this and the next few chapters, and by learning the tools available to you using XL Data Analyst™, you will gain an appreciation of what professional marketing researchers do every day.

Kevin Weseman, MSMR

Director of Analytics

DSS Research

*Kevin Weseman is Director of Analytics at DSS Research in Ft. Worth, TX. Kevin received his B.S. and MBA at the University of West Florida. After a stint in the retailing industry, Kevin enrolled in the Masters of Science Marketing Research program at the University of Texas, Arlington.[1] Upon graduation, Mr. Weseman received a job offer at DSS Research. Visit DSS Research at www.dssresearch.com*

This chapter describes the various ways a researcher summarizes the findings in a survey sample. It introduces the analyses—such as percentages and averages—to use, the proper or correct time to use them, and how to communicate them to sponsors or clients who are anxiously awaiting the findings of the survey. The chapter begins with a description of the various data analyses available to the marketing researcher. These devices convert formless data into meaningful information. These techniques summarize and communicate patterns found in the data sets that marketing researchers analyze. Some issues concerning data collection that affect data coding and the code book are discussed, as well as how to create a data set in Excel using our XL Data Analyst™.

# Errors Encountered in the Data Collection Stage

Regardless of the method of data collection, the data collection stage of a marketing research project can be the source of many **nonsampling errors**, errors in the research process involving anything except the sample size. If the researcher uses **fieldworkers**, or individuals hired to administer the survey to respondents, there are dangers of **intentional fieldworker errors**, meaning that interviewers deliberately falsify their work by, for example, submitting bogus completed questionnaires.[2] There are also dangers of **unintentional fieldworker errors**, meaning that interviewers make mistakes such as those caused by fatigue or lack of understanding of how to administer the questions. The best way to minimize fieldworker errors is to hire a reputable data collection company that has excellent training, good supervision, and built-in validation techniques.[3]

There are also **respondent errors**, which are errors committed by respondents when answering the questions in a survey. **Intentional respondent errors** are those committed when the respondent knowingly provides false answers or fails to give an answer. Tactics such as incentives, assuring anonymity, providing confidentiality, or follow-up validation are employed to reduce the level of intentional respondent error.[4] **Unintentional respondent errors**, on the other hand, occur when the respondent is confused, distracted, or otherwise inattentive. Good questionnaire design, adequate pretesting of the questionnaire, "no opinion" or "unsure" response options, negatively worded items, or prompters such as "Do you have any other things that come to mind?" minimize the amount of unintentional respondent error in a survey.

## Data Collection Errors with Online Surveys

In many ways, an online survey is similar to a self-administered questionnaire because there is no interviewer. Unless controls are in place, there can be misrepresentations in online surveys.[5] There are three data collection errors unique to online surveys: (1) multiple submissions by the same respondent, (2) bogus respondents and/or responses, and (3) misrepresentation of the population.

### Multiple Submissions
The typical online questionnaire is fast and easy to take. Unless controlled it is possible for a respondent to submit his or her completed questionnaire multiple times in a matter of minutes. If the person is free to submit multiple responses, an overrepresentation of that individual's views and opinions will cause respondent error. The customary control for **multiple submissions** is to ask the respondent for his or

Even with online surveys, marketing researchers must take precautions to reduce errors.

her email address, and an electronic block is activated if the email address is repeated. Of course, this control does not eliminate multiple email addresses from the same respondent.

### Bogus Respondents and Responses

The anonymity of the internet can inspire individuals to log into a questionnaire site as a fictitious person or to disguise themselves as another person. Under this guise, the individual may feel free to give nonsense, polarized, or otherwise false responses. Coupled with the multiple submissions error, a bogus response error has the potential to create havoc with an online survey. If this concern is great, researchers turn to online panels or other options where the respondents are pre-qualified or preidentified in some manner to control for bogus respondents.

### Population Misrepresentation

All consumers are not equally internet connected or web literate, a fact that can lead to **population misrepresentation** in surveys. Some segments of the population—such as elderly citizens, low-income families, people in remote areas where internet connection is sparse and/or expensive, or technophobic people—are not good prospects for an online survey. By the same token, some individuals are more connected than others in their respective market segments. For instance, a web-based survey of life insurance companies could result in a responding sample overrepresenting those people who are very comfortable with the web, and underrepresenting those individuals who use the internet infrequently.[6]

## Types of Nonresponse

**Nonresponse** is defined as a failure on the part of a prospective respondent to take part in the survey or to answer specific questions on the questionnaire. Nonresponse has been labelled the marketing research industry's biggest problem,

| Type | Description |
|------|-------------|
| Refusal | A prospective respondent declines to participate in the survey. |
| Break-off | A respondent stops answering somewhere in the middle of the survey. |
| Item omission | A respondent does not answer a particular question but continues to answer following questions. |

**Table 10.1** Three Types of Nonresponse Encountered in a Survey

it haunts the polling industry, and it is multinational in scope.[7–9] Some industry observers believe that nonresponse is caused by fears of invasion of privacy, skepticism of consumers regarding the benefits of participating in research, and the use of research as a guise for telemarketing.

There are at least three different types of potential nonresponse error: refusals to participate in the survey, break-offs during the interview, and refusals to answer specific questions, or item omission. Table 10.1 is a quick reference that describes each type of nonresponse.

### Refusals to Participate in the Survey

A **refusal** occurs when a potential respondent rejects the offer to take part in the survey. Refusal rates for telephone surveys are estimated to be as high as 50%.[10] The reasons for refusals are many and varied. The person may be busy, he or she may have no interest in the survey, something about the interviewer's voice or approach may have turned the person off, or the refusal may simply reflect how that person always responds to surveys. Some tactics found to reduce the refusal rate include making an offer to call back at a more convenient time, identifying the name of the research company (and client, if possible), making the interviews as short as possible, and emphasizing that the interviewer is not selling anything.[11]

### Break-Offs during the Interview

A **break-off** occurs when a respondent reaches a certain point and then decides not to answer any more questions for the survey. Reasons for break-offs are varied. The interview may take longer than the respondent initially believed; the topic and specific questions may prove to be distasteful or too personal; the instructions may be too confusing; a sudden interruption may occur; or the respondent may choose to take an incoming call on call-waiting and stop the interview. Sometimes with self-administered surveys, a researcher will find a questionnaire that the respondent has simply stopped filling out.

It is critical that well-trained interviewers be employed to carry out survey data collection. In a discussion on how to improve respondent cooperation, Howard Gershowitz, senior vice president of MKTG, said, "I think the interviewers have to be taken out of the vacuum and be included in the process. Companies that are succeeding right now realize that the interviewers are the key to their success."[12] Increasingly, research providers are focusing on improved training techniques and field audits.

### Refusals to Answer Specific Questions (Item Omission)

If a marketing researcher suspects ahead of time that a particular question, such as the respondent's annual income for last year, will have some degree of refusals, it is appropriate to include the designation "refusal" on the questionnaire. It is not wise to put these designations on self-administered questionnaires because respondents may use this option simply as a cop-out, when they might have provided accurate answers if the designation were not there. "**Item omission**" is the phrase often used to signify that some respondents refused to answer a particular question.

### Completed Interview

Researchers will experience both break-offs and item omissions. The researcher must make a judgment call as to what a **completed interview** is. If a sufficient number of questions are answered to allow the questionnaire to move into the data analysis stage, the interview can be considered completed. The determination will vary with each marketing research project. In some cases, it may be that the respondent must answer all of the questions. In others, there may be a decision rule to allow researchers to define completed versus not completed interviews. For example, in most research studies there are questions directed at the primary purpose of the study. Also, there are usually questions asked for purposes of gaining additional insights into how respondents answered the primary questions. Such secondary questions often include a list of demographic questions. Demographics, because they are more personal in nature, are typically placed at the end of the questionnaire. Because they are not the primary focus of the study, a "completed interview" may be defined as one in which all primary questions have been answered. Interviewers can then be given a specific statement as to what constitutes a completed survey, such as, "If the respondent answers through question 18, you may count it as a completion." (The demographics begin with question 19.) Likewise, the researcher must adopt a decision rule for determining how many and which item omissions invalidate a survey or a particular question.

# Coding Data and the Data Code Book

After questionnaires are scrutinized and completed questionnaires are identified, the researcher moves to the data entry stage of the data analysis process. **Data entry** refers to the creation of a computer file that holds the raw data taken from all of the completed questionnaires. A number of data entry options exist, ranging from manual keyboard entry of each and every piece of data to computer systems that scan entire sets of questionnaires and convert them to a data file in a matter of minutes. The most seamless data entry situations are integrated questionnaire design and analysis software programs, such as Websurveyor, that capture each respondent's answers and convert them to computer files almost immediately.

Regardless of the method, data entry requires an operation called **data coding**, defined as the identification of computer code values that pertain to the possible responses for each question on the questionnaire. Typically, these codes are numerical because numbers are quick and easy to input, and computers work with numbers more efficiently than they do with alphanumeric codes. In large-scale projects, and especially in cases in which the data entry is performed by a subcontractor, researchers use a **data code book** that identifies all of the variable names and code numbers associated with each possible response to each question that makes up the data set. With a code book that describes the data file, any analyst can work on the data set, regardless of whether that analyst was involved in the research project during its earlier stages.

Because precoded questionnaires have the response codes identified beside the various responses, it is a simple matter to create a code book. It is best to use the same code for missing data on completed questionnaires. The easiest and most acceptable code for a missing response is to use a blank, meaning that nothing is entered for that respondent on the question that was not answered. Practically all statistical analysis programs treat a blank as "missing."

With online surveys, such as the ones that use Qualtrics, the data file is built as respondents submit their completed online questionnaires. That is, with a web-based survey, the codes are programmed into the html questionnaire document, but they do not appear on the questionnaire as code numbers like those customarily placed on a paper-and-pencil questionnaire. Questions that are not answered are typically entered as a "blank" into the online survey's database unless the researcher preprograms the software to insert a different code number. In the case of web-based surveys, the code book is vital as it is the researcher's only map to decipher the numbers found in the data file and to match them to the answers to the questions on the questionnaire.

## Introduction to Your XL Data Analyst™

 You have downloaded and used a few of the features (such as sample size determination) in the XL Data Analyst that was created to accompany this textbook. It is now time to give you a formal introduction to the XL Data Analyst. The XL Data Analyst is a macro system for Excel. We created the XL Data Analyst so you can perform and interpret data analyses with ease. There are four reasons why we created the XL Data Analyst. First, practically everyone is acquainted with the Excel spreadsheet program that is included in Microsoft's Office Suite, so there is no need to learn a new software program. Second, commercial statistical analysis programs typically produce reams of output that are very confusing and unnecessary for basic marketing research. We have programmed our XL Data Analyst so that the findings of your analyses are plainly evident. You will need to understand some basic statistical concepts, but you will not need to memorize formulas or deal with statistical procedures. Third, the XL Data Analyst produces tables that can be copied and pasted into word processor applications such as Microsoft Word without the need for extensive reformatting into professional-looking tables. There are also graphs you can use or modify and copy, or you can make your own graphs in Excel. Finally, by creating a macro system for Excel, we have avoided the added cost of including a statistical program with this textbook.

*(Continued)*

## How to Get Your Data Code Book into XL Data Analyst

Your XL Data Analyst is a Microsoft Excel program with customized features designed to perform data analyses. We will systematically introduce you to these data analyses beginning in this chapter and continuing for the next three chapters of this textbook. We have set up the XL Data Analyst with a simulated data set pertaining to your "Student Life E-Zine" integrated case. The code book information for your "Student Life E-Zine" integrated case data set is in your XL Data Analyst.

You may wish to use a different survey data set such as a course team project or a data set provided to you by your instructor, so we will describe how to set up the XL Data Analyst with the code book information for any survey. In most data analysis situations, the code book information will be input to the data file so the analysis program can access it and apply it to whatever analysis is being performed. That is, a completed data set will include variable names, variable descriptions, data value codes (codes for each possible response to each variable) and data value names. There are two named worksheets in XL Data Analyst that are critical: the Data worksheet and the Define Variables worksheet. Both are described in Table 10.2.

**Table 10.2** Your Data and Code Book in XL Data Analyst

| Worksheet | Element | Description |
|---|---|---|
| *Data* | Variables | Each variable occupies a separate column. |
| | Variable labels | A unique descriptive word in row 1 of each variable column (e.g., Gender or Q1, Q2) |
| | Respondents | Rows of numbers in the various cells of each column, not including row 1 |
| | Data set | The matrix of rows and columns |
| *Define Variables* | Variable labels | Variable labels that are in row 1 of the Data worksheet are *linked* to the Define Variables worksheet beginning at cell B1. |
| | Variable descriptions | You can type in or paste a long variable description for each variable in the cell beneath its variable label (e.g., "Gender of the Respondent"). |
| | Value codes* | The related code values for each variable's possible answer (value label) are placed in row 3 with the codes separated by commas (e.g., 1, 2). |
| | Value labels* | The value labels for each set of variable's value codes are placed below them in row 4 with the value labels separated by commas and in the same order as your value codes (e.g., Male, Female). |

*With metric variables that do not have value labels such as the case of a respondent giving his actual age in years or other open-ended questions, the Value Codes and Value Labels cells are left blank.

The way you set up your code book in XL Data Analyst is through the "Define Variables" worksheet. When a researcher sets up the data set for the first time in XL Data Analyst, each variable can be defined in three ways. First, there *must* be a **variable label**, or a unique, short, single-word description for that variable placed in the first row on the Data worksheet. This row is then linked into the Define Variables worksheet: Copy the row in the Data worksheet and then Paste Special—Paste Link into the B1 cell of the Define Variables worksheet. (To ensure that information is correctly linked between the Data and Define Variables worksheets select Utilities—Clean-Up from the XL Data Analyst menu.)

The Define Variables worksheet accommodates the researcher's data code book as follows. There should be a **variable description**, which is a phrase or sentence that identifies the variable in more detail and is usually the question from the questionnaire, possibly condensed for readability. This is exactly how that variable will appear in all analyses, so it should be worded carefully and correctly. Then, depending on the nature of the variable, there can be **value codes** that are numerical values and **value labels**, which are responses that correspond to each data code number for that particular variable. You are not required to define your variables in XL Data Analyst; however, you will find that it will be much more convenient to use its menus and to read the various analyses results if you provide data labels and descriptions, and value codes and value labels where appropriate. Also, the data definition step is a one-time activity as XL Data Analyst will remember your data definitions as soon as you save your data set as an Excel file.

Figure 10.1 is a dual screen capture of Excel with the XL Data Analyst installed and a data set in the Data worksheet. We have pasted the Define

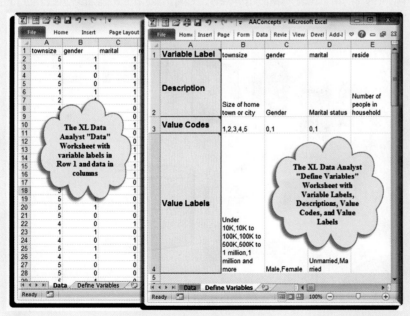

**Figure 10.1** The XL Data Analyst Data and Define Variables Worksheets Showing Variable Labels and Coded Data

*(Continued)*

Variables worksheet window so you can view both worksheets at the same time. As you can see in the Data worksheet, the columns include labels in the first row, meaning that each column pertains to a variable in the survey. Each row represents a respondent or a completed questionnaire. We also set up variable labels "townsize," "gender," "marital," and so forth with descriptions, value codes, and value labels.

Marketing Research in Action 10.1 discusses how Excel is used by OxGrid, a business applications company.

## MARKETING RESEARCH IN ACTION 10.1
# Microsoft Excel: A Useful Data Management Tool in Marketing Research

Marketing researchers have turned to Microsoft Excel to manage data, and OzGrid Business Applications is a good example. They not only teach and tutor in Microsoft Excel, but also use Microsoft Excel for marketing research on a daily basis. OzGrid has many clients who use their Excel add-ins to conduct marketing research. Their expert knowledge of Excel, combined with their industry experience, ensures clients that

OzGrid knows exactly the type of problems that are encountered in business today and how to properly analyze data to solve those problems. According to Raina Hawley of OzGrid, "Microsoft Excel is used widely in business for analyzing data for market research projects." Ms. Hawley states that "many businesses collect data to help them make better business decisions, and the use of Microsoft Excel can make the data analysis tasks simple

Raina Hawley oversees a staff member using Excel for a marketing research project at OzGrid.

and can automate what once took many labour-intensive hours of research."[13]

Microsoft Excel is specifically designed for these sorts of tasks and has many useful and extremely powerful features that can aid businesses in their efforts to become successful in the marketplace. Microsoft Excel not only has many useful built-in features that can make market research easy but also has many Microsoft Excel add-ins available on the market that have been or can be tailored to suit a company's needs. An add-in is a software product that adds extra functionality to an existing application, such as Microsoft Excel. The XL Data Analyst™ is an add-in that we developed to help make Microsoft Excel more useful to you for marketing research purposes. OzGrid Business Applications is far more extensive as it offers hundreds of Excel add-ins and business software designed for data analysis in all market areas through their website at **www.ozgrid.com**. OzGrid Business Applications provides training and tutoring in all aspects of Excel and Visual Basic Applications Excel, enabling their clients to become proficient users of this Microsoft Office tool.

# Types of Data Analyses Used in Marketing Research

The complementary processes of data coding and data entry result in a **data set**, defined as a matrix of numbers and other codes that includes all of the relevant answers of all respondents in a survey. (View part of a data set in Figure 10.1.) The researcher uses computer tools to perform various types of **data analysis**. Data analysis is defined as the process of describing a data set by computing a small number of measures that characterize the data set in ways that are meaningful to the client.[14] Data analysis accomplishes one or more of the following functions: (1) It summarizes the data, (2) it generalizes sample findings to the population, (3) it compares for meaningful differences, and (4) it relates underlying patterns.[15] Each data analysis function corresponds to one of four data analysis objectives. The appropriate types of data analysis a researcher uses are summed up in Table 10.3 on the next page.

It is important to have knowledge of what analyses are used by researchers, and under what conditions they are used. For example, credit card companies target post-secondary students and are quite successful for the most part.[16] However, one credit card company, Visa, lags far behind the other cards with respect to student market share. Pretend that Visa commissioned a survey to better understand the post-secondary student credit card market. The survey involves a representative sample of students from colleges and universities across Canada. In Table 10.3, an example of each data analysis type in the Visa survey is shown.

Before analyzing the data, the type of data needs to be identified so that the appropriate analysis is used. In Chapter 7, categorical and metric scales were discussed. Recall that categorical scales have a level of measurement such that they place respondents into groups such as gender (male versus female), buyer type (buyer versus nonbuyer), marital status (single, married, separated, divorced), yes/no, and the like. A metric scale is one where the respondent indicates an amount or quantity such as how many times, how much, how long, or his or her feelings on a synthetic metric scale such as a Likert scale (disagree–agree) or a five-point anchored scale. Recall also that the level of measurement dictates the *proper* data analysis.

**Table 10.3** Research Objectives and Appropriate Types of Data Analysis

| Research Objective | Description of Analysis Appropriate to Objective | Hypothetical Visa Post-Secondary Student Survey Example |
|---|---|---|
| Description | Summarizing the sample data with:<br>■ Percentages and Percentage Distribution (categorical data)<br>■ Averages, Range, and Standard Deviation (metric data)<br>(Chapter 10) | A total of 74% of the respondents used a credit card in the past month, and the average total credit card charge was $350. |
| Generalization | Generalizing the sample findings to the population with:<br>■ Hypothesis Tests<br>■ Confidence Intervals<br>(Chapter 11) | Visa managers believed that 40% of post-secondary students own a Visa card, but this was not supported. Actually, between 18% and 28% own one. |
| Differences | Comparing averages or percentages in the sample data to see if there are meaningful differences with:<br>■ Percentage Difference Tests<br>■ Averages Difference Tests<br>(Chapter 12) | A total of 25% of male post-secondary students own a Visa card, which was significantly different from 20% of female post-secondary students. However, female post-secondary students charged an average of $120, significantly more than male students, who charged an average of $100 on their Visa card last month. |
| Relationships | Relating variables to each other in a meaningful way with:<br>■ Cross-tabulations<br>■ Correlations<br>■ Regression Analysis | Post-secondary students who own Visa cards were more likely to be attending programs that result in medical, law, or business degress or diplomas and living off campus. They earned more income than nonowners. |

Visa may want a summary of students who are likely to own and use its credit card.

## Summarizing the Sample Data

For description research objectives, the researcher summarizes the data with the use of percentages or averages. Recall from Chapter 7 that if the variable under consideration is categorical, the proper summary analysis is a percentage distribution. If the variable is metric the proper summary analysis is an average. Turning to the Visa example, two of its description objectives might be: (1) Do students use credit cards and (2) if so, how much do they spend on credit card purchases per month? To summarize the data, the researcher would determine the following in the sample: (1) the percentage of students who own a certain credit card and (2) the average amount of purchases on their credit cards per month. Percentage is appropriate for question 1 since the data is yes/no. Average is appropriate for question 2 since the data is metric.

*[handwritten margin note: Categorical % of ppl married]*

*[handwritten margin note: metric average of pple who "agree"]*

## Generalizing the Findings

The researcher will need to generalize the findings of the sample data to the population. Generalization means that the researcher will conduct hypotheses tests and/or compute confidence intervals. Returning to our Visa survey example, the researcher could test the actual percentage of students who own a Visa credit card against what the Visa executives believe is the actual percentage. That is, if the Visa executives believe that 40% of students currently own a Visa credit card, the researcher could test his or her sample percentage of respondents against 40% to see if the executives' belief is supported or refuted. If this hypothesis is refuted, the researcher can compute a confidence interval as to the actual percentage of ownership of the Visa card. Table 10.3 shows that the researcher found no support for the Visa executives' belief and, in fact, the researcher estimated that between 18% and 28% of post-secondary students own a Visa credit card.

## Seeking Meaningful Differences

Often clients are very interested in finding meaningful differences between groups in the sample. Such differences, when found, can offer important marketing strategy insights. With differences analysis, the researcher identifies a categorical variable (such as gender) and compares the groups represented by that variable (males versus females) by analyzing their differences on a second variable. If the second variable is categorical (use or nonuse of our brand), then the researcher will perform a percentages differences analysis; but if the second variable is metric (how many purchases in the past month), the researcher will perform an averages differences test of some sort. In the Visa survey example, the Visa executives may be interested in determining differences between male and female students, so the researcher would perform a differences test for Visa card ownership (categorical) and one for dollars spent per month (metric), comparing males to females (categorical). In Table 10.3, more male post-secondary students own Visa cards than female students, but the female students spend more per month than the male students using their Visa card.

## Identifying Relationships

Finally, a client may wish to have a better understanding of the topics under study. The researcher can tackle relationship analysis in one of two ways. For one, the researcher isolates two variables, and if the two variables are categorical, then a cross-tabulation analysis is performed. If the two variables are metric, correlations must be used. Or the researcher may select several variables to see how they are related to a single critical variable, such as how demographics and lifestyle influence the client's target market definition. In this case, the researcher will use regression analysis. Relationship analysis could be used to investigate student gender and Visa recognition (crosstabulation), credit card dollar expenditures, and number of credit cards owned (correlation) or perhaps to determine the post-secondary student demographic and/or lifestyle factors that relate to how appealing Visa's credit card is to students (regression). Table 10.3 notes some relationships: Student Visa cardholders tend to be majoring in professional school curricula, to live off campus, and to earn more income.

Figure 10.2 is a handy visual aid and a reference figure for data analyses. The horizontal axis relates to the complexity of the analysis. Data analyses range from those that are very simple to those that are fairly complex. Figure 10.2 reveals that percentages are the most elementary, while regression analysis is the more complicated type of analysis. The vertical axis is labelled "Value of Findings." Findings of the analysis are more valuable with complicated data analyses, while simple analyses are less valuable. This is not to say that the simple analyses are not useful. As you move up the analysis balloons in Figure 10.2, the findings are typically more valuable to managers as they uncover patterns and relationships.

**Figure 10.2** Research Objectives and Data Analyses Used in Marketing Research

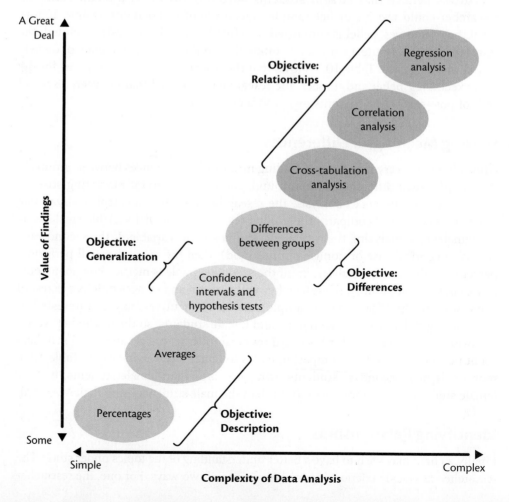

Regardless of the analysis level used, it is critical that the results are truthfully represented. Ethics in Marketing Research 10.1 on page 341 examines this issue.

# Summarizing Your Sample Findings

Summarization analysis is the type of data analysis appropriate for description research objectives. The basic data analysis goal with all summarization is to describe the most typical response to a question. It is vital to summarize the degree to which all of the respondents share this typical response. The typical response is referred to as the **central tendency**, while the degree to which respondents are typical is referred to as **variability**.[17]

For example, the average score on a class test can be 75%. If most students in the class scored around 75%, there is little variability. If the scores ranged from many students with 50%, and many who scored 90%, then the variability is greater. When summarizing sample findings, it is more useful to state both the measure of central tendency and the variability.

Depending on whether the data level of measurement is categorical or metric, the summarization analysis is different. Table 10.4 shows what analysis is appropriate for central tendency and variability of categorical versus metric variables.

## Summarizing Categorical Variables    nonmetric

When the researcher is working with a variable that is at the categorical level of measurement, the appropriate measure of central tendency is the mode. The **mode** is a summarization analysis measure defined as the value that occurs most often. Scanning a list of numbers in a column for a categorical variable in a data matrix, the mode would be the number that appeared more than any other.

Note that the mode is a relative measure of central tendency, for it does not require that a majority of responses occurred for this value. It simply specifies the value that occurs most frequently, and there is no requirement that this occurrence is 50% or more. It can take on any value as long as it is the most frequently occurring number. If a tie for the mode occurs, the distribution is considered to be "bimodal." Or it might even be "trimodal" if there is a three-way tie.

A summary of the mode (or modes) is not very informative about how typical the mode is. Occasionally, a **frequency distribution**, a summary of the *number* of times each and every category appears for the entire sample, is used. It is better to

| Type of Scale | Central Tendency (characterizes the most typical response) | Variability (indicates how similar the responses are) |
| --- | --- | --- |
| **Categorical Scale** (indicates a group) | Mode | Frequency or Percentage Distribution |
| **Metric Scale** (indicates an amount or quantity) | Average | Range and/or Standard Deviation |

**Table 10.4** Appropriate Summarization Analyses by Type of Scale

Variability indicates how different respondents are on a common topic such as buying fresh vegetables.

summarize the variability of responses to a categorical question, using a **percentage distribution**, or a summary of the percentage of times each and every category appears for the entire sample. A percentage distribution is much more intuitive, since all of its categories will sum to 100%. Frequencies themselves are raw counts and are easily converted into percentages by dividing the frequency for each value by the total number of observations for all of the values. Glancing at a percentage distribution, a researcher or a client can easily assess the mode and the variability.

A frequency or percentage distribution summarizes the responses to categorical data in a data set. It quickly communicates all of the different answers in the set, and it expresses how much agreement or disagreement there is among the respondents (the variability of their responses). The percentage distribution is often used because percentages are intuitive and easy to work with. Figure 10.3 illustrates how quickly percentage distributions communicate variability when they are converted to bar charts. For instance, if percentage distribution happened to have a great deal of agreement in it, it would appear as a very steep, spike-shaped histogram such as the one for "little variability" bar graph (drinking coffee); however, if the set happened to be made up of many dissimilar numbers, the bar graph would be much more spread out, with small peaks and valleys. This is the case with the "much variability" bar graph (drinking tea).

**Figure 10.3** A Bar Chart Shows Variability

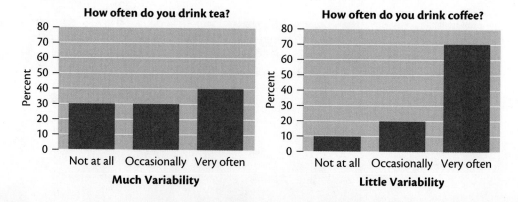

# How to Summarize Categorical Variables with XL Data Analyst™

To access the XL Data Analyst menu, simply click on the XL Data Analyst option on your Excel program menu, and move your cursor over "Summarize." This will activate the drop-down menu under Summarize to reveal two options: "Percents" and "Averages." Since we are now dealing with categorical variables, the correct selection is "Percents." As you can see in Figure 10.4, a click on the Percent menu item will open up a selection window that you can use to select variables from a data set. Note that you can use the check box to have a pie graph or cylinder graphs generated along with the tables for the variables you select. After completing the selection by highlighting or blocking the desired variables, a click on the "OK" button will cause XL Data Analyst to perform the percents summarization analysis.

Figure 10.5 shows the a pie graph and percents table generated by XL Data Analyst for the variable "Size of home town or city." The pie chart clearly shows the breakdown of different sized cities represented in the sample. Under this graph is a table with this variable's description included in the table heading, the value labels such as "1 million and more," "500K to 1 million," and so forth noted, and the frequencies and percentages displayed. The table is formatted with a professional appearance and can be copied and

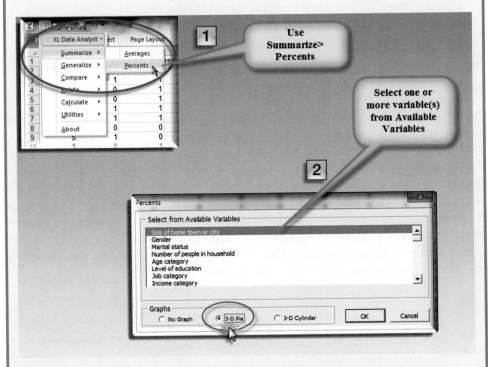

**Figure 10.4** Using the XL Data Analyst to Select Variables for Percentages Analysis

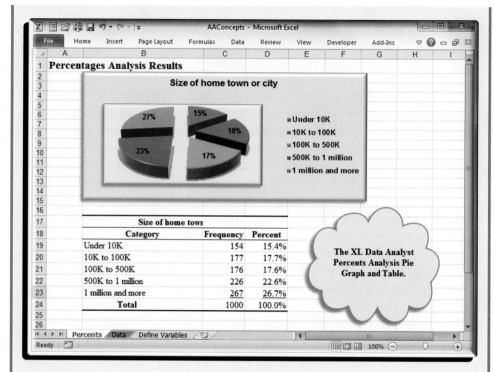

**Figure 10.5** XL Data Analyst Percentages Analysis Table

pasted into a research report or a presentation software program such as Microsoft PowerPoint. You can use Excel chart features or a chart template to create a stunning graphical presentation of the findings with any XL Data Analyst percentage analysis.[18] This can also be copied into a final report, PowerPoint, or any other compatible Windows program of your choice.

## Summarizing Metric Variables

With metric variables, the numbers are more than mere codes. They represent real amounts reflecting quantities rather than categories. Even working with a synthetic metric variable where a labelled or number scale is used, the researcher knows that the numbers express amounts of feelings, evaluations, or opinions on the parts of the respondents. To identify the central tendency number that typified all of the responses to a metric variable, the best measure would be the **average**. The average is computed by summing all of the numbers and dividing that sum by the number of respondents whose responses were included in that sum. The resulting number is the average or mean, a measure that indicates the central tendency of those values. It approximates the typical value in the set.

$$\bar{x} = \frac{\sum\limits_{n}^{i=1} x_i}{n}$$

**Formula for an average** ▶

where:     $x_i$ = each individual value
          $n$ = total number of cases (sample size)
          $\Sigma$ = signifies that all $x_i$ values are summed

The average is a very useful central tendency measure because when the same scale is used to measure various characteristics, the averages can be compared with quickly ascertain similarities or differences. If the mean house value in Saskatoon is $350 000 and the mean house value in Toronto is $450 000, one can say that Toronto has more expensive homes then Saskatoon.

There are two summarization analyses that describe the variability of respondents with respect to the mean. These are the range and the standard deviation. The **range** identifies the distance between the lowest value (minimum) and the highest values in a set of numbers. The range does not tell how often the maximum and minimum occurred, but it does provide some information on the dispersion by indicating how far apart the extremes are found. If the range is very narrow, the average is typical of many respondents, but if the range is very wide, it signals that the average is probably not typical of most respondents. For example, if the range of houses in Saskatoon is $100 000, then there are houses valued at $300 000 and $400 000. If the range of house prices in Saskatoon is $100 00, then most house

## ETHICS IN MARKETING RESEARCH 10.1
# How to Lie Using Statistics

In 1954, Darrell Huff wrote a popular book on statistics, entitled *How to Lie with Statistics*. It has become one of the most widely read statistics books in history, with over 1.5 million copies sold in the English language. It has also been widely translated.

The book focuses on the interpretation of statistical analysis for the purpose of influencing interested parties. It examines such common errors in data collection as using biased (nonrandom) samples and generalizing the results to the population as a whole. For example, if customers disappointed with a product were the only ones who posted their feelings on a social network site, it would be inaccurate to say that all customers are unhappy with that product. Also discussed are common errors in analysis, including comparing the averages between two unconnected samples. For example, it is inappropriate to compare the class average of a course in statistics for graduating students with the class average in a social studies course for first-year students as a means of evaluating the ease of the statistics course. The argument is made that many of these "misinterpretations" are intentional.

The book also describes how reporters give false impressions with summary graphs. For example, shortening the bottom of the $y$ axis on a line graph by starting at a higher value than originally researched can exaggerate the slope of the line and distort the relationship between the $x$ and $y$ variables.

Another book on the "unethical" use of statistics is Joel Best's 2001 book *Damned Lies and Statistics: Untangling Numbers from Media, Politicians, and Activists*.[19] He discusses methods for distorting numbers to make an incorrect point, as well as the common practice of making inappropriate comparisons between two or more unrelated groups (comparing apples to oranges). Best identifies the worst reporting of data as the following statement: "Every year since 1950, the number of American children gunned down has doubled." The original source reported that there were twice as many child deaths from guns in 1994 as there were in 1950—quite a different statement than the one quoted!

Although the Marketing Research and Intelligence Association (MRIA) in Canada continues to uphold the ethical use of statistics, it is still possible to *unintentionally* skew the interpretation of statistics.

prices probably are worth around \$350 000 (the average). While the range is informative about the variability of responses to a metric question, it is very ambiguous as it does not tell anything about how respondents are spread across the range. For instance, are there a great many respondents whose answers are near or at the outer limits? Are there very few of them at the limits? What about the intervals between the mean and the minimum and the maximum: How are respondents situated in their answers in these intervals?

Another variability measure of metric data is the **standard deviation**. The standard deviation is a measure of variability that uses a normal or bell-shaped curve interpretation. Although marketing researchers do not always rely on the normal curve interpretation of the standard deviation, they often encounter the standard deviation on computer printouts, and they usually report it in their tables.

A standard deviation is calculated using the following formula:

**Formula for a standard deviation** ▷

$$\text{Standard Deviation} = \sqrt{\dfrac{\sum\limits_{n}^{i=1}(x_i - \bar{x})^2}{n-1}}$$

where:

$x_i$ = each individual value
$\bar{x}$ = average
$n$ = total number of cases (sample size)

First calculate the average, then compare each respondent's value to the average by subtracting the average from it, and square that difference. If the differences were not squared, there would be positive and negative values; and if they were summed, there would be a cancellation effect. That is, large negative differences would cancel out large positive differences, and the numerator would end up being close to zero. But this result is contrary to what we know is the case with large differences. The formula remedies this problem by squaring the subtracted differences before they are summed. Squaring converts all negative numbers to positives and, of course, leaves the positives positive. Next, all of the squared differences are

## ONLINE APPLICATION 10.1
## Examine Real Reports

Go to **www.statcan.gc.ca**. In the "Search the Site Box", click on "Articles" to view a list of reports.

   Click on a report of your choice. Examine the report, paying special attention to the report highlights.

## Questions

1.   How were the data collected?

2.   Find examples of descriptive statistics in the report. Include examples of percentages as well as examples of central tendency.

3.   Why do you think the report uses simple descriptive statistics rather than more complicated analysis?

| Number of Standard Deviations from the Mean | Percent of Area Under Curve[a] | Percent of Area to Right (or Left)[b] |
|:---:|:---:|:---:|
| ±1.00 | 68% | 16.0% |
| ±1.96 | 95% | 2.5% |
| ±2.58 | 99% | 0.5% |

**Table 10.5** Normal Curve Interpretation of Standard Deviation

[a] This is the area under the curve with the number of standard deviations as the lower (left-hand) and upper (right-hand) limits and the mean equidistant from the limits.
[b] This is the area left outside of the limits described by plus or minus the number of standard deviations. Because of the normal curve's symmetric properties, the area remaining below the lower limit (left-hand tail) is exactly equal to the area remaining above the upper limit (right-hand tail).

summed and divided by 1 less than the number of total observations in the string of values (1 is subtracted from the number of observations to achieve what is typically called an "unbiased" estimate of the standard deviation). We now have an inflation factor to worry about because every comparison has been squared. To adjust for this, the equation specifies that the square root be taken after all other operations are performed. This final step adjusts the value back down to the original measure (e.g., units rather than squared units). If you did not take the square root at the end, the value would be referred to as the "variance." In other words, the variance is the standard deviation squared.

Table 10.5 shows the properties of a bell-shaped or normal distribution of values. The usefulness of this model is apparent when you realize that it is a symmetric distribution: Exactly 50% of the distribution lies on either side of the midpoint (the apex of the curve). With a normal curve, the midpoint is also the average. Standard deviations are standardized units of measurement that are located on the horizontal axis. They relate directly to assumptions about the normal curve. For example, the range of one standard deviation above and one standard deviation below the midpoint includes 68% of the total area underneath that curve. Because the bell-shaped distribution is a theoretical or ideal concept, this property never changes. Moreover, the proportion of area under the curve and within plus or minus any number of standard deviations from the mean is perfectly known.

For the purposes of this presentation, normally only two or three of these values are of interest to marketing researchers. Specifically, ±2.58 standard deviations describes the range in which 99% of the area underneath the curve is found, ±1.96 standard deviations is associated with 95% of the area underneath the curve, and ±1.64 standard deviations corresponds to 90% of the bell-shaped curve's area. Figure 10.6 is a visual aid to the ±1.96 standard deviations case that accounts for 95% of the area under the curve.

Whenever a standard deviation is reported along with an average, a specific picture should appear. Assuming that the distribution is bell shaped, the size of the standard deviation number helps envision how similar or dissimilar the typical responses are to the average. If the standard deviation is small, the distribution is greatly compressed. On the other hand, with a large standard deviation value, the distribution is stretched out at both ends. If the researcher says, "The average grade point average was 2.6," the manager might think that most or all of the respondents

**Figure 10.6** A Normal Curve with Its 95% Properties Identified

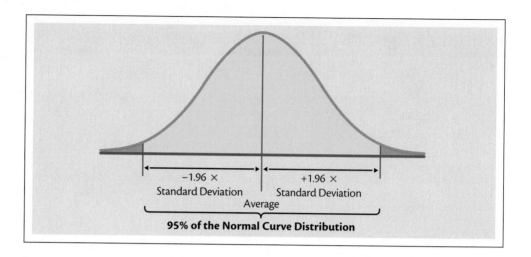

−1.96 ×
Standard Deviation

+1.96 ×
Standard Deviation

Average

**95% of the Normal Curve Distribution**

gave this answer. When the researcher says, "The standard deviation was 0.4," it appears that most students achieved the 2.6 GPA.

Ethical research companies may use any or a combination of the following to ensure that their client managers understand the analysis terminology used by its researchers: (1) prepared handbooks or glossaries defining marketing research terms, (2) appendices in reports that illustrate analysis concepts, (3) definitions of analysis terms embedded in reports when the manager first encounters them, or (4) footnotes or annotations with tables and figures that explain the analysis concepts used.

# How to Summarize Metric Variables with XL Data Analyst™

The procedure for summarizing metric variables in XL Data Analyst is identical to the one for summarizing categorical variables, except you will select "Averages." Click on the XL Data Analyst option on your Excel program menu, and move your cursor over "Summarize." This will activate the drop-down menu under Summarize to reveal "Percents" and "Averages." Since we are now dealing with metric variables, the correct selection is "Averages." A click on the Averages menu item opens a standard Excel selection window that you can use to select one or more metric variables. When you have completed your selection, a click on the "OK" button will cause XL Data Analyst to perform the Averages Summarization analysis. In other words, the XL Data Analyst selection procedure for Averages is identical to that for Percents, and the variables selection window looks the same as the selection window for percents that you saw in Figure 10.4, but without the graphing option.

Figure 10.7 shows the Averages tables generated by XL Data Analyst for a survey with the metric variable "Gasoline emissions can contribute to

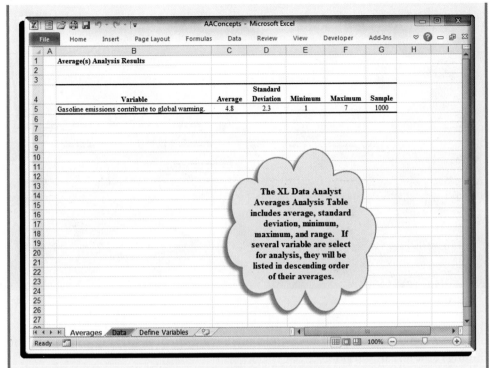

**Figure 10.7** XL Data Analyst Average Analysis Table

global warming," measured on a 7-point scale, where 1 = very strongly disagree and 7 = very strongly agree. This table is quite different from the Percents table because metric data summarization involves the average, standard deviation, and range (minimum and maximum). The table in Figure 10.7 reveals that the average response of 1000 respondents is 4.8, while the standard deviation is 2.3, and the minimum and maximum are 1 and 7, respectively. Thus, the typical respondent's 4.8 corresponds to "agree" on the 7-point scale. If you select more than one metric variable, the variables will be included in the same table, as it is most efficient to present them in this format, and the variables will be sorted in descending order with the variable that has the highest average listed first, and the variable with the lowest average listed last. If you want to make a graph, say, comparing the means of selected metric variables, you can easily create one with the Excel chart feature and use the averages in the Averages table.

# The Six-Step Approach to Data Analysis and Presentation

While summarization analysis is straightforward and simple to understand, the data analyses described in subsequent chapters are a bit more complicated. A step-by-step process that can be applied to all data analyses is a good approach. Even when students do select the proper data analysis, they are always challenged by

What is the average GPA of our E-Zine survey respondents?

the intepretation of the findings, and they have difficulties trying to present the findings in a research report.

In the six-step approach to data analysis, research objectives, data analysis, interpretation, and presentation of the findings are linked. The approach is presented in Table 10.6. It is important that the level of analysis leads to satisfying the research objective. The data collected in the first place was done with this end in mind.

**Table 10.6 The Six-Step Approach to Data Analysis for Description Objectives**

| Step | Explanation | Example from Your E-Zine Integrated Case |
|---|---|---|
| **1. What is the research objective?** | Determine that you are dealing with a Description objective.* | We want a profile of our sample. |
| **2. What questionnaire question(s) is/are involved?** | Identify the question(s), and for each one specify if it is categorical or metric. | Where do you live? (categorical) How many hours do you work per week? (metric) |
| **3. What is the appropriate analysis?** | For Description objectives, use Percents (categorical) or Averages (metric). | LIVE is categorical, so we will do percents. WORKHRS is metric, so we will do the average. |
| **4. How do you run it?** | Use the proper XL Data Analyst analysis: With Description objectives, use Summarize—Percents or Summarize—Averages. | |

**Table 10.6** (*Continued*)

| 5. How do you interpret the findings? | For Description objectives, report the central tendency and the variability (XL Data Analyst Averages table or Percentages table(s)). | Where does respondent live? |
|---|---|---|

Where does respondent live?

| Category | Frequency | Percent |
|---|---|---|
| On Campus | 97 | 16.2% |
| Off Campus | 503 | 83.8% |
| Total | 600 | 100.0% |

| Variable | Average | Standard Deviation | Minimum | Maximum | Sample |
|---|---|---|---|---|---|
| How many hours worked per week? | 10.1 | 11.9 | 0 | 40 | 600 |

| 6. How do you write/ present these findings? | With percents, paste the Percents table and/or an Excel graph for each categorical variable you want to report. With averages, modify the table with the metric variables as you see fit. |
|---|---|

**Where does respondent live?**

16% On Campus

84% Off Campus

| Variable | Average | Standard Deviation | Sample |
|---|---|---|---|
| How many hours worked per week? | 10.1 | 11.9 | 600 |

\* You will learn about other analyses in subsequent chapters.

Follow the instructions given in Online Application 10.1 on page 342 to examine real reports of marketing research.

# Summary

## 1. Recognize types of errors made in data collection.

Regardless of how data were collected, many errors can occur. Nonsampling errors are those involving anything other than sample size. For example, intentional or unintentional fieldworker errors are a danger when people are hired to collect data. There are also respondent errors committed by subjects answering questions in a survey. Again, these can be intentional or unintentional. Online surveys present a heightened risk of data collection error including multiple submissions by a respondent, bogus respondents and responses, and population misrepresentation. Nonresponse errors such as refusals to participate in a survey, break-offs during an interview, and item omissions can also occur.

## 2. Describe data entry.

Once collected data have been scrutinized, the researcher moves to the data entry stage of data analysis. Data entry is defined as creation of a computer file that holds the raw data taken from all completed questionnaires. Data coding is required. This process involves identification of computer code files that relate to possible answers for each question on the questionnaire. Often a data code book, which identifies all of the variable names and code numbers, is used.

3. **Discuss summarization analysis.**

Once the data have been entered, it is important to describe it. Summarization analysis is used for this purpose. If the variable being summarized is categorical, then the proper summary analysis is a percentage distribution. The mode describes the most frequent, typical response. If the variable is metric, then the proper summary analysis is an average. The standard deviation and range are used to sense the variability of the responses. XL Data Analyst™ performs summarization analysis as well as providing bar and pie graphs for visual presentation.

4. **Identify steps in data analysis.**

To simplify data analysis and interpretation, a six-step approach is introduced: (1) Identify the type of research objective; (2) identify the questions involved in the analysis; (3) identify the appropriate analysis for the type of objective and the type of data; (4) identify the proper XL Data Analyst™ analysis to use; (5) interpret the results generated by XL Data Analyst™; and (6) generate tables and graphs to use in your report.

# Key Terms

Average   (p. 340)
Break-off   (p. 327)
Central tendency   (p. 337)
Completed interview   (p. 328)
Data analysis   (p. 333)
Data code book   (p. 329)
Data coding   (p. 328)
Data entry   (p. 328)
Data set   (p. 333)
Fieldworkers (p. 325)
Frequency distribution   (p. 337)
Intentional fieldworker errors
   (p. 325)
Intentional respondent errors
   (p. 325)
Item omission   (p. 328)
Mode   (p. 337)
Multiple submissions   (p. 325)

Nonresponse   (p. 326)
Nonsampling errors   (p. 325)
Percentage distribution   (p. 338)
Population misrepresentation
   (p. 326)
Range   (p. 341)
Refusal   (p. 327)
Respondent errors   (p. 325)
Standard deviation   (p. 342)
Unintentional fieldworker errors
   (p. 325)
Unintentional respondent errors
   (p. 325)
Value codes   (p. 331)
Value labels   (p. 331)
Variability   (p. 337)
Variable description   (p. 331)
Variable label   (p. 331)

# Review Questions

1.1 Characterize types of errors commonly made during data collection.

1.2 In a survey on advertising, respondents are asked to describe the print ads they like best. Describe the types of data collection errors that can be made in this survey.

1.3 Describe the various kinds of nonresponse that a researcher may encounter with a survey.

**2.1** How does data coding relate to data entry?

**2.2** A survey on consumer preferences of food options on campus contained several open-ended questions. Outline how the researcher can deal with entering the responses to these questions.

**3.1** Define and differentiate each of the types of data analysis used in summarization.

**3.2** A professor asks his students how many hours they studied for the last exam. He finds that the class average is 10.5 hours and the standard deviation is 1.5 hours. The minimum is 2 hours, and the maximum is 20 hours. How would you describe the typical student's study time for this professor's last exam?

**4.1** Why is the central tendency an incomplete summarization of a variable?

**4.2** In a survey, Valentine's Day rose buyers are asked to indicate what colour of roses they purchased for their special friends. The following table summarizes the findings:

What colour of roses did you purchase last Valentine's Day?

| Category | Frequency | Percent |
|---|---|---|
| Yellow Roses | 66 | 17.1% |
| White Roses | 78 | 20.3% |
| Red Roses | 159 | 41.3% |
| Mixed colours | 82 | 21.3% |
| **Total** | 385 | 100.0% |

Describe the central tendency and variability apparent in this analysis. Include reasons for your choices.

**4.3** What is the proper measure of central tendency for summarizing a metric variable? Why do you say this?

**4.4** An entrepreneur is thinking about opening an upscale restaurant. To help access the market size, a researcher conducts a survey of individuals in the geographic target market who patronize upscale restaurants. The findings of the analysis for two questions on the survey are as follows:

| Variable | Average | Standard Deviation | Minimum | Maximum | Sample |
|---|---|---|---|---|---|
| Total amount spent in upscale restaurants per month | $150.11 | $32.72 | $5 | $250 | 400 |
| Average price expected to pay for an entree in an upscale restaurant | $28.87 | $5.80 | $16 | $60 | 340 |

Describe the central tendency and variability apparent in this analysis. Give reasons for your choices.

4.5 When summarizing a metric variable, what is the proper measure of variability? Give reasons for your answer.

4.6 What is the relationship between a standard deviation and a normal curve?

# Case 10.1

# Chatters Improvement Survey

Mary Yu graduated from college in June 2009. Upon graduation, she took a job as a marketing research assistant with Chatters, headquartered in Halifax, Nova Scotia. Chatters is a family restaurant with locations in all major cities in Canada. When Mary began working, the marketing research department was in the middle of a huge telephone survey of Chatters customers. The objectives of the survey included determining (1) how often and at what time of day people eat at Chatters, (2) how satisfied they are with selected aspects of Chatters, (3) how satisfied they are overall with Chatters, (4) what Chatters advertising they recall, and (5) the demographic profile of the respondents.

Mary was assigned the responsibility of data analysis because she was fresh out of college. She was informed that Chatters headquarters uses a statistical analysis program called SYSStats for its data analysis. All of the 5000 respondents' answers have been put into the computer, and all that is left is for someone to use SYSStats to perform the necessary analyses. Of course, someone has to interpret the results, too. It is Mary's responsibility to do the analysis and to interpret it. The questionnaire designers created a code sheet of the scales used in the survey. This code book is duplicated in the following table:

| Variable | Response Scale Used (data code) |
|---|---|
| Age | Actual age in years |
| Family income | Ranges in $10 000 increments |
| Gender | Male/Female |
| Marital status | Single (1), married (2), other (3) |
| Family size | Number of adults; number of children under 18 living at home |
| How often they eat at Chatters | Estimated number of times per month |
| Time of day they are most likely to use Chatters | Early morning (1), midmorning (2), late morning (3), noontime (4), early afternoon (5), mid-afternoon (6), late afternoon (7), early evening (8), late evening (9), around midnight (10), in the wee small hours (11) |
| Satisfaction with aspects of Chatters | "Poor," "Fair," "Good," "Very Good," or "Excellent" (coded 1, 2, 3, 4, 5, respectively) |
| Overall satisfaction with Chatters | "Extremely satisfied," "Somewhat satisfied," "Neither Satisfied nor Dissatisfied," "Somewhat Dissatisfied," or "Extremely Dissatisfied" (coded 5, 4, 3, 2, 1, respectively) |
| Recall of Chatters advertising | Yes/no for each of eight different advertising media: television, radio, internet, billboards, coupons, store sign, flyer, and/or phone book ad. (coded 0 = "No," 1 = "Yes") |

### Questions

1. What type of descriptive data analysis should Mary instruct SYSStats to perform to determine basic patterns in the factors listed on the code sheet? For each variable, identify the type of descriptive analysis, describe its aspects, and indicate why it is appropriate.

2. Give an example of what each analysis result might "look like" and how it should be interpreted.

## CASE 10.2

# Marketing Research

(The following case is fictional.)

Sally was starting her new job as a fieldworker for one of the largest marketing research companies in Canada. Her job required collecting data for a variety of clients and projects. Some of the projects required Sally to go to a large Toronto mall where her company had a research facility. Sally would approach potential subjects who looked like they had the criteria she was looking for, then ask them to follow her to the research facility where she would proceed with the interview. The questions were on a typed sheet and Sally had to enter responses by hand. Other projects required telephone interviewing. Sally would call people using a randomized telephone dialling system, then read the questions presented on her computer screen, and enter the responses as she received them, on the computer. The nice thing about this Computer Assisted Telephone Interviewing (CATI) system was that the computer would automatically go to the next question in the sequence depending on the response given by the subject. Sally preferred the telephone interviewing over the mall intercept method because the telephone would automatically find respondents required for the survey.

### Questions

1. What are the potential errors Sally can make in the mall intercept method of collecting data?

2. What are the potential errors Sally can make using the CATI system?

3. Which of the two methods is likely to generate higher respondent error? Give reasons for your answer.

## Case 10.3 YOUR INTEGRATED CASE

# The Student Life E-Zine Survey Summarization Analysis

Bob Watts was happy to inform Sarah, Anna, Wesley, and Don that the Student Life E-Zine survey data were collected and ready for analysis. Bob had other marketing research projects and meetings scheduled with present and prospective clients, so he called in his marketing intern, Lori Baker. Lori was a senior marketing major at City U, and she had taken marketing research in the

*(Continued)*

previous semester. Lori had "aced" this class, which she enjoyed a great deal. Her professor had invited Bob Watts to give a talk on "a typical day in the life of a market researcher," and Lori had approached Bob the very next day about a marketing research internship. Like every dedicated marketing major, Lori had kept her marketing research basics textbook and her XL Data Analyst™ software for future reference. Bob called Lori into his office and said, "Lori, it is time to do some analysis on the survey we did for the Student Life E-Zine project. For now, let's just get a feel for what the data look like. I'll leave it up to your judgment as to what basic analysis to run. Let's meet tomorrow at 2:30 p.m. and see what you have found."

Your task in Case 10.3 is to take the role of Lori Baker, marketing intern. As we indicated in this chapter, the Student Life E-Zine data set is included with your XL Data Analyst™ software that accompanies this textbook. We have used this data set in some of the examples of various types of descriptive analysis in this chapter. Now, it is time for you to use the XL Data Analyst™ on these and other variables in the Student Life E-Zine survey data set.

## Questions
1. Determine what variables are categorical, perform the appropriate descriptive analysis, and interpret it.
2. Determine what variables are metric, perform the appropriate descriptive analysis, and interpret it.

# Population Estimates and Hypothesis Testing

**Ipsos Reid**

**LEARNING OBJECTIVES**

1. Discuss generalization.

2. Estimate a confidence interval for a percentage or an average.

3. Test a hypothesis about a population percentage or an average.

## Answering Clients' Questions about the Applicability of Research Findings

Clients can benefit by understanding the basics of some of the tools of statistical inference you will learn about in this chapter. For example, let's suppose you've conducted some research and measured likelihood to purchase your proposed new product. You've set an action standard that if the mean on the 7-point scale is above 5.5, you will take the product to the next stage of product development. The results come in and the mean is 6.0. That's great news! This means you can start planning for that next stage in the development of this product.

But, a wise client would ask: "What would that number be if we did the research over again tomorrow?" This is indeed a wise question to ask because every measure we take in research is subject to sampling error. We will always have sampling error; it is inherent in the sampling process. This means the answer to the client's question is, "Yes, that number will likely vary if we conducted the research study over again tomorrow." In fact, because sampling error exists in every sample, that number is going to vary virtually every time we conduct a study. This is where confidence intervals can be very important to the client. A confidence interval will give the client a range within which we can expect the sample statistic, in this case, a mean, to vary if we conducted the study over many, many times. A confidence interval would allow us to make a statement such as, "If we conducted this study over 100 times, 95 times out of the 100 studies, the mean to this question will fall between 5.7 and 6.3." Now, our client has some measure of the reliability of our first estimate. Even if we did many, many studies, it is not likely that the mean will fall below 5.7. Since this is above our action standard of 5.5, the client can feel more assured in the decision to move forward in developing the new product.

> While the tools of statistical inference can be helpful, we must remember that other errors, nonsampling errors, must be controlled in order for us to have valid and reliable results. A good marketing research professional will know what the sources of those errors are and will have taken the steps necessary to control them. Also, clients should understand the impact of sample size on confidence intervals. The smaller the sample size, given the same variance in the data, the wider the confidence interval, and the larger the sample size, the more narrow the confidence interval. You will learn about confidence intervals and other tools of statistical inference in this chapter.
>
> Richard Homans
> Senior Vice President, Ipsos Forward Research

**Where We Are**

1. Establish the need for marketing research
2. Define the problem
3. Establish research objectives
4. Determine research design
5. Identify information types and sources
6. Determine methods of accessing data
7. Design data collection forms
8. Determine sample plan and size
9. Collect data
10. Analyze data
11. Prepare and present the final research report

Measures of central tendency and measures of variability adequately summarize the findings of a sample survey. However, whenever a probability sample is drawn from a population, it is not enough simply to report the sample's descriptive statistics. Along with reporting a measure of central tendency in the sample, reporting a range that the client understands defines the true population value or what would be found if a census were feasible. It is necessary to see the extent to which the sample represents the population.

Every sample provides some information about its population, but there is always some sample error that must be taken into account. In this chapter, the concept of "generalization" and the relationship between a sample finding and the population fact that it represents are explained. Further, how an estimate of the population fact is more certain with larger samples and with more agreement in respondents is shown. From an intuitive approach, parameter estimation, in which the population value is estimated with a confidence interval using specific formulas and knowledge of areas under a normal or bell-shaped curve, is described. Specifically, how to estimate a percentage confidence interval and how to estimate an average confidence interval are illustrated. Lastly, procedures and computations for a hypothesis test for a percentage or an average where the sample's finding is used to determine whether a hypothesis is supported or not are described.

## The Concept of Generalization

Researchers draw samples because they do not have the time or budget necessary to conduct a census of the population under study. A sample should be representative of its population but, by being a sample, has a degree of error. The determination of a probability sample's size is based on the amount of error that is acceptable to the manager.

A **sample finding** is a percentage or average or some other value computed with a sample's data. A **population fact** is defined as the true value when a census of the population is taken and the value is determined using all members of the population. When a researcher follows proper sampling procedures and ensures that the sample is a good representation of the target population, the sample findings are *best* estimates of their respective population facts. Sample findings are always estimates that are hindered by the sample error.

**Generalization** is the act of estimating a population fact from a sample finding.[1] Generalization is a form of logic in which an inference about an entire group is made based on some evidence about that group. When one generalizes, a conclusion is drawn from the available evidence. For example, if two friends each bought a new Ford and they both complained about their cars' performances, one might generalize that all Fords perform poorly. On the other hand, if one of the friends complained about his Ford, whereas the other one did not, one might generalize that the unhappy friend bought a lemon. Generalizations are influenced by the amount of evidence. So, if 20 friends bought new Fords, and they all complained about poor performance, the inference would be stronger or more certain than it would be in the case of only two friends complaining.

Generalization about any population's facts is a set of procedures where the sample size and sample findings are used to make estimates of these population values. The sample percentage, $p$, is the sample finding used to estimate the population percentage, $\pi$. Suppose that Ford suspected that there are some dissatisfied Ford buyers. The company commissions two independent marketing research surveys to determine the amount of dissatisfaction that existed in its customer group. (Of course, our Ford example is entirely fictitious. We do not mean to imply that Ford performs in an unsatisfactory way.)

In the first survey, 100 customers who purchased a Ford in the last six months are randomly chosen for the telephone survey. They are asked, "In general, would you say that you are satisfied or dissatisfied with the performance of your Ford since you bought it?" The survey finds that 33 respondents (33%) are dissatisfied. This finding could be generalized to the total population of Ford owners who had bought one in the last six months, and we would say that there is 33% dissatisfaction. However, our sample is a probability sample, and it must contain some sample error. Therefore, it is more correct to say that there is *about* 33% dissatisfaction in the population. In other words, it might actually be more or less than 33% if a census was done because the sample finding provides us with only an estimate.

In the second survey, 1000 respondents—that's 10 times more than in the first survey—are called on the telephone and asked the same question. This survey finds that 35% of the respondents are "dissatisfied." Again, the 35% is an estimate containing sampling error, so it would also be more accurate to say that the population dissatisfaction percentage is *about* 35%.

How do we translate our answers (remember they include the word "about") into more accurate numerical representations? One could say "33% plus or minus $x$%" for the sample of 100 and "35% plus or minus $y$%" for the sample of 1000 are dissatisfied. How would $x$ and $y$ compare? To answer this question, think back on how the generalization was stronger with 20 friends than it was with 2 friends regarding Fords. With more evidence there is more certainty that the sample finding was accurate with respect to estimating the true population fact. In other words, with a larger sample size, the range used to estimate the true population value is smaller. Intuitively, the range for $y$ should be smaller than the range for $x$ because $y$ has a large sample and less sampling error. Table 11.1 illustrates how to generalize the sample findings to the population of all Ford buyers in the case of the 100 sample versus the 1000 sample.

**Table 11.1** A Larger Sample Size Gives You More Precision When You Generalize Sample Findings to Estimate Population Facts*

| Sample | Sample Finding | Estimated Population Fact |
|---|---|---|
| 100 randomly selected respondents | Sample finding: 33% of respondents report they are dissatisfied with their new Ford. | Between 24% and 42% of all Ford buyers are dissatisfied.<br><br>24% ———————— 42%<br>33% |
| 1000 randomly selected respondents | Sample finding: 35% of respondents report they are dissatisfied with their new Ford. | Between 32% and 38% of all Ford buyers are dissatisfied.<br><br>32% ———— 38%<br>35% |

*Fictitious example

As these examples reveal, when estimates of population values are made, the sample finding is used as the beginning point, and then a range is computed in which the population value is estimated, or generalized, to fall. The size of the sample plays a crucial role in this computation. The larger the sample, up to a point, the less sampling error there is.

# Generalizing a Sample's Findings: Estimating the Population Value

Estimation of population values is a common type of generalization used in marketing research survey analysis. This generalization process is often referred to as "**parameter estimation**" because the proper name for the population fact, or value, is the **parameter**. Population parameters are designated by Greek letters such as $\pi$ (percent) or $\mu$ (mean or average), while sample findings are relegated to lower-case Roman letters such as $p$ (percent) or $\bar{x}$ (average or mean). As indicated earlier, generalization is largely a reflection of the amount of sampling error believed to exist in the sample finding. When *The Globe and Mail* conducts a survey and finds that readers spend an average of 45 minutes daily reading *The Globe*, or when McDonald's determines through a nationwide sample that 60% of all breakfast buyers buy an Egg McMuffin, both companies may want to determine more accurately how close these sample findings are to the actual population parameters.

## How to Estimate a Population Percentage (Categorical Data)

### Calculating a Confidence Interval
As the two examples just noted reveal, sometimes the researcher wants to estimate the population percentage (McDonald's example) and, at other times, the researcher will estimate the population average (*Globe and Mail* example). A **confidence interval** is a range (lower and upper boundary) into which the researcher believes the population parameter falls with an associated degree of confidence (typically 95% or 99%). Recall that percentages are proper when summarizing categorical variables.

Research can estimate how many minutes people read a particular newspaper each day.

The general formula for the estimation of a population percentage is written in notation form as follows:

$$p \pm z_\alpha s_p$$

◀ **Formula for a population percentage estimation**

where

$p$　= sample percentage

$z_\alpha$ = z value for 95% or 99% level of confidence ($\alpha$ [alpha] equals either 95% or 99% level of confidence)

$s_p$ = standard error of the percentage

Typically, marketing researchers rely only on the 95% or 99% levels of confidence, which correspond to ±1.96 ($z_{.95}$), and ±2.58 ($z_{.99}$) standard errors, respectively. By far, the **most commonly used level of confidence** in marketing research is the 95% level, corresponding to 1.96 standard errors. In fact, the 95% level of confidence is usually the default level found in statistical analysis programs. To be 95% confident that the sample range was included in the true population percentage, multiply the standard error of the percentage, $s_p$, by 1.96 and add that value to the percentage, $p$, to obtain the upper limit. Then subtract this value from the percentage to find the lower limit. Note that the sample statistic, $p$, the variability that is in the formula for $s_p$; the sample size, $n$, which is also in the formula for $s_p$; and the degree of confidence in your estimate were all considered.[2] For a 99% confidence interval, substitute 2.58 for 1.96.

Table 11.2 contains the formula and lists the steps used to estimate a population percentage. This table shows that estimation of the population percentage uses the sample finding to compute a confidence interval that describes the range for the population percentage. *In order to estimate a population percentage, all that is needed is the sample percentage, p, and the sample size, n.*

**Table 11.2 How to Estimate the Population Value for a Percentage**

Here is the formula for a 95% confidence interval estimate of a population percentage. Note that we have used the formula for $s_p$ to show how the sample percent, $p$, and the sample size, $n$, are used in this estimation procedure.

**Formula for 95% confidence interval estimate of a population percentage ▷**

$$95\% \text{ confidence interval } = p \pm 1.96 \sqrt{\frac{p \times q}{n}}$$

where

$p = $ sample percent
$q = 100\% - p$
$n = $ sample size

Calculation of 95% confidence interval to estimate the population value range is as follows:

| Step | Description | Ford Example ($n = 100$) |
|------|-------------|--------------------------|
| Step 1 | Calculate the percentage of times respondents chose one of the categories in a categorical variable, call it $p$. (This procedure is described on page 338.) | The sample percentage is found to be 33%, so $p = 33\%$ |
| Step 2 | Subtract $p$ from 100%, call it $q$. | $100\% - 33\% = 67\%$, so $q = 67\%$ |
| Step 3 | Multiply $p$ times $q$, divide the product by the sample size, $n$, and take the square root of that quantity. Call it the *standard error of the percentage*. | Standard error of the percentage $= \sqrt{\dfrac{pq}{n}}$ $= \sqrt{\dfrac{(33 \times 67)}{100}}$ $= 4.7\%$ |
| Step 4 | Multiply the standard error value by 1.96. Call it the *limit*. | Limit $= 1.96 \times 4.7\%$ $= 9.2\%$ |
| Step 5 | Take $p$; subtract the limit to obtain the *lower boundary*. Then take $p$ and add the limit to obtain the *upper boundary*. The lower boundary and the upper boundary are the 95% *confidence interval* for the population percentage. | Lower boundary: $33\% - 9.2\% = 23.8\%$  Upper boundary: $33\% + 9.2\% = 42.2\%$  The *95% confidence interval* is 23.8% to 42.2% |

In the McDonald's survey, 60% of the 100 respondents were found to order an Egg McMuffin for breakfast. Here are the 95% and 99% confidence interval calculations: the sample percent, $p = 60\%$, and the sample size, $n = 100$.

$$p \pm z_\alpha s_p$$

$$p \pm 1.96 \times \sqrt{\frac{p \times q}{n}}$$

$$60 \pm 1.96 \times \sqrt{\frac{60 \times 40}{100}}$$

$$60 \pm 1.96 \times 4.9$$
$$60 \pm 9.6$$
$$50.4\%\text{--}69.6\%$$

Therefore, one could say with 95% confidence that the population parameter is between 50.4% (60.0% − 9.6%) and 69.6% (60.0% + 9.6%), or 60% ±9.6%.

$$p \pm z_\alpha s_p$$

$$p \pm 2.58 \times \sqrt{\frac{p \times q}{n}}$$

$$60 \pm 2.58 \times \sqrt{\frac{60 \times 40}{100}}$$

$$60 \pm 2.58 \times 4.9$$
$$60 \pm 12.6$$
$$47.4\%\text{--}72.6\%$$

Therefore, one could say with 99% confidence that the population parameter is between 47.4% (60% − 12.6%) and 72.6% (60% + 12.6%), or 60% ±12.6%.

Note that the only thing that differs between the 95% confidence interval computations and the 99% confidence interval computations is $z_\alpha$. As we noted earlier, $z$ is 1.96 for 95% and 2.58 for 99% of confidence. The confidence interval is always wider for 99% than it is for 95% when the sample size is the same and variability is equal.

### Interpreting a 95% Confidence Interval

The interpretation is based on the normal curve or bell-shaped distribution that you are familiar with. The **standard error** is a measure of the variability in a population based on the variability found in the sample. There usually is some degree of variability in the sample: Not everyone orders an Egg McMuffin, nor does everyone order coffee for breakfast. Examining the formula for a **standard error of the percentage** (Step 3 in Table 11.2), the size of the standard error depends on two factors: (1) the variability, denoted as $p$ times $q$, and (2) the sample size, $n$. The standard error of the percentage is large with more variability and smaller with larger samples. This is the same as the Ford example: The more Ford owners disagree (more variability), the less certain one is about their generalization, and the greater the number of Ford owners heard from, the more confident one is about their generalization.

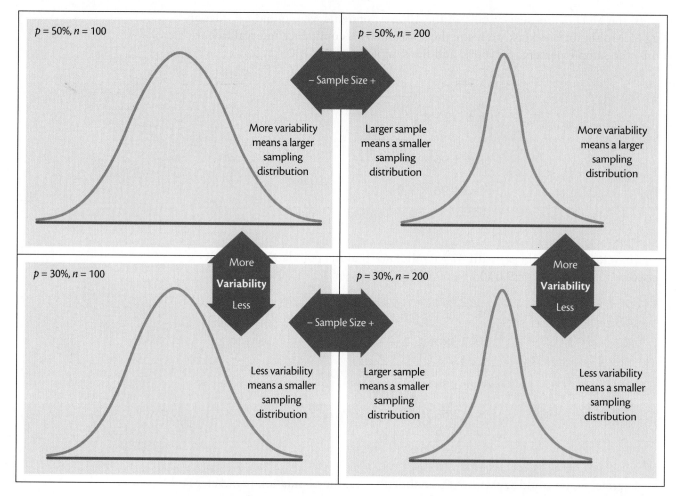

**Figure 11.1** How Variability and Sample Size Affect the Sampling Distribution

If many, many samples were taken and the sample percentages for all of these samples were plotted as a frequency distribution, it would approximate a bell-shaped curve called the **sampling distribution**. The standard error is a measure of the variability in the sampling distribution based on what is believed would occur if a multitude of independent samples were taken from the same population. Figure 11.1 helps understand how variability and sample size affect the sampling distribution.

Start with the upper left-hand quadrant, where the bell-shaped curve represents the case of $p = 50\%$ and $n = 100$. Move clockwise to the upper right-hand case of $p = 50\%$ and $n = 200$. Note that the curve has become more compressed due to the increase in sample size. Now, move down to the lower right-hand case, where $p = 30\%$ and $n = 200$. The curve is even more compressed due to the reduced variability and large sample size. A move to the left of this quadrant is the case of $p = 30\%$ and $n = 100$, where the bell-shaped curve is less compressed due to the smaller sample size. Finally, moving to the upper left-hand quadrant, the curve is less compressed due to the smaller sample size ($n = 100$) and more variability ($p = 50\%$).

To illustrate how confidence intervals work, Figure 11.2 compares two cases. In the first case, the standard error of the percentage is 5%, while in the second case

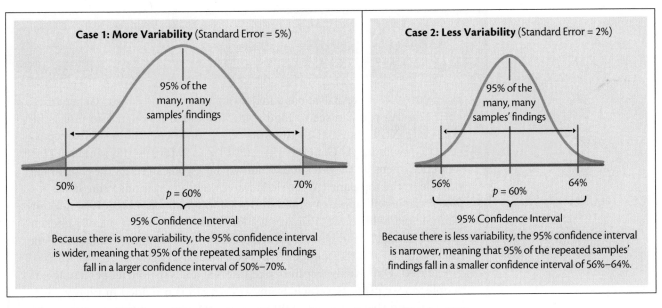

**Figure 11.2** The Variability Affects the Sampling Distribution Reflected in the 95% Confidence Interval for a Percentage

the standard error is 2%. Note that the two bell-shaped normal curves reflect the differences in variability, as the 5% curve with more variability is wider than the 2% curve that has less variability. The 95% confidence intervals are 50% to 70% and 56% to 64%, respectively. The larger standard error in case 1 has a larger interval, and the smaller standard error in case 2 has a smaller interval. If repeated many, many times (thousands of times) and each $p$, or percentage, found for each were plotted on a frequency distribution curve, it would look like a bell-shaped curve, and 95% of the percentages would fall in the confidence interval defined by the population percentage ± 1.96 times the standard error of the percentage. In other words, one can be 95% confident that the population percentage falls in the range of 50% to 70% in the first case. Similarly, because the standard error is smaller (perhaps the sample is larger in this case), one would be 95% confident that the population percentage falls in the range of 56% to 64% in the second case.

Obviously, a marketing researcher would take only one sample for a particular marketing research project, and this restriction explains why estimates of population parameters must be used. Furthermore, it is the conscientious application of probability sampling techniques that allows researchers to make use of the sampling distribution concept. Thus, generalization procedures are direct linkages between probability sample design and data analysis. Recall that one had to grapple with accuracy levels when determining sample size. Now, the sample size is used for our inference procedures. Confidence intervals must be used when estimating population values. The size of the random sample used is always reflected in these confidence intervals.

When making a nonstatistical generalization, judgment can be swayed by subjective factors, and may not be consistent. In statistical estimates, the formulas are objective and perfectly consistent, and are based on accepted statistical concepts.

# How to Obtain a 95% Confidence Interval for a Percentage with XL Data Analyst™

XL Data Analyst has a major menu command called "Generalize." As you can see in Figure 11.3, the menu sequence to direct the XL Data Analyst to compute a confidence interval for a percentage is Generalize—Confidence Interval—Percentage. This sequence opens up the selection window where you can select the categorical variable in the top pane (Available Variables) and the various value labels for that variable will appear in the bottom pane (Available Categories). In our example, we will select "Primary vehicle type: SUV or van" as our chosen variable in the top and bottom panes. Clicking "OK" will prompt the XL Data Analyst to perform the confidence interval analysis.

The XL Data Analyst confidence interval analysis for the percentage of people whose primary vehicle is an SUV or van is provided in Figure 11.4. You will find that a total of 1000 respondents answered this question, and 258 of them indicated that their primary vehicle is an SUV or van. This computes to a 25.8% value (258/1000 × 100%). The table reports the lower boundary of 21.3% and the upper boundary of 28.5%, defining the 95% confidence interval for this percentage. The interpretation of this

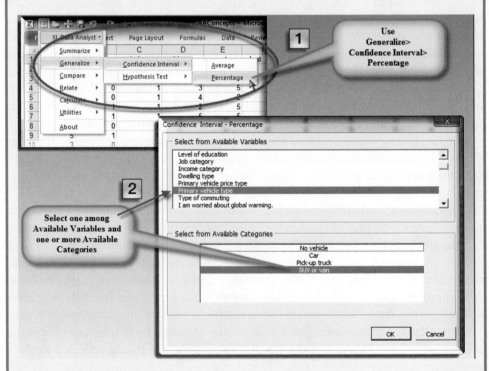

**Figure 11.3** Using the XL Data Analyst to Select a Variable Value for a Percentage Confidence Interval

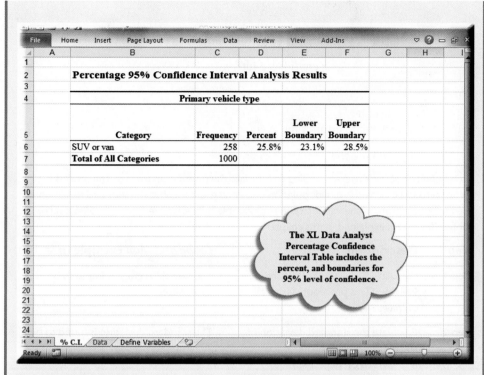

**Figure 11.4** XL Data Analyst Percentage Confidence Interval Table

boundary is that if we repeated our survey many, many times, 95% of the population percentages found for an SUV or van would fall between 23.1% and 28.5%. The boundaries are so narrow for two reasons: (1) SUV or van accounts for only about one-quarter of the sample, so there is very little variability, and (2) the sample size is fairly large.

## How to Estimate a Population Average (Metric Data)

### Calculating a Confidence Interval for an Average

If the data are metric, the population average is an appropriate measure of central tendency. The formula for the estimation of a population average is:

$$\bar{x} \pm z_\alpha s_{\bar{x}}$$

◀ **Formula for a population average estimation**

where:

$\bar{x}$ = sample average

$z_\alpha$ = z value for 95% or 99% level of confidence

$s_{\bar{x}}$ = standard error of the average

Table 11.3 describes how to calculate a 95% confidence interval for an average using *The Globe and Mail* reading example. The sample averaged 45 minutes of reading time per day.

**Table 11.3 How to Estimate the Population Value for an Average**

**Formula for 95% confidence interval estimate of a population average** ▶

Here is the formula for a 95% confidence interval estimate of a population average:

$$95\% \text{ confidence interval} = \bar{x} \pm 1.96 s_{\bar{x}}$$

where:

$\bar{x}$ = average

$s_{\bar{x}}$ = standard error of the average

$n$ = sample size

To generalize a sample average finding to estimate the population average, the process is identical to the estimation of a population percentage, except that the standard deviation is used as the measure of the variability. In the example below, we are to use the 95% level of confidence that is explained in this chapter.

| Step | Description | *Globe and Mail* Example ($n = 100$) |
|---|---|---|
| **Step 1** | Calculate the average of the metric variable. (This procedure is described on page 340.) | The sample average is found to be 45 minutes. |
| **Step 2** | Calculate the standard deviation of the metric variable. (This procedure is described on page 342.) | The standard deviation is found to be 20 minutes. |
| **Step 3** | Divide the standard deviation by the square root of the sample size. Call it the *standard error of the average*. | Standard error of the average $= \dfrac{s}{\sqrt{n}}$ $= \dfrac{20}{\sqrt{n}}$ $= \dfrac{20}{\sqrt{100}}$ $= 2$ |
| **Step 4** | Multiply the standard error value by 1.96, call it the *limit*. | Limit $= 1.96 \times 2 = 3.9$ |
| **Step 5** | Take the average; subtract the limit to obtain the *lower boundary*. Then take the average and add the limit to obtain the *upper boundary*. The lower boundary and the upper boundary are the 95% *confidence interval* for the population average. | Lower boundary: $45 - 3.9 = 41.1$ minutes  Upper boundary: $45 + 3.9 = 48.9$ minutes  The 95% *confidence interval* is 41.1 to 48.9 minutes. |

The procedure is parallel to the one for calculating a confidence interval for a percentage, except that the standard deviation is used, as it is the correct measure of variability for a metric variable. The formula for the **standard error of the average** is provided in Table 11.3. The standard error of the average is larger with more variability (standard deviation) and smaller with large samples ($n$).

In the fictional sample of 100 *Globe and Mail* readers, it was found that in the sample the average reading time was 45 minutes with a standard deviation of 20 minutes. The 99% confidence interval estimate is calculated as follows:

$$\bar{x} \pm z_\alpha s_{\bar{x}}$$
$$45 \pm 2.58 \times \frac{20}{\sqrt{100}}$$
$$45 \pm 2.58 \times 2$$
$$45 \pm 5.2$$
$$39.8 \text{ minutes–} 50.2 \text{ minutes}$$

Again, as with the percentage confidence intervals, the 99% confidence interval is wider because the standard error is multiplied by 2.58, while the 95% one is multiplied by the lower 1.96 value. Follow the instructions in Online Application 11.1 to calculate confidence intervals using an online tool.

### Interpreting a Confidence Interval for an Average

The interpretation of a confidence interval estimate of a population average is virtually identical to the interpretation of a confidence interval estimate for a population percentage: If the survey was repeated many, many times (thousands of times) and your average number of minutes of reading *The Globe and Mail* for each sample was plotted on a frequency distribution, it would look like a bell-shaped curve, and 95% of the sample averages would fall in the confidence interval defined by the population percentage ± 1.96 times the standard error of the average. In other words, one can be 95% confident that the population average falls in the range of 41.1 to 48.9 minutes. Of course, if the standard error is large (for example, there is a smaller sample in this case), one would be 95% confident that the population average falls in the larger confidence interval that would result from the calculations.

## ONLINE APPLICATION 11.1
# Calculate a Confidence Interval

Dimensions Research, Inc. is a marketing research company that specializes in analysis. Go to **www.dimensionresearch.com**. Click on "Use Our Market Research Tools and Resources." Then click on "Confidence Interval for Means" located on the left-hand navigation bar. Assuming you have a sample of 1000 completed interviews, an observed mean of 25, and an observed standard deviation of 10, calculate the confidence interval at the 95% level of confidence using this webpage.

### Questions

1.  Why is the mean value you obtain for a question on your survey different than the mean value for this question as it pertains to the population as a whole?

2.  What does the confidence level tell you about the results?

3.  What assumptions must you make about your sample in order to use this webpage?

# How to Obtain a 95% Confidence Interval for an Average with XL Data Analyst™

Figure 11.5 illustrates the two options possible from "Generalize—Confidence Interval." One is for a percentage confidence interval, while the other is for an average confidence interval. The Average option opens up a Selection window that can be seen in Figure 11.5. You select your metric variable(s) by highlighting it from among the Available Variables. When you click on "OK," the XL Data Analyst performs confidence interval analysis on the chosen metric variables.

In this data set example, we have selected the statement "Gasoline emissions contribute to global warming," which was responded to with a 7-point scale (very strongly disagree to very strongly agree). The results are shown in Figure 11.6. The average response for the 1000 respondents is 4.8, and the standard deviation is 2.3. The table here also reports the 95% confidence interval boundaries of 4.7 and 5.0. Thus, we have found that for the entire population of households, our estimate of the average response to the statement, "Gasoline emissions contribute to global warming" is this range, which translates to "agree" on the labelled scaled.

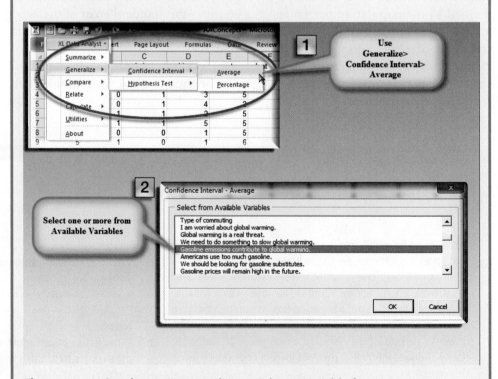

**Figure 11.5** Using the XL Data Analyst to Select a Variable for an Average Confidence Interval

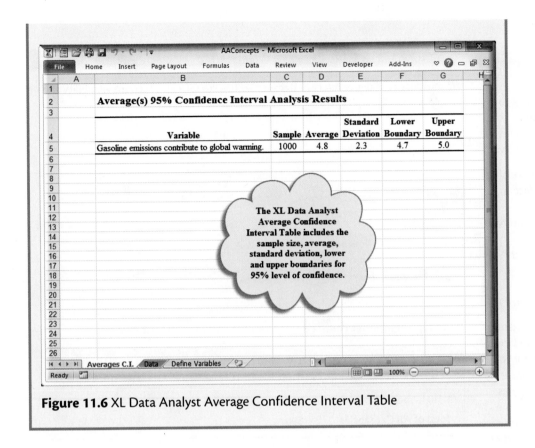

**Figure 11.6** XL Data Analyst Average Confidence Interval Table

## Using the Six-Step Approach to Confidence Intervals Analysis

Table 11.4 specifies how to apply the six-step analysis approach to confidence intervals.

**Table 11.4** The Six-Step Approach to Data Analysis for Generalization: Confidence Intervals

| Step | Explanation | Example (A is a categorical variable; B is a metric variable) |
|---|---|---|
| **1. What is the research objective?** | Determine that you are dealing with a Confidence Interval Generalization objective. | **A.** We want to *estimate* what percentage of students at this campus have high-speed modem internet access.<br><br>**B.** We want to *estimate* how much students at this campus who make purchases on the internet will spend on internet purchases in the next two months. |
| **2. What questionnaire question(s) is/are involved?** | Identify the question(s), and for each one specify whether it is categorical or metric. | **A.** "What type of internet connection do you have where you live?" "High speed" is *categorical*.<br><br>**B.** "To the nearest $5, about how much do you think you will spend on internet purchases in the next two months?" This is a *metric* measure. |

**Table 11.4** (*Continued*)

| Step | Explanation | Example (A is a categorical variable; B is a metric variable) |
|---|---|---|
| **3. What is the appropriate analysis?** | To generalize a sample finding to estimate the population value, use confidence intervals. | We must use confidence intervals because we have to take into account variability and sample error. |
| **4. How do you run it?** | Use XL Data Analyst™ analysis: Select "Generalize—Confidence Intervals—Percentage" (categorical) or "Generalize—Confidence Interval—Average" (metric). | |

**5. How do you interpret the findings?**

The 95% confidence interval boundaries are such that if you repeated your survey many, many times and calculated the average or percentage under study, 95% of the repeated findings would fall between the confidence interval boundaries.

**What type of internet connection do you have where you live?**

| Category | Frequency | Percent | Lower Boundary | Upper Boundary |
|---|---|---|---|---|
| 1. High-Speed Cable | 252 | 42.7% | 38.7% | 46.7% |
| **Total of All Categories** | 590 | | | |

| Variable | Sample | Average | Standard Deviation | Lower Boundary | Upper Boundary |
|---|---|---|---|---|---|
| To the nearest $5, about how much do you think you will spend on internet purchases in the next two months? | 143 | $63.71 | $18.13 | $60.73 | $66.68 |

Note that the values have been reformatted to currency with dollars and cents.

**6. How do you write/present these findings?**

For a single percentage or average, simply report that the 95% confidence interval is ##.# to ##.#.

**A.** It was determined from the sample of respondents that 42.7% of those students with internet access have high-speed cable modem connections. The 95% confidence interval estimate for the percentage of students in the population who have internet access with a high-speed cable modem connection is 38.7% to 46.7%.

**B.** For those respondents who make purchases on the internet, the average expected amount of purchase in the next two months was found to be $63.71. The 95% confidence interval for the expected average dollar expenditure for students in the population who make internet purchases is $60.73 to $66.68.

Generalizations of survey sample findings to describe the population are useful in many ways. One important application of confidence intervals is to generate market-potential estimates. Marketing Research in Action 11.1 shows how the Student Life E-Zine survey findings can be used to estimate the online-purchasing market potential of City University students.

## MARKETING RESEARCH IN ACTION 11.1
# How to Estimate Market Potential Using a Survey's Findings

A common way to estimate total market potential is to rely on the definition of a market. A market is people with the willingness and ability to pay for a product or a service. This definition can be expressed somewhat like a formula, in the following way:

*Market potential = Population base × percent willing to buy × amount they are willing to spend*

Magazines and e-zines depend greatly on the revenues of their advertising affiliates. That is, the subscription price of *People* magazine, for instance, is a mere pittance compared with the amount of money paid by the various companies that advertise their products and services in *People*. The potential advertising affiliates for the Student Life E-Zine might be persuaded to advertise in it if there is evidence that students make purchases on the internet. Our survey findings can be used to estimate how much students spend this way.

In the Student Life E-Zine case, we know that the City University population base is 35 000 students. We know that not all students make online purchases. In fact, we found that only 24.2% of them intend to make a purchase on the internet in the next two months. This translates to 8470 students. When asked how much they expect to spend on internet purchases in that time period, we found the average to be $63.71. We can use the lower and upper boundaries of the 95% confidence interval for this average to calculate a pessimistic (lower boundary) and an optimistic (upper boundary) estimate as well as a best estimate (average) of the annual internet-purchasing market potential of City U's student body. The calculations follow.

Using the 95% confidence intervals and the sample percentage, the total annual market potential for internet purchases by students is found to be between about $3.1 million and $3.4 million per year. The best annual estimate is about $3.2 million. It is "best" because it is based on the sample average, which is the best estimate of the true population average expenditures by students who make internet purchases. Of course, we realize that these are very conservative estimates for next year, as the percentage of students buying on the internet will surely increase, and the average amount they spend will most likely increase as well. We now have some convincing findings that can be used to approach potential advertising affiliates and to recruit them to use the Student Life E-Zine as an advertising vehicle that will effectively target college students.

### Estimation of Internet Purchases by City University Students

| Pessimistic Estimate | Best Estimate | Optimistic Estimate |
|---|---|---|
| | 8470 | |
| | (students who intend to make an internet purchase in the next 2 months) | |
| × $60.73 | × $63.71 | × $66.68 |
| = $514 383 each 2 months | = $539 624 each 2 months | = $564 780 each 2 months |
| | × 6 | |
| = $3 086 298 per year | = $3 237 744 per year | = $3 388 680 per year |

Bill's hyphothesis about seat belt use is about to be tested.

# Testing Hypotheses about Percentages or Averages

A statement about the population parameter based on prior knowledge, assumptions, or intuition is called a **hypothesis**. A hypothesismost commonly takes the form of an exact specification as to what the population value is. **Hypothesis testing** is a statistical procedure used to "support" (accept) or "not support" (reject) the hypothesis based on sample information.[3] With all hypothesis tests, the sample is the only source of current information about the population. Because the sample is a probability sample and therefore representative of the population, the sample results are used to determine whether or not the hypothesis about the population parameter has been supported.

Here is an example to show how hypothesis testing occurs. Your friend Bill does not wear his seat belt because he thinks only a few drivers actually wear them. But Bill's car breaks down, and he has to ride with his co-workers to and from work while it is being repaired. Over the course of a week, Bill rides with five different co-workers, and he notices that four out of the five buckle up. When Bill begins driving his car the next week, he begins fastening his seat belt. Marketing Research in Action 11.2 discusses a typical hypothesis test that students commonly perform.

**MARKETING RESEARCH IN ACTION 11.2**
## Intuitive Hypothesis Testing
### We Do It All the Time!

People do intuitive hypothesis testing all the time to reaffirm their beliefs or to reform them to be consistent with reality. The diagram below illustrates how people perform intuitive hypothesis testing.

Here is an everyday example. As a student taking a marketing research class, you believe that you will ace the first exam if you study hard the night before the exam. You take the exam, and you score a 70%. Ouch! It sure looks like your score does not support your belief that one cram session will be enough to earn an A grade in this course. You now realize that your belief (your hypothesis) was wrong, and you need to study more for the next exam. Because your hypothesis was not supported, you have to come up with a new one.

You ask the student beside you, who did ace the exam, how much study time he put in.

He says he studied for three solid nights before the exam. Note that he has found evidence (his A grade) that supports his hypothesis, so he will not change his study-habits belief. You, on the other hand, must change your hypothesis or suffer the consequences. Read the boxes and follow the arrows in the diagram below to see how your intuitive hypothesis testing comes out.

**Your Hypothesis**

| I believe that a single-night cram session is enough to ace the exam. This is my hypothesis. | I now believe that I need to study harder, say three solid nights, to ace the next exam. This is my revised hypothesis. | I will hold this belief (hypothesis) as long as I continue to ace the exams. |

**The Evidence**

| I score a 70 on the exam. Ouch! I definitely need to change my belief (hypothesis) because it is not supported by the evidence. | I score 95 on the next exam. Great! I will hold on to this hypothesis because it is supported by the evidence. |

This is intuitive hypothesis testing in action; Bill's initial belief that few people wear seat belts was his hypothesis. **Intuitive hypothesis testing** (as opposed to statistical hypothesis testing) is when someone uses something he or she has observed to see if it agrees with or goes against the belief about that topic.

Before his car went into the repair shop, Bill might have said that only a small percentage of drivers, perhaps as low as 30%, wear seat belts. His week of car rides is equivalent to a sample of five observations, and he observes that 80% of his co-workers buckle up. Because Bill's initial hypothesis is not supported by the evidence, he realizes that his hypothesis is in error, and it must be revised. Bill's estimated percentage of drivers wearing seat belts after his week of observations undoubtedly would be a much higher percentage than his original estimate. The fact that Bill began to fasten his seat belt suggests that he perceives his behaviour to be out of the norm, so he has adjusted his belief and his behaviour as well. His hypothesis was not supported, so Bill revised it to be consistent with what he now generalizes to be the "actual" case. The logic of statistical hypothesis testing is very similar to this process that Bill has just undergone.

## Testing a Hypothesis about a Percentage (Categorical Data)

Here is the formula for a percentage hypothesis test.

$$z = \frac{p - \pi_H}{s_p}$$

◀ **Formula for a hypothesis test of a population percentage** where

$$p = \text{sample percent}$$
$$\pi_H = \text{hypothesized population percentage}$$
$$s_p = \text{standard error of the percentage}$$

Table 11.5 provides formulas and lists the steps necessary to test a hypothesis about a percentage. Basically, hypothesis testing involves the use of four ingredients: the sample statistic ($p$ in this case), the standard error ($s_p$), the hypothesized population parameter value ($\pi_H$ in this case), and the decision to "support" or "not support" the hypothesized parameter based on a few calculations. The first two values were discussed in this chapter's section on percentage parameter estimation. The hypothesis is simply what the researcher hypothesizes the population parameter, $\pi$, to be before the research is undertaken. When these are taken into consideration by using the steps in Table 11.5, the result is a significance test for the hypothesis that determines its support (acceptance) or lack of support (rejection).

In Table 11.5, the sample percent ($p$) is compared with the hypothesized population percent ($\pi_H$). "Compared" means "difference." They are compared because in a hypothesis test, one tests the **null hypothesis**, a formal statement that there is no

**Table 11.5 How to Test a Hypothesis for a Percentage**

To test a hypothesis for a percentage, you will assess how close the sample percentage is to the hypothesized population percentage. The following example uses Bill's seat belt hypothesis and tests it with a random sample of 1000 automobile drivers.

| Step | Description | Seat Belt Example ($n = 1000$) |
|---|---|---|
| Step 1 | Identify the percentage that you (or your client) believe exists in the population. Call it $\pi_H$, or the "hypothesized percentage." | Bill believes that 30% of drivers use seat belts. |
| Step 2 | Conduct a survey and determine the sample percentage; call it $\pi$. (This procedure is described on page 338.) | A sample of 1000 drivers is taken, and the sample percentage for those who use seat belts is found to be 80%, so $\pi = 80\%$. |
| Step 3 | Determine the *standard error of the percentage*. (This procedure is described on page 364.) | $s_p = \sqrt{\dfrac{pq}{n}}$ $= \sqrt{\dfrac{(80 \times 20)}{1,000}}$ $= 1.26\%$ |
| Step 4 | Subtract $\pi_H$ from $\pi$ and divide this amount by the standard error of the percent. Call it $z$. | $z = \dfrac{p - \pi_H}{s_p}$ $= \dfrac{(80 - 30)}{1.26}$ $= 39.7$ |
| Step 5 | Using the critical value of 1.96, determine whether the hypothesis is supported or not supported. | The computed $z$ of 39.7 is greater than the critical $z$ of 1.96, so the hypothesis is not supported. |

(or null) difference between the hypothesized population $\pi$ value and the $p$ value found in our sample. This difference is divided by the standard error to determine how many standard errors away from the hypothesized parameter the sample percentage falls. All relevant information about the population as found by our sample is included in these computations. Knowledge of areas under the normal curve then comes into play to translate this distance into a determination of whether the sample finding supports (accepts) or does not support (rejects) the hypothesis.

The example provided in Table 11.5 uses Bill's hypothesis that 30% of drivers buckle up their seat belts. To move this example from intuitive hypothesis testing into statistical hypothesis testing, Bill reads about a Harris Poll and finds that 80% of respondents in a national sample of 1000 wear their seat belts. This is a 50% difference from Bill's intuitive hypothesis, but it must be translated into the number of standard errors, or $z$. In Step 4 of Table 11.5, this difference is translated into the calculated $z$, 39.7.

The crux of hypothesis testing is the sampling-distribution concept. There is a greater probability of finding a sample result close to the hypothesized population mean, for example, than of finding one that is far away. But there is a critical assumption working here. If our sample mean turns out to be within ±1.96 standard errors of the hypothesized mean, it supports the hypothesis maker at the 95% level of confidence because it falls within 95% of the area under the curve. As Figure 11.7 illustrates, the sampling distribution defines two areas: the acceptance region that resides within ±1.96 standard errors and the rejection region that is found at either end of the bell-shaped sampling distribution and outside the ±1.96 standard errors boundaries. The hypothesis test rule is simple: If the $z$ value falls in the acceptance region, there is support for the hypothesis, and if the $z$ value falls in the rejection region, there is no support for the hypothesis.

## What Significance Level to Use and Why

Most researchers prefer to use the 95% significance level. The critical $z$ value for the 95% level is ±1.96. Compare the computed $z$ value with the critical value. If the computed $z$ is inside the acceptance region, the hypothesis is supported. If it falls in the rejection region, the sample fails to support the hypothesis. In Bill's seat belt case, 39.7 is greater than 1.96 or 2.58. Bill's hypothesis is not supported.

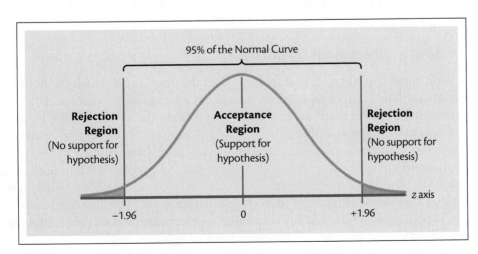

**Figure 11.7** 95% Acceptance and Rejection Regions for Hypothesis Tests

95% of the Normal Curve

Rejection Region (No support for hypothesis)

Acceptance Region (Support for hypothesis)

Rejection Region (No support for hypothesis)

$z$ axis

−1.96    0    +1.96

## How Do We Know That We Have Made the Correct Decision?

What if Bill does not agree with the rejection? Which is correct: the hypothesis or the researcher's sample results? The answer to this question is always the same: Sample information is invariably more accurate than a hypothesis. Of course, the sampling procedure must adhere strictly to probability sampling requirements and ensure representativeness. Bill was greatly mistaken because his hypothesis of 30% of drivers wearing seat belts was 39.7 standard errors away from the 80% finding of the national poll. Bill can dispute a national sample finding reported by the Harris Poll organization, but he will come to realize that his limited observations are much less valid than the findings of this well-respected research industry giant.

    Consider the following example. What percentage of Canadian post-secondary students own a major credit card? Let's say that you think 2 out of 3 (or 66% of) post-secondary students own a MasterCard, Visa card, or some other major credit card. A recent survey by Statistics Canada found that 1 in 3 or 33% of post-secondary students have a major credit card ($n = 1000$). The computations to test your hypotheses of 66% are as follows:

$$z = \frac{p - \pi_H}{s_p}$$

$$= \frac{p - \pi_H}{\sqrt{\dfrac{p \times q}{n}}}$$

$$= \frac{65 - 75}{\sqrt{\dfrac{65 \times 35}{6,000}}}$$

$$= \frac{-10}{0.62}$$

$$= -16.13$$

    The hypothesis that 66% of Canadian post-secondary students own a credit card is not supported because the computed $z$ value exceeds the critical value of 1.96. The sign of the $z$ value is irrelevant, since the absolute value of the computed $z$ is compared with the critical value of 1.96.

## Testing a Directional Hypothesis

A **directional hypothesis** is one that indicates the direction in which the population parameter falls relative to some hypothesized average or percentage. If testing a directional ("greater than" or "less than") hypothesis, the critical $z$ value is adjusted downward to 1.64 and 2.33 for the 95% and 99% levels of confidence, respectively. The hypothesis test formula does not change; it is only the critical value of $z$ that is changed when testing a directional hypothesis. This adjustment is because only one side of the bell-shaped curve is involved in what is known as a "one-tailed" test. Of course, the sample percentage or average must be in the right direction away from the hypothesized value, and the computed $z$ value must meet or exceed the critical one-tailed $z$ value in order for the hypothesis to be supported.

# How to Test a Hypothesis about a Percentage with XL Data Analyst™

Again, we are interested in generalizing our findings to see if they support or reject our percentage hypothesis. The menu sequence to direct the XL Data Analyst to accomplish this is Generalize—Hypothesis Test—Percentage (see Figure 11.8). This sequence opens up the selection window where you can select the categorical variable in the top pane, and the various value labels for that variable will appear in the bottom pane. Note the entry box at the bottom of the selection window where we will enter our hypothesized percentage.

In our example, we will select "Dwelling type" as our chosen variable, and then highlight the "Single family" category. We have hypothesized that 50% of households live in single-family dwellings. Clicking "OK" will prompt the XL Data Analyst to perform the hypothesis test.

Figure 11.9 is an annotated screenshot of an XL Data Analyst percentage hypothesis test analysis. This analysis produces a more detailed output than you have encountered thus far. There is a table that reveals that 45.2% of our 1000 respondents answered "Single family" to this question. The table also shows our hypothesized percentage of 50% has been entered correctly. Immediately following the table are the results of three hypotheses

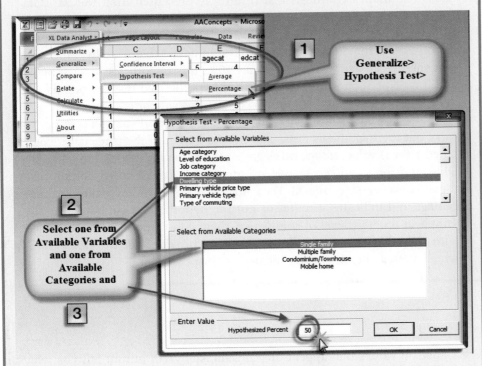

**Figure 11.8** XL Data Analyst Selection Menu for a Percentage Hypothesis Test

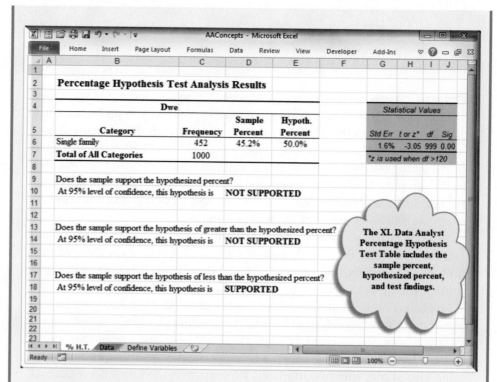

**Figure 11.9** XL Data Analyst Output Table and Results for a Percentage Hypothesis Test

tests. The main hypothesis test finding is presented first: the XL Data Analyst finds insufficient support for our hypothesis of 50%, signalling that our hypothesis is "Not Supported." Next, in case we had directional hypotheses in mind, the XL Data Analyst indicates that if we hypothesized that the percentage was greater than 50%, this hypothesis lacks support and it is "Not Supported," but if we had hypothesized that the population percentage is less than 50%, this hypothesis is "Supported."

Note that XL Data Analyst provides the statistical values necessary to carry out the hypotheses tests. The standard error of the percentage, computed $z$ (or $t$) value, associated degrees of freedom for using a $t$-distribution table, and the significance level are reported in case a user wishes to use them. However, since the XL Data Analyst assesses the hypothesized percentage and indicates whether or not the hypothesis is supported by the sample at the 95% level of confidence, there is little need to be concerned with the other statistical values. These are provided for the rare case in which a researcher might feel the need to inspect them.

## Is It $t$ or $z$?

The statistical values that appear on XL Data Analyst™ output tell you whether or not the hypothesis is supported. Note that there is reference to a "$t$" value and no reference to a "*z*" value. The *t* value is agreed by statisticians to be more proper than the *z* value when the sample is small, but the *t* value does not have set critical values such as 1.96.[4] When the sample size is large enough to represent population parameters with a high degree of confidence, *z* values are used. Whenever XL Data Analyst™ performs analysis, it uses the agreed-upon best approach, and its findings are correct based on the best approach. The *z* value is used in explanations because there are only a very few fixed critical values of *z* to deal with. Also, it is customary in marketing research books to use the *z* value formulas.

## Testing a Hypothesis about an Average (Metric Variables)

The procedure to test a hypothesis about an average is identical to that for testing a hypothesis about a percent. A *z* value is calculated using the following formula:

$$z = \frac{\bar{x} - \mu_H}{s_{\bar{x}}}$$

◀ **Formula for the test of a hypothesis about an average**

where:

$\bar{x}$ = sample average
$\mu_H$ = hypothesized population average
$s_{\bar{x}}$ = standard error of the average

Consider this example. Northwestern Mutual Life Insurance Company in the United States has a post-secondary student internship program. The program allows students to participate in an intensive training program and to become field agents for one academic term. Arrangements are made with various post-secondary schools in the United States whereby students will receive credit if they qualify for and successfully complete this program. Rex Reigen, district agent for Idaho, believed, based on his knowledge of other programs in the country, that the typical student agent will be able to earn about $2750 in his or her first semester of participation in the program. He hypothesized that the population parameter—that is, the average—would be $2750. To check Rex's hypothesis, a survey was taken of current student agents, and 100 of these individuals were contacted through telephone calls. Among the questions posed was an estimate of the amount of money made in their first semester of work in the program. The sample average is determined to be $2800, and the standard deviation is $350.

The amount of $2750 is the hypothesized average of the sampling distribution of all possible samples of the same size that can be taken of the student agents in the country. The unknown factor, of course, is the size of the standard error in dollars. It is assumed that the sampling distribution will be a normal curve, with the average of the entire distribution at $2750. The only information available that would help to determine the size of the standard error is the standard deviation obtained from the sample. This standard deviation can be used to determine a standard error by application of the standard error formula encountered in Step 2 of Table 11.3.

How much can a post-secondary student make selling insurance during the summer?

The amount of $2800 found by the sample differs from the hypothesized amount of $2750 by $50. Is this amount a sufficient enough difference to cast doubt on Rex's estimate? Using the formula for the standard error of the average in the second step, the $z$ value is evaluated as follows:

$$
\begin{aligned}
z &= \frac{\bar{x} - \mu_H}{s_{\bar{x}}} \\[2mm]
&= \frac{\bar{x} - \mu_H}{\dfrac{s}{\sqrt{n}}} \\[2mm]
&= \frac{2,800 - 2,750}{\dfrac{350}{\sqrt{100}}} \\[2mm]
&= \frac{50}{35} \\[2mm]
&= 1.43
\end{aligned}
$$

The sample variability and the sample size have been used to determine the size of the standard error of the assumed sampling distribution. In this case, one standard error of the average is equal to $35. When the difference of $50 is divided by $35 to determine the number of standard errors away from the hypothesized average the sample statistic lies, the result is 1.43 standard errors. As is illustrated in Figure 11.10, 1.43 standard errors is within $\pm 1.96$ standard errors of Rex's hypothesized average. The hypothesis is supported because it falls in the acceptance region.

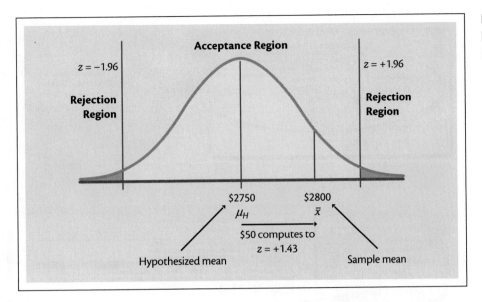

**Figure 11.10** The Sample Findings Support the Hypothesis in This Example

## How to Test a Hypothesis about an Average with XL Data Analyst™

If a car company's introduction of fuel-efficient models is to be successful, there must be attitudes in place that hybrid and/or alternative fuel vehicles will have some impact on carbon dioxide levels that may be contributing to global warming. Let's test the hypothesis that these attitudes exist among the target population. We will take the statement, "Hybrid autos that use alternative fuels will reduce fuel emissions" and test the belief that people "agree" with it. On the 7-point scale, "strongly agree" corresponds to a "5," so we will use the XL Data Analyst to see if the sample findings support this hypothesis.

To test the hypothesis that the average will be 5, you use the Generalize—Hypothesis Test—Average menu sequence to open up the selection window. Unlike the percentage hypothesis window, the average hypothesis test window has only one selection windowpane. You will see in Figure 11.11 that we have selected the "Hybrid autos that use alternative fuels will reduce fuel emissions" variable and entered a "5" in the "Hypothesized Average" box. A click on "OK" completes our selection process.

Figure 11.12 reveals that 1000 respondents answered this question, and the average was found to be 5.1. Our hypothesis of 5 is supported.

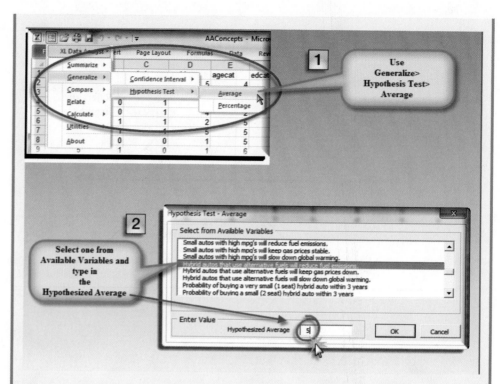

**Figure 11.11** XL Data Analyst Selection Menu for an Average Hypothesis Test

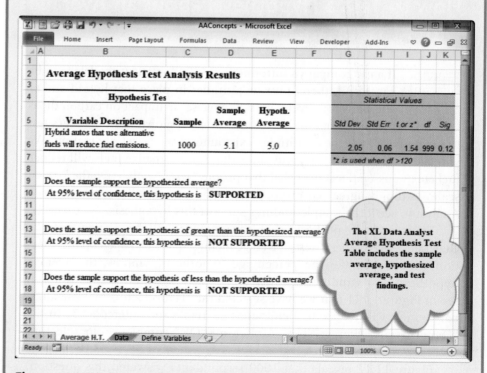

**Figure 11.12** XL Data Analyst Output Table and Results for an Average Hypothesis Test

> You should note that if we had specified directional hypotheses, the XL
> Data Analyst has tested them in this analysis as well. Also, the statistical
> values are present in case you wish to examine them.

## Interpreting Your Hypothesis Test

Regardless of whether a percentage hypothesis or an average hypothesis is being
used, the interpretation of a hypothesis test is directly linked to the sampling
distribution concept. If the hypothesis about the population parameter is correct
or true, then a high percentage of sample findings must fall close to this hypothesized value. If the hypothesis is true, then 95% of the sample results will fall
between $\pm 1.96$ standard errors of the hypothesized mean. On the other hand, if the
hypothesis is false, it is likely that the sample findings will fall outside $\pm 1.96$
standard errors.

In general, the further away the actual sample finding (percentage or average)
is from the hypothesized population value, the more likely the computed $z$ value
will fall outside the critical range, resulting in a failure to support the hypothesis.
When this happens, the XL Data Analyst™ tells the hypothesizer that his or her
assumption about the population is not supported. It must be revised in light of the
evidence from the sample. This revision is achieved through estimates of the population parameter discussed in a previous section. These estimates can provide the
manager or researcher with a new mental picture of the population through confidence interval estimates of the true population value.

## Using the Six-Step Approach to Test a Hypothesis

Table 11.6 lists the six-step approach to hypothesis testing and provides an example
of a hypothesis test for a percentage and one for an average using the Student Life
E-Zine survey data set.

**Table 11.6** The Six-Step Approach to Data Analysis for Generalization Objectives: Hypothesis Test

| Step | Explanation | Example (A is a categorical variable; B is a metric variable) |
|---|---|---|
| **1. What is the research objective?** | Determine that you are dealing with a Hypothesis Test Generalization objective.* | **A.** We hypothesize that 80% of college students will eat at a fast-food restaurant in the next week.<br><br>**B.** We hypothesize that those students who are likely (either very or somewhat likely) to subscribe to our Student Life E-Zine will "Somewhat Prefer" the "Instructor & Course Evaluations" feature. |
| **2. What question-naire ques-tion(s) is/ are involved?** | Identify the question(s), and for each one specify if it is categorical or metric. | **A.** Will you eat at a fast-food restaurant in the next week? The answer "Yes" is *categorical.*<br><br>**B.** The scale is 1 to 5, for "Strongly Do Not Prefer," "Somewhat Do Not Prefer," "No Preference," "Somewhat Prefer," and "Strongly Prefer," respectively. This is a synthetic *metric* measure. |

**Table 11.6** (*Continued*)

| Step | Explanation | Example (A is a categorical variable; B is a metric variable) |
|------|-------------|---------------------------------------------------------------|
| **3. What is the appropriate analysis?** | To test a hypothesis with a sample finding, use Hypothesis Test. | We must use a hypothesis test because we have to take into account variability and sample error. |
| **4. How do you run it?** | Use the proper XL Data Analyst™ analysis: Use "Generalize—Hypothesis Test—Percent" (categorical) or "Generalize—Hypothesis Test—Average" (metric). | *(XL Data Analyst menu screenshot: File, Home, Insert, Page Layout, Formulas, Data, Review, View — CollegeLifeE-zine.xlsm - Microsoft Excel. Menu: XL Data Analyst → Summarize, Generalize, Compare, Relate, Calculate, Utilities; Generalize → Confidence Interval, Hypothesis Test → Average, Percentage)* |

**5. How do you interpret the findings?**

Accept or reject the hypothesis, meaning that if you repeated the survey many, many times and conducted the hypothesis test every one of these times, the hypothesis would be accepted (or rejected, depending on your sample's finding) 95% of those times.

**A. Eat at fast-food restaurant in the next week?**

| Category | Frequency | Sample Percentage | Hypothesis Percentage |
|----------|-----------|-------------------|-----------------------|
| Yes | 429 | 72.7% | 80.0% |
| **Total of All Categories** | 590 | | |

Does the sample support the hypothesized percentage? At 95% level of confidence, this hypothesis is **NOT SUPPORTED**.

**B. Hypothesis Test for an Average**

| Variable Description | Sample | Sample Average | Hypothesis Average |
|----------------------|--------|----------------|--------------------|
| Course/Instructor Evaluator | 160 | 4.4 | 4.0 |

At 95% level of confidence, this hypothesis is **SUPPORTED**.

**6. How do you write/present these findings?**

You can report that for the variable under analysis, the hypothesis of ## is accepted (or rejected, depending on your sample's finding) at the 95% level of confidence. If rejected, it is proper to report the confidence interval for your sample's finding in order to estimate the true population value.

**A.** The hypothesis that 80% of college students will eat fast food in the coming week is not supported. The actual percentage is from 69.1% to 76.3% at the 95% level of confidence.

**B.** The (directional) hypothesis that those students who are likely to subscribe to our Student Life E-Zine will at least "Somewhat Prefer" the "Instructor & Course Evaluations" feature is supported.

*You will learn about other analyses in subsequent chapters.

# Summary

**1.  Discuss generalization.**
Generalization is a process used to estimate population values from a sample's findings. This process is often called "parameter estimation," since population values are called parameters. Generalization is a reflection of the amount of sampling error believed to exist in the sample finding.

**2.  Estimate a confidence interval for a percentage or an average.**
To estimate a population percentage or an average, a confidence interval is used. This is a lower and upper boundary into which the researcher believes the real population parameter value falls. The range is associated with a degree of confidence, typically 95% or 99%. In order to estimate a population percentage, the sample percentage and the sample size is plugged into the formula. In order to estimate a population average, the standard deviation is used as the correct measure of variability for a metric variable in the formula.

**3.  Test a hypothesis about a population percentage or an average.**
The researcher or manager may have a prior belief about what percentage or average value exists in the population. The sample findings can be used to access support or lack of support for this hypothesis. Formulas for testing hypotheses for a population percentage or a population average are provided in this chapter.

# Key Terms

Confidence interval    (p. 356)
Directional hypothesis    (p. 374)
Generalization    (p. 355)
Hypothesis    (p. 370)
Hypothesis testing    (p. 370)
Intuitive hypothesis testing
  (p. 371)
Most commonly used level of
  confidence    (p. 357)
Null hypothesis    (p. 372)

Parameter    (p. 356)
Parameter estimation    (p. 356)
Population fact    (p. 354)
Sample finding    (p. 354)
Sampling distribution    (p. 360)
Standard error    (p. 359)
Standard error of the average
  (p. 364)
Standard error of the percentage
  (p. 359)

# Review Questions

**1.1** Describe similarities and differences between sample findings and population facts and between parameter and parameter estimation.

**1.2** Define "generalization," and provide an example of what you might generalize if you moved to a new city and noticed that you were driving faster than most other drivers.

**2.1** Describe how a confidence interval can be used by a researcher to estimate a population percentage.

**2.2** Using the formula for a confidence interval for a percentage, indicate the role of
  **a.**  The sample finding (percentage)
  **b.**  Variability
  **c.**  Level of confidence

2.3 Indicate how a researcher interprets a 95% confidence interval. Refer to the sampling distribution in your explanation.

2.4 How is the standard error of the average affected by
   a.   The standard deviation
   b.   The sample size

2.5 It is reported in the newspaper that a survey sponsored by *Forbes* magazine with 200 Fortune 500 company top executives has found that 75% believe that the United States trails Japan and Germany in automobile engineering. What percentage of all Fortune 500 company top executives believe that the United States trails Japan and Germany?

2.6 Here are several computation practice exercises in which you must identify which formula should be used and apply it. In each case, after you perform the necessary calculations, write your answers in the blank column.
   a.   Determine confidence intervals for each of the following:

| Sample Statistic | Sample Size | Confidence Level | Your Confidence Intervals |
|---|---|---|---|
| Mean: 150 Std. Dev: 30 | 200 | 95% | |
| Percent: 67% | 300 | 99% | |
| Mean: 5.4 Std. Dev: 0.5 | 250 | 99% | |
| Percent: 25.8% | 500 | 99% | |

   b.   Test the following hypothesis and interpret your findings:

| Hypothesis | Sample Findings | Confidence Level | Your Test Results |
|---|---|---|---|
| Mean = 7.5 | Mean: 8.5 Std dev: 1.2 $n = 670$ | 95% | |
| Percent = 86% | $p = 95\%$ $n = 1000$ | 99% | |
| Mean = 125 | Mean: 135 Std dev: 15 $n = 500$ | 95% | |
| Percent = 33% | $p = 31\%$ $n = 120$ | 99% | |

3.1 How does statistical hypothesis testing differ from intuitive hypothesis testing? How are they similar?

3.2 When the person who posited a hypothesis argues against the researcher who has performed the hypothesis test and not supported it, who should win the argument, and why?

3.3 How does a directional hypothesis differ from a nondirectional one, and what are the two critical items to take into account when testing a directional hypothesis?

3.4 Hertz Rent a Car executives believe that Hertz accounts for about 50% of all Cadillacs that are rented. To test this belief, a researcher randomly identifies 20 major airports with on-site rental car lots. Observers are sent to each location and instructed to record the number of rental company Cadillacs observed in a four-hour period. About 500 are observed, and 30% are observed being returned to Hertz Rent a Car. What are the implications of this finding for the Hertz executives' belief?

# Case 11.1

# The Auto Online Survey

Auto Online is a website where prospective automobile buyers can find information about various makes and models. Individuals can also purchase a make and model with specific options and features online. Recently, Auto Online posted an online questionnaire on the internet, and it mailed invitations to the last 5000 automobile buyers who visited Auto Online. Some of these buyers bought their car from Auto Online, whereas the remaining individuals bought their autos from a dealership. However, they did visit Auto Online at least one time prior to that purchase. You may assume that the respondents to this survey are representative of the population of automobile buyers who visited the Auto Online website during their vehicle purchase process.

The Auto Online survey data set (and code book) is provided for you in an XL Data Analyst™ data file called **AutoOnline.xls**. Embedded in the questions below, we have provided copies of the relevant questions in the Auto Online survey. Your task is to use the six-step approach to data analysis that we have described in this chapter to perform and interpret the proper analysis for each question part.

1. In order to describe this population, estimate the population parameters for the following:
   a. For those who have visited the Auto Online website, what percentage found out about it from (1) an internet banner ad, (2) web surfing, and/or (3) a search engine?

5. *How did you find out about Auto Online? Indicate all of the ways that you can recall.*

   \_\_\_\_ *From a friend (0,1)*
   \_\_\_\_ *Web surfing (0,1)*
   \_\_\_\_ *Theater (0,1)*
   \_\_\_\_ *Billboard (0,1)*
   \_\_\_\_ *Search engine (0,1)*
   \_\_\_\_ *Newspaper (0,1)*
   \_\_\_\_ *Internet banner ad (0,1)*
   \_\_\_\_ *Television (0,1)*
   \_\_\_\_ *Other (0,1)*

   b. How often they make purchases online.
   2. *How often do you make purchases through the internet?*

   *Very Often  5*
   *Often  4*
   *Occasionally  3*
   *Almost Never  2*
   *Never  1*

   c. Number of visits they made to Auto Online.
   4. *About how many times before you bought your automobile did you visit the Auto Online website?*
   \_\_\_\_ *times*

   d. The percentage who actually bought their vehicle from Auto Online.
   7. *Did you buy your new vehicle on the Auto Online website?*
   \_\_\_\_ *Yes (1)*\_\_\_\_ *No (2)*

*(Continued)*

e. The percentage of those who felt it was a better experience than buying at a traditional dealership.

    a. *If yes, was it a better experience than buying at a traditional dealership visit?*
    _____ Yes (1)_____ No (2)

f. How do people feel about the Auto Online website?

    6. *What is your reaction to the following statements about the Auto Online website?*

| | Strongly Disagree | | Neutral | | Strongly Agree |
|---|---|---|---|---|---|
| The website was easy to use. | 1 | 2 | 3 | 4 | 5 |
| I found that the website was very helpful in my purchase. | 1 | 2 | 3 | 4 | 5 |
| I had a positive experience using the website. | 1 | 2 | 3 | 4 | 5 |
| I would use this website only for research. | 1 | 2 | 3 | 4 | 5 |
| The website influenced me to buy my vehicle. | 1 | 2 | 3 | 4 | 5 |
| I would feel secure buying from this website. | 1 | 2 | 3 | 4 | 5 |

2. Auto Online principals have the following beliefs. Test these hypotheses.

    a. People will "strongly agree" to each of the first four of the eight statements concerning use of the internet and purchase (question 3 on the questionnaire).

        3. *Indicate your opinion on each of the following statements. For each one, please indicate if you strongly disagree, somewhat disagree, are neutral, somewhat agree, or strongly agree.*

| | Strongly Disagree | | Neutral | | Strongly Agree |
|---|---|---|---|---|---|
| I like using the internet. | 1 | 2 | 3 | 4 | 5 |
| I use the internet to research purchases I make. | 1 | 2 | 3 | 4 | 5 |

| | | | | | |
|---|---|---|---|---|---|
| I think purchasing items from the internet is safe. | 1 | 2 | 3 | 4 | 5 |
| The internet is a good tool to use when researching an automobile purchase. | 1 | 2 | 3 | 4 | 5 |
| The internet should not be used to purchase vehicles. | 1 | 2 | 3 | 4 | 5 |
| Online dealerships are just another way of getting you into the traditional dealership. | 1 | 2 | 3 | 4 | 5 |
| I like the process of buying a new vehicle. | 1 | 2 | 3 | 4 | 5 |
| I don't like to hassle with car salesmen. | 1 | 2 | 3 | 4 | 5 |

    b. More than 90% of those buyers who say their Auto Online experience was better than buying at a traditional auto dealership will say that buying a vehicle online is "a great deal better" than buying it at a traditional dealership.

        b. *If yes, indicate how much better.*
        _____ *A great deal better (1)*
        _____ *Much better (2)*
        _____ *Somewhat better (3)*
        _____ *Just a bit better (4)*

    c. Those who visit the Auto Online will . . .
      i.  Be 35 years old,
          *13. What is your age? _____ years*
      ii.  Trade in autos that are worth $10 000.
      iii.  Buy cars with a sticker price of $15 000.
      iv.  Actually pay $12 000 for their new automobile.
          *10. If you traded in a vehicle, approximately how much was it worth? $ _____*
          *11. What was the approximate sticker price of your new vehicle? $ _____*
          *12. What was the approximate actual price you paid for it? $ _____*

# Case 11.2 YOUR INTEGRATED CASE

# The Student Life E-Zine Survey Generalization Analysis

*It will be useful to review the Student Life E-Zine integrated case description in Chapter 1 (Case 1.2) as a reference for the various research objectives referred to in Case 11.2.*

This was an exciting time for our four potential web entrepreneurs as Lori Baker, marketing intern working with Bob Watts at ORS Marketing Research, had just finished her PowerPoint presentation of the descriptive analysis results. "Wow," said Sarah, "I can see a lot of things that we can do with our e-zine now that we have found all of this positive feedback about the concept. Let's get a copy of Lori's PowerPoint file and take this to the bank."

Bob, who had been sitting behind the four prospective Student Life E-Zine originators during Lori's presentation, said, "Yes, the descriptive findings are impressive, and Lori's figures are certainly first-rate, but I need to remind everyone that we're dealing with a sample of City U students, so we need to take this fact into account. Do you remember our discussion about the sample size and the use of confidence intervals? We're going to need to perform generalization analyses of various sorts before you can take this survey to the bank. Specifically, we'll need to compute confidence intervals for percentages and averages, and we have some hypotheseses to test in order to feel confident about our break-even analysis."

Wesley took a quick look at Don, and then asked Bob, "Do we really need this? I mean, the descriptive findings that Lori presented are very impressive to me."

Bob answered, "I know that Lori's graphs are very professional, but part of my responsibility as a marketing researcher is to arm you with as much objective evidence as possible, and if we do the proper generalization analyses, and if they come out as we hope, your case will be airtight. No one will be able to shoot you down. My recommendation is that you take Lori's PowerPoint file and review the descriptive findings over the next week. You can discuss the many implications of these findings among yourselves. Meanwhile, Lori and I will do the necessary generalization analyses, and then you can see the findings as they pertain to the entire student body of City U. Let's meet a week from now so Lori and I can show you our findings then."

Sarah, Anna, Wesley, and Don thought about Bob's recommendation, and all quickly agreed when Anna said, "Come on, guys, we have plenty to think about, and we're a long way from launching our Student Life E-Zine, so I vote that we do as Bob recommends."

After the four budding entrepreneurs left the ORS building, Bob called Lori into his office and said, "Use the XL Data Analyst™ to perform the following generalization analyses on the Student Life E-Zine survey data set. Since you're a marketing intern, I've included some items that are not necessarily a part of our survey objectives, but which will give you some practice performing and interpreting generalization analyses.

"So, I want your interpretation of each finding. Oh, and some of these are a little vague, as I want you to figure out what type of scale you're working with and what the appropriate analysis is. Let's meet early next week to see what you've found."

1. Determine 95% confidence intervals for the relevant population for each of the following:
   a. High-speed cable access
   b. Use of coupons
   c. Whether they will purchase over the internet in the next two months
   d. How much they anticipate spending on internet purchases in the next two months

*(Continued)*

e.  Out of every $100 of internet purchases, how much do City U students spend on . . .
    i.   Books
    ii.  Gifts for weddings and other special occasions
    iii. Music/CDs
    iv.  Financial services (insurance, loans, etc.)
    v.   Clothing
    vi.  General merchandise for your home or car
f.  "Very likely" to subscribe to E-Zine
g.  Preference for the following possible E-Zine features:
    i.   Popcorn Favourites
    ii.  Student Government
    iii. What's Happen'n
h.  Living off campus

2.  Test the following hypotheses:
    a.  90% of City U students have some form of internet access.
    b.  50% of those with internet access have a dial-up modem connection.
    c.  70% of City U students will eat fast food in the coming week.
    d.  25% will purchase new clothes next month.
    e.  At least 18% of those who qualify are "very likely" to subscribe to the Student Life E-Zine at a price of $15 per month.
    f.  Those students who qualify will at least "somewhat prefer" the following possible E-Zine features:
        i.   On-Line Registrar
        ii.  Cyber Cupid
        iii. Weather Today
        iv.  My Advisor
    g.  "Quick Facts" on City U's website says that 15% of its students live on campus. Is our Student Life E-Zine survey sample consistent with this fact?
    h.  "Quick Facts" also states that the male/female student ratio at City U is 50/50. Is our Student Life E-Zine survey sample consistent with this fact?

# Testing of Differences

## Understanding Regional Differences in Work Hours

*By Andrew Heisz and Sébastien LaRochelle-Côté*

In recent years, international differences in work hours have been the focus of a substantial body of research. Much less attention has been paid to regional differences in working time in Canada in spite of regional differences in average work hours that are of a magnitude that is similar to that of the Canada–U.S. difference in work hours. In this paper, we document regional differences in work hours across 6 regions of Canada for 2004, using a representative sample of 19,500 workers from the Survey of Labour and Income Dynamics. We also examine potential explanations for these differences.

Average hours per worker were lower than the Canadian average in Quebec, the Atlantic and in British Columbia. In the Atlantic and in British Columbia, low working hours were mostly the result of a larger share of individuals working short years. In Quebec, the relative prevalence of the "low" full-year, full-time schedule (the equivalent of 29 to 37 weekly hours of work over 52 weeks) was the main difference between this province and the rest of the country (including Ontario). This suggests that Quebec–Ontario differences in average work hours, for the most part, were the result of differences in the middle of the hours distribution.

Average hours were higher than the Canadian average in Ontario, Manitoba–Saskatchewan, and in Alberta. While differences in average work hours were relatively small across these regions, men in Manitoba–Saskatchewan and Alberta were relatively more likely to work more than 2300 hours per year (long year), and women were relatively more likely to work fewer than 1500 hours (short year). Ontario had more individuals working between 1500 and 2300 hours per year (full-year, full-time schedule).

What explains regional differences in working hours? International studies of working time often point to a large pool of "observable" factors (factors that can be easily quantified in household surveys) and "unobservable" factors (factors that are difficult to observe in household surveys) to explain international differences in work hours, which may also apply to regional differences in work hours. Unobservable factors include differences in incentives related to wage inequality as well as differences in taxes, in macroeconomic conditions, in local preferences and tastes, and in the shape of institutions. Observable factors include compositional differences in union status, industrial structure, job conditions and demographic characteristics.

Using decomposition techniques, we determine how much of the differences in work hours between Ontario and five other regions of Canada can be explained by differences in union status, industrial structure, job conditions and demographic characteristics. While observable factors were relatively inefficient in explaining differences in average work hours, they were more efficient in explaining regional differences in the share of individuals working a short year (fewer than 1500 hours). For example, "observables" explain almost entirely why workers in Quebec and in Manitoba–Saskatchewan were more likely to work a short year than their Ontario counterparts. In addition, one third to two thirds of the differences in the share of individuals working between 1900 and 2300 hours a year could be attributed to observables. Of the observables, differences in union status and demographic characteristics explained very little of the differences in work hours. Differences in industrial structure and in job conditions (including firm size and management responsibilities) explained more of the differences. However, observables did not explain differences in long work hours, did not entirely explain the larger share of workers with short years in the Atlantic and in British Columbia, and did not explain the large incidence of the low full-year, full-time schedule in Quebec (between 1500 to 1900 hours per year). These remaining differences suggest that unobservable factors also contribute to exacerbate differences in regional work hours.

Source: Statistics Canada, *Analytical Studies Branch Research Paper Series: Understanding Regional Differences in Work Hours*, 11F0019MIE2007293 no. 293 Released January 22, 2007.

## Where We Are

It is possible to make generalizations about measures of central tendency such as averages and percentages found in a probability sample survey. These generalizations, or inferences, take the form of confidence intervals or tests of hypotheses. A different type of inference concerns differences between groups. For example, are college students more likely to buy a Red Bull energy drink than high school students are? In this chapter, the logic of differences tests and how to use XL Data Analyst™ to conduct various types of differences tests are presented.

The chapter begins with why differences are important to marketing managers. Next, differences (percentages or averages) between two independent groups, such as differences in satisfaction between high-speed cable versus DSL telephone internet users, are introduced. Following that, ANOVA, a simple way to compare the averages of several groups simultaneously and to quickly spot patterns of significant differences, is discussed. Finally, how to test whether a difference exists between the averages of two similarly scaled questions is presented. For instance, do buyers rate a store higher in "merchandise selection" than they rate its "good values"? Formulas and numerical examples are provided along with examples of XL Data Analyst™ procedures and output.

# Why Differences Are Important

One of the most vital marketing strategy concepts is market segmentation. **Market segmentation** holds that within a product market, there are different types of consumers with different requirements, and these differences can form the bases of marketing strategies. For example, the Iams Company, which markets pet foods, has more than a dozen different varieties of dry dog food geared to the dog's age (puppy versus adult), weight (normal versus overweight), and activity (active versus inactive). Toyota has many models, including the Camry Hybrid car, the four-door Avalon luxury sedan, the Highlander SUV, and the Tacoma truck. Even Boeing has several different types of commercial jets and a separate business jet division for corporate travel. The needs and requirements of each market segment differ greatly from others, and an astute marketer will customize his or her marketing mix to each target market's unique situation.[1]

Some differences, of course, are quite obvious, but as competition becomes more intense, with aggressive market segmentation and target marketing being the watchwords of most companies in an industry, there is a need to investigate differences among consumer groups. Market segmentation relies on the discovery of significant differences through the application of the proper data analysis. Of course, the differences must be meaningful and useful. For example, energetic, growing puppies need different nutritional supplements than do overweight, inactive, aging dogs with stiff joints, so Iams uses these different nutritional needs to formulate special types of dog food for these market segments.

In what might be considered an extreme example of market segmentation, Harrah's Entertainment Inc., the largest gaming corporation in the world—operating gambling casinos in the United States, the United Kingdom, Egypt, and South Africa—has analyzed its slot machine players and claims to have identified 90 different market segmentation types based on age, gender, game preference, casino location, and other variables.[2] This segmentation analysis has revealed that one of these segments amounts to about one-third of its customers, yet it represents 80% of revenues. Also, Harrah's claims that by custom-tailoring its marketing strategies to various market segments, it has significantly increased its market share and become more profitable.

Analyzing for significant and meaningful differences is a discovery process. The marketing researcher and manager formulate the research objectives with the goal of finding useful market segmentation differences in the total market, but there is no guarantee that significant and meaningful differences will be found. Data analysis is used to investigate for statistically significant differences, and there are rulesand guidelines about how to decide when significant differences are indeed found. This chapter discusses these rules, and how to spot and interpret differences easily.[3]

Harrah's uses market segmentation to target specific types of gamblers.

For example, there are three ways a researcher can analyze for differences in the service Rogers Communications' customers might want: (1) Compare one group to another group, such as comparing men to women customers; (2) compare three or more groups, such as people who are single, those who are married without children, those who are married with teenagers living at home, and those who are married with one or more children in college; or (3) compare how more important one service feature (such as rollover minutes) is than another service feature (such as sharing minutes with family members). How to perform differences tests for each of these three cases is covered in this chapter.

## Testing for Significant Differences between Two Groups

Often a researcher will want to compare two groups that exist in the same sample. The researcher may have identified two independent groups, such as disloyal versus loyal customers, men versus women, or coupon users versus those who never use coupons, and he or she may want to compare their answers to the same question. The question may use either a categorical scale or a metric scale. A categorical scale requires that the researcher compare the percentage for one group to the percentage for the other group, whereas averages among groups are compared when a metric scale is involved. The formulas differ depending on whether percentages or averages are being tested. However, the basic concepts involved in the formulas are identical.

### Differences between Percentages for Two Groups

When a marketing researcher compares two groups of respondents to determine whether or not there are statistically significant differences between them, the researcher thinks of them as two independent populations. It is as though two independent surveys were administered, one for each group. The question to be answered then becomes, "Are the respective parameters of these two independent populations different?" A researcher can work only with the sample results.

Therefore, the researcher falls back on statistical generalization concepts to determine whether the difference that is found between the two sample findings is a true difference between the two populations. The logic of differences tests is very similar to the logic of hypothesis testing discussed in the Chapter 11.

Gender is a demographic variable that is often used by marketers to segment their markets. Take the case of a DVD rental store that has added a line of candy, chips, pretzels, popcorn, and soft drinks. The manager pulls the sales slips from 100 randomly selected male customers and finds that 65% of them bought a snack item when they rented their movies. A different sample of 300 randomly selected female customers reveals that 40% bought a food item when they rented their movies. In other words, there are two surveys—a sample of males and a separate sample of females who rent from this store—and we have two percentages, 65% of the men and 40% of the women, who bought snacks with their movie rentals.

It appears that male movie renters are different than females movie renters with respect to buying snacks along with their movie rentals. There is a 25% arithmetic (65%–40%) difference. Is this difference a "true" difference between men and women movie renters or a reflection of sampling error? Sampling error is based on the sample sizes (100 men versus 300 women) and the variability of the percent of munchies buyers: 65% and 40%.

To test whether a true difference exists between two group percentages, the null hypothesis that the difference in their population parameters is equal to zero (i.e., there is no difference between the groups) is tested. The **alternative hypothesis** is that there is a true difference between the two group percentages (or averages) that are being compared. The alternative hypothesis is, of course, the crux of market segmentation differences, so a marketing researcher is always hoping for the null hypothesis to *not* be supported. In other words, the researcher would very much like to report that significant differences were found because this is the first of the two conditions for market segmentation that we described earlier—namely, a significant difference.

To perform the test of significance of differences between two percentages, each representing a separate group (sample), the first step requires a "comparison" of the two percentages. That is, there is an arithmetic difference between them. The second step requires that this difference be translated into a number of standard errors away from the hypothesized value of zero. Once the number of standard errors is known, knowledge of the area under the normal curve will yield an assessment of the support for the null hypothesis. This is almost exactly the same procedure used to test a hypothesis, except that in the present case, two percentages from two samples ($p_1$ to $p_2$) are compared, while in a hypothesis test for a percentage, the hypothesized percentage to the percentage in the sample ($p$ to $\pi_H$) were compared.

Here is the formula for the test of the significance of the difference between two percentages:

$$z = \frac{p_1 - p_2}{s_{p_1 - p_2}}$$

◁ **Formula for significance of the difference between two percentages**

where:

$p_1$    = percent for sample 1
$p_2$    = percent for sample 2
$s_{p_1 - p_2}$ = standard error of the difference between two percentages

Because there are two samples instead of the one that we worked with for a hypothesis test, the standard error term is calculated differently and called the **standard error of the difference between two percentages**. Here is its formula:

**Formula for the standard error of the difference between two percentages** ▷

$$s_{p_1-p_2} = \sqrt{\frac{p_1 \times q_1}{n_1} + \frac{p_2 \times q_2}{n_2}}$$

where:

$p_1$ = percent for sample 1, and $q_1 = (100 - p_1)$
$p_2$ = percent for sample 2, and $q_2 = (100 - p_2)$
$n_1, n_2$ = sample sizes for sample 1 and sample 2, respectively

Refer to Table 12.1 to follow, step-by-step, how to perform a test of the difference between two percentages.

The sampling distribution under consideration now is the assumed sampling distribution of the differences between the percentages. The assumption is that the differences have been computed for comparisons of the two sample percentages for many repeated samplings. If the null hypothesis is true, this distribution of differences follows the normal curve, with an average equal to zero and a standard error

**Table 12.1 How to Determine If One Group's Percentage Is Different from Another Group's Percentage**

Marketers are very interested in differences between groups because they offer potentially important market segmentation implications. As you might expect, the researcher assesses how close the percentage for one group is to the percentage for another group with a type of differences analysis. In this example, we are wondering if male movie renters differ from female ones with respect to purchases of candy, snack items, and soft drinks along with their rentals. The steps are as follows:

| Step | Description | Our Movie Rental Store Example |
|------|-------------|--------------------------------|
| Step 1 | Determine the percentage and sample size for each of your two samples. | The movie rental store manager has found that 65% of the 100 male customers buy food items, while 40% of the 300 female customers buy food items. |
| Step 2 | Compare the two percentages by taking their arithmetic difference. | The difference is 65% – 40%, or 25%. (The sign does not matter.) |
| Step 3 | Determine the *standard error of the difference between two percentages*. (This procedure is described above.) | $\text{Standard error} = \sqrt{\frac{(65 \times 35)}{100} + \frac{(40 \times 60)}{300}}$ $= 5.55\%$ |
| Step 4 | Divide the difference between the two sample percentages by the standard error of the difference between percents. Call it z. | $z = 25/5.55 = 4.5$ |
| Step 5 | Using the critical z value, determine whether the null hypothesis is supported or not supported at your chosen level of confidence* (95% is customary, meaning a z of 1.96). | In our example, 4.5 is much larger than 1.96, so the null hypothesis is not supported. In other words, male and female movie renters are different in their purchase of food items when they rent their movies. |

*The significance level is provided automatically by practically any analysis program that you use.

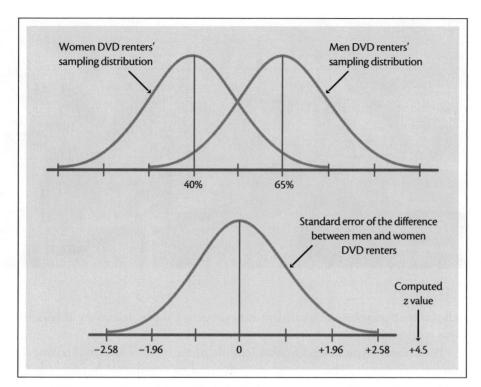

**Figure 12.1** Comparison of Women and Men DVD Renters Sampling Distributions for Purchase of a Snack Item with His/Her DVD

equal to one. The procedure requires acceptance of the (null) hypothesis as true until it lacks support from the statistical test. Consequently, the differences of (theoretically) hundreds of comparisons of the two sample percentages generated from many, many samplings would average zero. In other words, the sampling distribution is now the distribution of the difference between one sample and the other, taken over many, many times.

In Figure 12.1, the women's and the men's populations are represented by two bell-shaped sampling distribution curves. With the women movie renters' curve, the apex is at 40%, while the men's curve apex is at 65%. This shows that if the surveys were repeated many, many times, the central value for women movie renters would be 40%, and the central value for men movie renters would be 65% who purchase a snack item with their movie rentals. In Figure 12.1, there is also the sampling distribution of the difference between two percentages. Its apex is 0 to represent the null hypothesis that there is no difference between the two populations. The standard error of the difference curve has a mean of 0, and its horizontal axis is measured with standard errors such that it embodies the assumptions of a normal, or bell-shaped, curve.

If computing our differences test manually, the computed $z$ value is compared with our standard $z$ of 1.96 for a 95% level of confidence. The computed $z$ in Step 4 of Table 12.1 is 4.5. As you can see in Figure 12.1, 4.5 is larger than 1.96. A computed $z$ value that is larger than the critical $z$ value amounts to no support for the null hypothesis because it falls outside the 95% area of the standard error of the difference curve. Thus, there is a statistically significant difference between the two percentages. If this comparison was repeated many, many times with a multitude of

Do men differ from women with respect to buying snacks with their DVD rentals?

independent samples, a significant difference would be found in at least 95% of these replications.

Directional hypotheses are also feasible in the case of tests of statistically significant differences. The procedure is identical to directional hypotheses that are stipulated in hypothesis tests. First look at the sign of the computed $z$ value to check that it is consistent with the hypothesized direction. Then use a cutoff $z$ value such as 1.64 standard errors for the 95% level of confidence or 2.33 standard errors for the 99% level of confidence because only one tail of the sampling distribution is being used.

There are, of course, a great many differences between men and women, but a recent study that might be of interest to the Student Life E-Zine entrepreneurs compared the internet-usage differences between men and women.[4] The differences analysis found that men are typically in search of information. It was determined that men want objective and accurate information that is quite detailed, and they are often seeking answers to questions that they have about products, financial issues, software, or hobbies. An interesting counterintuitive finding is that men do not wish to search far for answers; in fact, one might characterize them as impatient information searchers. According to the same study, women internet users, on the other hand, tend to be searching general reference topics. They also check out e-books, seek medical information, surf for cooking hints and recipes, and click on government information. Women with families look at child-rearing websites, and other women gravitate toward social causes on the internet.

## Differences between Averages for Two Groups

The procedure for testing the significance of the difference between two averages from two different groups (samples) is identical to the procedure used in testing two percentages. However, the equations differ because a metric scale is involved. As with a percentages difference test, the average for one sample is "compared" with the average for the other sample. Recall that "compared" means "take the difference."

This value is then divided by the standard error of the difference between averages. Here is the formula:

$$z = \frac{\overline{x}_1 - \overline{x}_2}{s_{\overline{x}_1 - \overline{x}_2}}$$

◀ **Formula for significance of the difference between two averages**

where:

$\overline{x}_1$ = average found in sample 1
$\overline{x}_2$ = average found in sample 2
$s_{\overline{x}_1 - \overline{x}_2}$ = standard error of the difference between two averages

The standard error of the difference is easy to calculate and again relies on the variability that has been found in the samples and their sizes. The formula for the **standard error of the difference between two averages** is:

$$s_{\overline{x}_1 - \overline{x}_2} = \sqrt{\frac{s_1^2}{n_1} + \frac{s_2^2}{n_2}}$$

◀ **Formula for the standard error of the difference between two averages**

where:

$s_1$ = standard deviation in sample 1
$s_2$ = standard deviation in sample 2
$n_1$ = size of sample 1
$n_2$ = size of sample 2

## Using the XL Data Analyst™ to Determine the Significance of the Difference Between Two Group Percentages

The XL Data Analyst can easily compare two mutually exclusive groups with regard to their respective percentage on a category of some variable. (Note that this tool does not apply to metric variables.) Let us assume that we are interested in seeing if there is a difference between people who live in hometowns with dramatically different population sizes and their commuting type, specifically the percent that commute in their vehicle alone. That is, we want to know if the percentage of respondents living in huge cities (1 million and more residents) who commute alone is different from the percentage of those who live in very small towns (under 10,000) who commute alone.

Figure 12.2 shows the selection menu sequence for the XL Data Analyst to accomplish this test. Note that you use the command sequence of Compare—2 Group Percents, and then you select a Grouping Variable such as "Size of hometown or city," and then you select 2 categories such as "1 million and more" and "Under 10K." Next, you select "Type of commuting" as the Target Variable and highlight "Single occupancy" as the target group. We define a **grouping variable** as the variable that is used to identify

*(Continued)*

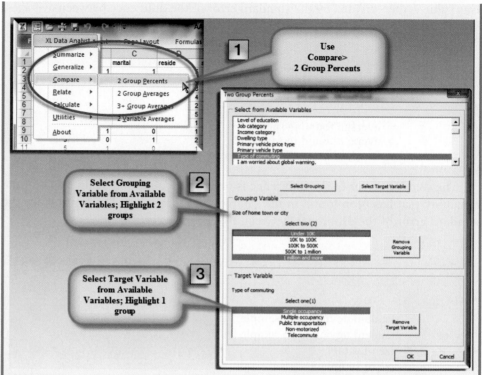

**Figure 12.2** Using the XL Data Analyst to Set Up a Two-Group Percentages Analysis

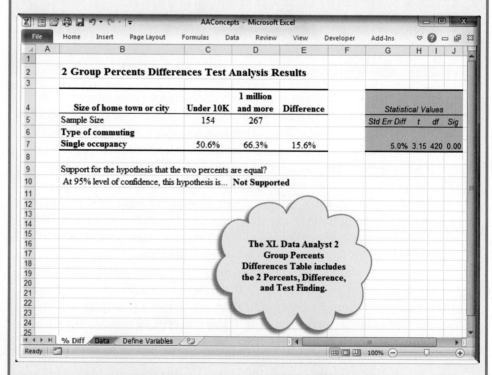

**Figure 12.3** XL Data Analyst Two-Group Percentages Differences Analysis Output

the groups that are to be compared with respect to differences. The **target variable** is the variable on which the groups will be compared. Here, size of hometown or city is the grouping variable, and the single occupancy category is the target variable's value.

The result of this difference analysis is found in Figure 12.3, and when you study this output, you will find that of the 267 large city respondents, 66.3% indicated "single occupancy," while of the 154 small town respondents, 50.6% responded identically as to type of commuting. The arithmetic difference is 15.6%, and at the bottom of the Difference Analysis Test Table, the XL Data Analyst has reported that the hypothesis of equal percentages (the null hypothesis) is "Not Supported." In other words, with respect to single occupancy commuting, proportionately more very large city dwellers commute this way. In relation to the examples from Chapter 11, we could argue that since large city commutes normally require large amounts of gasoline, it is possible that these individuals are looking for more efficient vehicles such as hybrid and/or alternative fuel vehicles.

To illustrate how significance of difference computations are made, consider the following example, which answers the question "Do male teens and female teens drink different amounts of sports drinks?" In a recent survey, teenagers were asked to indicate how many 20-ounce bottles of sports drinks they consume in a typical week. The descriptive statistics revealed that males consume 9 bottles on average and females consume 7.5 bottles of sports drinks on average. The respective standard deviations were found to be 2 and 1.2. Both samples were of size 100. Table 12.2 is a step-by-step explanation of the procedures used to test the null hypothesis that males and females consume an equal number of bottles of sports drink in a typical week.

As indicated earlier, Figure 12.1 illustrates how this analysis takes place. The two sampling distribution curves would be for the females' and males' averages, with the means of 7.5 and 9.0 under their respective apexes. The standard error of the difference curve would remain essentially as it appears in Figure 12.1, except that the computed $z$ value would now be 6.43.

Patrick M. Baldasare, former president and CEO of the Response Center, a Philadelphia research and consulting firm, and Vikas Mittel, a former research analyst at the Response Center, provide some useful insights on *statistical* versus *practical* significance.[5] They say that researchers often misuse and abuse the concept of significance, for they tend to associate statistical significance with the magnitude of the result. People often think that if the difference between two numbers is significant, it must be large and therefore *must* be considered important. To remedy this misuse of the concept of significance, Baldasare and Mittel suggest that when comparing numbers, we should consider two types of significance: *statistical significance* and *practical significance*. By understanding the difference between statistical and practical significance, we can avoid the pitfall that traps many in the research industry.

**Table 12.2** How to Determine If One Group's Average Is Different from Another Group's Average

When metric data are being used, the researcher compares the averages. The procedure and logic are identical to that used when comparing two percentages; however, the formulas differ, as averages and standard deviations are appropriate for metric data. In our example, we are investigating the possible differences between males and females with respect to the number of bottles of sports drink they drink in a typical week. The steps are described below:

| Step | Description | Our Sports Drink Example |
|------|-------------|--------------------------|
| **Step 1** | Determine the average, standard deviation, and sample size for each of your two samples. | We find that 100 males drink 9.0 bottles, while 100 females drink 7.5 bottles of sports drink per week, on average. The standard deviations are 2.0 and 1.2, respectively. |
| **Step 2** | Compare the two averages by taking their arithmetic difference. | The difference is (9.0 − 7.5) or 1.5. (The sign does not matter.) |
| **Step 3** | Determine the *standard error of the difference between two averages.* (This procedure is described on page 397.) | $$\text{Standard error} = \sqrt{\frac{2^2}{100} + \frac{1.2^2}{300}}$$ $$= \sqrt{0.04 + 0.0144}$$ $$= 0.233$$ |
| **Step 4** | Divide the difference between the two sample averages by the standard error of the difference between averages. Call it $z$. | $$z = \frac{1.5}{0.233}$$ $$= 6.43$$ |
| **Step 5** | Using the appropriate statistical table, determine whether the null hypothesis is accepted or rejected at your chosen level of confidence.* | In our example, the significance level would be 0.000, so the null hypothesis is rejected. In other words, males and females are different with respect to the number of bottles of sports drink they consume in a typical week. |

*The significance level is provided automatically by practically any analysis program that you use.

Researchers and executives discuss the meaning of data that are statistically significant.

A *statistical* significance level of, say, 95% implies that, if one were to do the study 100 times, 95 times out of 100 the difference observed would repeat itself in the sample data. But statistical significance does not reveal anything about how important the difference is, regardless of the size of the difference in the observed data. *Practical* significance depends on whether or not there is a useful managerial application that uses the difference. That is, when the researcher reports a significant difference, it is up to the manager or the researcher working with the manager to assess the practical usefulness of the difference.

# Using the XL Data Analyst™ to Determine the Significance of the Difference between Two Group Averages

Since differences analysis is so vital to marketing research, the XL Data Analyst performs a differences analysis for the comparison of one group's average to the average of a separate group. To illustrate the operation of this analysis, we will tackle the question of whether or not differences exist between males' versus females' preference for the "super cycle" one-seat hybrid vehicle under consideration by the company pursuing a new fuel-efficient line of cars. The survey asked the question, "What is your preference for the super cycle one-seat hybrid?" and respondents indicated their likelihood on a 7-point balanced symmetric scale where 1 = very undesirable and 7 = very desirable. To illustrate the operation of the XL Data Analyst's two-group-averages comparison analysis, let us see if the average for males is equal to the average for females. To direct the XL Data Analyst to perform this analysis, use the Compare—2 Group Averages menu sequence that will open up the selection window, as shown in Figure 12.4. First we select the Grouping Variable of Gender and the two groups: Male and Female will be automatically highlighted. Then we add the preference variable into the Target Variable window. Note that you can select multiple target variables if you desire; however, grouping variables must be categorical, while target variables must be metric to use the Compare, Two Group Averages tool.

Figure 12.5 contains the results of the XL Data Analyst's Two-Group Averages analysis. In the table, you can see that the Male and Female averages (3.5 and 3.1, respectively) are reported along with the number of respondents comprising each subsample (505 and 495, respectively). The arithmetic difference of 0.4 is indicated, and the hypothesis test outcome is also indicated. In this case, the "No" signifies that the null hypothesis that there is no difference between the two averages is not supported. That is, there is a significant difference between the two averages, with males showing more interest in the fuel-efficient car options than females in the target population.

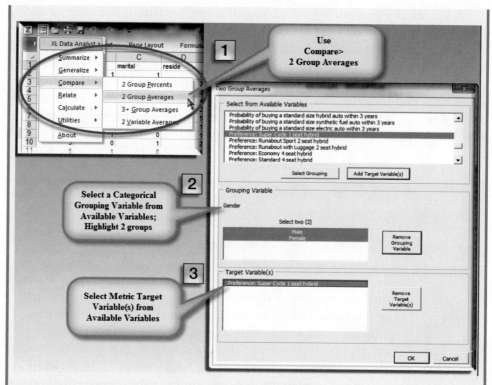

**Figure 12.4** Using the XL Data Analyst to Set Up a Two-Group Averages Analysis

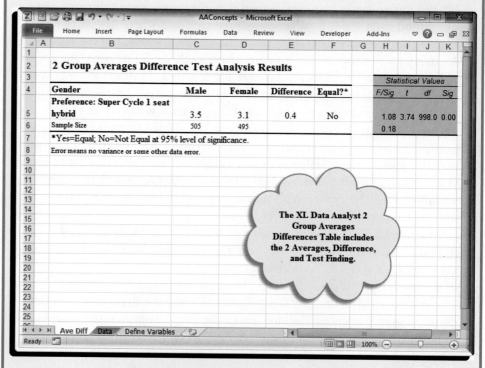

**Figure 12.5** XL Data Analyst Two-Group Averages Differences Analysis Output

# The Six-Step Process for Analyzing Differences between Two Groups

Thus far, how to perform analysis of differences between two groups in a sample—males versus females, 4th-year students versus 1st-year students, buyers versus nonbuyers, or any other two mutually exclusive groups that can be identfied in a survey—has been described. The type of analysis depends on the scaling assumptions of the test variable. If the test variable is categorical, the percentages are compared. When the test variable is metric, the averages are compared.

Table 12.3 details the six-step analytical process for differences analysis when two groups in the sample are being compared. Note that the scaling assumptions of

**Table 12.3** The Six-Step Approach to Data Analysis for Differences between Two Groups

| Step | Explanation | Example (A is a categorical test variable; B is a metric test variable) |
|---|---|---|
| **1. What is the research objective?** | Determine that you are dealing with a Two-Group Differences objective. | **A.** We want to determine whether students who use coupons are different from students who do not use coupons with respect to intended non–fast-food restaurant patronage in the coming weeks.<br><br>**B.** We want to determine if the average expected dollar internet purchases in the next two months differ for high-speed cable modem users versus DSL users. |
| **2. What questionnaire question(s) is/are involved?** | Identify the question(s), and for each one specify whether it is categorical or metric. | **A.** Use/nonuse (yes versus no) of coupons is *categorical*, and intend/do not intend (yes versus no) to purchase a non–fast-food meal is *categorical*.<br><br>**B.** High-speed modem versus DSL are *categorical* groups, while expected dollars spent on the internet is a *metric* measure. |
| **3. What is the appropriate analysis?** | To compare the percentages or averages of two groups, use two-group comparisons analysis. | We must use differences analysis because we have to take into account variability and sample error. |
| **4. How do you run it?** | Use XL Data Analyst™ analysis: Select "Compare—2 Group Percents" (categorical) or "Compare—2 Group Averages" (metric). | |

**Table 12.3** (*Continued*)

| Step | Explanation | Example (A is a categorical test variable; B is a metric test variable) |
|------|-------------|--------------------------------------------------------------------------|
| **5. How do you interpret the findings?** | The XL Data Analyst™ indicates that percentage differences are, indeed, true (supported), while the average dollar amounts are not significantly different. | (see below) |

**Two-Group Percents Differences Test Analysis Results**

| Do you typically use coupons . . . etc.? | Yes | No | Difference |
|------------------------------------------|-----|-----|-----------|
| Sample Size | 136 | 415 | |
| **Eat at a non–fast-food restaurant in the next week?** | | | |
| **Yes** | 70.6% | 32.3% | 38.3% |

Support for the hypothesis that the two percents are equal?

At 95% level of confidence, this hypothesis is **NOT SUPPORTED**.

**Two-Group Averages Difference Test Analysis Results**

| Variable Analyzed | High-Speed Cable | DSL | Difference | Equal?* |
|-------------------|------------------|-----|------------|---------|
| **Internet purchases in the next 2 months?** | $64.80 | $57.00 | $7.80 | Yes |
| Sample Size | 123 | 20 | | |

*Yes = Support; No = Not Supported at 95% level of significance

| Step | Explanation | Example |
|------|-------------|---------|
| **6. How do you write/ present these findings?** | When significant differences are found, present them with a graph or a table (see A). When differences are not significant, state this fact (see B). | (see below) |

A.

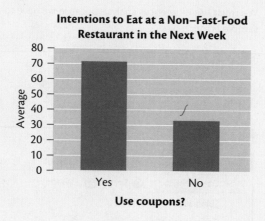

**Intentions to Eat at a Non–Fast-Food Restaurant in the Next Week**

B. No significant difference was found in the intended dollar amount of internet purchases over the next two months for high-speed modem users versus DSL users.

the target variable determine whether percentages are to be compared or whether averages are to be compared. A categorical target variable requires a percentages comparison, while a metric target variable requires a group averages difference analysis.

# Testing for Significant Differences between More Than Two Group Averages

When a researcher wants to compare the averages of several different groups, **analysis of variance**, sometimes called **ANOVA**, should be used. The use of the word "variance" is misleading—it is not an analysis of the standard deviations of the groups. To be sure, the standard deviations are taken into consideration, and so are the sample sizes, just as in all other statistical inference formulas. ANOVA is an investigation of the differences between the group averages to ascertain whether sampling errors or true population differences explain observed differences. That is, the word "variance" signifies differences between two or more groups' averages. Marketing Research in Action 12.1 illustrates how analysis among four cultural groups of students revealed differences in their ethical philosophies.

## MARKETING RESEARCH IN ACTION 12.1
## Analysis Reveals Ethical Philosophy Differences by Region of the Globe

Almost every day, we read in the newspaper, see on television, or find on the internet that the citizens of a particular country are angered by the policies or actions of other countries—sometimes to the point of committing violent acts. On a more subtle level, global business partnerships often encounter opposing beliefs as to what business practices or customs are acceptable. For instance, American businesspersons are sometimes frustrated by the deliberate nature of negotiations with prospective Asian or Arab buyers, and Latin American sellers are sometimes surprised by the quick, almost impulsive, decisions of American buyers.

In an attempt to understand the underpinnings of cultural differences such as these, researchers sought to measure and compare the basic ethical orientations of university students who represented four different global regions: Anglo-American, Latin American, Far Eastern, and Arab. They administered an instrument that categorized the ethical orientation of these students, and then

they compared the four groups. All four groups were found to have distinct and statistically significant differences. The ethical orientations they found are presented in the table on the next page.

These differences reveal that American businesspersons are basically pragmatic, and they attempt to grasp the opportunity of the moment, so to speak. At the other extreme, Arab businesspersons value consistency, tradition, and formality. Asian businessmen may appear to be confused or uncertain, but it is actually ethical orientation that fosters this appearance, for they neither value the opportunity nor adhere to precedents; hence, they ponder business decisions for a considerable time. Finally, Latin American businesspersons may be opportunistic, depending on the nature of the decision at hand. Obviously, Anglo-American and Arab businesspersons have the greatest ethical orientation distance between them, so one would predict more difficulties in the business relations between companies that reside in these two global regions.

| Global Region | Ethical Orientation | Description |
|---|---|---|
| Anglo-American | Flaming utilitarian | Considers every ethical decision to be unique, so past precedents and consistency are unimportant. |
| Latin American | Moderate utilitarian | Considers some ethical decisions to be unique, so past precedents may or may not be used. |
| Far Eastern | Independent neutral | Does not have a strong ethical orientation, so appears indecisive or a "fence sitter." |
| Arab | Moderate formalist | Considers past precedents to be important, so the uniqueness of each ethical decision is typically not considered. |

## Why Analysis of Variance Is Preferred over Multiple Two-Group Averages Analyses

When there are two group averages to compare, the average of one group is simply compared with the other's average. But when there are more than two groups, the comparisons are more involved. To illustrate, compare the averages of four different groups: A, B, C, and D. Six different comparisons are necessary: A:B, A:C, A:D, B:C, B:D, C:D. It would be tedious and difficult to keep track of all of these if the two-group averages differences test described above was used.

ANOVA is a very efficient, convenient analysis that does all of these tests simultaneously. Only one test is perfomed, and the results reveal where the significant differences are found. Researchers understand the basic purpose of ANOVA and can interpret ANOVA output. ANOVA's null hypothesis is that none of all of the possible group-to-group averages is significantly different: That is, there is not one single significant difference that exists between any possible pair of groups. The alternative hypothesis is that at least one pair is significantly different. When the null hypothesis is not supported in an ANOVA, follow-up analysis must be applied to identify where the significant differences are found.

Because multiple pairs of group averages are being tested, ANOVA uses the $F$ test statistic, and the significance value that appears on standard statistical output is the degree of support for the null hypothesis. The XL Data Analyst™ does the statistical interpretation of ANOVA. If it finds that the null hypothesis is not supported at the 95% level of confidence, it provides a table that shows you the various group averages plus identifies which ones are significantly different.

For example, a major department store conducts a survey, and one of the questions on the survey is, "At what department did you last make a purchase for over $250?" There are four departments where significant numbers of respondents made such purchases: (1) Electronics, (2) Home and Garden, (3) Sporting Goods, and (4) Automotive. Another question on the survey is, "How likely are you to purchase another item for over $250 from that department the next time?" The respondents

| Group Average** | Automotive | Electronics | Home and Garden | Sporting Goods |
|---|---|---|---|---|
| | 2.2 | 5.1 | 5.3 | 5.6 |
| **Automotive** | | Yes | Yes | Yes |
| **Electronics** | | | No | No |
| **Home and Garden** | | | | No |

Table 12.4 How Likely Are Customers to Return?*

*Significant differences are noted by "Yes."
**Based on a scale where 1 = very unlikely and 7 = very likely to purchase another item in this department.

indicate how likely they are to do this on a 7-point scale where 1 = very unlikely and 7 = very likely. To summarize the findings, the researcher calculates the average of how likely each group is to return to the department store and purchase another major item from that same department.

The researcher who is doing the analysis decides to compare these averages statistically with ANOVA. The findings are provided in Table 12.4. The Automotive Department is different from the other three departments in the store. Its average is only 2.2, while the other departments' averages range from 5.1 to 5.6. To indicate where significant differences are found, the researcher places a "Yes" notation in the cell where the group row and the group column intersect. A "No" is placed if no significant difference is found between the two group means. For instance, in Table 12.4, the "Yes" in the Automotive row reveals that the Automotive Department average of 2.2 is different from the Electronics Department average of 5.1. In fact, the "Yes" notations denote that the Automotive Department's average is significantly different from each of the three other departments' averages. The "No" entries denote that the averages for the other three departments are not significantly different from each other. In other words, there is a good indication that the patrons who bought an item for more than $250 from the department store's Automotive Department are not as likely to buy again as are patrons who bought from any of the three other departments.

Analysis of variance can be used to determine if shoppers have different experiences in different departments of the same store.

Again Figure 12.1's notions are relevant here, except that now there are four sampling distribution curves—one for each department. The Electronics, Home and Garden, and Sporting Goods sampling distribution curves would overlap a great deal, while the Automotive department curve would stand separately on the lower end of the scale. Because ANOVA takes on all groups simultaneously, Figure 12.1 would be modified by adding a separate standard error of the difference curve for each of the six possible group-to-group comparisons. The computed $z$ value was large for every comparison of the Automotive department average with each of the other three departments' averages.

The search for differences among more than two groups translates into partitioning a large market into a number of market segments. Marketing Research in Action 12.2 provides an example of how the province of Alberta's designated travel promotion agency came to identify five visitor market segments and to ascertain meaningful differences of various types among these groups.

## MARKETING RESEARCH IN ACTION 12.2
## Differences Analysis Reveals Five Market Segments for Alberta

Alberta is the fourth-largest Canadian province, and it is blessed with a huge variety of beautiful natural areas, including the Canadian Rockies, Banff National Park (and four other national parks), Dinosaur Valley, and hundreds of lakes and streams; an abundance of wildlife, including bighorn sheep, bison, and bears; and the attractive cities of Jasper, Edmonton, and Calgary. Alberta is an ecological wonderland in all four seasons. However, Travel Alberta, the agency charged with marketing Alberta to potential tourists, knew very little about the consumer behaviour of its visitors, so it commissioned a marketing research study to better understand its market.

The survey garnered a sample size of over 3000 respondents, and the analysts administered a number of statistical techniques. Ultimately, differences analysis revealed five separate travel-to-Alberta market segments that differed with respect to demographic factors and considerations that greatly influenced whether or not they visited Alberta. These factors also provided insight into the primary benefits each segment was seeking in its visit to Alberta. The segments and their unique profiles are summarized in the table below.

As happens with differences analyses, some differences were found, as can be seen in the demographic profiles and the key decision factors; however, no significant or meaningful differences were found in the core activities desired by the segments (experiencing Alberta's pristine mountains, forests, and many parks as well as venturing off and exploring these areas on their own). Nor were differences found for how the various segments learned about Alberta's many venues: word of mouth, meaning that they listened to friends, neighbours, co-workers, and relatives about Alberta, and they had also seen newspaper stories and advertisements about Alberta.

Using its knowledge of the five market segments in its market, Travel Alberta formulated and launched its "Alberta, Made to Order" campaign, which assured prospective visitors that in addition to delivering the core benefits of natural beauty and places to explore, their Alberta vacation could be customized to their particular desires and needs. The result of this campaign was that Alberta increased by 20% as a "top of the mind" travel destination over the year-long duration of the "Alberta, Made to Order" campaign.

| | The Young Urban Outdoor Market | The Indoor Leisure Traveller Market | The Children-First Market | The Fair-Weather-Friends Market | The Older Cost-Conscious Traveller Market |
|---|---|---|---|---|---|
| **Demographics** | • Youngest segment: mid-20s | • Early 40s | • Early 40s | • Mid-40s | • Oldest segment: mid-40s |
| | • 2/3 married, but 1/4 single | • 70% married | • 2/3 married | • 2/3 married, but 1/5 single | • > 60% married |
| | • > 50% with children | • > 60% with children | • 2/3 with children | • 1/3 with children | • Fewest with children |
| **Key travel decision factors** | • School holidays | • Safety and security | • Children's sports and competitions | • Visit family and friends | • Safety and security |
| | • Cost | • Cost | • Safety and security | • Weather conditions | • Cost |
| **Activities they desire** | | All segments | | • Mountains, forests, and parks | |
| | | | | • Want to explore and do new things | |
| **Information sources about vacation areas** | | All segments | | • Word of mouth | |
| | | | | • Newspaper | |

## Using the XL Data Analyst™ to Determine the Significance of the Difference among More Than Two Group Averages

Previously, we illustrated the use of a two-group averages differences analysis by comparing preferences of males versus females for the super cycle one-seat hybrid vehicle under consideration. There are five age categories—18–24, 35–34, 35–49, 50–64, and 65 and older—and all five classes are represented in a random sample of households. This is an instance where ANOVA applies. Figure 12.6 shows the menu commands and variable selection windows you use with the XL Data Analyst to set up three-plus–group averages analysis. Note that the menu sequence is "Compare—3+ Group Averages," and the grouping variable is "Age category," while the target variable is, "Preference: Super Cycle 1 seat hybrid." Also, remember that grouping variables must be categorical, while target variables must be metric for correct results from the Compare 3+ Group Averages tool.

Figure 12.7 reveals the XL Data Analyst ANOVA output. The ANOVA output table is arranged in ascending order based on the group averages. "Equal" or "Not equal" is placed in the intersection cell for each possible pair of averages. An "Equal" notation means that there is support for the

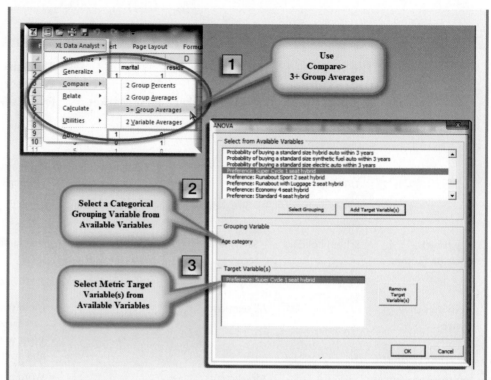

**Figure 12.6** Using the XL Data Analyst to Set Up a Three-Plus–Group Averages Differences Analysis

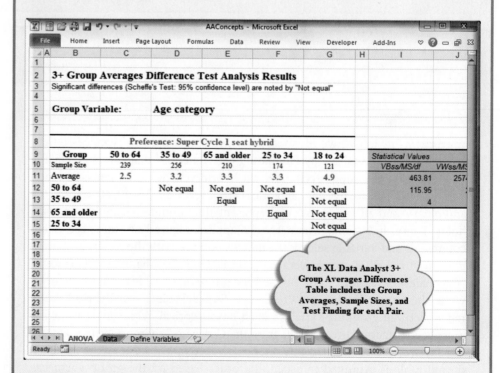

**Figure 12.7** XL Data Analyst Three-Plus–Group Averages Differences Analysis Output

null hypothesis that the two group averages are equal, while an "Not equal" designation indicates that there is no support for the null hypothesis that the two group averages are equal.

Examine the ANOVA table output in Figure 12.7. It is apparent that those in the 18–24 group have the highest preference for the super cycle one-seat hybrid, and their average (4.9) is significantly different from all other groups. Those in the 50–64 group, in turn, have an average (2.5) that is significantly different from that of all other age categories. Finally, the averages of 35–49 (3.2), 65 and older (3.3), and 25–34 (3.3) are not significantly different. As with other XL Data Analyst results, the relevant statistical values are included for users with expertise and interest in examining them.

## The Six-Step Process for Analyzing Differences among Three or More Groups

As indicated early in this chapter, differences analyses are important first steps in the investigation of possible market segments. Potential market segmentation variables are any factors that uniquely identify groups in the total market and that are related to some relevant consumer behaviour construct such as attitudes, perceptions, intentions, satisfaction, and so forth. With regard to the Student Life E-Zine, an internet connection with a high bandwidth is required so that graphics, pop-up ads, and other features can be experienced without lengthy loading times. Possible market segmentation variable of the type of internet connections currently used by City University students was used to compare the group averages as to how likely they are to subscribe to the Student Life E-Zine. Table 12.5 illustrates the application of the six-step analysis process to the investigation of market segmentation findings that can be relevant to the Student Life E-Zine entrepreneurs.

**Table 12.5** The Six-Step Approach to Data Analysis for Differences among Three or More Groups

| Step | Explanation | Example |
|---|---|---|
| **1. What is the research objective?** | Determine that you are dealing with a 3+ Group Differences objective. | We want to determine if there is a difference in the average likelihood of subscribing to the Student Life E-Zine among different types of internet access. |
| **2. What questionnaire question(s) is/are involved?** | Identify the question(s), and for each one specify whether it is categorical or metric. | The type of internet access (high-speed cable, dial-up, or DSL) is *categorical,* meaning that three separate groups are identified, and the intention to subscribe is on a 1 to 5 metric scale. |
| **3. What is the appropriate analysis?** | To compare the averages of three or more groups, use three-plus–group comparisons analysis. | We use ANOVA because it is much more efficient than a series of two-group averages comparisons. |

**Table 12.5** (*Continued*)

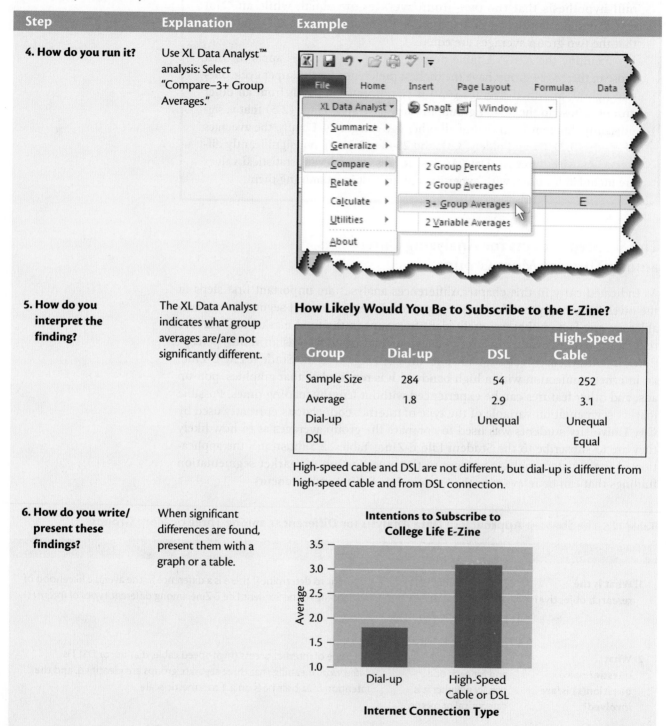

| Step | Explanation | Example |
|---|---|---|
| **4. How do you run it?** | Use XL Data Analyst™ analysis: Select "Compare–3+ Group Averages." | |
| **5. How do you interpret the finding?** | The XL Data Analyst indicates what group averages are/are not significantly different. | |
| **6. How do you write/ present these findings?** | When significant differences are found, present them with a graph or a table. | |

**How Likely Would You Be to Subscribe to the E-Zine?**

| Group | Dial-up | DSL | High-Speed Cable |
|---|---|---|---|
| Sample Size | 284 | 54 | 252 |
| Average | 1.8 | 2.9 | 3.1 |
| Dial-up | | Unequal | Unequal |
| DSL | | | Equal |

High-speed cable and DSL are not different, but dial-up is different from high-speed cable and from DSL connection.

**Intentions to Subscribe to College Life E-Zine**

*Note:* Because high-speed cable and DSL are not significantly different, a weighted average of these two group means was computed to determine the combined groups' mean of 3.1.

# Testing for Significant Differences between the Averages of Two Variables within One Group

The last differences analysis we will describe does not involve groups. Instead, it concerns comparing the average of one variable (question on the survey) to the average of another variable.[6] For this analysis, the entire sample is used, but two different variables are compared. For example, if a pharmaceuticals company wanted to improve its cold remedy medication, a survey could be used to answer the question: "How important is it that your cold remedy relieves your _____?" using a scale of 1 = not important and 10 = very important for each of several cold symptoms such as "congestion," "cough," or "runny nose." The question then becomes, "Are any two average importance levels significantly different?" Since the same respondents answer both questions, there are two independent questions within one group. When significant differences between the averages of two variables such as ratings of importance or performance are found, then levels of the ratings are truly different in the population that the sample represents. Of course, the variables should be measured on the same scale; otherwise, the comparison is invalid.

A graph of the test for the difference in the averages of two variables appears, as shown in Figure 12.1. Recall that the two bell-shaped curves are the sampling distributions of the two variables being compared, and the apex of each one is its average in the sample. When there is a small amount of overlap for the two curves, there is a true difference in the population averages. That is, if the survey were repeated many, many times, and the averages for all of these replications were graphed, they would appear similar to the bell-shaped curves in Figure 12.1, and the two averages would rarely, if ever, be equal (the null hypothesis). The formula for this statistical test is, in fact, similar to the one for the difference between two group averages. That is, the two averages are compared (take the difference), and this quantity is divided by the standard error of the difference to compute the $z$ value. Directional hypothesis tests are possible as well.

## Using the XL Data Analyst™ to Determine the Significance of the Differences between the Averages of Two Variables

As was indicated, the proper use of a differences test for two variables' averages requires that you select two metric variables that are measured with the same scale units. We might wonder if the overall preference of an economy hybrid vehicle differs from the preference for a standard model hybrid vehicle. Are these two averages significantly different, or is the arithmetic difference simply a reflection of sample size error and variability in the respondents'

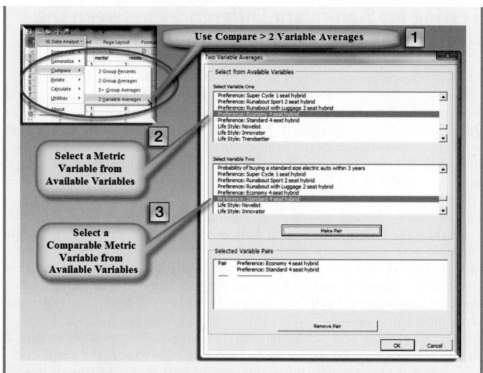

**Figure 12.8** Using the XL Data Analyst to Set Up a Two-Variable Averages Differences Analysis

answers? To answer this question, we can use the XL Data Analyst to perform a Two-Variables Averages comparison. The menu sequence is Compare—2 Variable Averages, which opens up the selection menu for this procedure. In Figure 12.8, you can see that two selection windows each list all of the available variables, so you must highlight a variable in the "Variable One" panel and another in the "Variable Two" panel to make a pair whose averages will be compared, and add this pair into the Selected Variables selection windowpane. You will see in Figure 12.8 that the "Preference: Economy 4 seat hybrid" and "Preference: Standard 4 seat hybrid" are selected, and they are identified as a "pair" in the selection windowpane. (Multiple pairs may be selected in a single analysis run, if desired.)

Figure 12.9 shows the resulting XL Data Analyst output for our Two-Variable Averages comparison analysis. A table that shows the averages of 3.5 and 5.0 for the two metric variables, and the arithmetic difference is provided. The XL Data Analyst has indicated in this table that the difference is a significant difference. In other words, the null hypothesis that there is no difference between these two averages is not supported. The standard size four-seat hybrid is preferred more by households than is the economy four-seat hybrid model.

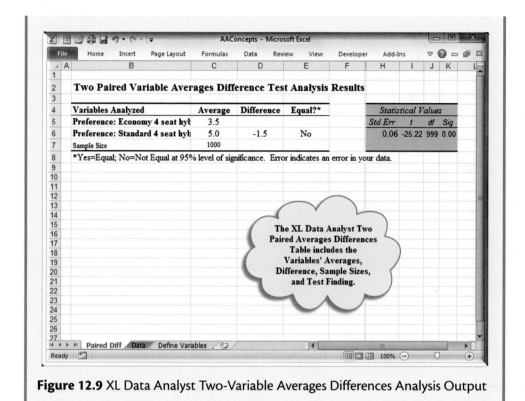

**Figure 12.9** XL Data Analyst Two-Variable Averages Differences Analysis Output

## The Six-Step Process for Analyzing Differences between Two Variables

When two variable averages are not significantly different, this means that the arithmetic difference between them is not a true one. If the survey were repeated many, many times, and these differences were tallied, the average of the differences would be 0. However, when the null hypothesis (of no difference between the two averages) is not supported, the researcher is assured that the relative sizes of the two averages exist in the population, and the researcher can confidently report this finding to the manager.

We have prepared Table 12.6 with explanations and an example of our six-step process for the assessment of the difference between the averages of two variables.

**Table 12.6** The Six-Step Approach to Data Analysis for Differences between Two Variables

| Step | Explanation | Example |
|------|-------------|---------|
| **1. What is the research objective?** | Determine that you are dealing with a Two-Variables Differences objective. | We want to determine if there is a difference in the estimated dollars out of every $100 in internet purchases for clothing purchases versus general merchandise purchases by City University students. |
| **2. What questionnaire question(s) is/are involved?** | Identify the question for each variable and verify that it is metric. | Respondents were requested to estimate the number of dollars out of every $100 of internet purchases that they typically spend on clothing and on general merchandise. This is a natural metric scale in dollars. |

**Table 12.6** (*Continued*)

| Step | Explanation | Example |
|------|-------------|---------|
| **3. What is the appropriate analysis?** | To compare the averages of the two variables, use two-variable averages analysis. | We use this procedure because the two variables are measured with the same scale, and we have one group (the entire sample) that answered both questions. |
| **4. How do you run it?** | Use XL Data Analyst™ analysis: Select "Compare—2 Variable Averages." | 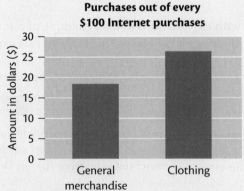 |

For step 4:

XL Data Analyst ▾   SnagIt   Window ▾

- Summarize ▸
- Generalize ▸
- Compare ▸ → 2 Group Percents
- Relate ▸      2 Group Averages
- Calculate ▸   3+ Group Averages
- Utilities ▸    2 Variable Averages
- About

| Step | Explanation | Example |
|------|-------------|---------|
| **5. How do you interpret the finding?** | The XL Data Analyst™ indicates the two variable averages and indicates whether or not they are equal. | **Two Paired Variable Averages Difference Test Analysis Results** |

| Variables Analyzed | Average | Difference | Equal? |
|--------------------|---------|------------|--------|
| **Internet purchases out of $100: Clothing** | $25.16 | | |
| **Internet purchases out of $100: General merchandise** | $18.13 | $7.03 | No |
| Sample Size | 143 | | |

Here, the clothing purchases average of $25.16 is different from the general merchandise average of $18.13. (The averages were reformatted in Excel to appear as currency with two decimal places in this table.)

| Step | Explanation | Example |
|------|-------------|---------|
| **6. How do you write/present these findings?** | When significant differences are found, you can report them with a graph or in the text of the report. | **Purchases out of every $100 Internet purchases** |

Bar chart: Amount in dollars ($), scale 0 to 30. General merchandise ≈ 18.5, Clothing ≈ 26.5.

City University students who make purchases over the internet typically spend about $25 out of every $100 on clothing, while they spend around $18 of every $100 on general merchandise.

Follow the instructions in Online Application 12.1 to see how Elections Canada uses testing of differences to explore many issues.

## ONLINE APPLICATION BOX 12.1
## See Testing of Differences by Elections Canada

Elections Canada examines many interesting issues. Go to **www.elections.ca**, and choose the language of your choice. In the search toolbar, type "40th general election"—the search results appear. Click #3. Here you will find many interesting surveys on this election. Download the report.

**Questions**
1. Identify the various groups that were analyzed.
2. What did the researchers do to analyze differences?
3. How were the results used by Elections Canada?

# Summary

**1.   Discuss differences analysis.**
Market segmentation is based on the notion that there are different types of consumers in a product market that have different needs. Such differences form the basis of marketing strategies. Such differences must be significant and meaningful to guide fruitful marketing activity. Data analysis is used to investigate for statistically significant differences. There are three types of differences analysis performed by marketing researchers: (1) comparing differences between one group and another group, such as men and women; (2) comparing three or more groups, such as people who are single, married people with children, and married people without children; (3) comparing the relative importance of one feature to another, such as taste compared to size in a soft drink.

**2.   Evaluate the significance of differences between two groups' percentages or averages.**
When a researcher compares two groups in a survey, it is as though a separate survey was conducted for each group. To test whether a real difference exists between two groups, the null hypothesis states that the difference in the population parameters is equal to zero. The alternative hypothesis is that there is a true difference between the two group parameters. To test the significance of differences, a difference test compares one group's percentage or average to the other group's by simple subtraction. Then this value is divided by the standard error of the difference. XL Data Analyst™ can perform the necessary difference tests to determine statistical significance of noted differences between two group averages or percentages.

**3.   Perform the analysis of variance (ANOVA).**
When a researcher has three or more groups and wishes to compare his or her various averages with the same variable, the analysis of variance, or ANOVA, is performed. ANOVA is a technique that tests all possible pairs of averages for all the groups involved and indicates which pairs are significantly different. For example, ANOVA can be used to determine if different coffee drinkers have different preferences in different locations of the same coffee retailer. ANOVA is also used to test the difference between the

averages of two variables within one group. For example, the significance of differences in importance of price compared to importance of performance in a sample of car buyers can be tested with ANOVA. XL Data Analyst™ is used to perform ANOVA.

## Key Terms

Alternative hypothesis    (p. 393)
Analysis of variance (ANOVA)
    (p. 405)
Grouping variable    (p. 399)
Market segmentation    (p. 391)

Standard error of the difference between
    two averages    (p. 397)
Standard error of the difference between
    two percentages    (p. 394)
Target variable    (p. 399)

## Review Questions

1.1 What are the three ways a researcher can investigate for differences?

1.2 How does the type of measurement scale (categorical or metric) affect a differences test?

1.3 Are the following two sample results significantly different? Draw the sampling distributions of each case—a, b, and c—in the format presented in Figure 12.1 on page 395.

|  | Sample 1 | Sample 2 | Confidence Level | Your Finding? |
|---|---|---|---|---|
| a. | Mean: 10.6<br>Std. dev: 1.5<br>$n = 150$ | Mean: 11.7<br>Std. dev: 2.5<br>$n = 300$ | 95% |  |
| b. | Percent: 45%<br>$n = 350$ | Percent: 54%<br>$n = 250$ | 99% |  |
| c. | Mean: 1500<br>Std. dev: 550<br>$n = 1200$ | Mean: 1250<br>Std. dev: 500<br>$n = 500$ | 95% |  |

2.1 When the percentages or the averages of two groups are compared, what is the nature of the comparison operation?

2.2 When a standard error of a difference between percentages or averages is computed, what two factors are taken into account, and how does each affect the size of the standard error?

2.3 A researcher is investigating different types of customers for a sporting goods store. In a survey, respondents have indicated how much they exercise in approximate minutes per week. These respondents have also rated the performance of the sporting goods store across 12 difference characteristics such as good value for the price, convenience of location, helpfulness of the sales clerks, and so on. The researcher used a 1 to 7 rating scale for these 12 characteristics, where 1 = poor performance and 7 = excellent performance. How can the researcher investigate differences in the ratings based on the amount of exercise reported by the respondents?

**3.1** How is a test of the difference between the averages of two variables different from a test of the difference between the averages of two groups with the same variable? How is it similar?

**3.2** A marketing manager of a web-based catalogue sales company uses a segmentation scheme based on the incomes of target customers. The segmentation system has four segments: (1) low income, (2) moderate income, (3) high income, and (4) wealthy. The company database holds information on every customer's purchases over the past several years, and the total dollars spent is one of the prominent variables. The marketing manager finds that the average total dollar purchases for the four groups are as follows:

| Market Segment | Average Total Dollar Purchases |
| --- | --- |
| Low income | $101 |
| Moderate income | $120 |
| High income | $231 |
| Wealthy | $595 |

Construct a table that is based on how the XL Data Analyst™ presents its findings for ANOVA that illustrates that the low- and moderate-income groups are not different from each other, but the other groups are significantly different from one another.

# Case 12.1

# The *Daily Advocate* Lost Subscribers Survey

(The following case is fictitious.)

The *Daily Advocate* is a newspaper serving the Capital City area, which accounts for about 350 000 households. The *Daily Advocate* has been the dominant daily newspaper in the area for the past 50 years. At one time, it was estimated that 9 out of 10 Capital City–area households subscribed or otherwise bought the *Daily Advocate*. In the past decade, Capital City has undergone a growth spurt due primarily to the development of three high-technology industrial "parks" where a great many internet, computer equipment, and biotechnology companies have located. However, the circulation of the *Daily Advocate* did not experience a corresponding spurt; in fact, the circulation peaked in 1998, and it has been slowly declining ever since. It is now estimated that only 7 out of 10 Capital City–area households subscribe to the *Daily Advocate*.

The circulation manager of the *Daily Advocate* commissions a market research study to determine what factors underlie the circulation attrition. Specifically, the survey is designed to compare current subscribers with those who have dropped their subscriptions in the past year. A telephone survey is conducted with both sets of individuals. Following is a summary of the key findings—using a 95% level of confidence—from the study.

*(Continued)*

| Variable Analyzed | Current Subscribers | Lost Subscribers | Difference | Equal? |
|---|---|---|---|---|
| Length of residence in the city | 20.1 years | 5.4 years | 14.7 years | No |
| Length of time as a subscriber | 27.2 years | 1.3 years | 25.9 years | No |
| Watch local TV news program(s) | 87% | 85% | 2.0% | Yes |
| Watch national TV news program(s) | 72% | 79% | −7.0% | Yes |
| Obtain news from the internet | 13% | 23% | −10.0% | No |
| Satisfaction* with . . . | | | | |
| Delivery of newspaper | 5.5 | 4.9 | 0.6 | Yes |
| Coverage of local news | 6.1 | 5.8 | 0.3 | Yes |
| Coverage of national news | 5.5 | 2.3 | 3.2 | No |
| Coverage of local sports | 6.3 | 5.9 | 0.4 | Yes |
| Coverage of national sports | 5.7 | 3.2 | 2.5 | No |
| Coverage of local social news | 5.8 | 5.2 | 0.6 | Yes |
| Editorial stance of the newspaper | 6.1 | 4.0 | 2.1 | No |
| Value for subscription price | 5.2 | 4.8 | 0.4 | Yes |

*Average, based on a 7-point scale where 1 = very dissatisfied and 7 = very satisfied

## Question

1. Why has the *Daily Advocate*'s circulation fallen in the face of a population boom in Capital City?

# Case 12.2 YOUR INTEGRATED CASE

# The Student Life E-Zine Survey
## Market Segmentation Analysis

Another week has passed, and Sarah, Anna, Wesley, and Don are again treated to a PowerPoint presentation by Lori Baker, marketing intern at ORS Marketing Research. Their excitement rises to a fever pitch with the good news that even when using the lower boundary of the 95% confidence interval for the percentage of students who are "very likely" to subscribe to the Student Life E-Zine at $15 per month, the expected number of City University students exceeds the required break-even point of 6000 subscriptions. In fact, the most likely estimate is about 7800, well above the 6000 critical value.

"I knew you would be very happy to hear Lori's generalization findings," said Bob Watts, "and I was very happy for you when Lori disclosed them to me a few days ago, for it means we are 'go' with the Student Life E-Zine. Plus, you've been studying the descriptive analyses that Lori presented to you last week, and I'm sure that you have come up with the basic features that all City U prospects for the e-zine want to see, and you no doubt have some preliminary targets for the e-zine's advertising affiliates, both national and local."

Wesley replied, "Yes, we certainly do, but I want to make it so that once we have a profile of each subscriber via his or her registration, we can custom-tailor the pop-up ads and other dynamic features of our Student Life E-Zine so they have the optimal effect."

"Ah," said Lori, "you must be talking about market segmentation. I recall Dr. Bush, who taught my marketing research course at City U, saying how useful various types of data analysis are in revealing meaningful market segment differences. I know the Student Life E-Zine data set very well from my work sessions with it, and I can refer to my class notes or even give Dr. Bush a call if I need help. I'd like to give it a try. Of course, Bob will be overseeing my work as well. Bob, if it's okay with you, I can get right on this and have it ready for a week from today."

Bob winked at the four e-zine entrepreneurs and said, "Are you sure you're up to it, Lori?"

Lori replied, "Absolutely!"

The very next day, Lori began her work at ORS by outlining the differences she intended to investigate.

Using Lori's questions, perform the proper data analysis on the Student Life E-Zine data set using the XL Data Analyst™. When you find differences, interpret them in the context of Wesley's vision for how the Student Life E-Zine can be optimally effective.

Lori's questions follow:

## Questions

1. Do male City U students differ from female ones with respect to expecting to make an internet purchase in the next two months?

2. Do on-campus City U students differ from off-campus ones with respect to expecting to make an internet purchase in the next two months?

3. Do working City U students differ from non-working ones with respect to expecting to make an internet purchase in the next two months?

4. Are there differences among the various City U classes with respect to:
   a.  Total internet purchases?
   b.  Internet purchases out of $100 (books, gifts, music, etc.)?
   c.  Preference for various possible e-zine features (Campus Calendar, Course/Instructor Evaluator, etc.)?

5. Are there differences among the various City U students by college with respect to:
   a.  Total internet purchases?
   b.  Internet purchases out of $100 (books, gifts, music, etc.)?
   c.  Preference for various possible e-zine features (Campus Calendar, Course/Instructor Evaluator, etc.)?

# Relationships between Variables

By permission, Maritz.

## Which Measure of Customer Loyalty Is Most Associated with Repeat Buying?

At the beginning of Chapter 7, three different ways of measuring customer loyalty were presented. One of these methods uses three questions: (1) overall satisfaction, (2) willingness to recommend, and (3) likelihood to return or buy again. The three questions are averaged to form an index of customer loyalty. We will call this the "Three-Question" method. A second method, developed by Reichheld, asks a single question about the likelihood that a respondent would recommend Company X to a friend or a colleague. We will call this the "Single-Question" method. Finally, Maritz Research's "Probability Allocation" measure asks, "Of the next 10 times you make a purchase of <insert product class here>, how many times will you buy <insert client's brand name here>?"

Which of these measurement methods results in a measure that is most highly associated with customer loyalty? A "high" score should be associated with a greater number of repeat purchases, and a "low" score should be associated with fewer repeat purchases. If one measure has a greater association with actual customer loyalty, then we should have greater confidence in using the measure as an indicator of actual customer loyalty.

One method of measuring the association between two variables is called correlation. The correlation coefficient is an index number ranging from +1.00 to −1.00. A positive association means that as one variable goes up (i.e., our measure of customer loyalty score) the other variable (actual repeat purchases) goes up as well. A negative association occurs when, as one variable goes up, the other goes down. A correlation of 1.00 is perfect association. We never expect to see perfect association, but the higher the correlation coefficient, the stronger is the association.

Researchers at Maritz Research wanted to determine which of the three measures was most highly associated with a measure of post-survey purchasing by conducting two separate studies. The first study tested nine different product and service categories with approximately 1000 respondents. The correlation coefficients for each method of measuring customer loyalty were:

Three-Question Method = 0.35

Single-Question Method = 0.26

Probability Allocation Method = 0.51

In a second study, conducted on mass merchandisers using a sample of approximately 600 respondents, Maritz Research found the following correlation coefficients for each method of measuring customer loyalty:

Three-Question Method = 0.47

Single-Question Method = 0.36

Probability Allocation Method = 0.71

The good news is that all three methods are associated with the construct they purport to measure: customer loyalty. However, the strongest measure in both studies is the probability allocation method. In this chapter, you will learn about correlation and the correlation coefficient.[1]

---

This chapter illustrates the usefulness of statistical analyses beyond generalization and differences tests. Often, marketers are interested in relationships among variables. For example, Frito-Lay wants to know what kinds of people, under what circumstances, choose to buy Doritos, Fritos, and any of the other items in the Frito-Lay line. A newspaper wants to understand the lifestyle characteristics of its prospective readers so that it is able to modify or change sections in the newspaper to better suit its audience. There are statistical procedures available, termed *relationship analyses*, that determine whether stable patterns exist between two (or more) variables.

The chapter begins by describing what a relationship is and why relationships are useful concepts. Then, Boolean relationships that can exist between two categorical variables are described, and the process of using cross-tabulation to determine whether or not a statistically significant relationship exists between the two variables is outlined. Next, a general discussion of correlation coefficients, a statistic that measures relationships involving metric variables, is presented. The remainder of the chapter is devoted to the subject of regression analysis, which is a powerful predictive technique. As in the previous analysis chapters, the processes of using the XL Data Analyst™ to perform these analyses and interpreting the resulting output are demonstrated throughout the chapter.

**Where We Are**

1. Establish the need for marketing research
2. Define the problem
3. Establish research objectives
4. Determine research design
5. Identify information types and sources
6. Determine methods of accessing data
7. Design data collection forms
8. Determine sample plan and size
9. Collect data
10. Analyze data
11. Prepare and present the final research report

# What Is a Relationship between Two Variables?

Every scale has unique descriptors, sometimes called levels, that identify the different labels of that scale. The term *levels* implies that the scale is metric, whereas the term *labels* implies that the scale is categorical. A simple categorical label is a "yes" or "no"—for instance, if a respondent is a buyer (yes) or nonbuyer (no) of a particular product or service. If the researcher measured how many times a respondent bought a product, the level would be the number of times, and the scale would be metric.

A **relationship** is a consistent and systematic linkage between the levels or labels for two variables. Relationships are invaluable tools for the marketing researcher because a relationship can be used for prediction and understanding of the phenomena under study. For example, if Canon finds that there is a relationship between its video camera buyers and children, it can predict that those families with children who are thinking about purchasing a video camera will be good prospects for its video camera models. Furthermore, it seems logical that parents are taking videos of their children, so Canon can use the promotional theme of "making memories" or "capturing special moments" because it understands that this is the primary purchasing motivation.

# Boolean Relationships and Cross-Tabulation Analysis

## Boolean Relationships

A **Boolean relationship** is one in which the presence of one variable's label is systematically related to the presence of another variable's label. Boolean operators are used with search engines. For instance, searching for "dog AND food" with Google will find all of the websites where the pet label "dog" and the product label "food" are both present. Note that labels are used—that is, specified categories, not numbers.

For a Boolean relationship, think about a Google search using "AND."

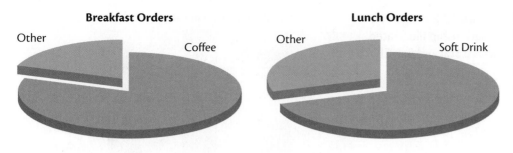

**Figure 13.1** Example of a Boolean Relationship for the Type of Drink Ordered for Breakfast and for Lunch at McDonald's

With a Boolean relationship present, the researcher often resorts to graphical or other presentation formats to "see" the relationship.

For example, McDonald's knows from experience that breakfast customers typically purchase coffee, whereas lunch customers typically purchase soft drinks. Here, we are using the meal variable and relating it to the choice-of-drink variable. Our labels are "morning" and "afternoon" to specify meal, and "coffee" and "soft drink" to specify drink. The relationship is in no way exclusive—there is no guarantee that a breakfast customer will always order coffee (breakfast AND coffee) or that a lunch customer will always order a soft drink (lunch AND soft drink). Figure 13.1 presents the Boolean relationship graphically. These Boolean relationship pairings are not 100% certainties, but 80% of breakfast buyers order coffee, and 90% of lunch buyers order a soft drink. Predictions of what type of drink would be ordered by the next McDonald's breakfast or lunch customer can therefore be made with some degree of confidence.

## Characterizing a Boolean Relationship with a Graph

Two pie charts are used in Figure 13.1 to depict the Boolean relationships in the McDonald's example. Pie charts are appropriate for categorical variables. However, it is cumbersome to create multiple pie charts in Excel and to present them as we have in Figure 13.1. An equally acceptable and more convenient graph is a stacked bar chart. With a **stacked bar chart**, two variables are shown simultaneously in the same bar graph. Each bar in the stacked bar chart stands for 100%, and it is divided proportionately by the amount of relationship that one variable shares with the other variable. In Figure 13.2 on the next page, there are three types (labels) of students: underclass, upperclass, and graduate. Underclass students are those in first and second year; upperclass students are those in third and fourth year; and graduate students are those who have finished their bachelor's degree and are working on a graduate degree. The figure also shows movie attendance for the three groups over the past month. As illustrated, 70% of the underclass students have attended a movie, while 50% of the upperclass students have done so, and only 10% of the graduate students have done so. In other words, one of the variables is student classification, with labels of "underclass student," "upperclass student," and "graduate student," and the other variable is attendance of a movie, with the labels of "yes" and "no." From the Boolean relationships depicted in Figure 13.2, one can predict that a first- or second-year student probably did attend a movie; a third- or fourth-year student may or may not have; and a graduate student very probably did not.

**Figure 13.2** A Boolean Relationship Illustrated with a Stacked Bar Chart

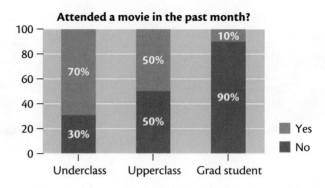

How do these relationships lead to understanding? Perhaps underclass students are not knuckling down on their studies, so they have more leisure time. Upperclass students are more likely getting serious about studying as they are deep into their major courses and they are trying to increase their grade point averages to be competitive in the job market or to be accepted into graduate school. Graduate students may not have leisure time because they are taking difficult graduate-level courses, so they rarely go to movies.

## Cross-Tabulation Analysis

A stacked bar chart provides a way of visualizing Boolean relationships and should be used only if the relationship is statistically significant. The analytical technique that assesses the statistical significance of Boolean or categorical variable relationships is **cross-tabulation analysis**. With cross-tabulation, the two variables are arranged in a **cross-tabulation table**, defined as a table in which data are compared using a row-and-column format. The intersection of a row and a column is called a **cross-tabulation cell**. A cross-tabulation analysis accounts for all of the relevant Boolean relationships and it is the basis for measuring the statistical significance of the relationships.

A cross-tabulation table for the stacked bar chart is presented in Table 13.1. Note that the various Boolean relationships within cross-tabulation cells are identified with rows and columns. The columns are in vertical alignment and are indicated in this table as "Underclass Student" or "Upperclass Student" or "Graduate Student," whereas the rows are indicated as "Yes" or "No" for movie attendance in the past month. In addition, there is a column for the Row Totals, and a row for the Column Totals. The intersection cell for the Row Totals column and the Column Totals row is called the Grand Total.

### Types of Frequencies and Percentages in a Cross-Tabulation Table

Table 13.1 is also a **frequencies table** because it contains the raw counts of the various Boolean relationships found in the complete data set. From the grand total, it can be seen that there are 370 students in the sample. From the row and column total cells, the number within each category of student classification (150, 170, and 50) and the number of "Yes" versus "No" movie attendees (195 and 175) in the sample can be seen. The intersection cell for "Underclass Student" and "Yes" movie attendance reveals that there are 105 underclass students who said "yes" to moviegoing. A cross-tabulation table contains the raw counts and totals pertaining to all of the relevant Boolean relationships for the two categorical variables being analyzed.

| | | Student Classification | | | |
|---|---|---|---|---|---|
| | | Underclass Student | Upperclass Student | Graduate Student | Row Totals |
| **Attended a Movie in the Past Month?** | Yes 105 | Underclass AND Yes | 85 Upperclass AND Yes | 5 Graduate AND Yes | 195 Underclass OR Upperclass OR Graduate AND Yes |
| | No | 45 Underclass AND No | 85 Upperclass AND No | 45 Graduate AND No | 175 Underclass OR Upperclass OR Graduate AND No |
| **Column Totals** | | 150 Underclass AND Yes OR No | 170 Upperclass AND Yes OR No | 50 Graduate AND Yes OR No | 370 Grand Total: Underclass OR Upperclass OR Graduate AND Yes OR No |

**Table 13.1** Cross-Tabulation Table with Boolean Relationships Identified

## Chi-Square Analysis of a Cross-Tabulation Table

**Chi-square ($\chi^2$) analysis** is the examination of frequencies for two categorical variables in a cross-tabulation table to determine whether the variables have a significant relationship.[2] The chi-square analysis begins when the researcher formulates a statistical null hypothesis that the two variables under investigation are *not* related—that is, there is no difference in response to moviegoing among the student groups. Actually, it is not necessary for the researcher to state this hypothesis in a formal sense, for chi-square analysis always explicitly takes this null hypothesis into account. Stated somewhat differently, chi-square analysis always begins with the assumption that no relationship exists between the two categorical variables under analysis.

**Observed and Expected Frequencies**   The raw counts in Table 13.1 are referred to as "**observed frequencies**," as they are the counts observed by applying the Boolean operators to the data set. Long ago, someone working with cross-tabulations discovered that if the row total is multiplied by the column total, and the product divided by the grand total for every cross-tabulation cell, the resulting "**expected frequencies**" would perfectly embody these cell frequencies if there was no significant relationship present. Here is the formula for the expected cell frequencies:

$$\text{Expected cell frequency} = \frac{\text{Cell column total} \times \text{Cell row total}}{\text{Grand total}}$$

◀ **Formula for an expected cell frequency.**

In other words, if the above formula was used to compute expected frequencies, and these were used to create stacked bar graphs, the percents of "Yes" and

"No" respondents would be identical for all three student classification types: There would be no relationship to see in the graphs. The expected frequencies are a baseline, and if the observed frequencies are very different from the expected frequencies, there is reason to believe that a relationship does exist.

**Computed Chi-Square Value**    The observed and expected cross-tabulation frequencies are compared, and the support or nonsupport of the null hypothesis is determined with the use of what is called the chi-square formula.

**Chi-square formula** ▷

$$\chi^2 = \sum_{i-1}^{n} \frac{(\text{Observed}_i - \text{Expected}_i)^2}{\text{Expected}_i}$$

where

$\text{Observed}_i$ = observed frequency in cell $i$
$\text{Expected}_i$ = expected frequency in cell $i$
$n$ = number of cells

The formula holds that each cross-tabulation cell expected frequency be subtracted from its associated observed frequency, and then that difference be squared to avoid a cancellation effect of minus and plus differences. Then the squared difference is divided by the expected frequency to adjust for differences in expected cell sizes. All of these are then summed to arrive at the computed chi-square value. A step-by-step description of this analysis is provided in Table 13.2.[3]

Whenever a statistician arrives at a computed value, it will be compared with a table value to assess its statistical significance. In Table 13.2, there is a computed chi-square value of 55.1. A chi-square value table is consulted to see if the computed chi-square value is greater than the critical table value. The chi-square distribution is not normal, so calculations of the *degrees of freedom* with the formula in Table 13.2 need to be done in order to know where to look in the chi-square table for the critical value. With higher degrees of freedom, the table chi-square value is larger, but there is no single value that can be memorized as in our 1.96 number for a normal distribution. A cross-tabulation can have any number of rows and columns. Since the degrees of freedom are based on the number of rows and columns, there is no single critical chi-square value that can be identified for all cases.

Table 13.2 indicates that the computed value of 55.1 is, indeed, greater than the table value of 5.99, meaning that there is no support for our null hypothesis of no relationship. In other words, when the calculated chi-square value exceeds the critical chi-square table value, there is a significant relationship between the two variables under analysis.

### How to Interpret a Significant Cross-Tabulation Finding
The best communication vehicle in this case is a graph. Pie charts or stacked bar graphs are recommended. Furthermore, raw counts (observed frequencies) should be converted to percentages for optimal communication.

When a significant relationship does exist (that is, there is no support for the null hypothesis of no relationship), two additional cross-tabulation tables can be

**Table 13.2** How to Determine If You Have a Significant Boolean Relationship Using Chi-Square Analysis

| Step | Description | Students Attending Movies Example ($n = 100$) |
|------|-------------|-----------------------------------------------|

**Step 1** — Set up the cross-tabulation table and determine the raw counts for the cell known as the *observed frequencies.*

**Student Classification**

| | | Underclass Student | Upperclass Student | Graduate Student | Row Totals |
|---|---|---|---|---|---|
| Attended a Movie? | Yes | 105 | 85 | 5 | 195 |
| | No | 45 | 85 | 45 | 175 |
| Column Totals | | 150 | 170 | 50 | 370 |

**Step 2** — Calculate the expected frequencies using the formula:

$$\text{Expected cell frequency} = \frac{\text{Cell column total} \times \text{Cell row total}}{\text{Grand total}}$$

**Student Classification**

| | | Underclass Student | Upperclass Student | Graduate Student | Row Totals |
|---|---|---|---|---|---|
| Attended a Movie? | Yes | 79.1 | 89.6 | 26.3 | 195 |
| | No | 70.9 | 80.4 | 23.6 | 175 |
| Column Totals | | 150 | 170 | 50 | 370 |

**Step 3** — Calculate the computed chi-square value using the chi-square formula noted above.

$$\chi^2 = (105 - 79.1)^2/79.1 + (85 - 89.6)^2/89.6 + (5 - 26.3)^2/26.3$$
$$+ (45 - 70.9)^2/70.9 + (85 - 80.4)^2/80.4 + (45 - 23.6)^2/55.3$$
$$= 55.1$$

**Step 4** — Determine the critical chi-square value from a chi-square table, using the following formula: (#rows − 1) × (#columns − 1) = degrees of freedom (df).

$$df = (2 - 1) \times (3 - 1)$$
$$= 2$$

You would need to use your computed *df* and a chi-square distribution table to find that the critical table value is 5.99.

**Step 5** — Evaluate whether or not the null hypothesis of *no* relationship is supported.

The computed chi-square value of 55.1 is larger than the table value of 5.99, so the hypothesis is not supported. There *is* a relationship between student status and going to a movie in the past month.

---

calculated that are very valuable in revealing underlying relationships. The **column percentages table** divides the raw frequencies by their associated column total raw frequency. That is, the formula is as follows:

$$\text{Column cell percentage} = \frac{\text{Cell frequency}}{\text{Cell column total}}$$

◀ **Formula for a column cell percentage**

The **row percentages table** divides the raw frequencies by their associated row total raw frequencies. That is, a row cell percentage is computed as follows:

$$\text{Row cell percentage} = \frac{\text{Cell frequency}}{\text{Cell row total}}$$

◀ **Formula for a row cell percentage**

In Figure 13.3, the calculated column percentages and the row percentages cross-tabulation tables, using the student movie attendance example, are shown. Stacked bar charts that portray these percentages are also provided. With regard to the column percentages, the chart is identical to Figure 13.2, while for the row percentages, the bar chart is different. The relationship that is significant is clear, regardless of which graph is inspected: Underclass students tend to go to movies, upperclass students may or may not go, and graduate students rarely take in a movie.

**Column Percentages Table and Graph**

|  |  | Underclass student | Upperclass student | Graduate student |
|---|---|---|---|---|
| Attend a Movie? | No | 30% | 50% | 90% |
|  | Yes | 70% | 50% | 10% |
| Column Totals |  | 100% | 100% | 100% |

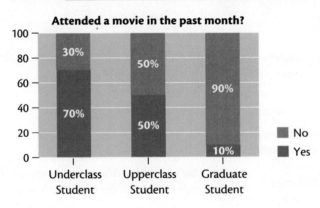

**Row Percentages Table and Graph**

|  |  | Underclass student | Upperclass student | Graduate student | Row Totals |
|---|---|---|---|---|---|
| Attend a Movie? | No | 26% | 48% | 26% | 100% |
|  | Yes | 53% | 44% | 3% | 100% |

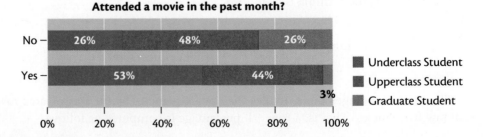

**Figure 13.3** Illustration of Column Percentages and Row Percentages in a Cross-Tabulation Table

# How to Perform Cross-Tabulation Analysis with the XL Data Analyst™

 The XL Data Analyst performs cross-tabulation analysis and generates row and column percentage tables so that users can see the Boolean relationship patterns when they encounter a significant cross-tabulation relationship. As an exercise, consider a survey question asking what types of magazines the respondent reads.

Do you think that there is a relationship to gender? In other words, what gender would you expect to be associated with reading what types of magazines? We will use the XL Data Analyst to investigate this question. Figure 13.4 illustrates the menu and selection window used to direct the XL Data Analyst to perform a cross-tabulation analysis. The menu sequence is Relate—Crosstabs, and this sequence opens up the selection window that you see in Figure 13.4. The Gender variable is selected as the Column Variable, and the Favorite Magazine Type variable is added into the Row Variable(s) pane. Actually, it does not matter which categorical variable is placed in which selection windowpane, as the XL Data Analyst will generate a row percentages table as well as a column percentages table.

Figure 13.5 is the resulting output in the form of three tables. The first table is the Observed Frequencies table along with grand totals for rows and columns. The XL Data Analyst uses these to perform chi-square analysis, the result of which is provided immediately below the frequencies table. In this

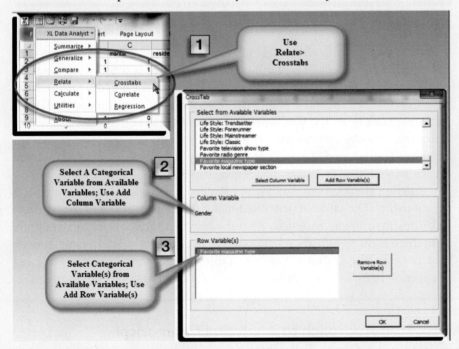

**Figure 13.4** Using the XL Data Analyst to Set Up a Cross-Tabulation Analysis

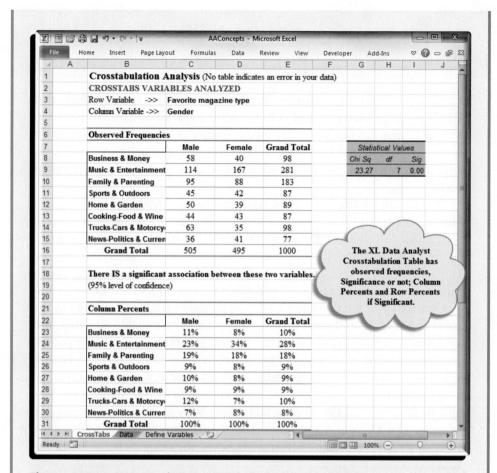

**Figure 13.5** XL Data Analyst Cross-Tabulations Analysis Output

example, there is a significant relationship. The determination of a significant relationship signals that it is worthwhile to inspect the row percentages and/or the column percentages table(s) to spot the pattern of the Boolean relationship. The Column Percents table shows the male/female readership distribution of each magazine type. The Grand Total percent refers to both genders, so departures from this percentage are informative. Specifically, Business & Money, Home & Garden, and Trucks-Cars & Motorcycle magazines are read more by males, while Music & Entertainment magazines are read more by females.

In sum, the XL Data Analyst has flagged a significant cross-tabulation relationship. The tables it generated make the identification of the Boolean relationship quite an easy task. By the way, when the XL Data Analyst finds that there is no significant relationship in the cross-tabulation table, it does not provide the Column Percents table or the Row Percents table, as inspecting these tables with a nonsignificant relationship is not productive.

## The Six-Step Approach to Analyzing Categorical Variables with Cross-Tabulation

Thus far, this chapter has introduced cross-tabulation, which is the appropriate analysis when investigating a possible relationship between two categorical variables.

**Table 13.3** The Six-Step Approach to Data Analysis for Cross-Tabulation Analysis

| Step | Explanation | Example |
|---|---|---|
| **1. What is the research objective?** | Determine that you are dealing with a Relationship Objective. | Is there a relationship between the dwelling location of City University students and their plans to purchase items on the internet in the next two months? |
| **2. What questionnaire question(s) is/are involved?** | Identify the question for the two variables and determine their scales. | Respondents indicated their residence (on-campus or off-campus) and they indicated "Yes," "No," or "Not sure" to a question as to whether or not they think they will make an internet purchase in the next two months. Both variables are categorical. |
| **3. What is the appropriate analysis?** | To assess the relationship between two categorical variables, use cross-tabulation analysis. | We use this procedure because the two variables are categorical, and cross-tabulation analysis is the proper one to investigate a possible Boolean relationship between them. |
| **4. How do you run it?** | Use XL Data Analyst™ analysis: Select "Relate—Crosstabs." | |
| **5. How do you interpret the finding?** | The XL Data Analyst™ indicates whether the relationship is significant and, if so, provides Row Percents and Column Percents tables that portray the Boolean relationship. | There is a significant association between these two variables (95% level of confidence). |

**Column Percents**

|  | Yes | No | Not Sure | Grand Total |
|---|---|---|---|---|
| On Campus | 61% | 0% | 14% | 16% |
| Off Campus | 39% | 100% | 86% | 84% |
| Grand Total | 100% | 100% | 100% | 100% |

**Row Percents**

|  | Yes | No | Not Sure | Grand Total |
|---|---|---|---|---|
| On Campus | 92% | 0% | 8% | 100% |
| Off Campus | 11% | 79% | 10% | 100% |
| Grand Total | 24% | 66% | 10% | 100% |

**Table 13.3** (*Continued*)

| Step | Explanation | Example |
|------|-------------|---------|
| **6. How do you write/ present these findings?** | When a significant relationship is found, you can create a graph that illustrates your finding. | 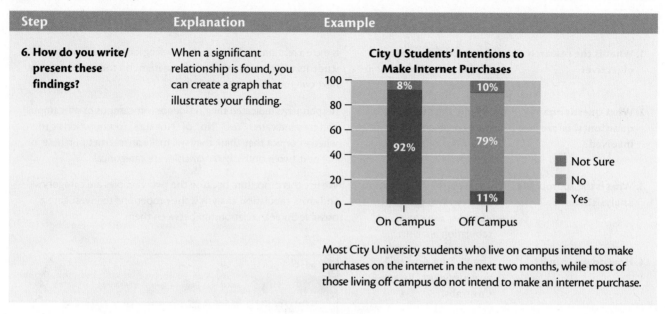 |

Table 13.3 outlines the six steps to perform a cross-tabulation analysis using the Student Life E-Zine data set.

## Linear Relationships and Correlation Analysis

Perhaps the most intuitive relationship between two metric variables is a linear relationship. A **linear relationship** is a straight-line relationship. Knowledge of the value of one variable will automatically yield knowledge of the value of the other variable when applying the linear or straight-line formula. In its general form, a **straight-line formula** is as follows:

**Formula for a straight line** ▷

$$y = a + bx$$

where:

$y$ = the variable being predicted
        (called the "dependent" variable)
$a$ = the intercept
$b$ = the slope
$x$ = the variable used to predict the
        predicted variable (called the "independent" variable)

As shown in Figure 13.6, the **intercept** is the point on the $y$-axis that the straight line "hits" when $x = 0$, and the **slope** is the change in the line for each one-unit change in $x$.

For example, Can-do Book Company (a hypothetical company), hires student representatives to work in the summer. These student representatives are put through an intensified sales training program and then are divided into teams. Each team is given a specific territory, and each individual is assigned a particular district within that territory. The student representative then goes from house to house in the district making cold calls, attempting to sell children's books. Assuming that

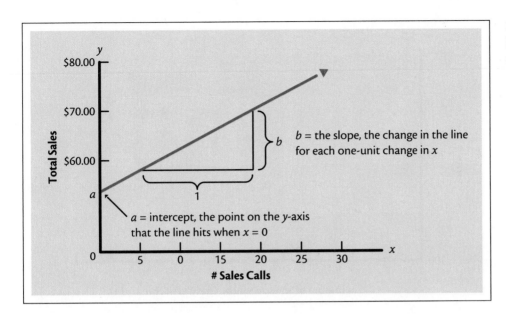

**Figure 13.6** The Straight-Line Relationship Illustrating the Intercept and the Slope

the amount of sales is linearly related to the number of cold calls made, then no cold calls determines zero sales, or $a = 0$ (the intercept when $x = 0$). If, on average, every tenth call resulted in a sale and the typical sale is $62, then the average per call would be $6.20, or $b$, the slope. The linear relationship between total sales ($y$) and number of calls ($x$) is as follows:

$$y = \$0 + \$6.20x$$

Thus, if the student salesperson makes 100 cold calls in any given day, the expected total revenues would be $620 ($6.20 times 100 calls). Certainly, the student sales rep would not derive exactly $620 for every 100 calls, but the linear relationship shows what is expected to happen on average.

## Correlation Coefficients and Covariation

The **correlation coefficient** is an index number falling between the range of $-1.0$ and $+1.0$. It communicates both the strength and the direction of the linear relationship between two metric variables. The amount of linear relationship between two variables is communicated by the absolute size of the correlation coefficient, whereas its sign communicates the direction of the association. A plus sign means that the relationship is positive and that as the $x$ variable increases, so does the $y$ variable and vice versa. This is called a positive or direct relationship. A negative sign means that as the $x$ variable increases, the $y$ variable decreases. This is called a negative or inverse relationship.

Stated in a slightly different manner, a correlation coefficient indicates the degree of "covariation" between two variables. **Covariation** is defined as the amount of change in one variable systematically associated with a change in another variable. The greater the absolute size of the correlation coefficient, the greater is the covariation between the two variables, that is, the stronger is their relationship regardless of the sign.

**Figure 13.7** A Scatter Diagram Showing Covariation

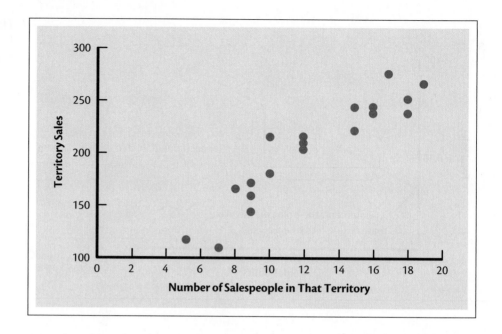

Covariation can be illustrated with a **scatter diagram**, which plots data pairs in an x- and y-axis graph. Here is an example: A marketing researcher is investigating the possible relationship between total company sales for CanPharm, a hypothetical pharmaceuticals sales company, in a particular territory, as well as the number of salespeople assigned to that territory. At the researcher's fingertips are the sales figures and number of salespeople assigned for each of 20 different CanPharm territories in Canada. It is possible to depict the raw data for these two variables on a scatter diagram such as the one in Figure 13.7. A scatter diagram plots the points corresponding to each matched pair of x and y variables. In this figure, the vertical axis (y) is CanPharm sales for the territory, and the horizontal axis (x) contains the number of salespeople in that territory.

The arrangement or scatter of points appears to fall in a long ellipse. Any two variables that exhibit systematic covariation will form an ellipse-like pattern on a scatter diagram. Of course, this particular scatter diagram portrays the information gathered by the marketing researcher on sales and the number of salespeople in each territory and only that information. In actuality, the scatter diagram could have taken any shape, depending on the relationship between the points plotted for the two variables concerned.[4]

A number of different types of scatter diagram results are portrayed in Figure 13.8. Each of these scatter diagram results indicates a different degree of covariation. For instance, the scatter diagram depicted in Figure 13.8a is one in which there is no apparent association or relationship between the two variables because the points fail to create any identifiable pattern. They are clumped into a large, formless shape. The points in Figure 13.8b indicate a negative relationship between variable x and variable y; higher values of x tend to be associated with lower values of y. In Figure 13.8c, the slope indicates a positive relationship between x and y, because larger values of x tend to be associated with larger values of y.

What is the connection between scatter diagrams and correlation coefficients? The answer to these questions lies in the linear relationship described earlier in this

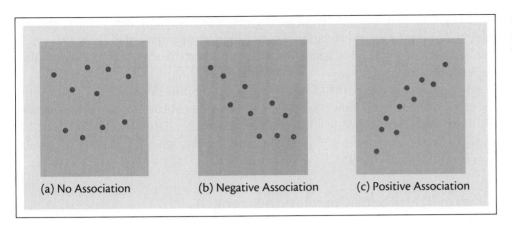

**Figure 13.8** Scatter Diagrams Illustrating Various Relationships

chapter. Look at Figures 13.7, 13.8b, and 13.8c. It can be seen that all of them form ellipses. Imagine taking an ellipse and pulling on both ends. It would stretch out and become thinner until all of its points fell on a straight line. If data points fall on the axis line, the correlation would be exactly 1.0 ($+1.0$ if the ellipse went up to the right and $-1.0$ if it went down to the right).

Now imagine pushing the ends of the ellipse until it became a ball-shaped pattern as in Figure 13.8a. There would be no identifiable straight line. Similarly, there would be no systematic covariation. The correlation for a ball-shaped scatter diagram is zero because there is no discernible linear relationship. In other words, a correlation coefficient indicates the degree of covariation between two variables. The form and angle of the scatter pattern are revealed by the size and sign, respectively, of the correlation coefficient.

In the two-variables averages analysis, the two variables must share the same scale: Both should be measured in dollars, number of times, the same five-point scale, and so on. Correlation analysis has the great advantage of relating two variables that are of very different measurements. For instance, a buyer's age can be correlated with the number of times he or she purchased the item in the past year; how many miles a commuter drives in a week can be correlated to how many minutes of talk radio he or she listens to; and how satisfied customers are can be correlated with how long they have been loyal customers. Correlation can be done with disparate metric scales because there is a standardization procedure in the computation of a correlation that eliminates the differences between the two measures involved.

## Statistical Significance of a Correlation

Working with correlations is a two-step process. First, the statistical significance of the correlation is measured. If it is significant, the second step, interpretation, is taken. If a correlation is not statistically significant, then it is a zero correlation regardless of its computed value. In other words, a correlation that is not statistically significant supports the **null hypothesis for a correlation**, which states that the population correlation coefficient is equal to zero. If this null hypothesis is rejected (that is, there is a statistically significant correlation), then a correlation other than zero will be found in the population.

Let us say that a correlational survey was repeated many, many times, and the computed average for a correlation was not significant across all of these surveys. If the correlation is not significant, the null hypothesis is true, and the population correlation is zero.

Tables exist that give the lowest value of the significant correlation coefficients for given sample sizes. However, most computer statistical programs will indicate the statistical significance level of the computed correlation coefficient. The XL Data Analyst™ evaluates the significance and reports whether or not the correlation is significant at the 95% level of confidence.

## Rules of Thumb for Correlation Strength

After you have established that a correlation coefficient is statistically significant, some general rules of thumb concerning the strength of the relationship and its interpretation should be considered. Correlation coefficients that fall between +1.00 and −0.81 or between −1.00 and −0.81 are generally considered to be "strong." Those correlations that fall between +0.80 and +0.61 or −0.80 and −0.61 generally indicate a "moderate" relationship. Those that fall between +0.60 and +0.41 or −0.60 and −0.41 denote a "weak" association. Any correlation that falls between the range of ±0.21 and ±0.40 is usually considered a "very weak" association between the variables. Finally, any correlation that is equal to or less than ±0.20 is typically uninteresting to marketing researchers because there is no meaningful association between two variables. Table 13.4 is a reference for these rules of thumb. First, we are assuming that the statistical significance of the correlation has been established. Second, researchers make up their own rules of thumb, so guidelines can differ slightly from those in this table.[5]

## The Pearson Product Moment Correlation Coefficient

The **Pearson product moment correlation** measures the linear relationship between two metric-scaled variables such as those depicted conceptually by our scatter diagrams. This correlation coefficient is a measure of the "tightness" of the scatter points to the straight line. The formula for calculating a Pearson product moment correlation is complicated, and researchers never compute it by hand, as they invariably are on computer output. However, some believe that students should understand the workings of the correlation coefficient formula. The components of this

**Table 13.4 Rules of Thumb about Correlation Coefficient Size**

| Coefficient Range | Strength of Association* |
|---|---|
| ±0.81 to ±1.00 | Strong |
| ±0.61 to ±0.80 | Moderate |
| ±0.41 to ±0.60 | Weak |
| ±0.21 to ±0.40 | Very weak |
| ±0.00 to ±0.20 | None |

*Assuming the correlation coefficient is statistically significant.

formula are briefly described here to show how the concepts discussed in this chapter fit in.

The formula is as follows:

$$r_{xy} = \frac{\sum_{c=1}^{n}(x_i - \bar{x})(y_i - \bar{y})}{ns_x s_y}$$

◀ **Formula for Pearson product moment correlation**

where:

$x_i$ = each x value
$\bar{x}$ = average of the x values
$y_i$ = average y value
$\bar{y}$ = average of the y values
$n$ = number of paired cases
$s_x, s_y$ = standard deviations of x and y, respectively

The numerator requires that the $x_i$ and the $y_i$ of each pair of (x, y) data points be compared (via subtraction) to its average, and that these values be multiplied. The sum of all these products is referred to as the "cross-products sum," and this value represents the covariation between x and y. Recall that covariation was represented on a scatter diagram in the introduction to correlation earlier in this section of the chapter.

The covariation is divided by the number of xy pairs, n, to scale it down to an average per pair of x and y values. This average covariation is then divided by both the standard deviation of the x values and the standard deviation of the y values. This adjustment procedure eliminates the measurement differences in the x units and the y units (x might be measured in years, and y might be measured on a 1 to 10 satisfaction scale). The result constrains the correlation, $r_{xy}$, to fall within a specific range of values, and this range is between −1.0 and +1.0, as we indicated earlier.

The larger the absolute size of a correlation coefficient, the stronger it is.

# How to Perform Correlation Analysis with the XL Data Analyst™

 A common application of correlation analysis with surveys is investigating relationships between lifestyle variables and consumer purchasing. Respondents were administered a 10-point scale anchored with "Does not describe me at all" and "Describes me perfectly," measuring their lifestyle as to the degree to which they are novelist, innovator, trendsetter, forerunner, mainstreamer, or classic. Is there a relationship between lifestyle orientation and preference for a certain model of the prospective hybrid vehicles?

Figure 13.9 shows the XL Data Analyst menu sequence for correlation analysis. The menu sequence is Relate—Correlate, which opens up the selection window. As you can see in Figure 13.9, Preference: Super Cycle One-seat Hybrid is chosen as the Primary Variable, while all six lifestyle types are clicked into the Other Variable(s) window pane. (Several "other variables" can be selected in a single analysis.)

Figure 13.10 shows the resulting XL Data Analyst output for correlation. The table reveals computed correlations and sample sizes (1000 in all cases), and all correlations are statistically significant from zero (the null

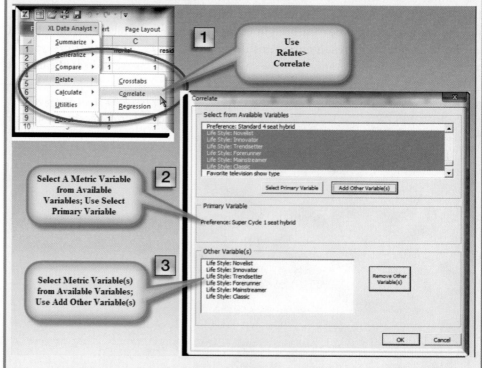

**Figure 13.9** Using the XL Data Analyst to Set Up a Correlation Analysis

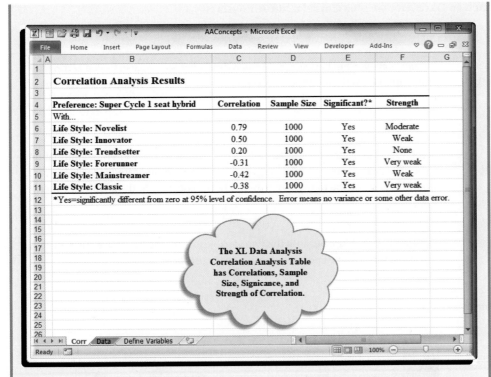

**Figure 13.10** XL Data Analyst Correlation Analysis Output

hypothesis). However, only one is stronger than weak according to our rules of thumb about correlation sizes. The +0.79 correlation for preference for the one-seat super cycle hybrid and the novelist lifestyle reveals that there is moderate positive association between these two variables. These two variables covary, suggesting that if the car company developed a one-seat hybrid super cycle, it would be useful to target the novelist lifestyle market segment, as this vehicle concept is definitely attractive to these individuals.

## The Six-Step Approach to Analyzing a Possible Linear Relationship between Two Metric Variables

While internet sites of all kinds are conceivable, an important aspect of the Student Life E-Zine is its intended delivery of all types of information to City University students. For instance, it has the potential to provide campus calendars, instructor evaluations, registration news, online specials, sports and entertainment news, weather, and more. There is an assumption by prospective e-zine entrepreneurs that post-secondary students are interested in obtaining information from the web. One of the lifestyle statements in the survey was, "I highly value the information I access from the internet." It is useful to correlate this variable with the subscription likelihood question. Table 13.5 describes the six-step analysis process used to investigate the relationship between these two variables.

**Table 13.5** The Six-Step Approach to Data Analysis for Correlation Analysis

| Step | Explanation | Example |
|------|-------------|---------|
| 1. What is the research objective? | Determine that you are dealing with a Relationship Objective. | Is there a relationship between how much City University students value getting information from the internet and how likely they are to subscribe to the Student Life E-Zine? |
| 2. What questionnaire question(s) is/are involved? | Identify the question for the two variables and determine their scales. | Respondents indicated their disagreement/agreement with the internet information value lifestyle statement using a five-point scale, and they indicated how likely they would be to subscribe to the e-zine using a five-point scale. Both variables are metric. |
| 3. What is the appropriate analysis? | To assess the relationship between two metric variables, use correlation analysis. | We use this procedure because the two variables are metric, and correlation analysis will assess the possible linear relationship that exists between them. |
| 4. How do you run it? | Use XL Data Analyst™ analysis: Select "Relate—Correlate." | |

| 5. How do you interpret the finding? | The XL Data Analyst™ indicates the significance and strength of the correlation. | **Correlation Analysis Results** |

| I highly value the information I access from the Internet | Correlation | Sample Size | Significant?* | Strength |
|---|---|---|---|---|
| **How likely would you be to subscribe to the E-Zine?** | 0.77 | 590 | Yes | Moderate |

*Yes = significantly different from zero at 95% level of confidence

**Table 13.5** (*Continued*)

| Step | Explanation | Example |
|------|-------------|---------|
| **6. How do you write/ present these findings?** | When a significant correlation is appreciable in its strength, you can report and interpret it in your findings. | Analysis revealed a moderately strong, significant positive correlation between City University students' value on the information they access from the internet and their likelihood of subscribing to the Student Life E-Zine. Thus, City U students who frequently use the internet to obtain information are good prospects for Student Life E-Zine. |

# Linear Relationships and Regression Analysis

**Regression analysis** is a predictive analysis technique in which two or more variables are used to predict the level of another by use of the straight-line formula, $y = a + bx$, that we described earlier. When a researcher wants to make an exact prediction based on a correlation analysis finding, regression analysis can be used. **Bivariate regression analysis** is a case in which only two variables are involved in the predictive model. When only two variables are used, one is termed *dependent* and the other is termed *independent*. The **dependent variable** is the one that is predicted, and it is customarily termed $y$ in the regression straight-line equation. The **independent variable** is the one that is used to predict the dependent variable, and it is the $x$ in the regression formula. Note that the terms *dependent* and *independent* are arbitrary designations and are customary to regression analysis. There is no cause-and-effect relationship or true dependence between the dependent and the independent variables.

## Computing the Intercept and Slope for Bivariate Regression

To compute $a$ and $b$, a statistical analysis program needs a number of observations of the various levels of the dependent variable $y$ paired with different levels of the independent variable $x$.

The formula for the slope, $b$, in the case of a bivariate regression is:

$$b = r_{xy} \frac{s_y}{s_x}$$

◀ **Formula for *b*, the slope, in bivariate regression**

That is, the slope is equal to the correlation of variables $x$ and $y$ times the standard deviation of $y$, the dependent variable, divided by the standard deviation of $x$, the independent variable. Note that the linear relationship aspect of correlation is translated directly into its regression counterpart by this formula.

Using data for slope $b$, calculate the intercept, $a$, with the following formula:

$$a = \bar{y} - b\bar{x}$$

◀ **Formula for *a*, the intercept, in bivariate regression**

When any statistical analysis program computes the intercept and the slope in a regression analysis, it does so on the basis of the "**least squares criterion.**"

The least squares criterion is a way of guaranteeing that the straight line that runs through the points on the scatter diagram is positioned to minimize the vertical distances away from the line of the various points. In other words, if a line is drawn where the regression line is calculated and the vertical distances of all points away from that line are measured, it would be impossible to draw any other line that would result in a lower total of all of those vertical distances, as shown in Figure 13.11. Regression analysis determines the best slope and the best intercept possible for the straight-line relationship between the independent and dependent variables for the data set that is being used in the analysis.

## Testing for Statistical Significance of the Intercept and the Slope

Simply computing the values for $a$ and $b$ is not sufficient for regression analysis, because the two values must be tested for statistical significance. The intercept and slope that are computed are sample estimates of population parameters of the true intercept, $\alpha$ (alpha), and the true slope, $\beta$ (beta). The tests for statistical significance are tests of whether the computed intercept and computed slope are significantly different from zero (the null hypothesis). To determine statistical significance, regression analysis requires that a $t$ test be undertaken for each parameter estimate. The interpretation of these $t$ tests is identical to other significance tests; that is, if the computed $t$ is greater than the table $t$ value, the hypothesis is not supported, meaning that the computed intercept or slope is not zero, it is the value determined by the regression analysis.

## Making a Prediction with Bivariate Regression Analysis

The fact that the line is a best-approximation representation of all of the points means a certain amount of error must be accounted for. The true advantage of a significant bivariate regression analysis result lies in the ability of the marketing researcher to use

**Figure 13.11** To Predict with Regression, Apply a Confidence Interval around the Predicted $Y$ Value(s)

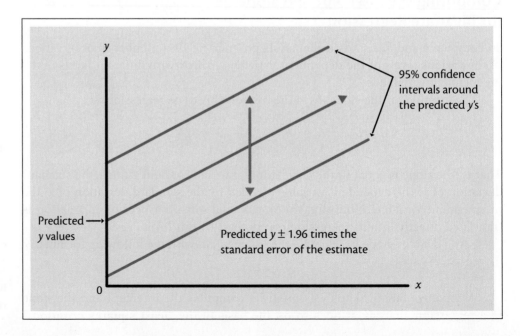

that information gained about the regression line through the points on the scatter diagram and to predict the value or amount of the dependent variable based on some level of the independent variable. In Figure 13.11, the regression prediction uses a confidence interval that is based on a standard error value. The scatter of points does not describe a perfectly straight line because a perfect correlation of +1.0 or −1.0 is almost never found. So the regression prediction can only be an estimate.

Generating a regression prediction is conceptually identical to estimating a population average. That is, it is necessary to express the amount of error by estimating a confidence interval range rather than stipulating an exact estimate for the prediction. Regression analysis provides for a **standard error of the estimate**, which is a measure of the accuracy of the predictions of the regression equation. This standard error value is analogous to the standard error of the mean used in estimating a population average from a sample. It is based on **residuals**, which are the differences between each predicted $y$ value for each $x$ value in the data set compared with the actual $x$ value.[6] In other words, regression analysis takes the regression equation and applies it to every $x$ value and determines the average difference from the associated actual $x$ value in the data set. The differences, or residuals, are translated into a standard error of estimate value. The standard error of the estimate is used to compute confidence intervals around the predictions made using the regression equation. The prediction process is accomplished by applying the following equations:

$$\text{Predicted } y = a + bx$$
$$\text{Confidence interval} = \text{Predicted } y \pm (1.96 \times \text{standard error of the estimate})$$

When making a prediction with a regression equation, use a confidence interval that expresses the sample error and variability inherent in the sample used to compute the regression equation.

One of the assumptions of regression analysis is that the plots on the scatter diagram will be spread uniformly and in accordance with the normal curve assumptions over the regression line. The points are congregated close to the line and become more diffuse as they move away from the line. In other words, a greater percentage of the points are found on or close to the line than are found further away.

The amount a family spends on groceries is related to the number of family members.

The great advantage of this assumption is that it allows the marketing researcher to use knowledge of the normal curve to specify the range in which the dependent variable is predicted to fall. Were the same prediction made many times and an actual result determined each time, the actual results would fall within the range of the predicted value 95% of these times.

The regression equation is used to make a prediction about the dollar amount of grocery purchases that would be associated with a certain family size. In this example, respondents were asked to provide their approximate weekly grocery expenditures and the number of family members living in their households. A bivariate regression analysis is performed. The regression equation is found to have an intercept of $75 and a slope of +$25. So, to predict the weekly grocery expenditures for a family of four, the computations are as follows:

$$y = a + bx$$
$$\text{Expenditures} = \$75 + (\$25 \times 4 \text{ members})$$
$$= \$75 + \$100$$
$$= \$175$$

The analysis finds a standard error of the estimate to be $20, and this value is used to calculate the 95% confidence interval for the prediction.

$$\$175 \pm 1.96 \times \$20$$
$$\$175 \pm \$39.20$$
$$\$135.8 - \$214.2$$

The interpretation of these three numbers is as follows: For a typical family represented by the sample, the expected average weekly grocery purchases amount to $175, but because there are differences between family size and grocery purchases, the weekly expenditures would not be exactly that amount.

In the grocery expenditures example, the average dollars spent on groceries per week may be predicted by the bivariate regression findings; however, if the survey was repeated many, many times, and the same prediction made every time—that a four-member household would spend on average $175 on groceries per week—95% of these predictions would fall between $136 and $214. There is no way to make this prediction range more exact because its precision is dictated by the variability in the data. Researchers sometimes refer to the **R-square value**, which is the squared correlation coefficient between the independent and dependent variables. The R-square value ranges from 0 to 1, and the closer it is found to 1, the stronger is the linear relationship and the more precise will be the predictions.

There are variations of regression analysis as well as a myriad applications. For example, researchers compared how university students in the United States and Greece felt when they learned of a deliberate overcharge.[7] In one situation, students learned that they had been overcharged for a new suit, by $5, $40, or $80, while in another situation students discovered they were overcharged for a year's membership in a health club by $25, $200, or $700. Using a form of regression called conjoint analysis, the researchers found that Greek and American college students are similar in many ways. For example, both groups felt that the suit purchase situation was more ethically offensive than the health club one. However, the Greek students saw the situations as more unethical than did the American students. Moreover, Greek students were more affected by the dollar size than were American students.

# Multiple Regression

**Multiple regression analysis** is an expansion of bivariate regression analysis such that more than one independent variable is used in the regression equation. The addition of independent variables makes the regression model more realistic because predictions normally depend on multiple factors, not just one.

The regression equation in multiple regression has the following form:

$$y = a + b_1 x_1 + b_2 x_2 + b_3 x_3 + ... + b_m x_m$$

◀ **Multiple regression equation**

where:

$y$ = the dependent, or predicted, variable
$x_i$ = independent variable $i$
$a$ = the intercept
$b_i$ = the slope for independent variable $i$
$m$ = the number of independent variables in the equation

Note that the addition of other independent variables has simply added $b_i x_i$'s to the equation. The basic $y = a + bx$ straight-line formula is still present, except that now there are multiple $x$ variables, and each one is added to the equation, changing $y$ by its individual slope. The inclusion of each independent variable in this manner preserves the straight-line assumptions of multiple regression analysis. This is sometimes known as **additivity** because each new independent variable is added on to the regression equation. Of course, it might have a negative coefficient, but it is added on to the equation as another independent variable.

## Working with Multiple Regression

Everything about multiple regression is essentially equivalent to bivariate regression except there is more than one independent variable. The terminology is slightly different in places, and some statistics are modified to take into account the multiple aspect, but for the most part, concepts in multiple regression are analogous to those in the simple bivariate case.

Let us assume that Toyota is trying to predict prospective customers' intentions to purchase a Lexus, given the negative publicity around Toyota (the parent company of Lexus). A survey is conducted that includes an attitude-toward-Lexus variable, a word-of-mouth variable, and an income variable. A multiple regression analysis is then applied, which shows that these three independent variables and the intercept are statistically significant.

Here is the result:

Intention to purchase a Lexus = 2
  + 1.0 × attitude toward Lexus (1–5 scale)
  − 0.5 × negative word of mouth (1–5 scale)
  + 1.0 × income level (1–10 scale)

This multiple regression equation says that a consumer's intention to buy a Lexus can be predicted if three variables are known: (1) attitude toward Lexus, (2) friends' negative comments about Lexus, and (3) income level using a scale with 10 income grades. Furthermore, the impact of each of these variables on Lexus purchase intentions can be seen. First, the average person has a "2" intention level, or some small propensity to want to buy a Lexus. Attitude toward Lexus is measured on a 1 to 5 scale and, with each attitude scale point, intention to purchase a Lexus goes up 1 point. Thus, an individual with a strong positive attitude of "5" has a greater intention than one with a weak attitude of "1." With friends' objections to the Lexus (negative word of mouth) such as "A Lexus is overpriced," the intention decreases by .5 for each level on the 5-point scale. Finally, the intention increases by 1 with each increasing income level.

Here is a numerical example for a potential Lexus buyer whose attitude is 4, negative word of mouth is 3, and income is 5:

$$
\begin{aligned}
\text{Intention to purchase a Lexus} &= 2 \\
&+ 1.0 \times 4 \\
&- 0.5 \times 3 \\
&+ 1.0 \times 5 \\
&= 9.5
\end{aligned}
$$

Multiple regression is a very powerful tool because it reveals which factors predict the dependent variable, which way (the sign) each factor influences the dependent variable, and even how much (the size of $b_i$) each factor influences it. Just as the case in bivariate regression analysis in which the correlation between $y$ and $x$ is used, it is possible to inspect the strength of the linear relationship between the independent variables and the dependent variable with multiple regression. **Multiple R**, also called the **coefficient of determination**, is a handy measure of the strength of the overall linear relationship. Just as was the case in bivariate regression analysis, the multiple regression analysis model assumes that a straight-line (plane) relationship exists among the variables. Multiple R ranges from 0 to +1.0 and represents the amount of the dependent variable "explained," or accounted for, by the combined independent variables. High multiple R values indicate that the regression plane applies well to the scatter of points, whereas low values signal that the straight-line model does not apply well.

Multiple R is like a lead indicator of the multiple regression analysis findings. It is often one of the first pieces of information provided in a multiple regression output. Many researchers mentally convert the multiple R into a percentage. For example, a multiple R of 0.75 means that the regression findings will explain 75% of the dependent variable. The greater the explanatory power of the multiple regression finding, the better and more useful it is for the researcher. However, multiple R is useful only when the multiple regression finding has significant independent variables. There is a process called "trimming" in which researchers make iterative multiple regression analyses, systematically removing nonsignificant independent variables until only statistically significant ones remain in the analysis findings.[8]

## Using "Dummy" Independent Variables

It is permissible to cautiously use a few categorical variables with a multiple regression analysis. A **dummy independent variable** is defined as one that is scaled with a categorical 0-versus-1 coding scheme. The 0-versus-1 code is traditional, but any two adjacent numbers could be used, such as 1-versus-2. The scaling assumptions that underlie multiple regression analysis require that the independent and dependent variables both be metric. However, there are instances in which a marketing researcher may want to use an independent variable that is categorical and identifies only two groups. It is not unusual, for instance, for the marketing researcher to wish to use a two-level variable, such as gender, as an independent variable, in a multiple regression problem. For instance, a researcher may want to use gender coded as 0 for male and 1 for female as an independent variable. Or a buyer–nonbuyer dummy variable may act as an independent variable. In these instances, it is usually permissible to go ahead and slightly violate the assumption of metric scaling for the independent variable to come up with a result that is in some degree interpretable.

## Three Uses of Multiple Regression

Bivariate regression is used only for prediction, whereas multiple regression can be used for (1) prediction, (2) understanding, or (3) as a screening device. Regression analysis for prediction is illustrated in the bivariate regression analysis example: Use the statistically significant intercept and beta coefficient values with the levels of the independent variables desired in the prediction, and then apply 95% confidence intervals using the standard error of the estimate.

However, the interpretation of multiple regression is complicated because independent variables are often measured with different units, so it is wrong to make direct comparisons between the calculated betas. For example, it is improper to directly compare the beta coefficient for family size to another for money spent per month on personal grooming because the units of measurement are so different (people versus dollars). The most common solution to this problem is to standardize the independent variables through a quick operation that involves dividing the difference between each independent variable value and its mean by the standard deviation of that independent variable. This results in what is called the **standardized beta coefficient**. When they are standardized, direct comparisons may be made between the resulting betas. The larger the absolute value of a standardized beta coefficient, the more relative importance it assumes in predicting the dependent variable. With standardized betas the researcher can directly compare the importance of each independent variable with others. Most statistical programs provide the standardized betas automatically.

For the Lexus multiple regression example, the unstandardized and standardized betas are as follows:

| Independent Variable | Attitude toward Lexus | Negative Word of Mouth | Income Level |
|---|---|---|---|
| Unstandardized beta | +1.0 | −0.5 | +1.0 |
| Standardized beta | 0.8 | −0.2 | −0.4 |

The unstandardized betas should not be compared, as they pertain to variables with very different scales, but the standardized betas can be compared. (Ignore the signs; just compare the absolute values.) Attitude toward Lexus is four times (0.8 versus 0.2) more important than negative word of mouth and twice (0.8 versus 0.4) as important as the income level. Income level is twice (0.4 versus 0.2) as important as negative word of mouth. These factors are related to intentions to purchase a Lexus. This leads Lexus to foster strong positive attitudes, as they are apparently instrumental to positive purchase intentions. Lexus does not need to worry about

Multiple regression can reveal factors related to the purchase of a Lexus automobile.

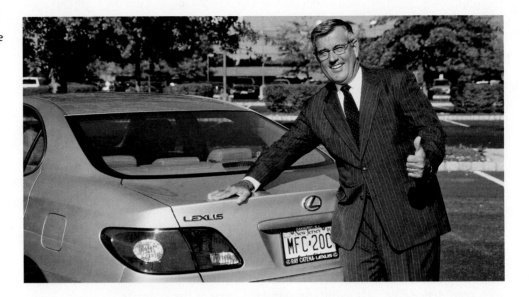

negative comments prospective buyers might hear from friends or co-workers about Lexus, as they are less important than attitudes and income level.

A third application of multiple regression analysis is as a **screening device**: Multiple regression analysis can be applied by a researcher to "narrow down" many considerations to a smaller, more manageable set. A marketing researcher may be faced with a large number and variety of prospective independent variables, and he or she may use multiple regression as a screening device or a way of spotting the salient (statistically significant) independent variables for the dependent variable at hand. In this instance, the intent is not to determine a prediction of the dependent variable; rather, it may be to search for clues about factors that help the researcher understand the behaviour of this particular variable. For instance, the researcher might be seeking market segmentation bases and could use regression to spot which demographic and lifestyle variables are related to the consumer behaviour variable under study.

Follow the instructions in Online Application 13.1 to experience the application of multiple regression analysis for understanding your learning style.

## ONLINE APPLICATION 13.1
# What's Your Learning Preference?

Have you ever completed the VARK survey? This survey identifies your learning preference based on the way you answer a series of questions. The four learning preferences are visual (V), auditory (A), reading (R), and kinesthetic (K). The website hosting the online survey provides the summarized results immediately after submitting the completed online questionnaire. It is an excellent website because it also offers some studying tips for each learning style preference.

Go to **www.vark-learn.com**. On the right-hand side of the page, click on "Questionnaire." Complete the survey. When you are finished, your results will appear.

**Questions**

1. What are possible errors that could be made in the data collection through this survey?

2. Outline in detail what you think happens to the data you submitted. How does VARK take the responses from each person completing the survey and turn them into VARK scores?

3. For what applications can the VARK results be used?

# How to Use the XL Data Analyst™ to Perform Regression Analysis

The XL Data Analyst has been developed to allow you to perform regression analysis. If you use only one independent variable, you are working with bivariate regression, whereas when you select two or more independent variables, you have moved into the domain of multiple regression analysis. To illustrate multiple regression analysis, we will take as our dependent variable "probability of buying a standard size hybrid auto within three years." Figure 13.12 shows the menu sequence and selection window for setting up regression analysis with the XL Data Analyst. Note that the menu sequence is Relate—Regression, which opens up the Regression selection window. We have selected our probability variable into the Dependent Variable windowpane, and we have selected some demographic factors (e.g., size of hometown or city, gender, number of people in household) and nine global warming and gasoline-related attitude items as the independent variables.

Figure 13.13 contains the results of this multiple regression analysis. There are two tables in Figure 13.13. First, the XL Data Analyst computes the full multiple regression analysis using all of the independent variables. It presents the beta coefficients, the standardized beta coefficients, and the result of the significance test for each independent variable's beta. Since one

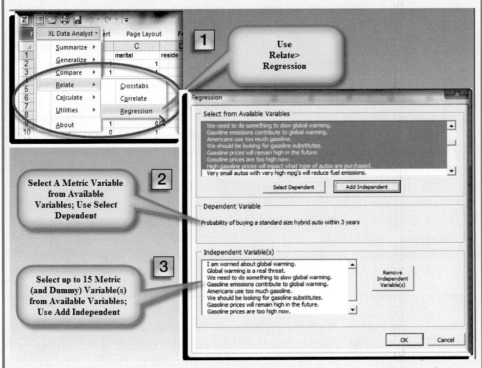

**Figure 13.12** Using the XL Data Analyst to Set Up a Multiple Regression Analysis

*(Continued)*

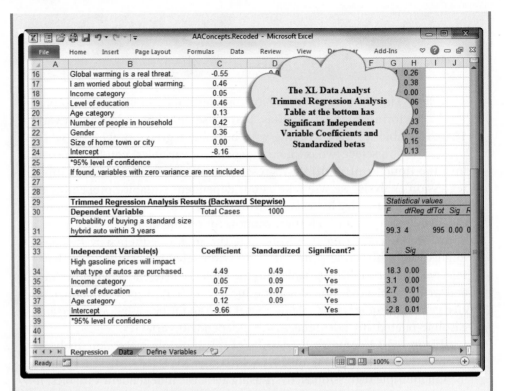

**Figure 13.13** XL Data Analyst Multiple Regression Analysis Output

or more independent variables resulted in a nonsignificant beta coefficient, meaning that even though a coefficient value is reported in the first table its true population value is 0, the XL Data Analyst reruns the analysis with the nonsignificant independent variables omitted from the analysis. The final result is in the second table, where all independent variables now left in the regression analysis results have significant beta coefficients.

We can now interpret our multiple regression finding. We will first use the signs of the beta coefficients as our interpretation vehicle. All four statistically significant independent variables have positive signs (no sign means positive), so as, for example, income and education increase, so does the probability of buying a standard size hybrid auto.

Next, we can use the standard beta coefficients to better our understanding of the demand for standard sized hybrid automobiles. The belief that high gasoline prices will impact the type of autos purchased in the future has a much larger value (.49) than any other variable, and it is five times more important than income, education, or age, which are approximately equal in importance.

Another application of multiple regression is to determine whether or not Las Vegas and Atlantic City compete for the same gambler market. A researcher compared the target market profile determined by multiple regression for Las Vegas gamblers to the one for Atlantic City gamblers.[9] The interpreted findings are given in the table on the next page.

The featured cells are the ones that distinguish the market segment profiles that differentiate Las Vegas from Atlantic City gamblers. Both Las Vegas and Atlantic City are drawing gamblers who live closer to their respective locations, and they both are attracting higher-income and higher-education groups. In addition, Las Vegas gamblers are more likely to be (1) homeowners, (2) Midwesterners, (3) retired or (4) students, and (5) Asian, not Northeasterners, Southerners, or African Americans. Atlantic City, in contrast, is attractive to Northeasterners and African Americans, but it is definitely not attracting Midwesterners or Southerners. Compared with Las Vegas, Atlantic City is not attracting homeowners, retirees, students, or Asians. According to this set of findings, the two main gambling destinations in the United States do not compete for the same gamblers.

| Characteristic | Las Vegas Gamblers | Atlantic City Gamblers |
|---|---|---|
| Income | More trips with higher income | More trips with higher income |
| Education | More trips with more education | More trips with more education |
| Distance to Las Vegas | More trips the closer he or she lives to Las Vegas | Fewer trips the closer he or she lives to Las Vegas |
| Distance to Atlantic City | Fewer trips the closer he or she lives to Atlantic City | More trips the closer he or she lives to Atlantic City |
| Own home | More trips with ownership | Not related |
| Home in Midwest | More trips by Midwesterners | Fewer trips by Midwesterners |
| Home in Northeast | Not related | More trips by Northeasterners |
| Home in South | Not related | Fewer trips by Southerners |
| Retired | More trips if retired | Not related |
| Student | More trips if a student | Not related |
| Asian | More trips if Asian | Not related |
| African American | Not related | More trips if African American |

## The Six-Step Process for Regression Analysis

Table 13.6 applies the six-step process to a phenomenon that is vital to the Student Life E-Zine's success—namely, anticipated internet purchases by City University students. Consult Table 13.6 to see the application of multiple regression analysis by the XL Data Analyst™ to gain an understanding of these purchases.

## Final Comments on Multiple Regression Analysis

There is a great deal more to multiple regression analysis, but it is beyond the scope of this textbook to delve deeper into the topic.[10] The coverage in this chapter introduces regression analysis, and it provides enough information about it for you to run uncomplicated regression analyses with XL Data Analyst™, identify the relevant aspects of the output, and interpret the findings. Note that there are many more assumptions, options, statistics, and considerations involved but not covered here. In fact, there is so much material that whole textbooks exist on regression. An introduction to multiple regression analysis is provided to help comprehend the basic notions, common uses, and interpretations involved with this predictive technique.[11]

**Table 13.6** The Six-Step Approach to Data Analysis for Regression Analysis

| Step | Explanation | Example |
|------|-------------|---------|
| **1. What is the research objective?** | Determine that you are dealing with a Relationship Objective. | We wish to understand the lifestyle and demographic factors that are related to City University students' purchases on the internet. |
| **2. What questionnaire question(s) is/are involved?** | Identify the question(s) for the variables and determine their scales. | Respondents indicated how much they expect to spend on internet purchases over the next two months. This is the metric dependent variable. The independent variables consist of the lifestyle questions (metric) and some metric demographic questions (GPA, class), as well as categorical questions (gender, living location, work status). |
| **3. What is the appropriate analysis?** | To assess the relationship among these variables, use regression analysis. | We use this procedure because the dependent variable is metric, and most of the independent variables are metric. The categorical questions can be treated as dummy independent variables. Multiple regression analysis will assess the linear relationship between the independent variables and the dependent variable, and it will identify the significant independent variables. |
| **4. How do you run it?** | Use XL Data Analyst™ analysis: Select "Relate—Predict (Regression)." | |

| **5. How do you interpret the finding?** | The XL Data Analyst™ indicates the significant independent variables and provides their standardized values. | |
|------|---|---|

| Independent Variable(s) | Coefficient | Standardized | Significant?* |
|-------------------------|-------------|--------------|---------------|
| Do you work? | −17.64 | −0.49 | Yes |
| Respondent's gender | −20.42 | −0.56 | Yes |
| Keeping up with sports and entertainment news is not important. | 2.05 | 0.14 | Yes |
| I shop a lot for "specials." | 4.68 | 0.24 | Yes |
| Even though I am a student, I have enough income to buy what I want. | 5.61 | 0.23 | Yes |
| I am a homebody. | −4.24 | −0.30 | Yes |
| Intercept | 87.09 | | Yes |

*95% level of confidence

**Table 13.6** (*Continued*)

| Step | Explanation | Example |
|---|---|---|
| **6. How do you write/ present these findings?** | With a significant regression finding, use the signs and sizes of the standardized beta coefficients as the basis of your interpretation. | City University students' anticipated internet purchases levels are related to certain demographic and lifestyle factors. Interestingly, the most important variable is gender, with males purchasing more than females, while those students who do not work purchase more than working students. Heavier internet purchasers tend not to be homebodies, they shop a good deal, and they feel they have sufficient income to buy what they want. Significant, but least important as a predictor of the anticipated level of internet purchases, is a desire to keep up with sports and entertainment news. |

# Summary

1.   **Evaluate a relationship between two categarical variables using chi-square analysis.**
This is the last data analysis chapter in the textbook, and it deals with relationships between two or more variables and how these relationships can be useful for prediction and understanding. The first type of relationship involves two categorical variables; the researcher deals with the co-occurrence of the labels that describe the variables. A Boolean operator approach is used, and raw counts of the number of instances are computed to construct a cross-tabulation table. This table is then used in the application of chi-square analysis to evaluate whether or not a statistically significant relationship exists between the two variables being analyzed. If so, then the research turns to graphs or percentage tables to envision the nature of the relationship.

2.   **Evaluate a relationship between two metric variables using correlation analysis.**
Correlation analysis can be applied to two metric variables, and the linear relationship between them can be portrayed in a scatter diagram. The correlation coefficient indicates the direction (by its sign) and the strength (by its magnitude) of the linear relationship. However, only statistically significant correlations can be interpreted, and by rules of thumb provided in the chapter, a correlation must be larger than $\pm0.81$ to be "strong."

3.   **Predict a relationship between two or more variables using regression analysis.**
Correlation leads to bivariate regression, in which the intercept and slope of the straight line are estimated and assessed for statistical significance. When statistically significant findings occur, the researcher can use the findings to compute a prediction. The prediction must be cast in a confidence interval because there is invariably some error in how well the regression analysis result performs. Multiple regression analysis is appropriate when the researcher has more than one independent variable that may predict the dependent variable under study. With multiple regression, the basics of a linear relationship are retained, but there is a different slope ($b$) for each independent variable, and the signs of the slopes

can be mixed. Generally, independent variables should be metric, although a few dummy-coded (e.g., 0,1) independent variables may be used in the independent variables set. A multiple regression result can be used to make predictions. With standardized beta coefficients, interpreting the relative importance of the various independent variables with respect to the behaviour of the dependent variable is possible.

## Key Terms

Additivity   (p. 448)
Bivariate regression analysis
   (p. 443)
Boolean relationship   (p. 424)
Chi-square analysis   (p. 427)
Coefficient of determination   (p. 449)
Column percentages table   (p. 429)
Correlation coefficient   (p. 435)
Covariation   (p. 435)
Cross-tabulation analysis   (p. 426)
Cross-tabulation cell   (p. 426)
Cross-tabulation table   (p. 426)
Dependent variable   (p. 443)
Dummy independent variable
   (p. 450)
Expected frequencies   (p. 427)
Frequencies table   (p. 426)
Independent variable   (p. 443)
Intercept   (p. 434)
Least squares criterion   (p. 443)
Linear relationship   (p. 434)

Multiple $R$   (p. 449)
Multiple regression analysis   (p. 448)
Null hypothesis for a correlation
   (p. 437)
Observed frequencies   (p. 427)
Pearson product moment correlation
   (p. 438)
Regression analysis   (p. 443)
Relationship   (p. 424)
Residuals   (p. 445)
Row percentages table   (p. 429)
$R$-square value   (p. 446)
Scatter diagram   (p. 436)
Screening device   (p. 451)
Slope   (p. 434)
Stacked bar chart   (p. 425)
Standard error of the estimate
   (p. 445)
Standardized beta coefficient
   (p. 450)
Straight-line formula   (p. 434)

## Review Questions

1.1 When a researcher finds a statistically significant chi-square result for a cross-tabulation analysis, what should the researcher do next?

1.2 A researcher has conducted a survey for Molson Canadian beer. There are two questions in the survey being investigated in the following cross-tabulation table:

|  | Molson Canadian | | |
|---|---|---|---|
|  | Buyer | Nonbuyer | Totals |
| White collar | 152 | 8 | 160 |
| Blue collar | 14 | 26 | 40 |
| Totals | 166 | 34 | 200 |

The computed chi-square value of 81.6 is greater than the chi-square table critical value of 3.8. Interpret the researcher's findings.

1.3 Following is some information about 10 respondents to a mail survey concerning candy purchasing. Construct the various different types of cross-tabulation tables that are possible. Label each table, and indicate what you find to be the general relationship apparent in the data.

| Respondent | Buy Plain M&Ms | Buy Peanut M&Ms |
|---|---|---|
| 1 | Yes | No |
| 2 | Yes | No |
| 3 | No | Yes |
| 4 | Yes | No |
| 5 | No | No |
| 6 | No | Yes |
| 7 | No | No |
| 8 | Yes | No |
| 9 | Yes | No |
| 10 | No | Yes |

2.1 Use a scatter diagram to illustrate the covariation for the following correlations:
   a. −0.99
   b. +0.21
   c. +0.76

2.2 Morton O'Dell is the owner of Mort's Diner, which is located in downtown Vancouver. Mort's opened up about 12 months ago, and it has experienced success, but Mort is always worried about what food items to order as inventory on a weekly basis. Mort's daughter, Mary, is an engineering student at the University of British Columbia, and she offers to help her father. She asks him to provide sales data for the past 10 weeks in terms of pounds of food bought. With some difficulty, Mort comes up with the following list:

| Week | Meat | Fish | Fowl | Vegetables | Desserts |
|---|---|---|---|---|---|
| 1 | 100 | 50 | 150 | 195 | 50 |
| 2 | 91 | 55 | 182 | 200 | 64 |
| 3 | 82 | 60 | 194 | 209 | 70 |
| 4 | 75 | 68 | 211 | 215 | 82 |
| 5 | 66 | 53 | 235 | 225 | 73 |
| 6 | 53 | 61 | 253 | 234 | 53 |
| 7 | 64 | 57 | 237 | 230 | 68 |
| 8 | 76 | 64 | 208 | 221 | 58 |
| 9 | 94 | 68 | 193 | 229 | 62 |
| 10 | 105 | 58 | 181 | 214 | 62 |

Mary uses these sales figures to construct scatter diagrams that illustrate the basic relationships among the various types of food items purchased at Mort's Diner over the past 10 weeks. She tells her father that the diagrams provide some help in his weekly inventory ordering problem. Construct Mary's scatter diagrams with Excel to indicate what assistance they are to Mort. Perform the appropriate correlation analyses with the XL Data Analyst™, and interpret your findings.

3.1 Papa's Pizza wants to predict how many of its pizzas customers order per month. A multiple regression analysis finds the following statistically significant results.

| Variable | Coefficient or Value |
|---|---|
| Intercept | 2.6 |
| Pizza is a large part of my diet.* | 0.5 |
| I worry about calories in pizzas.* | −0.2 |
| Gender (1 = female; 2 = male) | +1.1 |
| Standard error of the estimate | +0.2 |

*Based on a scale where 1 = "strongly disagree," 2 = "somewhat agree," 3 = "neither agree nor disagree," 4 = "somewhat agree," and 5 = "strongly agree."

Compute the predicted number of pizzas ordered per month by each of the following three pizza customers:

a. A man who strongly agrees that pizza is a large part of his diet but strongly disagrees that he worries about pizza calories.
b. A woman who is neutral about pizza being a large part of her diet and who somewhat agrees that she worries about calories in pizzas.
c. A man who somewhat disagrees that he worries about pizza calories and is neutral about pizza being a large part of his diet.

3.2 Segmentation Associates, a company that specializes in using multiple regression as a means of describing market segments, conducts a survey of various types of automobile purchasers. The following table summarizes a recent study's findings. The values are the standardized beta coefficients of those segmentation variables found to be statistically significant. Where no value appears, that regression coefficient was not statistically significant.

| Segmentation Variable | Compact Automobile Buyer | Sports Car Buyer | Luxury Automobile Buyer |
|---|---|---|---|
| **Demographics** | | | |
| Age | −0.28 | −0.15 | +0.59 |
| Education | −0.12 | +0.38 | |
| Family Size | +0.39 | −0.35 | |
| Income | −0.15 | +0.25 | +0.68 |

(Continued)

| Segmentation Variable | Compact Automobile Buyer | Sports Car Buyer | Luxury Automobile Buyer |
|---|---|---|---|
| **Lifestyle/Values** | | | |
| Active | | +0.59 | −0.39 |
| Canadian Pride | +0.30 | | +0.24 |
| Bargain Hunter | +0.45 | −0.33 | |
| Conservative | | −0.38 | +0.54 |
| Cosmopolitan | −0.40 | +0.68 | |
| Embraces Change | −0.30 | +0.65 | |
| Family Values | +0.69 | | +0.21 |
| Financially Secure | −0.28 | +0.21 | +0.52 |
| Optimistic | | +0.71 | +0.37 |

Interpret these findings for an automobile manufacturer that has a compact automobile, a sports car, and a luxury automobile in its product line.

# Case 13.1

# Friendly Market versus Circle K

Friendly Market is a convenience store located directly across the street from a Circle K convenience store. Circle K is a national chain, and its stores enjoy the benefits of national advertising campaigns, particularly the high visibility these campaigns bring. All Circle K stores have large red-and-white store signs, identical merchandise assortments, standardized floor plans, and they are open 24/7. Friendly Market, in contrast, is a one-of-a-kind "mom-and-pop" variety convenience store owned and managed by Billy Wong. Billy's parents came to Canada from Hong Kong when Billy was 10 years old. After graduating from high school, Bill worked in a variety of jobs, both full- and part-time, and for most of the past 10 years, Billy has been a Circle K store employee.

In 2002, Billy made a bold move to open his own convenience store. Don's Market, a mom-and-pop convenience store across the street from the Circle K, went out of business, so Billy gathered up his life savings and borrowed as much money as he could from friends, relatives, and his bank. He bought the old Don's Market building and equipment, renamed it Friendly Market, and opened its doors for business in November 2002. Billy's core business philosophy is to greet everyone who comes in and to get to know all of his customers on a first-name basis. He also watches Circle K's prices closely and seeks to have lower prices on at least 50% of the merchandise sold by both stores.

To the surprise of the manager of the Circle K across the street, Friendly Market has prospered. In 2003, Billy's younger sister, who had gone on to university and earned an MBA degree at Dalhousie University, conducted a survey of Billy's target market to gain a better understanding of why Friendly Market was successful. She drafted a

*(Continued)*

simple questionnaire and did the telephone interviewing herself. She used the local telephone book and called a random sample of over 150 respondents whose residences were listed within 3 kilometres of Friendly Market. She then created an XL Data Analyst™ data set with the following variable names and values:

| Variable Name | Value Labels |
|---|---|
| FRIENDLY | 0 = Do not use Friendly Market regularly; |
| | 1 = Use Friendly Market regularly |
| CIRCLE K | 0 = Do not use Circle K regularly; |
| | 1 = Use Circle K regularly |
| DWELL | 1 = Own home; 2 = Rent |
| GENDER | 1 = Male; 2 = Female |
| WORK | 1 = Work full-time; 2 = Work part-time; |
| | 3 = Retired or Do not work |
| COMMUTE | 0 = Do not pass by Friendly Market/ Circle K corner on way to work; |
| | 1 = Do pass by Friendly Market/ Circle K corner on way to work |

In addition to these demographic questions, respondents were asked if they agreed (coded 3), disagreed (coded 1), or neither agreed nor disagreed (coded 2) with each of five different lifestyle statements. The variable names and questions follow:

| Variable Name | Lifestyle Statement |
|---|---|
| BARGAIN | I often shop for bargains. |
| CASH | I always pay cash. |
| QUICK | I like quick, easy shopping. |
| KNOW ME | I shop where they know my name. |
| HURRY | I am always in a hurry. |

The data set is one of the data sets accompanying this textbook. It is named "FriendlyMarket.xlsm." Use the XL Data Analyst™ to perform the relationship analyses necessary to answer the following questions.

## Questions

1. Do customers patronize both Friendly Market and Circle K?
2. What demographic characteristics profile Friendly Market's customers? That is, what characteristics are related to patronage of Friendly Market?
3. What demographic characteristics profile Circle K's customers? That is, what characteristics are related to patronage of Circle K?
4. What is the lifestyle profile related to Friendly Market's customers?

# Case 13.2 YOUR INTEGRATED CASE

# Student Life E-Zine Relationships Analysis

Bob Watts of ORS Marketing Research and marketing intern Lori Baker are in an evaluation session. Bob has just told Lori that he is giving her the highest evaluation he has ever given to a marketing intern who has worked for him. "I am really impressed with your command of the several data analyses that you performed for our Student Life E-Zine project, and your PowerPoint presentations and report tables are among the best I have ever seen. You really have a good working knowledge of those analytical techniques. As you know, we have two weeks left for your internship, but I'm submitting my evaluation to your City U marketing internship supervisor today because you've done such an excellent job."

At this, Lori responds, "Thank you so much! I've really gained a lot of experience, and I'm very grateful that ORS has let me grow under your direction. I'm pretty sure that I want to be a marketing researcher, and I'll be devoting my senior year at City U to gearing up and applying to the Master of Marketing Research program."

"Oh?" says Bob. "That convinces me even more that you're the right person for the job I'm about to assign you for your last two weeks here. We need to do the final set of analyses for the Student Life E-Zine project, and I'm going to let you delve into it. It involves relationship analyses using correlations and regressions, so if you handle these—especially the multiple regression analyses—as well as I believe you can, you'll have

a really impressive 'bullet' to add to your application. Here are the relationship objectives that I proposed to our Student Life E-Zine entrepreneurs at the beginning of the project. What do you say?"

"I'll give it my very best," replies Lori.

Following are the Student Life E-Zine marketing research project relationship objectives provided to Lori by Bob Watts. Use your Student Life E-Zine survey data set and the XL Data Analyst™ to perform the appropriate relationship analyses, and interpret your findings in each instance.

## Questions

1. For each of the seven lifestyle dimensions, is it related to preference for any of the 15 possible Student Life E-Zine features?

2. Find those possible Student Life E-Zine features that are at least "somewhat preferred" (average of 4.0 or higher) by eligible City University students. For each one, what demographic and/or lifestyle factors are related to it, and how do you interpret these relationships?

# Communicating the Research Results

A well-known researcher in the industry, Michael Lotti of Eastman Kodak, believes that "even the best research will not drive the appropriate action unless the audience understands the outcomes and implications. Researchers must create a clear, concise presentation of the results."[1] Mr. Lotti's statement underscores the significance of the final research report. The **marketing research report** is a factual message that transmits research results, vital recommendations, conclusions, and other important information to the client, who in turn bases his or her decision making on the contents of the report. This chapter deals with the essentials of writing and presenting the marketing research report.[2]

Compiling a market research report is a challenging task that plays a significant role in determining how the research results are implemented. As a result of developments in technology, many organizations within the marketing research industry now offer online reports that are current and interactive. Readers can choose to see the information they need with a click of the mouse! An excellent example of this

**ONLINE APPLICATION 14.1**
## Examine Real Reports

**A.** To explore online reporting at Statistics Canada, follow these steps:

- Go to **www.statcan.gc.ca.** Select language of preference.
- In the "In the News" box on the homepage, click on *"The Daily." The Daily* is an online report released at 8:30 a.m. Eastern Time each day.
- Navigate your way according to your personal interests by clicking on hyperlinks you encounter.
- Note how the reporting of results is brief and uses a variety of communication techniques such as pictures and graphs.

**B.** For a tour of the online reporting offered by Burke, follow these steps:

- Go to **https://www.digitaldashboard.com**.
- Click on "Take a Tour."
- Once you click on the arrow to begin the tour, the program moves from screen to screen automatically. Review each screen as it is presented in order to see how Digital Dashboard works.

feature is the Statistics Canada website, which offers current information such as the consumer price index, unemployment rates, and retail trade statistics. Another example is **Digital Dashboard**, an online reporting service offered by Burke, a well-known marketing research firm. Online Application 14.1 provides directions to the online reports offered on the Statistics Canada and Burke websites.

## Importance of the Marketing Research Report

The communication of research results is the culmination of the entire research process. The marketing research report is the product that represents the efforts of the marketing research team, and it may be the only part of the project that the client will see. In order to have credibility and be useful to the client, the report must communicate effectively.

Marketing research users,[3] as well as marketing research suppliers,[4] agree that reporting the research results is one of the most important aspects of the marketing research process. Many managers will not be involved in any aspect of the research process but will use the report to make business decisions. Effective reporting is essential, and all of the principles of organization, formatting, good writing, and good grammar must be employed.

## Organizing the Written Report

Marketing research reports are tailored to specific audiences and purposes, and both must be considered in all phases of the research process, including planning the report. Before begining to write, then, some basic questions should be answered. What message do you want to communicate? What is the purpose? Who is the

**Where We Are**
1. Establish the need for marketing research
2. Define the problem
3. Establish research objectives
4. Determine research design
5. Identify information types and sources
6. Determine methods of accessing data
7. Design data collection forms
8. Determine sample plan and size
9. Collect data
10. Analyze data
11. Prepare and present the final research report

**Table 14.1 The Elements of a Marketing Research Report**

**A. Front Matter**
1. Title Page
2. Letter of Authorization
3. Letter/Memo of Transmittal
4. Table of Contents
5. List of Illustrations
6. Abstract/Executive Summary

**B. Body**
1. Introduction
2. Research Objectives
3. Method
4. Results
5. Limitations
6. Conclusions, or Conclusions and Recommendations

**C. End Matter**
1. Appendices
2. Endnotes

audience? Are there multiple audiences? What does the audience know? What does the audience need to know? What are the audience's interests, values, concerns?

When organizing the research report, it is often helpful to put oneself in the shoes of the reader instead of the writer. Doing so will help clarify things through the eyes of the audience and increase the success of communication.

Once these basic questions have been answered, the format of the document needs to be determined. Any specific guidelines given by the client on how to prepare the report should be followed. However, if no specific guidelines are provided, there are certain elements that must be considered when preparing the report. These elements can be grouped into three sections: front matter, body, and end matter (Table 14.1). Note that not all reports follow this format, or include all of the elements within each section.

## Front Matter

The **front matter** consists of all pages that precede the first page of the report: the title page, letter of authorization (optional), letter/memo of transmittal, table of contents, list of illustrations, and abstract/executive summary.

### Title Page

The **title page** (Figure 14.1) contains four major items of information: (1) the title of the document, (2) the organization/person(s) for whom the report was prepared, (3) the organization/person(s) who prepared the report, and (4) the date of submission. If names of individuals appear on the title page, they may be either in alphabetical order or in some other agreed-upon order; each individual should also be given a designation or descriptive title, if appropriate.

The document title should be informative. Some clients prefer extremely descriptive titles regardless of the length, including the purpose and the contents of the report. In the case of Figure 14.1, a more descriptive title would be "Student Life E-Zine: A Marketing Research Study to Determine Intention to Subscribe: Preferences

**Figure 14.1** A Title Page

**Student Life E-Zine**

MARKET POTENTIAL FOR
CANADIAN POST-SECONDARY STUDENTS

---

Prepared for:
Wesley Addington
Don Cooper
Anna Fulkerson
Sarah Stripling


Prepared by:
Bob Watts
ORS Research Inc.


June 2010

for Design; Online Access and Purchases; and Lifestyle and Demographics of Potential Subscribers." The title should be centred on the page. Many authors prefer to present the title in uppercase letters while other information on the page is in both upper- and lowercase letters. The title page is counted as page i of the front matter but the page number is not printed on the page. The next page of the report is numbered ii.

### Letter of Authorization

The **letter of authorization** is the marketing research firm's certification to do the project and is optional. It is particularly helpful in large organizations because it provides other users of the report with the name, title, and department of the individual(s) who authorized the project. It may also include a general description of the nature of the research project, completion date, terms of payment, and any special conditions of the research project requested by the client or research user. If conditions of authorization are in the letter/memo of transmittal, the letter of authorization is not necessary in the report. However, if the reader may not know the conditions of authorization, inclusion of this document is helpful.

### Letter/Memo of Transmittal

Use a **letter of transmittal** to release or deliver the document to a client organization. Use a **memo of transmittal** to deliver the document within your own organization. The letter/memo of transmittal describes the general nature of the research in a sentence or two and identifies the individual who is releasing the report. The primary purpose of the letter/memo of transmittal is to orient the reader to the report and to build a positive image of the report. It should establish rapport between the writer and reader. It gives the reader a person to contact if questions arise.

The writing style in the letter/memo of transmittal should be personal and slightly informal. Some general elements that may appear in the letter/memo of transmittal are a brief identification of the nature of the research, a review of the conditions of the authorization to do the research (if no letter of authorization is included), comments on findings, suggestions for further research, and an expression of interest in the project and further research. It should end with an expression of appreciation for the assignment, acknowledgment of assistance from others, and suggestions for following up. Personal observations, unsupported by the data, are appropriate.

### Table of Contents

The **table of contents** helps the reader locate information in the research report. The table of contents (Figure 14.2) should list all sections of the report that follow; each heading should read exactly as it appears in the text and should identify the number of the page on which it appears. If a section is longer than one page, list the page on which it begins. Indent subheadings under headings. All items except the title page and the table of contents are listed with page numbers in the table of contents. Front-matter pages are numbered with lowercase Roman numerals: i, ii, iii, iv, and so on. Arabic numerals (1, 2, 3) begin with the introduction section of the body of the report.

### List of Illustrations

If the report contains tables and/or figures, include in the table of contents a **list of illustrations** along with the page numbers on which they appear. All tables and figures should be included in this list by their respective titles; this helps the reader find specific illustrations that graphically portray the information. **Tables** are words or numbers that are arranged in rows and columns; **figures** are graphs, charts, maps, pictures, and so on. Because tables and figures are numbered independently, it is possible to have both a Figure 1 and a Table 1 in the list of illustrations. Give each a name, and list each in the order in which it appears in the report.

### Abstract/Executive Summary

A report may have many readers. Some of them will need to know the details of the report, such as the supporting data on which conclusions are based and

**Figure 14.2** A Table of Contents

**Table of Contents**

ii

recommendations. Others will not need as many details but will want to read the conclusions and recommendations. Still others may need only a general picture. Therefore, the **abstract** or **executive summary** is a "skeleton" of your report. It serves as a summary for the busy executive or a preview for the in-depth reader. It provides an overview of the most useful information, including the conclusions and recommendations. The abstract or executive summary should be very carefully written, conveying the information as concisely as possible. It should be single-spaced and should briefly cover the general subject of the research, the scope of the research (what the research covers/does not cover), identification of the type of methodology used (e.g., a mail survey of 1000 homeowners), conclusions, and recommendations.

## Body

The **body** is the bulk of the report. It contains an introduction to the report, a description of the methodology, a discussion of the results, a statement of limitations, and a list of conclusions and recommendations. Only a few people will read the report in its entirety. Most will read the executive summary, conclusions, and recommendations. Therefore, formal reports are repetitious. For example, the research objectives might be specified in the executive summary and again in the findings section as well as in the conclusions section. In lengthy reports, repetition can help the reader comprehend the volume of detail.

The first page of the body contains the title centred two inches from the top of the page; this page is counted as page 1, but no page number is printed on it. All other pages throughout the document are numbered sequentially.

### Introduction

The **introduction** to the marketing research report orients the reader to the contents of the report. It may contain a statement of the background situation leading to the problem, the statement of the problem, and a summary description of how the research process was initiated. It should contain a statement of the general purpose of the report and also the specific objectives for the research.

**Research objectives** may be listed either as a separate section (see Table 14.1) or within the introduction section. The listing of research objectives should follow the statement of the problem, since the two concepts are closely related. The list of specific research objectives often serves as a good framework for organizing the results section of the report.

### Method

The **method** describes, in as much detail as necessary, how the research was conducted, including a description of the sample plan and sample size determination, the method of gathering data, and how the data were analyzed. Supplementary information should be placed in the appendix. If secondary information was used, it is important to provide enough information so that the sources can be located.[5] It is not necessary to document facts that are common knowledge or can be easily verified. If in doubt, document! **Plagiarism** refers to presenting the work of others as one's own and is a serious offence. At one well-known university, 48 students recently either quit or were expelled from the university as a result of charges of plagiarism. The university was so diligent in prosecuting the offenders that it revoked the degrees of three of the students who had already graduated![6] Many people have lost their jobs over accusations of plagiarism. At the very least, plagiarists lose credibility.

In most cases, the method section does not need to be long. It should, however, provide the essential information the reader needs in order to understand how the data were collected and how the results were achieved. This section should be clear and detailed enough that other researchers could conduct a similar study for purposes of reliability.

### Results

The **results** section is the most important portion of the report. This section should present the findings of the research logically and be organized around the objectives for the study. The results should be presented in narrative form and be accompanied by tables, charts, figures, and other appropriate visuals that support and enhance the explanation of results. Tables and figures are supportive material; they should not be overused or used as filler. Each should contain a number and title and should be referred to in the narrative.

Outline the results section before beginning to write the report. The survey questionnaire itself can serve as a useful aid in organizing your results because the questions are often grouped in a logical order or in purposeful sections. Another useful method for organizing results is to individually print all tables and figures and arrange them in a logical sequence. Once the results are outlined properly, start to write the introductory sentences, definitions (if necessary), review of the findings (often referring to tables and figures), and transition sentences to lead into the next topic.

### Limitations

Do not attempt to hide or disguise problems in the research; no research is faultless. Always be honest and open regarding all aspects of the research. If one avoids discussing limitations, integrity and research are rendered suspect. Suggest what the limitations are or may be and how they affect the results. Also, suggest opportunities for further study based on the limitations. Typical **limitations** in research reports often focus on but are not limited to factors such as time, money, size of sample, and personnel. Consider the following example: "The reader should note that this study was based on a survey of students at City University. Care should be exercised in generalizing these findings to other university populations."

### Conclusions and Recommendations

Conclusions and recommendations may be listed together or in separate sections, depending on the amount of material reported. Note that conclusions are not the same as recommendations. **Conclusions** are the outcomes and decisions reached based on the research results. **Recommendations** are suggestions for how to proceed based on the conclusions. Unlike conclusions, recommendations may require knowledge beyond the scope of the research findings themselves—for example, information on conditions within the company, the industry, and so on. The researcher and the client should determine prior to the study whether the report is to contain recommendations. A clear understanding of the researcher's role will result in a smoother process and will help avoid conflict. Although a research user may want the researcher to provide specific recommendations, both parties must realize that the researcher's recommendations are based solely on the knowledge gained from the research report. Other information, if made known to the researcher, could completely change the researcher's recommendations.

If recommendations are required and if a report is intended to initiate further action, recommendations are the important map to the next step. Writing recommendations in a bulleted list and beginning each with an action verb help to direct the reader to the logical next step.

## End Matter

The **end matter** comprises the **appendices**, which contain additional information that the reader may go to for further reading. Appendices contain the "nice to know" information, not the "need to know" information. Therefore, that information should not clutter the body of the report but should instead be inserted at the end for the reader who desires or requires additional information. Tables, figures, additional reading, technical descriptions, data collection forms, and appropriate computer printouts are some elements that may appear in the appendix. (If they are critical to the reader, however, they may be included in the report itself.) Each appendix should be labelled with both a letter and a title, and each should appear in the table of contents. A reference page or endnotes (if appropriate) should precede the appendix.

# Following Guidelines and Principles for the Written Report

## Form and Format

Form and format concerns include headings, subheadings, and visuals.

### Headings and Subheadings

In a long report, readers need signals and signposts that help them find their way. Headings and subheadings perform this function. **Headings** indicate the topic of each section and **subheadings** should divide that information into segments. A new heading should introduce a change of topic. The form of heading should fit the research purpose and should be used consistently throughout the report. If subheadings are used within the divisions, the subheadings must be parallel to one another but not to the main headings. Marketing Research in Action 14.1 gives more detail on headings and subheadings.

### Visuals

**Visuals** are tables, figures, charts, diagrams, graphs, and other graphic aids. Used properly, they can dramatically and concisely present information that might otherwise be difficult to comprehend. Tables systematically present numerical data or words in columns and rows. Figures translate numbers into visual displays so that relationships and trends become more obvious. Examples of figures are graphs, pie charts, and bar charts.

Visuals should tell a story; they should be uncluttered and self-explanatory. Even though they are self-explanatory, the key points of all visuals should be explained in the text: Refer to visuals by number: ". . . as shown in Figure 1." Each visual should be titled and numbered. If possible, place the visual immediately below the paragraph in which its first reference appears. Or, if sufficient space is not available, continue the text and place the visual on the next page. Visuals can also be placed in an appendix.

## Style

Stylistic devices can make the difference in whether your reader gets the message as you intended it. Consider the following tips for the writer:

1. A good paragraph has one main idea, and a topic sentence should state that main idea. Writing a good paragraph is a good step toward becoming a good writer (see Marketing Research in Action 14.2).

## MARKETING RESEARCH IN ACTION 14.1
# How Headings Can Help You Write a Professional Report

Most students have difficulty organizing their reports. Yet, rarely will they take the time to outline their report as they were taught to do in grade school. There are few more effective methods to improving your writing skills than properly outlining before you begin writing. Below we provide you with some key ways to improve your writing skills through the proper use of headings.

First, before you can outline, you must do some basic planning. Go back to your research objectives. Make certain that your report addresses the research objectives that were identified at the beginning of the research project.

Second, read the information you have! Many students just start writing without reading over the information they have generated either from secondary data or even from analysis of the results in primary data collection.

Third, what information has been gathered for each of the research objectives? Organize your information into separate areas based upon how it addresses a particular research objective. For example, if one objective is to gather information on likelihood to subscribe to a new service, find that information and file it under the research objective. Was any other information gathered that addresses this objective?

Fourth, now that you are familiar with your research objectives and the information gathered for each, start outlining the information gathered by using headings. Headings are *the* most useful way a writer can organize a paper. Headings are very useful to readers in that they serve as guideposts telling readers where they are, where they have been, and where they are headed.

Fifth, understand your format for headings before you begin to write. We provide the following to help you with your headings. Read this and use it!

## Title

Titles are centred at the top of the page and are either boldfaced or underlined. Titles are normally in a larger font than the rest of the paper.

## First-Level Heading

First-level headings indicate what the following section, usually consisting of several subdivisions, is about.

Researchers at Burke, Inc., outline their client's report with headings and subheadings.

First-level headings are centred, bold, and all uppercase, and are usually in larger font sizes than the other material but smaller than the title.

## Second-Level Heading

Second-level headings are centred and bold, with uppercasing used only on the first letter of each word. Font size may be the same as that of the rest of the report. Try to always use more than one second-level heading if you are going to use them following a first-level heading.

## Third-Level Heading

Left-justified, third-level headings should be bold and in the same font size as the rest of the report.

## Fourth-Level Heading

These are left-justified and on the same line as the first sentence in the paragraph. Use bold and same-sized font as the remainder of the report.

## Fifth-Level Headings

These are in bold and are part of sentences. While this is generally the lowest level of outline you use, you can go further by indenting and numbering ideas or italicizing the first word in each item of the list.

Source: Portions of the above adapted from Bovée, C., and Thill, J. (2000). *Business communication today* (6th ed.). Upper Saddle River, NJ: Prentice Hall, p. 499.

# MARKETING RESEARCH IN ACTION 14.2
# Developing Logical Paragraphs

"A **paragraph** is a group of related sentences that focus on one main idea."[a] The first sentence should include a **topic sentence**, which identifies the main idea of the paragraph. For example, "To assess whether college students would subscribe to the e-zine, respondents were asked their likelihood of subscribing to an e-zine directed at college students." Next, the **body of the paragraph** provides the main idea of the topic sentence by giving more information, analysis, or examples. Continuing from the topic sentence example given above, the body of the paragraph might read something like this:

"A description of the student e-zine was read to all respondents. The description was as follows: . . . The respondents were then asked to indicate their likelihood of subscribing by selecting a choice on a five-point response rating scale ranging from 'Very likely to subscribe' to 'Very unlikely to subscribe.' The actual scale was as follows: . . ."

Paragraphs should close with a sentence that signals the end of the topic and indicates where the reader is headed. For example, "How respondents answered the likelihood-to-subscribe scale is discussed in the following two paragraphs." Note that this last sentence contains a **transitional expression**. A transitional expression is a word, or group of words, that tells readers where they are heading. Some examples include *following, next, second, third, at last, finally, in conclusion, to summarize, for example, to illustrate, in addition, so, therefore,* and so on.[b]

Controlling for the **length of paragraphs** should encourage good communication. As a rule, paragraphs should be short. Business communication experts believe most paragraphs should be under or around the 100-word range.[c] This is long enough for the topic sentence and three or four sentences in the body of the paragraph. The paragraph should never cover more than one main topic. For complex topics, break them into several paragraphs.

[a]Ober, S. (1998). *Contemporary business communication* (3rd ed.). Boston: Houghton Mifflin, p. 121.
[b]Ober, S. (1998). *Contemporary business communication* (3rd ed.). Boston: Houghton Mifflin, p. 123.
[c]Bovee, C., and Thill, J. (2000). *Business communication today* (6th ed.). Upper Saddle River, NJ: Prentice Hall, p. 153.

2. Avoid long paragraphs (usually those with more than nine printed lines). Using long paragraphs is a strategy for burying a message, not for communicating.

3. Capitalize on white space. The lines immediately before and immediately after white space (the beginning and the end of a paragraph) are points of emphasis. So are the beginning and the end of a page. Therefore, place more important information at these strategic points.

4. Use jargon sparingly. Some audience members may understand technical terms; others may not. When in doubt, properly define the terms for readers. If many technical terms are required in the report, consider including a glossary of terms in an appendix to assist the less-informed audience members.

5. Use strong verbs to carry the meaning of your sentences. Instead of "making a recommendation," "recommend." Instead of "performing an investigation," "investigate."

6. As a general rule, use the active voice. Voice indicates whether the subject of the verb is doing the action (active voice) or receiving the action (passive voice). For example, "The marketing research was conducted by Judith" uses

the passive voice. "Judith conducted the marketing research" uses the active voice. Active voice is direct and forceful and uses fewer words.

7. Eliminate extra words. Write the message clearly and concisely. Combine and reword sentences. Remove opening fillers and eliminate unnecessary redundancies. Instead of saying "the end results," say "the results."

8. Avoid unnecessary changes in tense. Tense tells if the action of the verb occurred in the past (past tense: *were*), is happening right now (present tense: *are*), or will happen in the future (future tense: *will be*). Changing tenses within a document is an error writers frequently make.

9. In sentences, keep the subject and verb close together. The farther apart they are, the more difficulty the reader has understanding the message and the greater is the chance for errors in subject/verb agreement.

10. Vary the length and structure of sentences and paragraphs.

11. Use faultless grammar. If grammar is in any way below par, take responsibility for finding ways to improve. Poor grammar can result in costly errors and loss of jobs. It can jeopardize the researcher's credibility and the credibility of the research. There is no acceptable excuse for poor grammar.

12. Maintain 2.5-centimetre side margins. If the report will be bound, use a 6.5-centimetre left margin.

13. Use the organization's preference for double or single spacing.

14. Edit carefully. The first draft is not a finished product; neither is the second draft. Edit work carefully, rearranging and rewriting until the intent of the research is communicated as efficiently and effectively as possible. Some authors suggest that as much as 50% of production time should be devoted to improving, editing, correcting, and evaluating an already written document.[7]

15. Proofread! Proofread! Proofread! After finishing, check the document carefully to make sure everything is correct. Double-check names and numbers, grammar, spelling, and punctuation. Although spell-checks and grammar-checks are useful, they cannot catch all errors. One of the best ways to proofread is to read a document aloud, preferably with a reader following along on the original. An alternative is to read the document twice: once for content and meaning and once for mechanical errors. The more important the document, the more time and readers you need to employ for proofreading.

## Using Visuals: Tables and Figures

Visuals assist in the effective presentation of numerical data. The key to a successful visual is a clear and concise presentation that conveys the message of the report. The selection of the visual should match the presentation purpose for the data. Common visuals include the following:[8]

*Tables*, which identify exact values.

*Graphs and charts*, which illustrate relationships among items.

*Pie charts*, which compare a specific part of the whole to the whole.

*Bar charts* and *line graphs*, which compare items over time or show correlations among items.

*Flow diagrams*, which introduce a set of topics and illustrate their relationships.

*Maps*, which define locations.

*Photographs*, which present an aura of legitimacy because they are not "created" in the sense that other visuals are created. Photos depict factual content. *Drawings,* which focus on visual details.

## Tables

Tables allow the reader to compare numerical data. Effective table guidelines are as follows:

1. Do not allow computer analysis to imply a level of accuracy that is not achieved. Limit the use of decimal places (12% or 12.2% instead of 12.223%).
2. Place items the reader needs to compare in the same column, not in the same row.
3. If there are many rows, darken alternate entries, or double-space after every five entries to assist the reader to accurately line up items.
4. Provide totals for columns and rows when relevant.

## Pie Charts

Pie charts are particularly useful for illustrating relative size or static comparisons. The **pie chart** is a circle divided into sections. Each section represents a percentage of the total area of the circle associated with one component. Today's data analysis programs make pie chartseasily and quickly. Marketing Research in Action 14.3 shows how to use XL Data Analyst™ and Excel to make pie charts.

The pie chart should have a limited number of segments (four to six). If the data have many small segments, consider combining the smallest or the least important into an "other" or "miscellaneous" category. Because internal labels are difficult to read for small sections, labels for the sections should be placed outside the circle.

---

## MARKETING RESEARCH IN ACTION 14.3
# How to Make a Pie Chart in Excel

You have collected your data, conducted your analysis using your XL Data Analyst™, and now have the output that you want. If you are like other marketing researchers, you may want to enhance your written report or presentation by using some of the improved graph features on Excel 2007. This Marketing Research in Action will show you step-by-step how to accomplish this goal. First, do a summarization analysis using percentages and request that the XL Data Analyst™ provide a graph. The graph is a pie chart.

Pie charts are useful when:

a. Data total to 100%,
b. You want to visually display proportions or percentages,
c. You do not have so many slices that the chart would be hard to interpret, and
d. You properly label your pie chart and include a legend for the slices.*

*For an excellent in-depth discussion on the use of pie charts, see: Fink, A. (2003). *How to report on surveys.* Thousand Oaks, CA: Sage Publications, pp. 5–9.

| Step in Excel | Illustration |
|---|---|

**Step 1: Use Excel to make an Exploded Pie chart.** Select an XL Data Analyst Summarize-Percents table and insert the pie chart. Be sure that you have correctly set up the value codes and the value labels. Here is the pie chart that is generated using the data set percent summarization analysis with the variable, "Primary vehicle price type."

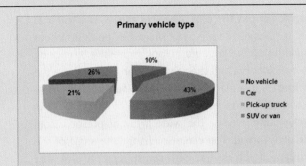

**Step 2: Change the pie chart.** If you want to change the pie chart type or use some other type of graph for this chart, click on the graph to activate it, and then use the Chart tools menu to open up the chart options. With the Design menu on, click on Change Chart Type to open up a menu of options. You can select any one of these displayed on the scrolling window menu for your chart. Of course some chart types, such as line charts, are not appropriate for a percentage summarization table.

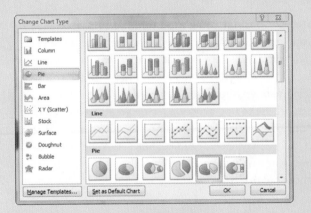

**Step 3: Make the pie slices look much better.** Assuming that the exploded pie chart is your choice, you can change the appearance of the slices. Just click on any one slice. Then left-click and choose "Format Data Series" to open up the Format Data Series Options window. The 3-D format option will assist you in choosing a bevel (the edge of each pie slice) and the material (texture or smooth surface) for the slices. Here, we have chosen the circle bevel for the top and bottom of the slices, and the metal material display.

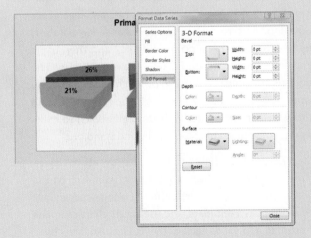

*(Continued)*

| Step in Excel | Illustration |
| --- | --- |

**Step 4: Format the plot area.** The plot area is the area that surrounds the pie chart slices. It is quite simple to make this part of your graph look impressive by clicking on the plot area and then right-clicking to bring up the Format Plot Area options. Here you can use Fill— Gradient fill, and then use the preset colors to select the background. Notice the wide array of preset colors available to you. You can also change the angle of the gradient. If you do not wish to use a preset plot area color, you can experiment with your own color and gradient stops.

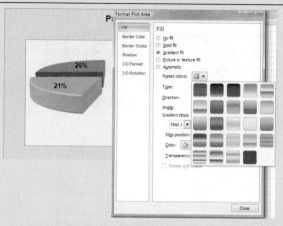

**Step 5: Consider using a picture file to personalize your graph.** Click on the outer chart area and then right-click and select Format Chart Area. The options are identical to those in step 4, and we chose to use "Picture or texture fill." By clicking the "File" button, you can browse to find a picture file on your personal computer. The picture in this example is a stock image that comes with Microsoft Office, but you could use your own photos, graphics from a website, or any other photo file that is appropriate.

**Step 6: Enhance the chart title, legend, and plot area.** If you used a picture or changed the chart area background, it is possible that the chart title and legend are now difficult to read. Both can be enhanced (separately) by selecting them via point-and-click and then using Format Chart Title or Format Legend Menus. The options are similar to those in other chart format menu windows. Of course, you can also use any of Excel's many format options (3-D, shadow, glow, etc.) to make aspects of your graph, title, and legend stand out.

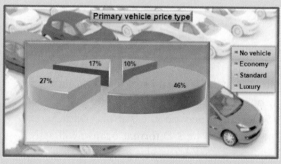

**Step 7: Save your chart as a template for future charts.** If you have a chart appearance that you want to use consistently in your report or presentation, you can save this format as a template, and use Excel's chart template feature to apply it to each of the XL Data Analyst's basic pie charts.

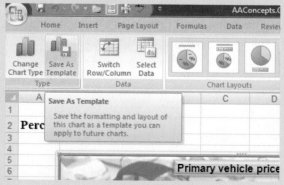

## Bar Charts

Several types of **bar charts** can be used and several different types are available in Excel. Bar charts are often used in reports because they present data in a way that is easily interpreted. They are also excellent for oral presentations. Specific keystroke instructions for making bar or column charts using XL Data Analyst™ and Excel are given in Marketing Research in Action 14.4.

**MARKETING RESEARCH IN ACTION 14.4**
# How to Make a Bar Chart in Excel

You have collected your data, conducted your analysis using your XL Data Analyst™, and you now have the output that you want. You may want to enhance your written or oral report with a figure in the form of a bar chart. Bar charts are often used in marketing research reports because they are easily interpreted. Consider using them when:

a.   You wish to display data on an *x*-axis and *y*-axis, and/or
b.   You want to compare groups or illustrate changes over time.

When you have a limited number of bars (six or less), use a vertical bar chart (called a *Column* chart in Excel). When you have seven or more bars, consider a horizontal bar chart (called a *Bar* chart in Excel). Finally, you should properly label your bar chart.

For our example we want to compare the averages of beliefs about hybrid vehicles' effects on gasoline prices, fuel emissions, and global warming.

## Steps in Making a Bar Chart in Excel

| Step in Excel | Illustration |
| --- | --- |
| **Step 1: Make a basic bar chart.** With your cursor, select the statements and averages in the XL Data Analyst table that results. Then use Excel's Insert menu to select the type of column chart you want to use. We used the 2-D column option. This will generate a basic bar chart. | 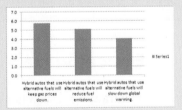 |
| **Step 2: Use "Chart Tools Design-Change Chart Type" to select a better bar chart appearance.** There are several options for bar-, cylinder-, or pyramid-shaped charts. We have selected the "clustered cylinder" one. | 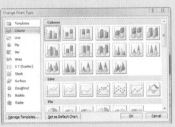 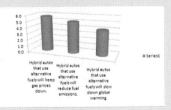 |

(Continued)

**Step 3: Use chart appearance features to greatly improve the appearance of your bars.** The "Design" tab opens with a great many Chart Styles options for the appearance of the bars in your graph. Some options provide for a dark or greyed plot background. Note that we have selected and applied the 3-D beveled metallic green appearance for the cylinders.

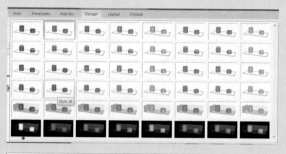

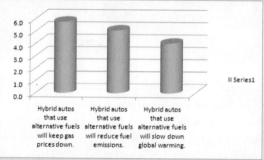

**Step 4: Use Excel's Chart features to create a professional final bar chart.** There are many enhancements available for backgrounds, fonts, labels, and other aspects of Excel charts. These enhancements are available on practically all Excel charts and you can use them to create a professional-quality final bar chart, such as the one shown here.

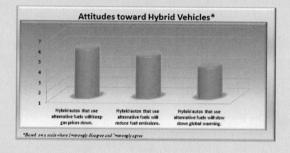

# Ethical Visuals

A marketing researcher should always follow the doctrine of full disclosure. An **ethical visual** is one that is totally objective in terms of how information is presented in the research report. Sometimes misrepresenting information is intentional (as when a client asks a researcher to misrepresent the data in order to promote his or her "pet project") or it may be unintentional. In the latter case, those preparing a visual are sometimes so familiar with the material being presented that they falsely assume that the graphic message is apparent to all who view it.

To ensure that visuals are objectively and ethically prepared, do the following:

1. Double- and triple-check all labels, numbers, and visual shapes. A faulty or misleading visual discredits the report and work.
2. Exercise caution if three-dimensional figures are used. They may distort the data by multiplying the value by the width and the height.
3. Make sure all parts of the scales are presented. Truncated graphs (having breaks in the scaled values on either axis) are acceptable only if the audience is familiar with the data.

# Presenting Research Orally

Often researchers are asked to present an oral summary of the recommendations and conclusions of the research. The purpose of the **oral presentation** is to present the information succinctly and to provide an opportunity for questions and discussion. The presentation may be accomplished through a simple conference with the client, or it may be a formal presentation to a roomful of people. In any case, says Jerry W. Thomas, CEO of Decision Analyst, research reports should "be presented orally to all key people in the same room at the same time." He believes this is important because many people do not read the research report and others may not understand all the details of the report. "An oral presentation ensures that everyone can ask questions to allow the researchers to clear up any confusion."[9] It also ensures that everyone hears the same thing.

The Interactive Advertising Bureau (IAB) of Canada conducts its Canadian Media Optimization Study (CMOST) annually, to research trends in Canadian media usage. The results are presented to marketers in Montreal and Toronto as part of Advertising Week. To view the PowerPoint presentation slides used to present the research orally, visit the IAB website: **www.iabcanada.com/resources/ CanMedUsageTrends_IABTotalCanada_ExecSumFINAL.ppt**

To be adequately prepared when presenting research orally, follow these steps:

1. Identify and analyze the audience. Consider the same questions addressed at the beginning of the research process and at the beginning of this chapter.
2. Find out the expectations the audience has for the presentation. Is the presentation formal or informal? Does the audience expect an electronic slide show?
3. Determine the key points the audience needs to hear.
4. Outline the key points, preferably on 3-inch $\times$ 5-inch index cards for quick reference.
5. Present points succinctly and clearly. The written report will serve as a reference for further reading.
6. Make sure visuals portray key points graphically and ethically.
7. Practise the presentation. Be comfortable with what will be said. The more prepared one is and the better one feels about oneself, the less need to worry about jitters.
8. Check out the room and media equipment prior to the presentation.
9. If relying on an electronic device such as a computer and projector for display of PowerPoint slides, it is always a good idea to have a backup such as overhead transparencies.
10. Arrive early.
11. Be positive and confident. Remember, the presenter knows more about the subject than anyone else does.
12. Speak loudly enough for all in the room to hear. Enunciate clearly. Maintain eye contact and good posture. Dress appropriately.

## Presenting Research to the Public (Online and to the Media)

Many research results are highly newsworthy because of the nature of the topic being researched. Of particular interest are the results of political polls and those reporting on attitudes toward controversial issues. With media hunger for news, and with the rise of online reporting, it is even more important to maintain high ethical standards when releasing research findings to the public on such topics. It is important to maintain high ethical standards when releasing such information to the public. Ethics in Marketing Research 14.1 outlines the MRIA's standards for the release of marketing research results to the public.

# ETHICS IN MARKETING RESEARCH 14.1
# The MRIA's Standards for the Public Release of Marketing Research Results

Members of the MRIA all have in common the single goal of encouraging excellence in the conduct of marketing, social, and opinion research in Canada and elsewhere. In addition, the MRIA promotes the responsible use of research for decision making in the public and corporate domains and works to increase public understanding of research methods.

In order to preserve public confidence in public opinion research—a science of mutual importance to the media and market research industries—please consider our following recommendations before releasing survey data to the public:

1. Please include the following key facts in the report:
   - Sample size, and population surveyed (who was included)
   - Sponsor of study (who commissioned the research)
   - Survey method (e.g., telephone, online, intercept)
   - Timing (when the survey was done)
   - Statement of sample error/margin of error (e.g., "±2.5% 19 times out of 20")
2. Please make the following facts available to the public upon request (if not included in report):
   - Name of practitioner (company conducting research)
   - Sampling method (e.g. random, custom list)
   - Weighting procedures (statistical weights, if used)
   - Exact wording and order of questions

3. Always differentiate between scientific (most public opinion polls) and nonscientific studies (reader/viewer polls or other "self-selection" methodologies).
4. Where appropriate, use the caveat that research is not necessarily predictive of future outcomes but rather captures opinion at one point in time.

## Additional Standards for Reporting on Qualitative Research

Additional considerations should be adhered to when reporting on qualitative research observations (such as focus groups, or other small sample in-depth research).

5. Clearly defined recruiting specifications (i.e., product usage, party affiliation, specific demographic specifications, etc.)
6. Inclusion of statement of nonprojectability. Results of qualitative research are not statistically projectable to the population at large.
7. Qualitative reporting should not include percentages or precise proportions. Expressions such as *some*, *most*, or *a few*, may be used.

Source: MRIA website, **www.mria-arim.ca/STANDARDS/ PublishResultsENG.asp**

# Summary

**1. Articulate the importance of the marketing research report.**

The final stage of the marketing research process is the preparation and presentation of the marketing research report. The marketing research report is a factual message that transmits research results, vital recommendations, conclusions, and other important information to the client, who, in turn, bases his or her decision on the contents of the report. The report-writing and presentation stage is a very important stage of the marketing research process. This importance is attributed to the fact that regardless of the care taken in the design and execution of the research project itself, if the report does not adequately communicate the project to the client, all of the effort has been to no purpose. In most cases, the report is the only part of the research process actually seen by the client.

Marketing research reports should be tailored to their audiences. Reports are typically organized into the categories of front matter, body, and end matter. Each of these categories has subparts, with each subpart having a different purpose. Conclusions are based on the results of the research, and recommendations are suggestions based on conclusions.

**2. Follow guidelines for writing effective marketing research reports.**

Guidelines for writing the marketing research report include proper use of headings and subheadings, which serve as signposts and signals to the reader, and proper use of visuals such as tables and figures. Style considerations include understanding the structure of paragraphs, sparse use of jargon, strong verbs, active voice, consistent tense, conciseness, and varied sentence structure and length. Editing and proofreading, preferably by reading the report aloud, are important steps in preparing the research report. Care should be taken to ensure that all presentations are clear and objective to the reader.

Report writers should understand the effective use of visuals such as tables and figures. Pie charts and bar charts can be used effectively to aid in communicating research results in a report. This chapter contains specific keystroke instructions on building pie charts and bar charts using XL Data Analyst™ and Excel. Many visual aids may be distorted so that they have a different meaning to the reader. This means that ethical considerations must be made in the preparation of the research report.

**3. Review guidelines for effectively presenting marketing research.**

In cases where research is made publically available, ethical guidelines should be followed to ensure honest and unbiased reporting.

In cases where marketing researchers are required to present the findings of their research project orally to the client, guidelines include knowing the audience, its expectations, and the key points to be made; correctly preparing visuals; practising; checking out presentation facilities and equipment prior to the presentation; having backup systems; and being positive.

# Key Terms

Abstract/executive summary  (p. 469)
Appendices  (p. 471)
Bar charts  (p. 479)
Body  (p. 470)

Conclusions  (p. 471)
Digital Dashboard  (p. 464)
End matter  (p. 471)
Ethical visual  (p. 480)

# Review Questions

**1.1** Discuss the relative importance of the marketing research report to the other stages of the marketing research process.

**2.1** Assume you have conducted a marketing research project for your school. You were asked to provide a descriptive study of the student population. You collected demographic information and information on student attitudes toward various campus services and student-life activities. Write a title page for the report.

**2.2** Go online and find three examples of marketing research reports. Compare them and describe:

- common sections,
- issues discussed in each section,
- information included in the methodology section,
- ways in which results were reported, and
- how recommendations differed from conclusions.

**2.3** Discuss challenges that marketing researchers face when reporting marketing research to the public (online or through the media).

**2.4** Using XL Data Analyst™ and Excel, prepare a pie chart and a bar chart from any data you have. How can you ensure that your charts represent the data ethically?

**3.1** You are asked to present your research findings to the executive of the company that hired you to do the research. The meeting will take place in the company boardroom with a total of six people, including you. Outline what you will do to plan this presentation. Describe in detail what the presentation will look like. What materials do you intend to bring? Give reasons for your choices.

# Case 14.1 YOUR INTEGRATED CASE

# Student Life E-Zine

## Organizing the Report

With all data collected and the analysis nearly completed, Bob Watts started working on the final report. He knew the report itself would be the instrument that would bear the burden of properly communicating the results of the months-long research project. Bob was very concerned about writing a report that Don, Sarah, Anna, and Wesley could easily read and understand.

Bob's first thoughts in preparing the report concerned proper organization. He had several options.

- **Organizing by Questionnaire Questions.** First, he could follow the questionnaire, making each separate question a separate division of the report. In fact, the questions themselves could serve as headings for each section. All the parties involved were thoroughly familiar with the questionnaire, and this familiarity could be an asset in organizing the report.
- **Organizing by Research Objective.** Bob considered a second alternative for organization: grouping questions in terms of a common research objective. For example, consider the following research objective: "To gather data reflecting potential adopters' purchases of selected products and services." Data for the questions dealing with purchases or planned purchases of soft drinks, restaurants, pizza delivery, automobiles, and so on could be organized under this research objective.

- **Organizing by Importance of Topic.** The most important topic in the survey deals with the likelihood that students will actually subscribe to the e-zine. Perhaps some of the less important questions deal with demographic issues such as age or gender.

## Questions

1. Write down the first five headings you would use in your report if you organized your paper by each one of the three methods Bob Watts is considering.
2. Which method of organization do you think Watts should use? Why?

# Case 14.2 YOUR INTEGRATED CASE

# Student Life E-Zine

## Appropriate Visuals

Bob Watts examined the questionnaire used to collect data in the Student Life E-Zine project (see Chapter 8, pages 287 to 290). His thoughts were now concerned with the choice of the appropriate visuals to use. Look back at the questionnaire and consider the following questions: (a) Do you have internet access? (b) What type of internet connection do you have where you live? (c) If you do purchase over the internet, please tell us how you allocate your expenditures. (d) If the subscription price for this e-zine was $15 per month for a minimum of 6 months, how likely would you be to subscribe to it? (e) All of the questions dealing with preferences for different types of features (i.e., Campus Calendar, Course/Instructor Evaluator, etc.). (f) Year born? (g) GPA. (h) Respondent's university.

## Questions

1. For each of the questions identified in the case, which visual, if any, do you believe Bob Watts should select?
2. Provide a justfication for your choice of visuals.
3. Are there any questions for which you believe multiple visuals should be used?
4. Can you identify some ethical issues that could arise in terms of how an entrepreneur could use visuals to represent survey data to potential investors or bankers?

## Case 14.3 YOUR INTEGRATED CASE

# Student Life E-Zine

### PowerPoint Presentations

Back in his office at ORS, Bob Watts was putting the final touches on the Student Life E-Zine project. He felt very pleased with the report, and now he was beginning to think about making an oral presentation. He wanted to begin the "Survey Results" part of the presentation with the question he felt was most important to the project: the one asking potential respondents about their likelihood of subscribing to the e-zine. He felt he should start to prepare for the oral presentation by writing out his notes on the results of that question and by preparing a PowerPoint slide to present the survey data on this question.

### Questions

1. Using Word, write out several of the statements that you think would be appropriate for an oral presentation to the four clients.

2. Import the statements you prepared in question 1 into PowerPoint by using copy and paste. Experiment with different text colours, font sizes, and styles.

3. Using your XL Data Analyst™ program, run a frequency distribution on the likelihood-to-subscribe question.

4. Using XL Data Analyst™, make a bar chart showing the percentage responses to each category in the question. Import the bar chart into PowerPoint.

# Endnotes

## Chapter 1

1. Bakker, G. (2003, January). Building knowledge about the consumer: The emergence of market research in the motion picture industry. Industry Overview. *Business History*, vol. 45, no. 1, p. 101 (29).

2. **www.CRA.org**, Regulations, Code of Ethics.

3. Vargo, S. L., and Lusch, R. F. (2004). *Journal of Marketing*, vol. 68, no. 1, pp. 1–17.

4. Drucker, P. (1973). *Management: Tasks, responsibilities, practices.* New York: Harper & Row, pp. 64–65.

5. Kotler, P. (2003). *Marketing management* (11th ed.). Upper Saddle River, NJ: Prentice Hall, p. 19.

6. **www.mria-arim.ca**, About the MRIA.

7. Bennett, P. D. (Ed.) (1995). *Dictionary of marketing terms* (2nd ed.). Chicago: American Marketing Association/NTC Books, p. 165.

8. Merritt, N. J., and Redmond, W. H. (1990). Defining marketing research: Perceptions vs. practice. *Proceedings: American Marketing Association*, pp. 146–150.

9. Clancy, K., and Krieg, P. C. (2000). *Counterintuitive marketing: Achieve great results using uncommon sense.* New York: Free Press.

10. Tracy, K. (1998). *Jerry Seinfeld: The entire domain.* Secaucus, NJ: Carol Publishing Group, pp. 64–65.

11. Marconi, J. (1998, June 8). What marketing aces do when marketing research tells them, "don't do it!" *Marketing News*. Also see Zangwill, W. (1993, March 8). When customer research is a lousy idea. *Wall Street Journal*, A12.

12. Heilbrunn, J. (1989, August). Legal lessons from the Delicare affair—1. United States, *Marketing and Research Today*, vol. 17, no. 3, pp. 156–160. Also see Frederickson, P., and Totten, J.W. (1990). Marketing research projects in the academic setting: Legal liability after Beecham vs. Yankelovich, in Capello, L. M., et al., (Eds.), *Progress in marketing thought: Proceedings of the Southern Marketing Association*, pp. 250–253.

13. See **www.Mintel.com**.

14. Scientific research pumps up new products: The benefits of health and wellness ingredients. (2003, March). *Stagnito's New Products Magazine*, vol. 3, no. 3, p. 30.

15. **www.howardforums.com/showthread.php/80169-Cosmic-moment-inspires-Telus-animal-ad-campaign**

16. Bruzzone, D., and Rosen, D. (2001, March). All the right moves. *Quirk's Marketing Research Review*, vol. 15, no. 3, pp. 56–76.

17. The description of the MIS is adapted from Kotler, P. (1997). *Marketing management: Analysis, planning, implementation, and control* (9th ed.). Upper Saddle River, NJ: Prentice Hall, 100ff.

18. **www.mria-arim.ca**, About the MRIA, Objectives/Mission.

19. Bartels, R. (1976). *The history of marketing thought* (2nd ed.). Columbus, OH: Grid, Inc., pp. 124–125.

20. Hardy, H. (1990). *The Politz papers: Science and truth in marketing research.* Chicago: American Marketing Association.

21. A.B. Blankenship, C. Chakrapani, & W. H. Poole. The History of Marketing Research in Canada, **HIS1269** Professional Marketing Research Society, Toronto, 1985.

22. **www.mria-arim.ca**, Research Buyers Guide.

23. Honomichl, J. (2006, June 15). Mixed bag of revenue growth.

24. Honomichl, J. (2006, August 15). No great growth. *Marketing News*, H3.

25. Malhotra, N. K. (1999). *Marketing research* (3rd ed.). Upper Saddle River, NJ: Prentice Hall, pp. 16–19.

26. Kinnear, T. C., and Root, A. R. (1994). *Survey of marketing research: Organization function, budget, and compensation.* Chicago: American Marketing Association, p. 38.

27. Opinion Research Corporation. (2001, August 27). *Marketing News*, 5.

28. Honomichl, J. (2003, June 9). Honomichl top 50, Company Profiles, Synovate. *Marketing News*, H6, H8.

29. These examples and the following paragraphs are based upon: Mahajan, V., and Wind, J. (1999, Fall). Rx for marketing research: A diagnosis of and prescriptions for recovery of an ailing discipline in the business world. *Marketing Research*, pp. 7–13.

30. **www.mediaincanada.com/articles/mic/20090327/marketing survey.html**

31. Clancy, K., and Krieg, P. C. (2000). Counterintuitive marketing: Achieve great results using uncommon sense. New York: Free Press.

32. Krum, J. R. (1978, October). B for marketing research departments. *Journal of Marketing*, vol. 42, pp. 8–12; Krum, J. R., Rau, P. A., and Keiser, S. K. (1987–1988, December–January). The marketing research process: Role perceptions of researchers and users. *Journal of Advertising Research*, vol. 27, pp. 9–21; Dawson, S., Bush, R. F., and Stern, B. (1994, October). An evaluation of services provided by the marketing research industry. *Service Industries Journal*, vol. 14, no. 4, pp. 515–526; also see Austin, J. R. (1991). An exploratory examination of the development of marketing research service relationships: An assessment of exchange evaluation dimensions. In M. C. Gilly, et al. (Eds.), *Enhancing knowledge development in marketing*, pp. 133–141, 1991 AMA Educators' Conference Proceedings; also see Swan, J. E., Trawick, I. F., and Carroll, M. G. (1981, August). Effect of participation in marketing research on consumer attitudes toward research and satisfaction with a service. *Journal of Marketing Research*, pp. 356–363; also see Malholtra, N. K., Peterson, M., and Kleiser, S. B. (1999, Spring). Marketing research: A state-of-the-art review and directions for the 21st century. *Journal of the Academy of Marketing Science*, vol. 27, no. 2, pp. 160–183.

33. What's wrong with marketing research? (2001, Winter). *Marketing Research*, vol. 13, no. 4.

34. Dawson, S., Bush, R. F., and Stern, B. (1994, October). An evaluation of services provided by the market research industry. *Service Industries Journal*, 144, pp. 515–526.

35. Bernstein, S. (1990, September). A call to audit market research providers. *Marketing Research*, vol. 2, no. 3, pp. 11–16.

36. Reidman, P. (2001, January 29). ABCi alliance begins. *Advertising Age*, vol. 72, no. 5, p. 38.

37. **www.mria-arim.ca**, VoxPox.

38. Kiecker, P. L., and Nelson, J. E. (1989). Cheating behavior by telephone interviewers: A view from the trenches. In P. Bloom, et al. (Eds.), *Enhancing knowledge development in marketing*, pp. 182–188. AMA Educators' Conference Proceedings.

39. **www.mria-arim.ca**, About the MRIA, Objectives/Mission.

40. **www.payscale.com/research/CA/Industry=Market_Research/Salary**

41. **www.payscale.com/research/CA/Industry=Market_Research/Salary**

42. **www.payscale.com/research/CA/Job=Marketing_Research_ Analyst/Salary**

## Chapter 2

1. Adapted from Adler, L. (1979, September 17). Secrets of when, and when not to embark on a marketing research project. *Sales & Marketing Management Magazine*, vol. 123, p. 108.

2. Adapted from Adler, L. (1979, September 17). Secrets of when, and when not to embark on a marketing research project. *Sales & Marketing Management Magazine*, vol. 123, 108.

3. The operative product word: Ambitiousness. (1996, December 21). *Advertising Age*, p. 14; Murtaugh, P. (1998, May). Consumer research: The big lie. *Food & Beverage Marketing*, p. 16; and Parasuraman, A., Grewal, D., and Krishnan R. (2004). *Marketing Research*. Boston: Houghton Mifflin, pp. 41–42.

4. Koten, J., and Kilman, S. (1985, July 15). Marketing classic: How Coke's decision to offer 2 colas undid 41/2 years of planning. *Wall Street Journal*, p. 1.

5. Personal communication with the authors by Lawrence D. Gibson. Also see: Gibson, L. D. (1998, Spring). Defining marketing problems: Don't spin your wheels solving the wrong puzzle. *Marketing Research*, vol. 10, no. 4, pp. 5–12.

6. Gibson, L. D. (1998, Spring). Defining marketing problems: Don't spin your wheels solving the wrong puzzle. *Marketing Research*, vol. 10, no. 4, p. 7.

7. Retrieved from **www.Dictionary.com** on November 13, 2003.

8. Kotler, P. (2003). *Marketing management: Analysis, planning, implementing, and control* (11th ed.). Upper Saddle River, NJ: Prentice Hall, p. 102.

9. For example, see: Gordon, G. L., Schoenbachler, D. D., Kaminski, P. F., and Brouchous, K. A. (1997). New product development: Using the salesforce to identify opportunities. *Business and Industrial Marketing*, vol. 12, no. 1, p. 33; and Ardjchvilj, A., Cardozo, R., and Ray, S. (2003, January). A theory of entrepreneurial opportunity identification and development. *Journal of Business Venturing*, vol. 18, no. 1, p. 105.

10. Personal communication with the authors by Lawrence D. Gibson. Also see: Gibson, L. D. (1998, Spring). Defining marketing problems: Don't spin your wheels solving the wrong puzzle. *Marketing Research*, vol. 10, no. 4, pp. 5–12.

11. Gibson, L. D. (1998, Spring). Defining marketing problems: Don't spin your wheels solving the wrong puzzle. *Marketing Research*, vol. 10, no. 4, p. 5.

12. For example, see: Tomas, S. (1999, May). Creative problem-solving: An approach to generating ideas. *Hospital Material Management Quarterly*, vol. 20, no. 4, pp. 33–45.

13. Kotler, P. (2003). *Marketing management: Analysis, planning, implementing, and control* (11th ed.). Upper Saddle River, NJ: Prentice Hall, p. 103.

14. Semon, T. (1999, June 7). Make sure the research will answer the right question. *Marketing News*, vol. 33, no. 12, p. H30.

15. Insights based on 30 years of defining the problem and research objectives in Burns, A.C. and Bush, R. F. (2006). *Marketing Research*, 5th edition. Upper Saddle River, NJ: Pearson Prentice Hall, pp. 92–93.

16. Dictionary, American Marketing Association. Retrieved from **www.marketingpower.com** on December 10, 2003.

17. Adapted from **Dictionary.com**. Retrieved on November 15, 2003. Also see Bagozzi, R. P., Phillips, L. W. (1982, September). Representing and testing organizational theories: A holistic construal. *Administrative Science Quarterly*, vol. 27, no. 3, p. 459.

## Chapter 3

1. Singleton, D. (2003, November 24). Basics of good research involve understanding six simple rules. *Marketing News*, pp. 22–23.

2. For an excellent in-depth treatment of research design issues, see Creswell, J. (2003). *Research design: Qualitative, quantitative, and mixed methods approaches*. Thousand Oaks, CA: Sage Publications.

3. http://en.wikipedia.org/wiki/1-800-GOT-JUNK%3F

4. Stewart, D. W. (1984). *Secondary research: Information sources and methods*. Newbury Park, CA: Sage Publications; and Davidson, J. P. (1985, April). Low cost research sources. *Journal of Small Business Management*, vol. 23, pp. 73–77.

5. Knox, N. (2003, December 16). Volvo teams up to build what women want. *USA Today*, p. 1B.

6. Bonoma, T. V. Case research in marketing: Opportunities, problems, and a process. *Journal of Marketing Research*, vol. 22, pp. 199–208.

7. Myers, J. Wireless for the 21st century. *Telephony*, vol. 231, no. 6, pp. 24–26.

8. Greenbaum, T. I. (1988). *The practical handbook and guide infocus group research*. Lexington, MA: D.C. Heath.

9. Stoltman, J. J., and Gentry, J. W. (1992). Using focus groups to study household decision processes and choices. In R. P. Leone and V. Kumar (Eds.), *AMA Educator's Conference proceedings. Vol. 3: Enhancing knowledge development in marketing*, pp. 257–263. Chicago: American Marketing Association.

10. Dictionary. American Marketing Association. Retrieved from **www.marketingpower.com** on December 16, 2003.

11. **www.cbc.ca/marketplace/2009/credit_card_catch/-poll.html**

12. **www.tns-cf.com/news/TNS-CCI-brochure.pdf**

13. Lohse, G. L., and Rosen, D. L. (2002, Summer). Signaling quality and credibility in Yellow Pages advertising: The influence of color and graphics on choice. *Journal of Advertising*, vol. 30, no. 2, pp. 73–85.

14. Campbell, D. T., and Stanley, J. C. (1963). *Experimental and quasi-experimental designs for research*. Chicago: Rand McNally.

15. Gray, L. R., and Diehl, P. L. (1992). *Research methods for business and management*. New York: Macmillan, pp. 387–390.

16. Doyle, J. (1994, October). In with the new, out with the old. *Beverage World*, vol. 113, no. 1576, pp. 204–205.

17. Brennan, L. (1988, March). Test marketing. *Sales Marketing Management Magazine*, vol. 140, pp. 50–62.

18. Miles, S. (2001, January 17). MyTurn is cutting back in unusual way. *Wall Street Journal*, Eastern edition.

19. Churchill, G. A., Jr. (2001). *Basic marketing research* (4th ed.). Fort Worth, TX: Dryden Press, pp. 144–145.

20. Clancy, K. J., and Shulman, R. S. (1995, October). Test for success. *Sales & Marketing Management Magazine*, vol. 147, no. 10, pp. 111–115.

21. Melvin, P. (1992, September). Choosing simulated test marketing systems. *Marketing Research*, vol. 4, no. 3, pp. 14–16.

22. Blount, S. (1992, March). It's just a matter of time. *Sales & Marketing Management*, vol. 144, no. 3, pp. 32–43.

23. Power, C. (1992, August 10). Will it sell in Podunk? Hard to say. *Business Week*, pp. 46–47.

24. Nelson, E. (2001, February 2). Colgate's net rose 10 percent in period, new products helped boost sales. *Wall Street Journal*, Eastern edition, p. B6.

25. Ihlwan, M. (2002, February 4). A nation of digital guinea pigs: Korea is a hotbed of such experiments as a cash-free city. *Business Week*, p. 50.

26. Kotler, P. (1991). *Marketing management: Analysis, planning, implementation, and control*. Upper Saddle River, NJ: Prentice Hall, p. 335.

27. Power, C. (1992, August 10). Will it sell in Podunk? Hard to say. *Business Week*, pp. 46–47.

28. Murphy, P., and Laczniak, G. (1992, June). Emerging ethical issues facing marketing researchers. *Marketing Research*, 6.

29. Saab plots device that detects early stages of tiredness. (2007, November 8) *Marketing Week, London*. Retrieved August 6, 2008 from ProQuest.

30. Ebenkamp, B. (2008, June 2). What can you do with a dollar? Go e.l.f. yourself. *Brandweek*, vol. 49, p. 22. Retrieved August 6, 2008 from ProQuest.

31. Wapshott, Nicholas (2008, April 14). My baby maybe. *New Statesman*, 137, 4892, p. 20. Retrieved August 27, 2008 fromProQuest.

32. Walkup, C. and Martin, R. (2007, October 15). McD thirsts for $1B in new beverage sales. *Nation's Restaurant News*, p. 41. Retrieved August 6, 2008 from ProQuest; Weird Facts. (2008, August 5). McDonald's tests changes. Retrieved August 6, 2008 from **weirdfactshere.blogspot.com/2008/08/mcdonalds-tests-changes-weird-facts.html.**

## Chapter 4

1. For a comparison of three search engines see: **www.lib.berkeley.edu/TeachingLib/Guides/Internet/SearchEngines.html.**

2. Ritchie, K. (2002). *Marketing to generation X*. New York: Simon and Schuster.

3. Kotler, P. (2003). *Marketing management* (11th ed.), Upper Saddle River, NJ: Prentice Hall, p. 53.

4. Senn, J. A. (1988). *Information technology in business: Principles, practice, and opportunities*. Upper Saddle River,NJ: Prentice Hall, p. 66.

5. Grisaffe, D. (2002, January 21). See about linking CRM and MR systems. *Marketing News*, vol. 36, no. 2, p. 13.

6.  www.mria-arim.ca/Education/DataMining.asp

7.  www.andersonanalytics.com/index.php?mact=News, cntnt01,detail,0&cntnt01articleid=52&cntnt01origid=16 &cntnt01detailtemplate=newsdetail.tpl&cntnt01dateformat= %m.%d.%Y&cntnt01returnid=46

8.  Lewis, L. (1996, November). Retailers begin tracking consumer purchases and recording consumer preferences and demographic data. *Progressive Grocer*, vol. 75, no. 11, p. 18.

9.  McKim, R. (2001, September). Privacy notices: What they mean and how marketers can prepare for them. *Journal of Database Marketing*, vol. 9, no. 1, pp. 79–84.

10.  See, for example, U.S. *Industrial Outlook 1999*. (1999). Washington, DC: International Trade Administration, U.S. Department of Commerce.

11.  These questions and much of the following discussion is taken from Stewart, D. W. (1984). *Secondary Research: Information Sources and Methods*. Newbury Park, CA: Sage.

12.  www.strategicbusinessinsights.com

13.  The information in this section was edited by Ms. Shelley L. Hughes, IRI, and communicated to the authors on January 15, 2009. Also see: Custom store tracking (2004). Retrieved on January 10, 2004 from **www.infores.com.**

## Chapter 5

1.  Ezzy, D. (2001, August). Are qualitative methods misunderstood? *Australian and New Zealand Journal of Public Health*, vol. 25, no. 4, pp. 294–297.

2.  Clark, A. (2001, September 13). Research takes an inventive approach, *Marketing*, pp. 25–26.

3.  DeNicola, N. (2002, March 4). Casting finer net not necessary. *Marketing News*, vol. 36, no. 5, p. 46.

4.  For some guidelines to direct observation, see Becker, B. (1999, September 27). Take direct route when data-gathering. *Marketing News*, vol. 33, no. 20, pp. 29, 31.

5.  Piirto, R. (1991, September). Socks, ties and videotape. *American Demographics*, p. 6.

6.  Fellman, M. W. (1999, Fall). Breaking tradition. *Marketing Research*, vol. 11, no. 3, pp. 20, 34.

7.  Modified from Tull, D. S. and Hawkins, D. I. (1987). *Marketing Research* (4th ed.), New York: Macmillan, p. 331.

8.  Rust, L. (1993, November/December). How to reach children in stores: Marketing tactics grounded in observational research. *Journal of Advertising Research*, vol. 33, no. 6, pp. 67–72; and Rust, L. (1993, July/August). Parents and children shopping together: A new approach to the qualitative analysis of observational data. *Journal of Advertising Research*, vol. 33, no. 4, pp. 65–70.

9.  Viles, P. (1992, August 24). Company measures listenership in cars. *Broadcasting*, vol. 122, no. 35, p. 28.

10.  Kephart, P. (1996, May). The spy in aisle 3. *American Demographics Marketing Tools*, **www.marketingtools.com/ Publications/MT/96_mt/9605MD04.htm.**

11.  http://brandsavant.com/social-media-monitoring-201- the-market-research-perspective/

12.  Last, J. and Langer, J. (2003, December). Still a valuable tool. *Quirk's Marketing Research Review*, vol. 17, no. 11, p. 30.

13.  Kahn, A. (1996, September 6). Focus groups alter decisions made in business, politics. *Knight-Ridder/Tribune Business News*, p. 916.

14.  Wellner, A. (2003, March). The new science of focus groups. *American Demographics*, vol. 25, no. 2, p. 29ff.

15.  Langer, J. (2001). *The Mirrored Window: Focus Groups from aModerator's Viewpoint*. New York: Paramount Market Publishing, p. 4.

16.  Greenbaum, T. L. (1993, March 1). Focus group research is not a commodity business. *Marketing News*, vol. 27, no. 5, p. 4.

17.  Greenbaum, T. L. (1991, May 27). Answer to moderator problems starts with asking right questions. *Marketing News*, vol. 25, no. 11, pp. 8–9; and Fern, E. F. (1982, February). The use of focus groups for idea generation: The effects of group size, acquaintanceship, and moderator on response quantity and quality. *Journal of Marketing Research*, pp. 1–13.

18.  Based on Henderson, N. R. (2000, December). Secrets of our success: Insights from a panel of moderators. *Quirk's Marketing Research Review*, vol. 14, no. 11, pp. 62–65.

19.  Zinchiak, M. (2001, July/August). Online focus groups FAQs. *Quirk's Marketing Research Review*, vol. 15, no. 7, pp. 38–46.

20.  Adapted from Zinchiak, Online focus group FAQs.

21.  Lonnie, K. (2001, November 19). Combine phone, Web for focus groups. *Marketing News*, vol. 35, no. 24, pp. 15–16.

22.  For interesting comments, see DeNicola, N. and Kennedy, S. (2001, November 19). Quality inter(net)action. *Marketing News*, vol. 35, no. 24, p. 14.

23.  Jarvis, S. and Szynal, D. (2001, November 19). Show and tell. *Marketing News*, vol. 35, no. 24, pp. 1, 13.

24.  Hines, T. (2000). An evaluation of two qualitative methods (focus group interviews and cognitive maps) for conducting research into entrepreneurial decision making. *Qualitative Market Research*, vol. 3, no. 1, pp. 7–16; Quinlan, P. (2008, June). Let themaps be your guide. *Quirk's Marketing Research Review*, vol. 22, no. 6, pp. 74, 76, 78.

25.  Berlamino, C. (1989, December/January). Designing the qualitative research project: Addressing the process issues. *Journal of Advertising Research*, Vol. 29, no. 6, pp. S7-S9; Johnston, G. (2008, June). Qualtitatively speaking. *Quirk's Marketing Research Review*, vol. 22, no. 6, pp. 18, 20; *Alert! Magazine*. (2007, September). Special Expanded Qualitative Research Issue, vol. 45, p. 9; Brownell, L. (2008, April). Chief executive column. *Alert! Magazine*, vol. 46, no. 4, pp. 11, 23.

26.  Reynolds, T. J. and Gutman, J. (1988). Laddering, method, analysis, and interpretation. *Journal of Advertising Research*, vol. 28, no. 1, pp. 11–21.

27.  Qualitative Research Services, Word Association Tests. Retrieved from **www.decisionanalyst.com** on May 20, 2005.

28. Qualitative Research Services, Sentence Completion Tests. Retrieved from **www.decisionanalyst.com** on May 20, 2005.

29. Miles, L. (2003, December 11). Market research: Living their lives. *Marketing. Market Research Bulletin.* Retrieved online from **www.brandrepublic.com** on May 20, 2005.

30. Marshall, S., Drapeau, T. and DiSciullo, M. (2001, July/August). An eye on usability. *Quirk's Marketing Research Review*, vol. 15, no. 7, pp. 20–21, 90–92.

## Chapter 6

1. Cleland, K. (1996, May). Online research costs about one-half that of traditional methods. *Business Marketing*, vol. 81, no. 4, pp. B8–B9.

2. See Macer, T. (2002, December). CAVI from OpinionOne. *Quirk's Marketing Research Review.* Retrieved on March 15, 2004 from **www.quirks.com**.

3. Jang, H., Lee, B., Park, M., and Stokowski, P. A. (2000, February). Measuring underlying meanings of gambling from the perspective of enduring involvement. *Journal of Travel Research*, vol. 38, no. 3, pp. 230–238.

4. Ericson, P. I., and Kaplan, C. P. (2000, November). Maximizing qualitative responses about smoking in structured interviews. *Qualitative Health Research*, vol. 10, no. 6, pp. 829–840.

5. See, for example, **www.uwf.edu/panel**.

6. Green, K., Medlin, B., and Whitten, D. (2001, July/August). A comparison of Internet and mail survey methodology. *Quirk's Marketing Research Review*, vol. 15, no. 7, pp. 56–59.

7. See Roy, A. (2003). Further issues and factors affecting the response rates of e-mail and mixed-mode studies. In Barone, M., et al., (Eds), *Enhancing knowledge development in marketing.* Proceedings: AMA Educator's Conference. Chicago: American Marketing Association, pp. 338–339; and Bachmann, D., Elfrink, J., and Vazzana, G. (1999). E-mail and snail mail face off in rematch. *Marketing Research*, vol. 11, no. 4, pp. 11–15.

8. Bush, A. J., and Grant, E. S. (1995, Fall). The potential impact of recreational shoppers on mall intercept interviewing: An exploratory study. *Journal of Marketing Theory and Practice*, vol. 3, no. 4, pp. 73–83.

9. Brown, S. (1987). Drop and collect surveys: A neglected research technique? *Journal of the Market Research Society*, vol. 5, no. 1, pp. 19–23.

10. Bush, A. J., and Hair, J. F. (1983, May). An assessment of the mall intercept as a data collection method. *Journal of Marketing Research*, vol. 22, pp. 158–167.

11. See, for example, Xu, M., Bates, B. J., and Schweitzer, J. C. (1993). The impact of messages on survey participation in answering machine households. *Public Opinion Quarterly*, vol. 57, pp. 232–237; and Meinert, D. B., Festervand, T. A., and Lumpkin, J. R. (1992). Computerized questionnaires: Pros and cons, in King, R. L., (ed.), "Marketing: Perspectives

for the 1990s." *Proceedings of the Southern Marketing Association*, pp. 201–206.

12. Bos, R. (1999, November). A new era in data collection, *Quirk's Marketing Research Review*, vol. 12, no. 10, pp. 32–40; and Fletcher, K. (1995, June 15). Jump on the omnibus. *Marketing*, pp. 25–28.

13. DePaulo, P. J., and Weitzer, R. (1994, January 3). Interactive phone technology delivers survey data quickly. *Marketing News*, vol. 28, no. 1, p. 15.

14. Jones, P., and Palk, J. (1993). Computer-based personal interviewing: State-of-the-art and future prospects. *Journal of the Market Research Society*, vol. 35, no. 3, pp. 221–233.

15. For a "speed" comparison, see Cobanouglu, C., Warde, B., and Moeo, P. J. (2001, Fourth Quarter). A comparison of mail, fax and Web-based survey methods. *International Journal of Market Research*, vol. 43, no. 3, pp. 441–452.

16. Bruzzone, D., and Shellenberg, P. (2000, July/August). Track the effect of advertising better, faster, and cheaper online. *Quirk's Marketing Research Review*, vol. 14, no. 7, pp. 22–35.

17. Greenberg, D. (2000, July/August). Internet economy gives rise to real-time research. *Quirk's Marketing Research Review*, vol. 14, no. 7, pp. 88–90.

18. Taylor, H., Bremer, J., Overmeyer, C., Siegel, J. W., and Terhanian, G. (2001, Second Quarter). The record of Internet-based opinion polls in predicting the results of 72 races in the November 2000 U.S. elections. *International Journal of Market Research*, vol. 43, no. 2, pp. 127–135.

19. **www.ipsos.ca/en/products-tools/public-affairs/omnibus-surveys-product/ipsos-reid-canadian-online-omnibus.aspx**

20. Brown, S. (1987). Drop and collect surveys: A neglected research technique? *Journal of the Market Research Society*, vol. 5, no. 1, pp. 19–23.

21. **www.infocanada.ca**

22. American Statistical Association (1997). *ASA Series: What is a survey? More about mail surveys.*

23. A large number of studies have sought to determine response rates for a wide variety of inducement strategies. See, for example, Fox, R. J., Crask, M., and Kim, J. (1988, Winter). Mail questionnaires in survey research: A review of response inducement techniques. *Public Opinion Quarterly*, vol. 52, no. 4, pp. 467–491. Also see Yammarino, F., Skinner, S., and Childers, T. (1991). Understanding mail survey response behavior, *Public Opinion Quarterly*, vol. 55, pp. 613–639.

24. Conant, J., Smart, D., and Walker, B. (1990). Mail survey facilitation techniques: An assessment and proposal regarding reporting practices. *Journal of the Market Research Society*, vol. 32, no. 4, pp. 369–380.

25. Jassaume Jr., R. A., and Yamada, Y. (1990, Summer). A comparison of the viability of mail surveys in Japan and the United States. *Public Opinion Quarterly*, vol. 54, no. 2, pp. 219–228.

26. Arnett, R. (1990, Second Quarter). Mail panel research in the 1990s. *Applied Marketing Research*, vol. 30, no. 2, pp. 8–10.

27. www.e-rewards.com

28. Gerlotto, C. (2003, November). Learning on the go: Tips on getting international research right. *Quirk's Marketing Research Review*, vol. 17, p. 44.

**Chapter 7**

1. Reichheld, F. (2006). *The ultimate question: Driving good profits and true growth*. Boston, MA: Harvard Business School Press, p. 31.

2. Turner, Michelle R. (2005, January). How do you best measure and grow customer loyalty? *The Research Report*, Vol. 18. Retrieved from www.maritzresearch.com on March 31, 2007.

3. Sometimes open-ended questions are used to develop closed-ended questions that are used later. See, for example, Erffmeyer, R. C., and Johnson, D. A. (2001, Spring). An exploratory study of sales force automation practices: Expectations and realities. *Journal of Personal Selling and Sales Management*, vol. 21, no. 2, pp. 167–175.

4. Fox, S. (2001, May). Market research 101. *Pharmaceutical executive*, Supplement: *Successful product management: A primer*, p. 34.

5. Honomichl, J. (1994). Satisfaction measurement jumpstarts survey research. *Marketing News*, vol. 25, no. 14, p. 15.

6. See, for example, Leigh, J. H. and Martin C. R., Jr. (1987). "Don't know" item nonresponse in a telephone survey: Effects of question form and respondent characteristics. *Journal of Marketing Research*, vol. 29, no. 3, pp. 317–339.

7. There are myriad other considerations that can factor into sample size calculation and are beyond the scope of this book. See, for example, Parker, R. A., and Berman, N. G. (2003, August). Sample size: More than calculations. *American Statistician*, vol. 57, no. 3, pp. 166–171.

8. See, for example, Wellner, A. S. (2002, February). The female persuasion. *American Demographics*, vol. 24, no. 2, pp. 24–29; Wasserman, T. (2002, January 7). Color me bad. *Brandweek*, vol. 43, no. 1, p. 2; or Wilke, M. and Applebaum, M. (2001, November 5). Peering out of the closet. *Brandweek*, vol. 42, no. 41, pp. 26–32.

9. Statements are taken from Wells, W. D. and Tigert, D. J. (1971). Activities, interests, and opinions. *Journal of the Advertising Research*, reported in Kassarjain, H. H. and Robertson, T. S. (1973). *Perspectives in Consumer Behavior*. Glenview, IL: Scott Foresman, pp. 175–176.

10. Other methods of brand image measurement have been been found to be comparable. See: Driesener, C. and Romaniuk, J. (2006). Comparing methods of brand image measurement. *International Journal of Market Research*, vol. 48, no. 6, pp. 681–698.

11. Another way to avoid the halo effect is to have subjects rate each stimulus on the same attribute and then move to the next attribute. See Wu, B. T. W. and Petroshius, S.

(1987). The halo effect in store image management. *Journal of the Academy of Marketing Science,* vol. 15, no. 1, pp. 44–51.

12. The halo effect is real and used by companies to good advantage. See, for example, Moukheiber, Z. and Langreth, R. (2001, December 10). The halo effect. *Forbes*, vol. 168, no. 15, p. 66; or Anonymous. (2002, March 11). Sites seeking advertising (the paid kind). *Advertising Age*, vol. 73, no. 10, p. 38.

13. Some authors recommend using negatively worded statements with Likert scales to avoid the halo effect; however, recent evidence argues convincingly against this recommendation. See Swain, S. D., Weathers, D. and Niedrich, R. W. (February, 2007). Assessing three sources of misresponse to reversed Likert items. *Journal of Marketing Research*, vol. 45, no. 1, pp. 116–131.

14. Garg, R. K. (1996, July). The influence of positive and negative wording and issue involvement on responses to Likert scales in marketing research. *Journal of the Marketing Research Society*, vol. 38, no. 3, pp. 235–246.

15. Scale development requires rigorous research. See, for example, Churchill, G. A. (1979, February). A paradigm for developing better measures of marketing constructs. *Journal of Marketing Research*, vol. 16, pp. 64–73, for method; or Ram, S. and Jung, H. S. (1990). The conceptualization and measurement of product usage. *Journal of the Academy of Marketing Science*, vol. 18, no. 1, pp. 67–76, for an example.

16. Semon, T. T. (2001, October 8). Symmetry shouldn't be goal for scales. *Marketing News*, vol. 35, no. 21, p. 9.

17. See, for example, Crask, M. R., and Fox, R. J. (1987). An exploration of the interval properties of three commonly used marketing research studies: A magnitude estimation approach. *Journal of the Market Research Society*, vol. 29, no. 3, pp. 317–339.

18. Some researchers claim the use of a 0–10 scale over the telephone is actually better than a 3-, 4-, or 5-point scale. See Loken, B., et al. (1987, July). The use of 0–10 scales in telephone surveys. *Journal of the* Market Research Society, vol. 29, no. 3, pp. 353–362.

19. See, for example, Bishop, G. F. (1985, Summer). Experiments with the middle response alternative in survey questions. *Public Opinion Quarterly*, vol. 51, pp. 220–232; or Schertizer, C. B. and Kernan, J.B. (1985, October). More on the robustness of response scales. *Journal of the Marketing Research Society,* vol. 27, pp. 262–282.

20. See also: Duncan, O. D. and Stenbeck, M. (1988, Winter). No opinion or not sure? *Public Opinion Quarterly*, vol. 52, pp. 513–525; and Durand, R. M. and Lambert, Z. V. (1988, March). Don't know responses in survey: analyses and interpretational consequences. *Journal of Business Research*, vol. 16, pp. 533–543.

21. Semon, T. T. (2001, October 8). Symmetry shouldn't be goal for scales. *Marketing News*, vol. 35, no. 21, p. 9.

22. de Jong, M. G., Steenkamp, J.-B. E. M., Fox, J.-P. and Baumgartner, H. (2008, February). Using item response theory to measure extreme response style in marketing

research: A global investigation. *Journal of Marketing Research*, vol. 45, no. 1, pp. 104–115. The figure in the Marketing Research Insight is an adaptation of Figure 3 in this article.

23. Ashley, D. (2003, February). The questionnaire that launched a thousand responses. *Quirk's Marketing Research Review*, electronic archive.

24. The topic of internal consistency of multiple-item measures is too advanced for this basic textbook. Also, recent research touts single-item measures in certain instances. See: Bergkvist, L. and Rossiter, J. (2007, May). The predictive validity of multiple-item versus single-item measures of the same constructs.

25. For example, bogus recall was found negatively related to education, income, and age, but positively related to "yea-saying" and attitude toward the slogan. See: Glassman, M. and Ford, J. B. (1988, Fall). An empirical investigation of bogus recall. *Journal of the Academy of Marketing Science*, vol. 16, pp. 3–4, 38–41; Raghav, S. Reliability andvalidity of survey research in marketing: the state of the art. In R. L. King, (Ed.), *Marketing: Toward the twenty-first century*. Proceedings of the Southern Marketing Association (1991), pp. 210–213; Milton, M. P., Strutton, H. D. and Dunn, M. G. Demographic sample reliability among selected telephone sampling replacement techniques. In R. L. King, (Ed.), *Marketing: Toward the twenty-first century*. Proceedings of the Southern Marketing Association (1991), pp. 214–219; Babin, B. J., Darden, W. R. and Griffin, M. A note on demand artifacts in marketing research. In R. L. King, (Ed.), *Marketing: Perspectives for the 1990s*. Proceedings of the Southern Marketing Association (1992), pp. 227–230; Dunipace, R. A., Mix, R. A. and Poole, R. R. Overcoming the failure to replicate research in marketing: A chaotic explanation. In T. K. Massey, Jr., (Ed.), *Marketing: Satisfying a diverse customerplace*. Proceedings of the Southern Marketing Association (1993), pp. 194–197; Malawian, K. P. and Butler, D. D. The semantic differential: Is it being misused in marketing research? In R. Achrol and A. Mitchell, eds., *Enhancing knowledge development in marketing*. A.M.A. Educators'Conference Proceedings (1994), p. 19.

26. Statistical analysis can sometimes be used to assist in estabishing face validity. See, for example, Wolburg, J. M. and Pokrywczynski, J. (2002, September/October). A psychographic analysis of Generation Y college students. *Journal of Advertising Research*, vol. 41, no. 5, pp. 33–52.

27. For an example, see: Russell, C., Norman, A. and Heckler, S. (2004, June). The consumption of television programming: Development and validation of the connectedness scale. *Journal of Consumer Research*, vol. 31, no. 1, pp. 150–161; or Terblanceh, N. S. and Boshoff, C. (2008). Improved scale development in marketing. *International Journal of Market Research*, vol. 50, no. 1, pp. 105–119.

## Chapter 8

1. Susan, C. (1994). Questionnaire design affects response rate. *Marketing News*, vol. 28, p. H25; and Sancher, M. E. (1992).

2. For a more comprehensive coverage of this topic, see Baker, M. J. (2003, Summer). Data collection—Questionnaire design. *Marketing Review*, vol. 3, no. 3, pp. 343–370.

3. Babble, E. (1990). *Survey research methods* (2nd ed.). Belmont, CA: Wadsworth Publishing, pp. 131–132.

4. www.ombrelle.com

5. Hunt, S. D., Sparkman, R. D., and Wilcox, J. (1982, May). The pretest in survey research: Issues and preliminary findings. *Journal of Marketing Research*, vol. 26, no. 4, pp. 269–273.

6. Dillman, D. A. (1978). *Mail telephone surveys: The total design method*. New York: John Wiley & Sons.

7. Loftus, E., and Zanni, G. (1975). Eyewitness testimony: The influence of the wording of a question. *Bulletin of the Psychonomic Society*, vol. 5, pp. 86–88.

8. Adapted and modified from Payne, S. L. (1951). *The art of asking questions*. Princeton, NJ: Princeton University Press. Current source is the 1980 edition, Chapter 10.

9. For memory questions, it is advisable to have respondents recontruct specific events. See, for example, Cook, W. A. (1987, February–March). Telescoping and memory's other tricks. *Journal of Advertising Research*, vol. 27, no. 1, pp. RC5–RC8.

10. Peterson, R. A. (2000). *Constructing effective questionnaires*. Thousand Oaks, CA: Sage Publications, Inc., p. 58.

11. Patten, M. (2001). *Questionnaire research*. Los Angeles: Pyrczak Publishing, p. 9.

12. Screens can be used to quickly identify respondents who will not answer honestly. See Waters, K. M. (1991, Spring–Summer). Designing screening questionnaires to minimize dishonest answers. *Applied Marketing Research*, vol. 31, no. 1, pp. 51–53.

13. Based on Sudman, S. and Bradhurn, N. (1982). *Asking Questions*. San Francisco: Jossey-Bass, pp. 219–221.

14. Webb, J. (2000, Winter). Questionnaires and their design. *Marketing Review*, vol. 1, no. 2, pp. 197–218.

15. Patten, M. (2001). Questionnaire research: A practical guide (2nd ed.) Los Angeles, CA: Pyrczak Publishing, p. 19.

16. Blunch, N. J. (1984, November). Position bias in multiple choice questions. *Journal of Marketing Research*, vol. 21, pp. 216–220; Welch, J. L. and Swift, C. O. (1992, Summer). Question order effects in taste testing of beverages. *Journal of Academy of Marketing Science*, pp. 265–268; Bickatt, B. A. (1993, February). Carryover and backfire effects in marketing research. *Journal of Marketing Research*, 52–62.

17. Dillman, D. A., Sinclair, M. D. and Clark, J. R. (1993). Effects of questionnaire length, respondent-friendly design, and a difficult question on response rates for occupant-addressed census mail surveys. *Public Opinion Quarterly*, vol. 57, pp. 289–304.

18. Question order may also affect responses. See, for example, Ayidiya, S. A. and McClendon, M. J. (1990, Summer).

Response effects in mail surveys. *Public Opinion Quarterly*, vol. 54, no. 2, pp. 229–247.

19. Carroll, S. (1994). Questionnaire design affects response rate. *Marketing News*, vol. 25, no. 14, p. 23.

20. Normally pretests are done individually, but a focus group could be used. See Long, S. A. (1991, May 27). Pretesting questionnaires minimizes measurement error. *Marketing News*, vol. 25, no. 11, p. 12.

21. Response latency, or subtle hesitations in respondents, can be used as a pretest aid. See, for instance, Bassili, J. N., and Fletcher, J. F. (1991). Response-time measurement in survey research. *Public Opinion Quarterly*, vol. 55, pp. 331–346.

**Chapter 9**

1. See Bradburn, N. M., and Sudman, S. (1988). Polls and surveys: Understanding what they tell us; Cantril, A. H. (1991). The opinion connection: Polling, politics, and the press; Cantril, A. H. Public opinion polling, retrieved from **Answers .com** on April 29, 2007; Landon in a landslide: The poll that changed polling. Retrieved from **www.historymatter.gmu .edu** on April 29, 2007.

2. See, for example, Lenth, R. (2001, August). Some practical guidelines for effective sample size determination. *American Statistician*, vol. 55, no. 3, pp. 187–193; Williams, G. (1999, April). What size sample do I need? *Australian and New Zealand Journal of Public Health*, vol. 23, no. 2, pp. 215–217; or Cesana, B.M, Reina, G., and Marubini, E. (2001, November). Sample size for testing a proportion in clinical trials: A "two-step" procedure combining power and confidence interval expected width. *American Statistician*, vol. 55, no. 4, pp. 288–292.

3. See, for example, Stephen, E. H., and Soldo, B. J. (1990, April). How to judge the quality of a survey. *American Demographics*, vol. 12, no. 4, pp. 42–43.

4. We use percents throughout this chapter because they are more intuitive than averages.

5. There are myriad other considerations that can factor into sample size calculation and are beyond the scope of this book. See, for example, Parker, R. A., and Berman, N. G. (2003, August). Sample size: More than calculations. *American Statistician*, vol. 57, no. 3, pp. 166–171.

6. See Shiffler, R. E., and Adams, A. J. (1987, August). A correction for biasing effects of pilot sample size on sample size determination. *Journal of Marketing Research*, vol. 24, no. 3, pp. 319–321.

7. Foreman, J., and Collins, M. (1991, July). The viability of random digit dialing in the UK. *Journal of the Market Research Society*, vol. 33, no. 3, pp. 219–227; and Hekmat, F., and Segal, M.(1984). Random digit dialing: Some additional empirical observations, in D. M. Klein and A. E. Smith, (Eds.), *Marketing comes of age: Proceedings of the Southern Marketing Association*, pp. 176–180.

8. For a somewhat more technical description of cluster sampling, see Carlin, J. B., and Hocking, J. (1999, October).

Design of cross-sectional surveys using cluster sampling: An overview with Australian case studies. *Australian and New Zealand Journal of Public Health*, vol. 23, no. 5, pp. 546–551.

9. See also Sudman, S. (1985, February). Efficient screening methods for the sampling of geographically clustered special populations. *Journal of Marketing Research*, vol. 22, pp. 20–29.

10. Bradley, N. (1999, October). Sampling for Internet surveys: An examination of respondent selection for Internet research. *Journal of the Market Research Society*, vol. 41, no. 4, p. 387.

11. Academic marketing researchers often use convenience samples of college students. See Peterson, R. A. (2001, December). On the use of college students in social science research: Insights from a second-order meta-analysis. *Journal of Consumer Research*, vol. 28, no. 3, pp. 450–461.

12. Wyner, G. A. (2001, Fall). Representation, randomization, and realism. *Marketing Research*, vol. 13, no. 3, pp. 4–5.

13. For an application of referral sampling, see Moriarity, R. T., Jr., and Spekman, R. E. (1984, May). An empirical investigation of the information sources used during the industrial buying process. *Journal of Marketing Research*, vol. 21, pp. 137–147.

14. For a detailed description of how to select a quota sample, see Baker, M. (2002, Autumn). *Marketing Review*, vol. 3, no. 1, pp. 103–120.

15. Paramar, A. (2003, February). Tailor techniques to each audience in Latin market. *Marketing News*, vol. 37, no. 3, pp. 4–6.

16. The nature of sample bias for online surveys is just becoming known. See, for example, Grandcolas, U., Rettie, R., and Marusenko, K. (2003, July). Web survey bias: Sample or mode effect? *Journal of Marketing Management*, vol. 19, no. 5/6, pp. 541–561.

17. See, as an example, Dahlen, M. (2001, July/August). Banner advertisements through a new lens. *Journal of Advertising Research*, vol. 41, no. 4, pp. 23–30.

18. For a comparison of online sampling to telephone sampling, see Cooper, M. P. (2000, Winter). Web surveys: A review of issues and approaches. *Public Opinion Quarterly*, vol. 64, no. 4, pp. 464–494.

19. Grossnickle, J., and Raskin, O. (2001, Summer). What's ahead on the Internet? *Marketing Research*, vol. 13, no. 2, pp. 8–13.

20. Miller, T. W. (2001, Summer). Can we trust the data of online research? *Marketing Research*, vol. 13, no. 2, pp. 26–32.

21. Based on: Lavrakas, P. J., Shuttles, C. D., Steeh, C. and Fienberg, H. (2007, Special Issue). The state of surveying cell phone numbers in the United States. *Public Opinion Quarterly*, vol. 71, no. 5, pp. 840–854.

## Chapter 10

1. www.uta.edu/msmr

2. These problems are international in scope. See Kreitzman, L. (1990, February 22). Market research: Virgins and groupies. *Marketing,* pp. 35–38, for the United Kingdom.

3. There is a move in the United Kingdom for interviewer certification. See Hemsley, S. (2000, August 17). Acting the part. *Marketing Week*, vol. 23, no. 28, pp. 37–40.

4. See also, Conrad, F., and Schober, M. (2000, Spring). Clarifying question meaning in a household survey. *Public Opinion Quarterly*, vol. 64, no. 1, pp. 1–28.

5. Miller, T. W. (2001, September 24). Make the call: Online results are mixed bag. *Marketing News*, vol. 20, no. 35, pp. 30–35.

6. To learn about how companies are attempting to resolve non-representativeness, see Johnson, D. W. (2002, December). Elections and public polling: Will the media get online polling right? *Psychology & Marketing*, vol. 12, no. 19, p. 1009.

7. Coleman, L. G. (1991, January 7). Researchers say non-response is single biggest problem. *Marketing News*, vol. 1, no. 25, pp. 32–33; Landler, M. (1991, February 11). The "bloodbath" in market research. *Business Week*, vol. 72, pp. 74; and Jarvis, S. (2002, February 4). CMOR finds survey refusal rate still rising. *Marketing News*, vol. 3, no. 4, p. 36.

8. Anonymous (2003, Spring). The case for caution: This system is dangerously flawed. *Public Opinion Quarterly*, vol. 67, no. 1, pp. 5–17.

9. Baim, J. (1991, June). Response rates: A multinational perspective. *Marketing & Research Today*, vol. 2, no. 19, pp. 114–119.

10. Mitchel, J. O. (2002, Fall). Telephone surveys: The next buggy whip? *LIMRA's Market Facts Quarterly*, vol. 4, no. 21, p. 39.

11. Jarvis, S. (2002, February). CMOR finds survey refusal rate still rising. *Marketing News*, vol. 36, no. 3.

12. Anonymous. (1993, August 16). The researchers' response: Four industry leaders tell how to improve cooperation. *Marketing News*, p. A12.

13. Personal communication, quoted by permission.

14. It is important for the researcher and client to have a partnership during data analysis. See, for example, Fitzpatrick, M. (2001, August). Statistical analysis for direct marketers— in plain English. *Direct Marketing*, vol. 64, no. 4, pp. 54–56.

15. For an alternative presentation, see Ehrnberg, A. (2001, Winter). Data, but no information. *Marketing Research*, vol. 13, no. 4, pp. 36–39.

16. Fitzgerald, K. (2003, June). They're baaaaack: Card marketers on campus. *Credit Card Management*, vol. 3, no. 16, p. 18.

17. Some authors argue that central tendency measures are too sterile. See, for example, Pruden, D. R., and Vavra, T. G. (2000, Summer). Customer research, not marketing research. *Marketing Research*, vol. 12, no. 2, pp. 14–19.

18. Gutsche, A. (2001, September 24). Visuals make the case. *Marketing News*, vol. 35, no. 20, pp. 21–23.

19. Joel Best (2001), *Damned lies and statistics: Untangling numbers from media politicians and activists*, Berkeley, CA: University of California Press.

## Chapter 11

1. In statistical jargon, one uses statistical inference (generalization) to estimate a population parameter (population fact) from the sample statistic (sampling finding).

2. Instructors may find this article useful when teaching confidence intervals: Blume, J. D., and Royall, R. M. (2003, February). Illustrating the law of large numbers (and confidence intervals). *American Statistician*, vol. 57, no. 1, pp. 51–57.

3. We are aware of the disconnect between applied statistical testing and classical statistical testing; however, we opt for the applied approach here. Refer to Hubbard, R., Bayarri, M. J., Berk, K. N., and Carlton, M. A. (2003, August). Confusion over measures of evidence (*p*'s) versus errors ([alpha]'s) in classical statistical testing. *American Statistician*, vol. 57, no. 3, p. 171.

4. Traditionally, statistics textbooks have advised the use of *t* over *z* when the sample size is 30 or less; however, since the variance is typically unknown in marketing research data, the *t* is preferable upto 120.

## Chapter 12

1. For a contrary view, see Mazur, L. (2000, June 8). The only truism in marketing is they don't exist. *Marketing*, p. 20.

2. Brandt, J. R. (2003, January/February). Meet your new market. *Chief Executive*, no. 185, p. 8.

3. Meaningful difference is sometimes called "practical significance." See Thompson, B. (2002, Winter). "Statistical," "practical," and "clinical": How many kinds of significance do counselors need to consider? *Journal of Counseling and Development*, vol. 30, no. 1, pp. 64–71.

4. Smith, S. M., and Whitlark, D. B. (2001, Summer). Men and women online: What makes them click? Marketing Research, vol. 13, no. 2, pp. 20–25.

5. Personal communication with the author.

6. This procedure is sometimes called a "paired samples" test. For an example of the use of paired samples *t* tests, see Ryan, C., and Mo, X. (2001, December). Chinese visitors to New Zealand: Demographics and perceptions. *Journal of Vacation Marketing*, vol. 8, no. 1, pp. 13–27.

## Chapter 13

1. Much of this material was adapted from Turner, M. R. (2005, January). How do you best measure and grow customer loyalty? *The Research Report*, vol. 18. Retrieved from **www.maritzresearch.com** on March 31, 2007.

2. For advice on when to use chi-square analysis, see Hellebush, S. J. (2001, June 4). One chi square beats two $z$ tests. *Marketing News*, vol. 35, no. 11, pp. 12–13.

3. Here are some articles that use cross-tabulation analysis: Burton, S., and Zinkhan, G. M. (1987, Fall). Changes in consumer choice: Further investigation of similarity and attraction effects. *Psychology in Marketing*, vol. 4, pp. 255–266; Bush, A. J., and Leigh, J. H. (1984, April/May). Advertising on cable versus traditional television networks. *Journal of Advertising Research*, vol. 24, pp. 33–38; and Langrehr, F. W. (1985, Summer). Consumer images of two types of competing financial institutions. *Journal of the Academy of Marketing Science*, vol. 13, pp. 248–264.

4. For a more advanced treatment of scatter diagrams, see Goddard, B. L. (2000, April). The power of computer graphics for comparative analysis, *Appraisal Journal*, vol. 68, no. 2, pp. 134–141.

5. See, for example, Branch, W. (1990, February). On interpreting correlation coefficients. *American Psychologist*, vol. 45, no. 2, p. 296.

6. Residual analysis can take many forms. See, for example, Dempster, A. P., and Gasko-Green, M. (1981). New tools for residual analysis. *Annals of Statistics*, vol. 9, pp. 945–959.

7. Based on Tsalikis, J., Seaton, B., and Tomaras, P. (2002, February). A new perspective on cross-cultural ethical evaluations: The use of conjoint analysis. *Journal of Business Ethics*, vol. 35, no. 4, part 2, pp. 281–292.

8. Our description pertains to "backward" stepwise regression. We admit that this is a simplification of stepwise multiple regression.

9. Reece, W. S. (2001, February). Travelers to Las Vegas and to Atlantic City. *Journal of Travel Research*, vol. 39, no. 3, pp. 275–284.

10. We admit that our description of regression is introductory. Two books that expand our description are Lewis-Beck, M. S. (1980). *Applied regression: An introduction.* Newbury Park, CA: Sage Publications; and Schroeder, L. D., Sjoffquist, D. L., and Stephan, P. E. (1986). *Understanding regression analysis: An introductory guide.* Newbury Park, CA: Sage Publications.

11. Regression analysis is commonly used in academic marketing research. Here are some examples: Callahan, F. X. (1982, April/May). Advertising and profits 1969–1978.

*Journal of Advertising Research*, vol. 22, pp. 17–22; Dubinsky, A. J., and Levy, M. (1989, Summer). Influence of organizational fairness on work outcomes of retail salespeople. *Journal of Retailing*, vol. 65, pp. 221–252; Frieden, J. B., and Downs, P. E. (1986, Fall). Testing the social involvement model in an energy conservation context. *Journal of the Academy of Marketing Science*, vol. 14, pp. 13–20; and Tellis, G. J., and Fornell, C. (1988, February). The relationship between advertising and product quality over the product life cycle: A contingency theory. *Journal of Marketing Research*, vol. 25, pp. 64–71. For an alternative to regression analysis, see Quaintance, B. S., and Franke, G. R. (1991). Neural networks for marketing research. In King, R. L. (Ed.), *Marketing: Toward the twenty-first century.* Proceedings of the Southern Marketing Association, pp. 230–235.

## Chapter 14

1. Lotti, M. (2003). Practitioner viewpoint. In Burns, A., and Bush, R., *Marketing research: Online research applications.* Upper Saddle River, NJ: Prentice Hall, p. 580.

2. The authors wish to acknowledge the assistance of M. R. Howard, Ed.D., and H. H. Donofrio, Ph.D., in preparing some of the material presented in this chapter. Both are experts in business communication and report writing, and we appreciate their insights.

3. Deshpande, R., and Zaltman, G. (1982, February). Factors affecting the use of market research information: A path analysis. *Journal of Marketing Research*, vol. 19, pp. 14–31.

4. Deshpande, R., and Zaltman, G. (1984, February). A comparison of factors affecting researcher and manager perceptions of market research use. *Journal of Marketing Research*, vol. 21, pp. 32–38.

5. To properly cite your sources, see *MLA handbook for writers of research papers* (7th ed.). New York: Modern Language Association of America; or *Publication manual of the American Psychological Association* (6th ed.). (2001). Washington, DC: American Psychological Association.

6. Hansen, B. (2003, September 13). Combating plagiarism. *CQResearcher.* Retrieved from **http://library.eqpress.com/eqresearcher/CQResearcher** on January 21, 2004.

7. Guffey, M. E. (2000). *Business communication: Process and product* (3rd ed.). Cincinnati: South-Western College Publishing, p. 103.

8. Tutee, E. R. (1983). *The visual display of quantitative information.* Cheshire, CT: Graphics Press.

9. Thomas, J. (2001, November). Executive excellence. *Marketing Research*, pp. 11–12.

# Credits

## Chapter 13

**p. 422** Courtesy of Maritz Research; **p. 424** Courtesy of Google; **p. 439** Bill Robbins/Stone/Getty Images; **p. 445** Erlanson-Messens, Britt J./Image Bank/Getty Images; **p. 451** Frank LaBua/Pearson Education/PH College

## Chapter 14

**p. 464** Statistics Canada, The Daily, Friday December 20, 2010, www.statcan.gc.ca/daily-quotidien/101018/tdq101018-eng.htm, accessed December 20, 2010; **p. 473** Courtesy of Burke, Inc.

# Name Index

# Subject Index